T0257894

IET COMPUTING SERIES 15

Big Data and Software Defined Networks

IET Book Series on Big Data – Call for Authors

Editor-in-Chief: Professor Albert Y. Zomaya, University of Sydney, Australia

The topic of Big Data has emerged as a revolutionary theme that cuts across many technologies and application domains. This new book series brings together topics within the myriad research activities in many areas that analyse, compute, store, manage and transport massive amount of data, such as algorithm design, data mining and search, processor architectures, databases, infrastructure development, service and data discovery, networking and mobile computing, cloud computing, high-performance computing, privacy and security, storage and visualization.

Topics considered include (but not restricted to) IoT and Internet computing; cloud computing; peer-to-peer computing; autonomic computing; data centre computing; multi-core and many core computing; parallel, distributed and high-performance computing; scalable databases; mobile computing and sensor networking; green computing; service computing; networking infrastructures; cyberinfrastructures; e-Science; smart cities; analytics and data mining; Big Data applications and more.

Proposals for coherently integrated International co-edited or co-authored handbooks and research monographs will be considered for this book series. Each proposal will be reviewed by the editor-in-chief and some board members, with additional external reviews from independent reviewers. Please email your book proposal for the IET Book Series on Big Data to: Professor Albert Y. Zomaya at albert.zomaya@sydney.edu.au or to the IET at author_support@theiet.org.

Big Data and Software Defined Networks

Edited by
Javid Taheri

The Institution of Engineering and Technology

Published by The Institution of Engineering and Technology, London, United Kingdom

The Institution of Engineering and Technology is registered as a Charity in England & Wales (no. 211014) and Scotland (no. SC038698).

First published 2018

The Institution of Engineering and Technology
Michael Faraday House
Six Hills Way, Stevenage
Herts, SG1 2AY, United Kingdom

www.theiet.org

British Library Cataloguing in Publication Data
A catalogue record for this product is available from the British Library

ISBN 978-1-78561-304-3 (hardback)
ISBN 978-1-78561-305-0 (PDF)

Typeset in India by MPS Limited

Contents

Dedication
To my love, Hadis

Foreword

Big Data and software-defined networking is the inaugural volume in our new *IET Book Series on Big Data*. This edited book is an exciting reference that deals with a wide range of topical themes in the field of software-defined networking (SDN).

Today we are witnessing many advances in SDN technologies brought about because of the convergence of computing and networking. This book explores the challenges imposed by Big Data issues, how the deployment of SDNs will impact the way we develop solutions and deploy applications and how a better resource allocation will help run smoother networks in large cloud data centres.

The publication of *Big Data and software-defined networking* is a timely and valuable achievement and an important contribution to the Big Data processing and networking literature. I would like to commend the book editor, Dr. Javid Taheri, for assembling a great team of contributors who have managed to provide a rich coverage of the topic.

I am sure that readers will find the book very useful and a source of inspiration for future research work and innovation. It should be well received by the research and development community and also be beneficial for graduate classes focusing on SDNs and Big Data research.

Finally, I would like to congratulate Dr. Javid Taheri on a job well done, and I look forward to a further fruitful collaboration.

Editor-in-Chief of the *IET Book Series on Big Data*
Professor Albert Y. Zomaya, University of Sydney, Australia

Preface

The increase of processing power is undoubtedly among the most prominent techno-logical achievements of the 21st century. Being able to process data on higher rates has opened many doors for both scientific and industrial communities to explore new areas. Big Data Analytic and Software Defined Networking (SDN) are among the methods and technologies that have directly contributed to such extraordinary achievements.

Big Data and SDN started for different reasons, and consequently advanced science and industry from different angles. Their collision is however imminent since both face ever growing Cloud Data Centres (CDCs). Big Data Analytics has entered CDCs to harvest their massive computing powers and deduct information that was never reachable by conventional methods. SDN entered this field to help CDCs run their services more efficiently.

This book, *Big Data and Software Defined Networks*, aims to investigate areas where Big Data and SDN could help each other in delivering more efficient services. SDN can help Big Data applications to overcome one of their major challenges: message passing among cooperative nodes. Through proper bandwidth allocation and prioritization, critical surges of Big Data flows can be better handled to effectively reduce their impacts on CDCs. Big Data, in turn, could also help SDN controllers to better analyse collected network information and make more efficient decisions about the allocation of resources to different network flows.

To mention several ways through which each technology can help the other, the book is sectioned into three parts. The first part (Introduction) serves as an intro-ductory section, providing crucial information about Big Data and SDN as well as their current state-of-the-art advancements and architectures. It also highlights gen-eral open issues in these vibrant fields. The second part (How SDN Helps Big Data) is focused on several ways that SDN helps Big Data applications run more efficiently. This section is further split into several chapters, each focusing on how SDN helps a specific "V" in the Big Data terminology. The third section (How Big Data Helps SDN) is focused on several Big Data Analytics that help SDN make better resource allocation decisions. Chapters in this section reveal current approaches in which large amount of collected network data can be processed to run smoother networks in large CDCs.

The book is intended to be a virtual round-table of several outstanding researchers from all corners of the globe. The number of chapters –and their sizes– was limited to keep the book within a single volume. Topics for chapters were carefully selected to provide a wide scope with minimal overlap and duplications. Although the list of topics is not exhaustive, most conclusions drawn here could be easily extended to similar problems.

To better serve the community, the content of this book is deliberately channelled to serve multiple stakeholders. Telco engineers, scientists, researchers, developers and practitioners developing and/or implementing cloud-based solutions are the first target audience for this book. Other groups that could also significantly benefit from topics of this book are marketing agencies with the aim of using Big Data for fast processing; academics working in networking and SDN, machine learning, Big Data analytics and optimization disciplines; and cloud infrastructure designers and cloud providers hosting Big Data services.

Javid Taheri

Acknowledgements

First and foremost, I would like to thank and acknowledge the contributors to this book for their support and patience, and the reviewers for their useful comments and suggestions that helped in improving the earlier outline of this book. I would also like to thank Prof. Zomaya for his guidance throughout this project. Last but not least, I would also like to thank the IET (Institution of Engineering and Technology) editorial and production teams for their extensive efforts during many phases of this project and the timely manner in which the book was produced.

Javid Taheri

Part I

Introduction

Chapter 1

Introduction to SDN

Ruslan L. Smelyanskiy* and Alexander Shalimov*

1.1 Data centers

1.1.1 The new computing paradigm

The rapid spread of the Internet, the World Wide Web, messaging (instant messenger) and the emergence of social networks presented new requirements to the computational infrastructure for support services. Users demand that services should always be available, when and where they need them. The stream of service requests is not uniform. For example, according to the Facebook Company report for 2010, the average number of on-line users all around the globe are in the system, estimated at 25 million [1]. However, at the rush hours, this number is several times higher than the average one and it drops to several thousand on-line users at night. Processing of such stream of requests required special features to scale computing performance allocated to a service, depending on its flow of requests, features to allocate processing power dynamically and depending on, for example, the time of the day and geographical positions of users.

The client–server architecture, developed in the 1980s and 1990s, did not meet these requirements. In this architecture, each application was bounded by the computing infrastructure, while the performance of the computing infrastructure was limited and not amenable to be quickly increased. Data centers (DCs) with fast communication channels (often wireless) and cloud computing had to break these limits [2,3]. The magic of a cloud is that its services are available anytime and anywhere. DC generates a stream of services on user's demands. Externally, DC looks like a warehouse, without any clues about what is in. There are the din of fans, cooling rack with servers inside. Each rack of a household refrigerator size forms a cluster. Clusters are woven into the "tapestry" of the electrical and optical cables that form a data communication network connecting servers in a cluster, clusters with each other and with the outside world. For example, Google's six DCs allocated across the world have more than 500 million of servers [4].

High-performance computing (HPC) system with massive parallelism consisting of thousands of machines have been available since the 1980s. HPC systems are

*Lomonosov Moscow State University, Faculty of Computational Mathematics and Cybernetics, Russia

based on the fast and efficient data communication system connecting computers and providing high-speed transmission of large amounts of small portions of data messages. This mad race for performance and for minimum delays is fueled by stock and financial institutions, where the delay of a fraction of a microsecond could dramatically change the value of transactions on the stock. In recent years, Ethernet-based computer networks have achieved the significant progress that helped to reduce the gap in performance and scalability between clusters of standard computers (COTS—commodity-off-the-shelf) and specialized problem-oriented HPC systems. This is evident from the growth of the share of supercomputers in the Top500 list of the most powerful computers (Top500.org), using Ethernet for interprocessor data communication. In the early 2000s, the high-speed interprocessor networks were made on demand, under the requirements of the user, based on proprietary technologies. Ethernet was used in only 2% of the Top500. In November 2011, more than 42% of the Top500 systems used Gigabit Ethernet in their networks. The second most common interprocessor communication system among supercomputers is InfiniBand data communication system, which is used in 40% of systems. As Ethernet, InfiniBand are standardized by industry. The presence of the industry standards, combined with simplicity of scalability, providing high cost-effectiveness has created a technological basis for DC [5,6]. Despite the fact that network plays a central part in the performance of the whole system, its cost usually amounts only 10%–15% of the cluster cost. Be careful not to confuse cost and value. Each cluster is homogeneous in the sense that all the servers are identical both in architecture and in performance. These thousands of servers are used for parallel query processing at the level of the processes of a special kind, the so-called threads. Each request is a task that is divided into subtasks. The process can involve all subtasks of a single query, or only one specific subtask. All tasks and subtasks are performed in parallel. Processing ends when all the subtasks of a single query are completed. With this organization of processing, maximum execution time of one sub-task will determine the response time to the user's request [7].

Even with massive parallelism at the processes level, the overhead for communication through the network and protocols stack can significantly limit the overall performance of applications due to the effect of Amdahl's law [8]. Thus, the architecture of DC and the architecture of software applications define how this application will be used and how it will operate. Delays and cost of access as to local memory as to remote memory in the cluster via the network is a trade-off between application code optimization and cluster architecture, e.g., DC architecture. The way to use a cluster determines the compliance with service level agreement (SLA) and, ultimately, on the performance of the application. Clusters can be used in a dedicated mode by only one application or in a shared mode by multiple applications. This requires certain control mechanisms and always affects application performance. On the other hand, many Web applications use services from many other clusters, where multiple applications may run simultaneously in order to increase the overall resources utilization for the entire system [4,9]. Therefore, DC, as systems of clusters, use virtualization and scalability to isolate applications by performance and by mutual influence of the error. Therefore, Web application architects always have to consider sharing of resources.

Various Web applications have planned resources to run in clusters, such as search engines, e-mail and shared documents development. Applications with a user-interface run in a soft real time mode—have a dozen of milliseconds to respond to a user request. Each request is allocated between multiple threads in a cluster. These threads generate responses, which send to users in aggregated form. If some threads do not complete their tasks in time, for example, because of network congestion, the delay may exceed the threshold, and the results of these threads will not be aggregated with the results of the remaining workflows. This will lead to the waste of computing and network resources, and can harm the results. To decrease the congestion, networks may be overprovisioned, which means that network resources can be requested to be the maximum. This is guaranteed to provide enough bandwidth for even the most intricate traffic patterns. However, overprovisioning in large-scale DC networks is extremely expensive. Another approach is to implement several QoS policies (quality of service) focused on different traffic classes. For guaranteed performance, traffic of different classes should be isolated from each other, using different techniques of traffic engineering. This ensures SLA requirements for applications. Most policies are implemented using hardware switches and NIC (network interface), where the traffic is shared on the basis of priorities, clearly indicated in the form of labels of routers or of hosts, or implicitly defined by the range of ports on the switch. The goal is only to provide a high-performance network with predictable latency and bandwidth for different traffic types.

1.1.2 DC network architecture

DC network topology describes relations between switches and cluster servers. A common representation of a network is a graph with switches and hosts as vertexes, and lines connecting them as arcs. Topology largely determines the cost and performance of the network [10]. It also effects on a number of design trade-offs, including performance, packaging, redundancy and diversity of the routes, which, in turn, affects fault-tolerance of a network, average and maximum cable length, and, of course, final costs. Cisco and its Data Center 3.0 Design Guide [11] caused the spread of the co-called tree topology, resembling early telephone networks offered by Clos [12] with bandwidth aggregation at different levels of a network. Leiserson [13] from MIT proposed fat-tree topology, shown in Figure 1.1, in 1985. Its total throughput capacity increases in proportion to the number of ports of all hosts. Network is scalable by increasing the number of ports, its throughput capacity grows up linearly with ratio 0.5. Scalability and reliability are inseparable, since with DC upsizing, network reliability also has to grow.

1.1.3 Traffic in DC

Traffic within a DC network is measured and characterized in terms of flows represented by a sequence of packets from a source–host to a destination–host. In Internet protocols, each flow is represented by the values in the additional fields of a packet header: destination port number and transport type, for example, UDP or TCP. Traffic is asymmetric. For example, traffic from a client to a server (client–server requests) is

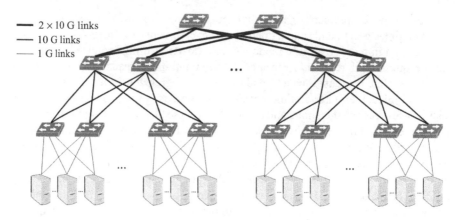

- 2 × 10 G links
- 10 G links
- 1 G links

Figure 1.1   Fat Tree topology

generally not heavy. Traffic from a server to a client (server–client requests) is usually significantly heavier. Inside a cluster, Internet traffic is very bursty, so the average figure for traffic flows is not very indicative. Because aggregated traffic is so volatile, it cannot be described by a normal distribution [14]. As a result, a network used for only 10% often discards packets. For better understanding the individual characteristics of a flow, applications use special "probe messages" to obtain information on the distribution of traffic flows. This information allows making a conclusion about the structure of network traffic and categorize its individual flows. The most common classification is to divide flows into two classes: "elephants" and "mice" [15].

"Elephants" have brought a large number of packets and have usually a long lifetime. Their behavior is irregular: they can "inject" (send) a large amount of packets into a network in a short period. Traffic in a flow is, typically, an ordered sequence of bytes. At the points of their intersection, traffic flows can make a congestion, which in its turn leads to the discards of the packets due to the buffer memory overflow in switches with weak congestion control mechanisms. "Elephants" can have a significant impact on system performance. Despite a relatively small number of "elephants," less than 1%, they may carry more than half the amount of data in a network.

The disbalance of a load, induced by an "elephant" flow, could adversely affect an innocent nearby flow, patiently waiting for a very busy channel, common for the routes of both flows. For example, the "elephant" flow from A to B can have a common (shared) part of the route with the flow from C to D. Any long-term competition for this shared route will increase the likelihood of discarding of the packets for the flow from C to D. This will lead to lack of confirmation at the transport level between a receiver and a sender, and to wait for a timeout and retransmission of packets discarded earlier. Since this timeout period is much longer than RTT time (Round Time Trip—time to deliver a package from a source to a destination and back), this additional delay can cause a significant loss of performance [16,17]. Usually, in DCs, bandwidth of a network inside a rack is almost the sum of links bandwidths between servers in rack and the TOR (Top Of the Rack) switch. The rack is in fact a computing cluster [18]. Bandwidth inside a rack can be much higher than bandwidth between racks, which reduces network costs and increases its load.

Intensity of traffic from each host is changed over time, which leads to the disbalance of a load. A disbalance may be caused by long competition for some channel that will discard packets. Traffic between clusters is usually less critical in time, and as a result can be scheduled, while inside a cluster, traffic consists of small packets with very irregular intensity. At the next level, between DCs, extensive connections with guaranteed high bandwidth are very expensive; a traffic has a more regular structure than inside a DC, which allows achieving high utilization of expensive channels. When congestion occurs, traffic of highest priority gets access to a channel. Understanding of the granularity of traffic flows and flow distributions in a network are essential for the allocation of the network capacity and for the use of traffic engineering methods.

1.1.4   Addressing and routing in DC

Addressing hosts as endpoints of a flow differs from the addressing of the middle switching elements on flow routes. It means that addresses can be considered as numeric equivalents of host names, similar to what we use in UNIX commands.

Address is unique and has a canonical form. In this form, it is used for routing to determine where the packet should be delivered to. A switch examines a packet header corresponding to the level where routing occurs, for example, IP address on the network level (L3) or Ethernet address on the data link level (L2). Ethernet switching uses ARP (Address Resolution Protocol) and RARP (Reverse Address Resolution Protocol), sending broadcast messages over a network on L2 to update the local caches for mapping between the addresses on L2 and the addresses on L3, and vice versa. L3 routing requires that each switch has to support, either statically or dynamically, the correspondence between a subnet mask and host IP addresses by Dynamic Host Configuration Protocol (DHCP).

In a network, each switch exchanges special messages with other switches and automatically fills in its routing table on Level 2. Each table can include up to 64k addresses. Beside all switches must support either Spanning Tree Protocol (STP), or Transparent Interconnect of Lots of Links (TRILL) protocol, which send each other the special service messages with characteristics of lines and corresponding ports thereby to avoid routing loops. However, TCP/IP legacy routing algorithms on L2 and L3 do not correspond to the DC requirements [19,20]. The special ones have been developed [9].

Routing algorithm determines the path by which the packet goes through the network. The route packet or the path in terms of graph theory, can be prescribed in advance while composing a message; it is called routing from the source. Either route can be formed while the package moves from switch to switch (hop). The routing from source implies that a sender knows in advance how to achieve each possible recipient. In this approach, each packet contains information about the entire route, which causes additional overhead and does not allow changing a route in case of errors. Source routing is usually used only for topology recognition and network initialization or during recovery after a failure, when the state of a switch is unknown. More flexible routing methods use hierarchy of the lookup tables on each switch.

For example, let us consider a standard Ethernet switch. When a packet arrives at an input port of the switch, it uses the fields from the packet header from lookup tables, and determine the next hop—the current output port of the switch. Good topology always has a variety of alternative paths that correspond to the different output ports of the switch. A variety of routes can be used by ECMP (equal-cost multipath protocol) to distribute the flow packets between several routes, or several switch ports. For uniform load distribution, the routing function on the switch makes a hash of several header fields, to determine the output port of the switch. In the case of the failures on line or on switch port, it can be fixed due to several alternative routes.

A route in network is called "minimal" if any shorter (i.e., with less hops) route in the network topology is not possible. Of course, there may be several minimum routes in network. For example, fat-tree topology has a plurality of minimum paths between any two nodes [13], while butterfly topology [10] has only one minimum or the shortest path between any two hosts. Sometimes it is better to choose not a minimal path, if this may help to avoid network overloading or any network problems. Minimal path length can range from minimal route + 1 to the length of the Hamiltonian path, where each switch is passed only once. In general, routing algorithm can consider not minimal paths that are minimal route + 1 long, but considering all nonminimum paths will cause unacceptable overhead costs.

1.1.5 Performance

Now, we will consider flow control and congestion control, which are the important aspects of network resources sharing, such as physical lines and buffer memory on switches. Flow control operates on different levels of the network stack: data link level, network level, transport level and for coordination of resources within applications as well. Its main purpose is to not allow the destination be flooded by a data flow from the source. In other words, the speed at which a source sends packets should match a speed at which the destination can process them. Sliding window technique can solve this problem. However, careful examination of the problem shows that in addition to the speed at which the destination can process packets from the source should also take into account the capabilities of communication lines and switches through which the packet flow goes. Even if a source sends packets at a speed that satisfied the ability of the destination to process them but exceeding the capacity of a switch on the flow route or the lowest bandwidth of a link on the route, packets will not reach destination due to network congestion.

Considering the problem of congestion, we should also take into account a packet scheduling and queuing policies in switches at the network level. This policy, for example, determines the policies for the input buffer of every switch. There are the following switching policies in DC: store and forward, virtual cut-through [14] and wormhole switching [21]. In order to understand the impact of these aspects on

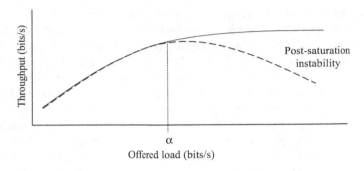

Figure 1.2   Throughput as load varies

network performance, let us consider first what is the end-to-end packet delay, which will denote as T:

$$T = \sum_{i=1}^{H} (t_i^p + L_i \times t_i^v + t_i^w),$$ (1.1)

where H is a number of hops, $L_i \times t_i^v$ is time needed to spread electric or electromagnetic signal through ith line with length L_i; t_i^w is packet delay in a switch, measured as the time interval from the moment when a packet arrives to the switch input port and till the moment when it leaves through the output port. The switches have multiple input ports with different packet flows going through them. In case of store-and-forward switching policy, different packets compete for space in buffer memory that affects t_i^w—time each packet spends in a switch.

The t_i^p denotes the transmission delay (also known as packetization delay), which is equal to the time required by the host network interface to push all bits of a packet into a line at the output port of a switch. For example, to push a 1,500-byte Ethernet packet into the line with a capacity of 1 Gbps, it will take about 12 μs. In case of store-and-forward switching, a packet will be buffered in a switch before being processed. Thus, transmission delay will occur at every hop. In case of virtual cut-through or wormhole switching, this delay will occur only at the destination point. Thus, store-and-forward switching can increase RTT delay for about 100 μs.

The t_i^v is a speed of a signal spreads along a line. It is proportional to the speed of light. In short lines (up to 10 m), electrical signal delay on the cupper cable is about to 5 ns, and in case of fiberglass cables it increase to 6 ns. However, for long line, fiberglass can provide shorter delays than electric cable, since it can be transmitted without reamplification over longer distances at high speed [22].

Increasing network load, the amount of data transmitted through this network will monotonically increase until network load reaches a saturation point (Figure 1.2) [1]. The saturation point means maximum amount of data in a network at the same time. Further load increasing will cause congestion. Congestion, in turn, will lead to packets discarding due to switch buffer overflows, which is quite common for Ethernet.

The packet discards will result in additional load on the transport level, responsible for detecting packet loss and retransmission. After a packet discard, the input queue of a switch will be exhausted for a while. It is noteworthy that packet loss due to transmission errors is a quite rare situation; therefore, packets are usually lost due to congestion, when network load exceeds the saturation point. Retransmission of the lost packets will only worsen the situation in the already congested network. Usually, the congestion control mechanisms in a network try to identify the symptoms of congestion as early as possible in order to block the injection of new packets into the network. For example, the congestion control mechanism in the TCP protocol uses the special window [23]. This protocol regulates the size of this window on the source side to adjust the speed of injection of new packets to the network.

1.1.6   TCP/IP stack issues

An important property of traditional (TCP/IP) protocol stack – the control of the data transmission, i.e., control of the network equipment, is not separable from the actual transmission of the data stream, so called control plane vs data plane. In the traditional TCP/IP protocol stack, the control plane and the data plane are not separable. This is the consequence of one of the fundamental principles of the network level organization assumed that each flow packet is routed independently; therefore, each packet must provide enough information to control its transmission properly [23]. This principle appeared because of the need for fail-safe data communication networks of any size and geographic extent. While the performance of computers and bandwidth of communication channels were not so high, it did not cause any problems. Over time, however, this principle has become a heavy burden. On the one hand, each network equipment (like a router or a switch) has to duplicate the same protocol stack software. On the other hand, each network equipment has to solve two unequal problems: the problem of choosing the optimal route and the problem of forwarding. The first problem is computationally heavy, very time-consuming task of optimization; the second one is a relatively not complicated task, which means modification of a packet header and transmitting this packet to a certain output port. The first task on each switch significantly increases the delay t_i^w. Moreover, because all network equipment operate independently, they spend many service messages for the coordination of the operation; this yields massive overheads. This is the price for the independence.

Another important feature of the TCP/IP protocols stack, which cause some problems was in a strict separation of packet header processing by level, i.e., at the transport level, only the part of a packet header corresponding to the transport level can be processed; at the network level, only network level header, etc. However, in many cases, we need to process the header fields all together. For example, this is useful to define flow types ("elephant" or "mouse"), and for security purposes. Finally, inseparability control plane from the data plane led to the fact that a hacker could launch attacks on the control plane from the data plane.

In the 1980s, the TCP/IP protocol stack developers have made another significant compromise: the same protocol stack used as for short-channels in several meters, as for channels in several kilometers. As long as processors and channels were slow, this compromise did not cause any problems, but later on, it has become a bottleneck and a source of significant delays compared to the time of the processor cycle. This was partly due to context switching in an operating system (OS) within TCP/IP/Ethernet stack operation, copying messages from application buffer to OS kernel space buffer and back again at the receiving side [17,18]. It took a lot of effort to decrease these costs. For example, bypassing the OS kernel, in order to reduce the cost of context switching for each message; the elimination of copying in memory, or by giving direct access from the network computer interface card to the application buffer. In order to reduce the impact on the performance of context switching between user space and kernel space, the OS bypassing is used where messages are immediately transmitted from the network interface to the application buffer. Just as a message arrives, the network interface card (NIC) copies this message into the application's buffer and release an interrupt, informing the application about the offset of the new message in its buffer. When a user process detects the updated value, the incoming message is processed entirely in the user space.

The mechanisms of interruption and direct access to application memory allow avoiding delays due to context switching, but processing time of an interrupt can be significant, especially when multiple interruptions take place. Therefore, although interruption helps to avoid delays on context switching, that also makes an access delay to a message volatile.

1.1.7 Network management system

As already noted, for routing purposes, each switch fills in its look-up table for packets routing by exchanging messages with other switches using special services. This approach led to the fact that the dissemination of information on any change in the network topology (line, switch or port failures) took a considerable time (also known as convergence time). Within this convergence time, all sorts of routing policies violations could occur. In traditional TCP/IP network, all network devices like routers, switches operate asynchronously. They just send to each other service messages to check if the neighbors are alive. This fact makes data communication network tolerant to the breakdown of a network device during network operation. However, this fact does not allow introducing the mathematically correct notion of network state in such asynchronous system, e.g. some devices just are in a process of state changing, the other ones have already finished this process, the rest ones even don't begin this process. Asynchronous control significantly restricts applying the formal methods to the network operation analysis. The good examples are BGP and DNS services where mostly the convergence time for a route announcement takes the hours. The asynchronous way of operation did not allow automatic identification and correction of failure during network operation. At the same time, it is clear that in DC, failure of any network element can cause avalanche of packets discards and of breaking already existed connections [24].

These features of the traditional protocol stack impose certain restrictions on the network infrastructure management system (NMS) [10]. In traditional networks, such systems collect, aggregate and analyze heterogeneous messages about states of network device and changes in their configuration. Thus, NMS systems can manage a network equipment configuration, provide monitoring their state and statistics about network traffic but do not allow managing the traffic flows directly. They normally use three main mechanisms: collection of statistics on network devices and their management through protocols such as SNMP and Telnet; standard mechanisms to collect statistics on the traffic using specialized protocols such as NetFlow, sFlow; specialized software agents located on network equipment to gather information. These monitoring systems support the collection of statistics only from ports of network device and only differentiated by the type of traffic such as unicast, broadcast and drop. Some network devices also support the collection of additional statistics for the specified IP source/destination addresses. However, as it has been said above, today in networks to support a given level of SLA, it needs the fine grain statistics, for example, about every user flow or every service. It is also noteworthy that NMS based on the SNMP protocol have significant limitations on the number of devices up to 50,000 and on the number of network interfaces up to 100,000.

1.1.8 Virtualization, scalability, flexibility

In cloud computing, generally there are two types of services: user interface, such as a Web service interface for Web pages, and internal services implemented by applications, such as indexing, searching, mapping, address translation (NAT), firewall, DPI, etc. As mentioned above, the flow of requests to the services is not uniform and very difficult to predict.

Strong binding an application software that deploy a particular service, to a particular physical server in DC causes several problems. First of all, this is fragmentation of computational resources, when server used partly does not allow running another application, even when the sum of the remains of the computational resources on other servers in DC let do this. The second, it is the problem of scalability of a computation: how to automatically run multiple instances of the same application with load balancing between instances to support the required performance of a service. In general, the application is a parallel system of interacting processes. What to do if not all processes of the application can be deployed on the same server?

To solve the above problems, we need virtualization and scaling of computing, storages and network resources [3,25]. Virtualization of computing and storage resources is used for a long time. All the issues of access to these resources and ensuring their safety still depends on the architecture and physical characteristics of DC network infrastructure. Virtual machines in DC can be prepared in minutes, but access to them is possible only through a network that needs to be deployed and secure enough, which takes a long time. Network infrastructure virtualization has been developed to solve this problem. Virtualization on a single physical network infrastructure, allows creating multiple isolated logical networks, where every network has its own topology and configuration, required by every individual DC customer. VXLAN and NVGRE protocols are examples that serve this task in traditional TCP/IP networks. Virtual eXtensible Local Area Network (VXLAN) [26] allows you to "overlay" networks on L2 over physical network on L3 level, with every such an overlay network as a separate segment of VXLAN. Therefore, VMs can be connected to each other only if they are in the same segment of VXLAN. Each VXLAN segment has a 24-bit ID called VXLAN Network ID (VNI), which enables to create up to 16 million VXLAN segments on a single physical network infrastructure. Using this technology, virtual machines send each other MAC-frames, so within the overlay networks of L2, there may not be VMs with identical MAC-addresses. VMs with the same MAC-address can run in different VXLAN segments, but the intersection of their traffic is excluded, as it is isolates based on VNI. VNI thus acts as the outer header of network packets that transmits a MAC-frame.

Another common network virtualization technology is Network Virtualization using Generic Routing Encapsulation (NVGRE) [27]. Network virtualization here refers to the creation of virtual topologies on L2 and (or) L3 levels over the physical network on L2 or L3 levels. In this virtual topology, connections are established by tunneling of Ethernet-frames through IP packets. Each virtual network of level L2 has a unique 24-bit identifier VSID (Virtual Subnet Identifier), which allows creating up to 16 million logical subnets within the same physical domain. Thus, each cloud services client can have a virtual subnet, uniquely defined by VSID, indicated in the outer header of a network packet and allowing various devices to communicate within a network.

It should be noted that virtualization of networks with the traditional TCP/IP architecture is not free of charge and brings additional overhead costs for packet encapsulation and additional software for every network devices, implementing the same relevant protocols. These overhead costs appear because all network devices are working independently and network management is not centralized. Moreover building an overlay, tunneling must be completed before the application on virtual machines will be launched and this procedure can take several minutes [3].

Using virtualization technics, it can effectively separate physical DC resources by isolating the virtualized entities. It is possible to clone virtual machines with identical application for the purposes of scaling the application to support the performance of the service implemented by the application and to ensuring availability of the service. For this purpose, each virtualized service in a cloud must have a performance monitor and an availability monitor. The first one should start scaling of a relevant application in case service performance goes down; the second one should restart a virtual machine with a proper application in case of the service shut down. The main thing is that everything a user gets in a cloud is a service. Virtual machine, virtual network, virtual storage, virtual NAT, virtual load balancer—all these just are services.

1.2 Software-defined networks

1.2.1 *How can we split control plane and data plane?*

Software-defined network or SDN is the response to the problems outlined above: the imbalance in the distribution and the duplication of tasks between data and control planes, complexity and duplication of software in network devices, TCP/IP stack limitations, overprovisioning of resources, inability to fully account SLA requirements, monitoring and management constraints, the complexity of the network virtualization and significant overheads, e.g., a large amount of broadcast messages (ARP, DHCP).

In SDN, control and data planes are separated to isolate management functions (routers, switches, etc.) from the forwarding devices to the applications running in a dedicated place (called controller). This reduces software complexity and its duplication in network devices, centralizes network management and control. The wide spread of such networks began in 2006 after Google's announcement about the success transition to the new approach. This approach developed rapidly in Stanford University and Berkeley University. Research topics widely conducted in the world found support not only in academic area, but also were actively perceived by the leading manufacturers of telco equipment. In March 2011, they formed an Open Networking Foundation (ONF) as a top organization to push SDN research toward to production. It was founded by Google, Deutsche Telekom, Facebook, Microsoft, Verizon and Yahoo. The ONF is rapidly growing and already includes companies such as Brocade, Citrix, Oracle, Dell, Ericsson, HP, IBM, Marvell, NEC and others. One of the first practical implementation of SDN Company offered Nicira, which became soon a part of VMware for $1.26B [28].

The main ideas of SDN are:

- Physical separation of control and data planes in network equipment. Forwarding devices transmit packets according to the rules that were laid down in them; thus all logics are migrated to a separate place called the controller.
- The transition from management of individual network devices to management of the entire network at once—logically centralized control.
- An open software programmable interface between the network applications and the transport network. The interface should allow not only to configure and to monitor the device, but also to give the possibility for programing a reaction to events in a network, to define the behavior we need on the different situations in the network.

The architecture of SDN can be divided on the following planes (see Figure 1.3):

- The infrastructure plane with a set of network devices (switches and links).
- The control plane with the controller that provides network services and application programing interface for managing the network.
- The application plane with a set of networking applications for flexible and efficient network management and control.

The API between the infrastructure plane and the control plane is called Southbound API, and the interface between the application plane and the control plane – is called Northbound API. Standardization of these interfaces is a key point to realize the ideas of SDN.

Today, the most promising and an actively developing standard for Southbound API of SDN is an OpenFlow (OpenFlow version 1.3+). It is an open standard that

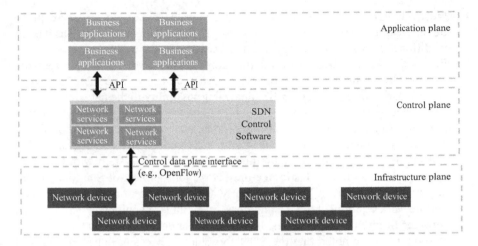

Figure 1.3 SDN architecture

describes the requirements for the switch that supports the OpenFlow protocol for remote management of network equipment. Northbound API standard still does not appear. This reduces applications portability between controllers. However, all controllers should have a set of mandatory functions. This is discussed more in the following chapters.

The advantages of SDN include the following:

- Facilitating network management by enabling centralized control and monitoring. SDN allows quickly configuring the services on the entire network at once other than configuring each device separately. For example, setting the single L2 broadcast domain for the ten's devices takes a couple of minutes compared to several hours in traditional approach. Configuring on backup paths in case of any failures in the network (link broken, etc.) and the dynamic rerouting in case of overloading previously require a lot of time and effort in order to configure each device separately. In SDN, the controller takes all complexity by automatic install appropriate rules on all devices.
- Centralization of control allows to define the term of the network state mathematically correctly. This opens the way to construct mathematical models of a network and to use the power of the mathematical technics for checking the correctness of the network operations, its topological properties such as cycles, the legitimacy of the traffic forwarding through a given network segment and an unauthorized packet loss.
- Network devices have become simpler. The routers as an independent network device are no longer needed in SDN networks. There are only programmable switches. Switch software does not duplicate the entire TCP/IP stack in each device, significantly reducing latency to packet processing, typical of the traditional network devices (this point was were discussed above).

- Network management becomes faster due to the possibility to configure all the devices along the traffic path simultaneously, rather than sequentially, as it is the traditional networks (learning switches/routers occurs at each hop).
- Forwarding devices becomes programmable by users and therefore open for innovation. Also ability to analyze packet headers at all levels from L2 to L4 at once significantly strengthen the traffic analyzing possibility in the network.
- SDN concept provides extensive capabilities for network monitoring and control the forwarding devices. This allows significantly to increase the flexibility of statistics granularity and diversity, e.g., per each client. SDN significantly simplifies the interoperability of the network management system with OSS/BSS systems. For example, ElasticTree project is a joint project of Stanford University and the Google [29]. It dynamically determines the workload of the server and network equipment in DC, and turns on/off unused equipment. All flows are rerouted through other switches. It reduces power consumption by 60%.
- It should also be noted that the SDN forwarding devices have become cheaper comparing with their traditional analogs. SDN switches do not include the management and control protocols like traditional ones.
- The new segment of the network market is opened that is the market of controllers and applications software, which is independent from network hardware market. High competition level and independent to the particular vendor's equipment (vendor lock) will bring the network to a new level.

The phrase "SDN means thinking differently about networking" well reflects the basic idea of SDN. Network technologies are no longer a craft art of engineering. Now, it is not necessary to think in terms of traditional approaches that do not keep up with the rapidly changing environment.

1.2.2   OpenFlow protocol and programmable switching: basics

As already mentioned, OpenFlow is one of the most popular and widespread implementation of the SDN concept. Other implementations will be discussed later.

The main components of software-defined network are (Figure 1.4):

- OpenFlow switch;
- Controller;
- Protected control channel for a switch controller communication.

An OpenFlow divides the network routing functions and the packet forwarding functions by leveraging OpenFlow protocol. Currently, the latest version of OpenFlow is 1.5, adopted in 2014 [30]. However, the most popular version is the OpenFlow 1.3.4, sold in most hardware. OpenFlow Controller that controls the communication paths and OpenFlow Switch that controls the packet forwarding are the elements that constitute a network. In an OpenFlow architecture, a data flow controlled on per-flow basis identifies packets as a flow with combinations of L2 header fields, IP header fields and TCP/UDP port field.

OpenFlow switch consists of one or more flow tables that are used for forwarding packets. Each flow table in the switch contains a set of records. Each record consists of

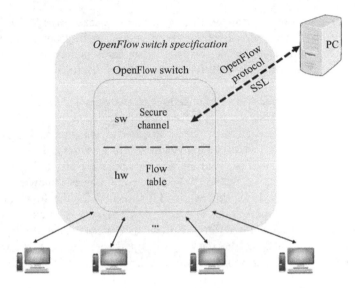

Figure 1.4   OpenFlow controller interacts with OpenFlow switch via OpenFlow protocol

attributes fields, counters and a set of instructions that apply to packet. Once a packet is received, the switch searches the appropriate record in the first flow table. If there is a flow entry that matches the packet, the packet is processed according to actions defined in the flow entry. Note that, even while Secure Channel is disconnected, if a flow entry exists, the same action is to be executed. If there is no appropriate flow entries in the tables, there are several options for the switches: search can be continued in the following tables, the unknown packet can be dropped or sent to the controller (packet_in event) for further understanding what to do with this new flow.

Typical actions include:

- Transmitting packets by specifying output interface. We can specify more than one output interface.
- Rewriting MAC addresses, VLAN tag or IP addresses, IEEE802.1p priorities or DSCP value in a VLAN tag, etc.
- Transmitting packets from the switch to the controller, and then the controller determine what action to take depending on the situation, and register flow entries to the flow table of the switch.

The controller uses OpenFlow protocol messages via Secure Channel to add, modify or delete a flow entry. It can also manage ports and configurations, or collect statistics information.

The switch also has single Group table. It consists of entries called groups that represent a set of common actions for flows: broadcast, multipath, fast rerouting, link aggregation. Each group record contains a list of actions containers with special semantics depending on the type of group. There are following four types of groups: (1) All—all containers are performed actions on packet (broadcast); (2) Select group executes only one randomly chosen set of actions in the group (multipath, link aggregation); (3) Indirect group performs a certain set of actions in the group; and (4) Fast failover group runs the first lived set of actions (liveness means whether the specified physical port is up).

OpenFlow also provides opportunities for QoS management for the network traffic. There are two ways. The first way is the priority queuing support. OpenFlow provides ability to specify for each traffic flow the queue to which its packets should go. Each queues has priority. The queue with highest priority is served first. For example, you can specify that Skype connection's packets have a high priority and have to go ahead the rest of the traffic. The second way is bandwidth metering support. It is possible to limit the bandwidth allocated for the flows in the network. For this purpose, OpenFlow has special meter counters that check how many packets per second have passed for the flow. If a predefined limit is exceeded (e.g., greater than 10 Mbps), the packet is dropped. For example, the traffic for photos backup on a cloud storage should spend no more than 5% of the channel bandwidth.

In SDN, the controller is a single point of failure. If it shuts down, the network will be out of service. In order to avoid this situation, OpenFlow opens the ability to use multiple controllers that control the same switch. Each controller has its own role in the set of running controllers. The master controller is always the single one controller that can control the equipment. The slave controllers can't change flow tables in the devices. In the slave role, there might be several controllers at the same time. The equal controllers have full access to the devices under their control. It's not possible to have both equal and master controllers for the forwarding device. It is not safe to use many equal controllers since there is no guarantee that controllers don't send inconsistency rules. The controllers can select by their own who the master controller is.

There are two alternative implementations of SDN other than OpenFlow. The first SDN implementation is about centralized management of an overlay networks based on tunneling approach (VXLAN, NVGRE, etc.). Virtual networking have been widely detailed in Section 1.8. Today, the OVSDB [31] is the most widely used protocol to configure virtual network in DC: tunnel configuration/termination and setting up routes between tunnels. This way doesn't allow to program reaction of network failures. The second SDN implementation relies on using traditional network equipment managing by protocols like NETCONF/YANG [32] or PCEP [33]. Vendors of network equipment provide an open API for configuration and monitoring capabilities of their devices. Note, it is important to recognize that all of these options resolve particular problems, while OpenFlow offers opportunities for extending the network functionality, rather than just using the same standard protocols and approaches to networking.

Above we just mentioned the problem of managing virtual networks. Existing approaches to manage virtual networks have high convergence time in case of network failures since they rely on traditional networks, do not allow to automatically add new tunneling termination points: consider the SLA requirements, and have additional overhead on packets size due to additional encapsulation header. OpenFlow allows to solve these problems more effectively through managing the whole network from a single point. If a link is broken, the controller can efficiently identify that overlay tunnels are affected and reroute them according to their SLA requirements. There are also approaches that have the ability to completely avoid the additional encapsulation: required information is encoded into optional or unused fields in the packets (e.g., src/dst mac) [34].

1.2.3 SDN controller, northbound API, controller applications

In SDN/OpenFlow, a controller is the central element, which consolidates all functionality to control the network services. The controller does not manage the network by its own, it provides programing interfaces (Northbound API) to manage the network. Thus, the actual network management tasks are done by network applications that use Northbound API to program their own protocol tasks. It should be noted that Northbound API has to support a wide spectrum of applications for network management tasks.

The controller's API has to cover the following main features:

1. The first, API provides the ability to create applications based on centralized programing model. That is, applications are written as if the entire network is presented on the same machine (we can use Dijkstra's algorithm to compute the shortest path, rather than Bellman–Ford). This requires the support of a network centralized state: the state of switches (the number of network interfaces/ports, their speed and the up/down status, the current state of the rules in the flow tables), topology [network graph is a set of pairs (<switch, port>, <switch, port>)], the actual loading of links (utilized bandwidth).
2. The second, the API provides the ability to operate in applications using high-level terms—e.g., user name and host name, rather than low-level settings—the IPs and MACs. This allows to setup the network behavior, regardless of the underlying network topology. In this case, the controller should support the mapping between the low-level and high-level terms e.g., host name "PC_hadoop" has IP address 10.172.15.78 and locates at the switch #50 and the port #1.

Thus, controller's applications are centralized programs using high-level abstractions as opposed to the development of distributed algorithms specifying low-level details as in traditional networks. The controller itself implements a basic set of functionality of OpenFlow protocol such as creating, editing and deleting rules in switches' flow tables.

Currently, there are a large number of open-source controllers written in different programing languages with a different set of applications. The most often used the controllers are Pox [35] (Stanford/Berkley, Python, for training and teaching), Ryu [36] (NTT, Python, to develop PoC projects, a wide range of applications), OpenDaylight [37] (Linux Foundation/Cisco, Java, enterprise/DC network management with using netconf/Yang, OVSDB), ONOS [38] (OpenNetworkFoundation/OnLab/Stanford, Java, backbone network of service providers, distributed controller), RunOS [39] (ARCCN/MSU, C++, research in SDN programing, service model for Metro Ethernet networks).

One of the key controller's indexes is its performance:

1. The maximum throughput in terms of the number of events occurring in the network that the controller can process and respond per second (i/o performance): turning off a switch or port, new packet arriving that does not match against any rules in the flow tables.
2. The delay or response time is the number of microseconds needed to process single event in the network.

These numbers strongly depend on the programing language and current CPU frequency [40]. The throughput varies by an order of magnitude for the controllers, written on Python, Java and C/C++: 10k, 100k, 1M, respectively (on 1 core 2.4 GHz). The delay is measured from 50 to 300 μs (fastest value is for C/C++). The conducted research about network characteristics in DC in US have shown that the peak load on the controller can reach 10M events per second [41].

Second key SDN controller's feature is programing. During developing the effective network applications, one has to keep in mind that the network can be programed all at the same time, avoiding unnecessary communication with the controller. For example, imagine an application supplies a tunnel with a client given MAC address from one switch to another one using a given path through the network. It can be implemented in two different ways. A packet comes to the first switch in the network. The switch does not know what to do with the packet and sends it to the controller in the packet_in message. The controller reads the MAC address and it knows where to send this packet based on the provided path, and finally sends the rule to the switch that moves all packet in this flow to the right port on the path. Then the packet arrives on next switch where the same steps repeat. This will happen again and again until the packet reaches the destination. This is not efficient implementation since the controller manages the entire network at once. Thus, we should install rules on all switched along the path immediately when we receive the packet on the controller first time.

There are two models for application implementation: first, when the controller adds rules in the reactive mode (in response to packet_in OpenFlow message with first seen packet); second, the controller fills the known rules for the service in advance of the proactive mode. For example, in the above example, the specified route can be directly installed on all switches in the network before any packets come. In this case, further communication with the controller would not be required.

It is worth noting that the development of applications is not an easy task for the programmer, and hides a lot of pitfalls. For example, applications running on the controller set rules on the switches without knowing anything about each other. Then they can install mutually contradictory rules on the switch and applications' tasks will not work correctly. The controller should resolve such conflicts. For example, Maple [42] defines rules that conflicts at the controller level, or Vermont [43], which operates as a proxy between the controller and the network and verifies the correctness of the installed rules.

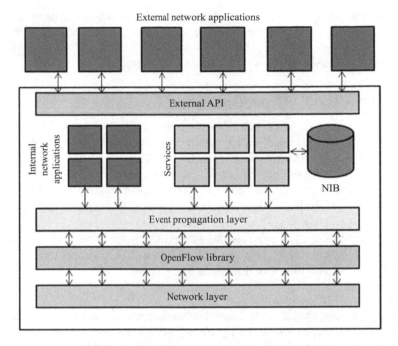

Figure 1.5   An OpenFlow controller architecture

Figure 1.5 shows the common OpenFlow controller architecture. At the bottom, the network layer is responsible for interaction with switches via TCP. The main task here is to listen incoming connections from new switches on port 6653. The Open-Flow level main task is to parse OpenFlow messages from the TCP stream (packet_in, feature reply, echo request/reply, etc.). Next, event propagation level is responsible for implementing a publisher/subscriber mechanism inside the controller. New OpenFlow events are distributed across subscribed modules. Further, the controller typically has two types of applications: services that implement commonly used functionality (e.g., routing or topology discovery) and ordinary applications that implement the necessary network services. All applications can use the database to store the information they need. At the top, it is one of the most important levels—an interface for communication with externally running applications. Typically, this layer implements REST interface to the controller [44]. Then, the level with external applications that can be developed in any programing language. These applications are well suited for the implementation of logic not requiring high interaction with the network, for example, monitoring. Implementing the same application inside the controller allows to quickly respond on events happened in the network.

The following applications for the DC are show as examples:

- Load balancing of requests to the server farm from end users. For example, CDN.
- Access control list to determine illegitimate user access to the network.

- Adjust the network to micro service architecture, when the communication between the most active services has to go through the dedicated links with minimum delay.
- Creating a virtual network to the needs of end users.

1.2.4   Open issues and challenges

OpenFlow is still tight to packet headers related to TCP/IP stack. The following versions of OpenFlow protocol should be able to configure devices by needed headers and protocols. Some tasks are covered by P4 [45], POF [46].

In the world of OpenFlow, it is not a well-considered integration with orchestration and management systems. For example, when deploying MapReduce service, there is no possibility to configure the DC's network for minimal delays between nodes.

Also, the SDN usually controls the single DC's network. In real case, data are often spread across multiple geographically distributed DC.

In the near future, the main directions are:

1.   Northbound API standardization.
2.   Extensive usage of systems to control network applications behavior, sandboxing, resolve conflicts, checking the legitimacy of their actions.
3.   Deeper integration with DC management systems and OSS/BSS.

1.3   Summary and conclusion

In today's networking world, there is a dire shortage of traditional networking capabilities. SDN offers a separation of data and control planes, increases the granularity of the data control, simplifies the network equipment, the integration with management systems and OSS/BSS. This automates and accelerates the development of new services.

For Big Data SDN can give the following:

- Simplify the process for Storing and Processing Big Data in cloud-computing environment.
- Improve the performance by dynamic load balancing and by fine-grain routing control.
- Make easy the adaptation of a tenant topology and tenant performance indexes to the application requirements.
- Support QoS aware application for Big Data.
- Simplify data management by SDN-based storage area network.
- Allow energy-efficient routing for Big Data services and energy-aware network provisioning.
- Improve fault tolerance for Big Data processing in DC.
- Increase the information security of cloud computing.

References

[1] Amazing Facebook statistics, demographic and facts – http://expanded ramblings.com/index.php/by-the-numbers-17-amazing-facebook-stats/, 2017.

[2] Hoelzle, U. and Barroso, L. A. The Datacenter as a Computer: An Introduction to the Design of Warehouse-Scale Machines (1st ed.). Morgan & Claypool Publishers, 2009.

[3] Mudigonda, J., Yalagandula, P., Mogul, J., Stiekes, B. and Pouffary, Y. Net-Lord: A scalable multi-tenant network architecture for virtualized datacenters. SIGCOMM Computer Communication Review 41, 4 (2011), 62–73.

[4] Barroso, L.A., Dean, J. and Holzle, U. Web search for a planet: The Google cluster architecture. IEEE Micro 23, 2 (2003), 22–28.

[5] Abts, D. and Felderman, R. A guided tour of data-center networking. Communications of the ACM 55, 6 (2012), 44–51.

[6] Al-Fares, M., Loukissas, A. and Vahdat, A. A scalable, commodity data-center network architecture. In Proceedings of the ACM SIGCOMM 2008 Conference on Data Communication (2008), 63–74; http://doi.acm.org/10.1145/1402958.1402967.

[7] Wilson, C., Ballani, H., Karagiannis, T. and Rowtron, A. Better never than late: Meeting deadlines in datacenter networks. In Proceedings of the ACM SIGCOMM 2011 Conference (2011), 50–61; http://doi.acm.org/10.1145/2018436.2018443.

[8] Amdahl's Law – http://en.wikipedia.org/wiki/Amdahl's_law, 2017

[9] Greenberg, A., Hamilton, J., Maltz, D.A. and Patel, P. The cost of a cloud: Research problems in data center networks. SIGCOMM Computer Communications Review 39, 1 (2008), 68–73; http://doi.acm.org/10.1145/1496091.1496103.

[10] Dally, W. and Towles, B. Principles and Practices of Interconnection Networks. Morgan Kaufmann Publishers, San Francisco, CA, 2003.

[11] Cisco Data Center Infrastructure 3.0 Design Guide. Data Center DesignIP Network Infrastructure; http://www.cisco.com/en/US/docs/solutions/Enterprise/Data_Center/DC_3_0/DC-3_0_IPInfra.html.

[12] Clos, C. A study of non-blocking switching networks. The Bell System Technical Journal 32, 2 (1953), 406–424.

[13] Leiserson, C.E. Fat-trees: Universal networks for hardware-efficient super-computing. IEEE Transactions on Computers 34, 10 (1985), 892–901.

[14] Kermani, P. and Kleinrock, L. Virtual cut-through: A new computer communication switching technique, Computer Networks 3, 4 (1976), 267–286; http://www.sciencedirect.com/science/article/pii/0376507579900321.

[15] Mori, T., Uchida, M., Kawahara, R., Pan, J. and Goto, S. Identifying elephant flows through periodically sampled packets. In Proceedings of the 4th ACM SIGCOMM Conference on Internet Measurement (2004); 115–120.

[16] Ballani, H., Costa, P., Karagiannis, T. and Rowtron, A. Towards predictable data-center networks. In Proceedings of the ACM SIGCOMM 2011 Conference (2011), 242–253.

[17] Protocol buffers: A language-neutral, platform-neutral extensible mechanism for serializing structured data http://code.google.com/apis/protocolbuffers/, 2017.

[18] Rumble, S.M., Ongaro, D., Stutsman, R., Rosenblum, M. and Ousterhout, J.K. It's time for low latency. In Proceedings of the 13th Usenix Conference on Hot Topics in Operating Systems (2011).

[19] Greenberg, A., Hamilton, J. R., Jain, N., *et al.* VL2: A scalable and flexible data center network. In Proceedings of the ACM SIGCOMM 2009 Conference on Data Communication (2009): 51–62; http://doi.acm.org/10.1145/1592568.1592576.

[20] Mysore, R.N., Pamboris, A., Farrington, N., *et al.* PortLand: A scalable fault-tolerant layer2 data center network fabric. SIGCOMM Computer Communication Review 39, 4 (2009), 39–50.

[21] Ni, L. M. and McKinley, P. K. A survey of wormhole routing techniques in direct networks. Computer 26, 2 (1993), 62–76.

[22] Vahdat, A., Liu, H., Zhao, X. and Johnson, C. The emerging optical data center. Presented at the Optical Fiber Communication Conference. OSA Technical Digest (2011); http://www.opticsinfobase.org/abstract.

[23] Cerf, V. and Icahn R.E. A protocol for packet network intercommunication. SIGCOMM Computer Communication Review 35, 2 (2005), 71–82.

[24] Gill, P., Jain, N. and Nagappan, N. Understanding network failures in data centers: measurement, analysis, and implications. In Proceedings of the ACM SIGCOMM 2011 Conference (2011), 350–361; http://doi.acm.org/10.1145/2018436.2018477.

[25] Vahdat, A., Al-Fares, M., Farrington, N., Mysore, R.N., Porter, G. and Radhakrishnan, S. Scale-out networking in the data center. IEEE Micro 30, 4 (2010), 29–41; http://dx.doi.org/10.1109/MM.2010.72.

[26] Virtual eXtensible Local Area Network (VXLAN): A Framework for Overlaying Virtualized Layer 2 Networks over Layer 3 Networks – https://tools.ietf.org/html/rfc7348, 2014.

[27] NVGRE: Network Virtualization Using Generic Routing Encapsulation – https://tools.ietf.org/html/rfc7637, 2015.

[28] Techcrunch, VMware Buys Nicira For $1.26 Billion And Gives More Clues About Cloud Strategy – https://techcrunch.com/2012/07/23/vmware-buys-nicira-for-1-26-billion-and-gives-more-clues-about-cloud-strategy/, 2012.

[29] Heller, B., Seetharaman, S., Mahadevan, P., *et al.* ElasticTree: saving energy in data center networks. In Proceedings of the 7th USENIX conference on Networked systems design and implementation (NSDI'10). USENIX Association, Berkeley, CA, USA (2010), 1–17.

[30] OpenFlow Switch Specification (version 1.5) – https://www.opennetworking.org/images/stories/downloads/sdn-resources/onf-specifications/openflow/openflow-switch-v1.5.0.noipr.pdf, 2014.

[31] OVSDB: The Open vSwitch Database Management Protocol – https://tools.ietf.org/html/rfc7047, 2013.

[32] YANG: A Data Modeling Language for the Network Configuration Protocol (NETCONF) – https://tools.ietf.org/html/rfc6020, 2010.

[33] PCEP: Path Computation Element Communication Protocol – https://tools.ietf.org/html/rfc5440, 2009.

[34] Al-Shabibi, A., De Leenheer, M., Gerola, M., *et al.* OpenVirteX: make your virtual SDNs programmable. In Proceedings of the Third Workshop on Hot Topics in Software Defined Networking (HotSDN '14). ACM, New York, NY, USA (2014), 25–30. http://ovx.onlab.us.

[35] Pox OpenFlow Controller – https://github.com/noxrepo/pox, 2013.

[36] Ryu OpenFlow Controller – http://osrg.github.com/ryu/, 2017.

[37] OpenDaylight SDN Controller – https://www.opendaylight.org/, 2017.

[38] Open Network Operating System – http://onosproject.org/, 2017.

[39] The Runos SDN/OpenFlow Controller – https://arccn.github.io/runos/, 2017.

[40] Shalimov, A., Zuikov, D., Zimarina, D., Pashkov, V. and Smeliansky, R. Advanced Study of SDN/OpenFlow controllers. Proceedings of the CEE-SECR13: Central and Eastern European Software Engineering Conference in Russia, ACM SIGSOFT, October 23–25, 2013, Moscow, Russian Federation.

[41] Benson, T., Akella, A., and Maltz, D. 2010. Network traffic characteristics of data centers in the wild. In Proceedings of the 10th ACM SIGCOMM conference on Internet measurement (IMC '10). ACM, New York, NY, USA, 267–280.

[42] Voellmy, A., Wang, J., Yang, Y. R., Ford, B. and Hudak, P. Maple: simplifying SDN programming using algorithmic policies. In Proceedings of the ACM SIGCOMM 2013 Conference on SIGCOMM (SIGCOMM '13). ACM, New York, NY, USA, 2013, 87–98.

[43] Altukhov, V. S., Chemeritskiy, E. V., Podymov, V. V. and Zakharov, V. A. Vermont – A Toolset For Checking SDN Packet Forwarding Policies On-Line. In Proceedings of the 2014 International Science and Technology Conference "Modern Networking Technologies: SDN&NFV". Moscow, Russia (2014), pp. 7–12.

[44] "Web Services Architecture". World Wide Web Consortium. 3.1.3 Relationship to the World Wide Web and REST Architectures. – https://www.w3.org/TR/2004/NOTE-ws-arch-20040211/#relwwwrest, 2004.

[45] Bosshart, P., Daly, D., Gibb, G., *et al.* P4: programming protocol-independent packet processors. SIGCOMM Computer Communication Review 44, 3 (July 2014), 87–95. http://p4.org/.

[46] Song, H. Protocol-oblivious forwarding: unleash the power of SDN through a future-proof forwarding plane. In Proceedings of the second ACM SIGCOMM workshop on Hot topics in software defined networking (HotSDN '13). ACM, New York, NY, USA (2013), 127–132. http://www.poforwarding.org/.

Chapter 2

SDN implementations and protocols

Cristian Hernandez Benet*,
Kyoomars Alizadeh Noghani*, and Javid Taheri*

Software-Defined Networking (SDN) aims to break the network paradigm by decoupling the network logic from the underlying devices. Nowadays, the use of SDN is rapidly expanding and gaining ground from data centres to cloud providers and carrier transport networks. Data centres, cloud providers and Internet service providers (ISP) have different challenges to overcome and the need to meet the contracted quality of service from their customers. Therefore, SDN implementation challenges vary depending on the area of the network and traffic properties. There is no doubt that SDN brings great benefits for providers and administrators by reducing expenses and network complexity, while improving the performance and flexibility. Academia and industry try to overcome the challenges and propose new solutions for the emerging SDN technology. Despite the progress already made for SDN implementation, there are still some open issues to be addressed. This chapter begins by explaining the main SDN concepts with the focus on a SDN controller. It presents the most important aspects to consider when we desire to go from traditional network to a SDN networks. We present an in-depth analysis of the most commonly used and modern SDN controllers and analyse the main features, capabilities and requirements of one of the presented controllers. OpenFlow is the standard leading in the market allowing the management of the forwarding plane devices such as routers or switches. While there are other standards with the same aim, OpenFlow has secured a position in the market and has been expanded rapidly. Therefore, an analysis is presented on a different OpenFlow compatible device for the implementation of an SDN network. This study encompasses both software and hardware solutions along with the scope of implementation or use of these devices. This chapter ends up presenting a description of OpenFlow protocol alternatives, a more detailed description of OpenFlow and its components and other well-known southbound protocols involved for the management and configuration of the devices.

*Department of Mathematics and Computer Science, Karlstads University, Sweden

2.1   How SDN is implemented

This section presents an in-depth analysis of the logical infrastructure of the SDN network and abstractions. Several abstractions are necessary since it helps to split the complex network paradigm under a list of sub-problems making it easier and more flexible to find an independent suitable solution for each sub-problem. As introduced in the previous chapter, SDN divides the network problem into three main abstractions: data plane, control plane and management plane. These planes are connected together through interfaces to allow the communication between the planes, exchange information and translate instructions and operations. This section focuses on the control plane abstraction concerning to the controller, which is responsible for conducting how the data plane elements behave. Such behaviour is usually leveraged by the applications developed on top of the controller, i.e. at the management plane. These applications in combination with the controller enforce the data plane devices to perform certain actions aiming to control and manage the network traffic. The controller or the 'network brain' has two main interfaces that allow the communication with the other two aforementioned planes. The first interface is the southbound interface that defines the set of instructions on the protocol responsible for exchanging information between the data plane devices and the controller(s). The second interface is the northbound interface that facilitates the interaction between the applications and the data plane devices.

All controllers provide a set of modules or functionalities, a.k.a. core-controller functions [1], designed to powerfully manage and control the network elements. These modules define the core of the controller that can be subsequently leveraged and extended by applications developed by the users in the management plane. Some of these functionalities are the network topology manager, network device manager, network device discovery, basic routing and forwarding protocols [2,3]. The network device discovery and manager define a set of instructions and methods to learn, gather information, configure and manage network devices such as switches and/or routers. Similarly, the network manager stores all the information related to the topology such as the connections between devices, ports, links, etc. A basic routing and forwarding module are usually provided to allow the communication between end-hosts within/inside or outside the network.

2.1.1   Implementation aspects

The implementation of the controller is not only structured around the selection of the controller operating system (OS) but also the design decisions such as its location and architecture [1]. The main idea of SDN revolves around its centralization since this provides a global view of the network. However, depending on the network size or the volume of incoming requests to handle, it may be necessary to use a group of controllers. This new paradigm opens a crucial debate on the network control plane architecture, centralized or distributed. However, when we talk about centralization we have to distinguish between logically or physically. Controllers can be physically distributed around the network and have a logically centralized control plane. On the other hand, placing several controllers connected to our topology in the same cluster can result in a physically and logically centralize architecture. In addition, hybrid solutions might be necessary for geographically distributed networks. These controllers can be configured to handle a set of devices to balance the load of the network. In the aforementioned scenario, two types of situation are possible: only one controller is active (taking the forwarding decisions of the network) or all are part of the decision-making.

The main challenges for the last approach are the synchronization of the controllers and the balanced distribution of the load. For this alternative, the controller should support east-west communication to exchange information about the network, statistics or applications. This information should be synchronized to take appropriate actions, e.g. by allowing or denying the communication to an incoming traffic in a firewall application or re-routing the traffic due to a link failure. The signalling between the controllers and the switches is another important design aspect that could impact on the performance of the network. There are two types of communication channel: in-band and out-band signalling. Sometimes, because of budget constraints, the control traffic is sent through the same physical connection between data plane devices. This process is referred as in-band signalling. In this case, it is recommended to have more than one connection between the controller and the data plane devices to avoid a single point of failure. Typically, data centres use out-signalling because of its reliability and security.

2.1.2   Existing SDN controllers

There are currently a large number of existing SDN controllers provided by vendors and open-source communities. Each controller has its own features, programming language and architecture. Some of these controllers are based on languages such as C, C++, Java and Python among many others. Depending on the scope of the controller, the solution provided for its architecture can be centralized or distributed. Despite the apparent drawbacks that centralized architecture may imply, some reasons such as achieving a high throughput and increase processing performance [1] may be behind the design decision. Although the apparent performance problems in the centralize architecture, the use of multithreading can significantly improve the controller performance. On the other hand, a distributed architecture can scale-up on-demand under certain requirements or improve the reliability of the system by operating with several controllers or designating a back-up controller. Some examples of the existing controllers are provided in Table 2.1. The standards supported and the external communication with the controller through the northbound interfaces depends on the controller platform. The majority of these controllers support other southbound standards than OpenFlow, for example, OVSDB or ForCES. Moreover, the northbound interfaces may be implemented in the same language of the controller such as Python/Java APIs or other solutions, for instance, REST API. Other features such as graphical user interface for managing the controller are also available in some of the controllers, e.g. OpenDaylight, Floodlight and ONOS.

Table 2.1   List of the most used controllers with some implementation features such as language, architecture and sort of licence

Controller	Programming language	Architecture	Licence
NOX	C++	Centralize	GPLv3
Opendaylight	Java	Distributed	EPL v1.0
ONOS	Java	Distributed	Apache 2.0/BSD
Ryu	Python	Centralized	Apache 2.0
Floodlight	Java	Centralized	Apache 2.0
POX	Python	Centralized	GPLv3/Apache
Beacon	Java	Centralized	GPLv2/BSD
Maestro	Java	Centralized	LGPLv2.1
Flowvisor	C	Distributed	–
Onix	C, Python	Distributed	Commercial
OpenContrail	Java	Distributed	Apache 2.0

2.2   Current SDN implementation using OpenDaylight

As part of this book chapter, we select and introduce a well-known controller: Open-Daylight. We provide an overview of the main benefits, available modules and features. This controller is selected due to the extensive support from the industry, e.g. CISCO, BROCADE, NEC and ERICSSON, among others, and a large SDN community.

2.2.1   OpenDaylight

OpenDaylight is an open source controller hosted by the Linux Foundation [4] and supported by many SDN vendors, industry and a SDN community with the commitment to collaborate and cooperate in building a uniquely SDN framework. The project is not only based on OpenFlow standard but on the extensive set of protocols aimed to encourage and give solutions towards the SDN and network function virtualization (NFV) technologies. The idea is based on a collaborative development of modules across the framework to both extend existing standards and create new standards and novelty solutions. Therefore, both industry and developers can benefit from working together by creating new technologies or enhancing existing products by developing new standards or solutions to mitigate current problems such as high energy consumption, low cross-section bandwidth, etc. At the time of this writing, boron was the last effort from the OpenDaylight community bringing its fifth release version.

OpenDaylight framework is composed of different technologies addressing different aspects of its management. These technologies and languages are briefly detailed below.

- **YANG:** It is a data modelling language aiming to model operation and configuration data. In addition, this language can be used for remote procedure calls (RPC) and notification between the modules. YANG as the modelling language specifies the functionalities, properties and APIs of the applications. Therefore, applications both internally and externally can use this data model by the northbound APIs.

- **Maven:** This tool aims to simplify, automatize and manage projects and their dependencies. The required plugins and dependencies as well as the configuration and information about the project are written using project object model (POM). This model results in an XML written file containing the aforementioned information to build the project applying the source code and resources from the specified directories or dependencies. Each project and sub-projects have their own POM file usually on the respective root directory. Therefore, the Maven archetypes build an initial project to develop applications providing the basic skeleton of the project, building files, structures and Java classes. All this content is packaged in JAR files describing the content of the project, which allows to be managed using Open Service Gateway Initiative (OSGi) in Karaf.
- **Karaf:** It is an OSGi-based container where modules or bundles can be dynamically installed, uninstalled, started or stopped on runtime. These bundles contain JAR files providing information through the manifest file about the necessary dependencies and information to be exported to other bundles.
- **Java:** It is the programming language used to develop all the functionalities/services and native applications (using OSGi interfaces).
- **Model-Driven SAL (MD-SAL):** MD-SAL provides a set of functions or services to adapt data transactions between consumers and providers, which can be both northbound and southbound plugins [5]. It emerges from the complexity and difficulties to re-use API from its predecessor, API-driven SAL (AD-SAL) [6,7]. The MD-SAL framework is based on the network configuration protocol (NETCONF), RESTCONF protocols and YANG, where each of them plays an important role [8]. RESTCONF protocol handles the iterations between the applications and data store (data tree described by YANG), while RESTCONF provides an HTTP interface to manage the data store information such as retrieve information via HTTP GET and store new data via HTTP POST. YANG is used as the modelling language for the applications and to generate APIs from models, RPC, data model definition, notifications, etc. The APIs and data stores created by YANG for each plugin are used to exchange information between providers and consumers.

2.2.1.1 Architecture

OpenDaylight framework has several layers and services [2]. The main architecture of the controller is depicted in Figure 2.1. These layers and services are described below in a top-down approach.

- **Applications, services and orchestration:** The OpenDaylight top layer consist of network and business applications that manage the network and influence its performance by managing operations on the data plane devices. Therefore, these

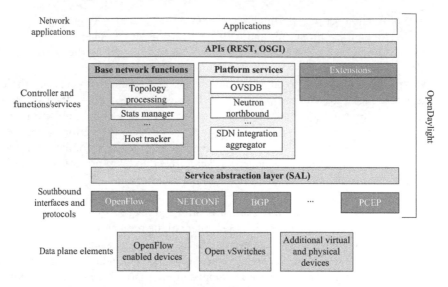

Figure 2.1   OpenDaylight architecture

applications run on top of the controller using all the available modules to control the network through routing algorithms, policies, control access applications, etc.

- **Northbound APIs:** OpenDaylight has a northbound interface which supports the OSGi framework and REST APIs. Applications can use any of both afore-mentioned interfaces to gather network information, perform operations or communicate with other modules. However, REST API can be used to remotely access to the controller and perform operations both by the user or applications.

- **Core modules:** The controller has basic functionalities, as described in Section 2.1, in charge of providing information about the network such as nodes, topology, statistics, etc. Each module is providing a basic functionality that can be extended or used by the network applications to provide network services. Besides these basic functionalities, OpenDaylight includes a collection of modules oriented to provide services and in most cases supported by vendors. One example of these oriented services to enhance SDN is the VTN component which provides L2/L3 networks isolation in a virtualized multi-tenant environment.

- **Service abstraction layer (SAL):** It provides an abstraction of the services in order to isolate the control plane from the southbound protocols and modules. This allows the management of services independently of the southbound protocols since SAL handles the requests and translates them to the proper module.

- **Southbound APIs:** These interfaces encompasses a set of protocols, such as OpenFlow, Border Gateway Protocol (BGP) and MPLS, in charge of the communication between the controller and the network devices, e.g. switches, routers or virtual switches. The SAL interacts with the core modules and the network applications to translate their requirements and handle the operations to the southbound modules.

Table 2.2 SDN control plane services for boron release

Feature	Description
Authentication Authorization Accounting (AAA)	It improves the security in OpenDaylight by providing authorization, authentication and accounting. Moreover, it provides a federation and allowing a single sign-on access with interoperability for OpenStack Keystone
Host Tracker	Similar to the Switch manager, it stores information about the end-hosts such as MAC address, IP address, etc. When the module receives traffic coming from an end-host, it stores the information related to that host
Infrastructure Utilities	Offer various utilities for projects such as counters management for debugging and statistics
L2Switch	It provides an implementation of Layer 2 switch aiming to interconnect, learn the MAC addresses, the location of the nodes and forward the traffic across the network
LISP Service	Provides a set of functionalities to use Locator/ID Separation Protocol technology
Link Aggregation Control (LAC)	It implements LAC protocol as an MD-SAL service to discover multiple links between OpenDaylight and switches. It improves resilience and bandwidth aggregation
OpenFlow Forwarding Rules Manager	It is in charge of tracking and managing the process of forwarding rules such as validate them, load them to the switch and resolve conflicts
OpenFlow Statistics Manager	It collects and request information about the network devices such as the number of ports, flows, meter, table and group statistics. These statistics can be collected every predefined interval
OpenFlow Switch manager	It provides all the information related to network devices such as supported features, datapath ID, the number of ports, etc.
Topology Processing	It provides a framework to manage and filter topology view according to certain specifications

2.2.1.2 Modules

OpenDaylight is composed of several modules that perform SDN-based services or functionalities. Besides the 10 modules that compose the basic network functions, OpenDaylight has around 50 different projects aiming to extend and enhance SDN functionalities. The scope of this book is not to cover all the available modules in OpenDaylight but to give a brief description of the basic network functions (Table 2.2).

2.3 Overview of OpenFlow devices

As in traditional networks, SDN architecture has forwarding devices in charge of forwarding the packets through the network. These devices need to be able to communicate with the controller to take appropriate decisions. Network decisions and

Table 2.3   OpenFlow switch products. Software and hardware vendors supporting OpenFlow capability

	Vendor	Products	OF version	Type
Hardware	HP	3800/5400	1.0 and 1.3	Hybrid switch
	Extreme Networks	X8/X670	1.0 and 1.3	Hybrid switch
	IBM/Lenovo	G8264	1.0 and 1.3	Hybrid switch
	Pica8	P-5401/P-5101	1.4	Hybrid switch
	Brocade	MLX	1.3	Hybrid router
Software	NEC	PF5240/PF5240	1.0	Hybrid switch
	Big Switch	Switch Light	1.3	Virtual switch
	CPqD/Ericsson	ofsoftswitch13	1.3	Virtual switch
	Linux Foundation	Open vSwitch	1.1–1.4[a]	Virtual switch

[a]OpenFlow 1.5 and 1.6 are supported with limited features

states are abstracted and conducted on the controller leaving only the forwarding capability to the network device. OpenFlow standard is positioned as the most used protocol between controller and network forwarding devices, although there are other standards that are assessed in detail in Section 2.4. Currently, many vendors provide OpenFlow-capable products, as illustrated in Table 2.3 [1,9], designed to be used in specialized hardware or in virtualized environments. These are therefore the two main OpenFlow products: software and hardware. Whereas the software switches are software programmes running on computers, the hardware switches are implemented in dedicated hardware.

2.3.1   Software switches

A software switch is a programming interface that performs packet switching and is purely implemented in software. In recent years, software switch has become more popular in data centres because of its virtualization and the main intention to implement network functions on a hypervisor. The software switch is in charge to process the packets between virtual machines (VMs) and to forward them to the destination accordingly. The packet can be forwarded internally between VMs belonging to the same machine or externally from the VM to the Internet and/or to another VM located on another physical machine.

Nowadays, the most well-known and used software switch in both industry and academy is Open vSwitch (OVS). Its main acceptance must be attributed to the open source software, extensive supported features and protocols. Some of these features [10] are STP, VM traffic policing, OpenFlow support, GRE, VXLAN tunnelling, kernel and user-space capabilities. This software is composed of several components: OVS-vswitchd, OVSDB-server and control and management cluster. The first module is a daemon, which implements the forwarding data plane together with the Linux kernel. It is possible to manually insert OpenFlow rules or connect it to an SDN controller. The OVSDB-server is a database that provides information about the OVS configuration such as ports, interfaces, flow tables and statistics. This database protocol is explained in more detail in Section 2.4. The last module is in charge of the communication between the OVSDB and the OVS.

The most recent achievement is the integration of OVS with the Intel Data Plane Development Kit (DPDK) technology [11] achieving higher performance in virtualized environments such as data centres. Previously, with the OVS architecture, the packets were copied to the kernel space for the switching *fastpath*, i.e. to be matched and forwarded according to the tables updated by the OVS daemon. If the packet does not match any entry of the existing tables, it is returned to the user space in order to take the first decision and subsequently insert the entry in the kernel space tables. Such handling could cause bottleneck issues due to copying packets from the user space to the kernel space and vice versa. Therefore, DPDK technology is used to boost the packet processing aiming to improve the throughput and processing performance. Intel is the first vendor to incorporate the DPDK technology in their Network Interface Card (NIC) chips. The use of the Intel-DPDK libraries enable to OVS to perform the *fastpath* switching in the user space by an optimized packet processing application where the packets are bypassed from the NIC to the user space through the poll mode drivers series. Therefore, this new OVS-DPDK architecture enhances the evolution of new services such as those offered by NFV [12].

2.3.2 Hardware switches

Currently, vendor's trend is positioned in two different areas: hybrid devices and only pure OpenFlow. These two types of products offer a number of advantages and disadvantages outlined in this chapter. The hybrid devices propose an approach of delegating some of the forwarding decisions to the devices itself rather than the controller. These devices reduce complexity and scalability problems to the controller by relaying only complex decisions to the controller. The rest of the other flows are forwarded according to the decisions taken in the data plane through distributed networking protocols. Some vendors identify the OpenFlow traffic by tagging its traffic with a specific VLAN tag [13]. Therefore, the hybrid devices can identify the traffic depending on the VLAN, performing both OpenFlow operations and routing the rest of the traffic based on routing local decision. However, the identification and filtering of OpenFlow traffic may be different depending on the implementation of the vendor. In addition, they are capable of making the decision over certain flows leading the other incoming packets to be forward to the controller for further inspection/decision. Applications such as firewalls, Dynamic Host Configuration Protocol (DHCP) or ARP are some use cases where hybrid devices can be used. However, depending on the vendor and models, they may support protocols under layers 2, 3, 4 and 7. Some of the most used and supported protocols of these devices are MPLS, VLAN, spanning tree (STP), LLDP, ARP resolution, TCP, SIP, UDP, etc. These devices substantially reduce the amount of data sent to the control plane for further analysis. This is a suitable solution for small or big companies to gradually replace their devices while moving to a SDN infrastructure.

On the other hand, pure OpenFlow devices, also called white boxes or bare metal switches, are switches with no default OS where the routing hardware and software are independent. For the OpenFlow device-capable, it is clear that the controller entity is performing the forwarding decision for every packet, which can lead to scalability problems. Therefore, the network OS (NOS) can be pre-loaded into the switches or can be purchased and installed. These devices are more flexible since they can be customized independently of the vendor; they are generally more reliable while cheaper. These devices are commonly used in an SDN environments, although they can run routing protocols such as BGP or Open Shortest Path First (OSPF) and be used a traditional devices. In a SDN scenario, these switches are configured to support OpenFlow protocol or any other standard or available feature. This results in a SDN-based solution flexible and vendor-independent. Some of the most extended NOS are PicOs, Switch Light OS and Comulus Linux that are all based on Linux distribution.

2.4   SDN protocols

SDN benefits from the data and control plane abstraction since it breaks down the network complexity into two main blocks giving flexibility and an effective management of the network. Different protocols have been proposed to manage efficiently the control plane functionalities and data plane resources through a secure configuration. This section aims to investigate the most well-known protocols in the different abstractions layers and analyse the main usage of these protocols. SDN can be used as a network orchestration where some protocols could be useful to manage and configure the network devices such as NETCONF.

2.4.1   ForCES

This chapter aims to explain briefly the forwarding and control element separation (ForCES) since this protocol was pioneer defining the interface and communication between the controller and the data plane devices. Since 2003, IETF aimed to define an open standard protocol interface and APIs [14]. Despite the bad impact in the commercial market, this protocol still remains in academia and with the view again towards the introduction of NFV [15–17]. The operating principle of ForCES is in a master–slave architecture where the forwarding elements (FEs) are slaves letting the master control element (CE) to control them [18]. These two models are implemented through an agent that includes the required protocols and models. Therefore, as with OpenFlow, the FE is in charge of packet processing and handling while the CE plans and executes the routing operations about how the packets should be treated. The main concept in this protocol is to forward the packets in the logical function blocks (LFBs), which resides in the FEs and defines how the FEs should process packets. This concept is similar to flow tables in OpenFlow protocol. The LFB is defined using XML to describe the components, capabilities and events supported by the FE. Therefore, each FE is built with one or more LFBs. The CE manipulates the configuration of the FEs through the ForCES protocol by managing one or more LFBs of a FE. There are two layers, defined in RFC 5810, in the communication ForCES Protocol between the FE and CE: protocol layer (PL) and transport mapping layer. The goals of PL are to maintain the link state, conduct the encapsulation and enable the CEs to configure LFB parameters. On the other hand, Transport Mapping Layer (TML) transports PL messages and defines the set of rules to achieve reliability, congestion control, etc. The FE capabilities are notified to the CE at the beginning of the communication selecting TCP or UDP among others as a transport protocol. Therefore, it is possible to specify the functionalities that the FE should perform and which capabilities are handled by the CE; for example CE handles all the traffic related to MPLS protocol but FE operates VXLAN. Moreover, it is possible to establish communication between two or more CEs and FEs. These interfaces and all available interfaces are listed in RFC 3746. The main advantage compared to OpenFlow is its protocol agnostic to the model; it gives flexibility to the vendor to use any protocol to communicate among FEs and CEs components. In addition, compared to OpenFlow, ForCES benefits from the separation of the protocol and the model enabling to change either one without affecting the other.

2.4.2 OpenFlow

This is the most well-known southbound protocol standardize by the open networking foundation (ONF). This section provides a comprehensive overview of the protocol with the intention of broadening the concepts covered in the last chapter. The OpenFlow architecture is composed of three components [9]: the OpenFlow tables, controller and secure channel. While the controller only has and needs the secure channel to communicate with the switch, OpenFlow switches have one or more flow tables, group tables and a secure channel. The protocol is used on both sides of the southbound interface, i.e. at the controller and network device (switch). The network traffic having the same set of packet header values are defined as flow. These flows traversing the network device ports are matched to the flow tables defined on the network device. Each OpenFlow port is a network interface where the packets are transmitted and operated by the network device. This interface can be mapped to either an Ethernet interface or logical interface depending on whether the port is logical or physical.

2.4.2.1 OpenFlow protocol

The OpenFlow protocol defines the set of messages exchanged between the OpenFlow controller and the OpenFlow network device. Therefore, the messages allow the controller to define the behaviour of the switch by specifying how the network traffic should be treated. There are three types of messages exchanged between the controller and the switch depending on who sends the message [2,19]. The first type of messages is sent from the controller to the switch used by the controller to manage or request information to the switch. The second type of messages, called asynchronous, are referred to the messages initialized by the switch to the controller to notify the network events such as a packet arrival or switch states, e.g. port down and error to process a message. The last group are the synchronous messages sent without solicitation by the switch or controller in order to keep the connection, initiate the connection, and for example, to provide other OpenFlow functionalities.

2.4.2.2   OpenFlow switch

The controller adds and deletes flow entries in the specific flow tables. The controller can be either an application that sets flow entries or more sophisticated applications monitoring the traffic to dynamically manage the flow entries of a network. The flows are matched according to the flow tables entries; otherwise, the flow can be dropped or sent to the controller to investigate a further action. In this case, the controller states flow entries for that flow to the network devices involved in the traffic. Once the flow entry is set, this describes the actions that all packets belonging to the flow should take. The three main actions that the switch can perform are forward the packet and/or edit the packet header, drop the packet, or send it to the controller.

2.4.2.3   Flow table

The flow table is the main concept of OpenFlow. It is possible to have multiple flow tables, each one with several numbers of flow entries. These flow entries are characterized by match fields, priority, actions, counters, timeouts and cookies. The headers of the incoming packet are extracted to match the matching fields of the flow entries together with the priority field. The flow entry that matches with the higher priority is selected to perform the action. Commonly, the Ethernet, IP or TCP/UDP header fields are utilized to match the flows. These actions can lead to a change in the packet header or pipeline processing such as 'go to a specific table', 'go to a pre-defined group', 'meter table', 'send the packet to an output port', etc. A number, starting from table 0, identifies each flow table. An incoming packet flows from the first table until the last one and stops when there is a match to one entry. Therefore, the match entry instruction is executed with the possibility to perform a *Goto Table* action. In this case, it is only possible to go to a table greater than its own and thereafter the pipeline processing continues on that table. Each time a flow is matched to a flow entry, the counter is increased and stored. While the aim of the counters is to keep track of the number of packets matched to a specific flow entry, the instructions define the set of actions that a switch should perform when a flow is matched to the entry. The liveliness duration of each flow entry before removing it from the flow table may be set by the timeouts. This time can be defined regarding (idle timeout) or regardless (hard timeout) of the packets hitting the entry. As a result, an entry must be deleted after the specified hard timeout independently of the flows matched to that entry or after a certain idle timeout if no flows were matched to the entry. However, if no timeouts are assigned, the flow entry remains permanently in the flow table. On the other hand, cookies are managed by the controller to organize the flows.

On the other hand, the packet flows from the first available table in the switch through the pipeline until it matches to a flow entry or until a table-miss event; the default action for this event is to either send it to the controller or to drop the packet. The controller can set the flow entries in response to a flow that is not matched to any flow entry or proactively when the controller is connected to the OpenFlow switch.

2.4.2.4   Group table

From OpenFlow 1.1, some operations are possible to perform such as multicast, broadcast or update faster a flow rule action by pointing some flow entries to a common action called group entry. This abstraction provides an efficient system to perform a common operation on a group of flows. There is only one group table with the possibility to add, update or delete group entries, which are uniquely identified by the group identifier. In order to add, modify or update a group entry, the controller sends the *OFTP_GROUP_MOD* message. Nevertheless, depending on the vendor there might exist some limitations when applying group tables, e.g. the impossibility to send the packet to meters or to flow tables.

Each group entry is uniquely identified by its group identifier, group type, counters and the set of actions to be executed. Each action also called bucket, define a set of actions (bucket list) to be performed on a packet. The group type defines to which of the four available groups the group entry belongs; two are required and must be supported (ALL and INDIRECT) while the other two are optional (SELECT and FAST FAILOVER). The applicability and specification of these group types are explained below.

- ALL group type is commonly used for multicast or broadcast since it executes all the actions defined in the group entry. This operation is performed by copying the packet to all the individual actions.
- SELECT group type is commonly used for load balancing. Besides the action, the bucket defines a weight parameter to select an operation to be executed each time. When an incoming packet is matched and sent to the group table, an algorithm is applied to execute one operation by selecting one bucket according to the applied algorithm such as weighted round robin or hash.
- INDIRECT group type executes only one action defined on the only available bucket. This group helps to optimize and perform an operation that affects a group of flow entries. This can also be applied for routing protocols which need to define the next-hop for several flows match.
- FAST FAILOVER group type monitors the liveliness of a port or group with the watch port/group parameter. Therefore, when the port status is down, the next bucket with 'up' status is selected. On the other hand, if the status of the bucket is up, the first bucket is selected to perform the action defined on this bucket. Moreover, if no bucket is up, the packet is dropped. This group type is in general adopted to configure back-up paths leading to the switch to change automatically the port in case of failure without the need to send the packet to the controller.

2.4.2.5   Meter table

From OpenFlow 1.3, meter tables are applied to provide QoS, shaping the traffic on the per-flow basis. This is not required and thereby not implemented on all OpenFlow switches. This feature allows defining the maximum bandwidth that a specific flow can have, differentiate ToS, flow burstiness, or others. Meters are not replacing the queues features, available on OpenFlow, but complement the queue framework aiming to reach a better granularity on the traffic and to create more complex systems. While queues are created and managed on a port basis, meters can be defined from OpenFlow protocol. Consequently, the meters can be created instantly from the controller and applied to a flow entry. Each meter entry is identifies by its uniquely 32-bit meter identifier that can be assigned to one flow or more flow entries independently of the flow table. Moreover, each meter has one or several bands utilized to define a threshold where a set of actions are executed depending on the packet rate and burst of the data. When the packet is sent to the meter, this selects only one band based on the measured rate and burst values. The meter typically measures the packet per second or kbps counting the number of packets traversing the pipeline to flow entry and hence, to the selected meter. When the rate exceeds the threshold set of the band, the meter assigns the band to the packet and consequently, the set of actions assigned to it. However, if the packet rate does not go beyond the threshold, no band is selected and therefore, no action is applied for that packet. There are two types of counters at the meter and the band level. The meter updates the meter counter when a packet is matched and processed. Similarly, the band counter updates its counter only when a packet is matched to a specific band. The first counter is used to measure the rate of the flow; the second counter can be used to measure the number of packets affected by the band such as dropped or remarked with DSCP.

When the measured rate exceeds the threshold set to one of the bands, the packet is applied to the meter band and the corresponding action is triggered. This allows a more granular set of actions to be applied to traffic flows depending on the match and measured rates.

2.4.2.6   Secure channel

The secure channel is an encrypted and thereby safe transport for data exchange between the OpenFlow devices, controllers and switches. The data exchanged between the controller and switches comprises the messages related to the switch management, packets in/out to the controller or any event triggered from the switch. The controller can have several secure channels established to diverse OpenFlow switches; similarly the switch can have several secure channels to enhance reliability using different controllers. There usually exists only a TCP – with or without TLS feature – connection between the controller and a particular switch. However, the controller may have multiple connections to each switch as identified by its Datapath ID. Since OpenFlow 1.3, besides the TCP connection, simultaneously connections over TCP/TLS/UDP/DTLS can also be established; they are called auxiliary connections, to carry packets between the controller and switches. These auxiliary connections are opened once the main connection is successfully established and thereby waiting until both sides receive the OFPT_HELLO message and proceed with the connection. Therefore, the main connection relies on TCP to provide reliable message delivery even though the processing or processing order in the device is not guaranteed. However, if the switch or controller cannot process the message because of long queues or long interval time between messages, they send an error message and close the connection. The switch runs in 'fail secure mode' or 'fail standalone mode' until the controller is connected to the switch. Moreover, if the connection is lost and there is no other controller, the switch returns to the defined fail mode. Switches are in charge of starting and keeping the connection with the controller. In the case of a connection failure, the switch retries to establish the connection again in different time intervals higher than the TCP timeout. At the same time, the switch informs other possible controllers about the channel status of the affected controller node. This allows the other controllers to take over the control of the switch and avoid the switch to return to the fail mode. However, the synchronization and handover between the controller and switches are taken independently and is not standardized in the OpenFlow protocol.

2.4.3   Open vSwitch database management (OVSDB)

OVSDB is a southbound API providing management capabilities intended to help developers and the controller to manage OVS entities in the hypervisor in virtualized environments. It was started from Nicira at 2012 and later acquired and finished by VMware at latest 2013. The controller or developer can create ports, interfaces or bridges depending on the network requirements through JSON-RPC. OVSDB also puts the controller in charge of each bridge (called OpenFlow datapath), collect statistics and apply QoS through queues. Therefore, it is important to distinguish between the OpenFlow protocol and the OVSDB protocol since the OpenFlow can only manipulate the forwarding device (e.g. creating matching rules) but cannot change the switch configuration (e.g. shutting down a port). Although it has been created with the intention of being utilized in virtualized environments, many vendors support this protocol in their hardware devices; Dell, Arista and Cumulus are vendors that incorporate this protocol in their products. Other vendors use proprietary configuration and use alternatives such as SNMP.

The OVSDB manager communicates with the OVSDB server located on the switch to accept and perform requested changes. Although the OVSDB server is isolated from the OpenFlow switch daemon, it is in charge of setting the data path in the switch; both are connected to enable the OpenFlow switch daemon to read and access to the configuration and state of the switch. This information is kept permanently in a JSON format database. Therefore, the main goal of this management protocol is to access the switch database. This works similar to SQL (e.g. storing the information in tables with rows and columns). It is possible to retrieve all the ports of a switch as illustrated in Example 1. While the data operations through JSON-RPC methods are defined in RFC 7047, the data structure is not defined to keep the flexibility of the protocol. The most well-known OVSDB schema is from OVS in which the tables' relationship, format, and usage are defined and analysed in-depth [10]. Therefore, each vendor can define its own data structure through the schema and use OVSDB to manage the network devices. In turn, this may also hinders the implementation of OVSDB in other vendors because of the need to change their databases format to also implement JSON and JSON-RPC.

OVSDB should not be confused with the OpenFlow configuration and management protocol (OF-CONFIG) that is intended to remotely control the configuration of the OpenFlow switch (Section 2.4.4).

Example 1:
$ ovsdb-client dump Port name –format json

```
{
"headings": ["name"],
"data" : [
   ["br0"],
   ["eth0"]
   ],
"caption": "Port table"
}
```

2.4.4 OpenFlow configuration and management protocol (OF-CONFIG)

This protocol is promoted by ONF to manage both physical and virtual switches. At the time of writing this book, the features, protocols and components of this protocol were based on OF-CONFIG 1.2. This protocol involves three main components (illustrated in Figure 2.2): OpenFlow configuration point (OFCP), OpenFlow capable switch (OFCS) and OpenFlow logical switch (OFLS). The first component is usually located in the controller or same server as the controller and is the entity issuing OF-Config commands. The OFCS is a switch device either physical or virtual with ports supporting the OpenFlow protocol and queues where the OFCP is able to configure and initiate tunnels such as VXLAN, NV-GRE or IP-GRE. An OFLS is an abstraction of an OpenFlow data path encompassing a subset of ports inside the OFCS that operates independently of the other logical switches. For that reason, the controller can manage each OFLS independently and configure its artefacts. The vendor preliminary decides about the resources allocated among each OFLS and the number of OFLS contained in each OFCS. The controller or OFCP can configure simultaneously several OFCS, while, at the same time, OFCS can be managed by more than one OFCP or controller, improving reliability and fault tolerance.

The communication between the OFCP and the OFCS is through NETCONF protocol (Section 2.4.5). At the beginning of the communication between these two entities, the OFCP shares the attributes supported and the protocol to be used such as SSH, TLS, SOAP and BEEP. In addition, with the introduction of OF-CONFIG 1.2, the configuration of certificates between OFLS and OpenFlow controller is possible to ensure a more secure communication. In contrast to JSON-RPC used in OVSDB, OF-Config performs XML-RPC for retrieving and pushing the configuration. OF-CONFIG can dynamically assign the resources associated with one or several OFLS allocated in one OFCS and get full control over those resources. Some controllers such as OpenDaylight, from Beryllium release, has already implemented OF-CONFIG

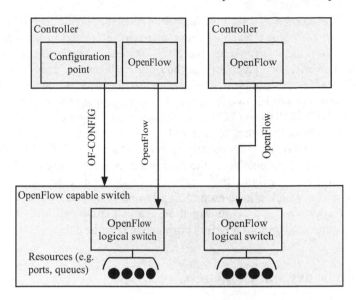

Figure 2.2   OF-CONFIG architecture and protocols

which enables the domain of physical and virtual devices over the same entity. On the other hand, OVSDB is an extended protocol implemented in the vast majority of controllers, e.g. since the hydrogen release in OpenDaylight.

2.4.5   Network configuration protocol (NETCONF)

This management protocol is defined in RFC 6241 and allows the management of a physical device by pushing or retrieving the specific configuration through RFC. While OpenFlow protocol operates at the control layer by modifying the flow tables, NETCONF operates at the management layer and provides the ability to configure and manipulate the network device configuration. This protocol defines a set of datastores (e.g. running, candidate and start-up) and operations (e.g. create, retrieve, update and delete) [20]. These set of datastores allow managing the network device operation without any impact on the currently used running configuration. In addition, information about the data state such as packet count can be retrieved from the controller. The datastores are created with different purposes, e.g. the running datastore is the running configuration of the device while the candidate is a temporal configuration. The start-up datastore, as its name implies, is the configuration to load when the device is restarted. The configuration can be applied during the running time, on start-up or at specific time periods/intervals. The configuration and messages between the controller and the network device are performed through XML-RPC [21]. Most vendors have started to standardize their configuration over YANG models to enhance the management of the devices and the inter-vendor operation, e.g. to create and validate a device configuration using the vendor-specific YANG modules before pushing it to the device. In addition, NETCONF is XML-based and vendors need to model the device structures with a language that facilitates the human comprehension such as YANG.

NETCONF protocol is split into four components: content, operation, message and secure transport layer. Each of these layers were created to provide a set of capabilities. The content layer states the XML data used both for configuration and notification. The operation layer defines the main available operations to manipulate the network device configuration. The message is in charge of encoding the RPCs and notification and send it over a secure transport through the next layer. This is possible since NETCONF uses TCP as a transport protocol in a combination of security protocols such as SSH and SSL. The NETCONF has two main entities: client and server. NETCONF client is usually referred also as a NETCONF southbound interface in charge of connecting to the networking devices acting as a NETCONG server to manage and configure them. One of the most prominent capabilities is the Rollback-on-error, which allows committing an operation and roll-back to the previous state if anything fails. Moreover, there is a validation capability that verifies misspelling in the configuration before committing it to the datastore.

2.5   Open issues and challenges

The decoupling of the control and data plane brings with it a series of challenges. We can split these challenges into three main areas depending on the direction of the efforts and the solutions provided: data plane, control plane and application. We will focus on the challenges of networking and applications, leaving aside the challenges associated with the security that can be affected by any of the decoupled planes.

The first challenge begins when different implementations of switches and protocols coexist. Vendors offer a number of features, performance enhancement and architectures completely different to the others with the aim to highlight the best hardware and software integration. This becomes a problem when the administrator or service provider has to lead with different network sources desiring to maximize the resources of the network. This is in addition to the complexity of dealing with switches or routers that support several OpenFlow versions and offering different management capabilities. Some research points to an API that abstracts the application layer from the switch. NOSIX [22] aim to provide an API to represent the network as a pool of resources meeting high-granulate configuration with driver development, whereas [23] provides a data model and interface to support the OpenFlow application development. Notwithstanding those positive strides, challenges remain in the complexity of the virtualization layer and the overheads of the abstraction layer. Other efforts are exerted to improve the OpenFlow devices performance trying to keep a low energy consumption by compressing and reducing the flow entries [24], new look-up models [25,26] or improve the processing power [27–29] by increasing the CPU capacity, the number of CPUs or changing the processors. DPDK is an example of recent efforts in Intel processors to enhance SDN capabilities by processing packets in the network card and therefore decreasing the processing time and providing high performance.

The second challenge tries to mitigate the scalability, resiliency and performance issues. The scalability issue arises when in a large-scale network the number of packets to be analysed by the controller exceeds its capacity. From here, two possible solutions arise: scaling vertically or horizontally. Scaling vertically is not an entirely effective solution because of its reliability and lack of flexibility. On the other hand, horizontal scaling with distributed controller platforms needs to address some issues such as synchronization, consistency and load balancing to name a few. It is complex to keep all the controllers synchronized, provide consistency under events such as a sudden failure of one controller and to balance the traffic efficiently between all the available controllers. Some research efforts are already geared toward providing a flexible and high reliability east/west bound APIs between vendor-independent controllers. This is necessary to provide interoperability between different SDN domains that may be isolated between service providers. In addition, research tried to reduce the latency induced by the controller by analysing and studying the proper location of the controller within a network [30]. Other efforts are directed toward an efficient and dynamically elastic solution to scale the number of controllers depending on the demand [31–33]. Another positive development is provided by the greater authority to data plane devices to undertake decisions and thereby reducing the overhead of the controller. DIFANE [34] or DevoFlow [35] are examples of the delegation of some decisions to the data plane devices.

The last challenge regards the development of applications for SDN. This has been a topic of discussion due to the difficulty of developing applications in the controllers with the need to learn the language and architecture of the selected controller. Beyond this, the difficulty of transferring application from one controller to another have not yet made much effort to improve the development of applications in this field. Some examples of efforts in this direction are portable programming languages such as Pyretic Frenetic and NetKat. However, other languages try to solve a particular problem such as QoS, fault tolerance or policy enforcement. Some challenges are also arising in the area of testing and implementation. In order to test new algorithms, applications or evaluate the performance of new prototypes, emulators and simulators are needed. One solution is to rent virtual servers on-demand in a cloud infrastructure but the lack of flexibility and control hinder the assessment. Some proposals aim to mitigate this problem by proposing large-scale SDN testbeds such as global environment for network innovation (GENI), OFELIA and OpenLab. However, this area needs to address a variety of common management plane challenges between testbeds such as between GENI, OFELIA and others. SDN is expanding beyond the data centres and spreading in some areas such as wireless, mobile networks and optical core networks. This implies considering the southbound protocols necessary to support these new areas.

2.6 Summary and Conclusions

Over time, networks have become a more complex problem and making the management and configuration difficult. On the one hand, the difficulty of implementing security policies, QoS, efficiently control network resources, has made the traditional networks a complex problem to be addressed. On the other, with the growth of traffic, the number of devices has also increased, making the management and configuration of these devices complicated. SDN emerges as a solution to these problems, not only to facilitate the management of the network but also to make the networks more vendor independent of devices and to a specific protocol. This allows the administrator of a network to easily and quickly configure the whole network regardless of the vendor switches or routers that have, models or protocols that are involved. This, in turn, accelerates the development of protocols and features without having to go through the tedious deploying cycle that affects both industry and academia. There is no doubt that SDN has brought a great number of benefits and opportunities for innovation and the creation of new business models. The decoupling of the control plane and data plane has allowed the manufacturers to leave aside the logic of the network and to focus on the hardware devices, leading to improve the device performance, efficiency and introduce new features. With the emergence of SDN, new protocols and technologies have appeared addressing different aspects of this new centralization concept. All this, along with the idea of centralization, brings with it new challenges and aspects still unresolved.

In this chapter, we have reviewed the main aspects to consider for implementing SDN. We have begun setting out briefly some of the most widely used controllers, both open-source and proprietary. Some aspects of implementation that any administrator should consider when implementing an SDN network have been discussed. In addition, one example of a controller have been described to give an insight of the power and potential of this controller. The two main sorts of OpenFlow devices were presented. On the one hand, the software OpenFlow switches are mostly used in virtualized environment such as data centres. On the other, physical switches are used as well in the data centre but typically as a top of the rack switch or for intra-data centre communication. In addition, some SDN protocols are presented and explained, given greater emphasis to OpenFlow protocol due to its major expansion in industry and academia. This protocol has had an extremely success and support from the industry and supported for almost all the SDN controllers. At the end of this section, we introduced some open issues still without a final solution and challenges to be mindful of SDN technology as well as some recent efforts.

References

[1] Kreutz D, Ramos FM, Verissimo PE, Rothenberg CE, Azodolmolky S, and Uhlig S. Software-defined networking: A comprehensive survey. Proceedings of the IEEE. 2015;103(1):14–76.

[2] Stallings W. Foundations of Modern Networking: SDN, NFV, QoE, IoT, and Cloud. Addison-Wesley Professional; 2015 Indianapolis (USA).

[3] Hoang DB, and Pham M. On software-defined networking and the design of SDN controllers. In: Network of the Future (NOF), 2015 6th International Conference on the. IEEE; 2015. p. 1–3.

[4] Linux Foundation Collaborative Project. OpenDaylight; [cited May 2017]. Available from: http://www. opendaylight. org.

[5] Medved J, Varga R, Tkacik A, and Gray K. Opendaylight: Towards a model-driven SDN controller architecture. In: A World of Wireless, Mobile and

Multimedia Networks (WoWMoM), 2014 IEEE 15th International Symposium on. IEEE; 2014. p. 1–6.

[6] Kondwilkar A, Shah P, Reddy S, and Mankad D. Can an SDN-based Network Management System use northbound REST APIs to communicate network changes to the application layer? Capstone Research Project. 2015; p. 1–10.

[7] Yamei F, Qing L, and Qi H. Research and comparative analysis of performance test on SDN controller. In: Computer Communication and the Internet (ICCCI), 2016 IEEE International Conference on. IEEE; 2016. p. 207–210.

[8] Ribes Garcia B. OpenDaylight SDN controller platform [B.S. thesis]. Universitat Politècnica de Catalunya; 2015.

[9] McKeown N, Anderson T, Balakrishnan H, *et al.* OpenFlow: enabling innovation in campus networks. ACM SIGCOMM Computer Communication Review. 2008 Mar 31;38(2):69–74.

[10] Linux Foundation Collaborative Project. Open vSwitch; [cited May 2017]. Available from: http://www.openvswitch.org.

[11] Intel. Data Plane Development Kit; [cited May 2017]. Available from: http://software.intel.com.

[12] Kourtis MA, Xilouris G, Riccobene V, *et al.* Enhancing VNF performance by exploiting SR-IOV and DPDK packet processing acceleration. In: Network Function Virtualization and Software Defined Network (NFV-SDN), 2015 IEEE Conference on. IEEE; 2015. p. 74–78.

[13] Juniper. Configuring OpenFlow Hybrid Interfaces on EX9200 Switches; [cited May 2017]. Available from: http://www.juniper.net.

[14] Kovacevic I. Forces protocol as a solution for interaction of control and forwarding planes in distributed routers. In: 17th Telecommunications Forum TELFOR. 2009; p. 529–532.

[15] Haleplidis E, Joachimpillai D, Salim JH, *et al.* ForCES applicability to SDN-enhanced NFV. In: Software Defined Networks (EWSDN), 2014 Third European Workshop on. IEEE; 2014. p. 43–48.

[16] Haleplidis E, Joachimpillai D, Salim JH, Pentikousis K, Denazis S, and Koufopavlou O. Building softwarized mobile infrastructures with ForCES. In: Telecommunications (ICT), 2016 23rd International Conference on. IEEE; 2016. p. 1–5.

[17] Haleplidis E, Salim JH, Denazis S, and Koufopavlou O. Towards a network abstraction model for SDN. Journal of Network and Systems Management. 2015;23(2):309–327.

[18] Doria A, Salim JH, Haas R, *et al.* Forwarding and control element separation (ForCES) protocol specification; 2010. RFC 5810.

[19] Morreale PA, and Anderson JM. Software Defined Networking: Design and Deployment. CRC Press; 2015 Boca Raton (USA).

[20] Yu J, and Al Ajarmeh I. An empirical study of the NETCONF protocol. In: Networking and Services (ICNS), 2010 Sixth International Conference on. IEEE; 2010. p. 253–258.

[21] Wallin S, and Wikström C. Automating network and service configuration using NETCONF and YANG. In: LISA. USENIX Association Berkeley, CA, USA; 2011. p. 22–22.

[22]   Yu M, Wundsam A, and Raju M. NOSIX: A lightweight portability layer for the SDN OS. ACM SIGCOMM Computer Communication Review. 2014;44(2):28–35.

[23]   Casey CJ, Sutton A, and Sprintson A. tinyNBI: Distilling an API from essential OpenFlow abstractions. In: Proceedings of the third workshop on Hot topics in software defined networking. ACM; 2014. p. 37–42.

[24]   Jia X, Jiang Y, Guo Z, and Wu Z. Reducing and balancing flow table entries in software-defined networks. In: Local Computer Networks (LCN), 2016 IEEE 41st Conference on. IEEE; 2016. p. 575–578.

[25]   Guerra-Perez K, and Scott-Hayward S. OpenFlow multi-table lookup architecture for multi-gigabit software defined networking (SDN). In: Symposium on Software-Defined Networking Research (SOSR). 2015; p. 1–2.

[26]   Li Y, Zhang D, Huang K, He D, and Long W. A memory-efficient parallel routing lookup model with fast updates. Computer Communications. 2014;38:60–71.

[27]   El Ferkouss O, Snaiki I, Mounaouar O, *et al.* A 100gig network processor platform for openflow. In: Network and Service Management (CNSM), 2011 7th International Conference on. IEEE; 2011. p. 1–4.

[28]   Suñé M, Alvarez V, Jungel T, Toseef U, and Pentikousis K. An OpenFlow implementation for network processors. In: Software Defined Networks (EWSDN), 2014 Third European Workshop on. IEEE; 2014. p. 123–124.

[29]   Bolla R, Bruschi R, Lombardo C, and Podda F. OpenFlow in the small: A flexible and efficient network acceleration framework for multi-core systems. IEEE Transactions on Network and Service Management. 2014;11(3): 390–404.

[30]   Philip VD, and Gourhant Y. Cross-control: A scalable multi-topology fault restoration mechanism using logically centralized controllers. In: High Performance Switching and Routing (HPSR), 2014 IEEE 15th International Conference on. IEEE; 2014. p. 57–63.

[31]   Lange S, Gebert S, Zinner T, *et al.* Heuristic approaches to the controller placement problem in large scale SDN networks. IEEE Transactions on Network and Service Management. 2015;12(1):4–17.

[32]   Sallahi A, and St-Hilaire M. Expansion model for the controller placement problem in software defined networks. IEEE Communications Letters. 2017;21(2):274–277.

[33]   Lange S, Gebert S, Spoerhase J, *et al.* Specialized heuristics for the controller placement problem in large scale SDN networks. In: Teletraffic Congress (ITC 27), 2015 27th International. IEEE; 2015. p. 210–218.

[34]   Yu M, Rexford J, Freedman MJ, and Wang J. Scalable flow-based networking with DIFANE. ACM SIGCOMM Computer Communication Review. 2010;40(4):351–362.

[35]   Curtis AR, Mogul JC, Tourrilhes J, Yalagandula P, Sharma P, and Banerjee S. DevoFlow: Scaling flow management for high-performance networks. ACM SIGCOMM Computer Communication Review. 2011;41(4):254–265.

Chapter 3

SDN components and OpenFlow

Yanbiao Li*, Dafang Zhang*, Javid Taheri**, and Keqin Li***

Today's Internet suffers from ever-increasing challenges in scalability, mobility, and security, which calls for deep innovations on network protocols and infrastructures. However, the distributed controlling mechanism, especially the bundle of control plane and the data plane within network devices, sharply restricts such evolutions. In response, the software-defined networking (SDN), an emerging networking paradigm, proposes to decouple the control and data planes, producing logically centralized controllers, simple yet efficient forwarding devices, and potential abilities in functionalities programming. This chapter presents a short yet comprehensive overview of SDN components and the OpenFlow protocol on basis of both classic and latest literatures. The topics range from fundamental building blocks, layered architectures, novel controlling mechanisms, and design principles and efforts of OpenFlow switches.

3.1 Overview of SDN's architecture and main components

In Internet Protocol (IP) networks, implementing transport and control protocols within networking devices indeed contributes to its great success in early days. However, its flexibility in management and scalability to emerging applications suffer from more and more challenges nowadays. What makes the situation worse is that the vertically integration becomes one of the biggest obstacles to fast evolutions and incessant innovations on both protocols and infrastructures. To this point, SDN [1] has been proposed, with a new architecture that decouples the control plane and the data plane of the network. Ideally, the underlying infrastructure could work as simple as an automate that processes received packets with pre-defined actions, according to polices installed by the logically centralized controller. Such a separation of control protocols from forwarding devices not only enable technologies in both sides evolve

*Computer Science and Electrical Engineering, Hunan University, China
**Department of Mathematics and Computer Science, Karlstads University, Sweden
***Department of Computer Science, State University of New York, USA

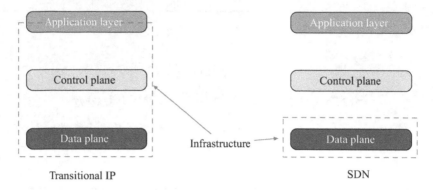

Figure 3.1   Comparison of layered architectures between IP and SDN

independently and much faster, but also simplifies the management and configuration of the whole network.

3.1.1   Comparison of IP and SDN in architectures

From the view of infrastructures, the network can be logically divided into three layers: (1) the data plane that processes network packets directly, (2) the control plane that controls the behaviour of the data plane and expresses the upper layer's requests of installing polices and applying resources, and (3) the application layer, which is composed of all applications that manages the infrastructure and that provides special network services on basis of the infrastructure. In traditional IP networks, the control plane and the data plane are tightly coupled within the same infrastructure, working as a whole middle box. Besides, some network applications, such as the Firewall, the Load Balancer, the Network Intrusion Detection System, etc., reside in the box as well.

While, as shown in Figure 3.1, SDN introduces a very different architecture. First of all, the control and data planes are completely decoupled, leaving the data plane in the network infrastructure only. By this means, networking devices are only required to play a very simple and pure role: the packet forwarding element. This will sharply simplify the design and implementation of devices, boosting technology evolution and product iteration as a result. Second, being outside the box, the control plane gains more power and flexibility. As a smart 'brain', the logically centralized controller manages all networking devices at the same time in a global view, which could balance network traffics in a fine-grained manner, improve resource utilizations globally, and provide more efficient management with desired intelligences. Last but not the least, decoupling control logics from the infrastructure also opens up the chance of implementing all network applications in software, producing more flexibility and scalability. Furthermore, with the help of potentially enabled high-level virtualization, the network becomes highly programmable. It's even possible to produce a network service by packaging a series of basic functionality elements, as simple as programming a software from modules. This is one of the simplest perspectives to understand essential differences between traditional IP and SDN.

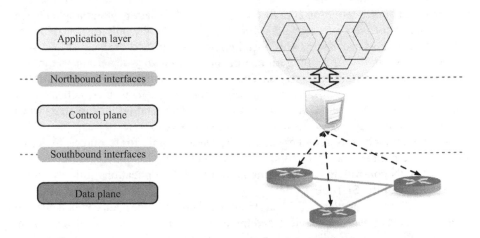

Figure 3.2   Overview of SDN's functionality layers and system architecture

3.1.2   SDN's main components

As for SDN, Figure 3.2 demonstrates its architecture more specifically. In addition to three functionality layers, there are two bridge layers, the southbound interface and the northbound interface respectively, connecting them one by one. The southbound interface layer defines the protocol associated with a series of programming interfaces for the communication between the data and the control planes. For instance, it should define the manner by which the data plane could be configured and re-configured by the control plane, the number and format of mandatory and optional arguments used in installing high level policies into the data plane, the right way and time of data plane's requesting higher level assistances, only to name a few.

Unlike the southbound interface that has clear basic responsibilities and many widely accepted proposals, the northbound interface is relatively unclear. It's still an open issue to clarify some common interfaces and standards. Learning from the development of the southbound interface, it must arise as the SDN evolves that being expected to describe some issues and solutions, manners and arguments for the communication between network applications and the controller. In the literature, there are already many discussions about northbound interfaces. Obviously, an initial and minimal standard is important for the development of SDN, a common consensus has been made out that it's too early to confine the specifications of the controller with a single abstraction right now. Although there are different application programing interfaces (APIs) provided by different implementations of the controller [2–9], we can summarize and conceive some key points here. First, it should be implemented within a software system to keep desirable flexibility. Besides, to explore all potential benefits from SDN, it should be abstracted to break the network applications' dependency to specific implementations. Last but not the least, it should support virtualization naturally, which reflects the basic motivation of SDN.

From the perspective of system design, the SDN's data plane is implemented as a series of software or hardware switches, which take the only responsibility of forwarding packets according to pre-installed polices. On the other hand, the network operating system (NOS) running on one or more commodity devices plays the role as the logically centralized controller. Through southbound interfaces, the controller initializes all switches at the beginning with some pre-defined rules, collects their statuses, controls their behaviours by updating rules, and handlers their requests when undefined events happen. While northbound interfaces can be treated as system APIs of the NOS, which is used by network applications to apply for resources, to define and enforce polices and to provide services. As those APIs may partially vary in different SDN controllers, the implementation of SDN applications still rely on the specification of the SDN controller.

Accordingly, in an classic SDN architecture, there are three main components: the controllers, the forwarding devices and the communication protocols between them. In next sections, they are discussed in detail. First, Section 3.2 introduces OpenFlow, the most popular and the most widely deployed southbound standard for SDN as of this writing. Then, Sections 3.3 and 3.4 review and analysis research topics as well as industrial attractions towards SDN controllers and forwarding devices respectively. At last, Section 3.5 concludes the whole chapter and discusses a series of open issues and future directions towards SDN's main components.

3.2   OpenFlow

As SDN's southbound interface proposals, there are already a number of protocols proposed towards different use cases [1,10–12]. ForCES [10] proposes an approach to flexible network management without changing the network architecture. OpFlex [11] distributes part of management elements to forwarding devices to add a little bit intelligence to the data plane. Protocol oblivious forwarding (POF) [12] aims at enabling the SDN forwarding plane be protocol-oblivious by a generic flow instruction set. Among them, OpenFlow, short for OpenFlow switch protocol, is no doubt the most widely accepted and deployed open southbound standard for SDN.

3.2.1   *Fundamental abstraction and basic concepts*

The fundamental abstraction of OpenFlow is to define the general packet forwarding process, how to install forwarding polices, how to track the forwarding process timely and how to dynamically control the process. Before stepping into details, a series of basic concepts are introduced below in groups according to the latest (as of this writing) OpenFlow specification [13].

3.2.1.1   Packet, flow and matching

A **Packet** is a series of consequent bytes comprising a header, a payload and optionally a trailer, in that order, which are treated as a basic unit to forward. Inside a packet, all control information is embedded as the **Packet Header**, which is used by forwarding devices to identify this packet and to make decisions on how to process it. Usually, parsing the packet header into fields, each of which is composed of one or more consequent bytes and expresses a piece of special information, is the first step of processing an incoming packet.

And **Flow** is a series of packets that follow the same pattern. A **Flow Table** contains a list of flow entries, where a **Flow Entry** is a rule that defines which pattern of packets applies to this rule and how to process those packets. Besides, each flow entry has a priority for the matching precedence and some counters for tracking packets. On this basis, **Matching** is defined as the process of checking whether an incoming packet follows the pattern defined in some flow entry. All parts of a flow entry that could be used to determines whether a packet matches it are called **Match Fields**.

3.2.1.2   Action and forwarding

An **Action** is an operation that acts on a packet. An action may forward the packet to a port, modify the packet (such as decrementing the time-to-live (TTL) field) or change its state (such as associating it with a queue). Both **List of Actions** and **Set of Actions** present a number of actions that must be executed in order. There is a minor difference. Actions in a set can occur only once, while that in a list can be duplicated whose effects could be cumulated. An **instruction** may contain a set of actions to add to the action set towards the processing packet, or contains a list of actions to apply immediately to this packet. Each entry in a flow table may be associated with a set of instructions that describe the detail OpenFlow processing in response to a matching of packet. Besides, an **Action Bucket** denotes a set of actions that will be selected as a bundle for the processing packet. While a **Group** is a list of action buckets and some means of selecting one or more from them to apply on a per-packet basis.

Forwarding is the process of deciding the output port(s) of an incoming packet and transferring it accordingly. Such a process could be divided into consequent steps, each of which includes matching the packet against a specified flow table, finding out the most matching entry and then applying associated instructions. The set of linked flow tables that may be used in forwarding make up the **Forwarding Pipeline**. While **Pipeline Fields** denote a set of values attached to the processing packet along the pipeline. The aggregation of all components involved in packet processing is called **Datapath**. It always includes the pipeline of flow tables, the group table and the ports.

3.2.1.3   Communication

A network connection carrying OpenFlow messages between a switch and a controller is called **OpenFlow Connection**. It may be implemented using various network transport protocols. Then, the basic unit sent over OpenFlow connection is defined as an **Message**. A message may be a request, a reply, a control command or a status event. An **OpenFlow Channel**, namely the interface used by the controller to manage a switch, always have a main connection and optionally a number of auxiliary connections. If an OpenFlow switch is managed by many controllers, each of them will setup an OpenFlow channel. The aggregation of those channels (one per controller) is called **Control Channel**.

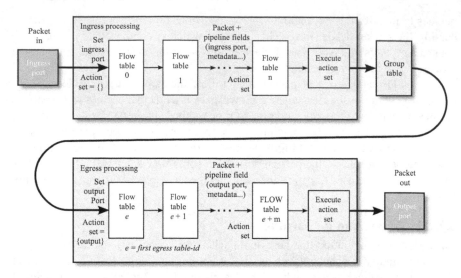

Figure 3.3   A simplified view of forwarding pipeline in OpenFlow (directly borrowed from the OpenFlow specification [13])

3.2.2   OpenFlow tables and the forwarding pipeline

This subsection describes the components of flow tables and group tables, along with the mechanics of matching and action handling.

As introduced above, an OpenFlow table contains one or more flow entries, which tells what packets could be matched and how to process them when matched. More specifically, an OpenFlow flow entry has three main components: (1) *match fields* that consists of ingress port, parts of packet headers and even metadata retrieved from previous steps, (2) *priority* that presents the matching precedence of this entry, and (3) *instructions* that may modify the action set associated with the processing packet or the forwarding process. Besides, a flow entry also has other fields for management, such as *timeouts* that denotes the time before it is being expired, *flags* that could be used to alter the way it is managed, and *cookie* that may be used by the controller to filter flow entries affected by flow statistics, flow modification and flow deletion requests. An OpenFlow table entry is uniquely identified by its match fields and priority. The flow entry wildcarding all fields (all fields omitted) and having a priority equal to 0 is called the table-miss entry, which will take effect when no other entries can match the processing packet.

During the forwarding process, all flow tables are traversed by the packet following a pipeline manner. Accordingly, they are numbered by the order they can be traversed, starting from 0. While, as Figure 3.3 depicts, pipeline processing happens in two stages, ingress processing and egress processing, respectively, which are separated by the first egress table. In another word, all tables with a lower number than that of the first egress table must be ingress tables and others works as egress tables.

Pipeline processing will start at the first ingress table (i.e. the table 0), other ingress tables may or may not be traversed depending on the outcome of the match in it. If the outcome of ingress processing is to forward the packet to some port, the corresponding egress processing under the context of that port will be performed then. It's noteworthy that egress tables are not mandatory. However, once a valid egress table is configured as the first egress table, packets must be performed on it, while other egress tables may be traversed according to the result of matching in it.

For the matching in one flow table, some header fields extracted from the processing packet, as well as some metadata transferred from previous steps, are compared to match fields of each table entry, to find out a matched entry with the highest priority. Then, the instructions associated with it are executed. The *goto-table* instruction is usually configured to direct packets from one flow table to another one whose table number is larger (i.e. the pipeline processing can only go forward). The pipeline processing will stop whenever the matched entry has not a *goto-table* instruction. Then, all actions associated with the processing packet will be applied one by one. While how to process a packet without any matching? The *table-miss* entry is configured for this purpose that defines whether miss-matched packets should be dropped, passed to other tables or sent to connected controllers.

3.2.3 OpenFlow channels and the communication mechanism

This subsection introduces types and components of OpenFlow channels, as well as underlying communication mechanisms.

As introduced earlier, an OpenFlow channel is defined, from the view of switches, as the interface connecting a switch to a controller that configures and manages it. Meanwhile, it's possible that multiple controllers manage the same switch at the same time. In this case, all channels, each of which connects the switch to one of those controllers, make up a **Control Channel**.

3.2.3.1 Control messages

OpenFlow protocol defines three types of messages exchanged between the switch and the controller: *controller-to-switch*, *asynchronous*, and *symmetric*. The essential difference among them is who is responsible for initiating and sending out the message.

As the name suggests, a *controller-to-switch* message is initiated and sent out by the controller. Those messages could be divided into two sub-groups further. One is to query status data from the switch, which therefore expects a response. For example, the controller may query the identity and basic capabilities or some running information of a switch via the **Features** requests and **Read-State** requests respectively. The other is to express control commands to the switch, which may or may not require a response. The most two popular messages in this group are **Modify-State** and **Packet-out**. Modify-State messages are primarily used to modify flow/group tables and to set switch port properties. While Packet-out messages indicate the switch to forward the specified packet along the pipeline, or to send it out on specified port(s). This type of message must contain a full packet or the identity that could be used to locate a packet stored locally. Besides, a list of actions to be applied are mandatory as well.

An empty list means 'to drop this packet'. Besides, there is an interesting message of this type named **Barrier** that does nothing on the switch, but ensuring the execution order of other messages.

On the contrary, *asynchronous* messages are initiated on and sent out from the switch. The most important message of this type is **Packet-in**. It is usually sent to all connected controllers along with a miss-matched packet, when a *table-miss* entry towards the **CONTROLLER** reserved port is configured. Besides, the switch will also initiatively report local status changes to controllers. For example, **Port-status** messages inform the controller of any changes on the specified port, such as being brought down by users. **Role-status** messages inform the controller of the change of its role, while **Controller-status** messages are triggered when the status of the channel itself has been changed.

Being much simpler than above two types of messages, most *Symmetric* messages could be sent without solicitation in either direction and are usually used to exchange lightweight information for special purposes. For instance, **Hello** messages are triggered when connection are established, **Error** messages are used to report connection problems to the other side, while **Echo** messages that require responses are very useful in verifying the connection and sometimes measuring its latency or bandwidth. Note that there is a special symmetric message named **Experimenter**, which provides a standard way of exchanging information between switches and controllers. This would be very useful in extending the OpenFlow protocol.

3.2.3.2 Communication mechanisms

An OpenFlow controller always manages multiple switches, via OpenFlow channels connecting it from each of them. Meanwhile, an OpenFlow switch could also establish multiple OpenFlow channels towards different controllers that shares the management on it, for reliability purpose. Note that the controller and the switch connected by an OpenFlow channel may or may not reside in the same network. While OpenFlow protocol itself provides neither error detection and recovery mechanisms nor fragmentation and flow control mechanisms to ensure reliable delivery. Therefore, an OpenFlow channel is always established over transport layer security (TLS) or plain transmission control protocol (TCP) and is identified in the switch by an unique **Connection uniform resource identifier (URI)** in the format of *protocol:name-or-address* or *protocol:name-or-address:port*. If there is no port specified, port 6653 is taken as the default.

The connection is always set up by the switch through a pre-configured URI. But it's also allowed to set up the connection from the controller. In this case, the switch must be able to and be ready to accept TLS or TCP connections. Once a connection is established, it works in the same manner no matter where it's initiated. To ensure both sides work under the same version of OpenFlow protocol, they must negotiate on the version number when the connection is firstly established, by exchanging the highest version they can support through *hello* messages. Then, the negotiated version number is set as the smaller of the one was sent and the one is received. A more complicated case is when bitmap is enabled in the negotiation, where the negotiated version number should be set as the one indicated by the highest bit of the interaction of the bitmap was sent and the bitmap is received. When the negotiated version of OpenFlow protocol is not supported in either side, the connection will be terminated immediately.

Once a connection is successfully established the version of OpenFlow protocol is negotiated, the employed transport protocol will take over on its maintenance. And all connections of a switch are maintained separately, protecting each of them being affected by the failures or interruptions on other connections. On receiving error messages, a controller or a switch can terminate the connection. Besides, whenever a connection is terminated unexpectedly, its originator is responsible to re-create it. But, in some cases such as the negotiated version of protocol is not supported, there should be no attempt to automatically reconnect.

SDN's core idea is decoupling the control and data planes, letting the logically centralised controller mange distributed switches to forward packets. But how will an OpenFlow switch work if all its connections to controllers are lost? The OpenFlow protocol also provides the answer. There are two modes of operations in that case. In the *fail secure mode*, the switch will work normally expect dropping mis-matched packets instead of forwarding them to controllers. While in the *fail standalone mode*, the switch, usually a hybrid switch, will work as a legacy Ethernet switch or router. Which one will take effect depends on the configuration.

3.3   SDN controllers

In SDN, the controller is the key component to enable highly elastic network management over networking infrastructures. It provides abstractions for connecting and communicating with forwarding devices, accessing underlying resources, generating and maintaining device configurations, and forwarding polices, to name only a few.

3.3.1   System architectural overview

From the perspective of the system architecture, SDN controllers can be divided into two main groups: centralized controller and distributed controllers.

As shown in Figure 3.4(a), a centralized controller is a single entity that manages all forwarding devices of the network. NOX [2] is the firstly proposed SDN controller that supports the OpenFlow protocol. It, especially its Python version (POX), plays an important role for prototyping SDN applications. Besides, it's the technical and architectural basis of many emerging controllers, such as NOX-MT [3] that improves NOX's performance by utilising the computing power of multi-core systems. To satisfy the ever-increasing requirements of throughput, especially for enterprise class networks and data centres, most centralized controllers [3,4] are proposed as highly concurrent systems, exploring the parallelism of multi-core platforms to boost the performance. As a popular instance, Beacon [4] has been widely adopted in both research experiments and industrial deployment (like Amazon), for its high performance, scalability, and stability. Its success owns to its modular and cross-platform architecture, as well as its easy-to-use programming model and stable user interfaces.

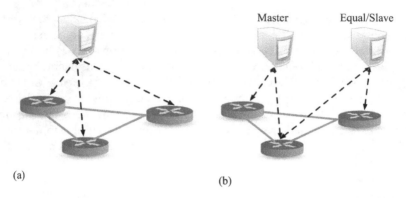

*Figure 3.4   System architectures of SDN controllers: (a) centralized architecture
and (b) distributed architecture*

Centralized controllers do contributed to SDN's deployment, development and application innovations in early days. However, they may have scaling limitations, which prevents them being adopted to manage a large number of data plane elements. First, the resources in one single entity is limited. Second, in a large-scale network, no matter where to deploy the controller there must be some forwarding devices suffering from long latencies, for configuration and real-time management. Last but not the least, the centralized controller also represents a single point of failure and the bottleneck of the security protection.

In contrast, distributed controllers could be more scalable to meet potential requirements of both small and large-scale networks. As shown in Figure 3.4(b), a distributed controller consists of a set of physically distributed elements, which therefore could be more resilient to different kinds of logical and physical failures. However, since any controller node within a distributed controller must maintain at least one connection to a forwarding device, to balance the load among all controller nodes is important. In view of this, some proposals [8,9] focus on balancing the load among distributed controllers. As an example, ElastiCon [8] proposes a series of novel mechanisms to monitor the load on each controller node, to optimize the load distribution according to the analysis of global status, and to migrate forwarding devices from highly loaded controller nodes to lightly loaded ones. But its distribution decisions are always made upon a pre-specified threshold, which cannot be guaranteed optimal as the network grows.

Another issue of distributed controllers is the consistency semantics. Most existing controllers, such as DIStributed SDN COntroller (DISCO) [5], all have low consistency. More specifically, within those controllers, different nodes may learn different values of the same property sometime, because data updates cannot spread to all nodes immediately. Currently, only a few proposals such as Onix [6], and SMaRt-Light [7] provide relatively strong consistency, which at least ensures all nodes read the latest value of some property after a write operation. But the cost is the performance.

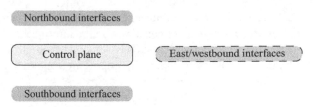

Figure 3.5   Overview of SDN controllers' components

3.3.2 System implementation overview

No matter what architecture the controller follows, there are some common components to implement. As shown in Figure 3.5, all controller systems consist of three mandatory components: northbound interfaces, the core control platform, and southbound interfaces. While for distributed controllers, there is another important component called east/westbound interfaces, which is used to exchange management information among all controller nodes within the same distributed controller system.

The core control system is made up by a series of service functions shared by network applications in building their systems, such as the topology discovery mechanism, notification streams, device management strategies, trust models and security mechanisms, and so on. Take security mechanisms as an example, they are critical components to provide basic isolation and security protection. For instance, rules generated by high priority services should not be overwritten with rules created by applications with a lower priority.

As mentioned above, there is no common standard for SDN's northbound APIs. In another word, how to implement the controller's northbound interfaces can vary completely. As a matter of fact, existing controllers implement a broad variety of northbound APIs according to application requirements and environment features, such as ad-hoc APIs, multi-level programming interfaces, file systems, among other more specialized APIs such as network virtualization platform (NVP) northbound API (NBAPI) [6]. Besides, there is another emerging type of northbound interfaces that focuses on building network applications from a series of basic functionality units, through specialized programming languages, such as Frenetic [14].

Southbound APIs of SDN controllers are implemented as a layer of device drivers, which provides unified interfaces to the upper layers, for deploying network applications onto existing or new devices (physical or virtual). By this means, a mix of physical devices, virtual devices (e.g. Open vSwitch (OVS) [15]) and a variety of device interfaces (e.g. OpenFlow, Open vSwitch database (OVSDB), NetConf, and simple network management protocol (SNMP)) can co-exist on the data pane. Although most controllers adopt OpenFlow as the southbound protocol, a few of them, such as OpenDaylight [16] and Onix [6], provide a range of southbound APIs and/or protocol plugins.

In a SDN controller, northbound and southbound interfaces are primarily used to communicate with network applications and forwarding devices, respectively. They work as bridges to entities in other layers. From this view, east/westbound interfaces are very different. They work between controller nodes within the same distributed controller system. General components of east/westbound interfaces may include, but not limited to, mechanisms of exchanging data between nodes, monitoring their status, and algorithms for ensuring data consistency. It's important to have some standards in constructing east/westbound interfaces. There are many research efforts contributing to this objective, such as Onix data import/export functions [6]. What are the differences between eastbound and westbound interfaces? The 'SDN compass' [17] makes a clear distinction, where westbound interfaces are treated as SDN-to-SDN protocols and controller APIs, while eastbound interfaces are used to communicate with legacy control planes.

3.3.3 Rule placement and optimization

From the perspective of the forwarding devices, the most frequent and important task of the controller is to install and update forwarding rules. Since a controller (or a controller node of a distributed controller) may manage two or more forwarding devices, how to distribute rules generated by high-level applications over the network becomes an issue. Improper solutions may not only raise traffic between the controller and the device, but also lead to highly frequent *table-miss* operations in the OpenFlow switch.

To split the set of all generated rules and to distribute them over the network efficiently, many approaches have been proposed with different optimization models, such as minimizing the total number of rules needed throughout the network [18,19]. For instances, the One Big Switch [19] abstracts all managed switches as a single one and proposes a flexible mechanism to split and place rules. Besides, an emerging proposal [18] presents a novel dependency graph to analysis the relationship between rules, where the node indicate a rule, while the edge connecting two nodes represents the dependency between corresponding rules. Then, the rule placement problem can be transformed into classic graph problems, which could then be solved via corresponding algorithms. On the other hand, the more rules the device can hold, the more packets will get matched within the device, and the less traffic will be produced between the device and controllers.

3.4   OpenFlow switches

Like all other Internet architectures, SDN's forwarding devices are the fundamental networking infrastructures. As OpenFlow is the first and the most popular southbound standard of SDN, this section only discusses OpenFlow switches, which communicate with SDN controllers following the OpenFlow protocol.

3.4.1   The detailed working flow

Figure 3.6 demonstrates the complete flowchart of a packet going through the OpenFlow switch. As depicted, when receiving a packet, an OpenFlow switch may perform

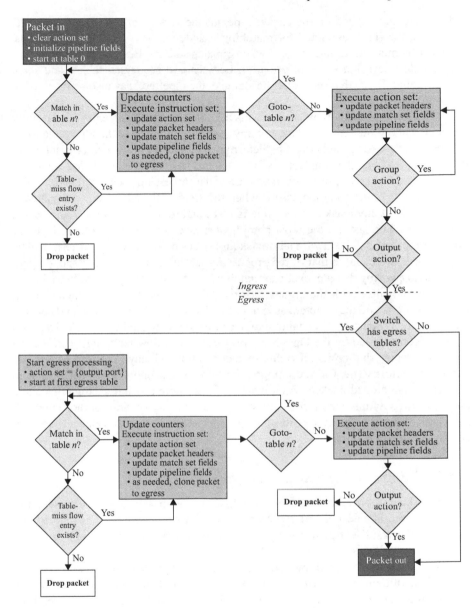

Figure 3.6   Detailed working flow of the OpenFlow switch (directly borrowed from the OpenFlow specification [13])

a series of functions in two similar pipelines: the ingress and egress pipelines, of which the latter is optional. Within each pipeline, a sequence of table lookups on different flow tables will be performed. To match a packet against a flow table, its header fields are extracted, as well as some pipeline fields. Which header fields should be used in the matching depend on the packet type and the version of OpenFlow protocols. Generally, the fields extracted for matching include various protocol header fields, such as Ethernet source address or IPv4 destination address. Besides, the ingress port, the metadata carrying some information between two sequential tables, and some other pipeline fields that represent the status of the pipeline, may also be involved in the matching process.

A packet matches a flow entry means all match fields of this entry are carefully checked and tell matchings at last. For any match field, there are three possible cases where the processing packet can be determined to match the flow entry being compared. The first and the simplest case is when this field of the entry being compared is an omitted field that can match any value of the processing packet at this field. The second and the most common case is when this field of the entry being compared is present without any mask and its value is just equal to that of the processing packet at this field. The last but the most complicated case is when this field of the entry being compared is present with a bitmask and values of all active bits, determined by the bitmask, are equal to that of the processing packet at this field correspondingly.

It's noteworthy that a packet can match two or more entries in one flow table. In this case, the entry with the highest priority will be selected as the matched entry, the instructions and the counters associated with which will be executed and updated respectively. When a packet cannot match any regular entries, this is a *table-miss*. As a rule recommended by the OpenFlow protocol, every flow table must configure a *table-miss* entry that omits all fields so that it can match any incoming packet and has lowest priority (i.e. 0). Accordingly, the *table-miss* is only used to define how to process mis-matched packets. As a matter of fact, there possible instructions could be configured with the *table-miss* entry according current versions of the OpenFlow protocol: dropping the processing packet, forwarding it to a subsequent table, or sending it to controllers.

3.4.2   Design and optimization of table lookups

In the working flow of the OpenFlow switch, table lookup is the basic and most important operation. The design and implementation of table lookup could be divided into two related parts: the structure design of flow tables and the design and optimization of lookup algorithms.

According to the OpenFlow protocol, the essential problem under table lookup is multi-filed rule matching, which shares the model with that of packet classification. But the number of fields and the scale of tables are much larger. If every match filed of a flow entry can be transformed into a prefix (namely the mask has consequent 1s), a hierarchical tree, based on the backtrack detecting theory, could be used to store all flow entries, enabling efficient lookups to find out the most matching entry. Deploying multiple copies of some rules onto some nodes can sharply reduce the time of backtracks, boosting the matching speed as a result [20]. Besides, multi-dimensional leaf-pushing technologies [21] can lead to further improvements on performance. On the other hand, as multi-field rules and the bundle of extracted packet header fields can be seen as super-rectangles and points in a multi-dimensional space, multi-filed rule matching can be transformed into a point locating problem. An efficient solution is to divide the space into lower dimensional spaces and then to solve simpler and similar problems recursively. For example, HiCuts [22] proposes to construct a decision tree to split the rule space, while HyperCuts [23] optimizes spatial and temporal efficiency by the multi-dimensional splitting mechanism and smart algorithms to migrate common rules. EffiCuts [24] presents a series of heuristic algorithms to achieve further memory compression. From the perspective of set processing, multi-filed rule matching can be solved by calculating the cross-products on the results of matching on rules with less fields [25]. The speed is fast, but memory consumptions will increase sharply as the number of fields increases, while HyperSplit [26] optimizes the splitting of rule projections to reduce memory consumption and utilizes the binary search to ensure processing speed.

Most existing approaches for TCP/IP packet classification suffer from the scalability issue that their comprehensive performance decreases as the number of fields increases, impeding their use in OpenFlow switches. One exception is the tuple-space-search (TSS) algorithm [27] that divides all flow entries into several groups according to the mask, ensuring that all entries in the same group share the same mask. Accordingly, the matching against any group is exact matching, which can be efficiently solved by hashing. Therefore, TSS has been adopted in the industrial level OpenFlow switches [15].

3.4.3   Switch designs and implementations

There are many types of OpenFlow switches available in the market or open source project communities. Typically, they vary in aspects, such as flow table size, performance, interpretation and adherence to the protocol specification, and architecture (e.g. hardware, software, or even heterogeneous implementations). This subsection will introduces some classic and main-stream switches grouped by the architecture.

3.4.3.1   Hardware switches

Thanks to its simple yet efficient processing logic, ternary content-addressable memory (TCAM) becomes a common choice of storing flow entries for fast lookup at early days. However, the TCAM is usually very small (can store 4k to 32k entries), costly and energy inefficient. All these drawbacks restrict its use in today's situation. That's why the open network foundation (ONF) forwarding abstraction working group works on table type patterns. In this area, most efforts focus on reducing the number of flow entries deployed onto TCAMs by novel compression techniques. Such as the Espresso heuristic algorithm [28] that can save up to 4k flow table entries by compressing wildcards of OpenFlow-based inter-domain routing tables. To keep updates consistent and rule tables away from space exhaustion, Shadow MACs [29] is proposed to employ opaque values to encode fine-grained paths as labels, which can be easily and cost-effectively implemented by simple hardware tables instead of expensive TCAM tables. Another trend of solutions is to combine many other hardware platforms with TCAMs, such as field-programmable gate array (FPGA), graphics processing units (GPUs), etc., in some specialized network processors.

3.4.3.2   Software switches

A software switch is a software programme that runs on the operating system to pull packets from the network interface cards, determine how to process them or where to forward them, and then send them out as expected. Though being a little bit slower than hardware implementations, software switches play an increasingly important role in SDN due to their scalability and flexibility, which are key factors to spread SDN's use in large, real-world networks. Open vSwitch [15] is such an software implementation of a multi-layer, open source virtual switch for all major hypervisor platforms. It is designed to enable massive network automation through programmatic extension, while still supporting standard management interfaces and protocols. Apart from operating as a software-based network switch running within the virtual machine hypervisors, it can work as the control stack for dedicated switching hardware; as a result, it has been ported to multiple virtualization platforms, switching chipsets, and networking hardware accelerators. Switch Light is a thin switching software platform for merchant silicon-based physical switches and virtual switches within hypervisors. It provides consistent data plane programming abstractions across merchant silicon-based physical switches and hypervisor vSwitches. Switch Light OS is developed by the Big Switch company to closely integrate with whitebox hardware, where OpenFlow-like functions work well on the current generation of switching silicon for data centres.

3.4.3.3   Industrial efforts

Microchip companies like Intel are already shipping processors with flexible SDN capabilities to the market such as the proposed data plane development kit (DPDK) that allows high-level programming of how data packets shall be processed directly within network interface cards (NICs). It has been shown of value in supporting high-performance SDN software switches. On the other hand, hardware-programmable technologies such as FPGA are widely used to reduce time and costs of hardware-based feature implementations. For example, NetFPGA has been a pioneering technology used to implement OpenFlow 1.0 switches [1]. Recent developments have shown that state-of-the-art System-on-chip platforms, such as the Xilinx Zynq ZC706 board, can also be used to implement OpenFlow devices yielding 88 Gbps throughput for 1k flow entries, supporting dynamic updates as well [30].

Besides, in order to improve the performance of software switches, off-loading some parts of the switch components onto specified hardwares become a trend according to recent industrial efforts. There are two representatives made contributions to this area. Netronome's Agilio software is dedicated to off-loading and accelerating server-based networking. Agilio software and the Agilio family of intelligent server adapters (ISAs) aim at optimizing Open vSwitch as a drop-in accelerator. Its use cases include computing nodes for IaaS or SaaS, network functions virtualization, and non-virtualized service nodes, among others. Netronome Agilio ISAs provide a framework to transparent off-load of OVS. With this solution, the OVS software still runs on the server, but the OVS datapath are synchronized down to the Agilio ISA via hooks in the Linux kernel. The Agilio software is derived from the OVS codebase and preserves all compatible interfaces. More specifically, it includes an exact match flow tracker that tracks each flow (or microflow) passing through the system. Such a system can achieve five to ten times improvement in performance. Another solution is provided by Mellanox. Mellanox's Accelerated Switching and Packet Processing (ASAP2) solution combines the performance and efficiency of server/storage networking hardware along with the flexibility of virtual switching software. There are two main ASAP2 deployment models: ASAP2 Direct and ASAP2 Flex. ASAP2 Direct enables off-loading packet processing operations of OVS to the ConnectX-4 eSwitch forwarding plane, while keeping intact the SDN control plane. While in ASAP2 Flex, some of the CPU intensive packet processing operations are off-loaded to the Mellanox ConnectX-4 NIC hardware, including virtual extensible local area network (VXLAN) encapsulation/decapsulation and packet flow classification. Evaluations demonstrates that the performance of ASAP2 Direct is three to ten times higher than DPDK-accelerated OVS.

3.5 Open issues in SDN

3.5.1 Resilient communication

For any Internet architecture, enabling resilient communication is a fundamental requirement. Accordingly, SDN is expected to achieve at least the same level of resilience as the legacy TCP/IP or other emerging architectures. However, its architecture with a logically centralized brain (i.e. the controller) is always questioned. Once such a brain is affected by kinds of faults or does not work due to some attacks, the data plane (i.e. switches) may step into a 'miss-control' state, where rules could not be updated and issues that need assistance could not be resolved timely. In this case, the whole system may become 'brainless'. Therefore, in addition to fault-tolerance in the data plane, the high availability and robustness of the (logically) centralized control plane should be carefully considered for resilient communication in SDN. In another word, there are more parts to deal with in SDN to achieve resilience, making this objective more challenging. Therefore, this topic calls for more and further research efforts in the near future to move SDN forward.

3.5.2 Scalability

For SDN, decoupling of the control and data planes contributes to its success, but also brings in more scalability concerns. Under some situations, i.e. processing a large number of tiny flows, many packets will be directed to the controller in short time periods, sharply increasing network load and make the controller a potential bottleneck. On the other hand, flow tables of switches are always configured by an outside entity, resulting extra latencies. These two issues could be ignored in small-scale networks. However, as the scale of the network becomes larger, the controller is expected to process millions of flows per second without compromising the quality of its service. Thus, in more real cases, above issues must be main obstacles to achieving the scalability purpose. Thus, improving the scalability is another hot topic now and in the future.

References

[1]   N. McKeown, T. Anderson, H. Balakrishnan, *et al.* OpenFlow: Enabling innovation in campus networks. *ACM SIGCOMM Computer Communication Review*, 38(2):69–74, 2008.

[2]   N. Gude, T. Koponen, J. Pettit, *et al.* NOX: towards an operating system for networks. *ACM SIGCOMM Computer Communication Review*, 38(3): 105–110, 2008.

[3]   A. Tootoonchian, S. Gorbunov, Y. Ganjali, M. Casado, and R. Sherwood. On controller performance in software-defined networks. *Hot-ICE*, 12:1–6, 2012.

[4]   D. Erickson. The beacon OpenFlow controller. In *ACM SIGCOMM Workshop on Hot Topics in Software Defined NETWORKING*, pages 13–18, 2013.

[5]   K. Phemius, M. Bouet, and J. Leguay. Disco: Distributed multi-domain SDN controllers. In *Network Operations and Management Symposium (NOMS), 2014 IEEE*, pages 1–4. IEEE, 2014.

[6]   T. Koponen, M. Casado, N. Gude, *et al.* Onix: A distributed control platform for large-scale production networks. In *OSDI*, volume 10, pages 1–6, 2010.

[7]   F. Botelho, A. Bessani, F. M. Ramos, and P. Ferreira. On the design of practical fault-tolerant SDN controllers. In *Software Defined Networks (EWSDN), 2014 Third European Workshop on*, pages 73–78. IEEE, 2014.

[8]   A. Dixit, F. Hao, S. Mukherjee, T. Lakshman, and R. Kompella. Towards an elastic distributed SDN controller. In *ACM SIGCOMM Computer Communication Review*, volume 43, pages 7–12. ACM, 2013.

[9]   Y. Hu, W. Wang, X. Gong, X. Que, and S. Cheng. Balanceflow: Controller load balancing for OpenFlow networks. In *IEEE International Conference on Cloud Computing and Intelligent Systems*, pages 780–785, 2012.

[10]   A. Doria, J. H. Salim, R. Haas, *et al.* Forwarding and control element separation (forces) protocol specification. Technical report, 2010.

[11]   M. Smith, M. Dvorkin, Y. Laribi, V. Pandey, P. Garg, and N. Weidenbacher. Opflex control protocol. *IETF*, 2014.

[12]   H. Song. Protocol-oblivious forwarding: Unleash the power of SDN through a future-proof forwarding plane. In *Proceedings of the Second ACM SIGCOMM Workshop on Hot Topics in Software Defined Networking*, pages 127–132. ACM, 2013.

[13]   OpenFlow specification. Version 1.5.1 (Wire Protocol 0x06). Open Networking Foundation. 2015.

[14]   N. Foster, R. Harrison, M. J. Freedman, *et al.* Frenetic: A network programming language. In *ACM Sigplan Notices*, volume 46, pages 279–291. ACM, 2011.

[15]   B. Pfaff, J. Pettit, T. Koponen, *et al.* The design and implementation of Open vSwitch. In *NSDI*, pages 117–130, 2015.

[16]   J. Medved, R. Varga, A. Tkacik, and K. Gray. Opendaylight: Towards a model-driven SDN controller architecture. In *A World of Wireless, Mobile and Multimedia Networks (WoWMoM), 2014 IEEE 15th International Symposium on*, pages 1–6. IEEE, 2014.

[17] M. Jarschel, T. Zinner, T. Hoßfeld, P. Tran-Gia, and W. Kellerer. Inter-faces, attributes, and use cases: A compass for SDN. *IEEE Communications Magazine*, 52(6):210–217, 2014.

[18] S. Zhang, F. Ivancic, A. G. C. Lumezanu, Y. Yuan, and S. Malik. An adaptable rule placement for software-defined networks. In *Proceedings of 44th Annual IEEE/IFIP International Conference on Dependable Systems and Networks*, pages 88–99, Jun 2014.

[19] J. R. N. Kang, Z. Liu and D. Walker. Optimizing the one big switch "abstraction in software-defined networks, one big switch" abstraction in software-defined networks. *Proceedings of 9th ACM Conference on Emerging Networking Experiments and Technologies*, pages 13–24, 2013.

[20] D. Decasper, Z. Dittia, G. Parulkar, and B. Plattner. Router plugins: A soft-ware architecture for next generation routers. In *ACM SIGCOMM Computer Communication Review*, volume 28, pages 229–240. ACM, 1998.

[21] J. Lee, H. Byun, J. H. Mun, and H. Lim. Utilizing 2-d leaf-pushing for packet classification. *Computer Communications*, volume 103, pages 116–129. Elsevier, 2017.

[22] P. Gupta and N. McKeown. Classifying packets with hierarchical intelligent cuttings. *IEEE Micro*, 20(1):34–41, 2000.

[23] S. Singh, F. Baboescu, G. Varghese, and J. Wang. Packet classification using multidimensional cutting. In *Proceedings of the 2003 Conference on Applications, Technologies, Architectures, and Protocols for Computer Communications*, pages 213–224. ACM, 2003.

[24] B. Vamanan, G. Voskuilen, and T. Vijaykumar. Efficuts: Optimizing packet classification for memory and throughput. In *ACM SIGCOMM Computer Communication Review*, volume 40, pages 207–218. ACM, 2010.

[25] V. Srinivasan, G. Varghese, S. Suri, and M. Waldvogel. *Fast and Scalable Layer Four Switching*, volume 28. ACM, 1998.

[26] Y. Qi, L. Xu, B. Yang, Y. Xue, and J. Li. Packet classification algorithms: From theory to practice. In *INFOCOM 2009, IEEE*, pages 648–656. IEEE, 2009.

[27] F. Baboescu and G. Varghese. Scalable packet classification. *ACM SIGCOMM Computer Communication Review*, 31(4):199–210, 2001.

[28] R. L. Rudell and A. Sangiovanni-Vincentelli. Multiple-valued minimization for PLA optimization. *IEEE Transactions on Computer-Aided Design of Integrated Circuits and Systems*, 6(5):727–750, 1987.

[29] K. Agarwal, C. Dixon, E. Rozner, and J. Carter. Shadow MACs: Scalable label-switching for commodity ethernet. In *Proceedings of the Third Workshop on Hot Topics in Software Defined Networking*, pages 157–162. ACM, 2014.

[30] S. Zhou, W. Jiang, and V. Prasanna. A programmable and scalable Open-Flow switch using heterogeneous SOC platforms. In *Proceedings of the Third Workshop on Hot Topics in Software Defined Networking*, pages 239–240. ACM, 2014.

Chapter 4

SDN for cloud data centres

Dimitrios Pezaros*, Richard Cziva*, and Simon Jouet*

4.1 Overview

The advent of virtualisation and the increasing demand for outsourced, elastic compute resources on a pay-as-you-use basis has stimulated the development of large-scale data centres (DCs) housing tens of thousands of physical servers and hundreds of network equipment. Of the significant capital investment required for building and operating such infrastructures, efficient resource utilisation is paramount in order to increase return on investment. As the vast majority of DC applications (e.g. big data processing, scientific computing, web indexing) continuously transmit data over the network, they are vulnerable to network inefficiencies and anomalies (e.g. overloaded links, routing issues, link and device failures) caused by the limited view and the decentralised, long timescale control of the network. Software-defined networking (SDN) has been proposed to manage DC networks by centralising the control plane of the network in order to have fine-grained visibility of flow tables, port and link statistics and temporal device status. By using temporal network statistics and a centralised view of the network topology, SDN controllers can react quickly and efficiently to changes, supporting applications with constantly changing, intense network requirements (such as Big Data processing).

In this chapter, we provide a technical overview of cloud DCs and their network infrastructure evolution and discuss how SDN has emerged as a prominent technology for configuring and managing large-scale complex networks in this space. After comparing and contrasting the most common DC network topologies (such as canonical and fat tree, B-cube, DCell, etc.), we discuss the main challenges that SDN can help addressing due to, among others, the fast and flexible deployment of advanced services it can facilitate, its inherent programmability, and its suitability for supporting measurement-based resource provisioning. We subsequently describe the benefits of using SDN for DC network configuration and management and briefly outline some prominent SDN deployments over large-scale DCs. We discuss the potential of SDN to play the role of the central nervous system for the converged management of server

*School of Computing Science, University of Glasgow, Glasgow, UK

Table 4.1   Number of physical servers owned by major operators

Company	Number of servers	Date
Facebook	>180,000	June 2013
Rackspace	94,122	March 2013
Amazon	454,400	March 2012
Microsoft	>1 million	July 2013
Google	>Microsoft	July 2013

and network resources over single-administrative DC environments and, finally, we highlight promising open issues for future research and development in this area.

4.2   Cloud data centre topologies

With the rise of the 'as-a-service' (*aaS) model, DCs have become among the largest and fastest evolving infrastructures. To cope with the ever increasing demand in compute, network, and storage resources, modern DCs have evolved into very large-scale infrastructures composed of tens to hundreds of thousands of servers that are interconnected by tens of thousands of (network) devices and hundreds of thousands of links. The complex task of deploying and managing such complex infrastructures is only exacerbated by the need for DC operators to provide very high reliability expressed as service level agreements (SLAs) to the customers with yearly downtime tallying up to less than a few hours. At the same time, operators are striving to keep the costs of the infrastructure and maintenance as low as possible. Table 4.1 shows an approximate number of servers from the main global DC operators that highlights the current scale of these infrastructures [1]. While DCs have traditionally been deployed in remote areas, recent studies report that, increasingly, DCs are being deployed in metropolitan areas with high-speed interconnect [2]. In order to improve aggregate bandwidth and reliability, and simplify the management, orchestration, and expansion of the infrastructure, DC operators have been focusing heavily on the network topologies to interconnect these servers in the most cost-effective way. In this section, we are describing the most prominent DC network topologies.

4.2.1   Conventional architectures

The first generations of DC networks have generally been designed following a multi-tiered canonical tree topology as shown in Figure 4.1(a). The canonical tree topology has the advantage of being very straightforward to implement, requiring a low number of (network) devices and links in order to interconnect a large number of servers. In a three-tier topology, the bottom-most layer consists of the racks of servers with each rack hosting a top-of-rack (ToR) switch. One step higher in the tree, the aggregation switches connect multiple ToR switches together and provide the uplink to the core switches responsible for forwarding traffic between the different branches. A typical deployment of this topology would likely use 1-Gbps links between the hosts, ToR, and aggregation switches and leverage the switches' uplink ports to provide 10 Gbps to the core layer.

While faster links are applied in higher layers of the topology, these conventional architectures are heavily oversubscribed. The term *oversubscription* is defined as the ratio of the worst case achievable aggregate bandwidth among the end hosts to the total bisection bandwidth of a particular communication topology. For instance, an oversubscription of 1:1 means that all hosts can communicate with arbitrary other hosts at full (link line-rate) bandwidth at any time and traffic load. An oversubscription ratio of 4:1 means that only the 25% of the host bandwidth is available for some communication patterns [3]. Traditional DC designs use oversubscription in order to reduce the cost of deployment but expose the network to congestion that results in increased latency, packet drops and decreased available throughput for servers and virtual machines [4].

Although conventional architectures are attractive due to their simplicity, they suffer from a number of drawbacks:

- The links at different layers of the topology can be highly oversubscribed, depending on the port density of the ToR switches, number of servers and capacity of the uplinks. A typical canonical tree topology can suffer from a 10:1 oversubscription at the aggregation layer and an oversubscription as high as 150:1 at the core [5].
- Traffic between servers in different racks must communicate through the aggregation or core layers, causing substantial east–west traffic across the DC in the worst case scenario and resulting in significantly different traffic characteristics depending on the server's locality.
- The lack of path diversity in the infrastructure can result in loss of a large portion of servers if a single switch or link fails. In the worst case scenario, the core switch can fail preventing access to all servers.
- In order to increase the size of the network, the topology must be modified to either deploy higher density ToR switches to host more servers per rack, or with higher density aggregation or core switches to increase the number of branches. In both cases, the expansion relies on replacing the existing devices with more expensive higher density ones, worsening oversubscription as the number of devices increases but the uplink remains the same.

4.2.2   Clos/Fat-Tree architectures

More recently, alternative topologies such as Clos-Tree [4] and Fat-Tree [3] have been proposed to address the oversubscription and path redundancy issues of canonical tree topologies. These architectures, as shown in Figure 4.1(b), promote horizontal rather than vertical expansion of the network through adding similar off-the-shelf commodity switches to the existing network instead of replacing with higher density devices. Dense interconnect in these new fabrics provides a large number of redundant paths between source and destination edge switches, resulting in better resilience in

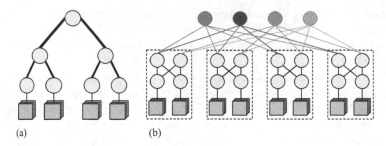

Figure 4.1   The two most common DC network topologies [3,5]: (a) canonical tree and (b) fat tree

case of link or device failure and greatly reducing oversubscription. In a Fat-Tree topology, the size of the network is defined by the number of pods, with each pod connecting to the core switches. Each pod contains two layers of switches with the bottom-most layer connecting the servers to the aggregation switches. Clos/Fat-Tree architectures have seen an increasing popularity in modern DCs but scaling limitations in the number of links and switches possible often results in partial deployments:

- The limiting size for a Fat-Tree topology is the number of ports on the switches. Fat-Tree requires uniform devices to be used with k ports, resulting in k pods to be connected each containing k switches. Each ToR switch is connected to $k/2$ aggregation switches, resulting in the remaining $k/2$ ports to connect to servers, summing up $k^3/4$ hosts supported. This level of multi-path networks results in a very large number of links and devices to be deployed to support a limited number of servers.
- The redundant paths require the topology to be configured manually to prevent network loops. It also relies on load balancing mechanisms such as Equal Cost Multi Path (ECMP) [6] or Valiant Load Balancing (VLB) [7] to uniformly distribute the traffic between links which are unfair at balancing unequal sized flows [8].
- Through the large number of redundant links, connectivity failures are less common, however, ToR failure can still result in the loss of connectivity to a rack, while aggregation or core switch failure can significantly reduce the overall available bandwidth.

The latest generation of DCs have focused on the design of very a high-performance network, instead of a hierarchically oversubscribed system of clusters as shown in Figure 4.2 [9,10]. In this model, the continuous evolution of the network and server infrastructure is paramount, allowing new servers and network links to be added without impacting the already deployed infrastructure. The main building block for this design is small-sized pods limited to 48 racks of servers to simplify the allocation of resources. To provide high bandwidth without oversubscription, each server is connected to the ToR switch with a 10-Gbps link, and 4 uplinks at 40 Gbps are connected to the aggregation switches, providing a total of 160-Gbps capacity

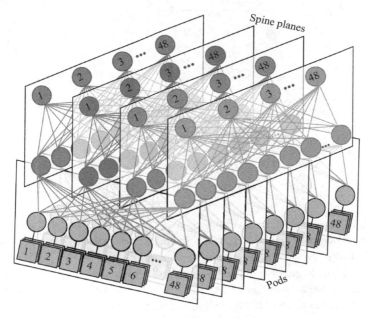

Figure 4.2   Facebook third-generation network topology

for each rack of servers. To interconnect all the pods, independent planes of spine switches operating at 40 Gbps are used. This design allows the deployment of new resources to be modular: if more compute capacity is required, new pods can be added and if more inter-pod connectivity is required new spine planes are deployed. However, path diversity results in some limitations which are similar to the Fat-Tree topologies:

- To distribute the traffic across the different paths, ECMP flow-based hashing is used which results in an unequal distribution of traffic across the different links when the size of the flows differs.
- The high number of switches and links required to provide a non-oversubscribed topology makes the deployment complex, especially in existing infrastructures. To mitigate this issue, careful building design and placement of the different planes can be done to reduce the length and number of links [9].

4.2.3   Server-centric architectures

To address some of the issues directly related to tree topologies, new research has been looking at clean-slate designs diverging from the standard multi-tier architectures. BCube [11] and DCell [12] have been proposed as server-centric topologies, in which the servers also participate in forwarding packets. The goal of server-centric topologies is to provide high reliability of the network infrastructure at a low equipment cost. The design approach of both these topologies is similar and relies on a simple

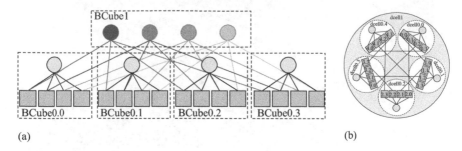

(a)   (b)

Figure 4.3   (a) BCube and (b) DCell topologies

building block repeated recursively to create large network infrastructures [13]. In BCube, as shown in Figure 4.3(a), a block contains n servers connected to a n-port switch. A BCube$_1$ consists of n BCube$_0$'s and n n-port switches [11]. In this approach, each BCube's local low port density switch can provide high bandwidth connectivity amongst the servers in the same BCube, and each server has an uplink to the higher level switches. The DCell design, shown in Figure 4.3(b), is very similar to BCube, a server is connected to a number of servers in other cells and a switch in its own cell, and large-scale infrastructures can be obtained by recursively creating new higher order DCells. The main difference between the two is that in DCell, the inter-connection between cells is performed only through the servers and not another set of switches. Server-centric architectures have shown that highly reliable networks can be designed without the multitude of high-density switches and links necessary for multi-tier topologies; however, they suffer a number of drawbacks preventing their adoption for mainstream networks:

- Server-centric architectures are designed around low density switches but delegate a portion of the packet forwarding logic to the servers. This design choice, requires new routing mechanisms to be used to leverage the topological properties of the architecture preventing easy deployment and backwards compatibility with existing networks.
- The recursive design of the network makes the topology complex and hard to maintain at large scale, requiring dedicated algorithms to generate a specific topology for a network of a certain size. This complexity in the topology makes the design and maintainability of the network harder as the network operators cannot rely on the inherent symmetry of the design like in multi-tier topologies.
- Relying on servers to provide packet forwarding has been viewed as an unreliable approach for large-scale networks. Switches have been designed to provide network connectivity over very long periods of time without maintenance; however, servers have not been designed as a critical aspect of the network and can therefore result in loss of connectivity during maintenance, reboot and degraded performance when highly utilised [14]. BCube and DCell mitigate this by rerouting traffic at the cost of a significantly increased path length [13].

4.2.4   Management network

The network infrastructure of DCs is regularly separated, physically or virtually, into two distinct networks, one carrying the production traffic between servers and the outside world and a second private network used by the operator to manage and orchestrate the servers and the switches. The management software within the infrastructure is responsible for checking the state of the servers and maintaining the accurate view of the overall resources utilisation, such as processor, memory, storage, and network load. The management network is also used to communicate with the hypervisors to start, stop, or migrate the VMs between hosts. Moreover, with the rise of SDN and the centralisation of the control plane logic, these networks are becoming even more important. In order for the switches to notify the controller to make a routing decision and send this decision back to the switches, the management network is used. Through this separation, the control logic can remain private to the network operator and can be transmitted without being impacted by the production traffic. As reported in a technical report from F5 networks [15], 5%–10% of the bandwidth during normal operation can be attributed to management traffic inside a DC.

While management networks can assume similar topologies to those described above (for the data-carrying network), these networks are typically designed for sparse and latency-sensitive traffic where maintaining high throughput is not as critical as for the data-carrying production network. The management network should therefore be designed to provide reliable and consistent performance regardless of the load over the production traffic. According to related literature, management networks can be one of three types:

1. In-band network: The simplest way is to use the same 'in-band' network for the management network as the one carrying production traffic of the tenants. In this scenario, there is no isolation between production and management traffic, therefore the management traffic is subjected to congestion or low bandwidth caused by production traffic. As a result, in-band management network is not recommended for production DCs.
2. Logical out-of-band (OOB) network: In this approach, the management network is logically separated using, for instance, VLANs or dedicated flow rules in the switches. Extending the in-band solution, this approach allows QoS enforcement to prioritise management traffic over tenant's traffic (by, for instance, assigning different queues in switches). However, as isolation can only happen in certain points of the network (at routers capable of QoS enforcement), logical OOB does not guarantee fully fledged isolation of management and user traffic.
3. Physical OOB network: A physically separated network can be set up solely for management purposes. While this incurs significant investment in new switches and network interfaces for hosts, this solution is preferred for critical environments. In fact, a physically separated management network is being deployed at many production cloud DCs [10], and it is the recommended solution for the OpenStack[1] open-source cloud software.

---

[1] https://www.openstack.org.

4.3 Software-defined networks for cloud data centres

In this section, we highlight the challenges in cloud DC network management that have led to the need and deployment of SDN. We show how SDN helps addressing these challenges, and we also present a number of production cloud DCs that have reportedly rely on SDN. At the end of this section, we show how SDN can be used as the basis for a converged resource management plane for DC networks that are under a single administrative authority.

4.3.1 Challenges in cloud DC networks

Cloud DCs are generic infrastructures designed to host many tenants with many types of applications, including web, database or image processing servers, or big data analytics clusters just to mention a few. As a result of the variety of applications running in the cloud, studies have found traffic patterns in DC networks to change rapidly and unpredictably [4] and found CPU, disk I/O, and network bandwidth to be highly variable [16] making it challenging to manage resources in an efficient way. In a prominent study [5], the authors have conducted empirical measurement of the network traffic in ten DCs belonging to different types of organisations (they examined university, private and commercial DCs) and presented the differences in traffic patterns in different clusters.

On the other hand, cloud DCs are challenged by the ever-increasing service-level expectations of tenants. Providers are competing to offer better SLAs than competitors, advertising high commitments for uptime. As a concrete example, Amazon EC2 offers an SLA of 99.95%,[2] giving only 4 h and 22 min downtime yearly. Considering the failure rates of today's commodity hardware (servers, disks, network links), this level of service can only be achieved with redundancy and more importantly efficient always-on control over the infrastructure. Some providers also host tenants with diverse QoS requirements, making resource management even more challenging.

The complex management of network services undoubtedly brings privacy and security considerations into attention. With thousands of services continuously migrating between hosts in geographically distributed cloud DCs, providers need to make sure that tenants' traffic is always forwarded to the right place and never gets exposed to other tenants or the outside world. Moreover, since cloud DCs are shared infrastructures, providers also need to identify and filter any malicious activity from harmful tenants to avoid privacy leaks and attacks such as Economical DDoS where attackers target the on-demand charging of resources for other users by generating unnecessary traffic to the other tenant services to increase their spending.

Energy consumption in cloud DCs accounts for a considerable slice of the total operational expenses. Reports from Gartner Group have estimated energy consumptions to account for up to 10% of the current OPEX, and this estimate is projected to rise to 50% in the next few years.[3] On top of expenses, national and international

---

[2] https://aws.amazon.com/ec2/sla/.
[3] http://gartner.com.

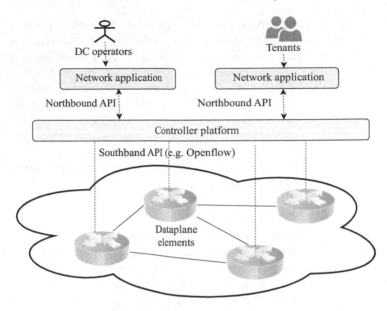

Figure 4.4   High-level view of SDN for cloud DCs

regulations are also forcing DC operators to cut back on unnecessary energy usage to reduce carbon emission.

4.3.2   Benefits of using SDN in cloud DCs

SDN has been proposed for cloud DCs as a centralised control plane and a clear abstraction between the physical network infrastructure and a virtualised network layer provided by a network operating system. The network operating system is usually implemented in an SDN controller, and it provides an interface to network applications for different entities in a cloud DC network. As shown in Figure 4.4, even tenants in a cloud DC network are users of the SDN infrastructure through SDN applications – this for instance allows tenants configure access control rules (and other advanced network services) for their VMs. DC operators are also users of such SDN platform with network-wide topology and utilisation information collected by the controller platform.

In the following sections, we highlight the most prominent benefits of using SDN in cloud DCs, reflecting on the challenges we detailed in the previous section.

4.3.2.1   Advanced services

To satisfy increasing user demands, clouds and their offerings for network services are evolving from year to year. While clouds used to only provide simple IP connectivity for users in the same data centre, with the help of SDN, they currently support various advanced network services, delivered at a world-wide scale. As a prominent example, Amazon's virtual private cloud (VPC)[4] lets tenants provision a logically isolated section of the Amazon web services (AWS) cloud where they can launch AWS resources in a tenant-defined virtual network. Tenants now have complete control over their virtual networking environment (including selection of their own IP address range, creation of sub-nets, and configuration of route tables and network gateways). These advanced network services require logically virtualised networks and flexible reconfigurations of the underlying infrastructure (routers, gateways, switches). Such virtualisation of the network can be achieved by for example FlowVisor [17], a network abstraction layer that allows a physical SDN infrastructure to be shared between multiple controllers.

4.3.2.2   Network programmability

On top of centralised control, many researchers have proposed new, higher level programming languages to interact with the network. These languages help formalising network-wide policies, such as access control or QoS enforcement. As an example, a high-level policy can be used to express that in case of congestion, lower priority flows are dropped to maintain QoS for specific users. In Frenetic [18], the authors proposed a declarative language designed to handle race conditions in an SDN-controlled network. Frenetic policies are then compiled to low-level OpenFlow flow rules that can be actioned by SDN switches. Flow-based management language [19] is another example language that has been designed for access control policies to be expressed in a high-level syntax. These advances help operators to overcome privacy and security issues, and flexibly implement complex, network-wide policy configurations.

4.3.2.3   Always-on measurement

In order to monitor the network status and identify potential faults or misbehaviour, it is important to continuously collect metrics from the switches throughout the infrastructure. Using the collected metrics, the normal operating network behaviour can be profiled and used to predict future trends as well as identifying anomalies as deviations from the modelled behaviour. This process of collection has been referred to as network telemetry and has been widely used to provide a fine-grained view of the network to the central controller and third-party management applications. Such insight into the network provides new means to adapt the infrastructure as the demand changes, allowing allocated resources to be optimised and improving policies to meet customers' SLAs.

SDN provides a simplified and cost-effective way to collect temporal performance indicators from the network devices through allowing the central controller to query the data from each individual device. Using this approach, SDN can also be used as an always-on measurement platform for DC networks. OpenFlow relies internally on the use of counters to monitor specific sets of metrics and exposes the value of these counters to the controller through simple OpenFlow commands. These

---

[4]https://aws.amazon.com/vpc/.

counters infer the traffic volume, number of packets, and liveliness of every port and flow currently allocated in the device. With the option to periodically collect and aggregate flow statistics from all network devices, a SDN controller can build up a real-time view of link utilisation and react to sudden changes (e.g. overloaded links, link failures, etc.) by re-directing traffic. The authors in [20] have collected flow counters to find sub-optimal VM placement in cloud DCs, while in [21], flow statistics have been collected to present an energy-efficient scheduler for cloud DCs.

4.3.2.4 Energy efficiency

The centralised control of networking equipment allows cloud DC services to be managed in an energy efficient way. As an example, routing policies can minimise the number of switches and links used in a multi-path topology and therefore allow some switches or transceivers to go to idle state, consuming less energy. A similar, SDN-based approach has been presented in [22], where the authors presented ElasticTree, a network-wide power manager, that dynamically adjusts the set of active network elements – links and switches – to satisfy the evolving data centre traffic loads and save up to 50% of network energy, while maintaining the ability to handle traffic surges. The benefit of careful traffic engineering on energy consumption has also been evaluated in DENS where the authors present a scheduling algorithm for DC networks that balances the energy consumption of a data centre, individual job performance, and traffic demands [21].

4.3.3 Current SDN deployments in cloud DC

SDN and its most prominent realisation, OpenFlow, have been deployed in many cloud DCs. In fact, all cloud networks nowadays apply the SDN principle in one way or another. One of the first reported deployments of SDN is accredited to Google, where the technology was used to interconnect private DCs across the globe. This deployment, called B4 [23], allows setting up bandwidth guarantees between any two hosts, even if the hosts are located in two different DCs. In their paper, they described how they support multiple routing protocols simultaneously and how they perform centralised traffic engineering with SDN. While the paper has been presented in 2013, at the time of publication B4 had already been deployed for three years, dating the first large-scale deployment of SDN back to ca 2010.

Apart from B4, Google has also presented the evolution of their data centre architecture and their approach to overcome the cost, operational complexity, and limited scale of data-centre networks. This recent paper highlights how multi-stage Clos topologies can support cost-effective deployments at Google's scale and how they have implemented centralisation of their network control over the years [10]. Jupiter, their latest generation of networking fabric, interconnects high-speed hosts (10G and 40G hosts) with simple, commodity switches that compute forwarding decisions on their own based on topology and link information distributed from a centralised controller on a reliable out-of-band control plane network. This operation presents how SDN's centralised view can be used in a distributed way, which provides scalability to network operations. Other large-scale operators have deployed OpenFlow as part of the neutron network module in OpenStack such as IBM with their Bluemix cloud infrastructure [24].

The Raspberry Pi Cloud, a scale-model of a cloud from the University of Glasgow has also applied the SDN principle [25]. In this work, Raspberry Pi devices are inter-connected through a canonical multi-root tree topology. Machines in the same rack are connected to a ToR switch, while ToR switches are connected to an OpenFlow-enabled aggregation switch. This provides control over the network to a SDN controller and allows creating SDN switching domains between any of the selected Raspberry Pi devices using network slicing provided by FlowVisor [17].

4.3.4 SDN as the backbone for a converged resource control plane

4.3.4.1 Network resource management

Most SDN controllers (e.g. OpenDaylight[5], Ryu,[6] or ONOS[7]) expose APIs to con-figure network components using OpenFlow, manage access control, collect traffic counters, etc. SDN controllers have also been widely used for diverse network-related operations such as to perform complete network migration [26], present new network management interfaces [27], implement QoS management [28], and introduce new concepts such as participatory networking [29]. However, SDN is network-centric and does not inter-operate with VMs, hypervisors, or other control interfaces to convey information of the temporal network state that could subsequently be exploited for admitting server resources without causing network-wide congestion and bandwidth bottlenecks [5,30,31].

4.3.4.2 Network-agnostic server resource management

Server resources account for up to 45% of the total investment of DCs according to [32]. These server resources are provisioned in the form of VMs in today's cloud DCs, using virtual memory, I/O, and CPU cores. It is apparent that in order to increase return-on-investment, server resources need to be used in an efficient way. However, the utilisation of a server can be as low as 10% [33], since most DCs are over-provisioned to handle occasional peak demand.

Server consolidation has been the most prominent activity for grouping and re-assigning VMs to new hosts in order to optimise server-side resource utilisation and to reduce OPEX. However, consolidation has been employed to optimise diverse objectives, such as server resource utilisation (CPU, RAM, disk I/O) [34], energy efficiency [35], or to meet SLA requirements which are often expressed as CPU or response time guarantees [36]. While these server-side metrics are useful to reduce the number of hypervisors required for a set of VMs, they do not take the resulting network

---

[5] http://opendaylight.org.
[6] https://osrg.github.io/ryu/.
[7] http://onosproject.org.

congestion into account (especially at the more expensive core layer links). Recent evidence suggests that server virtualisation can adversely impact cloud environments, causing dramatic performance and cost variations which mainly relate to networking rather than server bottlenecks. In particular, consolidation itself has a significant impact on network congestion [30,37], especially at the core layers of DC topologies which in turn become the main bottleneck throughout the infrastructure [4,5], limiting efficient resource usage and resulting in loss of revenue [32].

4.3.4.3 SDN-based converged server-network resource management

To overcome the aforementioned challenges of diverse control planes managing server and network resources in isolation and resulting in sub-optimal, network-wide usage patterns, research has been focused on designing unified resource management schemes and interfaces. For example, the authors in [20] extended a SDN controller to interface with hypervisors and manage VM migrations in a cloud DC in order to achieve network-aware, bandwidth-efficient placement of all communicating VMs. This work has built on top of S-CORE [38,39], a scalable communication cost reduction scheme that exploits live VM migration to minimise the overall communication footprint of active traffic flows over a DC topology. In brief, S-CORE measures VM-to-VM communication cost at the hypervisors and calculates the potential overall cost reduction for each active VM among different hypervisor alternatives. If the communication cost can be reduced by migrating the VM, the hypervisor initiates the migration. Otherwise, the system goes to the next VM selected by the orchestration algorithm.

The high-level system design of the SDN-enabled version of S-CORE is shown in Figure 4.5. Network resources are controlled by traditional OpenFlow messages. However, the SDN controller does not only manage the forwarding policy of the particular cloud DC, but also assigns link weights to individual links in the network topology and, based on various orchestration algorithms implemented centrally at the controller, it triggers VM migrations by calling the API of the hypervisors. The authors used the Ryu SDN controller which had most of the high-level network information readily available – such as the network topology (collected by the controller using link layer discovery protocol messages) which was essential in order to assign weights for different links, and the location of all hosts and VMs that were identified from traffic received from VMs/hosts. As a result, controlling server resources from a SDN controller has proven to significantly reduce congestion and increase overall throughput by over six times, while achieving over 70% cost reduction by migrating less than half of the VMs. For more information on this work, we refer interested readers to [20].

Apart from managing VMs, SDN can also serve as a backbone for other converged control logic, since SDN provides a high-level, centralised view of the network: the location of the hosts and VMs are known, and the entire network topology with accurate link utilisation is also readily available. SDN controllers on top of this are well tested software suites, providing a good starting point for similar control logic.

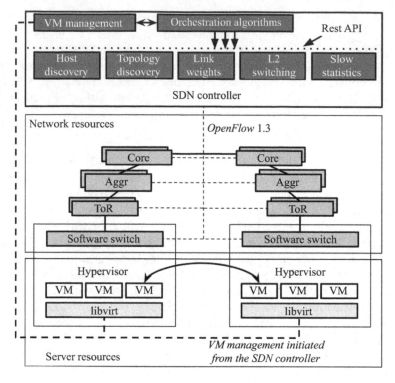

Figure 4.5   Controlling server resources from a SDN controller, example from [20]

4.4   Open issues and challenges

In this section, we describe a number of interesting open research issues. We shed light on two selected topics: how the emerging network function (NF) virtualisation (NFV) trend can be used alongside SDN in next-generation cloud DCs and also how experiences with SDN can be leveraged to unleash the potential of future network programmability.

4.4.1   Network function virtualisation and SDN in DCs

Traditional networks apply security and performance middleboxes (e.g. firewalls, caches, protocol analysers, deep packet inspection) to inspect and modify traffic. In fact, the number of middleboxes in traditional enterprise networks is estimated to be on par with the number of switches and routers [40]. With the rise of public cloud computing, enterprises have started outsourcing their formerly in-house ICT to cloud infrastructures. Despite the growing adoption of this paradigm, key challenges remain when migrating enterprise network services to the cloud – including performance, privacy and security issues [41].

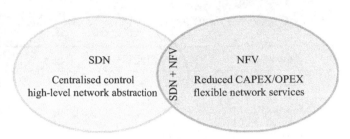

Figure 4.6   Relationship between SDN and NFV

NFV has been introduced in recent years to softwarise traditional middleboxes and handle them as virtual entities. NFV extends SDN by virtualising network services to reduce capital and operation expenditure. Several approaches have proposed merging the two technologies and essentially introducing the term software-defined NFV (SDNFV) to promote virtualised network services that are interconnected with software-defined networks, as shown in Figure 4.6.

As a concrete example of bringing NFV and SDN together in cloud DCs, in [42] the authors have introduced the Glasgow NFs (GNF) framework that provides cloud tenants advanced network services, such as rate limiters, firewalls and caches. GNF relies on container-based NFs that can be hosted on any virtualised physical server in the DC and uses a SDN controller to manage all traffic between NFs and hosts. Extending this work, GNFC (Glasgow network function in the cloud) has been evaluated in public cloud environments (Amazon AWS, Microsoft Azure, Google Compute Engine) [43]. In GNFC, the authors have created a virtualised network between a tenant's VMs (using VXLAN tunnels) in order to use OpenFlow 1.3 flow rules to steer selected traffic through container NFs, also running on VMs provided by the same cloud infrastructure. This study has not only shown a proof of concept of running container-based, virtualised NFs as tenants in the cloud, but also provided a way for tenants to create their own overlay SDNs [43].

Apart from supporting enterprise cloud adoption, NFV can play an important role in future big data DCs, since it allows new, network-focused services to be introduced for big data clusters without modifying the core data processing elements. As an example, new data transforming NFs such as protocol accelerators can be introduced between parts during each stage (partition or aggregate stage) of big data analyses to reduce unnecessary network utilisation and enhance the performance of big data processing [44].

4.4.2   The future of network programmability

OpenFlow was originally put forward as a balanced compromise between programmability and pragmatism, providing much more flexibility than the existing switches but limiting this flexibility to the capabilities of the vendors' existing chips. This pragmatism has been the main reason for OpenFlow to become the first widely

Table 4.2   Number of supported fields per OpenFlow protocol revision

OF version	Release date	Match fields	Depth	Size (bits)
<1.0	March 2008	10	10	248
1.0	December 2009	12	12	264
1.1	February 2011	15	15	320
1.2	December 2011	36	9–18	603
1.3	June 2012	40	9–22	701
1.4	October 2013	41	9–23	709
1.5	December 2014	44	10–26	773

deployed implementation of SDN by offering new capabilities to network operators and researchers, and allowing vendors to provide added value without the need
to re-design the underlying hardware. Building on the programmability offered by
OpenFlow, a wide range of research areas have progressed significantly, such as
routing, traffic engineering, quality of service and network virtualisation. Despite
its large-scale success, OpenFlow is only one partial implementation of SDN that is
limited by its pragmatic design choices. SDN as a concept is much broader and can
provide for significantly more flexibility than what is currently offered in order to
support new protocols, new metrics and the ability to deploy middlebox-like functions
to the devices required for next-generation DC networks.

In order to support new and changing requirements of networks operators, Open-
Flow evolved significantly between its first production release in 2008 and its current
revision. These revisions added support for matching packets on new protocol headers such as MPLS tags, IPv6 source and destination addresses, GRE, VxLAN and
STT, resulting in a significant growth in tuple size (depth) and memory requirements
as shown in Table 4.2. This continuous evolution of the OpenFlow specification to
support new protocols, per-packet actions and encapsulations, highlights the lack of
future-proofness of the current approach. These limitations, as well as the very limited
matching and per-packet actions that can be performed, results in seemingly simple
applications to be impractical due to flow-table size limitations or unfeasible without
redirecting all the traffic to the controller. Hence, it is worth considering OpenFlow
as a stepping stone in showcasing the benefits and possibilities of SDN.

To support the next generation of NFs and control for DCs, and provide
middlebox-like functions such as deep packet inspection, load balancing, telemetry and protocol offloading, network programmability must be extended beyond
OpenFlow. To address OpenFlow's restrictive match-action pipeline, switch architectures such as the Reconfigurable Match Table (RMT) [45] model, and commercial
chips such as Intel's FlexPipe [46] and Cavium's Xpliant [47] have been suggested.
These three chips follow a match-action pipeline that can be reconfigured dynamically to match over arbitrary packet headers while providing performance comparable
to fixed-functions chips. To express this architectural flexibility and allow network
operators to design the data plane function, domain specific languages such as P4,

POF and the BPF instruction set have been suggested [48–50]. Another influential work in this domain has been PISCES [51], which moves away from the hardware infrastructure to focus only on hypervisor-level software switches. PISCES justifies this decision based on the very large number of software switches deployed in modern DCs, often one per server, resulting in more software than hardware switches in the network.

This increased programmability allows DC operators to design and quickly iterate over network services, to improve resource utilisation and reduce OPEX. By deploying new network services directly onto the switches at runtime, expensive middleboxes such as load balancers or intrusion detection services can be avoided, hence reducing cost and improving maintainability. Using operator-specific telemetry modules, the network state can be monitored and reported to the central controller, highlighting the current operating behaviour of the infrastructure and raising alarms on deviation from the expected normal state. Finally, by providing support for new and custom network protocols, DC operators can deploy fine-tuned transport and overlay network protocols to better utilise the available network resources without impacting the connectivity or the end users.

4.5 Summary

In this chapter, we have provided a general introduction to the infrastructure and topological characteristics of cloud DC networks and illustrated how SDN has penetrated cloud DCs in order to facilitate advanced networking capabilities and provide a fine-grained, network-wide configuration and management framework that can be exploited for flexible, cost-effective, and energy-efficient centralised control of DC networks. After discussing the prominent DC topologies and highlighting their configuration and management challenges, we have looked into how SDN can leverage its inherent programmable, flexible, and measurement-based characteristics for the efficient management of resources over increasingly converged and centralised ICT environments. We have discussed prominent SDN deployments over cloud DCs, and highlighted SDN research to address, among others, VPCs, QoS enforcement and measurement-based resource provisioning. Finally, we have highlighted open research issues in using SDN as an enabling technology for the deployment of virtualised NFs over cloud DCs, and in extending the SDN paradigm for enabling truly programmable next generation networks.

Acknowledgements

The work has been supported in part by the UK Engineering and Physical Sciences Research Council (EPSRC) projects, EP/L026015/1, EP/N033957/1, EP/P004024/1 and EP/L005255/1, and by the European Cooperation in Science and Technology (COST) Action CA 15127: RECODIS – Resilient communication services protecting end-user applications from disaster-based failures.

References

[1]   R. Miller, "Who has the Most Web Servers." http://www.datacenterknowledge
.com/archives/2009/05/14/whos-got-the-most-web-servers/, 2013.

[2]   I. Research, "Rise of high-capacity data center interconnect in hyper-scale
service provider systems." 2014 ACG Research.

[3]   A. L. Mohammad Al-Fares and A. Vahdat, "A scalable, commodity data center
network architecture," in *SIGCOMM 2008*, SIGCOMM '08, (New York, NY,
USA), pp. 63–74, ACM, 2008.

[4]   A. Greenberg, J. R. Hamilton, N. Jain, *et al.*, "VL2: a scalable and flexible data
center network," in *Proc. ACM SIGCOMM'09*, pp. 51–62, 2009.

[5]   T. Benson, A. Akella, and D. A. Maltz, "Network traffic characteristics of data
centers in the wild," in *Proc. ACM SIGCOMM Internet Measurement Conf.
(IMC'10)*, pp. 267–280, 2010.

[6]   D. Thaler and C. Hopps, "Multipath issues in unicast and multicast next-hop
selection," RFC 2991, RFC Editor, November 2000.   http://www.rfc-
editor.org/rfc/rfc2991.txt.

[7]   R. Zhang-Shen and N. McKeown, *Designing a Predictable Internet Backbone with Valiant Load-Balancing*, pp. 178–192. Berlin, Heidelberg: Springer
Berlin Heidelberg, 2005.

[8]   S. Ghorbani, B. Godfrey, Y. Ganjali, and A. Firoozshahian, "Micro load bal-
ancing in data centers with drill," in *Proceedings of the 14th ACM Workshop on
Hot Topics in Networks*, HotNets-XIV, (New York, NY, USA), pp. 17:1–17:7,
ACM, 2015.

[9]   Facebook, "Introducing data center fabric, the next-generation Facebook
data center network." https://code.facebook.com/posts/360346274145943/.
Accessed 14 November 2014.

[10] A. Singh, J. Ong, A. Agarwal, *et al.*, "Jupiter rising: a decade of clos topologies and centralized control in Google's datacenter network," *ACM SIGCOMM
Computer Communication Review*, vol. 45, no. 4, pp. 183–197, 2015.

[11] C. Guo, G. Lu, D. Li, *et al.*, "Bcube: a high performance, server-centric network
architecture for modular data centers," *SIGCOMM Computer Communication
Review*, vol. 39, pp. 63–74, Aug. 2009.

[12] C. Guo, H. Wu, K. Tan, L. Shi, Y. Zhang, and S. Lu, "Dcell: a scalable
and fault-tolerant network structure for data centers," *SIGCOMM Computer
Communication Review*, vol. 38, pp. 75–86, Aug. 2008.

[13] R. D. Couto, S. Secci, M. E. Campista, and L. H. Costa, "Reliability and
survivability analysis of data center network topologies," *Journal of Network
and Systems Management*, vol. 24, pp. 346–392, Apr. 2016.

[14] T. Wang, Z. Su, Y. Xia, and M. Hamdi, "Rethinking the data center networking:
architecture, network protocols, and resource sharing," *IEEE Access*, vol. 2,
pp. 1481–1496, 2014.

[15] P. Stalvig, "Management networks – living outside of production. Management
networks segregate non-production traffic off production networks." Technical
Report, F5 Networks, Inc., 2008.

[16] J. Schad, J. Dittrich, and J.-A. Quiané-Ruiz, "Runtime measurements in the cloud: observing, analyzing, and reducing variance," *Proceedings of the VLDB Endowment*, vol. 3, no. 1–2, pp. 460–471, 2010.

[17] R. Sherwood, G. Gibb, K.-K. Yap, *et al.*, "Flowvisor: a network virtualization layer," in *OpenFlow Switch Consortium, Tech. Rep*, pp. 1–13, 2009.

[18] N. Foster, R. Harrison, M. J. Freedman, *et al.*, "Frenetic: a network programming language," in *ACM Sigplan Notices*, vol. 46, pp. 279–291, ACM, 2011.

[19] T. L. Hinrichs, N. S. Gude, M. Casado, J. C. Mitchell, and S. Shenker, "Practical declarative network management," in *Proceedings of the 1st ACM Workshop on Research on Enterprise Networking*, pp. 1–10, ACM, 2009.

[20] R. Cziva, D. Stapleton, F. P. Tso, and D. P. Pezaros, "SDN-based virtual machine management for cloud data centers," in *Cloud Networking (CloudNet), 2014 IEEE 3rd International Conference on*, pp. 388–394, Oct. 2014.

[21] D. Kliazovich, P. Bouvry, and S. Khan, "DENS: data center energy-efficient network-aware scheduling," *Cluster Computing*, vol. 16, no. 1, pp. 65–75, 2013.

[22] B. Heller, S. Seetharaman, P. Mahadevan, *et al.*, "ElasticTree: saving energy in data center networks.," in *Nsdi*, vol. 10, pp. 249–264, 2010.

[23] S. Jain, A. Kumar, S. Mandal, *et al.*, "B4: experience with a globally-deployed software defined wan," *SIGCOMM Computer Communication Review*, vol. 43, pp. 3–14, Aug. 2013.

[24] I. L. Lundquist, "The power of openstack." https://www.ibm.com/blogs/bluemix/2016/07/the-power-of-openstack/. Accessed on 19 July 2016.

[25] F. P. Tso, D. R. White, S. Jouet, J. Singer, and D. P. Pezaros, "The Glasgow raspberry pi cloud: a scale model for cloud computing infrastructures," in *Distributed Computing Systems Workshops (ICDCSW), 2013 IEEE 33rd International Conference on*, pp. 108–112, IEEE, 2013.

[26] E. Keller, S. Ghorbani, M. Caesar, and J. Rexford, "Live migration of an entire network (and its hosts)," in *Proceedings of the 11th ACM Workshop on Hot Topics in Networks*, pp. 109–114, ACM, 2012.

[27] D. Mattos, N. Fernandes, V. da Costa, *et al.*, "Omni: Openflow management infrastructure," in *Network of the Future (NOF), 2011 International Conference on the*, pp. 52–56, Nov. 2011.

[28] H. E. Egilmez, S. T. Dane, K. T. Bagci, and A. M. Tekalp, "OpenQoS: an OpenFlow controller design for multimedia delivery with end-to-end Quality of Service over Software-Defined Networks," in *Signal & Information Processing Association Annual Summit and Conference (APSIPA ASC), 2012 Asia-Pacific*, pp. 1–8, 2012.

[29] A. D. Ferguson, A. Guha, C. Liang, R. Fonseca, and S. Krishnamurthi, "Participatory networking: an API for application control of SDNs," in *Proceedings of the ACM SIGCOMM 2013 Conference on SIGCOMM*, pp. 327–338, ACM, 2013.

[30] G. Wang and T. Ng, "The impact of virtualization on network performance of Amazon EC2 data center," in *Proc. IEEE INFOCOM'10*, pp. 1–9, Mar. 2010.

[31]   S. Kandula, S. Sengupta, A. Greenberg, P. Patel, and R. Chaiken, "The nature of data center traffic: measurements & analysis," in *Proc. ACM SIGCOMM Internet Measurement Conference (IMC'09)*, pp. 202–208, 2009.

[32]   A. Greenberg, J. Hamilton, D. A. Maltz, and P. Patel, "The cost of a cloud: research problems in data center networks," *SIGCOMM Computer Communication Review*, vol. 39, pp. 68–73, Dec. 2008.

[33]   L. A. Barroso, J. Clidaras, and U. Hölzle, "The datacenter as a computer: an introduction to the design of warehouse-scale machines," *Synthesis Lectures on Computer Architecture*, vol. 8, no. 3, pp. 1–154, 2013.

[34]   T. Wood, P. Shenoy, A. Venkataramani, and M. Yousif, "Black-box and gray-box strategies for virtual machine migration," in *USENIX NSDI'07*, 2007.

[35]   V. Mann, A. Kumar, P. Dutta, and S. Kalyanaraman, "VMFlow: leveraging VM mobility to reduce network power costs in data centers," in *Proc. IFIP TC 6 Networking Conf.*, vol. 6640 of *LNCS*, pp. 198–211, Springer Berlin Heidelberg, 2011.

[36]   N. Bobroff, A. Kochut, and K. Beaty, "Dynamic placement of virtual machines for managing SLA violations," in *Integrated Network Management, 2007. IM '07. 10th IFIP/IEEE International Symposium on*, pp. 119–128, 2007.

[37]   A. Li, X. Yang, S. Kandula, and M. Zhang, "CloudCmp: comparing public cloud providers," in *Proc. ACM SIGCOMM Internet Measurement Conf. (IMC'10)*, pp. 1–14, 2010.

[38]   F. P. Tso, G. Hamilton, K. Oikonomou, and D. P. Pezaros, "Implementing scalable, network-aware virtual machine migration for cloud data centers," in *Cloud Computing (CLOUD), 2013 IEEE Sixth International Conference on*, pp. 557–564, Jun. 2013.

[39]   F. P. Tso, K. Oikonomou, E. Kavvadia, and D. P. Pezaros, "Scalable traffic-aware virtual machine management for cloud data centers," in *Distributed Computing Systems (ICDCS), 2014 IEEE 34th International Conference on*, Jun. 2014.

[40]   J. Sherry, S. Hasan, C. Scott, A. Krishnamurthy, S. Ratnasamy, and V. Sekar, "Making middleboxes someone else's problem: network processing as a cloud service," *ACM SIGCOMM Computer Communication Review*, vol. 42, no. 4, pp. 13–24, 2012.

[41]   M. Hajjat, X. Sun, Y.-W. E. Sung, *et al.*, "Cloudward bound: planning for beneficial migration of enterprise applications to the cloud," in *ACM SIGCOMM Computer Communication Review*, vol. 40, pp. 243–254, ACM, 2010.

[42]   R. Cziva, S. Jouet, K. J. S. White, and D. P. Pezaros, "Container-based network function virtualization for software-defined networks," in *2015 IEEE Symposium on Computers and Communication (ISCC)*, pp. 415–420, Jul. 2015.

[43]   R. Cziva, S. Jouet, and D. P. Pezaros, "Gnfc: towards network function cloudification," in *2015 IEEE Conference on Network Function Virtualization and Software Defined Network (NFV-SDN)*, pp. 142–148, Nov. 2015.

[44]   SDxCentral, "Definition of SDN & NFV big data optimization use case." https://www.sdxcentral.com/sdn-nfv-use-cases/data-center-optimization/big-data-optimization/, accessed at: 28/02/2017.

[45] P. Bosshart, G. Gibb, H.-S. Kim, *et al.*, "Forwarding metamorphosis: fast programmable match-action processing in hardware for SDN," in *Proceedings of the ACM SIGCOMM 2013 Conference on SIGCOMM*, SIGCOMM '13, (New York, NY, USA), pp. 99–110, ACM, 2013.

[46] R. Ozdag, "Intel ethernet switch fm6000 series – software defined networking." http://www.intel.co.uk/content/www/uk/en/ethernet-products/switch-silicon/ethernet-switch-fm5000-fm6000-series.html, 2012.

[47] Caviant, "XPliant: Ethernet Switch Product Family." http://www.cavium.com. Accessed on 14 November 2017.

[48] P. Bosshart, D. Daly, G. Gibb, *et al.*, "P4: programming protocol-independent packet processors," in *SIGCOMM*, Jul. 2014.

[49] H. Song, "Protocol-oblivious forwarding: unleash the power of SDN through a future-proof forwarding plane," in *Proceedings of the Second ACM SIGCOMM Workshop on Hot Topics in Software Defined Networking*, HotSDN '13, (New York, NY, USA), pp. 127–132, ACM, 2013.

[50] S. Jouet, R. Cziva, and D. P. Pezaros, "Arbitrary packet matching in openflow," in *High Performance Switching and Routing (HPSR), 2015 IEEE 16th International Conference on*, pp. 1–6, IEEE, 2015.

[51] M. Shahbaz, S. Choi, B. Pfaff, *et al.*, "Pisces: a programmable, protocol-independent software switch," in *Proceedings of the 2016 ACM SIGCOMM Conference*, SIGCOMM '16, (New York, NY, USA), pp. 525–538, ACM, 2016.

Chapter 5

Introduction to big data

Amir H. Payberah* and Fatemeh Rahimian*

The amount of data generated during the last few years has been unprecedented. This is not only due to the prevalence of online social networks and the ubiquitous devices connected to the Internet but also as the result of the advances in technology across other fields, for instance, whole genome sequencing. Hence, it is fair to say that we are living in the era of *big data*. Big data refers to large datasets or data flows that have outpaced our capability to store and process and cannot be analyzed by traditional means. More specifically, challenges arise mainly due to one or several of the following reasons:

- *Volume*: when we encounter massive data in size, e.g., data from crawling the web, or genome sequencing data, traditional storage and processing systems fall short. We, thus, need to build new systems, techniques, and algorithms that efficiently store, retrieve, and process huge volumes of data.
- *Velocity*: big data is not only about the size. High rate of data generation is also important. For example, data generated in Twitter or communication networks come in form of continuous streams of data at a very high rate. Many systems require to analyze this kind of data in real time.
- *Variety*: sometimes, data comes from multiple sources and in a variety of forms, for example, as a combination of structured, semi-structured, and unstructured data. It is, therefore, important to have systems that handle diverse data models without compromising performance.

In the presence of these challenges, traditional platforms fail to show the expected performance, and thus, new systems for storing and processing large-scale data are crucial to emerge. In this chapter, we explore some of the new trends of technology for handling big data.

5.1 Big data platforms: challenges and requirements

A big data platform should provide means to efficiently store, retrieve, and process massive amount of data. One of the main challenges a big data platform should address

*The George Institute for Global Health, University of Oxford, UK

is *scalability*. More specifically, the platform should allocate as much resources as required for handling big data. There are two possible solutions to make a system scalable: (i) to *scale up* (or *scale vertically*), by adding more resources to a single machine, or (ii) to *scale out* (or *scale horizontally*), by adding more machines in a network and use all their collective resources. Buying an extremely strong machine for scaling up is probably less challenging, but it is very costly. More importantly, you can scale up a system only to a certain degree, i.e., there is a limit in how much resources you can add to a single machine, and this limit is far less than what most big data processing applications require. In contrast, exploiting the collective resources of a network of commodity machines is an economically and technically attractive solution, and thus, scaling out is the approach taken by almost all the existing platforms. Nevertheless, due to the distribution of data and computation over a network, new challenges and requirements arise.

- *Fault tolerance*: one or several machines may fail while running a job. Assume a machine can stay up for 1,000 days. If there are 1,000 machines in a network, we expect to observe one failed machine per day, on average. When there are millions of machines in a network, like in Google sites, we may have 1,000 machine failures per day. It is, therefore, crucial for the platform to be resilient to the failures.

- *Transparency*: while resources of a platform are distributed, it is widely agreed that users should get an illusion of working with one single machine. More precisely, the details of resource management, including resource allocation and load balancing, should be hidden from an ordinary user of the platform. This is one of the requirements of any big data processing platform.

- *Parallel programming model*: traditional programming models assume that code, data, and all the required resources for executing the code (e.g., CPU and memory) are available locally. This assumption is not valid anymore in horizontally scalable platforms. In the new model, data and/or operations should be parallelized, so that different parts of the data can be processed in parallel. Moreover, since transferring large amounts of data over network is costly, it is often the code that is sent over to where the data is stored. This paradigm shift calls for the development of many new parallel and distributed algorithms.

- *Shared-nothing communication model*: processes can communicate over a network in three different ways: via storage, memory, or network. These models are known as shared storage, shared memory, and *shared nothing*, respectively [1]. For scalability reasons, the shared-nothing architecture has become the de-facto communication model in building big data platforms.

Currently, there exist several big data platforms that provide the above features. The diversity of these platforms can make it difficult to choose the best one for carrying out a task. Some platforms are designed for a specific type of processing, for example, GraphLab [2] for graph processing and Storm [3] for stream processing, while some others are more generic and handle a wider range of processing types. Example of such platforms includes MapReduce [4], Spark [5], and Flink [6]. While the overall architecture of these platforms share many common features, the platforms

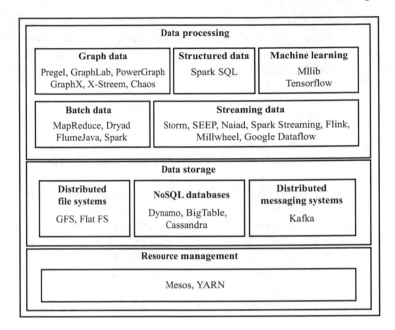

Figure 5.1   Big data platforms stack

themselves can be integrated in a stack, depicted in Figure 5.1, which consists of the following layers:

- *Resource management*: this layer contains platforms that are used to manage resources of a cluster and share them among the platforms in the upper layers.
- *Data store*: the platforms in this layer are used to store and retrieve massive data. They include distributed file systems that maintain data on distributed disks, messaging system for handling real-time data, and databases to maintain structured data at scale.
- *Data processing*: this layer contains the platforms for parallel processing of data across a large number of commodity computers. These platforms are categorized into a few subgroups, based on their target application and input model, for example, for batch data, streaming data, graph data, structured data, or for higher level analysis, e.g., machine-learning algorithms.

Due to lack of space, we chose to skip the platforms in the resource management layer. We will, however, explore some of the well-known platforms in the two top layers of Figure 5.1 that answer two main questions: (i) how to *store* big data and (ii) how to *process* it.

5.2   How to store big data?

When the size of data exceeds the capacity of one disk, we have to use multiple disks in a distributed environment. To build a distributed storage system, we need to take into account the nature of data that we are going to store. We could be dealing with batch or streaming data, and the data could be structured or unstructured. Based on these characteristics and also on the target application, data can be stored in either a file system, a messaging system, or a database. In this section, we will explain some of the well-known storage systems.

5.2.1   Distributed file systems

In operating systems (OS), a *file system* refers to a collection of methods and data structures to store files on a disk and retrieve them. In Unix-like file systems, for instance, a file is divided into small data blocks, which are stored on a disk. The OS, then, uses a data structure, called *inode* to maintain the file's metadata, e.g., ownership and access mode, as well as the location of the file's data blocks on disk. The inode structure is originally designed for a single disk and does not work over multiple and distributed disks. We, thus, need to design a *distributed file system* that makes it possible to store and retrieve files on/from distributed disks, without involving users in details and complexity of the system. Several distributed file systems have been designed and developed, e.g., GFS [7], FlatFS [8], and Ceph [9], among which GFS and its open source implementation HDFS [10] are the most popular ones.

5.2.1.1   GFS and HDFS

In GFS, a file is split into a number of *chunks*. A chunk is a single unit of storage, which is transparent to users. Size of chunks is chosen relatively big (64MB or 128MB), compared to block size in OSs, to reduce the read/write time. From the architectural perspective, GFS has three main components: *master*, *chunk server*, and *client*. The master (similar to inode) stores metadata about files and the location of their chunks, while chunk servers store chunks as regular files on their local file systems. The clients, then, find the location of chunks by contacting the master, and continue the rest of operation, e.g., read and write, by communicating directly with the respective chunk server(s).

The GFS master maintains the file system namespace as a key-value table, with file full pathname as key and the metadata as value. It also manages the access control to files by acquiring a set of read/write locks on files in the namespace. For example, in the path `/foo/bar/test.txt`, the master can apply a read lock on internal nodes, e.g., `/foo` or `/bar`, to prevent the deletion or renaming of them and their descendant subtrees. Similarly, it can apply a read/write lock on the leaf nodes, e.g., `test.txt`, to protect them from further read and write operations, while they are opened by one client.

In GFS, each chunk is replicated on a number of chunk servers to increase data reliability and availability. The master decides on replica placement, by placing the replicas on chunk servers with below-average disk usage. It also creates new replicas when the number of available replicas falls below a predefined threshold. To provide consistency among replicas of a chunk, one replica is designated as the *primary* for that chunk, and the other replicas are maintained as *secondaries*. The primary replica decides the update order, and the secondaries follow this order.

GFS does not provide POSIX-based APIs for interaction, but it provides function-alities to read, write, and delete files. To read a chunk, the user application originates a read request and delivers it to a GFS client, who sends the request to the master. Upon receipt of a read request, the master responds with the address of replicas (over chunk servers). The client selects one of these chuck servers and sends it the read request. Finally, the chunk server sends the requested data back to the client, and the client forwards it to the application. Similarly, to write a chunk, the application sends a write request to a client, which in turn forwards the request to the master. Once more, the master replies with the address of existing replicas on the chunk servers. When the client receives this information, it pushes data to all the corresponding chunk servers, both primary and secondaries. The chunk servers keep the received data in their internal buffers, without writing them to their disk. When the client issues a write command, the primary serializes data instances, that is, it writes the updates to chunks in a specific order. It then sends the data instance order to the secondaries, so that they apply the update in that same order. The delete function, is however, a metadata operation, meaning that when a user calls it, the master just marks the name of the file as deleted, but the actual data will remain on disks. After a certain time, the master deletes the data of all the marked files.

Since all the metadata information about the file system is on the GFS master, the system cannot work if the master fails. To make the system robust, the master state is also replicated on multiple machines. If the master fails, a new master takes over and continues from the latest replicated state.

5.2.2 Messaging systems

Sometimes, the complete data is not available in the beginning of a process, and instead, it is received as streaming data gradually over time. For example, a web server, as a data provider, continuously sends events every time someone requests a page. The consumers, then, can use this data for different purposes, e.g., to store in HDFS, trigger an alert, or send a notification email. A *messaging system* is a middleware that facilitates a near real-time asynchronous computation by decoupling all consumers works from the actual data provider services. When a new event takes place at a provider, messages are added to the messaging system, and consumers can read them based on their demands. Several messaging systems exist, e.g., Kafka [11], ActiveMQ [12], RabbitMQ [13], and Flume [14]. Among this list, we will briefly explain Kafka.

5.2.2.1 Kafka

Kafka [11] is a distributed topic-oriented log service, which was designed originally in LinkedIn. It categorizes feeds of messages into multiple groups, called *topics*, each containing a stream of messages of a particular type. Each topic is divided into a number of *partitions*, each being an append-only and immutable file on disk. Messages generated by a producer to a particular topic partition are appended in the same order they are sent, and consumers see them in the same order they are stored.

To increase the reliability of the system, partitions of a topic are replicated on several servers, called *brokers*, where one broker becomes the leader of a partition, and all writes and reads are managed through it. Kafka uses Zookeeper [15] to manage its system on a cluster of machines. Zookeeper detects the addition and the removal of brokers and consumers, maintains the consumption relationship, and keeps track of the consumed offset of each partition.

5.2.3   NoSQL databases

File systems store any type of data, whether it is structured or unstructured, but they provide no means to take advantage of the structure in data in the former case. This is where database systems can play an important role. Databases are built on top of file systems to deal with well-formatted data and perform efficient read, write, update, and delete operations. Among the existing databases, relational database management systems (RDBMSs) are the dominant ones for maintaining structured data. RDBMSs guarantee certain properties, commonly known as the *ACID properties*, with the following descriptions: (i) *Atomicity*: either all or none of the operations in a *transaction* are executed, where a transaction is a single unit of work and consists of a sequence of operations in a database, (ii) *Consistency*: database should be in a consistent state before and after a transaction, (iii) *Isolation*: uncommitted changes in the databases should not be visible to other transactions, and (iv) *Durability*: changes should be written to a disk before a transaction is marked as committed, so that any updated data could be later recovered in case the system fails.

With the emergence of big data in various domains, for example, over the Web 2.0 applications, data management technologies are entering a new phase. The big data applications have special demands, such as *scalability* and *availability*, which are not necessarily in-line with the ACID properties provided by RDBMSs. For example, when we are dealing with a high rate of read/write operations, treating each operation as a transaction and locking the data to provide ACID guarantees, may hinder the scalability of the system. One way out of this problem is to relax some of the unnecessarily strong properties, for instance consistency and isolation. In fact, a new set of properties have been defined for such scenarios. These properties, known as *BASE properties*, are introduced to trade consistency and isolation of ACID properties for achieving scalability and availability. The BASE properties are: (i) *Basic Availability*: faults may happen, but they should not obstruct the functioning of the whole system, (ii) *Soft state*: different copies of a data piece may be inconsistent, and (iii) *Eventually consistent*: all copies of a data piece eventually become consistent at some point in future, if no more updates happen to that data piece. The BASE properties have become the baseline in all the emerging databases, known as *NoSQL (Not Only SQL)* databases that deal with big data.

To put the two sets of properties in perspective, it is perhaps useful to recall the famous *CAP theorem*, which states that in any distributed system, it is impossible to provide consistency (C), availability (A), and partition tolerance (P) properties all at the same time. In other words, a distributed database system can have only two of these properties simultaneously. While most RDBMSs have chosen to provide consistency and availability, without providing partition tolerance, NoSQL databases are always partition tolerant but provide either consistency or availability, not both at the same time.

NoSQL databases can have different data models, that is, they can store data in different ways. There exist four popular data models in use, namely *key value*, *column based*, *document based*, and *graph based*. Key-value data model is the simplest data model, where data is stored in form of pairs of key and value, and values could be any arbitrary data. Column-based data model enhances the key-value model by adding some schema to values. The document-based databases are similar to column-based store, except that values can have a flexible schema (e.g., XML or JSON), instead of a fixed schema. Finally, graph databases model data and its interdependencies as a graph and store it in form of graph nodes, edges, and properties.

In this part, we introduce two different NoSQL databases, Dynamo [16] and BigTable [17], where the former is a key-value store that provides P and A properties, and the latter is a column-based storage that provides P and C properties.

5.2.3.1 Dynamo

Dynamo [16] borrows the idea of *consistent hashing* [18] from distributed hash tables for partitioning and distributing data across multiple machines. Each machine is given an *identifier (id)*, using a hash function, and the machines are ordered along a ring by their ascending ids. The same hash function is also applied on data to give each data item an id in the same id space. Each machine, then, stores data items with ids between its own node id and its *predecessor* id in the ring. The predecessor of a node *B* would be a node *A*, whose id is the previous id anticlockwise in the ring before the *B*'s id. In this case, node *B* is the *successor* of node *A*. To achieve high availability and durability, Dynamo replicates data on multiple machines, listed on a *preference list* per data item, which are usually the *n* successor machines of an id along the ring.

Although consistent hashing is an efficient way to distribute data over machines, it may end up with imbalanced load on machines, due to several reasons, such as nonuniform distribution of data ids (keys) over the ring, various popularity and hit rate of the keys, or the heterogeneous power of machines. To overcome these challenges, Dynamo uses *virtual nodes*, meaning that each physical machine picks multiple random ids, where each id represents a virtual node. Hence, we can assume that each physical machine runs multiple virtual nodes over different parts of the ring, where each virtual node covers the range of keys between its id and its predecessor virtual node id.

To read and write data, Dynamo provides two APIs: `get`, which returns a single item or list of items with conflicting versions, and `put`, which stores an item under a given key. These operations are handled by a *coordinator* for each item, which is the first node on its preference list. As mentioned earlier, Dynamo does not guarantee strong consistency but provides eventual consistency, which enables asynchronous updates of data items. More precisely, multiple versions of a data item may exist in the system, but replicas of each item eventually become consistent. Dynamo tracks the causality of events over different replicas, and if it identifies an order among them, it replaces the older version of replica with the new one; otherwise, it raises a conflict, in which case, reconciliation is required. A conflict may happen due to node or network failures. If multiple versions of a data item exist, the system delegates the reconciliation to users. Such a scenario can happen in online shopping, for example, when a user finds inconsistent shopping baskets in her profile. The system never refuses to add new items to the basket, but a user may find some already removed items, back in the basket again.

Machines can be added to or removed from Dynamo by an administrator. After new machines are added/removed, the membership change is propagated in the system using a gossiping protocol [19], such that eventually all machines acquire a consistent view of the system. When a new machine joins, it gets an id, and thus, a key range for which it is responsible. Then, the data items that fall into that range are transferred to the new machine. For example, assume a new machine X is added to the system between two existing machines A and B, where B was the successor of A and responsible for the key range $[A, B)$. After adding X, the data items for the key range $[A, X)$ should be transferred to X, and B would be responsible for the new key range $[X, B)$. When a machine is removed, for example, the newly added X, a reverse process will take place, during which data items on X are transferred to its successor B. This is how the number of machines in Dynamo can dynamically change.

5.2.3.2 BigTable and HBase

BigTable [17], introduced by Google, is another NoSQL database. While BigTable is built on top of GFS, the open source version of it, that is HBase [20], is part of the Hadoop ecosystem and is built over HDFS. BigTable uses a column-based data model to store data. A *table* is the highest abstraction to store data. Each table consists of multiple rows, where each row has one or more columns. Rows are ordered lexicographically by their key. A group of columns with the same type can build a *group family*, which are the basic units of access control. Each cell in the table can have multiple values, distinguished by their timestamps. When a table becomes too large, the system splits it into *tablets*, which are contiguous rows stored together.

BigTable has three main components: *master server*, *tablet server*, and *client library*. In each cluster, there exists only one master server, which assigns tablets to tablet servers. The master server also balances the load among tablet servers and conducts garbage collection of useless files in GFS. Moreover, it handles the changes to the schema, e.g., creates new tables or adds new column families. Management of tablets are done by the tablet servers. Multiple tablet servers exist in a cluster, and they can be added or removed dynamically. Each tablet server is in charge of a set of tablets and all the read and write operations that apply to those tablets. Each tablet is assigned to only one tablet server. Note that the data of tablets are stored in GFS, and tablet servers only handle the read and write requests for their assigned tablets. Since files are replicated in the GFS layer, there is no need to replicate tablets separately. Client libraries provide methods to communicate with the master and tablet servers and cache the tablet locations. Clients can work with BigTable through these libraries.

BigTable takes advantage of other existing platforms internally. For example, it uses GFS to store log and data files, and Chubby lock service [21] to manage the deployed system. Chubby is responsible for the following tasks: (i) to ensure only one master is active in cluster, (ii) to store the location of the *root tablet* that contains the location of all other tablets, (iii) to discover tablet servers, (iv) to store tables' schema, and (v) to store access control lists. When a master starts, it communicates with Chubby and grabs a lock to prevent any other master claiming the system. It, then, gets the list of available tablet servers from Chubby and communicates with them to discover their already assigned tablets.

BigTable uses a three-level hierarchical structure to maintain the address of tablets: (i) Chubby stores a file that contains the address of a metadata tablet, called *root tablet*, (ii) the root tablet contains the location of all other metadata tablets, and (iii) each metadata tablet maintains the address of a set of user tablets. Each tablet, internally, is divided into a number of *SSTables*, which are the fundamental components of BigTable for storing data. An SSTable is a set of immutable sorted key-value pairs, stored as a file in GFS.

When a user commits some update to a tablet, first the commit logs are stored in GFS. Then, the responsible tablet server for that tablet keeps the most recent updates in an in-memory structure, called *memtable*. When the size of a memtable exceeds some threshold, it is written to an SSTable, and consequently to GFS. This can eventually result in having a large number of SSTables in GFS, and thus, the system periodically merges the SSTables of each tablet into a single SSTable, to optimize the disk usage. To read data from a tablet server, both memtable, which contains the latest updates, and the sequence of recent SSTables are used.

BigTable guarantees strong consistency, because each tablet is managed by one tablet server only, and all concurrent queries for a tablet are serialized in that tablet server. However, if a tablet server fails, the availability of its part of data is violated until a new server is assigned. In other words, BigTable provides consistency but cannot guarantee availability.

5.3 How to process big data?

The next big challenge while dealing with massive data is how to process it. Various platforms and tools have been recently developed for this purpose, and choosing the right tool is essential. The existing tools can be categorized based on the kind of data they process, for example, batch data, streaming data, graph (linked) data, and structured data. In this section, we explore some of the state-of-the-art tools from each of these categories.

5.3.1 Batch data processing platforms

Processing batch data, also known as *data-at-rest*, is the traditional way of data processing. Building a single machine system for batch processing is simple and well studied since the first generation of computers emerged. When dealing with batch data, we know that all the data is available at the processing time, but in case of big data, it may be too big to be loaded into the memory all at once. Hence, when the size of data exceeds the capability of one machine, then new solutions are required.

To provide a practical example, assume there is a text file and the goal is to count the number of distinct words in this file. Also, assume the size of the file is small enough to be loaded into the memory of one machine. In this case, a simple bash script command can count the number of words.

```
words (file) | sort | uniq - c
```

where `words (file)` splits the words of the given file by space and returns a list of words. However, if the file does not fit in the memory of one machine, the above script does not work any longer. A possible solution to scale up the system is to divide the file and distribute it across several machines and process them in parallel. However, new challenges arise with such a system, including parallelization, fault tolerance, data distribution, and load balancing.

5.3.1.1 MapReduce

MapReduce [4] is one of the first batch data processing systems that addressed the above challenges, while providing users with a new programming model that enables them to implement their code easily. In other words, MapReduce is both (i) a programming model for big data processing, inspired by functional programming, and (ii) an execution framework to run parallel algorithms on clusters of commodity machines.

Programming in MapReduce model boils down to writing two main functions: a *map* function that processes data and generates a set of intermediate key-value pairs and (ii) a *reduce* function that aggregates all the intermediate values associated with the same intermediate key. There is also a *shuffle* step that takes place between the execution of these two functions. During the shuffle step, the key-value pairs that are generated by the map function are sorted and prepared for the reduce function.

To implement the "word count" — the process of listing the words accompanies with the number of their occurrences in a file — example using this model, the following three steps can be performed: (i) `words (file)` extracts words from `file`, (ii) `sort` shuffles and sorts the words, and (iii) `uniq -c` aggregates the intermediate results and generates the final output. This code can be perfectly modeled with MapReduce, where each command corresponds to one of the phases of MapReduce. If the sample input file contains `Hello World, Hello Life`, then the map function reads the words and for each one generates a key-value pair with value 1, e.g., `(Hello, 1), (World, 1), (Hello, 1)`, and `(Life, 1)`. The shuffle phase between map and reduce phase creates a list of values associated with each key, e.g., `[Hello, (1, 1)], [World, (1)]`, and `[Life, (1)]`. Finally, the reduce function sums up the counts per key and generates the final result, e.g., `(Hello, 2), (World, 1)`, and `(Life, 1)`. Note that the user needs only to implement the map and reduce functions, and the system takes care of the shuffle phase.

An important notion here is that, while the code is very small, the data can be big and possibly distributed over multiple machines in a network. A traditional computation model will move the data over the network to be read and processed by the code. In contrast, the MapReduce computation model suggests that we keep data where it is and instead move the computation close to data. The small piece of code can then be executed in parallel on each machine, and the result will be aggregated and reported. More specifically, the following steps are taken to execute a program in MapReduce:

1. The input files are read and divided into a number of *splits*. The size of splits is typically the same as the size of chunks in HDFS.
2. The MapReduce library in the user program, then, sends a copy of the program to each of the machines, among which one becomes the *master*, and the others become *workers*. The master assigns tasks (map or reduce) to the workers, who become mappers and reducers, accordingly.
3. Each mapper takes a set of splits as input and performs the map function on them. The result of the map function is generated as intermediate key-value pairs, which are buffered in the memory of the mapper.
4. Each mapper periodically writes the buffered data to its local disk and sends their addresses to the master. Then, the master forwards these addresses to the reducers.
5. Each reducer reads the corresponding intermediate data from the local disks of the mappers. When a reducer reads all the required key-value pairs, it sorts and groups them by their keys.
6. Each reducer, then, iterates over the list of intermediate keys and their corresponding values and performs the reduce function on them. The result of reduce functions is appended to the final output file in HDFS.
7. When all map and reduce tasks have been completed, the master informs the user program that the final result is ready.

The master monitors workers liveness via periodic heartbeats. If it detects the failure of an in-progress map or reduce task, it reexecutes it (possibly on a different worker). If it detects a completed map task has failed, it again needs to reexecute the map task, because the output is stored on the local disk of the failed mapper. However, if a reducer with a completed task fails, the master does not reexecute the task, because the output is stored in HDFS. The state of the master is periodically checkpointed. Hence, upon failure, a new master starts and resumes the work from the last check-pointed state.

5.3.1.2   Spark

Although MapReduce facilitates an easy implementation of batch data processing over a cluster, it is very rigid in nature and cannot be used for building complex, interactive, or iterative programs. Sometimes, adding only a little complexity can render the whole MapReduce model infeasible. For example, let us add a few steps to the word count example:

```
words (doc.txt) | grep | sed | sort | awk
```

This is a job that requires more than one map and reduce round, and each two consecutive rounds can only communicate through HDFS. That is, the reducer of one round writes the result in HDFS, and the mapper of the next round reads that data from HDFS. However, reading from and writing to HDFS is a slow process.

To overcome this problem, we need to reduce the interaction with HDFS as much as possible, for example, by keeping the intermediate results in memory, when there are multiple consecutive rounds of map and reduce functions. Replacing a stable storage with volatile memory is challenging, and the question is how to make such a memory model efficient and fault tolerant.

Spark [5] provides an answer to this question. It is a batch processing engine for massive data, which exploits in-memory processing by presenting a distributed memory abstraction, called *Resilient Distributed Datasets (RDD)*. RDD is an immutable collections of objects spread across a cluster. An RDD is divided into a number of *partitions* (atomic pieces of information), where each partition can be stored on a different machine in a cluster.

Spark works based on the master–worker model. The main program, the *driver*, runs on a master machine and coordinates the execution of the whole application. When a Spark application is executed, the driver connects to the cluster manager and acquires *executors* on worker machines to run tasks and store data (one or more partitions of RDDs). The driver, then, sends the application code, as well as tasks to the executors. The entry point to Spark functionalities is through a `SparkContext` object in the driver that defines how Spark can access the cluster, e.g., run locally, run as a stand-alone cluster, or run on cluster via a resource management system, such as Mesos [22] or YARN [23].

There are two types of operators that can be applied on RDDs: *transformations* and *actions*. Transformations are *lazy* operators that are applied on RDDs and create new RDDs. They are called lazy, because they do not compute the result right away. Instead, they build a chain (graph) of operations over RDD, called *lineage graph*. Actions, on the other hand, launch a computation on RDDs and return a value. When an action is called on an RDD, all the transformations in its lineage graph are executed, and then the final result is computed. More specifically, upon calling an action, RDDs are broken down into multiple partitions and are loaded by the Spark executors on worker nodes. Then, transformations are executed, and finally the result are calculated. When multiple actions are called on an RDD, all the transformations in its lineage graph are recomputed per action. To reduce the overhead of recomputation, however, the transformed RDDs can be *cached* in memory. The caching, if needed, should be explicitly done by the programmer.

The lineage graph is also used to recover from failures in an efficient way. Unlike MapReduce that replicates data to make the system resilient, Spark keeps track of the lineage information, by which it can reconstruct the lost partitions. If a partition fails, Spark backtracks on the lineage graph until it finds a correct partition and then recomputes the lost partitions of RDDs. If an RDD becomes unavailable, all its missing partitions are recomputed in parallel. If a task fails, it is reexecuted on another machine, providing that its parent RDDs on the lineage graph are available.

5.3.2　Streaming data processing platforms

Some applications need to process streams of live data and provide results in real time. Wireless sensor network services, traffic management systems, and stock markets are examples of such applications. Stream processing systems (SPS) are a group of platforms that process such streaming data [24]. In contrast to batch processing systems and database management systems (DBMS), which are used to analyze data at rest, an SPS processes *data in motion*. Typically, batch processing systems and DBMSs store and index data before computation and process them only when explicitly asked by users. However, an SPS processes data as it arrives, without having to store it persistently.

An SPS receives streaming data as an unbounded sequence of individual data items, called *tuples*. A tuple is the atomic data item in a streaming data, which is equivalent to a row in table. The tuples can be either structured in a predefined schema, semi-structured with self-describing tags (e.g., XML), or totally unstructured in custom formats (e.g., video and/or audio).

The programming model for an SPS is normally based on defining *jobs* in form of *dataflows* to represent the *logical plan* of the work. A dataflow is a *directed acyclic graphs (DAG)* composed of data sources, *processing elements (PE)*, and data sinks. A PE is the basic functional unit in a dataflow that reads some input tuples, applies a specific function on them, and outputs new tuples.

Two fundamental questions regarding the dataflow programming model are (i) how to compose a dataflow and (ii) what functions to use. Dataflow composition is the process of creating a DAG associated with a job. DAG composition can be *static* or *dynamic*. If all the PEs and their relation in the DAG are known in advance, they can be connected statically; otherwise, the dynamic composition is used. The PEs that are put in a DAG in this step are higher order functions that belong to one of the following operation categories: (i) *aggregation*, to collect and summarize a subset of tuples, (ii) *merge/split* to combine/partition input streams, (iii) *logical* and *mathematical* operations, (iv) *sequence manipulations*, to reorder or delay tuples, or (v) any other custom data manipulations, e.g., data mining algorithms. Each of these categories includes many different functions, and thus, the next step is to decide which function should be used inside each PE.

A PE can be either *stateless* or *stateful*. In a stateless model, a PE processes tuples independent of each other and then forgets about them, whereas in a stateful model, a PE is a *synopsis* of the already received tuples, meaning that it maintains an internal state with the footprint of the processed tuples. In this case, a PE also keeps a subset of the most recent tuples in a buffer, namely a *window*. There exist two popular window models: *tumbling* and *sliding*. Both models keep a certain number of tuples, defined by the window size. When the buffer is full, a tumbling window will remove all the buffered tuples at once, while a sliding window only removes the oldest ones from the buffer. The tumbling window model is usually used for batch operations, while the sliding window model fits better in scenarios with incremental operations.

More specifically, the semantics of a window model is defined by its *eviction policy* and *trigger policy*, where the eviction policy determines the properties of tuples that are to be removed, and the trigger policy defines when the buffered tuples should be processed. In general, four different policies are available: (i) *count based*, which defines the maximum number of tuples the buffer can hold (for an eviction policy) or the number of tuples that should be received before the tuples can be processed (for a trigger policy), (ii) *delta based*, which is specified by a delta threshold in a tuple attribute, for eviction or trigger, (iii) *time based*, which defines a time interval for eviction or trigger, and (iv) *punctuation based*, which triggers processing or eviction of tuples, upon receipt of a punctuation. Any combination of these policies can be used independently for eviction and trigger. For example, a count-based eviction policy could coexist with a time-based trigger policy.

The dataflow that a user defines is a *logical plan* that should be converted to a *physical plan* at run time and deployed over a cluster. Vertices and edges of a logical plan correspond to PEs and their connections, respectively. Whereas, in a physical plan, vertices represent the OS processes, and edges denote the data communication medium (e.g., network connection and/or shared memory). The physical plan is not unique, and the transformation task is not straightforward. A decent physical plan takes into account the workload of each PE and the amount of data transfer between different PEs, when partitioning the logical plan and deciding if a partition or a set of PEs should be located on a single machine or multiple ones. These are, however, similar to the challenges of parallelization in general.

Parallelization enables the SPSs to remain efficient with the increasing number of queries and the high rate of incoming data. There are different ways to parallelize an SPS. The first approach is *pipelined parallelization*, where sequential PEs of a dataflow run concurrently on different tuples of a stream. For example, if A and B are sequential PEs, represented as $(A \rightarrow B)$, then B can start processing a `tuple1`, as soon as A completes processing it and moves on to process `tuple2`. The second model is *task parallelization,* in which, independent PEs are executed concurrently on the same or distinct tuples. For example, if A and B are independent PEs, they can run in parallel on the same tuple, e.g., `tuple1`. *Data parallelization* is the third model, where the same PE runs in parallel on different parts of a tuple. For example, if `tuple1` is a big data item, it can be divided into a number of parts, and different instances of a single PE, e.g., A, can be executed concurrently on different parts of the tuple. In the data parallelization model, the incoming tuples can be distributed randomly between PEs, or they can grouped by some keys and divided between PEs, or all tuples can be sent to all PEs.

Since failures are inevitable in a distributed system, data recovery becomes an important challenge for any SPS. A popular technique for avoiding data loss is *rollback recovery*, which can benefit from either an *active backup*, *passive backup*, or *upstream backup*. In the active backup, a backup node is associated with each processing node (called *primary*), and the same input is given to both primary and backup nodes. However, the output of the backup node is logged and is not sent downstream. Once the primary fails, the backup node takes over and sends the logged tuples to all downstream nodes and remains active afterwards. In the passive backup, the state of each node is periodically checkpointed in a shared storage. If a node fails, it will be replaced by a new node to take over from the latest checkpoint. Finally, in the upstream backup, upstream nodes (the parent node in DAG) store and keep the tuples until the downstream nodes acknowledge that the tuples are not needed any longer.

If a node fails, a new node takes over by rebuilding the latest state of the failed node from the logged tuples at the upstream node.

In the rest of this section, we will explain three SPS, Spark Streaming [25], Storm [3], and Flink [6]; Spark Streaming uses a *minibatching* processing model, while the other two use a *tuple-at-a-time* processing model. In the minibatching processing model, the streaming data is divided into small batches, and the streaming process is run as a series of deterministic computations over the batches. In the tuple-at-a-time processing model, stateful PEs process every incoming tuple, update their internal state, and emit new tuples.

5.3.2.1 Spark Streaming

Spark Streaming [25] is an SPS built on top of Spark that runs a streaming computation as a sequence of small and deterministic batch jobs. The incoming streaming data is divided into batches of *n* seconds, and each batch of data is treated as one RDD. A continuous sequence of RDDs is called *Discretized Stream* or *DStream*. DStream supports different operations, including standard RDD operations (such as `map` and `join`), as well as other operation specifically developed for DStream (such as window operations). When an operation is applied on a DStream, it will be applied on all its RDDs, and the final result would be a new DStream.

Spark Streaming supports the sliding window model and allows to apply a transformation over a set of RDDs collected in a window. A sliding window is defined by two parameters: *window length* that declares the size of window in time, and *slide interval* that defines how much a window should slide every time. Note that if we need to apply a function over all the received RDDs, then the sliding window is not enough. In this case, we should checkpoint and maintain the computation state, while continuously updating it with new incoming data. To enable checkpointing, user should create a directory in a reliable storage where the check-pointed states will be saved. Given the check-pointed data, user can apply a function over the state as well as on the new incoming data.

Spark Streaming architecture follows a master–worker model, where the master keeps track of DStream dataflow graph and schedules tasks on worker nodes, and workers keep partitions of RDDs and execute tasks. Moreover, workers receive data from client libraries or load them periodically from an external storage. The master, then, tracks the location of data items and helps clients to find the required data. To make the system fault tolerant, Spark Streaming takes advantage of the *lineage graph* used in the core of Spark by remembering the sequence of transformations over RDDs. If some data is lost due to a worker failure, it can be recomputed using the parent RDDs in the lineage graph. Moreover, the input data stream is replicated in memory of multiple worker nodes, so that in the worst case, when all the transformations should be recomputed from scratch, the original data is accessible.

5.3.2.2 Storm

While Spark Streaming is a non-native SPS, meaning that it discretizes the input stream into minibatches and applies short-lived batch tasks over them, Storm [3] and

Flink [6] are two native SPSs. In these systems, we have long-lived task execution, where each task maintains its own state. Storm is a distributed SPS for real-time processing of streaming data. There are two types of PEs in Storm: *spouts* as sources of streams and *bolts* that contain the main computation functions. Each bolt receives tuples from spouts and/or other bolts, processes them, and emits new tuples. In the Storm terminology, the DAG of spouts and bolts is called *topology*. To execute a topology, Storm runs spouts and bolts in parallel on different machines of a cluster. It is through the data and task parallelization models that Strom provide scalability.

Storm provides two types of *delivery* semantic guarantees: *at most once*, where each tuple is either processed once, or dropped if a failure happens, and *at least once* (also called *reliable* processing), in which, each tuple is processed at least once even if failures happen. To guarantee the reliable delivery, Storm uses a number system level bolts, called *acker bolts*, which keep track of the tuples of every spout in a topology. When a bolt successfully executes its function on a received tuple, it notifies the acker bolt by sending an ack message to it. When the acker bolt receives an ack message for all tuples in a *tuple tree*, it sends a final ack to the spout that emitted the tuple. A tuple tree refers to all the tuples emitted by subsequent bolts starting from a spout tuple. A spout also assigns a time-out for each tuple, and the acker bolt keeps track of these time-outs. If the ack message for a tuple does not arrive by the time-out, the tuple is considered to be failed, and thus, it is replayed by the spout.

The Storm cluster consists of two main components: (i) one master, called *nimbus*, that distributes and coordinates the execution of topologies, and (ii) a number of worker nodes that carry out the actual stream processing. A worker node executes one or more *worker processes*. Every worker process, in turn, runs one or more *executors*, each containing one or more tasks (spouts or bolts). Each worker node also runs a *supervisor* that receives assignments from nimbus and spawns worker processes for those assignments. The supervisor periodically contacts nimbus and informs it about the topologies the worker node is currently running, as well as the available resources for running more assignments and topologies. To coordinate the interaction between nimbus and the supervisors, Storm takes advantage of Zookeeper [15] coordination service. Zookeeper also provides fault tolerance, by maintaining the state of both nimbus and supervisors.

5.3.2.3   Flink

Flink is a distributed dataflow processing system that unifies stream and batch processing. Similar to previous systems, a job in Flink is defined as a DAG of PEs and their connections. In addition to the basic transformations, e.g., `map`, `reduce`, and `filter`, Flink provides binary stream transformations, e.g., `coMap` and `coReduce`, flexible window operations, and native iterations. It also supports several different windowing policies, including time-based, count-based, and delta-based windows.

Flink uses a master to schedule tasks, coordinate checkpoints, and perform recovery in case of failures. Jobs are submitted to the master in form of a dataflow graph (*job graph*). The master first transforms the job graph to an *execution graph*, which consists of information on job scheduling along with the tasks. Then, it sends the tasks to the workers, which perform the real computations by running one or more processes that carry out the assigned tasks.

As we explained, the fault tolerance in Spark Streaming is *coarse grained*, based on RDD recomputation. On the other hand, the recovery in Storm is *fine grained*, as it keeps track of each tuple individually. The fault tolerance in Flink is something in between: instead of asking an acknowledgment per tuple, a sequence of tuples are acknowledges together. Flink uses asynchronous *barrier* snapshotting for globally consistent checkpoints, inspired by Chandy–Lamport snapshot algorithm [26]. In this model, data sources periodically inject checkpoint barriers into the data stream that flows through the connections of the DAG. Upon receipt of a barrier at a PE, it emits all the tuples that only depend on the tuples before the barrier. Once a PE receives barriers from all it input links, it checkpoints its state and then emits barrier and continues its computations.

5.3.3 Graph data processing platforms

Graph is a well-known flexible abstraction for describing linked data, and a natural way of modeling a variety of problems across various domains. Although graph theory is well studied in mathematics, physics, and computer science over the years, the traditional graph algorithms often fail to provide a good performance when applied to big graphs. In fact, processing of large graphs that cannot fit in the memory of a single machine brings about new challenges.

While the intuitive approach to overcome the size limitation is to partition the data and parallelize the computation, data partitioning in a graph is not straightforward, because each vertex of a graph should be processed in the context of its surrounding vertices. Hence, the *data parallelism* in systems, like MapReduce and Spark, does not necessarily show a good performance for large-scale graphs. *Graph-parallel* processing model is an alternative to data-parallel model and has proven efficient and effective for large graph processing. In data-parallel computation, there is a *record-centric* view of data, and computation is done in parallel on separate and independent data records. On the other hand, in graph-parallel computation, a *vertex-centric* view of graphs is used, and the computation is done in parallel on all the vertices, each having access to its neighboring vertices.

In this section, we present four different graph processing platforms, i.e., Pregel [27], GraphLab [2], PowerGraph [28], and GraphX [29].

5.3.3.1 Pregel

Pregel is a large-scale graph processing system, developed at Google, and inspired by the *bulk synchronous parallel (BSP)* model [30]. In the BSP model, there exists a set of processor–memory pairs that are communicating in a point-to-point manner, and there is a barrier mechanism to synchronize them. Giraph [31] is the open source counterpart of Pregel, developed as an Apache project.

Pregel executes an applications as a sequence of iterations, referred to as *super-steps*. In a superstep, a vertex receives all the messages sent to it in the previous superstep, updates its local state, and sends messages to its neighbors, to be delivered in the next superstep. Vertices use *message passing* to communicate directly with each other. A vertex can be either *active* or *inactive*. Initially, all the vertices are in the active state, but if they do not receive any message during a superstep, they become inactive. Note that an inactive vertex becomes active again, as soon as it receives some messages in the subsequent supersteps. The algorithm terminates when all vertices are simultaneously inactive, and there are no messages in transit.

Pregel uses the master–worker model, where the master coordinates workers, decides the number of partitions, and assigns partitions to workers. Each worker maintains the state of its partitions, executes the process of its vertices, and handles the message exchange with other workers. As mentioned earlier, graph partitioning is a crucial step in all the graph processing platforms that deal with huge graphs. Nevertheless, Pregel uses a naïve graph partitioning, by assigning vertices randomly to different machines. The random partitioning is expected to impose a high net-work traffic, because neighbors of a vertex are most likely not located on the same machine (especially if the number of partitions is large) and thus cannot be accessed locally.

Fault tolerance in Pregel is achieved by checkpointing, meaning that master asks the workers to save their states at start of every k supersteps. This state includes the value/state of all the vertices and edges, as well as the incoming messages. If the master detects the failure of a worker, it tells all workers to revert to the last checkpoint and resume the work from there.

5.3.3.2 GraphLab

Although Pregel makes large-scale graph processing possible, it is limited in effect by its rigid synchronization mechanism. Considering the fact that the workload is not necessarily evenly distributed (due to the random partitioning) and taking into account the heterogeneous power of worker machines, the runtime of each superstep in Pregel is determined by the slowest machine in that superstep.

GraphLab utilizes an asynchronous model for graph processing. In this model, vertices can read and modify the data in their *scope* directly, instead of sending read/update requests through messages passing. The scope of a vertex is the data stored in that vertex and in all its adjacent vertices and edges. All vertices, then, run in parallel, and the user-defined function in each vertex has access to all the data in its scope. Note that vertex scopes are overlapping, meaning that vertices are shared among each other's scope. The overlapping scopes may cause a race condition when two update functions execute simultaneously on the same vertices.

To solve this problem, GraphLab defines three levels of consistency: (i) *full consistency*, where during the execution of a function at vertex v, no other vertices can read or modify data within the scope of v, (ii) *edge consistency*, where during the execution of a function at vertex v, no other function can be applied to v and its adjacent edges, but the data in its adjacent vertices can be read, and (iii) *vertex consistency*, during the execution of a function v, no other vertices can read or modify data at v. The stronger consistency level is used, the lower level of parallelization takes place. In the full consistency model, which is the strongest level, only vertices in the nonoverlapping scopes can run in parallel, while in the vertex consistency level, all vertices can execute their functions in parallel.

To make GraphLab fault tolerant, two synchronous and asynchronous checkpointing models are proposed. In the synchronous model, the master periodically signals all workers to store their cached data, i.e., data that has been modified since the last checkpoint, to disk. The asynchronous model, however, is inspired by the Chandy–Lamport algorithm [26]. In this model, the checkpoint function is implemented as a function in all vertices with higher priority than all other functions, and the edge consistency model is used among them. The checkpoint function, then, is called periodically by each vertex to save its current vertex state, as well as the state of all the edges connected to not-checkpointed vertices.

GraphLab uses *two-phase partitioning* to split the input graph. In this model, the input graph is first turned into a smaller graph, called *metagraph*, by grouping neighboring vertices and replacing them with a super node. Since the size of the metagraph is much smaller than the original one, a fast balanced partition algorithm can be easily applied on it. When the metagraph is divided into a number of partitions, each called an *atom*, the workers become responsible for one or more atoms each.

5.3.3.3 PowerGraph

PowerGraph improved on GraphLab, by: (i) introducing a new graph programming model and (ii) employing a new *vertex-cut* partitioning. It factorizes the user-defined functions in GraphLab into three steps of *gather, apply, and scatter (GAS)*. In the gather step, a vertex accumulates data from its neighbors. Then, in the apply step, the user-defined function is applied on the accumulated data, and the vertex state is updated accordingly. Finally, in the scatter step, the vertex updates its adjacent edges and vertices. Initially, all the vertices are active, and once a vertex function completes the scatter phase, it becomes inactive. A vertex can become active again and then activate its neighboring vertices. The order in which active vertices are processed is up to the PowerGraph execution engine.

Two synchronization modes can be used in PowerGraph. First is the synchronous mode, similar to Pregel, which uses the BSP model by defining supersteps. In each superstep, it executes the gather, apply, and scatter for all the active vertices with a barrier at the end. When all the workers complete their tasks, then updates made to the vertices and edges are committed and will be visible in the subsequent supersteps. Next mode is the asynchronous mode, in which, changes made to vertices and edges during the apply and scatter functions are immediately committed to the graph and are visible to the neighboring vertices.

The second big improvement of PowerGraph over GraphLab is replacing the *edge-cut* partitioning with *vertex-cut* partitioning. A vertex-cut partitioning divides edges of a graph into equal size clusters. The vertices that hold the endpoints of an edge are also placed in the same cluster as the edge itself. However, the vertices are not unique across clusters and might have to be replicated, due to the distribution of their edges across different clusters. A good vertex cut is one that requires minimum number of replicas. Both theory and practice [32,33] prove that power-law graphs can be efficiently processed in parallel, if vertex cuts are used instead of edge cuts, which is mainly due to unbalanced number of edges in each cluster in the edge-cut partitioning. PowerGraph takes this partitioning model into account and presents a new greedy algorithm for vertex-cut partitioning. The graph is read as a sequence of edges, and the master decides where to put the endpoint vertices of the received edge, based on their current membership in the existing partitions.

5.3.3.4 GraphX

GraphX is a graph processing platform, implemented on top of Spark, that unifies data-parallel and graph-parallel models. GraphX introduces the *property graph*, a new data structure and API that blurs the distinction between tables and graphs. In other words, the property graph makes it possible to express both table and graph views of the same physical data. Each table and graph view, then, has its own operators that exploit the semantics of the view to achieve efficient execution. This characteristic makes GraphX very efficient for running a pipeline of graph analytic tasks, where we have to switch between table and graph views frequently. The property graph is represented using two RDDs for vertices and edges, and an auxiliary table, which is a logical map from a vertex to the set of partitions that contain edges adjacent to that vertex. To partition the input graph, GraphX uses a vertex-cut partitioning, similar to PowerGraph.

5.3.4 *Structured data processing platforms*

In the systems, we have seen so far, data structure or schema is not considered. However, there are systems that are developed to exploit data schema in order to achieve an even better performance and ease of use. In this section, we introduce two of these systems, Hive [34] and Spark SQL [35].

5.3.4.1 Hive

Hive, initially developed at Facebook, is a system for managing and querying struc-tured data. It is built on top of MapReduce and converts a query to a series of map and reduce tasks to run. Hive reuses the table data model in RDBMS, where a table is a set of rows with the same schema (columns). In Hive, each table corresponds to a HDFS directory. To work with tables, Hive uses HiveQL, a SQL-like query language that supports data definition language (DDL) operations, e.g., `create`, `alter`, `drop`, as well as data manipulation language (DML) operations, e.g., `load` and `insert` (overwrite), and also data retrieval query operations, e.g., `select`, `filter`, `join`, `group by`. It does not, however, support any operation for updating and deleting data items (rows).

To execute a query, Hive processes HiveQL statements and generates the execu-tion plan in three phases: (i) parsing query that is to transform a query string to a parse tree representation, (ii) generating a logical plan from the parse tree representation, and optimizing the plan, and (iii) generating a physical plan by splitting the optimized logical plan into multiple map and reduce tasks.

5.3.4.2   Spark SQL

Hive conducts some optimizations in the logical plan generation to improve the performance; however, Shark [36] pushes the performance improvement further, by replacing the MapReduce physical execution engine with Spark. More specifically, Shark is built on the Hive code base, but the physical execution engine part of Hive is replaced with Spark. Although Shark enables users to speed up their queries, the complicated code base that it inherits from Hive brings about many challenges for query optimization. This is due to the fact that the optimization techniques used in Hive were designed for the MapReduce engine, not the Spark engine. Consequently, Spark SQL [35] was developed that borrowed data loading process from Hive, and in-memory column-oriented data store from Shark. Moreover, Spark SQL introduces some new features, for example, it enables adding schema to RDDs and uses an RDD-aware optimizer, called catalyst optimizer.

Spark SQL introduces *DataFrame*, a distributed collection of rows with a homogeneous schema. DataFrame is equivalent to a table in a relational database, but it can also be manipulated in similar ways to RDDs. To have access to the functions of Spark SQL, we need to build an `SQLContext`, just like we used an `SparkContext` as the entry point into Spark functionalities. By using an instance of `SQLContext`, one can build DataFrames from an existing RDD, from a Hive table, or from other data sources. Spark SQL provides a rich set of domain-specific languages for structured data manipulation with DataFrames.

Another feature added by Spark SQL is the catalyst optimizer, which is used in four phases: (i) to analyze the logical plan and resolve attribute references by tracking tables in data sources, (ii) to optimize the logical plan by applying standard optimization rules, e.g., null propagation, constant folding, boolean and filter simplifications, push predicate through joins and projection, etc., (iii) to generate several physical plans using Spark physical operators and to select a plan using some cost model, e.g., based on join algorithms, and finally (iv) to generate Java bytecode to run on workers.

5.4   Concluding remarks

The unprecedented growth of data we have witnessed in recent years has brought about new challenges. This big data is commonly characterized by its extreme dimensions in terms of volume, the speed with which it is updated or produced, or the heterogeneity of its representation schemes. These properties have caused the traditional platforms fall short to store and process data efficiently, and thus, several new solutions are developed, among which, we briefly explored a few of the state-of-the-art platforms. Each of these systems, of course, deserve more elaborated descriptions, but we kept it short, because our main goal was to position each system relative to other systems in the big data ecosystem. These systems and platforms are continuously evolving, but even if the tools and technologies for dealing with big data change over time, the main challenges and requirements that this chapter touched upon will remain the same. As opposed to many other technology hypes that go out of fashion in a few years, big data is here to stay.

References

[1] D. DeWitt and J. Gray, "Parallel database systems: the future of high performance database systems," *Communications of the ACM*, vol. 35, no. 6, pp. 85–98, 1992.

[2] Y. Low, D. Bickson, J. Gonzalez, C. Guestrin, A. Kyrola, and J. M. Hellerstein, "Distributed graphlab: a framework for machine learning and data mining in the cloud," *Proceedings of the VLDB Endowment*, vol. 5, no. 8, pp. 716–727, 2012.

[3] A. Toshniwal, S. Taneja, A. Shukla, *et al.*, "Storm@ twitter," in *Proceedings of the 2014 ACM SIGMOD International Conference on Management of Data.* ACM, 2014, pp. 147–156.

[4] J. Dean and S. Ghemawat, "Mapreduce: simplified data processing on large clusters," *Communications of the ACM*, vol. 51, no. 1, pp. 107–113, 2008.

[5] M. Zaharia, M. Chowdhury, T. Das, *et al.*, "Resilient distributed datasets: a fault-tolerant abstraction for in-memory cluster computing," in *Proceedings of the 9th USENIX Conference on Networked Systems Design and Implementation.* USENIX Association, 2012, pp. 15–28.

[6] P. Carbone, K. Asterios, E. Stephan, M. Volker, H. Seif, and K. Tzoumas, "Apache flink: stream and batch processing in a single engine." Bulletin of the IEEE Computer Society Technical Committee on Data Engineering vol. 36, no. 4, pp. 28–38, 2015.

[7] S. Ghemawat, H. Gobioff, and S.-T. Leung, "The google file system," in *ACM SIGOPS Operating Systems review*, vol. 37, no. 5. ACM, 2003, pp. 29–43.

[8] E. B. Nightingale, J. Elson, J. Fan, O. Hofmann, J. Howell, and Y. Suzue, "Flat datacenter storage," in *Presented as part of the 10th USENIX Symposium on Operating Systems Design and Implementation (OSDI 12)*, 2012, pp. 1–15.

[9] S. A. Weil, S. A. Brandt, E. L. Miller, D. D. Long, and C. Maltzahn, "Ceph: a scalable, high-performance distributed file system," in *Proceedings of the 7th Symposium on Operating Systems Design and Implementation.* USENIX Association, 2006, pp. 307–320.

[10] K. Shvachko, H. Kuang, S. Radia, and R. Chansler, "The hadoop distributed file system," in *2010 IEEE 26th Symposium on Mass Storage Systems and Technologies (MSST).* IEEE, 2010, pp. 1–10.

[11] J. Kreps, N. Narkhede, J. Rao, *et al.*, "Kafka: a distributed messaging system for log processing," in *Proceedings of the NetDB*, 2011, pp. 1–7.

[12] Apache activemq. [Online]. Available: http://activemq.apache.org. Accessed on November 2017.

[13]   A. Richardson, "Introduction to rabbitmq," *Google UK,* available at http://www.rabbitmq.com/resources/google-tech-talk-final/alexis-google-rabbitmq-talk.pdf, accessed on Mar 30, 2012, p. 33.

[14]   Apache flume. [Online]. Available: https://flume.apache.org. Accessed on November 2017.

[15]   P. Hunt, M. Konar, F. P. Junqueira, and B. Reed, "Zookeeper: wait-free coordination for internet-scale systems." in *USENIX Annual Technical Conference,* vol. 8, 2010, p. 9.

[16]   G. DeCandia, D. Hastorun, M. Jampani, *et al.*, "Dynamo: amazon's highly available key-value store," *ACM SIGOPS Operating Systems Review*, vol. 41, no. 6, pp. 205–220, 2007.

[17]   F. Chang, J. Dean, S. Ghemawat, *et al.*, "Bigtable: a distributed storage system for structured data," *ACM Transactions on Computer Systems (TOCS)*, vol. 26, no. 2, p. 4, 2008.

[18]   I. Stoica, R. Morris, D. Karger, M. F. Kaashoek, and H. Balakrishnan, "Chord: a scalable peer-to-peer lookup service for internet applications," *ACM SIGCOMM Computer Communication Review*, vol. 31, no. 4, pp. 149–160, 2001.

[19]   S. Boyd, A. Ghosh, B. Prabhakar, and D. Shah, "Randomized gossip algorithms," *IEEE/ACM Transactions on Networking (TON)*, vol. 14, no. SI, pp. 2508–2530, 2006.

[20]   M. N. Vora, "Hadoop-hbase for large-scale data," in *Computer Science and Network Technology (ICCSNT), 2011 International Conference On*, vol. 1. IEEE, 2011, pp. 601–605.

[21]   M. Burrows, "The chubby lock service for loosely-coupled distributed systems," in *Proceedings of the 7th Symposium on Operating Systems Design and Implementation*. USENIX Association, 2006, pp. 335–350.

[22]   B. Hindman, A. Konwinski, M. Zaharia, *et al.*, "Mesos: a platform for fine-grained resource sharing in the data center." in *NSDI*, vol. 11, 2011, pp. 295–308.

[23]   V. K. Vavilapalli, A. C. Murthy, C. Douglas, *et al.*, "Apache hadoop yarn: yet another resource negotiator," in *Proceedings of the 4th Annual Symposium on Cloud Computing*. ACM, 2013, p. 5.

[24]   H. C. Andrade, B. Gedik, and D. S. Turaga, *Fundamentals of Stream Processing: Application Design, Systems, and Analytics*. New York, NY, USA: Cambridge University Press, 2014.

[25]   M. Zaharia, T. Das, H. Li, T. Hunter, S. Shenker, and I. Stoica, "Discretized streams: fault-tolerant streaming computation at scale," in *Proceedings of the Twenty-Fourth ACM Symposium on Operating Systems Principles*. ACM, 2013, pp. 423–438.

[26]   K. M. Chandy and L. Lamport, "Distributed snapshots: determining global states of distributed systems," *ACM Transactions on Computer Systems (TOCS)*, vol. 3, no. 1, pp. 63–75, 1985.

[27]   G. Malewicz, M. H. Austern, A. J. Bik, *et al.*, "Pregel: a system for large-scale graph processing," in *Proceedings of the 2010 ACM SIGMOD International Conference on Management of Data*. ACM, 2010, pp. 135–146.

[28]   J. E. Gonzalez, Y. Low, H. Gu, D. Bickson, and C. Guestrin, "Powergraph: distributed graph-parallel computation on natural graphs," in *Presented as part of the 10th USENIX Symposium on Operating Systems Design and Implementation (OSDI 12)*, 2012, pp. 17–30.

[29]   J. E. Gonzalez, R. S. Xin, A. Dave, D. Crankshaw, M. J. Franklin, and I. Stoica, "Graphx: graph processing in a distributed dataflow framework," in *11th USENIX Symposium on Operating Systems Design and Implementation (OSDI 14)*, 2014, pp. 599–613.

[30]   L. G. Valiant, "A bridging model for parallel computation," *Communications of the ACM*, vol. 33, no. 8, pp. 103–111, 1990.

[31]   C. Avery, "Giraph: large-scale graph processing infrastructure on hadoop," *Proceedings of the Hadoop Summit. Santa Clara*, vol. 11, 2011.

[32]   A. Abou-Rjeili and G. Karypis, "Multilevel algorithms for partitioning power-law graphs," in *Proceedings 20th IEEE International Parallel & Distributed Processing Symposium*. IEEE, 2006, p. 10.

[33]   K. Lang, "Finding good nearly balanced cuts in power law graphs," Technical Report YRL-2004-036, Yahoo! Research Labs, 2004.

[34]   A. Thusoo, J. S. Sarma, N. Jain, *et al.*, "Hive: a warehousing solution over a map-reduce framework," *Proceedings of the VLDB Endowment*, vol. 2, no. 2, pp. 1626–1629, 2009.

[35]   M. Armbrust, R. S. Xin, C. Lian, *et al.*, "Spark sql: relational data processing in spark," in *Proceedings of the 2015 ACM SIGMOD International Conference on Management of Data*. ACM, 2015, pp. 1383–1394.

[36]   R. S. Xin, J. Rosen, M. Zaharia, M. J. Franklin, S. Shenker, and I. Stoica, "Shark: Sql and rich analytics at scale," in *Proceedings of the 2013 ACM SIGMOD International Conference on Management of data*. ACM, 2013, pp. 13–24.

Chapter 6

Big Data processing using Apache Spark and Hadoop

Koichi Shirahata* and Satoshi Matsuoka**

6.1 Introduction

In this section, we introduce overview of what is Big Data processing and how Big Data is processed using Apache Hadoop and Spark, mostly in distributed computing platforms.

Data in the world will grow to 40 Zetta Bytes (40,000 Exa Bytes or 40 trillion Giga Bytes) in 2020 [1]. Processing Big Data requires techniques to handle data efficiently. This chapter describes how to process Big Data using Apache Spark [2] and Hadoop [3] as well as discuss recent research activities including open issues and challenges.

Research scientists generate and use Big Data in many domains including genomics, biology, meteorology, and complex physical simulations such as large-scale particle collider. Big Data is generated and used also in industry such as Internet web search, finance, and other digitalized business information data. Consumers also generate Big Data through communicating between IoT devices and between IoT devices and servers, and logging and sending processed data from devices to servers, using devices such as mobile phones, cameras, watches, wireless censor networks, and RFID tags.

Amount of the data is different between small- and large-scale data. In small-scale environments, the amount of data might be in the order of Tera-byte. We do not call these data as Big Data because the data can be processed using traditional relational database and can be stored in a single local disk in a computer. On the other hand, in many situations, the amount of data can be Tera-bytes, Peta-bytes, or Exa-bytes. For instance, networks in real world, such as health care, social networks, intelligence, system biology, and electric power grid, can be modeled as big graph data with millions to trillions of vertices and 100s millions to 100s trillions of edges, whose structure has the following characteristics: scale-free (power-law degree distributions), small-world (6 degree of separation), clustering, etc. For these situations, it is hard to process

*Fujitsu Laboratories Ltd., Japan
**Global Scientific Information and Computing Cener, Tokyo Institute of Technology, Japan

the data using the traditional database because the amount of data is too large to store in a single local disk and requires distributed storage consisting of multiple disks, and processing the data requires more computing power than that of a single computer in order to process the data within a realistic time. We call the latter type of data as Big Data, and we target this type of data in this chapter.

There are many types of data in the domains mentioned above. We can categorize Big Data into structured and unstructured data. The structured can be structured using relational database, object database, or other types of database and graph-structured data such as World Wide Web, which is consisting of web pages (i.e., nodes) and their links (i.e., edges). The unstructured data is raw digitalized data, such as list of numbers, documents, images, voices, audios, movies, and other signal data including medical heart rate data.

Big Data processing is to transform unstructured data into structured data or structured data into other structured data and analyze the structured data. Transforming unstructured data into structured data is required for the unstructured data because it is hard to analyze unstructured data directly; we can analyze the structured data more efficiently than the unstructured data. For example, by transforming documents into tagged documents by analyzing the contents of the documents, the tagged documents can be categorized. Analyzing the structured data includes discovering trends from documents or web data, deciding future behavior from past accumulated data, discovering rules from scientific simulation data, finding a structure from many documents, finding inappropriate contents, and real-time traffic analysis. Big Data analyzing techniques include searching important contents from a large amount of documents such as web search engine and statistical analyses using machine learning (ML) techniques such as finding correlations and categorizing many data into a several number of large clusters and nonlinear data modeling by training neural networks using a large number of data.

We categorize Big Data processing into several types, including batch processing, real-time processing, stream data processing or processing growing data, and graph processing. Batch processing is a type of Big Data processing where the whole data is collected in a place and process the whole data. The processing can be a series of processing. An example of the batch processing is tabulation of the log data. The batch processing typically takes several hours to days. On the other hand, in real-time processing, data is processed within the expected elapsed time, typically in a short time such as several minutes or seconds. An example of the real-time processing is processing of an automated teller machine. Stream data processing is to process continuously incoming data. An example of the stream data processing or processing growing data is analyzing continuously generated data in a social network service. Graph processing is to analyzing graph-structured data. We describe graph processing models in Section 6.2.1.

There are several Big Data processing models. MapReduce (MR) is a batch-based Big Data processing model which can utilize multiple compute nodes and multiple disks using distributed computing and distributed file system efficiently. MR [4] is developed by Google originally for large-scale web search indexing by constructing inverted index of web pages. Although MR is used for a specific purpose, MR can also be applied to wide range of applications including statistical log data analysis, distributed sorting, graph processing, and ML, because MR is a generalized Big Data processing model. Google also proposed Google File System [5], which is a distributed file system for Big Data and can be used with MR. Other data flow processing models using Directed Acyclic Graph (DAG) have been also proposed [6]. For graph processing, Bulk Synchronous Parallel (BSP) based model is proposed in the Pregel system [7] and widely used in existing graph processing frameworks including Apache Giraph, and GraphLab [8] also uses a similar graph processing model. We describe the MR model and other Big Data processing models in Section 6.2.

There are several Big Data processing software implementations using the Big Data processing models mentioned in the last paragraph. Apache Hadoop [3] is Java-based open source software framework for MR-based Big Data processing with distributed storage. Hadoop is inspired by Google MR [4] as well as Google File System [5], and originally developed by Yahoo! for using MR and distributed file system as an open source software. Hadoop provides Hadoop MR, Hadoop Distributed File System (HDFS), Hadoop Scheduler [Yet Another Resource Negotiator (YARN)], and external libraries for Hadoop. There are many MR implementations optimized for specific computing platforms including using GPU including Mars [9] and using Intel Many Integrated Core Architecture which is also known as Xeon Phi. We describe the Hadoop architecture, as well as recent activities on Hadoop in Section 6.2.3. Apache Spark [2] is a distributed computing framework developed by UC Berkeley's AMPLab. Spark supports more generalized Big Data processing using a DAG-based model than MR and provides fast in-memory Big Data processing in distributed file systems. Spark provides its distributed dataset called Resilient Distributed Dataset (RDD) as well as the Spark scheduler, but Spark works with Hadoop by using HDFS and optionally using YARN. We describe the Spark architecture, as well as recent activities on Spark in Section 6.2.3. There are other software frameworks using DAG-based processing model such as Dryad/LINQ [6].

There are several open issues and challenges in Big Data processing using Hadoop and Spark, including programing model choice, software framework choice (Hadoop, Spark, or another framework), hardware platform choice (clouds or supercomputers), data processing model choice (batch processing, real-time processing, dynamic data processing model for growing data, or another data processing model), how to utilize data, software, and hardware efficiently, how to optimize performance applications such as emerging ML or artificial intelligence applications such as image recognition using deep learning.

6.2   Big Data processing

In this section, we introduce MR-based distributed Big Data implementations of Google MR, Hadoop, Spark, and some other implementations such as Massage Passing Interface (MPI)-based MR. We also briefly introduce other Big Data processing models such as distributed graph processing models for such as social web search (e.g., Google Pregel, GraphLab, ScaleGraph), and a distributed processing model for training deep neural networks (e.g., Google DistBelief). Then, we briefly describe recent computing platforms for MR-based Big Data processing including cloud data centers and supercomputers.

6.2.1   Big Data processing models

Big Data processing models have been proposed for general-purpose and specific applications. MR is a general purpose batch-based Big Data processing model. The MR model can utilize multiple compute nodes and multiple disks using distributed computing and distributed file system efficiently. The model handles distributed computing platforms inside a MR system so that a user does not have to think about how to parallelize computation and how to utilize distributed file system. MR is a two-stage data flow model consisting of Map stage and Reduce stage. The Map stage computes an embarrassingly data parallel operation on distributed computing platforms. The Map stage receives key-value pairs of input data and output key-value pairs are computed for each input data. After the Map stage, Shuffle operation is conducted. The Shuffle operation exchanges the Map output based on the output keys among all the compute nodes. The Shuffle operation outputs a list of values for each key. After the Shuffle operation, The Reduce stage does an operation to the list of values for each key and outputs computed key-value pairs. The detail of MR is described in Section 6.2.3.

DAG-based Big Data processing model is also proposed. The DAG-based model is an extension of the two-stage model of MR to more generalized and flexible data flow, by computing each stage on a vertex of a DAG. The DAG-based model is used for complicated data flow applications that are difficult to express using MR. There is also iterative processing model, by extending MR or the DAG-based model. The iterative processing model is useful for ML applications, which require a large number of iterative computations using such as gradient descent-based algorithms.

In the graph processing, there exist a wide range of graph processing algorithms: breadth-first search, Shortest path, PageRank, connect component, minimal spanning Tree, finding graph center, bipartite matching, etc. Breadth-first search is a strategy for searching a graph. Breadth-first search can be used to solve many problems such as finding all nodes within one connected component, finding the shortest path, computing maximum flow in a flow network. Breadth-first search is also used in Graph500 benchmark.

Shortest path algorithms are applied to automatically find directions between physical locations, such as driving directions on road networks. The shortest path problem is categorized into two variations: single-source shortest path problem and all-pairs shortest path problem. There have been a lot of efforts on developing efficient shortest path algorithms; such as Dijkstra's algorithm, Bellman–Ford algorithm, A* algorithm for solving the single-source shortest path problem, as well as Floyd–Warshall algorithm and Johnson's algorithm for solving all-pairs shortest path problem.

PageRank is an algorithm developed and used by Google Search to rank websites in their search engine results. PageRank is a way of measuring the importance of website pages. PageRank works by counting the number and quality of links to a page to determine an estimate of how much the website is important, with an underlying assumption that more important websites are likely to have more incoming links from other websites.

There are several Big Data processing models for graph processing. BSP based graph processing model is proposed in the Pregel system [7]. The BSP model is an iterative computation and computes all the vertices of a graph in parallel at each iteration. The BSP model is useful for graph processing because MR and the DAG-based model require synchronizations and data exchanges for each stage, while the BSP model does synchronizations and data communications based on the graph structure which results in less synchronizations and data communications. The BSP model is useful for static graphs, whereas it is redundant for BSP to computing to only changes values of a graph. To this end, asynchronous graph processing model is also proposed.

There are application specific Big Data processing models. For example, there are Big Data processing models for ML, such as clustering, recommendation engines, classification, similarity matching, neural networks, Bayesian networks. For real-time stream data processing, Apache Storm is proposed as a data flow model for stream data processing. The details of Storm will be described in the next chapter.

6.2.2 Big Data processing implementations

There are several Big Data processing software implementations. Big Data processing software implementations using batch processing include Apache Hadoop and Apache Spark. Hadoop and Spark scale well to hundreds to thousands of compute nodes. However, note that Hadoop and Spark are sometimes not suitable for computations with smaller data than TBs, since the Hadoop MR model and the Spark's computational models require to handle computations using some specific workflows.

Graph processing implementations can be categorized into three types: pure implementation of a graph algorithm, MR-based framework, and BSP-based framework. Pure implementation of a graph algorithm is developed for achieving high performance for a specific graph algorithm. Implementations of Graph500 are instances of pure implementations of breadth first search algorithm. A graph processing framework consists of some built-in graph processing algorithms but also provides API to build new algorithms and extend the framework. An instance of MR-based graph processing framework is PEGASUS [10], a framework implemented on top of Hadoop. Shirahata *et al.* proposed a scalable MR-based graph processing framework on GPUs [11,12]. As for BSP-based graph processing frameworks, Pregel [7] is proposed as a first BSP-based graph processing framework as an alternate graph processing framework to MR, since not all graph algorithms can be solved with MR efficiency. There exist a number of BSP-based graph processing implementations, such as Apache Giraph and Apache GraphLab [8]. Giraph and Hama both work on top of HDFS, and Giraph is implemented on top of Hadoop MR while pure BSP framework is implemented in Hama. GraphLab is a high performance distributed graph processing framework written in C++.

There are several formats to store graphs: (1) in a flat file as pairs of vertex id and connected vertices ids to the vertex, (2) in a relational database using referencing tables or join tables, or (3) using a specialized format for graphs. A flat file is typically stored as an adjacency list for sparse graph and an adjacency matrix for dense graph. Main difference between relational database and graph database is that graph database has direct pointers from a vertex to its any adjacency vertices.

There exist graph databases for storing graph dataset in specialized formats, such as Neo4, InfiniteGraph, FlockDB. Neo4j is a disk-based Java persistence graph database. InfiniteGraph is a distributed graph database in Java designed to handle very high throughput. FlockDB is a distributed fault-tolerant graph database for managing wide but shallow network graph, initially used by Twitter to store relationships between users.

There exists MR-based large-scale graph processing including Hadoop-based implementations and MPI-based implementations. PEGASUS [10] is a Hadoop-based graph mining system written in Java. Graph mining algorithms that PEGASUS provides include PageRank, Random Walk with Restart (RWR), connected components, degree, and radius. PEGASUS implements the GIM-V (Generalized Iterative Matrix-Vector multiplication) graph processing algorithm, which can compute various graph processing algorithms such as PageRank, Random Walk with Restart, and Connected Components using MR. MR-MPI [13] also implements several graph algorithms such as PageRank, triangle finding, connected component identification, Luby's algorithm for maximally independent sets, and single-source shortest path calculation.

As for ML, Dean *et al.* developed a software framework called DistBelief that utilizes computing clusters with thousands of machines to train deep neural networks [14]. After four years from DistBelief, TensorFlow is proposed as an open source software for fast deep neural network training on GPU [15].

As for other applications, there have also been a lot of efforts on MR-based large-scale bioinformatics computing. CloudBLAST [16] provides MR-based bioinformatics applications, which integrates Hadoop, virtual machine, and virtual network technologies to deploy the commonly used bioinformatics tool NCBI BLAST on a WAN-based test bed consisting of clusters. Zhang *et al.* conducted performance analysis of existing MR implementations including Hadoop, Spark, and MPI-based MR implementation developed by Shirahata *et al.* [11,12] on biological homology search.

6.2.3   *MapReduce-based Big Data processing implementations*

MR [4] is a programing model with associated software tool chains proposed by Google. MR is used for large data sets effectively through distributed algorithm across a cluster. MR is composed of two major functions. The Map function takes in the input and emits key-value pairs that represent useful information from the input. These key-value pairs are later passes to reduce function to process the final results. The Reduce function produce zero or more outputs based on the values associated with each different key. An advantage of MR is that it can handle large-scale data even when the data is larger than host memory capacity by handling memory overflow automatically.

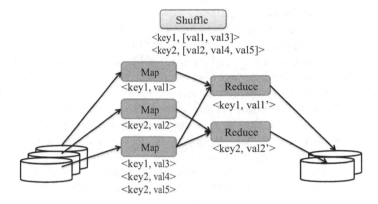

Figure 6.1   MapReduce workflow

Another characteristic is that MR can also handle compute node failures by applying techniques of fault tolerance. MR is suitable for large-scale data processing and its implementations are widely used.

Figure 6.1 shows execution workflow of MR. First, input data files are divided into multiple chunks (also called splits) whose size is typically 16–64 MB per split. The master assigns each map task to workers. Then, each worker reads the contents of the corresponding input split. A worker parses key/value pairs out of the input data and passes each pair to the user-defined map function. The intermediate key/value pairs produced by the map function are buffered in memory or written to local disk. After that, the intermediate key/value pairs are transferred to workers (possibly via network) who are responsible to process the key in reduce phase, which is defined by a partitioning function. Reduce workers read the transferred intermediate data sent from map workers. When a reduce worker has read all intermediate data for its partition, the worker sorts the data by the intermediate keys so that all occurrences of the same keys are grouped together. The sorting is needed since typically many different keys map to the same reduce task. If the amount of intermediate data is too large to fit in memory, an external sort is used. After the reduce worker iterates over the sorted intermediate data and for each unique intermediate key encountered, the worker passes the key and the corresponding set of intermediate values to the user-defined reduce function. The output of the reduce function is appended to a final output file for this reduce partition. Google MR [4] is the original implementation, which includes a distributed file system and a MR framework itself.

Hadoop, inspired by the original Google MR, is a now-popular open-source software framework implemented in Java for storing and processing large data distributive on clusters. Hadoop is consisted of Hadoop Common, HDFS, Hadoop YARN, and Hadoop MR. HDFS is a highly fault-tolerant distributed system, designed for applications with large data sets. Hadoop YARN manages the compute resources in the file system and schedule jobs. A master node, called NameNode, manages information related to file system namespace, such as directory tree and metadata of stored files, etc., while worker nodes, called DataNodes, accommodate actual file data. A single file is divided into several chunks (typically 64 MB). Then, the divided chunks are stored across DataNodes and replicated to different DataNodes (typically three replicas). On the other hand, Hadoop MR provides a MR execution environment on top of HDFS, whose environment also employs master-worker model.

There exists in-memory MR implementations that intended higher performance compared with Hadoop. Phoenix [17] provides programing APIs and runtime systems for shared memory systems, such as systems employing multicore processors. Spark is intended to perform faster than Hadoop by in-memory computing on distributed memory computing environments.

MPI-based MR has been studied for multinode execution for utilizing the fast network data transfer. The MR-MPI library [13] is an open-source implementation of MR written for distributed-memory parallel machines on top of standard MPI massage passing for processing terabyte-scale data sets on large-scale graph algorithms. MR-MPI can handle out-of-core execution by off-loading intermediate data on local disks. MR-MPI exhibits good scalability up to 1,024 processors on various graph processing algorithms. Their experimental results also showed that a distributed-memory matrix-based implementation using linear algebra toolkits performs an order of magnitude faster than MR-MPI when the input data fits on CPU host memory, while MR-MPI can handle out-of-core execution.

There exist MR implementations for GPU. A MR implementation using a single GPU is proposed, which is called Mars [9]. As for multi-GPU MR implementations, GPMR [18] is a multi-GPU MR library supporting out-of-core GPU execution on distributed computing platforms. Mars is also extended for multi-GPU by integrating with Hadoop. For computing platforms that equips Xeon Phi, MR implementations for utilizing Xeon Phi have been proposed. MPI-based MR for GPU-based clusters for large-scale graph processing has been also proposed [11,12].

6.2.4   Computing platforms for Big Data processing

Originally, Hadoop is built for exploiting performance of computer clusters consisting of dozens to thousands of compute nodes using commodity hardware, since performance on a single computer had been limited by maturity of frequency and the number of cores of CPUs. Hadoop is designed with an assumption that hardware failures occur frequently because the computer clusters are usually composed of more than one thousand compute nodes. After Hadoop has been developed, compute clusters became more common and currently cloud-computing platforms and super computers are widely used.

Public cloud based on cloud data centers is service of infrastructure, platform, and software based on large-scale compute clusters open for public use. Users use multiple compute nodes with prebuild platform and software without spending time for building and preparing Big Data processing environments. Widely used cloud vendors' public cloud services include Amazon Web Services (AWS), Microsoft Azure, Google Could Platform, VMware vSphere, IBM Bluemix, and Fujitsu Cloud Service S5. Private cloud is cloud service of infrastructure, platform, and software for a single organization. Users can build their own computing platforms based on their computing resource requirements and the users can use their computing platforms proprietary.

Supercomputer is computing infrastructure with multiple compute nodes where performance is highly optimized. Supercomputers had been used for specific purposes that require a large number of numerical computations. However, recently supercomputers are also used for general-purpose processing including Big Data processing which requires a large number of memory operations or I/O operations. Recent some supercomputers employ many-core processors such as GPU and Xeon Phi in addition to general CPUs, since many-core processors can provide high peak performance and high memory bandwidth for applications with specific computation patterns, while CPUs offer flexibility and generality over wide-ranging classes of applications. These supercomputers are called heterogeneous supercomputers since these supercomputers employ two different types of processors. A large number of heterogeneous super-computers have been ranked high order in terms of the TOP500 list. For instance, Tianhe-2 at National Super Computer Center in Guangzhou, China, which employs Intel Xeon Phi many-core processors ranked 1st in June 2014. As for GPU-based het-erogeneous supercomputers, Titan at Oak Ridge National Laboratory, United States ranked 3rd, Piz Daint at Swiss National Supercomputing Centre, Switzerland ranked 8th, and TSUBAME2.5 at Tokyo Institute of Technology, Japan ranked 13th, as of November 2016.

6.3 Apache Hadoop

In this section, we introduce Apache Hadoop. First, we briefly explain the overview of Hadoop architecture and Hadoop is suitable for batch job processing using Big Data. Then, we explain the architecture of HDFS, and Hbase, with examples. We also introduce research activities on Hadoop acceleration and Hadoop extensions, such as applying Hadoop to GPU-based supercomputers and supporting application-specific algorithms and data structures on Hadoop.

6.3.1 Overview of Hadoop

The core of Hadoop is composed of Hadoop MR and HDFS, which are inspired by Google MR [4] as well as Google File System [5] respectively. Figures 6.2 and 6.3 show overviews of Hadoop architecture. The original version of Hadoop (originally Hadoop version 0, which has been upgraded to version 1) consists of mainly MR and HDFS. Figure 6.2 describes the basic Hadoop architecture of Hadoop version 1. MR processes Big Data by scaling out using multiple compute nodes, and HDFS stores Big Data on distributed storage composed of local disks on multiple compute nodes. Also, on top of MR and HDFS, application specific libraries for Hadoop are available, such as a graph processing library called Apache Giraph, a ML library called Apache Mahout, SQL-like data analysis library called Apache Hive, and real-time processing library called Apache Storm. A database storage library called Apache HBase is used

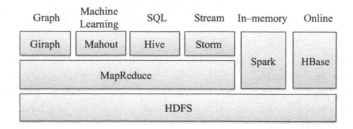

Figure 6.2   Overview of Hadoop architecture (Hadoop version 1)

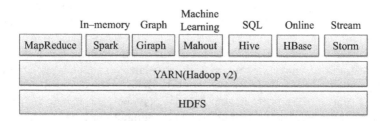

Figure 6.3   Overview of Hadoop architecture (Hadoop version 2)

on top of HDFS, which is inspired by Google Big Table [19]. Also, Apache Spark is used as fast in-memory Big Data processing on top of HDFS, and Spark can be also used on top of Hadoop MR. We describe Spark in Section 6.4.

Figure 6.3 describes the basic Hadoop architecture of Hadoop version 2. The biggest difference of Hadoop version 1 from Hadoop version 2 is that it supports DAG computation flow, which is an extension of Hadoop MR. Supporting the DAG computation flow allows users to express more complicated workflow including branch and divergence as well as iterations. The DAG computation flow is realized by using Apache YARN. YARN handles resource management including job scheduling and monitoring. MR as well as the other libraries for Hadoop can be processed on top of YARN and HDFS.

6.3.2   Hadoop MapReduce

Hadoop MR provides a MR execution environment on top of HDFS, whose environment also employs master-worker model, JobTracker as a master node and TaskTrackers as worker nodes, in Hadoop version 1. Hadoop scheduler and resource manager are included in MR in Hadoop version 1. In Hadoop version 2, Hadoop scheduler is divided into individual resource management in YARN. Thanks to the localized data accesses provided by HDFS, Hadoop achieves scalable data processing for large computer clusters.

Figure 6.4 shows how MR job scheduling works in the Hadoop framework version 1. JobTracker is responsible to manage submitted jobs, while TaskTrackers

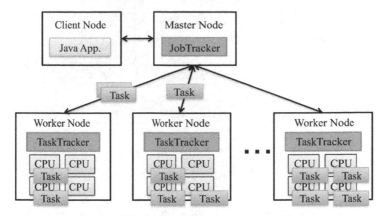

Figure 6.4   Overview of MapReduce job scheduling in Hadoop

execute actual map and reduce tasks in the submitted jobs. When a MR job, typically written in Java, is submitted to the system, the JobTracker schedules map and reduce tasks in the MR job to idle CPU slots on the TaskTrackers, then the tasks are run on the assigned CPU slots. JobTracker assigns map and reduce tasks onto TaskTrackers. A heartbeat is sent from TaskTrackers to JobTracker every few seconds (3 s in default) to check its status. For example, if a TaskTracker does not have any assigned tasks, JobTracker is notified that status by heartbeat, and JobTracker assigns next task to the TaskTracker. Each TaskTracker has Mapper and Reducer. Mappers are used in the Map phase and Reducers are used in the Reduce phase, respectively. When a job is executed, first, tasks are allocated into Mapper. Mapper executes map tasks using map function implemented by user. When all the map tasks are finished, the results of the map tasks are stored in HDFS, and then the Shuffle phase is executed. The Shuffle phase is implemented in Hadoop, therefore users do not have to care about how the Shuffle phase is implemented. After the Shuffle phase finished, the Shuffle phase output is stored in HDFS, and then passed as input of Reduce phase. In the Reduce phase, Reducer executes reduce tasks using a reduce function implemented by user. After the Reduce phase finished, the Reduce phase output is stored in HDFS and the job is completed.

6.3.3   Hadoop distributed file system

HDFS is a distributed file system designed for handling data on Hadoop MR efficiently with fault-tolerance. HDFS enables compute clusters to be used as storage pool extensible to large-scale. HDFS is suitable for Big Data processing that requires scalability, flexibility, and high throughput.

Figure 6.5 describes the overview of HDFS. HDFS is a distributed file system that employs a master-worker model. A master node, called NameNode, manages information related to file system namespace, such as directory tree and metadata of stored files, etc., while worker nodes, called DataNodes, accommodate actual file

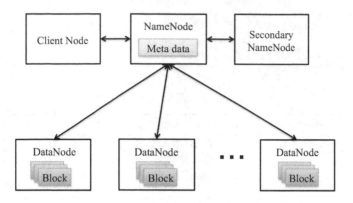

Figure 6.5   Overview of Hadoop distributed file system (HDFS)

data. A single file is divided into several chunks (also called blocks) of typically 64 MB. Then, the divided chunks are stored across DataNodes and replicated to different DataNodes, typically three locations including a replica in the same rack and the other replica in a different rack. Secondary NameNode generate snapshots of the NameNode's memory structures, in order to prevent file-system corruption and loss of data caused by failures of NameNode. Note that since both MR and HDFS employs master-worker model and HDFS is utilized by storing data into local disks on slave nodes, usually both JobTracker in MR and NameNode in HDFS are located in the same node as well as TaskTrackers in MR and DataNodes in HDFS are located in the same nodes.

6.3.4 YARN

YARN is in charge of resource management and job scheduling of Hadoop clusters. In Hadoop version 1, resource manager tightly works with MR, it is hard to handle more flexible jobs such as DAG workflow. YARN enables users to allocate and manage resources more flexible manners, therefore users can run not only MR but also more complicated job structure such as DAG workflow. Also, by using YARN, users can run multiple applications simultaneously in the same Hadoop system, sharing the same resource management.

Figure 6.6 describes overview of YARN. YARN divides JobTracker and TaskTracker into ResourceManager, ApplicationMaster, NodeManager, and Container. ResourceManager has authority to assign and manage resources among all the applications in Hadoop. ResourceManager invokes ApplicationMaster per application. ApplicationMaster requests resources to ResourceManager and manages and monitors the application as being the master and assigns tasks onto NodeManagers. NodeManager works as a slave of ResourceManager and launches applications' Containers. NodeManager also monitors the resource usage on the slave node and reports the usage to ResourceManager. Container grants rights to an application to use a specific amount of resources on a specific ApplicationMaster.

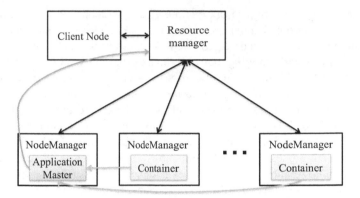

Figure 6.6   Overview of YARN scheduler and resource manager

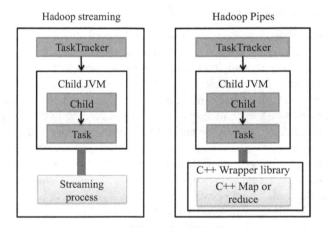

Figure 6.7   Hadoop streaming (left) and Hadoop pipes (right)

6.3.5   Hadoop libraries

The Hadoop framework, including HDFS and Hadoop MR, is currently implemented in Java. Thus, user applications are also typically implemented in Java by using the Hadoop libraries. If we want to run programs written in other languages, we have to translate the programs to a Java code. There are several solutions to invoke C/C++/CUDA codes from the Hadoop framework, including Hadoop Streaming and Hadoop Pipes.

Hadoop Streaming (Figure 6.7 left) is an API that allows application users to write their map and reduce functions in languages other than Java. Using Unix standard streams as the interface between Hadoop and user's program, application users can use any languages with standard I/O operations to implement their MR programs.

Hadoop Pipes (Figure 6.7 right) is a C++ interface to Hadoop MR. Unlike Streaming, Pipes uses sockets as the channel over which the TaskTracker communicates with the process running the C++-based map and reduce functions without using JNI. Hadoop Streaming supports wide-ranging map and reduce programs written in any languages with the standard I/O; however, application users have to write parser codes of the standard I/O manually, which may introduce complex programmability. By contrast, Hadoop Pipes does not require parsing data via the standard I/O, since the runtime can communicate with key-value abstractions by using the Hadoop Pipes library.

As mentioned in Section 6.3.1, extension libraries on Hadoop for a wide range of Big Data processing applications are available, such as Apache Giraph for graph processing, Apache Mahout for ML, Apache Hive for SQL, Apache Storm for stream processing, Apache HBase for database storage, and Apache Spark for in-memory processing.

6.3.6 Research activities on Hadoop

GPU-based heterogeneous computer clusters can be used for a MR execution environment; however, scheduling map and reduce tasks onto CPU cores and GPU devices for efficient execution depends on running task characteristics and underlying computing environments. For example, tasks that contain data parallelism may suit for GPU execution, while tasks that contain many branches or synchronizations may not. The performance of task execution may also vary according to the resource configurations: the number of CPU cores and GPU devices, memory size and bandwidth, local I/O performance to secondary storage systems. Ad hoc scheduling strategies, such as allocating tasks to only GPU devices, or to idle CPU cores and GPU devices in a FIFO manner, may not achieve optimal job throughput and may cause inefficient resource utilization and energy consumption.

To address this problem, a hybrid map task scheduling technique for GPU-based heterogeneous computer clusters has been proposed [20]. When a client submits a MR job whose tasks can run on both CPU cores and GPU devices, a master job scheduler assigns the map tasks onto CPU cores and GPU devices in order to minimize the overall MR job execution time by using profiles collected from dynamic monitoring of map task's behavior. Worker nodes execute the scheduled map tasks on CPU cores or GPU devices. This scheduling technique has been implemented to Hadoop, and they evaluated the proposed technique on the GPU-based supercomputer called TSUBAME, by using a K-means cluster analysis application. The results show that the proposed technique achieves 1.93 times faster than the Hadoop original scheduling at 64 nodes with 1,024 CPU cores and 128 GPUs.

A lot of application and algorithms on Hadoop have been studied. Collaborative-Filtering recommendation algorithms on Hadoop have been proposed for scalable recommender systems. Supports for other file systems than HDFS, such as Amazon S3, OpenStack Swift, Microsoft Azure from cloud vendors, and other file systems such as Gfarm, PVFS, Ceph and file systems which are accessible via FTP, HTTP, or HTTPS have been also studied. Also, there have been a lot of efforts on improving storage performance and usability including RAID support for Hadoop, metadata management, energy saving for HDFS.

6.4　Apache Spark

In this section, we introduce Apache Spark. First, we briefly explain the Spark architecture and that Spark is suitable for fast in-memory iterative computing using Big Data such as ML. Then, we explain the Spark architecture, including RDD and Spark DSL. We explain that Spark supports more generalized programing model than Hadoop, and Spark can be used cooperatively with Hadoop. We also introduce recent research activities on Spark, including acceleration of some applications using Spark such as acceleration of training deep neural networks.

6.4.1　Overview of Spark

Apache Spark [2] is a fast open-resource cluster computing framework written in Scala, developed by AMPLab of UC Berkeley. Currently, Spark has been enhanced as an Apache project. Spark runs on Hadoop, Mesos, standalone, or in the cloud. It can access diverse data sources including HDFS, Cassandra, HBase, and S3. Mesos is an open source global resource manager for an entire data center, while YARN is in charge of resource management and job scheduling of Hadoop.

Spark has more generalized computational models than Hadoop. Basically, Hadoop can handle jobs that can be expresses as MR, while Spark may be able to handle other types of jobs that cannot be expresses as MR. Spark can handle not only batch jobs but also other types of processing such as interactive analyses using SQL queries, in-memory processing, streaming processing, graph processing, and ML processing. For example, Spark can compute iterative processing such as PageRank much more efficiently than Hadoop, since Spark can handle intermediate data in memory during iterations while Hadoop stores intermediate data onto local disks for every iteration. In this case, Spark can sometimes perform over $100\times$ faster than Hadoop, because in-memory bandwidth (about 10GB/s using DRAM) is about $100\times$ faster than that of local disks (about 100MB/s using SSD) for data-intensive Big Data applications.

Spark is built on top of HDFS and YARN. Spark manages jobs by a standalone task scheduler or YARN. Spark can also create RDDs from any other storage source supported by Hadoop, including your local file system, Cassandra, HBase, and Amazon S3.

6.4.2　Resilient distributed dataset

The main abstraction Spark provides is a RDD, which is a fault-tolerant collection of elements that can be persistent in memory and operated in parallel in a distributed manner. Spark uses RDDs for storing and manipulating datasets. Spark can distribute datasets automatically by using RDD methods; therefore, application developers do not have to think about how to distribute data and how to parallelize computations.

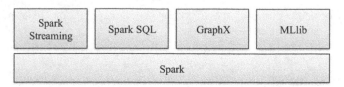

Figure 6.8 Spark libraries

RDDs support two types of operations, which correspond to map and reduce operations is Hadoop. Transformations create a new dataset from an existing one, including the map operation that passes each dataset element through a function and returns a new RDD representing the results. Actions return a value to the driver program after running a computation on the dataset, including the reduce operation that aggregates all the elements of the RDD using some function (e.g., plus for receiving the sum) and returns the final result to the driver program. All the transformations optimize data management of RDDs automatically in Spark by avoiding storing temporal results of the transformations before actions. Spark just remembers the transformations applied to some base dataset and the transformations are only computed when an action requires a result to be returned to the driver program.

Spark also supports Shuffle operations for re-distributing data for grouping key-value data into value lists for each corresponding key, in the same way as the Shuffle operation in MR and Hadoop. The Shuffle operation involves disk I/O, data serialization and network data transfer, since the Shuffle operation needs to exchange data across multiple nodes in a distributed computing environment.

One of the most important capabilities of RDD is persisting (or caching) a dataset in memory, which allows future access to the persisted RDDs much faster (often by more than 10×). This optimization works efficiently for iterative algorithms such as PageRank used in graph processing, since the persisting avoids storing the re-computed results of the RDD operations to the reallocated memory region or disk region.

6.4.3 Spark libraries

Spark powers a stack of libraries including Spark Streaming, Spark SQL, GraphX, and MLlib for ML (Figure 6.8). The users can combine these libraries seamlessly in the same application.

Spark Streaming is a Spark library for scalable, high-throughput, fault-tolerant streaming processing of real-time streaming data. Spark Streaming brings Apache Spark's language-integrated API to stream processing, letting users write streaming jobs the same way the users write batch jobs. Spark Streaming supports Java, Scala, and Python. Data can be ingested from many sources like Kafka, Flume, Kinesis, or TCP sockets and can be processed with high-level functions such as map, reduce, join, and window. Finally, processed data can be pushed out to file systems, databases, and live dashboards. Users can apply graph processing and ML algorithms on data streams. Spark Streaming provides a high-level abstraction called discretized stream of DStream, which represents a continuous stream of data internally represented as a sequence of RDDs.

Spark SQL is Apache Spark's module for working with structured data. Unlike the basic Spark RDD API, the interfaces provided by Spark SQL provide Spark with more information about the structure of both the data and the computation being performed. Internally, Spark SQL uses this extra information to perform extra optimizations. There are several ways to interact with Spark SQL including SQL and the Dataset API. One use of Spark SQL is to execute SQL queries. Spark SQL can also be used to read data from an existing Hive installation. When running SQL from within another programing language the results will be returned as a Dataset or DataFrame. You can also interact with the SQL interface using the command-line or over JDBC or ODBC.

GraphX is Apache Spark's API for graphs and graph-parallel computation. GraphX extends the RDD by introducing a Graph abstraction, which is a directed multigraph with properties attached to each vertex and edge. To support graph computation, GraphX exposes a set of fundamental operators such as subgraph, joinVertices, and aggregateMessages as well as an optimized variant of the Pregel API. In addition, GraphX includes a growing collection of graph algorithms and builders to simplify graph analytics tasks.

MLLib is a ML library which runs on Spark. MLlib provides common ML algorithms such as classification, regression, clustering, and collaborative filtering. The primary ML API for Spark is currently the DataFrame-based API instead of RDD-based API. The benefits of DataFrames include Spark Datasources, SQL/DataFrame queries, Tungsten and Catalyst optimizations, and uniform APIs across languages.

There are many other efforts on third-party projects that can work with Spark. As for infrastructure projects, REST interface, R frontend called SparkR, ML research project, cluster management system, memory speed virtual distributed storage system, Cassandra connector, have been supported.

6.4.4   *Using both Spark and Hadoop cooperatively*

Although Hadoop and Spark are both Big Data frameworks, their functions are different. Hadoop is a distributed data infrastructure which supports not only data processing using MR but also distributing data across multiple nodes using HDFS and scheduling multiple jobs onto the multiple nodes using YARN. On the other hand, Spark is specialized to data processing on distributed data collections.

Hadoop can run jobs without using other frameworks such as Spark. Conversely, Spark can also run without Hadoop. However, Spark does not have its own file system; therefore, Spark needs a distributed file system including HDFS or another one such as the Lustre-distributed file system or Cassandra. Spark uses Mesos or YARN as backend for cluster resource management and job scheduling. Spark also provides a simple standalone deploy mode. You can launch a stand-alone cluster either manually, by starting a master and workers by hand, or use provided launch scripts.

6.4.5 Research activities on Spark

There are a lot of efforts on performance improvements of Spark. Spark won the 2016 CouldSort Benchmark sorting by a joint team from Nanjing University, Alibaba Group, and Databricks Inc. They developed a distributed sorting program called built on top of Spark, and set a new world record as the most cost-efficient way to sort 100 TB of data. Their developed sorting implementation called NADSort is able to complete the 100-TB Daytona CloudSort in 2,983.33 s on random nonskewed datasets at an average cost of $144.22. There is an effort on accelerating the Spark execution engine by utilizing hardware such as SIMD-based parallel computation and GPU [21], which removes Java Virtual Machine overhead from many of Spark code paths by using code generation and nongarbage-collected memory.

There are performance optimizations on specific type of applications. There is a work on matrix computation optimizations on CPU and GPU for applications such as singular value decomposition, linear programs and other convex programs, which has been merged into Spark. There is an integrated graph processing system called GraphFrames that lets users combine graph algorithms, pattern matching and relational queries, and optimized workload across them. Near-optimal fair memory cache sharing in order to utilize memory for multiuser shared environments such as the cloud platforms, called FairRide. A deduplication framework [22] aims to solve large-scale deduplication problems on arbitrary data tuples. There is work on improvements of real-time stream computation, including a fault-tolerant streaming computation called Discretized Streams, and a generalized on-line aggregation for interactive analysis called G-OLA. There is an effort on improving job scheduling performance and usability [23]. They proposed delay scheduling, which avoids conflict between locality and fairness for multiusers on a shared cluster. There is a proposal on low-latency scheduler called Sparrow, which is a stateless decentralized scheduler that provides near optimal performance [24]. There are works on application studies, including drug discovery and genome search.

6.5 Open issues and challenges

In this section, we discuss open issues and challenges in Big Data processing. Since the amount of data will grow exponentially, there will be a demand for storing and processing the Big Data efficiently by utilizing data processing systems. We classify the challenges into four categories: storage, computation, network, and data analysis.

6.5.1 Storage

In recent years, the size of data has grown exponentially since Internet and cloud services have become widespread. The data size is expected to continue increasing as a large number of IoT devices generate data and communicate with servers. Although the size of data storage has been also increasing, the increase speed of the data size is faster than that of the storage size. Therefore, how to store the exploding size of Big Data and how to access and manage the data efficiently are challenging. If the data size becomes larger than the storage size, we need to select data to use and delete some portion of data to fit in the storage. Issues caused by the challenge include fast large memory and storage, data structure transformation, data compression and selection, data sharing, and real-time processing of growing data.

If the data size becomes much larger, there will be a demand for fast processing of the large data. In recent years, there are a lot of efforts on developing high speed non-volatile memory (NVM), such as flash memory, ReRAM, MRAM, and PCM. These memories are expected to be used for high-speed storage. Utilizing these emerging fast memory as Big Data storage is an open issue.

There are two types of data in the real world: structured data and unstructured data. While a large amount of data has been generated, about 80 percent of the data is considered to be unstructured data. Therefore, extracting information from the unstructured data is a key for utilizing the Big Data. Efficient transformation from the unstructured data to structured data is an open problem. Also, when we consider the amount of data exceeds the total capacity of data storage, data compression and selection techniques without losing important information will become important.

There is a movement of open data, which is an idea that some data should be freely available to public without restrictions, similar to the movements of open source software, open hardware, and open access. Also, some organizations accept sharing their data in some restricted geometrical region or accept sharing if the data is anonymized. Sharing the data has a great value for accelerating data analysis such as cancer detection with image processing using large number of patient data. Storage systems that store and process open data and shared data efficiently is an important research direction.

Real-time streaming processing is required in many domains such as network monitoring, intelligence and surveillance, risk management, e-commerce, fraud detection, network routing, transaction cost analysis, pricing, algorithmic trading, data warehouse augmentation, and autonomous car driving. Data grows rapidly in these application domains, therefore processing and storing growing data in real time is required. Existing real-time data processing frameworks and libraries using Hadoop include Apache Hive, Apache Drill, and Cloudera Impala for SQL, and Summingbird for streaming MR with Hadoop and Storm. However, it is unclear how to manage real time and growing in terms of which framework should be used for a specific application and data.

6.5.2   Computation

For the last several decades, computational power has been increased exponentially according to Moore's law. Shrinking transistors have powered the advances, however, the shrinking becomes slowing and is going to plateau due to physical limitation of the scaling of semiconductor lithography. Therefore, it becomes challenging to improve performance of hardware and software for Big Data processing in the post-Moore era. Issues caused by the challenge include distributed processing, utilizing many core processors, efficient processing by utilizing memory and saving arithmetic computational resource, Rack-Scale Architecture (RSA) and disaggregated computing, and memory-driven computing.

Since the improvement of arithmetic computational resource per processing unit slows down, performance improvements in other directions are required. One way is to improve efficiency of distributed computing, using hundreds to thousands of compute nodes simultaneously with high utilization. However, utilizing distributed computing platform has several issues including scalability of compute nodes by utilizing network communication, power efficient computing in order to avoid excessing electric power constraint. Also, many-core processors such as GPU and Intel Xeon Phi are useful for Big Data processing especially ML which conducts a lot of matrix and vector arithmetic operations.

Previously, the increase of arithmetic computational resource is faster than the increase of memory throughput. However, since the increase of arithmetic computational resource slows down, utilizing memory performance becomes more important. Investigating Big Data processing algorithms which utilize memory throughput and consume less computational resource is an open issue. Also, RSA is proposed by Intel, in which a rack consisting of multiple compute nodes, storage, and network is regarded as a computer. As a result, a big computer consisting of thousands of cores and ten to thousand TB of memory can be utilized depending on application requirements. Hewlett-Packard also proposed similar concept called The Machine. Utilizing a rack level architecture will become more important.

There are two ways in scaling of computation: scale-out and scale-up approaches. The scale-out approach is adding more compute nodes and using distributed computing. In the distributed computing, higher performance can be achieved if the larger number of compute nodes is used. However, since the scaling of the number of compute nodes has a limitation due to network overhead of throughput and latency, adding more computational resource on a node and assigning larger data per node for using fewer number of nodes may improve performance. The scale-up approach is adding more computational resource in a node and improving performance per node. In the scale-up approach for Big Data processing, utilizing local storage such as NVM is required if the processing data size is larger than the memory size of the compute node. In this way, the both approaches have the advantages and drawbacks. Therefore, optimizing balance between scale-up and scale-out approaches in terms of using larger data per node (scale-up) and increasing the number of node (scale-out) can improve performance based on balance between bandwidth of off-loading to external memory such as NVM and network bandwidth.

6.5.3 *Network*

IoT allows objects of the physical world to be sensed or controlled remotely across existing network infrastructure. The number of IoT devices is expected to increase to 50 billion by 2020, thanks to innovation that enables to reduce cost such as commoditization of sensors and communication equipment for data collection. The widespread use of highly developed wireless networks and cloud services also accelerates cost reduction and realization of IoT. Data-processing performance on the IoT edge devices has been also increasing.

If the large number of IoT edge devices is connected through Internet, the amount of network data transfer between the edge devices and cloud servers, as well as computational cost in cloud servers will be much larger. Since processing the large amount of computation in the cloud servers may become bottleneck, processing some amount of computation on the edge devices will be required. When considering networking speed and data processing performance between edge device and cloud server, where to process data and how to communicate between the large number of devices and cloud servers are challenging. Some data will be processed on edge devices instead of sending data to servers in order to avoid sending data to the servers or reduce the amount of data to send by doing data compression. Also, utilizing emerging high speed network such as Wavelength Division Multiplexing (WDM), which is $100\times$ higher bandwidth than existing data center network, as well as real-time data processing with the large number of devices are open issues.

6.5.4   Data analysis

Big Data processing requires parallel programing models since Big Data processing requires computing power using multiple machines and distributed storage where the Big Data can be read and written. There are multiple levels of parallel programing model, including MR, DAG, and MPI. Also, a wide range of application specific programing models have been proposed for application domains such as graph processing, iterative processing, ML, real-time streaming processing, and relational database. Selecting optimal algorithm, programing model, and framework for Big Data processing considering characteristics of data and computing platform is challenging.

Thanks to the huge improvement of computational power using many-core-based highly parallel processors such as GPU as well as availability of Big Data in recent years, we have seen a focus on technologies that use many-core processors for high-speed ML to support the huge volume of calculations necessary for deep learning processing. Especially, in recent years, deep learning has been gaining attention as a ML method that emulates the structure of the human brain. In deep learning, the more layers there are in a neural network, the more accurate it performs tasks, such as recognition or categorization.

There are several libraries and frameworks for optimized processing of ML applications using Hadoop and Spark, such as Apache Mahout, and MultilayerPerceptronClassifier in Spark MLlib. A large number of ML and deep learning frameworks have been actively developed, including Caffe, TensorFlow, Torch, MXNet, Chainer, and Microsoft Cognitive Toolkit. Some of the frameworks can be run on multiple machines for fast processing using Spark or MPI. Also, cloud-computing environments for ML have been actively developed from cloud vendors including Microsoft AzureML, Amazon ML, Google Cloud ML, Nervana Cloud, IBM Watson, and Fujitsu Zinrai.

6.6   Summary

There is great demand for processing many types of Big Data of TB to EB or ZB for a wide range of applications such as statistical log data analysis, distributed sorting, graph processing, and ML. In order to process such Big Data efficiently using recent software and hardware environments, distributed computing frameworks such as Hadoop and Spark are widely used. Hadoop and Spark supports not only distributed computing but also distributed job/task scheduling and distributed file system for managing distributed computing and distributed data storage management utilizing hardware including processors, disks, and network. There are a lot of activities on improving Big Data processing in a wide range of aspects including performance optimizations and extensions of application domains and computing platforms.

References

[1]   John Gantz and David Reinsel. The digital universe in 2020: Big data, bigger digital shadows, and biggest grow in the far east. https://www.emc.com/collateral/analyst-reports/idc-the-digital-universe-in-2020.pdf, 2012.

[2]   Matei Zaharia, Mosharaf Chowdhury, Michael J. Franklin, Scott Shenker, and Ion Stoica. Spark: cluster computing with working sets. In *Proceedings of the 2nd USENIX Conference on Hot Topics in Cloud Computing*, 2010.

[3]   Andrzej Bialecki, Michael Cafarella, Doug Cutting, and Owen O'Malley. Hadoop: a framework for running applications on large clusters built of commodity hardware. *Wiki at http://lucene. apache. org/hadoop*, 2005.

[4]   Jeffrey Dean and Sanjay Ghemawat. MapReduce: simplified data processing on large clusters. In *OSDI '04, Sixth Symposium on Operating System Design and Implementation*, pages 137–150, 2004.

[5]   Sanjay Ghemawat, Howard Gobioff, and Shun-Tak Leung. The Google file system. In *ACM SIGOPS Operating Systems Review*, volume 37, pages 29–43. ACM, 2003.

[6]   Yuan Yu, Michael Isard, Dennis Fetterly, *et al.* Dryadlinq: a system for general-purpose distributed data-parallel computing using a high-level language. In *OSDI'08, 8th USENIX Symposium on Operating Systems Design and Implementation*, volume 8, pages 1–14, 2008.

[7]   Grzegorz Malewicz, Matthew H. Austern, Aart J.C. *et al.* Pregel: a system for large-scale graph processing. In *Proceedings of the 28th ACM Symposium on Principles of Distributed Computing*, pages 135–146, New York, NY, USA, 2009. ACM.

[8]   Yucheng Low, Joseph Gonzalez, Aapo Kyrola, Danny Bickson, Carlos Guestrin, and Joseph M. Hellerstein. Graphlab: a new framework for parallel machine learning. *arXiv preprint arXiv: 1408.2041*, 2014.

[9]   Bingsheng He, Wenbin Fang, Qiong Luo, Naga K. Govindaraju, and Tuyong Wang. Mars: a MapReduce framework on graphics processors. In *Parallel Architectures and Compilation Techniques*, pages 260–269, 2008.

[10] U. Kang, Charalampos E. Tsourakakis, and Christos Faloutsos. PEGASUS: a peta-scale graph mining system implementation and observations. In *Proceedings of the 9th IEEE International Conference on Data Mining*, ICDM'09, pages 229–238, Washington, DC, USA, 2009.

[11] Koichi Shirahata, Hitoshi Sato, Toyotaro Suzumura, and Satoshi Matsuoka. A scalable implementation of a MapReduce-based graph processing algorithm for large-scale heterogeneous supercomputers. In *Proceedings of the 2013 IEEE/ACM 13th International Symposium on Cluster, Cloud and Grid Computing*, CCGrid '13, pages 277–284, May 2013.

[12] Koichi Shirahata, Hitoshi Sato, and Satoshi Matsuoka. Out-of-core GPU memory management for MapReduce-based large-scale graph processing. In *Proceedings of the IEEE Cluster 2014*, pages 277–284. IEEE, 2013.

[13] Steven J. Plimpton and Karen D. Devine. MapReduce in MPI for large-scale graph algorithms. *Parallel Computing*, 37(9):610–632, September 2011.

[14] Jeffrey Dean, Greg Corrado, Rajat Monga, *et al.* Large scale distributed deep networks. In *Advances in Neural Information Processing Systems*, pages 1223–1231, 2012.

[15] Martín Abadi, Paul Barham, and Jianmin Chen. TensorFlow: A System for Large-Scale Machine Learning. In OSDI'16, 12th USENIX Symposium on Operating Systems Design and Implementation, pages 265–283, November 2016.

[16] Andréa Matsunaga, Maurício Tsugawa, and José Fortes. CloudBLAST: combining MapReduce and virtualization on distributed resources for bioinformatics applications. In *eScience'08, IEEE Forth International Conference on eScience*, pages 222–229. IEEE, 2008.

[17] Colby Ranger, Ramanan Raghuraman, Arun Penmetsa, Gary Bradski, and Christos Kozyrakis. Evaluating MapReduce for multi-core and multiprocessor systems. In *HPCA 2007, IEEE 13th International Symposium on High Performance Computer Architecture*, pages 13–24, February 2007.

[18] Jeff A. Stuart and John D. Owens. Multi-GPU MapReduce on GPU clusters. In *Proceedings of the 25th IEEE International Parallel and Distributed Processing Symposium*, IPDPS '11, May 2011.

[19] Fay Chang, Jeffrey Dean, Sanjay Ghemawat, *et al.* Bigtable: a distributed storage system for structured data. *ACM Transactions on Computer Systems (TOCS)*, 26(2):4, 2008.

[20] Koichi Shirahata, Hitoshi Sato, and Satoshi Matsuoka. Hybrid map task scheduling for GPU-based heterogeneous clusters. In *The 1st International Workshop on Theory and Practice of MapReduce (MAPRED'2010)*, 2010.

[21] Reynold Xin and Josh Rosen. Project tungsten: bringing apache spark closer to bare metal. https://databricks.com/blog/2015/04/28, 2015.

[22] Niklas Wilcke. Ddup-towards a deduplication framework utilizing apache spark. In *BTW Workshops*, pages 253–262, 2015.

[23]   Matei Zaharia, Dhruba Borthakur, Joydeep Sen Sarma, Khaled Elmeleegy, Scott Shenker, and Ion Stoica. Delay scheduling: a simple technique for achieving locality and fairness in cluster scheduling. In *Proceedings of the 5th European Conference on Computer Systems*, pages 265–278. ACM, 2010.

[24]   Kay Ousterhout, Patrick Wendell, Matei Zaharia, and Ion Stoica. Sparrow: distributed, low latency scheduling. In *Proceedings of the Twenty-Fourth ACM Symposium on Operating Systems Principles*, pages 69–84. ACM, 2013.

Chapter 7

Big Data stream processing

Yidan Wang*, M. Reza HoseinyFarahabady**, Zahir Tari*,
and Albert Y. Zomaya**

7.1 Introduction to stream processing

7.1.1 Background and motivation

At the beginning of twenty-first century, the research interest of a new model of
streamlined data processing has been arising, involving a huge volume of data in
today's market that makes it impossible to store and process data along with the
traditional way. Data stream processing (DSP) is a data computational paradigm that
enables the real-time processing of continuous data streams instead of maintaining
the static relationship among them. In this model, a large volume of raw tuple of data
enters in a rapid, continuous, and streaming manner to the ecosystem. Such a set of
streams is unbounded in size, while the data arrival time and data processing time
have an online nature.

More specifically, performing queries in such a model can be made by targeting at
either relational data or streaming data. As a result, the format of a stream processing
output mainly depends on the expected operations. New streaming data may produce
for further processing, or data could accordingly store in some place to maintain the
persistent relationships in a traditional database management system (DBMS). Also,
the continuous querying requires constant processing along with the arrival of the
data to the system.

Unlike the DBMS model, in which only the most recently measured data is
precious, a stream processing system (SPS) values the data over the history observations the most. Moreover, because DBMS mainly acts as a data repository, a human
user often can initiate a query in DBMS. But a user could only passively involve in
the computational task of stream processing applications. In this way, she might be
informed when a certain event has been triggered. In a SPS, transactions are normally
performed whenever a new tuple of data arrives to the system without any human
interventions. Consequently, approximation result is more desirable instead of exact
answers which are produced by specific queries.

*School of Science, RMIT University, Australia
**School of Information Technologies, University of Sydney, Australia

Stream-processing applications are running in a long-term pattern unless it is terminated by users. Also, for a dedicated SPS, a new job can be submitted at any time. It may accordingly lead to various weight or priorities assignment, and even the priorities can be dynamically changing over time. Considering, the continuous and online nature of SPS, the computation in stream processing application would call for a proportion of data. Therefore, it provides a roughly estimated result derived from the existing data.

The goal of a DSP model is to process the flying data timely and accurately. In such a model, the inputs of the system are not stored unless a special analysis is demanded to cover the history data set for the sake of space saving. New knowledge and information are delivered from a series of logic computations of input data. In most cases, the applications are fed with potentially unsteady flows of information in the format of chunks with semantics and relationships. Due to the long-running nature, these applications performances are easily affected by highly variable arrival rate of data or exhibit abrupt changes in their workload characteristics.

Examples of stream processing applications can be found in a variety of domains ranging from anomaly detection, stocking market, and social media (finance, secure, sensing networks, network monitoring, and manufacturing). In such domains, data is no longer serving just for the storage and/or retrieving purposes. Users need to gather, process, and analyse these data streams to extract insights and knowledge or to detect emerging patterns or outliers. The main objectives of such system include having a low latency, scalable, and fault tolerance platform. Moreover, a fast recovery mechanism that ensures an effective and efficient processing of streaming data is highly desirable. SPS application aims to be robust and flexible for the provision of resources to deal with a variety of streaming workloads.

7.1.2   Streamlined data processing framework

Streamlined data processing paradigm enables continuous data streams to be processed in a scalable and fault-tolerant manner. More specifically, streaming data that comes continuously would be divided into different sets of simple tuples, where a tuple is regarded as the anatomic data item. The tuples can be considered as a row in the traditional DBMS system, which consists of the name and associated property values. Normally, tuples in the same stream are sharing same attributes, also known as "schema." The different scheme could apply to the same data source to the target specific system.

A wide range of distributed sensors might be involved as the streaming data source. Sensors data can collect and formalise data to ensure that it is capable of processing by the system. Moreover, the data in the form of a tuple is usually labelled with a timestamp, to represent the time of data generated or transferred. The consumer of the streaming data, normally a real-time application, would receive the processed streaming data in the same format of the input data. As a result, streaming data can either directly get delivered to an algorithm or temporarily stored for the later retrieval.

Before initiating the entire system, the end-user needs to submit some computing components to the platform. For example, let us assume that a cloud data centre is expected to sustain the execution of a large-scale SPS. Then, the initial phase would allocate the computing resources, dedicated physical hosts, or virtual machines (VMs) based on either a computing component- or a stream-manner. The way of allocating entirely depends on the scheduling and resource management algorithm. After that, the raw data, in the format of continuous tuples, starts to be fed to the system, while it might keep running for a long period. The results are delivered just after a new data is arrived to the system or a certain regular job is triggered. However, only approximation results can be provided based on the range of data recently arrived.

Another essential component in a stream processing application is the computing unit. By combining the core logic computing units, a wide variety of functions can be implemented. In general, the basic logic operators are similar to the operations in a traditional database. Below, we list some typical functions along with some examples.

1. Aggregation: Merely grouping of a subset of tuples that have the same temporal or logical conditions.
2. Splitting: Dividing the entire stream data into small blocks and exploring parallelism levels.
3. Merging: Collecting data from different input channels subject to some specific conditions in serving the purpose of summarizing.
4. Ranking: Reordering the tuples based on certain principles.

In this way, a complicated system can be simplified into several independent units. By manipulating the individual components, existed modules can be easily attached to other applications. This allows the system to capture the computing conditions and deliver the expected level of performance on a segment basis.

A directed acyclic graph (DAG) is often used to present the workflow of operations happening in an application. The arrows in such a model illustrate how the data flows through the system along with all kinds of the logics which are embedded at individual computing component. The input and the output units can be identified as the one with no incoming data and the one with no outgoing data, respectively. Upstream and downstream are then introduced to differentiate the flow direction of data input and data output. For any set of data tuple, such a graph is generated by the unit of entry and then can be processed and transferred through the connected components. Finally, the data that is generated at the output unit can be gathered as the ultimate output of the system.

7.1.3 Stream processing systems

With the emergence of stream processing paradigm, several different implementations can be found in both industry and academic worlds. In fact, there are a myriad of solutions that provides application program interfaces (APIs) to comply with different particular programming models and runtime environments based on the clients' requirements. We describe two example systems in this section to provide an overview of computing mechanism of stream processing applications. A more detailed explanation of the popular open-source system, e.g. Apache Storm, can be found in the next section.

7.1.3.1 Aurora [1]

As a general DSP system, Aurora is derived from an imperative language called "SquAL." It visually interprets the operators and workflow as a DAG. Moreover, two types of workers are involved in "SquAL" as "windowed operator" and "single-tuple operators." For a windowed operator, the function fixed with a moving window that is continuously updating the data flow. A single-tuple operator, in contrast, only operates on a single information unit while the data itself can be reused for a different operation.

Aurora allows a user to define output data with a specific quality of service (QoS) level that accordingly enables the user to customise the configuration of the system with her own performance expectation. Since data might get lost due to a higher demand of responding time, shedding policies are introduced based on the QoS specifications. Therefore, it targets at achieving a better trade-off between latency and throughput.

To recover the failed operator, Aurora provides a temporary storing procedure to keep the historical data. The mechanism allows the system to be retrieved later if such a recovering is required. Also, the scheduler would allocate the computing resources based on the operator load and predefined QoS constraints.

In 2005, a more advanced system, namely Borealis, has been proposed to address the requirement of dynamic query modification and optimization [2].

7.1.3.2 Yahoo S4 [3]

S4 is a distributed stream processing engine that is inspired by the MapReduce model. It is a general-purpose and scalable platform that allows the extension of the system to process continuous unbounded streams of data in a partial fault-tolerant manner. The S4 is designed to solve searching problems with the assistant of online data mining and machine learning algorithms.

Processing element (PE) can be regarded as the essential computing items in S4. There are four attributes associated with each PE as follows:

1. Functionality and configuration,
2. Type of events,
3. Keyed attributes in events, and
4. The value of keys attributes.

These four factors help the user to identify the instance of a PE. In addition, there are some other PEs that is known as "keyless PE's," where no keys attribute or value is attached to them. Keyless PEs appear in the input layer and can consume any kind of event. In S4, a computation can be performed on the PE layer with data flowing through them in the context of events. However, unlike Aurora where the message transferring is guaranteed by the system, S4 lacks the ability to store historical information, and therefore, is unable to recover any kind of data transmission act.

7.2 Apache storm [8,9]

Along with the increasing need for data flow applications, Apache Storm has been proposed as an efficient open-source framework for dealing with real-time streaming data that can be used as an effective solution in different domains such as the financial market, manufacturing, security, network monitoring, and the Internet of Things.

Based on the conceptual working mechanism of the generic SPS, Apache Storm has been implemented widely in industrial sections, as either a proportion or the core system of a Big Data processing framework (e.g. Twitter, Yahoo!, Groupon, and Baidu).

Apache Storm makes itself famous as one of the most reliable open sources distributed real-time computational system. It can deal with an unbounded stream of data in a fast, scalable and fault-tolerant manner. Therefore, it is beneficial for both researchers and industry practitioners to study and explore the processing paradigm of real-time streaming data in more details.

7.2.1 Reading path

To get a full appreciation of the working mechanism of Apache Storm, we will deep dive into its design details in this section. We start by picturing an overall structure of Apache Storm which is followed by describing its composing components. Then, we present the data model, the concept of topology, and the way that the processing data flows within the Storm framework. Section 7.2.4 gives a further exploration of the parallelization of topology, which is the key point for performance tuning. In Section 7.2.5, we illustrate the categories of stream grouping strategy and the logic behind them. Finally, Section 7.2.6 describes the discipline of message processing, which potentially helps to enhance the reliability of message exchanging in a storm cluster.

7.2.2 Storm structure and composing components

Following the structure of a master–slave scheme, the set of hosts that are involved in a Storm cluster can be seen as a "master" node or a "worker" node. A master node is regarded as the administrator of a cluster. It takes the responsibility of acknowledging job submission and task assignment. In practise, the majority of nodes involved in a Storm cluster are worker nodes that are receiving jobs from the master node and executing programmes that are submitted by users. The service maintained by Storm and those invisible activities within the cluster are all enabled by some daemons which are running at each actively running host.

More specifically, a particular daemon called "Nimbus" runs in a master node. Nimbus plays the role of an administrator, and all of the jobs submitted to the Storm cluster must be led to it directly. Accordingly, whenever a topology is successfully uploaded to the Storm cluster, the Nimbus acknowledges such a request and it can normalize the necessary configurations to set up the static state of the submitted topology. The concept of topology will be further explained in the next section. Jobs will be assigned among the available worker nodes which can be managed by either the default scheduler or a customized schedule policy based on the cluster configurations.

Similarly, a particular daemon, called "Supervisor" is running in each worker node that manages the execution of working processes. Theoretically, any number of working processes can be placed at a worker node. However, in practise, this number should be determined by the capacity of available worker nodes and the scale of tasks. There is another type of node in a Storm cluster that runs a Zookeeper daemon. The availability of storm cluster is ensured by the set of active worker nodes and also their cooperation with a Zookeeper service. Apache Zookeeper is proposed as a solution to enable highly reliable distributed coordination. In other words, the Zookeeper daemon provides high throughput and low-latency coordination among distributed processes along with a shared in-memory namespace.

The scalability and fault-tolerance of Apache Storm have been widely studied through a vast body of research works in the past. Such features are supported by a bunch of services running in the Storm cluster. More specifically, group's collaboration data (e.g. the configurations and the status information of each working host) are stored in the memory space of Zookeeper. Therefore, the Storm cluster is secured with regard to the reliability and availability issues as long as enough amount of Zookeeper services run normally. Moreover, both the Nimbus and the supervisor daemons are designed as the stateless and fail-fast components, which means the daemons can be promptly enabled upon self-destructing.

There is an increasing concern about the failure of Nimbus daemon in some studies published recently. Let us consider a scenario that the Nimbus node becomes unavailable. Then, all new requests are unable to be submitted to the cluster, although there are several topologies that work in a regular status. Also, if one of the supervisors suddenly goes offline, the rescheduling for the failed messages or any new incoming data flows is not possible until the Nimbus daemon is relaunched.

7.2.3 Data stream and topology

In a typical stream processing application, the data that flows across the entire system can be abstracted as flow of data-tuples, also known as data streams. Each stream must be continuously processed by applying some predefined functionalities. Such a stream typically can be constituted as an unbounded sequence of tuples, where each tuple is an atomic data model.

Following the tradition of the complex event processing system, each application is structured as a DAG. Such a representation not only provides a clear overview of the computation components (or operators) but also illustrates how a set of streams flows across adjacent components. More specifically in Apache Storm, a topology is introduced as a calculation model of real-time stream processing. As opposed to the batch processing model, e.g. Hadoop, that executes once only and then terminates itself after the execution of the job, a topology in the storm must be implemented in an event-based manner. In other words, it will not terminate until a particular interrupting operation is performed by end users.

For every topology, the source point of the data stream is labelled as a "Spout." These are the starting points that retrieve data from either integrated data generators

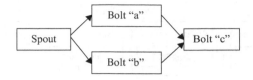

Figure 7.1   A sample topology in Apache Storm

or external data repositories. They transform the data into a set of normalized tuples that are acceptable by a streaming application in the next steps.

Once a topology is fed with the input data, the Spout module can emit multiple streams along the edges of the directed graph. The processing nodes which are receiving the tuples from the Spout are labelled as bolt, accordingly. These bolts consume the tuples that are sent by the spout or upstream bolts and following up with some predefined functions. Tuples exploration, join, or aggregation operations are considered as the set of standard functions deployed at each bolt. A new stream in the format of a sequence of tuples can be generated for further processing.

Figure 7.1 shows a simple example of a topology in Apache Storm. Spout emits data in the stream format from the external data source to both "Bolt a" and "Bolt b." Supposing that the topology aims to count the number of words for a given stream, a tuple with the same index is allocated to either "a" or "b," and the counting process is processed locally. Then, the results of these two bolts are emitted to "Bolt c," which produces the system output for either storing or reporting purpose.

7.2.4   *Parallelism of topology*

Increasing the parallelization level is an efficient approach for improving the throughput in a SPS. As suggested by most of the recent studies, the total performance cannot be continuously improved by merely increasing the number of machines without the expansion of parallelism degree.

Apache Storm allows the parallelization degree to serve as a mean to provide both high throughput and fault-tolerance. Hence, any level of parallelism can be maintained for components in a topology that is derived from the expected functionality or performance. Particularly, a data processing operation in a storm topology, sometimes referred to as a "task," can be an instance of a spout or a bolt node. Also, an "executor" runs tasks as a single thread. These threads are executed as the part of a topology and are identified as a "worker" process. Each worker process hosts a Java virtual machine (JVM) to sustain some level of isolation between different topologies.

The parallelism of Storm topology can further be implemented by configuring the number of tasks, the number of executors, and the number of worker processes. In particular, the number of executors is mostly determined based on its execution priority or critical level of operation.

For a topology, several JVMs are provisioned as the worker processes. They can be coordinated across the actual physical machines. Inside each worker process, the executor is executed as a thread (often there is only one task). Multiple tasks

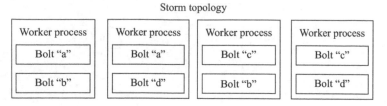

Figure 7.2   *A sample topology with four working processes*

can allocate to a worker by explicit defining of parallelism of tasks. The number of executors is determined at the time of instantiating the bolt or spout nodes. Figure 7.2 shows a sample topology with four working processes. They may execute at either same or distinct hosts, while two executors are included in each process. For instance, we can define two tasks for "Bolt c" which possess an identical function and each is executed as a separate thread. Consequently, the capability of processing of "Bolt c" can be improved to some extent by increasing the number of tasks.

Unfortunately, the current Storm solution only grants the privilege of determining instance numbers of an executor to users, who might not be well aware of varying QoS objectives. Therefore, having a mechanism for dynamic self-adjustment of parallelism level in a Storm cluster for meeting a wide variation of QoS expectations merits a future investigation.

7.2.5   Grouping strategies

There can be different grouping strategies to be applied for each stream; each can aim for locating a target task for tuples. Partitioning principles, which are decided by the grouping strategies in each bolt, can declare the upstream data source as an input. In Apache Storm, there are eight different stream-grouping mechanisms that can be customised to define a grouping policy based on the specific user's requirement. In the following section, we give a brief introduction for each of the grouping strategies and possible scenarios.

7.2.5.1   Shuffle grouping

In this policy, stream tuples are equally distributed to each downstream bolt's tasks based on the workload balance across bolts. The tuples are randomly assigned in a round robin (RR) fashion. This policy usually works best for atomic operations.

7.2.5.2   Fields grouping

In this policy, a set of specific fields can be defined beforehand, and tuples are allocated based on the value of a particular field. This policy promises that the set of tuples with the same value for a particular field is always directed to the same destination. It can be used for calculating based on particular fields, like words counting or sorting.

7.2.5.3 Partial key grouping

This policy essentially works in a similar manner as the field grouping policy works. It assigns the tuples based on the value of a specific field. However, the level of resource utilization will be taken into consideration as well when making the allocate decisions. For storm clusters with a limited resources provisioning, this policy can ensure the maximum utilization of the computing resources is achieved.

7.2.5.4 All grouping

In this policy, every tuple will be copied and delivered to the rear bolts. In other words, the entire stream is replicated and targeted at every downstream bolt. It is suitable for broadcast messages and/or join operations. This policy normally incurs an extra overhead of performance that might lead to delays in the entire system, especially in peaking hours.

7.2.5.5 Global grouping

In this policy, instead of sending tuples to multiple tasks, the entire stream with global grouping strategy will be targeted at one downstream bolt. The bolt is usually the one with the lowest id. This policy guarantees the integrity of the streaming data that is commonly found in one to one data flow patterns.

7.2.5.6 None grouping

This policy makes no preference policy in terms of grouping policies, which lead to shuffle grouping as the default setting.

7.2.5.7 Direct grouping

The direct grouping is dedicated to working with streams that are declared as the direct streams. The tuple producer has the right to decide the particular consumer, among the downstream bolts. This grouping policy requires a higher computing cost mainly due to this fact that for each tuple of data, the destination has to be checked and directed, respectively.

7.2.5.8 Local or shuffle grouping

This policy makes a difference when a bolt has multiple tasks in the same working process, and therefore, the tuple will target on the in-process tasks.

7.2.6 Reliable message processing

There are three different levels of delivery guarantee that are provided by the Apache Storm, namely "at most once," "at least once," and "exactly once" level. The "at most once" ensures that tuples are processed in the order of emitting; hence, the tuples are only dropped if the entire network or the system is failed. The "at least once" level enables re-transferring of failed tuple, hence, the tuple might be processed out of order or be processed more than once. The "exactly once" guarantee level only works with Trident that as a third-party tool which is sitting on the top of the Storm service.

Every tuple has to be linked with its original tuples to achieve the "at least once" guarantee level, and it should acknowledge the successful or failure of an execution. Therefore, a unique ID will be assigned to each tuple to serve as the purpose of tracking and constructing of the tuple trees. Such a tree structure makes it possible to divide a message into individual components. In this way, the tuples are markable; hence, their associated timeout is configurable. For the failed part of streams, they can be quickly retrieved and replayed by the topology manager. The integrity of the message is ensured unless the explicit requirement is claimed (this might occur to save the bandwidth and/or to increase the throughput by sacrificing processing qualities).

7.3   Scheduling and resource allocation in Apache Storm

Resource management and scheduling for cloud-based applications attract a huge interest since past decades. From the performance enhancement to resource aware-ness, scheduling strategies are designed to fulfil a variety of objectives. However, the variation of the working mechanism of target applications makes it more complicated to define a generic solution for scheduling and resource management problem.

We begin this section by providing an overview of scheduling schemes that are widely adopted nowadays for cloud-based applications. Then, the limitations of Storm default scheduler are illustrated. We then analyse the specific requirements for an effective scheduling policy in the Apache Storm, based on its nature and the most known challenges. The last part describes some advanced scheduling schemes that have been proposed to solve specific issues in an Apache Storm platform.

7.3.1   Scheduling and resource allocation in cloud [4–7]

The work related to resource management and scheduling can categorize as a reactive or proactive approach. The reactive methodology works based on threshold rules, that passively adjusts the number of physical machines or VMs when the predefined threshold is achieved. However, the proactive manner enables dynamic adjustment of resource provisioning, according to the predicted workload or resource demand. It helps to either increase or decrease the resource allocation (RA) in advance of workload changes is observed. Moreover, a desirable result can be expected with no time delay in line with accuracy guaranteed prediction algorithms.

There is a considerable body of researches on scheduling strategies that are designed based on the concept of threshold rules, which frequently require a higher and a lower limit for the particular type of computing resource. Whenever the usage comes to the limits, reactions are taken to serve the purpose of cost minimiza-tion or resource saving. These thresholds in most cases are chosen from intensive experiments. Threshold-instructed algorithms allow light weight calculation regard-ing threshold violation, and it is easy to deal with conventional processing. However, it is not well suitable for the system with unstable performance, especially in a case of burst workload that happens often.

Most recently, researchers tend to propose resource management scheme in a proactive manner. For instance, control theory and reinforcement learning have applied in some of the studies as ways to automate the scheduling processes. Without a thorough understanding of the system properties, the scheduling scheme is capable of making optimal decisions by observing the measurements or delivered performance. Note that more complexities will incur due to the online learning and estimation. In the meantime, however, it expands the working scenario with the fluctuating and varying workloads.

Under-provisioning, over-provisioning, and oscillation are three most common challenges for the existing scheduling algorithms to cope with. More specifically, when the capacity of resources is not affordable for user demanding, it will lead to service-level agreement violations. Meanwhile, the over-provisioning causes the resource wastage and may incur extra cost. Typically, service providers tend to provide more resources than required that attempts to avoid performance degradation. Also, the time of monitor and reconfigure should keep enough since the scaling configurations might happen so frequently without able to detect the impact of reconfigurations.

Nowadays, the scheduling question in the scope of cloud computing tends to allocate resource to given tasks instead of only map jobs to the specified computing resources. In other words, RA, in its way, is taking advantage of the heterogeneous computing resources.

7.3.2 Scheduling of Apache Storm [8,9]

The default scheduler of a Storm cluster is defined by "nimbus" daemon, which is located at the master node and it is implemented in a RR manner. At any given point in time, the scheduler aims to distribute the number of executors among worker processes evenly and fairly allocate worker processes across activate physical machines. Such a scheduler scheme is proposed to balance the resource usage among active hosts directly. But it accordingly results in less awareness of computation capability and resource demanding.

The data flow between connected components in a topology indicates the importance of network conditions when making scheduling decisions. Network bandwidth may become the bottleneck when even the computing resources are fully offered. Also, heterogeneity is prevalent in storm clusters as all cloud-based frameworks. It is an essential requirement for the efficient scheduler to take both resource and task heterogeneity into consideration when making decisions.

Despite the fact that customised scheduler is possible to integrate with Storm implementation, the different QoS objectives might not well aware from a user's perspective. Especially, the benefits of software-as-a-service or infrastructure-as-a-service providers, concerning the energy consumption or economic scaling, should be respected all the time.

Typically, there are two types of operators involved in stream processing application: "stateless" and "stateful" operators. While stateless operators process each tuple independently, stateful operators maintain an internal state for the processing of stream data for either complex pattern exploration or rescheduling purpose. Hence, sustaining the state and migration of such stateful operators make the design of scheduling algorithm of the Storm much more complicated. For the default scheduler, the storm does not support such a general state management mechanism. Therefore, scheduling efficiency in the context of rescheduling strategies of stateful operators heavily depends on developers' implementation.

7.3.3　Advanced scheduling schemes for Storm

The design of dedicated scheduling scheme for real-time distributed stream processing received significant attention along with the increasing popularity of streaming processing applications. Most of the studies in the past addressed the limitations of the default RR scheduler of Apache Storm.

Generally, the past projects related to SPS scheduling can be categorised as the two broad "online" or "offline" approaches. In an offline scheduling, components carefully placed by exploring the parallel partition and data dependencies for the given topology. It aims to minimize the communication cost between connected components as network conditions play a significant role in streaming processing application performance.

The offline algorithm proposed by Aniello [10] successfully reduces the processing delays of streams comparing with Storm default scheduler. However, such offline scheduling decisions always require executing beforehand, instead of making schedule decisions during execution. Hence, its limitation is quickly revealed as it fails to adapt to varying traffic conditions in runtime. An online scheduling is also suggested in this work, in order to deal with dynamic traffic conditions in particular.

Another notable work is presented by Gedik [11], where an online mechanism is devised to automatically explore the parallel level of a given topology based on measured congestion status and throughput. This work also allows the migration of stateful operators.

The T-Storm [12] uses an online approach to allow the dynamic adjustment of schedule parameters to support running fewer worker nodes while speeding up the overall time for data processing. It is also concerned with the run-time traffic patterns. R-storm [13] implements a resource-aware scheduling scheme in Storm that respecting to CPU and memory constraints. In the meantime, network distance between connected components and the variety of resource types have taken into consideration. Two steps are included in the scheduling process, task selection and node selection. Tasks sorted in an ordering list, and node selection executed for each item of the ordered list. For choosing the node, Euclidean distance between job demand and node capability calculated and predefined hard constraints should be never violated.

As we mentioned before, "control theory" is regarded as an efficient approach in achieving dynamic adjustment of resource provisioning. Some studies imply a control loop to automatically adjust resources for stream processing applications by effective monitoring and analysis of resource consumption. As a notable example, van der Veen [14] implemented such a control system to deal with both under- and over-provisioning of resources in a virtualized environment. As they suggested, the number of processing nodes can be self-configured by continuous monitoring of the performance of Storm components, especially the size of queues.

More recently, De Matteis [15] proposed a set of proactive strategies that can dynamically adjust Storm's configurations. In particular, they adopted model predictive control (MPC) to explore the optimal configuration of target applications (i.e. latency-sensitive applications) under ever changing operational conditions. This model-based controller not only enables the prediction of arrival rate for incoming data, but it also forces the system to follow a set-point trajectory through adjustment of some controllable factors, which includes parallelism degree of an operator, CPU frequency, and the distribution scheme. The algorithm also imposes a greater penalty to measured latencies that exceed defined threshold subject to QoS objectives. Compared to previous studies, this work provides a more efficient elastic scaling mechanism, with flexible and dynamic reconfigurability.

7.4 Quality-of-service-aware scheduling

7.4.1 Performance metrics [16]

Fair allocation of available resources among submitted topologies seems as an efficient strategy to ease the imbalance resource usage; however, careful observations revealed that fairness cannot always lead to a desirable output as expected in practise.

More specifically, applications can tolerate delays at different levels, e.g. from the response time point of view. Some applications, such as high-frequency trading or health monitoring systems, are highly sensitive to any delays. While others, like applications in social media, environmental monitoring, or network intrusion detection, might be less sensitive to such problem. Even for applications in the same domain, users might enforce different service levels and charge individually by the service provider.

Therefore, devising an efficient mechanism to respond differently to QoS violation is essential. It is suggested that a fair allocation of resources among applications in a sharing environment does not necessarily provide an appropriate QoS satisfaction level. The ideal situation is if a data stream experiences some amount of QoS violation, other data streams should also experience almost the same level of QoS violation.

Considering a scenario where the input rates of several streams suddenly go up, the scheduler struggles to assign enough resources to all streams. It may decide to give fewer resources to arbitrary streams. As a result, if the objective function only worries about minimizing the total number of QoS violation incidents, it might end up allocating fewer resources to those streams that are more important than others.

A metric that reflects the QoS violations for a set of streaming data during each time interval is essential to evaluate SPS. It is suggested that a desirable RA/scheduling (S) algorithm is capable of minimizing the variance of desired performance and monitored performance across a number of streams. However, one can argue that trying to reach such an objective, that equalize the QoS violation that each stream experiences has a serious defect.

To address this deficiency, we define an alternative metric that models the amount of QoS violations from another perspective. The owner of each data stream is asked to submit the required QoS level ("Qs") as a real number in (0,1], referred as the QoS enforcement level of streams. We also need to design a truthful mechanism rule to force users reporting the desired value of QoS for each stream. To relax such a requirement, we allow the RA/S algorithm to violate QoS level now and then.

Equipped with the above statements, we introduce the new metric QoS detriment to quantify the amount of QoS violation happening during an interval $T = (t, t+\Delta t)$:

$$DT = \sum_{s \in S} I_S \tag{7.1}$$

where S represents all streams that experience QoS violation during time T. I_s is the factor to illustrate the importance of an individual stream s. In other words, if a stream s imposes a high QoS requirement Q_s, then this contributes more in the system's QoS detriment metric if it experiences a violation. At any given interval, the controller adjusts the system input variables so as to reduce the overall value of QoS detriment metric among all server nodes.

7.4.2   Model predictive control-based scheduling

MPC-based scheduling scheme can enable the system to predict future workload and resource utilization. The basic concept of MPC lies in using a dynamic model to forecast future system's behaviour and optimize the system to produce the best possible decision.

MPC helps to illustrate the non-linear operations of a complex system and ensures optimization of the controlling variables repetitively within short intervals, with the considering of future states. While applications of MPC controller are ubiquitous in the manufacturing industries, its usage in complex computer systems is still in the early stage.

The authors in [17] designed a controller to maximize the total revenue of cloud providers, subject to capacity, QoS availability, and migration constraints. For a comprehensive tutorial review in the theory and design of MPC systems, the reader can refer to predictive control with constraints [18].

The basic idea of a predictive controller is that at any time, t, the system output, denoted as Z_t, should follow an ideal trajectory, indicated as S_t. Such a reference signal is professionally known as set-point trajectory. The major goal of the designer is to establish a mechanism to force the system's output follows the set-point trajectory within the near short periods.

In a typical MPC controller, the designer needs to determine the values of a three-dimension vector:

1. An internal state vector, shown by X;
2. An input vector, shown by U; and
3. An output vector, shown by Z.

In most cases, the input variable U itself consists of two disjoint sets of both controllable and uncontrollable variables. In a general discrete-time MPC model, the relationship maintained among X, U, and Z at any time t, can be shown as

$$X_{(t+1)} = g_1(X_t, U_t) \tag{7.2}$$

$$Z_t = g_2(X_t) \tag{7.3}$$

where g_1 and g_2 are some non-linear functions that are determined by the system models.

With the MPC works, the system moves forward with the following steps iteratively till the controlling is no more required:

1. Obtaining the measurement of Z_t,
2. Predicting the values for noncontrollable input values,
3. Computing the best possible values of the controllable input vector, and
4. Applying the derived one step input to the system.

Specifically, at time $t+1$, MPC measures the latest values of output vectors as the feedback signal and repeat the whole cycle of prediction, trajectory determination, and optimization process. Moreover, the prediction of the future values, saying noncontrollable input vectors is imperative in MPC controllers.

7.4.3 Experimental performance analysis

In this section, we introduce a study which provides a concrete MPC for Storm scheduling. More details can be found in [16].

7.4.3.1 Experimental setting

We build a local virtualized cluster that consists of three machines which have Xen release 4.2.0-42-generic running with total 96 cores and 304 GB RAM. One of them composed of four 2.40 GHz Intel®Xeon®E7-8870 CPUs, with 30 Mb LLC, 256 GB of RAM. The other two have a 3.40 GHz i7 CPU, 16 GB of RAM, and 8 MB LLC, respectively. A fixed amount of 3 GB of RAM and one dedicated core is provision for Ubuntu 14.04.1 that ran on Dom0 during all experiments. The rests of resources used exclusively by Apache Storm cluster.

Controllable factors in this proposed controller include:

1. The number of worker nodes,
2. The amount of CPU/RAM resources that each worker node should receive.

Consider a scenario that there are initially 32 worker nodes deployed to handle some streams (each worker node has access to use one CPU core and 2 GB of RAM, at the beginning). After running for a while, assume that two new events triggered:

1. The arrival rate of an important (with high QoS demand) stream, say "s1," increases abruptly,
2. Three new data streams, with high QoS enforcement, submitted to the system.

Then, for the MPC controller, it has two options:

• Assign more resources (cores and RAM amount) to those worker nodes which are responsible for serving stream "s1,"
• Create more worker nodes to serve requests generated by the new streams.

We evaluated the performance of the underlying system concerning different scenarios with two metrics: the average latency experienced by emitted event and the amount of QoS detriment metric (as an indicator of QoS violations occurred in the entire system).

All evaluations performed on a Storm cluster with "k" worker nodes. The number of slots in each worker node is a variable which is set by the MPC controller, with a maximum value of five. We also assigned one node hosting the Nimbus and Zookeeper services exclusively.

7.4.3.2   Topology and workload attributes

We compared this solution against the default setting of Apache Storm. The default Storm scheduler uses a RR policy to balance the load amongst the resources. In essence, the scheduler aims to distribute the existing executors evenly among worker processes and allocate worker processes across active hosts in a fair manner.

The general topology used in this study is compatible with the one introduced in work [10]. Each component "c" in the topology has an associated stage number, "s," which represents the longest path length where a tuple should pass, from a spout to a component. Components that have the same stage number will not communicate with each other, while components at stage "s" can only receive tuples from its upstream components.

Such a topology can be characterized by two factors: the number of stages and the replication parameter for each stage. The spout executor sets its tuple rate from either a Poisson or Weibull distribution. Parameters of lambda in [1,4,6] for Poisson or in [1,4,6] and beta in [1,3,5] for Weibull distribution. In the Poisson process, lambda represents the average number of events per millisecond. And in Weibull model, lambda and beta are the scale and shape parameters of a standard Weibull distribution.

To imitate the QoS patterns of real applications, we have used two mainstreams, "UniQoS" and "NormQoS," to represent the probability distribution of QoS enforcement requested. In the UniQoS (NormQoS) scheme, the QoS requirement of each stream derived from a uniform (standard normal) probability distribution over the unit interval with an average at 0.5. By switching the above parameters, we have created 54 scenarios that represent different possible generated workloads.

7.4.3.3   Evaluation

In the experimental evaluation, we have three performance metrics included:

1.   The average event latency,
2.   The average resource (CPU) utilization, and
3.   The total amount of QoS violation.

As suggested by the evaluation result, both the latency and CPU utilization become larger with the increasing of stages. It is reasonable as each tuple of data naturally requires more processing time, and each worker node demands to do more work as the total number of nodes is fixed.

The proposed controller can quickly adapt to the alternation of replication factor by assigning more resources to the workers that almost become a bottleneck. But without the controlling mechanism, the system experienced performance degradation as the effectiveness of schedule scheme drops down.

In general, a larger arrival rate leads to the longer latencies for any solutions. However, the controller can adaptively prevent longer response time by either provision more worker nodes or assign more resources to available ones, enabled by the traffic predictor.

A significant achievement by applying MPC controller is its ability to keep the utilization of CPU at an ideal level. This can leverage by switching off or putting other nonworking cores into the deep sleeping mode to save the total power usage. To find out the QoS detriment value, we need to identify the average latency achieved by tuples in each data stream. If the observed latency of a stream is higher than the expected value, we count it as a QoS violation.

From the result, the QoS-aware controller keeps the QoS violations below 18% even under the most extreme cases. Specifically, it tries to avoid collocating data streams with a high level of QoS enforcement in same worker node. Furthermore, if a continuous set of QoS violation incidents is detected, it dynamically makes more CPU/memory resources available to the worker node that is recognized as the bottleneck.

7.5   Open issues in stream processing

State management in SPS is one of the open challenges that has been well acknowledged. It deserves further research efforts. Instead of migrating operations along from one worker node to another with rescheduling procedure, certain computations are requiring state maintained align with the reconfiguration. Moreover, the efficiency of migration policy is critical in terms of time cost and resource cost. Therefore, the aim is to ensure that the system can run smoothly even experiencing state migration, and the mechanism of dealing with data loss due to migration should be well designed.

For some of the implementations of stream processing, like Apache Storm, the level of parallelism can only be defined manually. In other words, the system is not able to reconfigure with increase or decrease of parallel degree adaptively and automatically. It suggests that the overall throughput is unable to further improve unless the level of parallelism is enlarged.

Devising an efficient and effective scheduling algorithm is extremely challenging due to the nature of stream processing. The problem of exponential growth of energy consumption in data centres has been pointed out as one of the outstanding challenges of scheduling schemes research. It is much more complex when a high volume of streaming data is flowing from large-scale, multisite applications with an integrated fashion and demanded to interpret for further processing.

Therefore, the limitations of existing solution make it difficult to approach to the desired performance, and the more advanced implementation of DSP is essential towards an efficient SPSs.

7.6   Conclusion

With the increasing requirement of real-time data processing, a new data model has proposed in recent years. DSP is capable of dealing with high volume of data incoming continuously in the format of streams with varying arrival rate. The streams are unbounded in size and processing is expected in an online fashion.

The query of this data model is accordingly changed in the term of triggering rules and operating mechanism. Since the frequency of data updating in SPS is tend to be much higher than they do in traditional DBMS, the content of a group of data within a certain time frame or the meaning behind the continuous data has significant roles in stream processing applications. Newly data can trigger the events by itself instead of manually operation required. As a consequence, only estimated results are expected based on a proportion of data.

In general, the goal of DSP model is to process the flying data timely and accurately. Users are demanding to gather, process, and analyse these data streams to extract insights and knowledge as well as to detect emerging patterns or outliers. The objectives of this application normally include low latency, scalable and fault tolerance.

Resources in contemporary cloud-based data centres are allocated in the form of VM and mapped onto the physical hosts. Scheduling algorithm in a given platform would either define the policy of assigning tasks to VM with better matching solutions between resource requirement and computing capability or designs the rules of dynamically adjusting resources allocation to each VM to meet the tasks' demand. Moreover, the VM configurations commonly include the number of CPU core and the amount of main memory.

More recently, as one of the most popular stream processing frameworks, Apache Storm has been applied widely from scientific research to industries. It is an open-source real-time computation framework that works with continuous streaming data. With the addressing of uncertainty and complexity of stream processing, along with the deficiency of the default scheduling mechanism, studies tend to provide more advanced scheduling scheme in order to improve the overall performance. Controller based methodologies enable the system to configure itself along with a set-point trajectory and actions would be taken before the changes of workload observed. The distributed computing resource managed in such ways can benefit more comparing with the traditional reactive approach.

However, in the meantime, there are still challenges and limitations concerning about stream processing deployment and implementation. More sophisticated computation model or framework is expected so that the data centre resource can be fully utilized and the system can deliver more desirable output.

Acknowledgement

This work is supported by ARC (Australian Research Council) LP150101213 "Contention-Aware Scheduling in Cloud Data Centres."

References

[1]   D. J. Abadi, D. Carney, U. Çetintemel, *et al.*, "Aurora: a new model and architecture for data stream management," *The VLDB Journal—The International Journal on Very Large Data Bases,* vol. 12, pp. 120–139, 2003.

[2]   D. J. Abadi, Y. Ahmad, M. Balazinska, *et al.*, "The design of the borealis stream processing engine," in *CIDR*, 2005, pp. 277–289.

[3]   L. Neumeyer, B. Robbins, A. Nair and A. Kesari, "S4: Distributed stream computing platform", in Data Mining Workshops (ICDMW), 2010 IEEE International Conference on, 2010, pp. 170–177.

[4]   P. Padala, K.-Y. Hou, K. G. Shin, *et al.*, "Automated control of multiple virtualized resources," in *Proceedings of the 4th ACM European Conference on Computer Systems*, 2009, pp. 13–26.

[5]   I. Pietri and R. Sakellariou, "Mapping virtual machines onto physical machines in cloud computing: a survey," *ACM Computing Surveys (CSUR),* vol. 49, p. 49, 2016.

[6]   B. Jennings and R. Stadler, "Resource management in clouds: survey and research challenges," *Journal of Network and Systems Management,* vol. 23, pp. 567–619, 2015.

[7]   T. Lorido-Botran, J. Miguel-Alonso, and J. A. Lozano, "A review of auto-scaling techniques for elastic applications in cloud environments," *Journal of Grid Computing,* vol. 12, pp. 559–592, 2014.

[8]   A. Toshniwal, S. Taneja, A. Shukla, *et al.*, "Storm@ twitter," in *Proceedings of the 2014 ACM SIGMOD International Conference on Management of Data*, 2014, pp. 147–156.

[9]   N. Marz, "Storm: Distributed and fault-tolerant realtime computation," 2011, https://www. infoq, com presentations/Storm-Introduction.

[10] L. Aniello, R. Baldoni, and L. Querzoni, "Adaptive online scheduling in storm," in *Proceedings of the 7th ACM International Conference on Distributed Event-based Systems*, 2013, pp. 207–218.

[11] B. Gedik, S. Schneider, M. Hirzel, and K.-L. Wu, "Elastic scaling for data stream processing," *IEEE Transactions on Parallel and Distributed Systems,* vol. 25, pp. 1447–1463, 2014.

[12] J. Xu, Z. Chen, J. Tang, and S. Su, "T-storm: traffic-aware online scheduling in storm," in *Distributed Computing Systems (ICDCS), 2014 IEEE 34th International Conference on*, 2014, pp. 535–544.

[13] B. Peng, M. Hosseini, Z. Hong, R. Farivar, and R. Campbell, "R-storm: resource-aware scheduling in storm," in *Proceedings of the 16th Annual Middleware Conference*, 2015, pp. 149–161.

[14] J. S. van der Veen, B. van der Waaij, E. Lazovik, W. Wijbrandi, and R. J. Meijer, "Dynamically scaling apache storm for the analysis of streaming data," in *Big Data Computing Service and Applications (BigDataService), 2015 IEEE First International Conference on*, 2015, pp. 154–161.

[15]   T. De Matteis and G. Mencagli, "Proactive elasticity and energy awareness in data stream processing," *Journal of Systems and Software,* vol. 127, pp. 302–319, 2017.

[16]   M. R. Hoseiny Farahabady, H. R. D. Samani, Y. Wang, A. Y. Zomaya, and Z. Tari, "A QoS-aware controller for Apache Storm," in *Network Computing and Applications (NCA), 2016 IEEE 15th International Symposium on*, 2016, pp. 334–342.

[17]   E. Casalicchio and L. Silvestri, "Mechanisms for SLA provisioning in cloud-based service providers," *Computer Networks,* vol. 57, pp. 795–810, 2013.

[18]   J. M. Maciejowski, *Predictive control: with constraints*, Pearson Education Limited, Prentice Hall, London, 2002, pp. IX+331, ISBN 0-201-39823-0.

Chapter 8
Big Data in cloud data centers
Gunasekaran Manogaran* and Daphne Lopez*

Big Data refers to a collection of massive volume of data that cannot be processed by conventional data processing tools and technologies. In recent years, the data production sources are enlarged noticeably, such as high-end streaming devices, wireless sensor networks, satellite, wearable Internet of Things devices. These data generation sources generate massive amount of data in continuous manner. Nowadays, Big Data analytics plays a significant role in various environments it includes business monitoring, healthcare applications, production development, research and development, share market prediction, business process, industrial applications, social network analysis, weather analysis and environmental monitoring. A data center is a facility composed of networked computers and storage that businesses or other organizations use to process, analyze, store and distribute huge volume of data. In recent years, cloud data centers have been used to store and process the Big Data. This chapter reviews various architectures to store and process the Big Data in cloud data centers. In addition, this chapter also describes the challenges and applications of Big Data analytics in cloud data centers.

8.1 Introduction

Big Data is defined as a collection of large volume of data that becomes complex to process by using traditional data processing techniques and platforms. In other words, a data set can be named Big Data if it is difficult to store, process and visualize using state-of-the-art technologies. Nowadays, data generation sources are increased dramatically, such as streaming machines, high-throughput instruments, sensor networks, telescopes and streaming machines, and these environments produce large amount of data [1]. In recent years, Big Data has been playing a vital role in many environments such as public administration, scientific research, business organization, healthcare, industry, social networking and natural resource management. For example, more number of researchers suggests that Big Data is one of the best research frontiers [2]. Big Data is ranked in both "Top 10 Critical Tech Trends for the Next Five Years" and "Top 10 Strategic Technology Trends For 2013" by Eric Savitz [3,4].

*School of Information Technology and Engineering, VIT University, India

Table 8.1   Difference between traditional data center and cloud data center

	Traditional data center	Cloud data center
Servers	Colocated dependent failure	Integrated fault-tolerant
Resources	Partitioned performance interrelated	Unified performance isolated
Management	Separated manual	Centralized full control with automation
Scheduling	Plan ahead over provisioning	Flexible scalable
Renting	Per physical machines	Per logical usage
Application/ Services	Fixes on designated servers	Runs and moves across all VMs

A data center is a facility composed of networked computers and storage that businesses or other organizations use to process, analyze, store and distribute huge volume of data. Cloud computing is the practice of using a network of remote servers hosted on the Internet to manage, store and process data rather than a personal computer and local server. In other words, cloud computing is a type of computing and is used for the delivery of hosted services over the Internet to manage the real-time applications. Virtualization is playing a major role in implementation of both Big Data and cloud computing. It provides facilities such as storing, accessing, analyzing and managing the distributed computing components in Big Data analytics. In other words, virtualization is also used to increase IT resource utilization, scalability and efficiency. The main goal of the virtualization is to increase the consumption of physical servers and efficiently saving on infrastructure costs. Cloud computing is one of the most powerful techniques used to perform large-scale computing, parallel processing, complex computing, security and data service integration with scalable data storage. In the recent years, cloud application integration is growing at a high speed. Organizations used variety of integrations in cloud services especially for mobile apps that need to exchange messages and Big Data. The software deployed in cloud-computing environment and the data stored in the cloud data centers are connected virtually to communicate each other asynchronously or synchronously by fetching, transferring and storing the data. Table 8.1 represents the difference between traditional data center and cloud data center.

8.2   Needs for the architecture patterns and data sources for Big Data storage in cloud data centers

Nowadays, many organizations have started use of cloud computing. Though cloud computing provides possible storage space, there is a need to process such huge amounts of data. In order to overcome this issue, Big Data analytics are used in many organizations such as government and private institutes, healthcare industries and research and development organizations are also interested in using Big Data

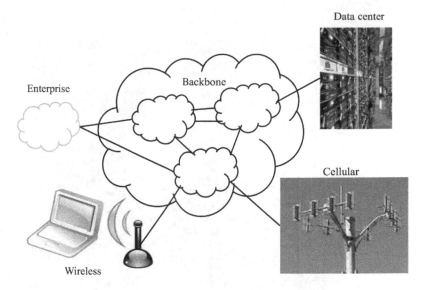

Figure 8.1   Cloud data center for networking application

analytics. Cloud-deployment models provide various cloud architectures to store and process Big Data such as private cloud, public cloud and hybrid cloud. A private cloud is a type of cloud-computing model that involves a distinct and secure cloud-based environment in which only the authorized users can operate. A public cloud is a type of cloud-computing model, in which a service provider makes resources, such as storage, computing resources and applications available to the all users or general public over the Internet. Hybrid cloud is a type of cloud-computing model which uses a mix of on-premises, private cloud and third-party, public cloud services. Figure 8.1 represents the cloud data center for networking application.

There is a need to develop an architecture that process a wide variety of data sources and formats (such as CSV, text, XML, images, and other formats). The analytics solution is used to provide various services such as preprocessing, converting, analyzing, transforming, pre-analytic processing and more. The cloud provider must provide various tools and technologies to process such huge data stored in the various cloud deployments models. The cloud provider tools should perform the following operations such as connectivity, load balancing, transformation, resource sharing, routing, and the like, or hardware supplies such as appropriate storage, process, analyze, compute and networking. The cloud provider should enable the security features to prevent unwanted access from the malicious user and also capable of handling various compliance rules, processes and audit trails to meet privacy, security and IP protection guidelines for organizations in different industries. Provider cloud components are used to provide features for data analysis, data storage and processing or analyze the results of the system. The following elements that are playing a vital role in provider cloud include: API management, Streaming computing, Data integration,

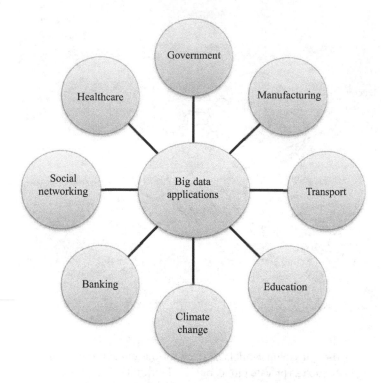

Figure 8.2   Big Data application

Data repositories, Analytics discovery and exploration, Deployed analytics, Security, Information governance, Transformation and connectivity.

8.3   Applications of Big Data analytics with cloud data centers

Big Data have been playing a significant role in various fields and increased much concentration from government sectors, business enterprises and research centers. Cloud data centers used to store the huge volume of data. This section elaborates how Big Data is expected to rise in the future and how Big Data is used to solve our various issues in the day-to-day environment (Figure 8.2). Recently, Big Data analytics are significantly used to gain more important hidden values from various environments it includes healthcare analytics, environment and natural resource management, public sector units, business enterprises, government organizations, social networking and computational platforms [5].

8.3.1   Disease diagnosis

The data generation sources in healthcare departments are increased dramatically. These data generation sources generate a variety of data such as pharmaceutical data, electronic medical records, scanned images, data on individual food and dietary preferences, data on exercise patterns, financial details and so on. The combination of all these data produces Big Data. Nowadays, cloud-computing technologies are used to store the large volume of medical records. This data is used to take a better decision in disease diagnosis, healthcare services, drug recommendation, healthcare delivery and drug interventions.

8.3.2   Government organizations

Nowadays, government and public sector units are started using of Big Data analytics and cloud data centers to process and store the massive records. These massive records are stored as structured and unstructured format in distributed environment to gain more useful and high-value insights. For example, AWS GovCloud is developed to store the large volumes of administration files and business transaction details.

8.3.3   Social networking

In the recent years, the users of the Internet and social-networking sites such as Facebook, Twitter and LinkedIn are increased significantly. Antoniadis *et al.* [6] have reported that above two billion people are aggressively using social networking sites each month. Big Data analytics is used in social networking to analyze people emotions, take better decision based on the people opinions, conduct the general survey, and spared the hot news and topics.

8.3.4   Computing platforms

Computing environments and high throughput instruments are started using cloud-based Big Data analytical tools to gain more useful hidden information. Especially, quantum mechanical simulation, astrophysical modeling, geo-spatial environment uses scalable and distributed Big Data platforms to analyze the huge volume of data.

8.3.5   Environmental and natural resources

In the recent years, Big Data analytics are also used to save the natural resources and environmental modeling. For example, Big Data analytics are used to process high resolution satellite images to take better decision when emergency situation arise; examples are deforestation [7], water resources supervision [8], extreme weather events, biomass monitoring [9], urban encroachment [10], land slide, climate change, green gas emission, global warming [11], landslide and earthquake.

8.4   State-of-the-art Big Data architectures for cloud data centers

Currently, there is no generic architecture available for analytical "Big Data" systems. However, a number of small-scale architectures have been proposed by various organizations to fulfill their own requirements [12]. Most architectures are developed only for specific purposes such as batch processing, stream processing, security

Table 8.2   State of-the-art tools and technologies to handle Big Data

S. No.	Task	Tool
1.	Data storage and management	Hadoop Cloudera MongoDB Talend
2.	Data cleaning	OpenRefine DataCleaner
3.	Data mining	RapidMiner IBM SPSS Modeler Oracle data mining Teradata FramedData Kaggle
4.	Data analysis	Qubole BigML Statwing
5.	Data visualization	Tableau Silk CartoDB Chartio Plot.ly Datawrapper
6.	Data integration	Blockspring Pentaho
7.	Data languages	R Python RegEx X Path
8.	Data collection	Import.io

and storage. This product-oriented architecture, thereby, is limiting the scope to the specific products from a company, while other architectures are technology oriented, thereby skipping a functional view and mappings of technology to functions. This section discusses about different Big Data architecture and it use cases [13].

8.4.1   Lambda architecture

Marz and Warren [14] originally developed the Lambda Architecture to implement the Big Data systems (Figure 8.3). Nathan Marz implemented the Lambda Architecture on distributed data processing systems for Twitter data analytics [15]. This architecture contains three layers: batch, speed and serving.

8.4.1.1   Batch layer

Batch layer performs two main functions namely master dataset management and batch views pre computation. Apache Hive is used to manage the master data in the

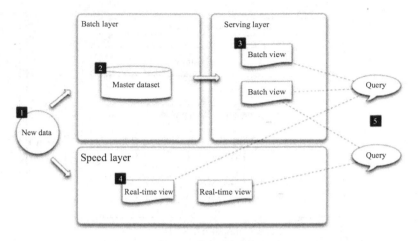

Figure 8.3 Lambda architecture [14]

batch layer whereas Hadoop MapReduce framework is used compute the batch views. The above-mentioned functions continuously maintains a balance between what will be precomputed at first and what will be computed during execution time to complete the ad-hoc query.

8.4.1.2 Speed layer

It usually takes few hours to complete the batch views. These views will be stale during the scanning period of large system record, but user continuously generates the transaction information without any break. In order to compute results for the most recent user's query, the transaction file should be combined and stored into the real-time view. The real-time layer is used compute results for the most recent incoming stream of data. After query results are computed, they results will be stored to answer the most recent user's query.

8.4.1.3 Serving layer

The serving layer is always connected with the batch layer to store the batch views. In general, due to high latency, the batch views always out of date. This latency issue can be solved by speed layer, because the speed layer always responsible for any data that is not yet available in the serving layer. As batch layer does not display batch views, the batch views should be stored in a distributed database that stores batch views and makes the batch views efficiently queryable and always makes changes in updated versions of a batch view as they are provided by the batch layer. Due to the high volume of data stored in the batch layer, it will take a few hours to update a single batch view, whereas the serving layer takes within an hour to complete its updates.

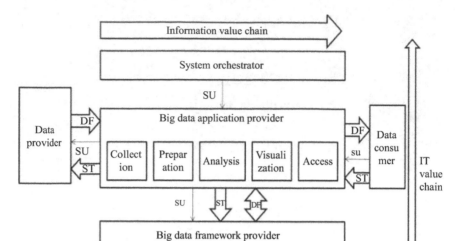

Figure 8.4   NIST Big Data Reference Architecture (16)

8.4.2   NIST Big Data Reference Architecture (NBDRA)

NIST [16] originally developed the Big Data Reference Architecture (NBDRA) to enable data scientists, software developers, data architects, engineers and senior decision makers to develop solutions to issues related to Big Data characteristics. NBDRA is shown in Figure 8.4, and it describes a Big Data ecosystem consisting of various functional layers that are interconnected by interoperability surfaces. NBDRA consist of five layers, namely, System Orchestrator, Data Provider, Data Consumer, Big Data Application Provider and Big Data Framework Provider.

8.4.2.1   System Orchestrator

System Orchestrator is developed to define and integrate all the activities of the data applications into a set of vertical system. The vital role of the System Orchestrator is to provide high-level design, system requirements and monitoring of the data system.

8.4.2.2   Data provider

A data provider makes user's data available to various functional blocks. In other words, it broadcasts the new data or information feeds into the all functional blocks of the Big Data ecosystem. In addition, data provider also creates an abstract view for various data sources.

8.4.2.3   Data consumer

The data consumer continuously receives the value output from the Big Data Application Provider. Data consumer layer also uses the interface to obtain the results of the Big Data system. The essential roles of data consumer are follows: searching, querying, exploring and retrieving the data, creating and analyzing reports, importing and processing data for storage, converting information into business rule.

8.4.2.4   Big Data Application Provider

The Big Data Application Provider always executes the data lifecycle to meet privacy and security requirements. In addition, it also executes the requirements identified by the System Orchestrator. The essential functionalities of the Big Data Application Provider as follows: collecting data from various sources, data cleaning, data standardizing, removing outliers, data optimization, data aggregation, data visualization, data security and privacy.

8.4.2.5   Big Data framework provider

Big Data Framework Provider provides general services or resources for Big Data Application Provider to carry out certain transformation applications, while preserving data integrity and privacy. It contains three subcomponents such as infrastructure frameworks, data platforms and processing frameworks. This Block also provides infrastructure related to computing framework such as system hardware, storage structure, networking structure and computing platform.

8.4.3   Big Data Architecture for Remote Sensing

Rathore *et al.* [17] have proposed this architecture for real-time Big Data analysis, especially for remote sensing applications. The proposed architecture (Figure 8.5) can efficiently process and analyze both offline and real-time remote sensing data to make better decisions in future. It consists of three major blocks, namely, Remote Sensing Big Data Acquisition Unit (RSDU), data processing unit (DPU) and data analysis decision unit (DADU). These units have algorithms depending on the required analysis. Algorithms proposed in each unit are used to analyze satellite remote sensing data, which helps user to understand the current situation of land and sea areas.

8.4.3.1   Remote sensing Big Data Acquisition Unit

RSDU is used to obtain data from various satellites around the globe. Relational data preprocessing techniques such as data integration, data cleaning and redundancy elimination are used in the RSDU unit to process the raw satellite data. Once the preprocessing task is finished, the preprocessed data is transferred to a ground station using downlink channel with appropriate antenna and wireless communication link. The data processing task is split into two steps: offline Big Data processing and real-time Big Data processing. In offline data processing, once the processed data is ready then Earth Base Station transfer the data to the data center storage block. This data is used further for analyses and report generation. However, in real-time DPU, the streaming data are directly transmitted to the filtration and load balancer server (FLBS).

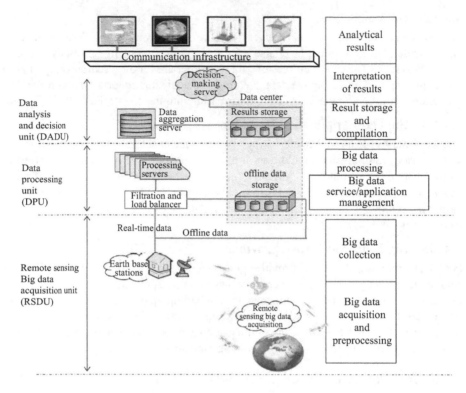

Figure 8.5   Big Data architecture for remote sensing [17]

8.4.3.2 Data processing unit

DPU is used filtration, load balancing and parallel processing functions to process the real-time Big Data. DPU consists of FLBS to filter the unwanted data and load balancing of processing power, respectively. Load balancing block divides the whole filtered data into different blocks and shares them to various processing servers. Finally, the results gathered from each server are aggregated for further processing.

8.4.3.3 Data analysis and decision unit

DADU is the upper layer unit, and it contains three major functions: aggregation and compilation server, results storage server and decision-making server. DPU sends the partial results to the aggregation and compilation server. Aggregation and compilation server consists of various algorithms that compile, organize, store and transmit the results. Aggregation server first aggregates the results, then transfers to the storage block; while aggregation server send a same copy to the decision-making server to process the result for making decision in near future. The decision-making algorithm finally produces the decisions at real time to make the development in the organization.

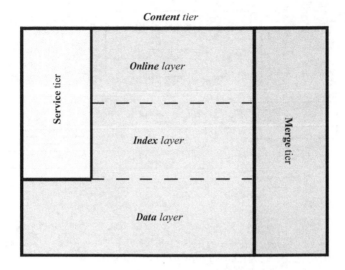

Figure 8.6   The Service-On-Line-Index-Data (SOLID) architecture [18]

8.4.4   The Service-On Line-Index-Data (SOLID) architecture

Martínez-Prieto *et al.* [18] have identified Service-On-Line-Index-Data (SOLID) architecture (Figure 8.6) to manage big semantic data in real-time. SOLID uses large size of data storage block for storing big semantic data, which indexed to allow high-speed querying. SOLID is developed as a multitiered, layered architecture to solve the main requirements of big semantic data. It consists of three tiers, namely, Service Tier, Content Tier and Merge Tier. Content Tier is further classified into three layers: Data Layer, Index Layer and Online Layer.

8.4.4.1   Content tier

The content tier consists of three data-centric layers and all are developed for data storage responsibilities. This tier stores both big semantic data and new run-time generated data.

8.4.4.2   Data layer and index layer

The data layer is responsible for big semantic data storage; it follows the same principles as the batch layer of Lambda architecture [19]. It stores raw data considering the immutability principle, so this layer can never be deleted or altered; only insertions are possible. The index layer works with the data layer and responsible for efficient querying.

8.4.4.3   Online layer, merge tier and service tier

The online layer is responsible for complexity of managing runtime data. The temporary data store is used in this layer to manage the flow of real-time data. The merge tier plays a connection role between online and data layers. This layer is also responsible

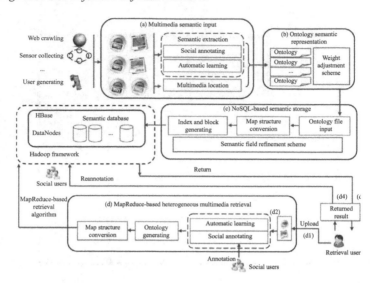

*Figure 8.7   Semantic-based Architecture for Heterogeneous Multimedia
Retrieval [19]*

for run-time data integration of big semantic data. The service tier is responsible for connection between online and index layers. The main function of this tier is to query their corresponding datasets.

8.4.5   Semantic-based Architecture for Heterogeneous Multimedia Retrieval

Guo *et al.* [19] have developed the Semantic-based architecture (Figure 8.7) used to store and retrieve semantic information from heterogeneous multimedia data. This architecture consists of four blocks, namely, Multimedia Semantic Input, Ontology Semantic Representation, No Structured Query Language (NoSQL)-base Semantic Storage and MapReduce-based Heterogeneous Multimedia Retrieval.

8.4.5.1   Multimedia semantic input

This block collects the multimedia content from different sources such as sensor, web crawling, and user generating. The data types include images, videos, audios or text documents. This semantic information will be initialized in this block by two ways namely social annotating and automatic learning.

8.4.5.2   Ontology semantic representation

Ontology Semantic Representation is used to combine the semantic fields with the multimedia location. During the information retrieval process, higher weights are assigned to more frequently used semantic fields. This process is used to efficiently access the most recent information.

8.4.5.3 NoSQL-base Semantic Storage

NoSQL-base Semantic Storage is used to store the semantic fields combined with multimedia location which are represented as the highly optimized map <key-value> format. Apache HBase is used in this architecture to store the semantic fields and multimedia locations.

8.4.5.4 MapReducebased Heterogeneous Multimedia Retrieval

Once the Apache HBase is stored (the semantic fields and multimedia locations), then it can be processed by distributed & parallel mode with MapReduce-based retrieval algorithm. In this proposed MapReduce algorithm, user query is divided into <QueryId, Query Ontology> pairs. Mapper Function finds every pair Query-Ontology with the Record Value, then it will catch all the matching records. Reducer function sorts the records with greater similarity value.

8.4.6 LargeScale Security Monitoring Architecture

Marchal *et al.* [20] have developed Large-Scale Security Monitoring Architecture (Figure 8.8) to detect and prevent intrusion and malicious user of a local company network. This architecture collects the honeypot data, DNS data, HTTP traffic and IP-flow records and stores them into a heterogeneous distributed storage system. Correlation algorithms will be used to detect the intrusion and malicious user. This architecture consists of two main functions: Data presentation and Data correlation.

8.4.6.1 Data presentation

Nowadays, almost all the network communications are initiated via Domain Name System (DNS). Hence, continuous monitoring of DNS ensures that identify malicious domains. Proposed architecture use Apache Cassandra database to store every observed domain along with its extracted information. Cisco NetFlow is used in this architecture to monitor the flow records by observing routers. Flow records are valuable to detect botnet communications and intrusions. SQLite database is used in this architecture to monitor several vulnerable network services (HTTP, FTP, MSSQL, SMB, etc.).

8.4.6.2 Data correlation

Distributed data correlation system function is used to identify the level of risk for communications. When a client fetches the domain, the fetch request will go to the local Recursive DNS server. It solves the request by consulting its authoritative DNS servers to resolve the domain. All the authoritative DNS replies are stored into the Cassandra database. Finally, the following operations are performed to check whether the domain is malicious or not: (1) Domains are checked against three publicly available blacklists, (2) Automated classification techniques relying on DNS data are used to identify malicious domains and (3) Every IP address appearing in DNS resource records are checked against IP addresses logged by the honeypot.

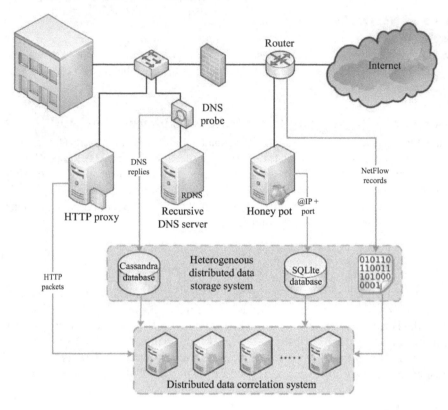

Figure 8.8   Large-Scale Security Monitoring Architecture [20]

8.4.7   Modular software architecture

Kramer *et al.* [21] have identified the Modular Software Architecture (Figure 8.9) for processing of large-scale geospatial datasets in the cloud. Proposed architecture is flexible and it supports variety of recent Big Data frameworks such as MapReduce, in-memory computing or agent-based programing. A web-based user interface is developed in this architecture so that GIS analysts or urban system user can describe high-level processing workflows using a domain-specific language. The web-based interface consists of three components such as data upload form, a data browser and the workflow editor. Data upload form is used to store new geospatial data together with related metadata, while data browser is used to search the existing data sets based on a spatial metadata. Once the GIS analysts identified the workflows, then it passed through a number of blocks such as parser, interpreter and job manager to process the user query. Job manager creates a new entry in the data catalogue; it contains generated result set for the user query. Finally, the result set are send to the user interface.

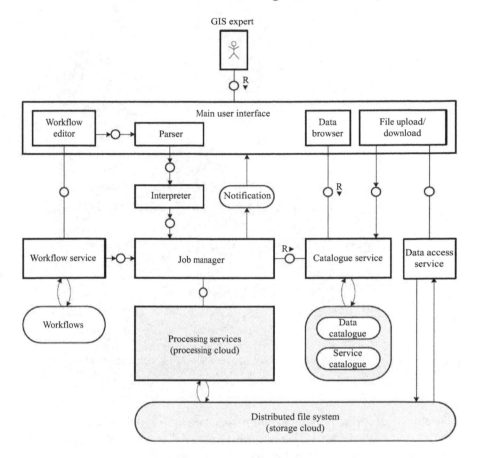

Figure 8.9   Modular Software Architecture [21]

8.4.8   MongoDB-based Healthcare Data Management Architecture

Gorton *et al.* [22] have developed the MongoDB-based Healthcare Data Management Architecture (Figure 8.10) to increase availability and reduce latency for globally distributed users. MongoDB is used in this prototype to illustrate the architecture drivers and identify the decisions. Proposed architecture maintains data across three shards and replicates data across two data centers. MongoDB implement the master-slave architecture, in master system serves write requests and propagates changes to other replicas, while in slaves read from any replica. MongoDB uses parameter option to maintain the tradeoff between consistency and latency on each read and write operation. When doing write operation, MongoDB maintains so that they can be unacknowledged, durable on the master replica, or durable on the master and one or more replicas. While doing read operation, it uses closest replica, restricted to the master replica or require most replicas to agree on the data value before it is read. In this proposed architecture, when writing demographic data of each patient, it must

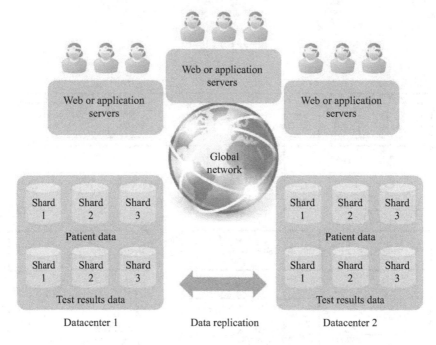

Figure 8.10   MongoDB-based Healthcare Data Management Architecture [22]

be durable on the primary replica, but reading the demographic data can be directed to the closest replica for low latency. This ensures that patient demographic reads insensitive to other partitions in the network.

8.4.9   Scalable and Distributed Architecture for Sensor Data Collection, Storage and Analysis

Aydin *et al.* [23] have developed the end-to-end sensor data lifecycle-based architecture (Figure 8.11) for Sensor Data Collection, Storage and Analysis. Proposed architecture uses open source software's and provides a distributed and scalable infrastructure for tracking many sensors. The system architecture consists of three main blocks: Data Harvesting Subsystem, Data Storage Subsystem and Data Analysis Subsystem.

8.4.9.1   Data Harvesting Subsystem

QuickServer is used in this block to collect the real-time data sent by the GPS servers. Generally, QuickServer supports multiclient TCP server connections, secure services such as SSL and TLS, thread per client and nonblocking communications. After collecting the real-time data sent by the GPS servers, Data Harvesting Subsystem uses data filtering and parsing technique to extract useful information.

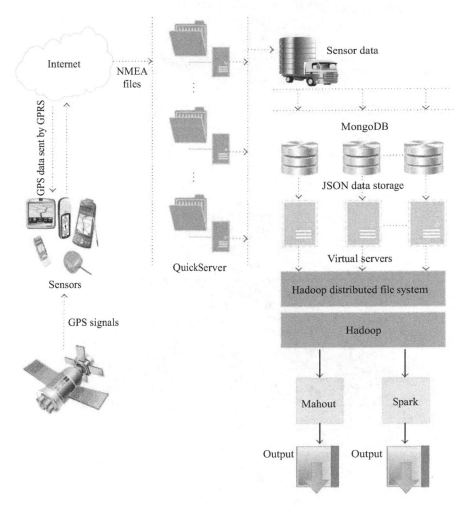

Figure 8.11   Scalable and Distributed Architecture for Sensor Data Collection,
Storage and Analysis [23]

8.4.9.2   Data Storage Subsystem

In Data Storage Subsystem, MongoDB is used to store filtered data sent by the
Data Harvesting Subsystem. MongoDB provides high-performance write support
for QuickServer and also allows users to easily scale the databases for store a large
number of sensor data.

8.4.9.3   Data Analysis Subsystem

In Data Analysis Subsystem phase, a scalable and distributed data analysis subsystem is created using Big Data technologies to find important information such as
early warning messages and fault messages. Finally, cloud-computing framework is

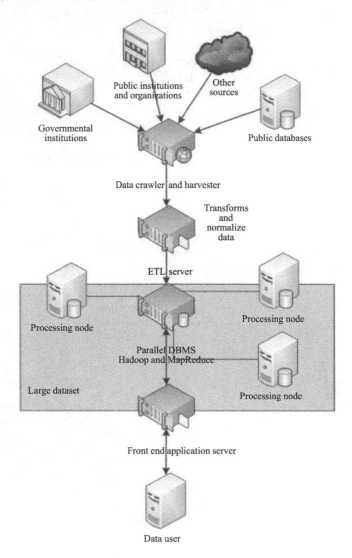

Figure 8.12   Distributed parallel architecture for "Big Data" (24)

developed using OpenStack. It provides a web-based GUI for management of the system and creating/deleting VMs. Proposed architecture uses private cloud using OpenStack platform and run six virtual machines as Hadoop cluster nodes.

8.4.10   Distributed parallel architecture for "Big Data"

Boja *et al.* [24] have developed the distributed parallel architecture (Figure 8.12) to process large financial datasets. It consist of three layers namely input layer, data layer and user layer.

8.4.10.1 Different layers

Input layer collects data from various sources such as reports, data repositories. Data layer stores and process large datasets of economic and financial records using distributed, parallel processing platforms. The extract, transform and load (ETL) intermediary layer is used in this data layer to convert a normal data into new form and loads it in the parallel DBMS data store. In addition, ETL also normalize the data; convert into predefined structure and discards unwanted information. User layer consist of front end application server that will allow the user to query the data and manage requests for analysis and reports. Table 8.2 depicts the state-of-the-art Big Data architectures and its merits and demerits.

8.5 Challenges and potential solutions for Big Data analytics in cloud data centers

Traditional tools and technologies are not applicable to store Big Data in cloud data centers. It requires advance scalable storage and processing platforms to get useful information [25]. Big Data has following challenges as well as the potential solution such as (Figure 8.13).

Data processing: Data preprocessing is the fundamental process to be done before the data analysis in cloud data center. Preprocessing of Big Data is becoming a complex problem in day-to-day life. Nowadays, data generation sources generate a large amount of data in a continuous manner. This data consists of unwanted noise and dirty; hence, there is a need to preprocess the Big Data before the data analysis process. The traditional data preprocessing tools and technologies are not applicable to process such huge amount of data stored distributed cloud data center. For example, it takes 635 years to preprocess 1k petabytes of data. Hence, there is a need to use parallel processing platforms and algorithms such as CUDA, MPI, Spark Streaming, and Hadoop MapReduce to remove the unwanted noise present in the Big Data.

Data storage: Data storage is another complex issue in cloud data center. Traditional databases are not capable of handling the massive size of data in cloud data center. Moreover, the variety of data types is also considered as a complex issue in Big Data. As a Relational Database Management System follows structured query language, the Big Data is not possible to store in SQL databases. Thus, NoSQL databases are identified in cloud data center to store the variety of unstructured data. In the recent years, various scalable NoSQL databases are developed by Apache and Yahoo developers namely Apache HBase, Mongo DB and Apache Hive and so on.

Data stream: Streaming machines and high throughput instruments are considered as major challenges in real-time data processing. These devices are continuously generating the huge amount of data with high speed. Hence, the traditional data processing methods and technologies are not applicable to store and process such

Table 8.3 Comparison of state-of-the-art Big Data architectures in cloud data centers

S. No.	Name of the architecture	Application	Merits	Demerits
1.	Lambda Architecture [14]	Social networking	It merges both streaming data and offline data so that up-to-date information can be process	Immutability in nature; variety of data (it processes only text data)
2.	NIST Big Data Reference Architecture (NBDRA) [16]	Applicable to tightly integrated enterprise systems or loosely coupled vertical industrial systems	Various data sources and variety of data can be process	Due to the rapid emergence of new Big Data techniques, framework provider need to be updated consciously
3.	Big Data Architecture for Remote Sensing [16]	Remote sensing in satellite application	Tested with real-time data	Streaming Big Data tools are not used in data-collection phase and assumption made as streaming data in structured format
4.	The Service-On-Line-Index-Data (SOLID) Architecture [18]	Weather data modeling	Address the main requirements of Big Semantic Data and real-time data management	Graphical processing unit is not available
5.	Semantic-based Architecture for Heterogeneous Multimedia Retrieval [19]	Processing of heterogeneous multimedia data	NoSQL and MapReduce frameworks are used for better scalability	Experimental dataset acquisition is from some specific websites such as Flickr, Wikipedia and YouTube not tested with real Internet environment and increasing the retrieval speed
6.	Large-Scale Security Monitoring Architecture [20]	Preventing and detecting intrusion	Proved that Spark and Shark appear to be the best performers in all scenarios	Architecture computes score with few delay
7.	Modular Software Architecture [21]	Processing of big heterogeneous geospatial data	It supports multiple algorithm design paradigms such as MapReduce, in-memory computing or agent-based programing	Applicable only to specific domains
8.	MongoDB-based Healthcare Data Management Architecture [22]	Processing of big patient data (demographical data i.e. name, address, personnel details) across distributed system	Achieved increase availability and reduce latency for globally distributed users	Streaming data are not considered
9.	Scalable and Distributed Architecture for Sensor Data Collection, Storage and Analysis [23]	Discovering hidden and interesting information using location data collected from GPS vehicles	High performances are achieved when working with sensor data	Only K-means algorithm is discussed
10.	Distributed Parallel Architecture for "Big Data" [25]	Processing large financial datasets	Graphical processing unit provides user friendly interface	Streaming data are not considered

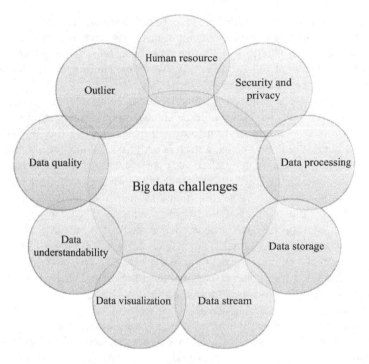

Figure 8.13   Big Data challenges

huge amount of data. To overcome this issue, various stream processing tools and technologies are developed by Apache and Yahoo developers namely Apache Spark Streaming, Apache Strom, Samza, Hadoop Yarn and Cassandra and so on. Furthermore, In-memory databases are also used to store the large amount of data.

Data visualization: As volume, velocity and variety exceed its standard value, the traditional visualization tools and technologies are not used to represents the Big Data. The visualization methods play a vital role in identifying more useful hidden information. eBay is one of the business organization, developed the scalable visualization tool called Tableau. This tool is capable of converting massive and composite data sets into insightful images. The results generated from the Tableau software is in the form of graphs, charts and scatter plots. Moreover, Tableau software is more often used to observe responses of the most recent users and perform sentiment analysis.

Data understandability: Understanding of data is vital to get meaningful information. Though advanced visualization tools are available to represent the Big Data; there is a need to have a proper domain expert to express the knowledge. To overcome this issue, modern business organizations must have various domain experts to describe the knowledge about the origin and application of the data.

Data quality: Data quality decides the level of understandability and accuracy. Data quality plays a significant role in decision-making process. Business organization and data scientists face this challenge when processing the Big Data. To solve this issue, a data control method or an information administration system is used to clean and improve the accuracy of the data.

Outlier detection: Outlier detection is used to detect the unnecessary or unused data. The important cause of outlier is inconsistency in the investigation or measurement. As modern data generation sources increased rapidly, the Big Data have a large number of outliers. Visualization is one of the valuable solutions to detect the outlier in Big Data. In general, 5% of outliers are always present in the massive size of raw data. In the Big Data context, detecting 5% of outliers itself is a complicated task. In recent years, various outlier detection charts are introduced to remove the huge volume of outliers present in the Big Data. However, removing the large size of outlier itself reduces the accuracy of the event prediction.

Human resource: The traditional human resource is not capable of handling Big Data. Big Data analytics requires the individuals who are good in not only programing knowledge but also research and development. Hence, various training programs and skill-development methods are needed to develop the knowledge for handling Big Data in an enterprise environment.

Security and privacy: Security and privacy play a significant role in Big Data. The traditional privacy and security methods are not sufficient to protect and prevent the Big Data. For example, the personal information of customers such as name, age, sex, address and blood group are complex to protect in the Big Data environment. The leakage of the personal information may create complex issues for the customers. In order to overcome this problem, the enterprise environments and organizations have to maintain a Big Data security platform to protect and prevent the more sensitive details of the users. For example, the Vormetric framework provides security and privacy services for Big Data. This framework consists of encryption, access control, and key management features to prevent and protect the Big Data against the unauthorized or malicious users.

8.6   Conclusion

Data generation speed and amount of data has increased over the past 20 years in different fields. A report published in 2011 from International Data Corporation states that, the overall generated and stored data size in the globe was 1.8 ziga bytes which enlarged by almost nine times within 5 years. Due to the enormous growth of world data, the name of Big Data is essentially used to express massive datasets. In general, Big Data analytics is requires advance tools and techniques to store, process and analyze the large volumes of data. Big Data consists of large unstructured data that require advance real-time analysis. Thus, many of the researchers are interested in developing advance technologies and algorithms to solve such issues when dealing with Big Data. This chapter gives a detail survey on Big Data characteristics for cloud data centers, Big Data application, and Big Data opportunities and challenges.

In addition, this paper also compares the state-of-the-art Big Data architecture for cloud data centers in terms of merits and demerits.

References

[1] Lynch, C. (2008). Big data: How do your data grow? Nature, 455(7209), 28–29.

[2] Khan, N., Husain, M. S., and Beg, M. R. (2015). Big Data classification using evolutionary techniques: a survey. In Proc. of IEEE International Conference on Engineering and Technology (ICETECH) (pp. 243–247).

[3] Savitz, E. (2014). Gartner: 10 critical tech trends for the next five years. *Forbes*. Retrieved from http://www.forbes.com/sites/ericsavitz/2012/10/22/gartner-10-critical-tech-trends-for-the-next-five-years (accessed on January 8, 2016).

[4] Savitz, E. (2015). Gartner: Top 10 strategic technology trends for 2013. *Forbes*. Retrieved on http://www.forbes.com/sites/ericsavitz/2012/10/23/gartner-top-10-strategic-technology-trends-for-2013 (accessed on January 8, 2016).

[5] Chen, C. C., Lee, K. W., Chang, C. C., Yang, D. N., and Chen, M. S. (2013, October). Efficient large graph pattern mining for big data in the cloud. In Big Data, 2013 IEEE International Conference on (pp. 531–536).IEEE.

[6] Antoniadis, I., Koukoulis, I., and Serdaris, P. (2017). Social Networking Sites' Usage in a Period of Crisis. A Segmentation Analysis of Greek College Students. In *Strategic Innovative Marketing* (pp. 73–79). USA: Springer International Publishing.

[7] Wang, X., and Sun, Z. (2013). The Design of Water Resources and Hydropower Cloud GIS Platform Based on Big Data. In *Geo-Informatics in Resource Management and Sustainable Ecosystem* (pp. 313–322). USA: Springer Berlin Heidelberg.

[8] Gijzen, H. (2013). Development: big data for a sustainable future. Nature, 502(7469), 38.

[9] Howe, D., Costanzo, M., Fey, P., *et al.* (2008). Big data: The future of biocuration. Nature, 455(7209), 47–50.

[10] Hampton, S. E., Strasser, C. A., Tewksbury, J. J., *et al.* (2013). Big data and the future of ecology. Frontiers in Ecology and the Environment, 11(3), 156–162.

[11] Jang, S. M., and Hart, P. S. (2015). Polarized frames on "climate change" and "global warming" across countries and states: Evidence from twitter big data. Global Environmental Change, 32, 11–17.

[12] Thota, C., Manogaran, G., Lopez, D., and Vijayakumar, V. (2016). Big Data Security Framework for Distributed Cloud Data Centers. In *Cybersecurity Breaches and Issues Surrounding Online Threat Protection* (p. 288), IGI Global, USA.

[13] Pääkkönen, P., and Pakkala, D. (2015). Reference architecture and classification of technologies, products and services for big data systems. Big Data Research, 2(4), 166–186.

[14]   Marz, N., and Warren, J. (2015). *Big Data: Principles and Best Practices of Scalable Realtime Data Systems*. USA: Manning Publications Co.

[15]   Manogaran, G., and Lopez, D. (2017). Disease surveillance system for big climate data processing and dengue transmission. *International Journal of Ambient Computing and Intelligence (IJACI)*, 8(2), 88–105.

[16]   NIST Big Data Reference Architecture, DRAFT Version 1, NIST Big Data Public Working Group Reference Architecture Subgroup (NBD-WG), April 6, 2015.

[17]   Rathore, M. M. U., Paul, A., Ahmad, A., Chen, B. W., Huang, B., and Ji, W. (2015). *Real-Time Big Data Analytical Architecture for Remote Sensing Application*, IEEE, USA.

[18]   Martínez-Prieto, M. A., Cuesta, C. E., Arias, M., and Fernández, J. D. (2015). The Solid architecture for real-time management of big semantic data. Future Generation Computer Systems, 47, 62–79.

[19]   Guo, K., Pan, W., Lu, M., Zhou, X., and Ma, J. (2015). An effective and economical architecture for semantic-based heterogeneous multimedia big data retrieval. Journal of Systems and Software, 102, 207–216.

[20]   Marchal, S., Jiang, X., State, R., and Engel, T. (2014, June). A Big Data Architecture for Large Scale Security Monitoring. In Big Data (BigData Congress), 2014 IEEE International Congress on (pp. 56–63). IEEE.

[21]   Kramer, M., and Senner, I. (2015). A modular software architecture for processing of big geospatial data in the cloud 49, 69–81. Computers & Graphics.

[22]   Gorton, I., and Klein, J. (2014). Distribution, data, deployment: Software architecture convergence in big data systems. IEEE Software, 32, 3, 78–85.

[23]   Aydin, G., Hallac, I. R., and Karakus, B. (2015). Architecture and implementation of a scalable sensor data storage and analysis system using cloud computing and big data technologies. Journal of Sensors, 501, 834217.

[24]   Boja, C., Pocovnicu, A., and Batagan, L. (2012). Distributed parallel architecture for Big Data. *Informatica Economica*, 16(2), 116–127.

[25]   Chen, C. P., & Zhang, C. Y. (2014). Data-intensive applications, challenges, techniques and technologies: A survey on Big Data. *Information Sciences*, 275, 314–347.

Part II

How SDN helps Big Data

Chapter 9

SDN helps volume in Big Data

Kyoomars Alizadeh Noghani*, Cristian Hernandez Benet*, and Javid Taheri*

During the last decade, businesses invested remarkable effort to convert the vast collections of disparate data to a precious resource using Big Data applications and analytics, which help businesses to value their insights, create a competitive advantage, inspire new innovations, and drive more revenue. The significance of Big Data analytics continues to grow, and many enterprises (e.g., Netflix and Facebook) base their entire business models on the results of data analytics. Therefore, the importance of delivering data quickly and efficiently is higher than ever.

In this context, the network plays a critical role. The existence of Big Data applications (especially real-time or near-real-time applications) with their extremely large volume and computing complexity depends on the proper support from the underlying network. The network upon which Big Data applications operate should have the following key features:

1. Agile and efficient: The network should continuously deliver a substantial volume of data from sources to destinations in a fast, smooth, and reliable way with minimum impact on other ongoing traffic.
2. Dynamic: The network should react in real time to changes in traffic loads and adopts a suitable routing strategy in order to meet requirements of applications and to enhance the network performance.
3. Fair: The network is obliged to satisfy its customers by fulfilling the service-level agreement and delivering consistent bandwidth to all flows with the same priority, while it serves other traffic in addition to Big Data applications traffic.
4. Resilient: The network should be resilient against failures to avoid packet loss and unnecessary retransmissions when a failure occurs.
5. Scalable: The network should scale easily and linearly to thousands of compute and storage nodes. Traditional network designs (e.g., three-tier Data Center (DC) design) are optimized for "North–South" traffic while the volume that Big Data delivers includes what is commonly referred to as "East–West" traffic within a DC.

*Department of Mathematics and Computer Science, Karlstad University, Sweden

Considering the aforementioned features, a new network design in conjunction with a new network architecture is needed. Recently, software-defined networking (SDN) [1] vigorously attracted attentions as an important networking paradigm. Future networks may benefit from features that SDN architecture provides in terms of immediate deployability, scalability, and updatability. Additionally, the programmability feature in SDN helps to allocate network resources optimally, avoid congestion, and enhance Quality of Service (QoS) by reprogramming the data plane dynamically from a centralized controller. Thanks to its features, SDN may have a significant impact on the performance of Big Data applications and greatly facilitate the acquisition, transmission, storage, and process of data [2].

Both Big Data and SDN are described in detail in previous chapters. This chapter investigates how SDN architecture can leverage its unique features to mitigate the challenges of Big Data volume. Accordingly, first, we provide an overview of Big Data volume, its effects on the underlying network, and mention some potential SDN solutions to address the corresponding challenges. Second, we elaborate more on the network-monitoring, traffic-engineering, and fault-tolerant mechanisms which we believe they may help to address the challenges of Big Data volume. Finally, this chapter is concluded with some open issues.

9.1   Big Data volume and SDN

"Big Data" is tied to the term "volume." According to the literature (e.g., [3]), volume is one of the main characteristics of Big Data. However, it is inconceivable to define a certain value for data size in order to be considered as Big Data. Among a variety of definitions, herein, we have selected the widely quoted definition of Big Data by McKinsey [3].

What is Big Data?
Big Data refers to datasets whose size is beyond the ability of typical database software tools to capture, store, manage, and analyze.

The aforementioned definition of Big Data truly implies the enormous volume of data without stating a certain threshold for the dataset. In fact, as technology advances over time, the size of datasets that qualify as Big Data will also increase. The volume of the dataset has been rapidly increased during the last decade and will continue escalating in the future. It is predicted [4] that approximately 40 zettabytes of data will be created by 2020, an increase of 300 times since 2005.

Data volume is one of the main challenges that any network must be able to cope with. Transferring a massive-scale data volume leads to increase in congestion and packet loss probability which degrade the network performance, respectively. In this regard, three following mechanisms may assist network providers to confront the challenges of Big Data volume:

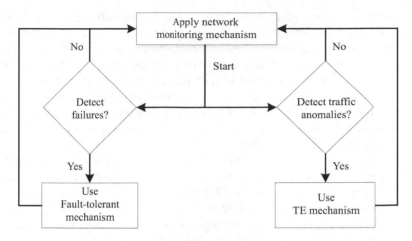

Figure 9.1   How SDN helps volume in Big Data

1. Traffic engineering (TE): TE is an important mechanism to increase the network performance by dynamically analyzing, predicting, and regulating the behavior of the transmitted data [5]. TE results in an improvement in the overall use of network resources and smoother service delivery. Although TE techniques have been widely exploited in the past, the proposed solutions do not mitigate the recently emerged problems in today's networks. Thanks to distinguishing characteristics of SDN, TE mechanisms can be implemented in more efficient, dynamic, and intelligent ways in comparison with legacy solutions.
2. Fault tolerance methods: A failure in the network causes packet loss which in turn leads to packet retransmission and network performance deterioration. SDN-based fault tolerance mechanisms aid to enhance the network resiliency against failures and react appropriately to manage the failure circumstance by leveraging OpenFlow (OF) resiliency methods.
3. Network monitoring: A frequent and consistent monitoring helps to track and detect all changes in the network including instant failures and congestion. Network monitoring is the prerequisite to deploy an effective TE as well as fault-tolerant methods. SDN architecture may help to develop next generation of monitoring solutions.

The aforementioned components and their main functionalities are depicted in Figure 9.1.

9.2   Network monitoring and volume

A network transferring a large volume of data has to be steadily monitored to illuminate potential bottlenecks and network changes. Therefore, network monitoring (i.e., device and traffic monitoring) is crucial to assure that networking systems function properly. Device monitoring helps network providers to ensure continuous communication throughout the network by detecting failed and malfunctioned devices at the right time. The extensive view over the network topology in SDN architecture helps to detect failures in a shorter period of time than legacy networks and subsequently react faster to conceal the failure effects. On the other hand, traffic monitoring allows network providers to support fundamental network management tasks such as user application identification, forensic analysis, security issues, and anomaly detection (e.g., protocol and traffic problems).

The right traffic monitoring tools enable persistent congestion to be identified and workloads to be rebalanced. The effective monitoring tools should fulfill five requirements: (1) being precise and accurate, (2) being affordable, (3) being easy to manage and fast to operate, (4) being persistent and supply on-demand visibility throughout the whole network, and (5) being resilient to ensure continuous monitoring. Furthermore, traffic monitoring tools should provide the aforementioned requirements, while imposing minimum overhead to the network. However, there is an everlasting trade-off between some of these features. For example, the accuracy in traffic monitoring is attained at the cost of increased overhead in the network. In the context of Big Data volume, pooling network traffic every 1 s or longer indicates missing congestion when the link rates are 10 Gigabits or higher. In addition, network entities are almost occupied by transferring a massive volume of data. Consequently, traffic monitoring tools for Big Data applications and analytics should be highly accurate and fine granular without causing overhead.

In this section, we discuss how SDN architecture may improve the traffic monitoring methods for Big Data networks. First, legacy monitoring solutions are investigated, and the reasons for not being appropriate for Big Data networks are elaborated. Second, this section studies SDN-based monitoring solutions and discusses how they mitigate the legacy monitoring solution problems.

9.2.1 Legacy traffic monitoring solutions

In legacy networks, traffic is monitored in different ways. The first group of monitoring methods is based on port counters. Simple Network Management Protocol (SNMP)[1] and Remote Network MONitoring (RMON)[2] are examples of this approach and are utilized by many internet service providers to assess link utilization. SNMP counters are used to gather information about packet and byte across every individual switch interface. A poller periodically sends requests to every device in a network and retrieves information from the counters. The obtained information is then available on a central structure.

Flow-based methods are another group of monitoring techniques that rely on packet sampling. For instance, in sFlow,[3] network nodes collect periodic samples for

---

[1] RFC 1157: https://tools.ietf.org/html/rfc1157.
[2] RFC 3577: https://tools.ietf.org/html/rfc3577.
[3] RFC 3176: https://tools.ietf.org/html/rfc3176.

every flow per interface and send them to a centralized collector for further analysis. However, both foregoing methods fall short to meet the requirements for an ideal monitoring solution. While some are not accurate or granular enough, others impose additional load to the network and are not scalable.

Some other types of monitoring mechanisms are based on sending a copy of the traffic to an analyzing tool. Switched Port Analyzer (SPAN) is a tool which allows network operators to mirror traffic from source port(s) to destination port(s) for the purpose of collecting and analyzing the traffic by a separate analyzer. There are three main drawbacks to this approach. First, the administrator cannot select traffic; second, the switch can be overloaded with the volume of traffic being mirrored; and third, the mirrored port feeds traffic to another port, so it uses extra ports on the switch. In response to these issues, the industry developed dedicated devices called Network Packet Brokers (NPBs). Using NPBs, network administrators can select the traffic being monitored (e.g., based on IP address or application type) and forward that to analytical tools. Although NPBs do a great job to select and forward the traffic for analysis, they are too expensive to be deployed in typical networks. The need for box-by-box configuration and lack of scalability are other problems of using NPBs as monitoring methods.

Consequently, due to lack of accuracy, granularity, scalability, and considering the imposed overhead, the legacy traffic monitoring solutions are indeed inappropriate for Big Data networks.

9.2.2 SDN-based traffic monitoring

SDN architecture provides traffic monitoring solutions in three different ways: (1) by collaborating with existing legacy traffic monitoring tools, (2) by using OF protocol to query switches for the number of packets or bytes in flows, and (3) by deploying SDN-based monitoring frameworks which operate out of band.[4]

The first approach has been the topic of extensive research such as sFlow using SDN [6]. However, SDN architecture may not cover the drawbacks of legacy solutions; this makes the first approach inefficient for Big Data networks. The second approach is based on the OF protocol features; it supports the functionality to query switches for the number of packets or bytes in flows matching a specific rule or passing a specific port. Although this approach imposes additional overhead, the dynamic and programmable nature of SDN makes it possible to control overhead while achieving desired accuracy. In this regard, various mechanisms are proposed for efficient statistics collection using OF. For example, PayLess [7] is an SDN-based monitoring framework that utilizes the variable rate adaptive sampling technique to gather highly accurate information in real time without incurring significant network overhead. To achieve this goal, instead of letting the controller to continuously poll switches, an adaptive scheduling algorithm for polling is proposed to achieve the same level of accuracy as continuous polling with much less communication overhead. Moreover,

---

[4]This way of data monitoring does not lead to contention between data and control packets sharing the same medium.

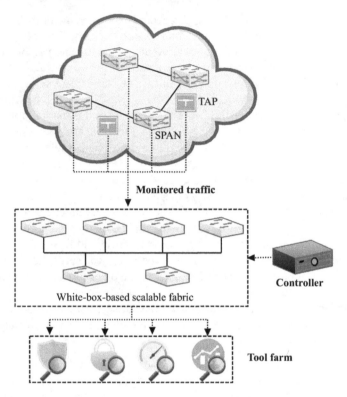

Figure 9.2   Big switch SDN-based monitoring fabrics

PayLess provides a high-level RESTful API so that it can be accessed by other pro-gramming languages. Therefore, it is easy for network applications to develop their own monitoring mechanisms and access the collected data from the PayLess data stored at different aggregation levels [5]. Like PayeLess, other SDN-based moni-toring solutions are proposed to implement accurate monitoring systems using OF protocol while decreasing the monitoring overhead [8–10].

The third approach is to develop an out-of-band SDN-based monitoring frame-work; it benefits from monitoring solutions in the legacy networks (TAP and SPAN) while covering their disadvantages. Big Switch Networks and Microsoft already paved a way in this direction and developed their own network monitoring tools: Big Moni-toring (Big Mon) fabric and Distributed Ethernet Monitoring (DEMON), respectively. According to Big Mon description [11], network traffic is replicated using TAPs or port mirroring (SPAN) on network nodes; it is directed to the monitoring framework made of white box switches instead of expensive NPBs. The white box switches (con-figurable via a controller) send the traffic to the farm of analyzing tools based on the policy defined by network administrators. The Big Mon architecture is depicted in Figure 9.2.

Out-of-band SDN-based monitoring solutions have several key benefits:

1. Since an SDN monitoring fabric operates out of band, it does not affect network applications performance.
2. An SDN monitoring network can operate with essentially zero impact on network traffic, using traffic from network TAPs and SPAN ports.
3. This architecture delivers the same level of traffic control granularity as NPBs, but at a lower cost.
4. Network analysis tools are typically used in groups due to the lack of capacity to handle a large amount of traffic. The proposed SDN framework is able to balance the load among the analyzing tools in numerous ways based on policies.

Based on such summary, SDN may help network providers to design and implement a variety of more affordable, scalable, and fine granular traffic monitoring solutions with comparatively lower overhead as compared with legacy solutions.

9.3   Traffic engineering and volume

TE encompasses a wide range of mechanisms designed and developed to enhance the network and application performance. In the context of Big Data, TE methods may significantly help to manage Big Data volume.

Network congestion is the most important challenge in transferring an enormous volume of data. Particularly, traffic patterns of Big Data applications (such as Hadoop) including bulk transfer and data aggregation/partitioning increase the congestion probability. The congestion may take place due to following reasons:

*   Inadequate provisioning of overall network resources.
*   Suboptimal traffic routing mechanism.
*   Lack of adaptivity in the allocation of available network resources.
*   Microburst or TCP incast.
*   Interface speed mismatch.

Network congestion has a destructive effect on the performance of Big Data applications and analytics, for example, by causing a delay in the data movement between compute nodes in the shuffle phase of a Map-Reduce job, increasing the total run time required and consequently degrading overall performance. With the aim to reduce the consequences of congestion in the network, effective load balancing, congestion avoidance, and flow scheduling techniques can be exploited. However, the proposed techniques in the legacy network are confined to the inflexible nature of such networks and may not deal with the requirements of future or recently emerged applications (e.g., Big Data applications). SDN may leverage enhanced TE methods to address the challenges raised by Big Data volume in the following ways:

*   Anticipate network traffic and change the network configuration dynamically.
*   Classify traffic types and provide a suitable strategy for each traffic type in a very short time period. Each source/destination may generate/consume data with

different volume and importance. The SDN controller can classify, segregate, and prioritize network traffic in order to avoid congestion and ensure a reliable performance of Big Data applications.

- Leverage variety of congestion control, traffic management schemes, and admission control policy rules to support various traffic types from different applications with distinctive QoS requirements for both real-time and non-real-time applications.
- Locate Big Data sources, steer the traffic generated by them in an appropriate way, and avoid congestion in the network.
- Update network policies timely to react to the current traffic status.

First, this section discusses how SDN-based flow scheduling methods can help the network providers against Big Data volume. Then, SDN solutions to solve the TCP incast problem are elaborated. Finally, this section investigates how SDN collaboration with other frameworks may alleviate the problem of transferring a large volume of data. It is noteworthy to mention that the solutions discussed herein are merely examples on how SDN may mitigate the challenges of transferring an enormous volume of data.

9.3.1 Flow scheduling

Traffic in a network is dispatched based on the following ways [12]:

1. Application-aware: Traffic in the network is treated variously depends on the application generating or consuming the traffic.
2. Traffic-aware: Traffic in the network is served according to its characteristics such as size, duration, etc.
3. Hybrid: Traffic in the network is routed by considering both its characteristics and the source/destination application.

9.3.1.1 Application-aware

To avoid the network being the main bottleneck for Big Data applications, network operators may leverage various routing policies/techniques to specifically treat Big Data applications. For instance, Map-Reduce applications generate a large volume of data in shuffling stage that consumes large amounts of bandwidth. Network may facilitate the shuffling procedure by reserving resources for the Map-Reduce application or prioritizing the traffic originated/consumed by such application. To this end, network operators should be able to classify the traffic according to the intrinsic characteristics of each service or application using the network. Despite fundamental drawbacks, Differentiated Services (Diffserv)[5] and Resource Reservation Protocol (RSVP)[6] serve as the two most common legacy solutions for traffic management and classification.

On the contrary, SDN has the ability to interact with Big Data applications (or application controller) directly. Therefore, it improves the network performance

---

[5]RFC 2475: https://tools.ietf.org/html/rfc2475.
[6]RFC 2205: https://tools.ietf.org/html/rfc2205.

by scheduling flows according to the application-level inputs, outputs, and requirements. To this extent, a number of SDN-based methods are proposed to manage the network traffic according to the characteristics and the current state of the Big Data application. Although each method performs distinctively by utilizing different SDN features, the common aim is to assess the state of the Big Data applications and their flows.

OFScheduler [13] is a dynamic network optimizer for heterogeneous clusters to mitigate the network traffic during the execution of Map-Reduce jobs. OFScheduler first assesses the network traffic using a controller. Afterward, the SDN controller offloads heavy loaded links by prioritizing load-balancing and larger flows to decrease the finishing time of Map-Reduce jobs. The simulation results of OFScheduler demonstrate that it increases bandwidth utilization and improves the performance of Map-Reduce for most of the jobs in a multi-path heterogeneous cluster.

Ferguson *et al.* [14] designed an API, which can be used directly by users, hosts, or applications, to communicate with a centralized SDN controller named PANE to dynamically and autonomously request network resources. Applications can issue queries to the PANE controller to improve the user experience. For example, Hadoop can use the *network weather service*[7] to place reducers away from currently congested parts of the network. PANE includes a compiler and verification engine to ensure bandwidth requests to not exceed the limits set by the administrator and avoiding starvation.

A number of techniques utilize OF to improve data transportation through better provision of available bandwidth. Narayan *et al.* [15] have observed that by using OF protocols transportation of critical traffic such as Hadoop shuffle traffic can be expedited by giving it a higher priority in network flows. Such higher priority traffic is directed through links having a higher throughput, and thus the overall performance of Hadoop system in terms of job completion time is further reduced. Qin *et al.* [16] proposed an SDN-based and bandwidth-aware scheduler to flexibly assign tasks in an optimal manner and reduce the time taken by the data to reach the distributed data nodes from the mappers. It first utilizes SDN to manage the network bandwidth and allocates it in a time slot manner; then their proposed scheduler decides whether to assign a task locally or remotely depending on the completion time. Therefore, this approach can guarantee data locality from a global view; meanwhile, it can efficiently assign tasks. The key point of this approach is that the scarce network bandwidth from an SDN/OF controller is not only taken into account but also regarded as a vital parameter for task scheduling.

9.3.1.2   Traffic-aware

Big Data applications usually coexist with a variety of different applications and services in the same network. As a result, optimizing the network for Big Data applications may degrade the other application performance and violate the network fairness

---

[7]"Network weather service" provides coarse information about current traffic conditions.

principle. Hence, some TE techniques are proposed based on distributing the traffic load in the network independent of the traffic source and destination. Load-balancing protocols require schemes for splitting traffic across multiple paths at a packet or flow granularity.

Splitting traffic at the packet granularity significantly ameliorates the effectiveness of load-balancing mechanisms. However, the improvement is achieved at the expense of several problems such as packets reordering within a TCP flow, TCP congestion control confusion, and unnecessary shrinkage of TCP send window. In contrast, splitting traffic at the flow granularity avoids packet reordering. In what follows, the flow-based traffic scheduling solutions are discussed since the per-packet solution is no longer utilized in the network.

Traffic flows have disparate characteristics and are always competing for the network resources. Hence, it is possible that some of the flows abuse resources, while the rest fairly share them. Network traffic mainly consists of two types of flows: (1) elephant flows that extensively use network resources (high bandwidth) without a strict completion deadline and (2) mice flows that are often very sensitive to latency and do not consume many resources. Big Data applications may generate/consume thousands of elephant flows or millions of mice flows. The existence of other mice and elephant flows belonged to other applications in addition to Big Data flows clearly shows the fatal pressure over the underlying network.

The hash-based equal-cost multi-path (ECMP) is a legacy load-balancing solution that splits flows across available paths using flow hashing techniques when multiple paths exist between any two nodes. ECMP does not account for either current network utilization or flow size, therefore, two or more elephant flows may collide on their hash values and being forwarded to the same path. As a result, ECMP may lead to imbalance loads, bandwidth waste, and low end-to-end network goodput even when there is available bandwidth in an alternate path. The main advantage of load balancing in the SDN is that forwarding decision calculations are centralized; it allows to consider network status more comprehensively and plan a better load-balancing strategy. Several SDN-based solutions are proposed to mitigate problems that ECMP is facing. Their main idea is to identify elephant flows first and then to choose the right path by the controller.

Hedera [17] is a scalable and dynamic flow scheduling system to avoid the limitations of ECMP. In order to effectively utilize multiple paths between DC servers, elephant flows should be detected and managed. Based on this viewpoint, the scheduling strategy of Hedera contains three steps: (1) collecting flow information from the aggregation layer switches, (2) computing nonconflicting paths for elephant flows, and (3) instructing switches to reroute traffic accordingly to fulfill the requirements of DC applications including Map-Reduce jobs.

Unlike Hedera that detects elephant flows by polling per-flow statistics from edge switches, Mahout [18] monitors and detects elephant flows at the end host via a shim layer in the operating system of the back-end server. The main motivation of using shim layer in back-end servers is to avoid enforcing more pressure on edge switches. The shim layer is responsible for monitoring local traffic by a socket buffer. When the buffer exceeds a specified threshold, it determines that the flow is an elephant.

Then, it marks subsequent packets of that flow using an in-band signaling mechanism. Mahout defines high and low priorities for rules of the flow table. By default, packets matching the low priority rules are forwarded using the ECMP. On the other hand, the packets of an elephant flow that match the high priority rules are sent to Mahout controller to calculate optimal routing.

Although SDN is a great architecture to simplify the network and traffic management in large-scale networks, its central control and global visibility require the controller to set up all flows for the critical path in the network. Considering the volume of data traversing over the network in shape of elephant flows or millions of mice flows, the controller may be a bottleneck and consequently increases the latency in the network. To encounter such problem, some studies such as DevoFlow [19] are proposed to reduce the number of interactions between the controller and switches. This mechanism implements wildcard OF rules so that the switches can make local routing decisions with matching mice flows. At the same time, DevoFlow introduces a method of traffic statistics to identify elephant flows in which they need help of the controller to be rerouted.

9.3.1.3   Interface mismatch: a use case of flow scheduling

Despite the fact that network operators may prefer homogeneous network, having a multivendor environment with different configurable and capable entities in large-scale networks such as DC is inevitable. The difference between capabilities of network components leads to numbers of problems such as packet retransmission. Interface speed mismatch is a common problem in heterogeneous environments that severely affect the application performance. Consider a scenario where a compute node with 1-Gigabit network bandwidth is communicating with a storage node with 10-Gigabit network bandwidth. In such circumstances, the network must buffer the burst as it serializes the data out at the lower interface rate. The problem is depicted in Figure 9.3.

In the legacy network, the interface mismatch problem is primarily addressed by using deep packet buffering techniques in the network nodes. The idea is to capture the packets in large buffers, which network nodes may have, and feed the packets to the destination according to its capability to serve. Lack of deep buffering capabilities causes packet loss which as a result decreases TCP transmission rate; it has a direct and negative impact on application performance. However, as a side effect, deeper buffers induce large delays, retransmission synchronization, unpredictable end-to-end RTT and prevent the congestion control algorithms to react in a timely fashion [20]. The comprehensive view of SDN architecture over the underlying network mitigates this problem by deploying adaptive flow scheduling. The controller may be informed or learnt by the network operator about a specific condition in the network. Consequently, the controller schedules flows in a way to reach the network node with lower interface capacity smoothly, for example, via sending traffic through different paths. By performing in this way, the controller may avoid packet loss and TCP throughput degradation. Furthermore, queues in network elements may not need to capture an enormous number of packets which in turn decreases their resource usage.

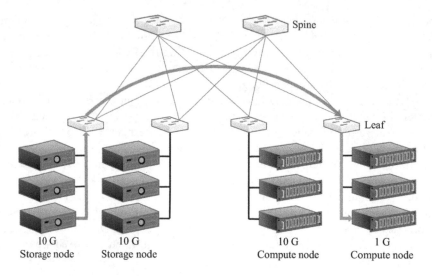

Figure 9.3   Interface mismatch

9.3.2   TCP incast

In distributed Big Data applications such as Hadoop, a single host requesting for data can simultaneously be served by tens of storage nodes that oversaturates the capacity on the host interface when all storage nodes reply at the line rate. As the number of concurrent senders increases, the perceived application-level throughput at the receiver collapses and the receiver achieves goodput that is, in the orders of magnitude lower than the link capacity. This phenomenon is known as TCP incast or microburst problem. TCP incast has also been observed by others in distributed storage, and web-search workloads. The problem is illustrated in Figure 9.4.

Although a variety of algorithms are proposed in the literature to mitigate the TCP incast problem in the legacy network, they lack adaptability to network conditions. While some studies alleviate the problem by lowering the packet injection rate into the network through assigned congestion control parameters statically, some others have tackled the problem by using deep-buffered switches. In addition to previously mentioned (Section 9.3.1.3) deep packet buffering problems, hiding the congestion event by utilizing the large buffers prevents the end hosts from adapting their sending rate to recover from congestion. Consequently, deep packet buffering artificially increases the bandwidth-delay product of the network and introduces high and variable latency for soft real-time flows.

Contrary to the proposed solutions in legacy networks to avoid TCP incast, SDN empowers network administrators to control and manage network parameters in real time and seems to be an appropriate solution to the TCP incast problem. This notion is further strengthened as the SDN controller continuously monitors congestion in the network. SDN-based solutions to tackle TCP incast problem are recently addressed in a number of studies. Lu *et al.* [21] proposed to implement an SDN-based TCP

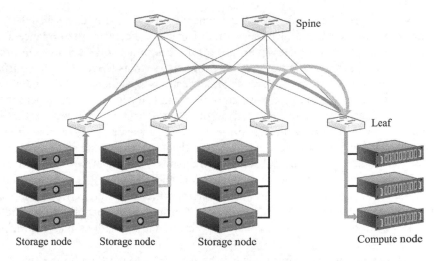

*Figure 9.4   TCP incast occurs when multiple senders (e.g., storage nodes) start
serving a client (e.g., compute node) simultaneously*

(SDTCP) congestion control mechanism, which modifies the TCP receive window
of an ACK packet, to reduce the transmission rate of the sender, at the controller
level. The OF-switch notifies the controller when congestion occurs by monitoring
a queue and triggering an alert upon reaching a threshold value. In response to such
a notification from the OF-switch, the controller modifies the receive window of an
ACK packet for a selected long-lived flow. In another study, Jouet *et al.* [22] proposed
to exploit SDN to tune TCP parameters for the operating environment. The authors
show that the bursty nature of DC traffic combined with large buffers and statically
assigned congestion control parameters can significantly delay and slow down the
transfer of new incoming flows [23]. Although reducing the buffer sizes is necessary
to gain low-latency transmissions, it can hinder achieving high throughput if the
default value of minimum retransmission timeout is used. As a result, their proposed
architecture centrally collects the network infrastructure properties and subsequently
computes and distributes congestion control parameters suitable to the end hosts for
the operating environment.

9.3.3   Dynamically change network configuration

The ability to program/reconfigure the network at run time can elevate the performance of Big Data applications significantly. Ideally, changing the network
configurations should be automated with relatively small overhead and a minimum
number of box-by-box configurations.

SDN is able to configure both OF-enabled and legacy network entities from the
central controller. The capabilities of SDN to reprogram OF-enabled network entities

are previously described in Section 9.3.1 where the SDN controller reschedules or reroutes the flows through a different path to increase the network performance and avoid potential congestion. However, not all devices in networks support OF protocol. As a result, network infrastructure providers (such as Cisco, Juniper, Arista, etc.) have developed their network management entities to facilitate the configuration and management tasks for a network administrator. The network management tool in the legacy network can be replaced by the controller in an SDN architecture if the controller can interact with network elements in a standard way. Model-driven network management (described in previous chapters) is developed to provide a standard communication protocol for network nodes. Recall that, YANG is a data-modeling language used to model configuration, and NETCONF is used to install, manipulate, and delete the configuration of network devices. Herein, we investigate how unique features in NETCONF in conjunction with SDN capabilities may help network providers to configure the network beforehand to handle a massive traffic volume.

A various traffic-analyzing tools can be developed to work with the controller in the SDN architecture. The analyzing tools can anticipate traffic pattern in the near future based on the previous traffic records. Moreover, the administrator may interact with the analyzing tools through available APIs to inject information about future circumstances of the network. The analyzing tools can therefore provide various solutions to the controller (e.g., in terms of network configuration) to supervise events in the underlying network. On the other hand, NETCONF has two key features: (1) it can schedule the configuration to be deployed at a specific time and (2) it can apply changes for a specific duration and roll back to the previous configuration when the time has expired.[8]

Using the aforementioned features, SDN can schedule the configuration when it is aware of traffic pattern in the future. Consider a scenario (depicted in Figure 9.5) where the controller knows that a given Big Data application at a specific time needs (e.g., at 11 PM every day) to receive or send a large volume of data, and this event lasts for 30 min. Moreover, a number of network nodes (herein switch 1 and 2) have extra (or backup) ports (X and Y, respectively) which are turned off to save energy. In such a case, the SDN controller creates appropriate configurations and informs involved elements to turn on the corresponding ports at the specific time (in this case 11 PM) using NETCONF protocol. Then, the responsible nodes deploy the new configuration at the time specified and roll back to their previous configurations in 30 min. Correspondingly, during the given time, the network configuration facilitates the transmission of large data volume for Big Data applications.

9.4   Fault tolerant and volume

There are numbers of different ways in which a network fails to provide the desired level of service such as a given end-to-end delay or level of availability. Failures may be

---

[8]RFC 7758: https://tools.ietf.org/html/rfc7758.

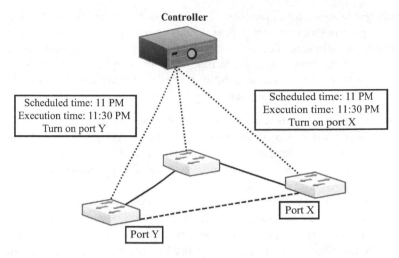

Figure 9.5   How SDN and NETCONF configure network to handle new events

incurred by several sources such as malicious attacks or natural disasters. Additionally, network systems may include hardware and software faults that can similarly result in failures, if triggered. Failure in the network leads to packet loss and calls the need for packet retransmission in return. The packet retransmission procedure incurs waste of network resources and creates additional overhead on the network. Furthermore, packet loss makes TCP to deploy congestion avoidance mechanisms that affect the network performance. In the network where a massive data volume transfers at a link rate, each instant failure leads to lose many packets.

Ideally, the network should detect failures in a short period of time and be resilient against them. Approaches to network resilience aim to protect the network and overcome a degradation in the performance of services when confronted with challenges and faults. Detection of failure in the network at the right time helps to transfer the workload of applications in a reasonable time and avoid performance degradation. This section mainly investigates how SDN may provide the fault-tolerant methods to ensure continued operation in case of failures in the network topology. For a comprehensive survey on the variety of network challenges and existing resilient methods, we refer the reader to [24].

The failure detection and resiliency come with the following problems in legacy networks:

- Inefficient: Resiliency is usually provided by redundancy in a legacy network. Network operator deploys extra network nodes and links to provide resiliency in case of disruption in the network hardware. In such network configuration, extra elements are in the standby mode and become active when a failure occurs; this method is not resource efficient and induces extra costs to network operators.
- Long convergence time: When a failure occurs in the network, the adjacent elements may inform other nodes to update their routing tables and converge. The

convergence procedure may take a long time to be accomplished depending on various parameters (e.g., network size, nodes performance, and algorithm used).

*   Suboptimal solution: The adjacent nodes are usually responsible for failure handling, if multiple paths are available for them to bypass the point of failure. However, the outcome solutions may be suboptimal by, for example, oversaturating the alternate links.

Contradictorily, comprehensive view over the network in SDN architecture may assist to enhance network resiliency and reliability by detecting failures and deploying various solutions to transparently recover the failure(s). In what follows, we present a short overview of mechanisms that allow an SDN-based solution to rapidly detect and repair failures.

In principle, a robust network needs to encompass redundant paths and controllers. While there are several proposals for redundant controller design, we focus on the relevant SDN mechanisms for topology failure recovery and protection. SDN may react to failures in the network using reactive and proactive methods. In reactive failure recovery mode, the SDN controller detects and recovers from link/node failures by installing appropriate rules to forward ongoing traffic through alternative paths. The problem of these approaches is that once a link fails, the controller has to be notified, react based on preconfigured alternative paths, and install new forwarding rules; this may require around 150 ms. Although the aforementioned reaction time is considerably small in comparison to average convergence time in a legacy network, yet many packets are dropped in this short period.

On the other hand, in proactive protection schemes, protection is applied locally to the switch by using preprogrammed actions in order to avoid costly communication to the controller. One technology that can enable fast local path restoration is fast failover (FF), which was introduced along with the group tables in the OF 1.1 specification [25]. FF works by executing the first live bucket in the group, meaning it sends the packet to the first port in the group where the port state is "up." This allows the switch to perform a local failover instead of the SDN controller performing a centralized failover. For detecting the link state, Bidirectional Forwarding Detection (BFD)[9] is a commonly used supporting technology. It determines the state of a port by establishing a connection using a three-way handshake and subsequently sending periodic control messages over the link. If no response message is received within a specified interval, the link is considered down. By using a low-control message interval, a fast reaction to the change of link state is possible [26]. Utilizing both BFD and FF, the current link state can be quickly detected and local forwarding decisions can be made.

An important point for these approaches is to consider that, during the link failure protection process, the network may result in suboptimal topologies since failures are repaired locally; this typically leads to longer paths. After the controller is notified of the repair, it can later reconfigure the network to its optimal state without service

[9]RFC 5880: https://tools.ietf.org/html/rfc5880.

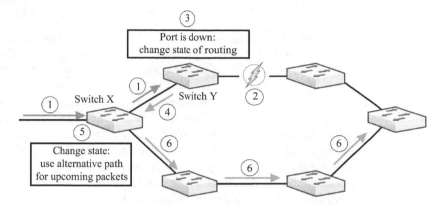

Figure 9.6 How OpenState reacts in link failure

interruption. However, these schemes only work if the local node can be configured with an alternative route or link.

Although the situation is much improved with centralized network management, achieving fast failure recovery is still very challenging in SDN because the central controller in restoration should calculate new routes and notify all the affected switches about the recovery actions immediately. Moreover, relying purely on centralized controller introduces longer delays in reaction to such events severely limiting the use of SDN. Additionally, a potential weakness of using BFD and FF is that they can only perform local failover. If no local path is available, crankback forwarding should be performed [26]. Crankback forwarding can potentially have large impacts on the latency in certain network configurations. Introducing a small amount of logic into the SDN switch can solve the crankback forwarding problem. Therefore, some intelligence in the forwarding plane of SDN is of great importance for Big Data applications.

Recently, stateful forwarding has been proposed to augment the OF data-plane using, for example, OpenState [27]. Such stateful forwarding can be used for fast path restoration even if the node does not have a backup path available, leading to more optimized routing during link failures. As depicted in Figure 9.6, for example, if packets arrive at the switch Y that does not have a next hop toward the destination because that link went down, the node sends back the packet toward the source. As it reaches a switch X with a backup path preconfigured, the state of that forwarding rule at switch X will be changed so that arriving packets traverse the backup path already at the node X. As a consequence, with the stateful forwarding suboptimal paths may exist just for some packets because once the state changes at intermediate nodes, packets get rerouted without controller involvement.

9.5 Open issues

This section investigates a number of problems which should be tackled to make SDN a proper solution to manage Big Data volume.

9.5.1   Scalability

Scalability, both in data and control plane, is the main challenge that SDN encounters in managing a large volume of data. According to initial idea for SDN, the controller is in charge of making decisions for all flows in the network. In other words, no data preprocessing is done in the switches, which results in heavy load in the controller. However, a single centralized controller cannot work efficiently and becomes another performance bottleneck if a large number of new flows are aggregated at the end of switches or if the whole network grows. Moreover, one controller is a single point-of-failure and should be avoided to not endanger the resiliency and reliability of the network. The scalability issue is tackled using two different approaches: (1) decreasing the network nodes dependability to the controller by moving a portion of logic to data plane (like OpenState) and (2) leveraging multiple controllers.

In the latter approach, multiple controllers split the workload among each other according to different strategies, e.g., in the hierarchy order. However, the load-balancing schemes for control plane are largely unexploited. The control plane load-balancing solutions need to solve a set of fundamental problems such as finding the optimal number of controllers, their locations, and workload distribution among them. There are very few papers that address the controller load-balancing problem in the literature. For instance, the controller placement problem is investigated in [28] where the distance between a controller and switches is adopted as the performance metric. In another study, Hu *et al.* [29] tackled controller placement and number by proposing a heuristic solution with the objective to minimize the flow setup time and communication overhead. Furthermore, the authors proposed a heuristic algorithm to adjust the workload of each controller dynamically. Nevertheless, these efforts only look for quantitative analysis or even heuristic results rather than qualitative assessment. In addition, there is a lack of thorough studies to bring traffic statistics into control message load balancing.

9.5.2   Resiliency and reliability

The importance of being fault tolerant is discussed earlier in Section 9.4. In SDN architecture, the controller is playing a critical role in amending the failures and making network resilient against all possible types of threats. However, the controller itself must be also resilient to failures. In this regard, several solutions are proposed including the primary backup controller and distributed controller clusters in an equal mode with a logical central view. Needless to mention, the coordination among controllers and how to handover the workload in case of controller failure are the examples of challenges that have to be addressed in more detail.

9.5.3   Conclusion

Transferring large volume of data brings different anomalies such as congestion to the network. Moreover, it is possible that while a part of the network is oversaturated, the other parts are underutilized. Thereby, mechanisms are required to flexibly distribute the load through the network and resolve the aforementioned problems. Furthermore, network providers clearly want to avoid traffic retransmission that is needed in response to failure and congestion in the network. The prerequisite to have a mature traffic-engineering and fault-tolerant mechanisms is to continually and accurately monitor the network and detect the anomalies at the shortest possible time. The accuracy in monitoring can be achieved at the cost of imposing more overhead, although there is no room for doing so since the network elements are already overloaded by excessive transfer of a large volume of data.

This chapter discussed how problems caused by a large volume of data can be managed using SDN architecture. First, we investigated how SDN architecture may help to provide accurate monitoring solutions without imposing additional overhead to the network. Then, traffic management using SDN was elaborated. Also, a number of solutions proposed to balance the load, avoid congestion, and elevate the performance of Big Data applications were studied. We also explained the importance of resiliency and fault tolerance in case of transferring a large volume of data and investigate a number of SDN-based resilient solutions. Finally, this chapter was concluded by introducing open issues and challenges for SDN architecture in order to deal with large volumes of data.

References

[1]   Open Networking Foundation, "Software-defined networking: The new norm for networks," *ONF White Paper*, Apr. 2012.

[2]   L. Cui, F. R. Yu, and Q. Yan, "When big data meets software-defined networking: SDN for big data and big data for SDN," *IEEE Network*, vol. 30, pp. 58–65, Jan. 2016.

[3]   J. Manyika, M. Chui, B. Brown, *et al.*, "Big data: The next frontier for innovation, competition, and productivity," *Report*, Jun. 2011. Available at https://www.mckinsey.com/business-functions/digital-mckinsey/our-insights/big-data-the-next-frontier-for-innovation

[4]   J. Gantz and D. Reinsel, "The digital universe in 2020: Big data, bigger digital shadows, and biggest growth in the far east," *IDC iView: IDC Analyze the Future*, vol. 2007, pp. 1–16, Dec. 2012.

[5]   I. F. Akyildiz, A. Lee, P. Wang, M. Luo, and W. Chou, "A roadmap for traffic engineering in SDN-openflow networks," *Computer Networks*, vol. 71, pp. 1–30, 2014.

[6]   K. Giotis, C. Argyropoulos, G. Androulidakis, D. Kalogeras, and V. Maglaris, "Combining openflow and sflow for an effective and scalable anomaly detection and mitigation mechanism on SDN environments," *Computer Networks*, vol. 62, pp. 122–136, 2014.

[7]   S. R. Chowdhury, M. F. Bari, R. Ahmed, and R. Boutaba, "Payless: A low cost network monitoring framework for software defined networks," in *Network Operations and Management Symposium (NOMS)*, pp. 1–9, IEEE, May 2014.

[8]   A. Tootoonchian, M. Ghobadi, and Y. Ganjali, *OpenTM: Traffic Matrix Estimator for OpenFlow Networks*, pp. 201–210. Berlin, Heidelberg: Springer, 2010.

[9]   M. Yu, L. Jose, and R. Miao, "Software defined traffic measurement with opensketch," in *Symposium on Networked Systems Design and Implementation (NSDI)*, (Lombard, IL), pp. 29–42, USENIX, 2013.

[10]   J. Suh, T. T. Kwon, C. Dixon, W. Felter, and J. Carter, "Opensample: A low-latency, sampling-based measurement platform for commodity SDN," in *International Conference on Distributed Computing Systems (ICDCS)*, pp. 228–237, IEEE, Jun. 2014.

[11]   Big Switch Networks, "Big monitoring fabric: Next-generation visibility and security." November 2017. Available at http://www.bigswitch.com/sdn-products/sdn-products/big-monitoring-fabric/overview/.

[12]   S. Yu, M. Liu, W. Dou, X. Liu, and S. Zhou, "Networking for big data: A survey," *IEEE Communications Surveys Tutorials*, vol. 19, no. 1, pp. 531–549, 2017.

[13]   Z. Li, Y. Shen, B. Yao, and M. Guo, "Ofscheduler: A dynamic network optimizer for mapreduce in heterogeneous cluster," *International Journal of Parallel Programming*, vol. 43, pp. 472–488, Jun. 2015.

[14]   A. D. Ferguson, A. Guha, C. Liang, R. Fonseca, and S. Krishnamurthi, "Participatory networking: An API for application control of SDNs," *ACM SIGCOMM*, vol. 43, pp. 327–338, Aug. 2013.

[15]   S. Narayan, S. Bailey, and A. Daga, "Hadoop acceleration in an openflow-based cluster," in *SC Companion: High Performance Computing, Networking Storage and Analysis (SCC)*, (Washington, DC, USA), pp. 535–538, IEEE, Nov. 2012.

[16]   P. Qin, B. Dai, B. Huang, and G. Xu, "Bandwidth-aware scheduling with SDN in hadoop: A new trend for big data," *IEEE Systems Journal*, vol. 11, no. 4, pp. 2337–2344, 2017.

[17]   M. Al-Fares, S. Radhakrishnan, B. Raghavan, N. Huang, and A. Vahdat, "Hedera: Dynamic flow scheduling for data center networks," in *Conference on Networked Systems Design and Implementation (NSDI)*, (Berkeley, CA, USA), pp. 19–19, USENIX, 2010.

[18]   A. R. Curtis, W. Kim, and P. Yalagandula, "Mahout: Low-overhead datacenter traffic management using end-host-based elephant detection," in *IEEE INFOCOM*, pp. 1629–1637, IEEE, Apr. 2011.

[19]   A. R. Curtis, J. C. Mogul, J. Tourrilhes, P. Yalagandula, P. Sharma, and S. Banerjee, "Devoflow: Scaling flow management for high-performance networks," *ACM SIGCOMM*, vol. 41, pp. 254–265, Aug. 2011.

[20]   J. Gettys and K. Nichols, "Bufferbloat: Dark buffers in the internet," *Queue*, vol. 9, pp. 40:40–40:54, Nov. 2011.

[21]   Y. Lu and S. Zhu, "SDN-based TCP congestion control in data center networks," in *International Performance Computing and Communications Conference (IPCCC)*, pp. 1–7, IEEE, Dec. 2015.

[22] S. Jouet, C. Perkins, and D. Pezaros, "OTCP: SDN-managed congestion control for data center networks," in *Network Operations and Management Symposium (NOMS)*, pp. 171–179, IEEE, Apr. 2016.

[23] S. Jouet and D. P. Pezaros, "Measurement-based TCP parameter tuning in cloud data centers," in *International Conference on Network Protocols (ICNP)*, pp. 1–3, IEEE, Oct. 2013.

[24] A. S. da Silva, P. Smith, A. Mauthe, and A. Schaeffer-Filho, "Resilience support in software-defined networking: A survey," *Computer Networks*, vol. 92, Part 1, pp. 189–207, 2015.

[25] OpenFlow Switch Specification, "Openflow switch specification (version 1.1.0)." Available at http://archive.openflow.org/documents/openflow-spec-v1.1.0.pdf.

[26] N. L. Van Adrichem, B. J. Van Asten, and F. A. Kuipers, "Fast recovery in software-defined networks," in *European Workshop on Software Defined Networks*, pp. 61–66, IEEE, Sep. 2014.

[27] G. Bianchi, M. Bonola, A. Capone, and C. Cascone, "Openstate: Programming platform-independent stateful openflow applications inside the switch," *ACM SIGCOMM*, vol. 44, pp. 44–51, Apr. 2014.

[28] B. Heller, R. Sherwood, and N. McKeown, "The controller placement problem," in *Workshop on Hot Topics in Software Defined Networks (HotSDN)*, (New York, NY, USA), pp. 7–12, ACM, 2012.

[29] Y. Hu, W. Wang, X. Gong, X. Que, and S. Cheng, "Balanceflow: Controller load balancing for openflow networks," in *International Conference on Cloud Computing and Intelligence Systems (CCIS)*, vol. 2, pp. 780–785, IEEE, Oct. 2012.

Chapter 10

SDN helps velocity in Big Data

Van-Giang Nguyen*, Anna Brunstrom*, Karl-Johan Grinnemo*, and Javid Taheri*

As discussed in the previous chapters, we are now in the era of Big Data where we are witnessing the growth of data being exponentially generated from a massive number of Internet-enabled devices such as phones, wearable devices, sensors, etc. This tremendous amount of datasets imposes many challenges in processing. However, Big Data is not just about the growth in the amount of generated data (i.e., volume) but the speed of data being generated also increases, for example, the data from social media networks, live streaming services, etc. The speed of data being generated is one of main features of the velocity dimension of Big Data. The other feature of the velocity dimension is how fast data is processed. This feature is becoming crucial nowadays for many applications such as system monitoring, fraud detection, security, etc., which require reacting to changing conditions in a real-time manner. Recently, the real-time data processing has gained a lot of attention in Big Data analytics because it allows companies to make a better decision and take meaningful actions at the right time, thus helping them respond to customer demands more effectively.

Currently, improving the performance of Big Data in general and velocity in particular is challenging due to the inefficiency of current network management, and the lack of coordination between the application layer and the network layer to achieve better scheduling decisions, which can improve the Big Data velocity performance. In this chapter, we discuss the role of recently emerged software defined networking (SDN) technology in helping the velocity dimension of Big Data. We start the chapter by providing a brief introduction of Big Data velocity and its characteristics and different modes of Big Data processing, followed by a brief explanation of how SDN can overcome the challenges of Big Data velocity. In the second part of the chapter, we describe in detail some proposed solutions which have applied SDN to improve Big Data performance in term of shortened processing time in different Big Data processing frameworks ranging from batch-oriented, MapReduce-based frameworks to real-time and stream-processing frameworks such as Spark and Storm. Finally, we conclude the chapter with a discussion of some open issues.

*Department of Mathematics and Computer Science, Karlstad University, Sweden

10.1　Introduction

For years, Big Data has been one of the hottest buzzwords in both academia and industry. With the ever-increasing number of devices being digitalized and Internet-enabled, we are witnessing a significant increase in the amount of data being generated; the increase is likely to continue with the advent of the next-generation (5G) mobile network. As mentioned in [1,2], 28 billion devices are expected to be connected to the ecosystem by 2021, and the Internet of Things (IoT) is one of the key contributors with around 16 billion devices. Additionally, mobile devices, e.g., smartphones, are becoming smarter and smarter, which allows user to do multiple tasks at the same time (e.g., live streaming and online purchasing at the same time), which together with data generation from IoT devices is largely contributing to the explosive increase of the global data, or Big Data datasets. Although Big Data is bringing a lot of new opportunities to many companies to gain new values from analyzing such a tremendous amount of dataset, it also imposes tremendous challenges. Challenges are not only coming from the extremely large volume of datasets, but also due to the rate at which data is being generated, and the time required to process them. With the two latter challenges, we are referring to the second dimension of Big Data velocity.

10.1.1　Big Data velocity

In Big Data, the velocity is characterized by the increasing rate of data being generated, and the increasing rate at which the data can be processed, stored, and analyzed. The former is also known as the streaming of data from various data sources such as market data, IoT devices, live streaming, financial transactions, social media tweets, etc., which are arriving at a Big Data processing framework. The latter is about how fast the data is processed and analyzed by this framework. Depending on different requirements of Big Data applications, the speed of data processing can vary from batch, real-time, and stream as shown in Figure 10.1. Recently, the demand for real-time and stream processing is increasing noticeably, and shortening the processing time of data is becoming one of the key requirements in Big Data analytics. It is because reducing the response time of data processing phase has a significant impact on the decision making of organizations. It allows organizations to react to changing business conditions, or allows an application to produce meaningful results in a real-time or a near real-time manner. Any late decisions can result in missing opportunities. In other words, the faster the data is processed, the more competitive advantages an organization can gain. Some typical use cases which require real-time processing include fraud and intrusion detection, system monitoring, e-commerce, intelligence, and surveillance.

10.1.2　Type of processing

As shown in Figure 10.1, while the volume means different size of data coming and to be processed, the velocity means the speed at which data is received and processing speed (batch, real-time, stream, etc.). Typically, data processing in Big Data can be classified into three main categories: batch processing, real-time processing, and

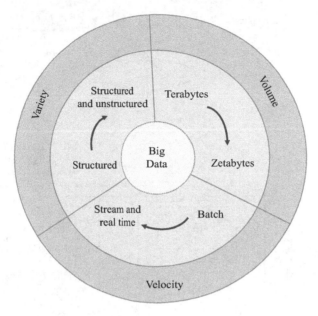

Figure 10.1   Big Data velocity representation among other key Big Data dimensions

stream processing [3]. In the following, we will briefly discuss these three processing types and their corresponding practical implementation platforms and/or frameworks.

10.1.2.1   Batch processing

This type of data processing has been used for many years in Big Data analytics where the whole dataset is collected over a period of time. The collected data is then stored in a distributed file system such as the Hadoop Distributed File System. Next, the data is processed, and the output is produced based on the well-known programing model, e.g., MapReduce [4]. Figure 10.2 shows the data flow in MapReduce. As follows, the data must be processed in two phases. In the mapping phase, computation nodes, so-called Mappers, take input data and produce intermediate results. These results are used as input to the reducing phase composing of computation nodes, so-called Reducers. These results are transported from the Mapper to the Reducer through an intermediate phase, called the Shuffle phase. Apache Hadoop [5] is the most notable open source Big Data processing framework which follows the MapReduce programing model. Due to its nature of "storing-before-processing," batch processing often takes time to process the data and produce outputs, thus it is not suitable for many recent applications which require extremely short processing time (e.g., many times less than a minute) or even requires real-time processing. However, the advantage of batch processing is the accuracy of the produced output. A more detailed description of MapReduce model and Apache Hadoop is found in Chapter 6.

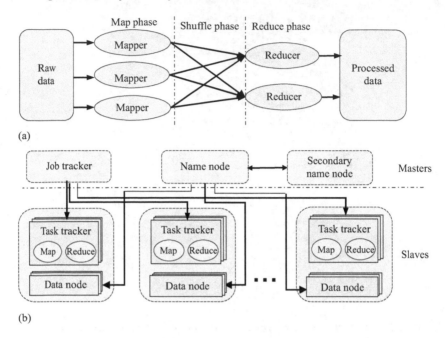

Figure 10.2   System architecture of Hadoop MapReduce. (a) Data flow between Mappers and Reducers; (b) physical view of MapReduce in a Hadoop Cluster

10.1.2.2   Near real-time and real-time processing

Real-time or near real-time processing of a system denotes the ability to process the data and produce the results strictly within certain time constraints [3]. In this regard, the real time often means the time for producing an output is in the order of milliseconds, or even microseconds, depending on the application and user requirements. This cannot be achieved by the conventional Hadoop system, which is less time sensitive. Apache Spark [6] is one of the most notable open source platforms which can be used for real-time processing. Although Spark also employs the MapReduce programing model, it allows the input data to be stored in-memory by using the concept of resilient distributed dataset (RDD), thus making Spark much faster than a traditional Hadoop (up to 100 times [7]).

10.1.2.3   Stream processing

In contrast to batch processing, stream processing is the system's ability to process the input data which is continuously flowing through the system without being stored. In other words, it requires that the data should be processed as it arrives. Although, the results produced by a stream-processing system are not always constrained by the processing time, it is currently more common that stream processing is also considered to be real-time. Apache Storm [8] is one of the most popular open source platforms for

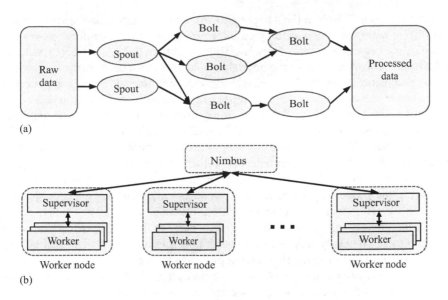

Figure 10.3 System architecture of Storm. (a) Storm data flow between Spouts and Bolts and (b) physical view of Storm Cluster

stream processing and is currently used by the Twitter. Figure 10.3 shows the logical and physical views of the Storm-based stream processing platform. There are two main computation components within Storm [8], namely Spout and Bolt. The Spouts are the sources of the stream which normally read the input data and generate tuples. These tuples are then forwarded to the Bolts, which are responsible for processing the tuples and produce a number of output streams, or pass the output towards other Bolts for further processing. Interested readers can seek more detail about the Apache Storm in Chapter 7.

10.2 How SDN can help velocity?

SDN [9] is a recently emerged networking paradigm which features the separation of the control and data planes of the network and moves the network intelligence to a centralized controller. This controller has a global view of all network states and its controlled devices; it is able to program the underlying network through an open interface (e.g., OpenFlow [10]). With many benefits such as network programmability, flexibility, traffic engineering, etc., SDN has been proven to be a promising solution for many aspects of networking ranging from wired campus and data center networks to wireless communication networks.

Big Data processing often relies on distributed frameworks which are deployed in data centers or cloud environments [11]. During the processing phase, the data often moves from one computation node to another (e.g., Mapper to Reducer in the Apache

Hadoop or Spout to Bolt in the Apache Storm), which are either on the same rack or in different racks interconnected by an intermediate network. Therefore, networking is one of the key components of any Big Data ecosystem [12]. Any problem with the underlying network can cause the degradation of the overall performance, especially the job completion time (JCT), which is the key factor to assess the processing speed of a Big Data framework. According to a study that analyzed a data trace from Facebook's Hadoop cluster [13], the shuffle phase (for delivering data from the mapping phase to reducing phase) accounts for 33% of the total running time.

As discussed earlier, the time constraints are very important factors of the velocity dimension. Solving the challenge of velocity means to focus on reducing the data processing time. Although several approaches have been proposed in the past to shorten the processing time, these approaches only exploited either scheduling computation at application level or scheduling flow (e.g., Hedera [14]) at networking level. Thus, there is still a lack of coordination between these two approaches, which can lead to significantly reduced processing time. In this regard, SDN will be considered as a great enabler for Big Data applications in coping with the challenges of velocity by providing a tool the Network Orchestrator, which dynamically programs and orchestrates the underlying network at run-time. With the logical centralization of network control and global view of network state, SDN can help accelerating the data delivery [15].

In summary, the answer to the question "How can SDN increase the velocity?" is to utilize the network programing capability of SDN together with the application-level information (e.g., job, task information) to derive a better scheduling decision on both application-level (i.e., optimal job/task allocation), and networking level (i.e., optimal flow allocation, optimal path computation), thus shortening the processing time of a Big Data application, and consequently meeting velocity requirements. The detailed answers will be addressed in Sections 10.3 and 10.4 through a survey of successfully launched projects.

10.3   Improving batch processing performance with SDN

In this section, we highlight some of the most influential research works that use SDN to improve the processing time for batch-oriented Big Data processing frameworks, in particular Map/Reduce.

10.3.1   FlowComb

FlowComb [16] is a network-management framework that helps Big Data processing applications such as Hadoop to achieve high utilization and low data processing times. The overall architecture of FlowComb is shown in Figure 10.4. There are three main modules implemented in the FlowComb framework: a Predictor, a Scheduler, and a Controller. The Predictor is responsible for the flow prediction and collects the information about data transfers within the Hadoop cluster reported from agents running on each Hadoop node. The agent periodically scans the local Hadoop log

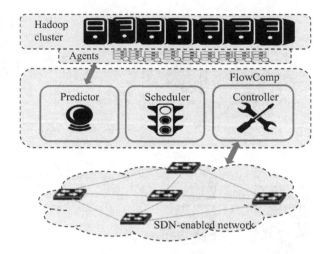

Figure 10.4 FlowComb architecture

files to learn whether a transfer has already started or not. The Scheduler module uses the information sent from the Predictor, such as a list of current or pending data transfers, to perform flow scheduling. Particularly, the Scheduler chooses a flow to schedule, decides whether it needs another path and, if so, chooses a new one for the flow. It is the responsibility of the Controller to install flow rules in the underlying programmable switches when it receives the decision from the Scheduler. Based on a prototyped experimentation, FlowComb has demonstrated its ability to reduce the average processing time by reducing the time to sort 10 GB of data (Sort application) by 35% compared with traditional Hadoop; it also performs 28% faster than the Hadoop which uses Equal-Cost Multi-Path (ECMP) routing scheme. The flow prediction task is able to detect around 28% of data transfers before they start, and 56% before they finish.

10.3.2 Pythia

Pythia [17] is another solution which also employs SDN to reduce the JCT for a Hadoop application. The overall architecture of Pythia is shown in Figure 10.5. Similar to the FlowComb architecture, Pythia has the concept of a monitoring agent, a so-called instrumentation middleware, which are installed in every Hadoop node that hosts a TaskTracker. The middleware constantly monitors its local TaskTracker and predicts the future shuffle transfers at MapReduce level. The monitored information and predictive knowledge are forwarded to the Pythia Runtime Collector/Predictor module. The Collector performs information collection, analysis, and some extra tasks such as flow aggregation and then forwards the analyzed information to the Pythia Flow Allocation module. This module is responsible for flow and path allocation computed by using shortest path routing algorithms, and path allocation algorithms such as ECMP [18]. The network-level information collected from the Orchestration

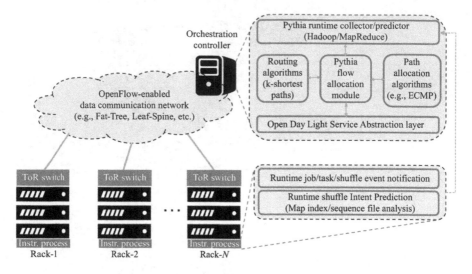

Figure 10.5   Pythia architecture

Controller is combined with the communication intention information collected by the middleware and the knowledge of the application-level transfers to heuristically find optimal flow allocations. Pythia is evaluated by using two different Hadoop applications: Sort and Nutch indexing. By employing Pythia, the time to sort 240 GB of input data is reduced by up to 43% as compared with an ECMP-based scheme. The Nutch JCT with 8 GB of input data using Pythia is reduced by up to 46% as compared with an ECMP-based scheme. The flow prediction of Pythia is able to timely predict flows well in advance with an over-estimating factor as low as 3%–7%. In comparison with FlowComb, Pythia claims that it can consistently detect 100% of shuffle flows before they start, while FlowComb can predict up to 28%.

10.3.3   Bandwidth-aware scheduler

Qin *et al.* [19] proposed a heuristic bandwidth-aware task scheduler called BASS (bandwidth-aware scheduling with SDN), which utilizes the SDN technology to improve task scheduling for Hadoop applications. With its ability of having the global view of the entire network state, SDN can provide information such as network traffic and available bandwidth in a real-time manner. With the information of available link bandwidth, the authors propose a scheme to allocate bandwidth in a time-slot manner. A time slot is described as the occupation time of each link's residue bandwidth. The BASS will decide whether to assign a task locally or remotely depending on the completion time. Qin *et al.* [19] analyses the BASS algorithm analyzes the BASS algorithm and how to efficiently and optimally assign tasks in detail (e.g., in local nodes or remote nodes). The BAAS is evaluated by using two different Hadoop applications: Wordcount and Sort. The experiment results show that the BASS scheduler can significantly reduce the JCT compared to two other schemes, namely Hadoop

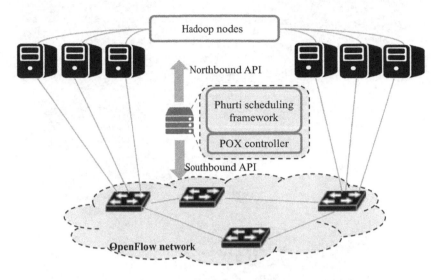

Figure 10.6 Phurti architecture

Default Scheduler and balance-reduce scheduler. More specifically, with BASS the JCT of the wordcount application is reduced by up to 10%, while the JCT of the sort application is reduced by up to 15%. In comparison with Pythia and FlowComb, the BASS scheduler mainly relies on the network-level information (e.g., available link bandwidth) without exploiting the application-level information or implementing the flow prediction concept. That explains why BASS scheme has less improvement in terms of JCT as compared with Pythia [17] and FlowComb [16]. However, it still proves the role of SDN in accelerating the Hadoop jobs.

10.3.4 Phurti

Phurti [20] is a centralized scheduling framework which uses the concept of SDN to decrease the completion time for Hadoop MapReduce jobs. Figure 10.6 depicts the concept of Phurti. The key idea of Phurti is to enable applications and Open-Flow switches to pass the information about the system through APIs to enable global network traffic coordination. Similar to previously described approaches, the Phurti controller uses a southbound API (e.g., OpenFlow) to collect information about the underlying network topology, flow information, etc. A northbound API is used between the Phurti controller and the Hadoop cluster to collect information about the shuffling phase traffic of each MapReduce job, the number of concurrent flows in a job, etc. The use of this information is similar to the Pythia and FlowComb approaches, however, the Phurti scheduling module does not seem to use any the Phurti does not mention any monitoring agent in its architecture. The Phurti scheduling module is the main contribution of this work which implements a heuristic-based scheduling algorithm called Smallest Maximum Sequential-traffic First (SMSF). The basic idea of SMSF is that a maximum sequential-traffic which is defined as the traffic

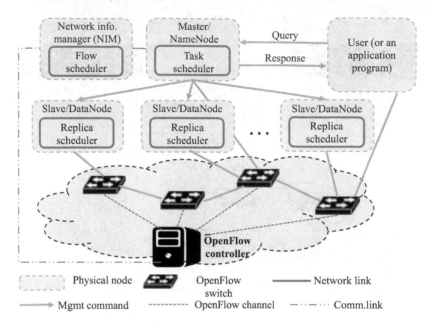

Figure 10.7   Cormorant system architecture

it needs to transmit between a host pair (e.g., Mapper and Reducer) is calculated for each MapReduce job. The flow scheduling function of Phurti will allocate network bandwidth to the flows of MapReduce jobs in an increasing order with respect to the maximum sequential-traffic values. A job with smaller maximum sequential-traffic has higher priority. Phurti is evaluated through the use of both microbenchmarks, and a realistic workload trace from Facebook. For the microbenchmark scenario, the experiment results show that Phurti can reduce the JCT by 36% compared to a FIFO scheduling scheme, and 15% compared to a Fair Scheduling (FS) scheme—FIO and FS are default MapReduce Schedulers. For the realistic workload scenario, the experiment results show that Phurti can improve the completion time for 95% of the jobs and decrease the average completion time by 20% for all jobs and 23% for small jobs compared with the FS scheme. Although Phurti has illustrated its ability to reduce the JCT, its scheduling algorithm is quite simpler compared with BASS [19], and it does not have the concept of flow prediction like FlowComb [16] and Pythia [17].

10.3.5   Cormorant

Xiong *et al.* [21] proposed Cormorant, a Hadoop-based query processing system built on top of a collaborative SDN. Similar to previously described works, Cormorant also attempts to bridge the gap between application and networking so as to accelerate the data processing in MapReduce Hadoop framework. Figure 10.7 shows the overall architecture of Cormorant. In this architecture, the OpenFlow Controller is responsible for managing the OpenFlow switches, collect all the flow information,

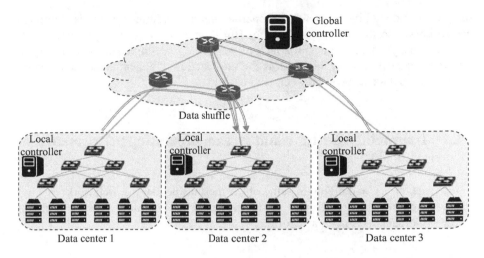

Figure 10.8   *Two-layer architecture for SDN-enabled Hadoop for social TV analytics*

and periodically generate a snapshot of the current network status. The information is then stored at the network information manager (NIM) in such a way that it is easily accessed by the task scheduler, the replica scheduler, and the flow scheduler. These schedulers collaborate with each other to improve the scheduling decision, which is similar to many of the previously described schemes. More specifically, on the basis of the network status, the task scheduler chooses the best task with the most available bandwidth. The flow scheduler schedules data on the physical path that has maximum available bandwidth corresponding to the task scheduler's choice. The performance of Cormorant is evaluated using TPC-H query benchmarking under different scenarios such as with or without background traffic, task scheduler only, collaborative scheduler, etc. The experiment results show that by enabling the collaboration between the task and flow scheduler, Cormorant is able to reduce the execution time by almost 22.5% as compared with the default Hadoop scheduler.

10.3.6 SDN-based Hadoop for social TV analytics

Hu *et al.* [22] proposed an SDN-enabled Hadoop platform for social TV analytics. In view of the current Hadoop does not support cross-site shuffle, the authors introduced the two-layer architecture (Figure 10.8). This architecture allows the data to be transferred between different data centers located at different IP segments. The first layer consists of several data centers are controlled by local controllers. The local controller is responsible for monitoring and configuring the network flow in order for local data to be transferred to other data centers. The global controller is in charge of managing the whole network and to interact with the local controllers. The performance of this proposed solution is evaluated by using the Sort application in which each server has to process 5 GB of tweets. The experiment results show that the JCT in the proposed solution is reduced by up to 30% compared with the traditional methods. Although the authors describe the use of SDN for Big Data processing in a specific application (TV analytics), there is still a lack of detailed scheduling algorithms. The most important contribution of this work is the introduction of a hierarchical architecture which allows data to move between data centers.

10.4   Improving real-time and stream processing performance with SDN

In this section, we will highlight some of the most influential research works that use SDN to improve the processing time for real-time and stream Big Data processing frameworks such as Spark and Storm.

10.4.1   Firebird

As discussed earlier in this chapter, Apache Spark [6] can reduce the processing time by up to 100 times compared with the traditional Hadoop, and it is considered as one of the solutions for real-time Big Data processing. In order to further improve the performance of Spark, He *et al.* [23] proposed a network-aware task scheduling for Spark called Firebird. The authors claim that the current delay scheduling method in Spark cannot perfectly solve the problem of data contention and network congestion, which cause the long processing time. The overall architecture of Firebird is shown in Figure 10.9. In this architecture, the computing nodes are connected to an OpenFlow-enabled network. The OpenFlow controller collects information from the network and update to the Network Information Manager (NIM). The information about the network status is shared between the flow scheduler module in the NIM and the task scheduler module at the master node. The Data Processing Rate (DPR) estimator module at the master node is responsible for estimating the data processing rate of a new task and its bandwidth requirements. The DPR estimates the amount of data that can be processed per second by the current CPU if the data I/O is unlimited. The task scheduler fetches the network status information from the NIM and uses this information in combination with the estimated DPR value from the estimator module to perform the task scheduling. Several scheduling methods are discussed and analyzed by He *et al.* [23] including local preferred scheduling, adaptive scheduling or network-aware scheduling, etc. The flow scheduler is based on the concept of flow scheduling in Hedera [14]. The performance of Firebird is evaluated by using three different applications including TPC-H query, *K*-means and Wordcount under two different scenarios: dedicated network and shared network with some background traffic. The experiment results show that Firebird can significantly reduce the execution time in all scenarios. More specifically, Firebird with the network-aware scheduler performs up to 39% better than the default scheduler in a dedicated network with a TPC-H query job, while performing up to nine times better than the default scheduler in the shared network.

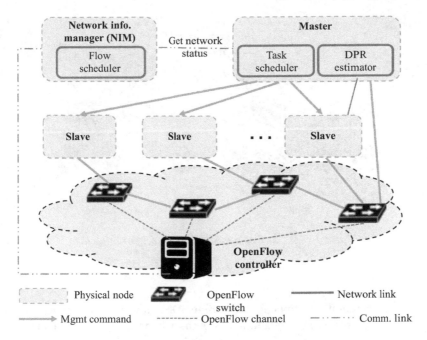

Figure 10.9 Firebird system architecture

10.4.2 *Storm-based NIDS*

Pamukchiev *et al.* [24] proposed the first solution which integrates SDN into a Storm-based Big Data processing framework. More specifically, the authors proposed a novel approach to develop an intrusion detection system (IDS) which detects the network anomaly in data centers by exploiting the Storm-based event processing framework with the assist of the SDN technology; it is called Storm-based NIDS, which is shown in Figure 10.10. In this architecture, the Storm Bolts are deployed on network switches and perform anomaly detection at line-rate on the traffic. The main roles of detection modules are to extract relevant fields from the packets processed and check them for anomalies. The controller is responsible for orchestrating the infrastructure by dynamically deploying the Bolts on all of the switches in the data center fabric. When a Bolt is instantiated, the controller establishes the connection between this Bolt and other Bolts to form a Directed Acyclic Graph or topology in Storm terminology. The controller controls the Bolts by using a southbound API, which allows the controller to push the latest configuration to the Bolts to make sure that the network anomaly detection is always evolved over the time as new threats emerge. The controller also performs other tasks such as monitoring Bolts' states and behavior over time so that it can quickly recover the Bolt upon failure. The performance of the Storm-based NIDS is evaluated under a realistic workload in terms of packet processing performance and the packet processing time. The experiment results show that all the packets are processed in less than 7 ms, while half of them being processed in only 4 ms. The

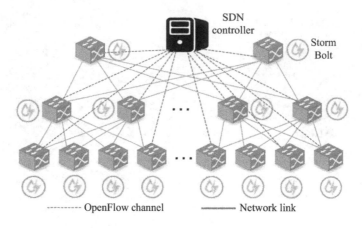

Figure 10.10   Storm-based NIDS system architecture

results indicate that it is promising to combine SDN with streaming event processing framework like Storm to detect anomalies in the network in a real-time manner.

10.4.3   Crosslayer scheduler

The crosslayer scheduler for Storm proposed by Alkaff *et al.* [25] is another approach which combines SDN and Storm for Big Data processing. Similar to the approaches described in Section 10.3, the key idea of this proposal is the coordination of application and networking layer to derive a better scheduling decision which is called crosslayer scheduling in this paper. The most noticeable contribution of this work is the introduction of a meta-heuristic algorithm namely Simulated Annealing [26] to find the optimal solution for both flow scheduling and task scheduling. The crosslayer scheduling framework is run whenever a new job arrives. The authors implement the concept by modifying Nimbus, which is a daemon process running on every master node in Storm (see Figure 10.3) to able to communicate with the SDN controller. The SDN controller provides the Nimbus information about the current status of the underlying network. At the beginning, when a job is initiated, the crosslayer scheduler will allocate the Spouts and the Bolts according to the output of Simulated Annealing algorithm. The scheduler then contacts the SDN controller which runs the Simulated Annealing algorithm for finding the best paths for each communicating computation node. The performance of this proposed framework is evaluated by using a self-generated synthetic Storm topology over two different data center topologies, namely Fat-Tree and JellyFish. The experiment results show that the crosslayer scheduler improves the Storm throughput with almost 35% with the Fat-Tree topology and up to 32% with the JellyFish topology depending on the number of computing nodes in the network. In addition, the crosslayer scheduler improve the Storm's JCT by 38% at 50th percentile and 42% at 75th percentile, respectively.

10.5   Summary

In this section, we first present the comparison table of all presented works on utilizing SDN to help the Big Data velocity, and then, we describe a proposed generic SDN-based Big Data processing framework.

10.5.1   Comparison table

Table 10.1 summarizes all existing approaches on using SDN to help the Big Data velocity. In this table, we compare these approaches based on what type of scheduling method are used, whether monitoring agent and flow prediction mechanism are used, what type of applications are used for the evaluation, and the maximum reduced JCT. It should be noted that the maximum reduction of JCT gained by each proposal in the last column are not comparable because they have different baseline scenarios.

10.5.2   Generic SDN-based Big Data processing framework

We have seen many proposed architectures and frameworks which integrate SDN with Big Data processing frameworks like Hadoop and Storm. There are several common components and functions which are necessary to make SDN be beneficial in a Big Data environment. In this section, we derive a generic SDN-based Big Data processing framework and describe its basic components. Figure 10.11 shows the logical overall architecture of an SDN-based, Big Data processing. The left side of the figure is the cluster of computation nodes interconnected by an SDN-enabled network. Monitoring agents are installed in each computing node (e.g., in worker nodes in Storm or TaskTracker nodes in Hadoop) and track information about data transfers. These agents can perform the prediction of any new data transfer like the function of the instrument process middleware in the Pythia architecture [17]. The upper part of the figure shows the generic processing framework which is composed of several components including an Application Controller, a Resource Manager, a Network Orchestrator, a Collector, and a Coordinator.

Application controller: This component is in charge of scheduling tasks over the computing cluster. It provides a southbound API interacting with the agents to collect the application-level information such as task information, data transfers on data being processed. The information is then passed to the Collector for analysis. The Application Controller later receives a command from the Coordinator to perform job/task scheduling over the cluster of computing nodes.

Resource manager: This component is in charge of managing the resources of both computing nodes and network devices (provided network devices are running as virtualized instances). It collects the resource related information such as processing capabilities of nodes and network devices and forwards the collected statistics to the Collector for analysis. The Resource Manager performs resources management tasks such as scheduling, migration, turning on/off unused nodes or network devices, etc., upon receiving the command from the Coordinator.

Table 10.1 Summary of SDN-based solutions for improving velocity of Big Data applications

Name	Type	Processing framework	Scheduling method	Monitoring agent	Flow Prediction	Evaluated applications	Reduced JCT
FlowComb [16]	Batch	Hadoop	Cross-layer	Yes	Yes	Sort job	Up to 90%
Pythia [17]	Batch	Hadoop	Cross-layer	Yes	Yes	-Nutch indexing -Sort job	Up to 46%
BASS [19]	Batch	Hadoop	Bandwidth-aware	No	No	Wordcount Sort job	Up to 15%
Phurti [20]	Batch	Hadoop	Cross-layer	No	No	-Terasort jobs -Facebook trace	Up to 36%
Cormorant [21]	Batch	Hadoop	Cross-layer	No	No	TPC-H query	Up to 22.5%
Hu et al. [22]	Batch	Hadoop	Bandwidth-aware	Yes	No	Sort job	Up to 30%
Firebird [23]	Real-time	Spark	Cross-layer	No	No	-TPC-H query -Wordcount -Kmeans	Up to 39%
NISD [24]	Stream	Storm	Network-aware	Yes	No	Realistic workload	Less than 7 ms
Alkaff et al. [25]	Stream	Storm	Cross-layer	Yes	No	Self-generated workload	Up to 42%

JCT = job completion time.

Network orchestrator: This component is in charge of managing the underlying SDN-enabled network infrastructure. It collects network-level statistics about the network such as topology information, flow information, devices, links, port status, etc., via a southbound API and forwards to the Collector. Upon receiving the information about the allocation of flow and path computed by the Coordinator, the Network Orchestrator then performs the flow installation and path setup.

Collector: As expected from its name, this component collects the information forwarded from the Application Controller, the Resource Manager, and the Network Orchestrator and analyzes them resource information, topology information, etc. It then sends the analyzed information to the Coordinator, which uses it as the input for computing job/task allocation, or flow and path allocation. The collected information can be used to predict whether there is congestion in the underlying network.

Coordinator: This component is the "brain" of the framework which is responsible for computing all job/task allocation, flow path, and resource allocation based on the information sent from the Collector. Some optimization algorithms can also be included to find optimal solutions for the allocation and scheduling of the above metrics. For example, a meta-heuristic Simulated Annealing algorithm [26] is used in the crosslayer scheduler [25] (discussed in Section 10.4). Outputs of the computation are executed by sending the control command to the corresponding lower level components, i.e., the Application Controller, the Resource Manager, and the Network Orchestrator. It can also perform the computation based on specific policies specified by the users.

10.6 Open issues and research directions

From the preceding description of the state-of-art works, we can see that SDN has been proven to be a promising candidate to cope with the challenges of Big Data velocity. However, there are still some open issues that have not been considered in the proposed solutions. In the following, we will discuss some of the main issues and offer a perspective on the future research directions on this topic.

Scalability and reliability: The principle of SDN is to move all the network control into a centralized controller, which indeed results in the scalability issue. When the controller fails, the whole network will fail. There are many other solutions that have been proposed to tackle this problem by using multiple controllers including distributed (flat) controller design, hierarchical controller design, and hybrid controller design [27]. Nevertheless, when it comes to using SDN to help Big Data analytics, most solutions simply ignore scalability and/or reliability issues of SDN. In order to fully exploit the benefit of SDN in the Big Data world, it is necessary to guarantee the reliability of the controller because it periodically provides the current network state such as network topology,

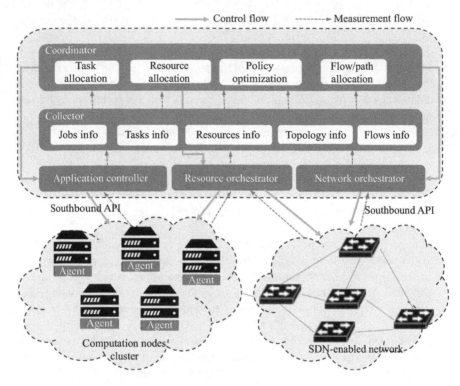

Figure 10.11   Big Data processing with SDN

flow information, etc. This information is used together with other information such as current task information, resource information to derive a better
scheduling decision which helps reduce the total processing time as discussed in
Section 10.2.

Monitoring and prediction: As shown in Figure 10.11 and discussed in Section 10.3, the monitoring and prediction are important tasks because they provide
the essential information for scheduling. In other words, it influences the scheduling decision either task scheduling or flow scheduling. In addition, the velocity
of Big Data means data is sent with a high rate; this would be a big challenge for
the monitoring task. We believe that the accuracy of monitoring and precision of
prediction must be addressed in more detail.

Network virtualization: SDN is not only beneficial in terms of network programmability but it is also a great tool for network virtualization. Using this feature,
when integrating SDN with Big Data, we can create multiple tenants for running multiple Big Data applications under the same physical infrastructure in an
isolated manner. Depending on service-level agreements and quality-of-service
requirements, each tenant can be allocated appropriate network resources that
do not conflict with other tenants. The flexibility of SDN allows it to create the

virtualized network on demand and terminate it when the tenant finishes its tasks. To date, there is only one work proposed by Akhthar [28] that implements tenant-aware scheduling for Big Data applications with the use of SDN. However, this work has not shown benefit of tenant-aware scheduling on the Big Data velocity. Thus, there are still avenues for the future research.

Optimization: As addressed in Section 10.2, some optimization algorithms can be used to find optimal solutions for task scheduling, flow scheduling and resource allocation. For example, Alkaff *et al.* [25] has used Simulated Annealing meta-heuristic for finding the optimal set of tasks and flows to be allocated. When running Big Data analytics in a cloud environment, computing nodes are virtual machines (VMs). Finding the optimal placement of VM not only helps better resource utilization but also improves the data processing performance. For example, Gu *et al.* [29] proposed a communication-aware optimization solution to place VMs and balance the network flow for Big Data processing. We believe that by combining the optimal flow allocation and the optimal placement of the computing nodes (which corresponds to the flow allocation and resource allocation modules shown in Figure 10.11), the performance of the Big Data velocity can be further improved.

10.7 Conclusion

In this chapter, we have discussed how SDN can cope with the velocity challenges in Big Data analytics caused by the high arrival rate of data and the requirements of shortening the processing of data so that valuable outputs can be produced in a near real-time and real-time manner. We explained why SDN is a promising solution to reduce the processing time in Big Data and how SDN is able to provide such advantages. We derive a generic architecture which provides an overview of how SDN is implemented in the context of Big Data analytics to help the processing phase to be faster. Then, we elaborated the benefits of SDN in Big Data applications by providing a summary of the major proposals with detailed design and the extent to which they reduced the processing time as compared with traditional non-SDN approaches. According to the surveyed study, it is obvious that SDN is truly helping in processing Big Data in general and especially in terms of velocity.

References

[1]   Erricsson, "Ericsson mobility report", 2016. https://www.ericsson.com/assets/local/mobility-report/documents/2016/ericsson-mobility-report-november-2016.pdf. [Online; accessed 12-February-2017]

[2]   V.-G. Nguyen, A. Brunstrom, K.-J. Grinnemo, and J. Taheri, "5G mobile network: Requirements, enabling technologies, and research activities," in *Comprehensive guide to 5G security* (M. Liyanage, A. Gurtov, M. Yliantilla, I. Ahmed, and A. B. Abro, eds.), ch. 2, pp. 1–28, UK: Wiley Publishers, 2017.

[3]   S. Shahrivari, "Beyond batch processing: Towards real-time and streaming big data," *Computers*, vol. 3, no. 4, pp. 117–129, 2014.

[4]   J. Dean and S. Ghemawat, "Mapreduce: Simplified data processing on large clusters," *Communications of the ACM*, vol. 51, no. 1, pp. 107–113, 2008.

[5]   Apache Hadoop, 2017. http://hadoop.apache.org. [Online; accessed 2017].

[6]   Apache Spark, 2017. http://spark.apache.org. [Online; accessed 2017].

[7]   M. Zaharia, M. Chowdhury, T. Das, *et al.*, "Resilient distributed datasets: A fault-tolerant abstraction for in-memory cluster computing," in *Proceedings of the 9th USENIX conference on Networked Systems Design and Implementation (NSDI)*, pp. 1–14, USENIX Association, 2012.

[8]   Apache Storm, 2017. http://storm.apache.org. [Online; accessed 2017].

[9]   Open Networking Foundation, "Software-defined networking: The new norm for networks." https://www.opennetworking.org/images/stories/downloads/ sdn-resources/white-papers/wp-sdn-newnorm.pdf, 2012. [Online; accessed 6-July-2016].

[10]   N. McKeown, T. Anderson, H. Balakrishnan, *et al.*, "Openflow: Enabling innovation in campus networks," *ACM SIGCOMM Computer Communication Review*, vol. 38, no. 2, pp. 69–74, 2008.

[11]   M. Chen, S. Mao, and Y. Liu, "Big data: A survey," *Mobile Networks and Applications*, vol. 19, no. 2, pp. 171–209, 2014.

[12]   S. Yu, M. Liu, W. Dou, X. Liu, and S. Zhou, "Networking for big data: A survey," *IEEE Communications Surveys & Tutorials*, vol. 19, no. 1, pp. 531–549, 2017.

[13]   M. Chowdhury, M. Zaharia, J. Ma, M. I. Jordan, and I. Stoica, "Managing data transfers in computer clusters with orchestra," *ACM SIGCOMM Computer Communication Review*, vol. 41, no. 4, pp. 98–109, 2011.

[14]   M. Al-Fares, S. Radhakrishnan, B. Raghavan, N. Huang, and A. Vahdat, "Hedera: Dynamic flow scheduling for data center networks," in *Proceedings of the 7th USENIX Conference on Networked Systems Design and Implementation (NSDI)*, pp. 1–15, USENIX, 2010.

[15]   L. Cui, F. R. Yu, and Q. Yan, "When big data meets software-defined networking: SDN for big data and big data for SDN," *IEEE Network*, vol. 30, no. 1, pp. 58–65, 2016.

[16]   A. Das, C. Lumezanu, Y. Zhang, V. K. Singh, G. Jiang, and C. Yu, "Transparent and flexible network management for big data processing in the cloud," in *Proceedings of the 5th USENIX Workshop on Hot Topics in Cloud Computing (HotCloud)*, pp. 1–6, USENIX Association, 2013.

[17]   M. V. Neves, C. A. De Rose, K. Katrinis, and H. Franke, "Pythia: Faster big data in motion through predictive software-defined network optimization at runtime," in *Proceedings of the 28th IEEE International Symposium in Parallel and Distributed Processing*, pp. 82–90, IEEE, 2014.

[18]   C. E. Hopps, "Analysis of an equal-cost multi-path algorithm," RFC 2992, IETF, 2000.

[19] P. Qin, B. Dai, B. Huang, and G. Xu, "Bandwidth-aware scheduling with SDN in Hadoop: A new trend for big data," *IEEE Systems Journal*, vol. 11, no. 4, pp. 2337–2344, 2017.

[20] C. X. Cai, S. Saeed, I. Gupta, R. H. Campbell, and F. Le, "Phurti: Application and network-aware flow scheduling for multi-tenant mapreduce clusters," in *Proceedings of the 2016 IEEE International Conference on Cloud Engineering (IC2E)*, pp. 161–170, IEEE, 2016.

[21] P. Xiong, X. He, H. Hacigumus, and P. Shenoy, "Cormorant: Running analytic queries on mapreduce with collaborative software-defined networking," in *Proceedings of the 3rd IEEE Workshop on Hot Topics in Web Systems and Technologies (HotWeb)*, pp. 54–59, IEEE, 2015.

[22] H. Hu, Y. Wen, Y. Gao, T.-S. Chua, and X. Li, "Toward an SDN-enabled big data platform for social TV analytics," *IEEE Network*, vol. 29, no. 5, pp. 43–49, 2015.

[23] X. He and P. Shenoy, "Firebird: Network-aware task scheduling for spark using SDNs," in *Proceedings of the 25th IEEE International Conference on Computer Communication and Networks (ICCCN)*, pp. 1–10, IEEE, 2016.

[24] A. Pamukchiev, S. Jouet, and D. P. Pezaros, "Distributed network anomaly detection on an event processing framework," in *Proceedings of the 14th Annual IEEE Consumer Communications and Networking Conference (CCNC)*, pp. 1–6, IEEE, 2017.

[25] H. Alkaff, I. Gupta, and L. M. Leslie, "Cross-layer scheduling in cloud systems," in *Proceedings of the 3rd IEEE International Conference on Cloud Engineering (IC2E)*, pp. 236–245, IEEE, 2015.

[26] P. J. Van Laarhoven and E. H. Aarts, "Simulated annealing," in *Simulated Annealing: Theory and Applications*, pp. 7–15, Springer, 1987.

[27] M. Karakus and A. Durresi, "A survey: Control plane scalability issues and approaches in software-defined networking (SDN)," *Computer Networks*, vol. 112, pp. 279–293, 2016.

[28] T. Akhthar, "Tenant-aware big data scheduling with software-defined networking," Master's thesis, Instituo Superior Tecnico, 2016.

[29] L. Gu, S. Tao, D. Zeng, and H. Jin, "Communication cost effective virtualized network function placement for big data processing," in *Proceedings of the IEEE INFOCOM Workshop on Big Data Sciences, Technologies and Applications (BDSTA)*, pp. 1–6, IEEE, 2016.

Chapter 11

SDN helps value in Big Data

*Harald Gjermundrød**

Our modern society has entered the information age, which is heavily reliant on the extraction of knowledge from vast amounts of data. Raw data is collected from all kinds of devices, ranging from customer supplied information to sensors information in wearable devices. It is expected that the number of devices that will be able to collect data will grow exponentially in the next few years, as the IoT (Internet of Things) will become a reality. In order to address the numerous challenges regarding the storing of vast amount of data, its processing, and the extraction of knowledge (including generating value from the data), the term Big Data was coined [1].

In this chapter, we are investigating the ways that software-defined network (SDN) [2–5] facilitates the creation of value in Big Data [6–8]. We will use the term *value* inclusively, meaning that it refers to the monetary value that an organization could additionally generate from Big Data, as well as the extraction of knowledge, best practices, and transfer of knowledge resulting from Big Data. In order to cover the broad spectrum of the ways SDN accommodates generating extra value from Big Data, the discussion will focus on four deployment scenarios spanning over two dimensions: the infrastructure setting and type (i.e., centralized/decentralized, public/private) and the nature of the data (i.e., at rest/streamed and private/public). Below is a short description of the deployment scenarios, which are also depicted in Figure 11.1.

1. **Private centralized infrastructure:** The computing, storage, and network resources of the infrastructure are owned by one organization and they are centralized. For example, the organization has deployed its own private cloud infrastructure within one localized network zone.
2. **Private distributed infrastructure:** The computing, storage, and network resources of the infrastructure are owned by one organization and they are distributed. For example, the organization has deployed a private cloud consisting of multiple data centers connected as a WAN (could be a mixture of leased lines and using the common Internet backbone).
3. **Public centralized infrastructure:** The computing, storage, and network resources of the infrastructure are owned by a cloud provider that is renting

*Department of Computer Science, University of Nicosia, Cyprus

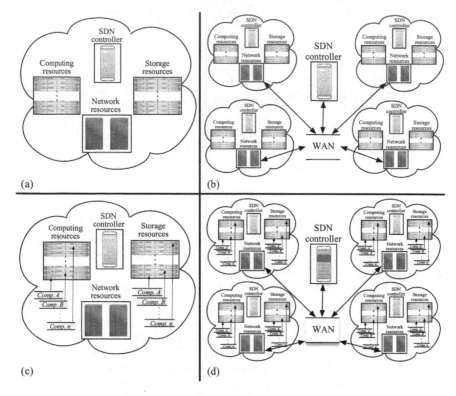

*Figure 11.1   Four deployment scenario: (a) private centralized infrastructure,
(b) private distributed infrastructure, (c) public centralized
infrastructure, and (d) public distributed infrastructure*

out the resources to the general public. This scenario demonstrates how a SDN
could be deployed to control the "local" network within the cloud infrastructure.

4. **Public distributed infrastructure:** The computing, storage, and network
    resources of the infrastructure are owned by a cloud provider that is renting
    out the resources of multiple cloud deployments worldwide to the general public.
    In this case, there is a SDN that controls the WAN [9,10] interconnecting the
    cloud deployments as well as another SDN that controls the "local" network
    within each cloud infrastructure.

In the above-deployment scenarios, the nature of the data is also taken into consideration. A distinction between data at rest and streamed data is necessary as a SDN
could be utilized differently for data at rest compared to streamed data. Furthermore,
we also make the distinction between private and public data, since it determines the
data processing and handling procedures followed by the organization. As a result,
there are five data categories that are discussed throughout this chapter:

Private stored data: Data owned by one organization, not shared or be available for
    other organizations.

Private streamed data: Data collected by one organization and consists of a stream of data-points that are collected from various sensors or any other data generation source. The data-points from the streams may be filtered (could be done dynamically depending on available network resources) from the source to the sink if less fidelity of the data points are required at the processing entity. The processing entity could be a Stream Processing Engine [11], and the result of the processing could be further fed into Big Data processing engines. The result from the processing as well as the raw streamed data (potentially filtered to a lower fidelity) may be stored for future processing or future use.

Publicly accessible stored data: Data publicly accessible by anyone interested in obtaining the specific datasets. The providers are not obliged to offer any guarantees regarding the accuracy of the data or its availability.

Publicly accessible streamed data: Similar to the *private streamed data* except that the streams are publicly available. The format of the data in the streams and subscription to the streams details are made publicly available. The providers are not obliged to offer any guarantees regarding the accuracy of the data or its availability.

Dark data: Public or private stored data stored in long-term archiving. The reason behind storing the specific data or the actual data contents may not be known. Additionally, the data is most likely not indexed or directly searchable and that is why it is referred to as dark data [12].

Now that the landscape of the investigation is set, the next step is to establish the dimensions that will be examined to assess the way SDNs add value to Big Data. These are listed as follows:

Value of adaptable network platform: The processing of Big Data usually requires a Cloud Data Center (CDC). Utilizing SDN as the network platform within the CDC [13,14], will result in an adaptable platform to accommodate any future needs of the Big Data Application layer [15]. This is a more cost-effective solution for the CDC in the long run, with a prospect of improving scalability as well [16].

Value of adaptable data flows: When considering the velocity of the Big Data, it is observed that a large portion of the data flow is often filtered out, due to the fact that the underlying sensors generate more data than the back-end infrastructure can handle. In case that the value or accuracy of the knowledge that could be extracted from the Big Data requires different granularity for different data flows, then this will depend on the ability of the underlying network infrastructure to handle this shift [17,18]. A SDN accommodates adaptable data flows without the need to upgrade the underlying IT infrastructure.

Value of dark data: Given the vast amount of collected data, a significant percentage of data ends up as dark data with no immediate usage foreseen. Depending on the design of the IT infrastructure it may be challenging to restore dark data as active data flow in the analytical part of the infrastructure (i.e., if a future usefulness of the dark data is discovered). A SDN accommodates the dark data restoration without the need to upgrade the underlying IT infrastructure.

Data markets and ecosystems: A flexible, adaptable, and potentially scalable underlying network infrastructure could facilitate new markets for selling, sharing, and trading data. Given the monetary importance of data in the current information society, new ecosystems can be devised where all parties involved in the trade/sell of data are participating.

The rest of the chapter is organized as follows. Section 11.1 presents potential innovative ways of the deployment of a SDN within a private centralized cloud infrastructure, whereas Section 11.2 scales this up to the setting where a private organization connects its distributed cloud infrastructure using a SDN. Details on how a SDN adds value in the public Cloud infrastructures, where multiple organizations are cohosted within the same SDN-controlled infrastructure, are presented in Section 11.3. Section 11.4 leverages the setting in the previous section to the setting where multiple public Cloud infrastructures are connected together using a SDN. Current open issues and challenges are presented in Section 11.5. Finally, Section 11.6 concludes with a summary of the chapters discussions.

11.1   Private centralized infrastructure

The first deployment scenario that is investigated is the smallest and simplest one, namely the one for a private centralized infrastructure. It covers a single organization that hosts *all* its resources in either a data center or a private cloud (could also be a public cloud, but then the organization must have its resources controlled be a single SDN and have full control over its network operating system, i.e., controller). The value of adaptable network platform, the value of adaptable data flows, the value of dark data and lastly the data markets and ecosystems are examined in turn in order to assess the ways an SDN offers added value to Big Data.

11.1.1   Adaptable network platform

In a rapidly evolving digital world, the value placed on the various data types (including data streams of live data) could shift rapidly. The data that was essential for the organization yesterday may not be relevant today or in the near future. Nevertheless, the organization had to commit a large CAPEX expense for the installation and deployment of the underlying network infrastructure which is optimized to handle this specific data. As presented in Chapter 1, it is very challenging (almost impossible from a financial point-of-view) to rapidly change the underlying network infrastructure. In order to change the topology of the network using current technology requires a significant amount of human intervention, i.e., OPEX, in addition to the possibility of downtime due to the time it takes to change the topology and the possibility of various misconfigurations. In order to avoid this undesirable situation, NaaS (Network as a Service) must be used so that whenever new types of data or data streams are needed this can be done without any CAPEX, due to the feature of SDN.

The adaptive network platform is more relevant for an organization that owns its own IT infrastructure, as it has complete control of the infrastructure. During the deployment of the IT infrastructure the organization's current needs influence its architecture. Most likely, the IT architects try to envision future needs, but with varying success rates.

11.1.2   Adaptable data flows and application deployment

Development and deployment of Big Data applications must take into consideration the available computing, storage, and network resources. The introduction of virtualized computational resources has somewhat alleviated the considerations regarding computing resources. However, there will always be competing interest regarding the different resources allocation and which application gets to gather the most data. This is especially true for processing of Big Data, meaning that the raw data used as input may need to get filtered. Decisions are taken on determining the data flows that require very fine granularity and those that could produce good enough results with a much courser granularity. Depending on the various compromises and business needs the IT infrastructure will be set up or evolved over time as it scales up w.r.t. the amount of input data and computational resources.

One resource which is more difficult to scale, due to its more "hard-coded" nature is the network resource. This is where lies the benefit of using a SDN for the interconnection among the IT resources. Compromises that are currently enforced on the resource allocation scheme for Big Data application or on the selection scheme of data flows that are to be throttled back (i.e., filtering close to the source) are not fixed but could be changed in the future. An organization's priorities change or new/modified Big Data applications get developed, requiring the underlying network infrastructure be flexible and dynamic and be reconfigured to fit the current organization needs. This is similar with the way virtualization of computing resources changed the flexibility of computing resources.

Flexibility will also be given to application developers and deployers, as the placement of resources (including its cost of gathering the required data) will no longer need to be considered as a priority during this phase of the project. The added value of this is that it will give the developers and deployers much more freedom when developing and deploying these kinds of complex applications as one constraint is removed, and it may result in new kinds or usage patterns that were prohibited before due to the inflexibility of the network resources.

11.1.3   Value of dark data

Even it is not scientifically proven, one could assume that most medium to large organizations possess large datasets that fall into the dark data category. The nature and the amount of dark data vary greatly as it depends on the organization and the sector that it operates in. One example of dark data is data archived to comply with national regulations and/or internal policies. In addition, a large percentage of the continuous data flows collected by an organization and also tends to end up as dark data. Dark data has no foreseen direct use or value; thus, there are no provisions (especially with respect to the network architecture) to restore the dark data back to the computational resources of the data center.

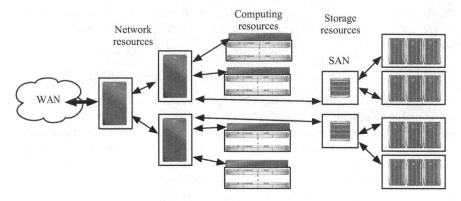

Figure 11.2   Data center architecture

In addition, if we classify dark data as Big Data (i.e., large datasets that are collected for various unrelated reasons), they may be stored in different storage units within the data center, due to the data size and variety. The dark data may be stored based on the location, application, time, expected value at the time of collection, or any other deciding factor. If future potential value or usefulness of combining/mining dark data is revealed, it will prove cumbersome to provide the appropriate network infrastructure for the analysis of the data. This is due to fact that dark data will most likely be spread at different storage units, the network is optimized for data to flow one way making it challenging to revert the direction to accommodate the introduction of dark data into the Big Data applications.

A common architecture for an organization's IT infrastructure when deployed in a Cloud is depicted in Figure 11.2, where the storage of the data is at the back end. The network is usually configured for data to flow one way and the setting is "hard coded" to be optimized for the current usage of the Big Data. In order to start to search for new knowledge from the dark data, the data flows will be different; hence, a flexible and adaptive network infrastructure is needed. The reason to suspect that the archived data may contain information that could be extracted to new knowledge are numerous. Some examples are the following:

- New machine-learning algorithms that allow for new ways to process the data or allow for the combination of unrelated datasets in a novel way
- Improved computational resources that make it now possible to deploy applications that in the past were considered to be too computational intensive
- Emerging application domains that make this archived data relevant
- Relaxation of regulations that may allow various government (or any organization for that matter) entities to combine different records containing citizen data (or tax registered companies) to discover tax evasion or fraudulent use of government funds.

Different types of data may be stored as dark data depending on the nature of the organization that collected it. Some data that may be collected by the various organization types could be:

Businesses: Customer and business relation records including all the interactions and preferences, all kinds of proprietary information about their products and business domain.

Government organizations: All kinds of records about citizens and organizations operating within the state, all kinds of records about the governing of the state (including vast amounts of statistical data).

Research organizations: Enormous amounts of research data, some of which is also intended to be made publicly available.

An example of storage of large amounts of data that may or may not be useful in the future is the data collected from large scientific experiments in fields such as high energy physics, chemistry for drug discovery, and astronomy. An example is the Large Hadron Collider that generates about 50 Petabytes annually that must be stored, distributed and analyzed. The emergent need to handle the large amounts of data collected by these experiments motivated the creation of Grid Computing.

As pointed out earlier, today's network deployments are fairly static, even in the data center setting, and it requires a significant amount of human resources to reconfigure them. This is where using a SDN for the network infrastructure will allow the organization to rapidly use the dark data without upgrading the underlying IT infrastructure. It could also schedule the processing of dark data at time intervals when there are ample reserves of resources available. The added value by deploying a SDN for this scenario are the following:

1. Generate new value from archived data (e.g., research organization/groups extract new findings from stored research data).
2. Able to use the computational resources as efficiently as possible (i.e., when there is excess resource available, reconfigure the network setting as to feed the computational resources with data to process).

11.1.4 New market for the cloud provider

Consider the case where the organization is renting its IT infrastructure (computational and storage) from a public cloud. The cloud provider could then offer an additional service, namely NaaS, in addition to the IaaS (Infrastructure as a Service), PaaS (Platform as a Service), and SaaS (Software as a Service). The cloud provider would give to each organization complete control over the controller plus a set of forwarding engines that would provide the network topology needed for the rented computing and storage resources. Potentially, the forwarding engines (i.e., data plane) could be virtualized and the cloud provider would be able to optimize the usage of its physical network devices as it is optimizing its resources of the physical computing and storage devices.

Different layers of abstraction of the NaaS could be offered, depending on the requirements of the organization. The cloud providers are already offering preconfigured GNU/Linux based web service, email servers and could potentially offer pre-configured Network Operating Systems with minimal maintenance by the system administrators of the organization renting the service. Needless to say, organizations that want to customize their Network Operating Systems, they should be allowed to do so.

11.2   Private distributed infrastructure

A privately owned infrastructure that supports a SDN could anticipate added value for Big Data as shown in Section 11.1. In this section, we scale the IT infrastructure of the previous scenario to support multiple IT infrastructures distributed in various geographical locations that are interconnected with an underlying SDN. A private distributed infrastructure scenario will still enjoy the added value benefits of the private centralized one, in addition to new ones that contribute in extracting more value for its Big Data applications.

A real world deployment of such infrastructure is presented in [19], where Google reports the findings from utilizing SDN for the private network that interconnected its data centers. It was observed that the network utilization was close to 100% of its capacity, in contrast with the normal link utilization being in the range of 30%–40%, without incurring any interruption to its services. The motivation behind deploying the SDN for the data centers interconnection was the intention to increase the utilization of the private network links as its predicted cost of using its current technology would not be financial feasible for the future expected load. It was emphasized that almost full utilization of the links was achieved due to the fact that the end-points and all the applications using the links are under the control of Google. Hence, based on the semantic of the applications, various priorities for the data flows could be set and adapt at run time to provide assurances that the needs of the different application types would be satisfied.

11.2.1   Adaptable resource allocation

An organization could take advantage of a two-level SDN-controlled infrastructure to gain significant flexibility. The first level is the SDN-controlled interconnection among the various cloud deployments whereas the second level is the SDN-controlled network within a cloud infrastructure. This adaptability is examined from two different viewpoints: the computational resources aspect and the interconnected links aspect. In both cases, the focal point is to utilize them close to their full capacity, under the condition that the production systems (computation and network resources) should not be affected by stretching the resources to reach their limits. Thus, the aim is to use the excess resources (over-commissioned to handle failures) when available, but be able to pause these additional systems when resources are not available.

11.2.1.1   Maximizing usage of computing resources

There are numerous reasons for the under-utilization of data center computational resources, with varying duration. Below a few such reasons are listed:

1. Depending on the location and usage of the data center, there may exist peak seasons or peak hours. Each center must be designed to handle the peak requests, but as a side effect there are low seasons (or hours in the day) that the center witnesses excess resource capacity. These high-low peak cycles can be studied and potentially predicted, therefore data flows could be redirected to under-utilized data centers to off-load the ones reaching their capacity.
2. Each data center has redundancy of resources as a measure to handle various failures. There are organizations that downtimes are not an option, meaning that ample excess capacity to handle any contingency is required.
3. When a new data center is deployed it could be the case that initially it is expected to be underutilized, as it is designed to scale as the organization grows. During the adaptation period, the excess resources could be utilized by other data centers.

Needless to say, it is beneficial for an organization to utilize its resources at or close to their maximum, while at the same time having a contingency plan on scaling back schemes in case of failures. The SDN interconnected network among these potentially under-utilized data centers will facilitate a quicker adaptation. Examples of exploiting excess resource capacity are given below:

1. Precompute expected future needs; in case the prediction is false, there is no extra computational cost as the resources were already available.
2. Different scenarios could be precomputed and compared, instead of just opting for the predicted best scenario; these scenarios could take into consideration priorities and/or classified as *nice-to-have* vs. *need-to-have*.

11.2.1.2 Adaptable data flows and application deployment

During the time periods that excess resources capacity within certain cloud infrastructures are reported, various data-streams could be duplicated and forwarded to those under-utilized infrastructures. Different data mining/machine learning applications could run on the unused resources, allowing the manipulation of the same data stream in various ways, with benefits such the ones below:

1. Derive potentially new knowledge from the data-streams given some intuition of different algorithms. However, they would not be business critical and could be halted at any time if the resources could be used in a better way.
2. These scenarios could be used as a "fire drill" to verify that different data-streams could be forwarded to different centers and the applications would be able to run within these infrastructures.
3. Graceful degradation of the input to the various Big Data applications. In various failure situations, the Big Data applications can potentially reduce the granularity of the data streams that they receive, or reduce the number of streams that are used in the input. Similarly, the priority of the various Big Data applications should be pre-determined, hence when the failures take place. The different applications will pause in the order of priority, until the failures are rectified.

11.2.2   Value of dark data

With distributed data centers, an organization stores large amounts of data (potentially of different type of data) at different sites due to the regional usage pattern. By having a SDN controlling the links among the data centers, various data priority classes could be defined (similar to what was done in [19]). The normal data flows that deliver services for a center will have the highest priority. The reserve capacity of the interconnections could be used to move dark data between centers with very low priority. Since the organization owns all the edges that connect the data centers it could quickly drop the low priority traffic to assure that the high priority traffic will not be affected by low priority movement of data. Situations where an organization could take advantage of the reserve excess capacity of its interconnections are presented below:

1.   Data archived at the different sites may yield new knowledge when combined, however the envisioned usage may not justify the cost of moving large datasets between the centers and the labor cost involved in establishing these data transfers. In a SDN setting, the establishment of allowing these data transfers are relative straightforward and could be done in a way that will not influence the production systems.
2.   Instead of having a dedicated infrastructure to experiment on new applications, these applications can be deployed within the cloud infrastructures that have excess capacity. The transfer of the data needed for these experiments will be of low priority type, hence not affecting the production systems.

11.3   Public centralized infrastructure

One popular setting where the SDN could potentially generate additional value from Big Data is in the *Public Cloud* setting. We are presenting approaches that could potentially create an ecosystem in the public cloud, having the various organizations that are using/renting resources in the cloud collaborating in novel ways as well as allowing the service providers to offer new services such as *DaaS* (Data as a Service) [20]. Using/sharing the data in the public cloud will most likely require that the cloud provider supplies an API to the Application Network Controller and provide a pricing information service of the current available resources along with the price of using network resources. A dynamic pricing scheme for the usage of network resources based on resource availability is also envisioned.

11.3.1   Adaptable data flows and programmable network

An organization using the public cloud infrastructure to host and process their Big Data will be have the means to adapt its Big Data applications to maximize the perceived data value compared to the cost of deriving the specific knowledge from the data at a specific time. Having a SDN that is programmable and flow based, organizations could evaluate at run-time if it is in their benefit to either receive *all* data from a stream (due to the cost) or filter a number of streams (or receive streams with less fidelity, i.e., drop every x values.). Organizations, based on cost/benefit analysis of forwarding the data to the required nodes, will develop their Big Data applications by adjusting the fidelity of the data streams considering the aforementioned analysis.

There are cases where flows, such as live public streams (public stock prices, weather information), attract the interest of multiple organizations, but with perhaps different fidelity. A SDN could facilitate the data streams sharing (from the cloud provider's point of view). In this way, there are no duplicate *data packets* traversing the same network links within the cloud infrastructure. Additionally, the stream could be filtered as close to the sink as possible in case of different fidelity of the data [21]. The cloud provider could also aggregate common streams that are popular and provide these streams at various fidelity as a *Data as a Service*.

In addition to the adaptability of the data flows, an organization can also take advantage of the programmable network and the status information service that the cloud provider provides. The Big Data applications could be programed to deliver the extracted knowledge from the data as a *just-in-time* service. What that entails is having applications programed to move the required data when the cost of doing so is below a certain configurable threshold, given that the computational nodes will have enough time to derive the needed knowledge from the data and to deliver it on time. Certain applications focusing on not time-sensitive knowledge such as long-term trends, and deriving profiles could be scheduled to run when there are ample network resources and the cost is at its lowest. On the contrary, time-sensitive knowledge (buy/sell shares in the stock marked) applications will not take into consideration the cost of moving data.

A formulation of determining the time to schedule the execution of the application while staying within the available budget is shown in (11.1). The organization specifies the data needed, the predicted computational resources usage, the time the result should be available, and the budget willing to pay (according to an SLA). The cloud provider can then schedule network and computing resources to the application when those requirements are met. Hence, the provider should find an i such that the computation will be done in time, while at the same time minimizing the price, which must stay below the budget:

$$\min\{|\Phi_{[i,(i+\delta)]} + \Upsilon_{[i,(i+\delta)]}| : \tau \geq (i + \delta) \wedge \alpha \leq \beta\} \tag{11.1}$$

where α is the price, β is the available budget, δ is the expected duration to compute the result, τ is the time when the results must be available, $\Phi_{[i,(i+\delta)]}$ is the cost of computing starting at time i for duration δ, and $\Upsilon_{[i,(i+\delta)]}$ is the cost of gathering data starting at time i for duration δ.

Having a scheme to compute the optimal time to run an application gives the cloud provider the flexibility to curve the computational and network spikes as to approach full utilization of the resources. However, their scheduling will, without any doubt, be more complicated as all the requirements for all the organizations hosted within its infrastructure must be considered when devising a pricing scheme. The higher the resource usage optimization, the lower the prices the cloud provider will be able to offer. Organizations could take advantage of the low prices at underutilized periods, especially for Big Data applications where the search for knowledge from the data is not straightforward. The aim is to lower the network and computational resource usage while producing the most accurate result. In this case, different processing scenarios are allocated to execute at low utilization time, different intermediate results are precomputed, and the different mining/machine learning algorithms are compared. When the knowledge is really needed, the organization could use the intermediary results to apply the most appropriate mining/machine-learning algorithm.

11.3.2 Usage of dark data

In the public cloud domain, organizations could develop applications that only search for dark data when the cloud host is offering resources at low prices (during low peak hours). As soon as prices climb above a programmable threshold, the application halts until the prices are again favorable. In addition, to search for new knowledge in this dark data, other auxiliary actions would need to be performed that augment the dark data such as adding meta-data, indexing, and categorization. It is not considered a failure if no new knowledge was found during the augmentation of the dark data. By tagging the data with new meta-data (if any is derived), could be proven useful to future iterations (with improved algorithms) that attempt to derive new knowledge.

11.3.3 Data market

Numerous new markets can be envisioned with respect to data, which could be developed by deploying a SDN in the public cloud. The motivation behind these markets is the creation of a data sharing/trading ecosystem among the various organizations that are brokered/controlled by the cloud provider.

Given the scenario with the cloud provider as a broker, some of the trading could take place anonymously as an organization may not want to reveal that it possesses a certain type of information or that it is even interested in specific information; in both cases the disclosure could affect its future business strategy. By selling it anonymously, it does generate extra income for the seller, without revealing to the buyer that the seller indeed possess such datasets.

In some ecosystems, the cloud provider could also be an active participant (in the line with the organizations) while controlling the ecosystem. In this scenario, strict regulations must be in place to assure that the group within the cloud provider managing the market is separated from the group involved with the trading. This is a situation similar to the electric power market as well as the electronics industry where the fabrication entities of a company are separated from the entities developing end-products.

Below, two new market segments that we envisioned are described. The first market is the one handling stored data and the other one handles live data streams.

11.3.3.1 Market for stored data

Different organizations possess different datasets as they collect raw information from various sources like customer information, surveys, or from Network Processing Engines. These large datasets are stored within the cloud infrastructure and used for further processing and/or other purposes. Given the flexibility of SDN and the Cloud Provider role as a broker, further value could be generated from this stored data. Different scenarios for how this trading/selling of data could be envisioned, are presented below.

Cloud provider broker

The Cloud provider acts as an independent broker where the owners of the datasets publish information about the datasets that are willing to share. Various conditions and/or policies could dictate how the broker is to publicize the availability of these dataset, with even restrictions on access control and further disclosure/dissemination of the datasets outside the boundaries of the specific cloud provider.

Arrangements could also be provided where the buyer of the data doesn't actually get access to the data directly. The buyer submits to the broker the application for processing the data. The broker runs the application within the cloud infrastructure with the bought datasets as input. The results are given to the buyer, who at no time during the process have access to the raw data. Value could potentially further be yielded from the purchased result data since it could potentially be traded again. The original owner of the raw data may have offered the data at a discount price if the findings are also shared with that organization. Similarly, the cloud provider may offer the computational resource at a discount price if it will be allowed to resell the results from the processing.

Bilateral and multilateral agreements

Organizations within the same hosting environment could develop bilateral or multilateral agreements of data trading among them. In the network settings, the movement of large datasets, even within the same hosting environment, is nontrivial to accomplish. In this chapter, we will not go into the detail of all the different arrangements and trading abilities that could take place, but rather we emphasize that a SDN should alleviate most of the technical challenges. Given the flexibility of the network infrastructure, organizations could even collaborate by sharing storage and access to read-only data, resulting in greatly reducing their cost of using cloud infrastructure.

11.3.3.2 Market for data flows

Similar to the extra value generated from stored data, new opportunities are possible to generate new services and value for streamed data with an SDN cloud infrastructure. This includes scenarios where the cloud provider acts as a broker or where multiple organizations within the infrastructure develop *n*-lateral agreements. An additional scenario could exist when organizations are using stream data and are co-hosted within the same cloud infrastructure. The cloud provider, upon realization that numerous organizations within its hosing environment are receiving the same outside data streams, could provide this outside streamed data as DaaS, with varied fidelity, to its customer organizations. In addition, the provider may store durations of these streams and offer them as an auxiliary service to retrieve historical data from these streams.

For all the streamed data, it is possible to optimize the usage of network resources, in that only one data stream is actually entering the cloud infrastructure. The stream is only split on the last hop to the various organizations interested in this stream (similar idea is used in many Publish–Subscribe systems).

11.4   Public distributed infrastructure

The various services and collaborations envisioned for various organizations that are hosted within one cloud infrastructure using SDN as its network infrastructure as well as the benefits yielded could also be extended to a distributed public cloud infrastructure that is also interconnected using a SDN. Additional services and benefits are anticipated for the public distributed infrastructure that generate more value from Big Data.

Often global organizations are using cloud providers that offer infrastructure in various regions worldwide with the intention to serve the cloud clients as close to their location as possible. Benefits of this practice are, among others, the minimization of both the latency and network resources usage as well as redundancy. In the latter case, one infrastructure serves as a redundancy to another one. For example, in case the infrastructure in Asia should suffer downtime, the market could be supported by the infrastructure in Europe albeit with an increased latency and potentially reduced service. Due to the different time zones, the peak usage in the different worldwide regions will be different (of course this is a great generalization and depends on the usage scenario). One could assume that an organization using cloud infrastructures worldwide will always have infrastructures that are not operating at their peak. Due to the elasticity provided by the cloud provides, an organization may choose to scale down the number of virtual hosts that it is using during those hours. The downside though is the case where a large number of organizations decide to follow the same practice; cloud providers will have ample excessive resource available during non-peak hours. Using an SDN in the WAN environment that connects the various cloud infrastructures additional value could be generated by maximizing the usage of the infrastructure.

11.4.1   Usage of dark data

Extending the idea and motivation from Section 11.3.2, organizations having data stored in different geographical regions to serve specific markets, accumulate vast amounts of dark data in different centers. As already mentioned, the movement of these large datasets over the WAN and with the current network technologies is not trivial, especially if the intention is to accomplish the data transfer without disrupting "regular" traffic (unless leasing of dedicated resources).

Connecting the different cloud infrastructure using a SDN, numerous new opportunities are available to alleviate the above challenging scenario. The cloud provider could provide a service that allows an organization to specify the move of large amount of data between the could infrastructures. As these are considered to be low-priority searches for new value in the stored data, an organization could also specify the maximum budget willing to pay for the data move. The cloud provider, in turn, would schedule the data transfer when there is excess capacity in the WAN network between the involved cloud centers. The search for new knowledge is more complicated when the data is spread in different cloud centers. The data is copied to the destination center; thus, more storage capacity is required that incurs additional costs, not to mention the extra cost for using the computational resources needed to perform the knowledge search in the data.

If we were to formulate the relationship between these costs against the expected value of the data derived from dark data, three cost variables must be taken into consideration before performing such a search for new value in the dark data in a distributed infrastructure settings:

*t*Cost(set$_i$):   Cost for transferring the dataset$_i$ from center α to center β
*s*Cost(set$_i$):   storage cost of data dataset$_i$ in center β
*c*Cost(set$_i$):   computational cost of dataset$_i$ in center β.

The sum of these should be less than the expected value of the new knowledge yielded from this action. Hence:

$$\text{ExpectedValue} \geq \sum_{i=0}^{n} (t\text{Cost}_\alpha(\text{set}_i) + s\text{Cost}_\alpha(\text{set}_i) + c\text{Cost}_\alpha(\text{set}_i)) \qquad (11.2)$$

11.4.2 Data market

Regarding the data market, the ideas outlined in Section 11.3.3 could be extended for a WAN connected distributed set of cloud infrastructures. Different markets and ecosystems that are envisioned with a two-level SDN setting are presented next.

11.4.2.1   KaaS—trading markets

A new category of participants in the IT industry could be developed by the interaction of Big Data, Cloud Infrastructure, and SDN. The Big Data collected by various organizations could be resold to data wholesalers, thus creating a new market of processing second-hand data on demand in order to generate knowledge from it, namely *KaaS* (Knowledge as a Service). It could be envisioned that the wholesalers will not need to store their own copy of large datasets, but only one copy is stored within a cloud infrastructure with read-only access for the organization that originally collected the data and for the wholesalers that acquired the right to use the data. The wholesalers will, of course, own (the right-to-access) datasets in many different cloud infrastructure spread throughout the world.

The new marketplace spans through the datasets that wholesalers advertise as available for purchase. Furthermore, the marketplace could be enriched with other services such as:

Ready-made applications: Knowledge extraction from ready-made applications, which are deployed on demand by a customer. The customer is given the option/feature to customize the knowledge extraction by setting various options, etc.
Knowledge for group purchase: The wholesaler may anticipate that certain knowledge will always be in demand; hence, it will be running those knowledge

extraction applications continuously as COTS (commercially available off the shelf). The more customers that are interested and willing to pay for this knowledge, the more profits for the wholesaler and potentially lower selling prices. It is anticipated that this will be a very dynamic market; thus, it is vital that the applications are continuously updated along with the data streams needed for the knowledge extraction. It is of paramount importance that the underlying network infrastructure is flexible to be able to accommodate this dynamic environment. For instance, if new data streams are needed that must traverse the network in the opposite direction of that of the "normal" data flow, then the SDN should be able to accommodate this much better than what is possible in a "traditional" network setting.

The wholesaler could also set different requirements regarding the execution of the various knowledge extraction applications. They may only be scheduled to run during the off-peak hours when the wholesalers may be able to negotiate more favorable pricing schemes. Similarly, the cloud provider could itself become a wholesaler and use the excessive resources within their cloud infrastructures without actually incurring any additional cost. In this case, the cloud provide must already possess the required data. Various deals could be envisioned; one such deal is having the cloud provider offering an organization special pricing schemes and in exchange the cloud provider could use non-sensitive information belonging to the organization.

Bring your own data and application: The general knowledge that could be extracted from the datasets that the wholesaler is in possession of may not be adequate for an organization to derive the knowledge needed. It could be the case that a combination of the data that the wholesaler possess and some of its own private data is required. The wholesaler will then offer the customer to supply its own application, which will take as input the wholesaler's data as well as the customer's own datasets. The flexibility of an SDN-controlled intra cloud network is essential for the ability to combine all the required data sources and feed them to the needed computational resources. It is also important that there exist a trusted third party for these multilateral interactions. Each organization needs assurance that there will be no data leakage from these interactions and that the wholesaler only sells derived knowledge and not the raw data. The wholesaler also needs guarantees that the end-customer is not allowed to gather the knowledge from its datasets that it considers proprietary. Similarly, the end-customer must have assurances that the wholesaler will not gather its proprietary data that is used in this type of interactions.

Publicly available data and data stream: A possibility for sharing the cost of extracting knowledge from Big Data involves its extraction from publicly available data and data streams. Numerous organizations may be interested in extracting the same knowledge from publicly available data sources and data streams, however the expense is too high for any single organization to carry the cost alone. A consortium of organizations could be created (this could include research groups from universities, NGOs, and potentially companies) and a trading portal could be developed where interested parties express interest in obtaining specific knowledge and their monetary contribution. If there is a lack of trust between the organizations, a portal Distributed Autonomous Organization [22] could be established acting as the intermediary.

Competitive marketspace: In the spirit of free market and with the datasets being publicly available, new markets could be developed, where the "provider" sets a price of the cost of providing the knowledge from the datasets. As there will be multiple "providers" in this competitive space, they would not only compete on the price, but also on delivery time, and potentially fidelity of the knowledge being extracted. This would be similar to market research firms which are using datasets from state statistical services.

11.4.2.2 Cooperating of data sharing

Different organizations possess different datasets and streams or live data. Organizations could proceed with signing memoranda of understanding and share the cost of developing platforms. This is similar to the auto industry that develops common platforms and/or engines in order to share the expenses, but still each industrial entity produces products that are distinct from each another. A recent trend is the new sharing economy, like Airbnb, which with the help of SDN and Big Data could lead to the sharing knowledge industry, with something like "bring your own data" to be processes.

Example
An example illustrating the collaboration between organizations using the 2-level SDN architecture is now discussed and presented in Figure 11.3. Due to the complexity of the interactions, the figure only partially illustrates the entire setting. The entities involved along with their resource needs, stored data and data streams that they are willing to bring to the collaboration are given below:

Company A: Large multinational retailer
- Hosted mainly in Cloud infrastructure α
- Data stream *a.s.1*, *a.s.2* and stored dataset *a.d.1*, *a.d.2* (residing in Cloud infrastructure α)
- Interested in the result of the *A.App*, *C.App*, and *Z.App*

Company B: Regional telecommunication company
- Hosted mainly in Cloud infrastructure β
- Data stream *b.s.1*, *b.s.2* and stored dataset *b.d.1*, *b.d.2* (residing in Cloud infrastructure β)
- Interested in the result of the *B.App*, *A.App*, and *Z.App*

Company C: National investment bank
- Hosted mainly in Cloud infrastructure γ
- Data stream *c.s.1*, *c.s.2* and stored dataset *c.d.1*, *c.d.2* (residing in Cloud infrastructure γ)
- Interested in the result of the *C.App*, *B.App*, and *Z.App*

As it can be seen, all three companies are interested in *Z.App*, while for the other applications, at least two of the companies are interested in the result. For this example, we will only pick one application for each of these settings, namely

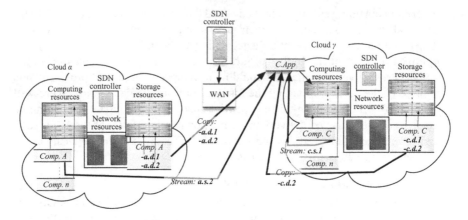

Figure 11.3   Example illustrating collaboration

the *C.App* (bilateral agreement) and *Z.App* (multilateral agreement). The Big Data applications have the following features and requirements:

C.App: Disposable income within a specific region
* Results can be provided as: ultra-fine granularity, fine granularity, and coarse granularity
* Needs data streams: *a.s.2* and *c.s.1*
* Needs stored datasets: *a.d.1*, *a.d.2*, and *c.d.2*

Z.App: Predicting smart phone market trends
* Results can be provided as: ultra-fine granularity, fine granularity, and coarse granularity
* Needs data streams: *a.s.1* and *c.s.1*
* Needs stored datasets: *c.d.1*, *b.d.2*, and *a.d.1*

The SDN controller that connects all the cloud infrastructures will orchestrate the movement of the data and allocation of the required computational services.

For *C.App*, the goal is to be placed at a cloud infrastructure that has excess computational resources, available storage for all required data, and available network resources to move all the required stored data as well as the data streams needed. As illustrated in Figure 11.3, the application will be placed in Cloud infrastructure *γ*.

This can be dynamically evaluated and in case of changes to cost (or availability of resources) the computation can be moved to another cloud infrastructure without the change to the underlying network infrastructure [23]. Further optimizations can also be considered. Although not fully supported currently by SDN, the idea of active networks would work well for the example above. Part of the streams and stored data could be filtered close to their source if the intersection of all apps within a cloud infrastructure does not need the specific data or needs the data with less fidelity.

In the previous example, the three organizations may also wish that their proprietary applications and data not to be shared (not shown in the example). However, nothing technically prevents them from sharing some of those applications in the future. This is the great advantage of the SDN, which the allocations of resources can be done in a dynamic and adaptable manner.

11.4.3   Data as a service

Ideas from the 1990s with active networks [24] that have already influenced SDN could also be used to form a future SDN with more processing power in the data plane [25]. In addition to the extra processing power to the data plane, it could also be envisioned that also data storage could be added to selected nodes in the data plane. Ideas of a complete software-defined environment (SDE) [26] have been proposed by IBM as per their SmartCloud Orchestrator. One of the SDs within this environment is the Software Defined Storage [27]. This complete ecosystem could result in storing publicly available data in the network. Similarly, organizations could rent services to store their streams of data for a specific period of time in the network. This would enable them to extract extra value of their data in numerous ways such as:

1. Reuse of the data from the streams, great flexibility to move the data to different cloud infrastructures for additional use.
2. Cost benefits to store it in the network for short term before archiving it somewhere (and in time it may become dark data).
3. Ability to offer the data for sale/trading using the various collaboration schemes presented above. This trading would make it possible to quickly offer the data with very low latency.

This can be elevated to the next level where computation can be done in the network. The organizations will submit their application to the SDN controller, which can then orchestrate the collection of the required data (streams and stored data) and arrange their transfer to appropriate location within the "cloud network" where the computation takes place and the results are delivered to the customers. Various hybrid schemes could be envisioned, where only light-weight computation is done in the network part of this "cloud network" and the more computational nonsensitive part of the application will then be moved out of the network to dedicated computational cloud resources. Synergies can be taken advantage of by the SDN controller where partial results common to multiple organizations only needs to be computed once and only one copy of the data needs to be stored within the network.

11.5   Open issues and challenges

Deployments of SDN within the cloud infrastructure are in their infancy, thus there are many open issues and challenges before deployments of SDNs will be commonplace for production systems. Throughout this chapter, we have introduced many conceptual scenarios that SDN can be deployed in production systems of Big Data applications in order to generate new value. However, numerous issues would need to be addressed before most of these scenarios could be realized. Below, are some issues and challenges that will need to be researched.

First, a rethinking of the Big Data application development life cycle needs to be done with the introduction of the SDN. The application architect must take into account the flexibility of the network level, similar to how the introduction of elasticity of computation and storage resource (cloud computing) influenced the deployment of cloud applications in the last decade. Specifically, *how will the application architect take advantage of the virtualization of the network layer to easily scale the network layer to accommodate changes in the data flows (both from stored data and data streams) in and out of the Big Data application?*

Second, the introduction of an elastic network layer results in numerous open questions on how this flexibility could be utilized by application developers, *i.e., how will the future Big Data applications be developed in order to use this flexibility?* However, it is important that the complexity/difficulty of developing these applications doesn't get any higher. New development frameworks, libraries, and tools must be devised to expose an appropriate and intuitive programing API. In order to further alleviate the difficulty for the application developers, a policy language could be introduced where the developer specifies (at a high level) that various tradeoffs depending on the availability of network resources. The characteristics of this language as well as the policy engine interpreter are nontrivial challenges that must be addressed. No matter the solution, it is of utmost importance that there is a clear separation between mechanisms and policies at all levels. The development of a new policy language and the advancements in the area of artificial intelligence may assist to solve a few of these challenges. Additional open research questions will follow if formal verification of the different "choices" that the processing engine may take is required. The advantage of the current "hard-coded" network infrastructure is that once it is configured "correct" for the current setting nothing unexpected should happen. With all of the "smartness" that can be done in a fully deployed and dynamic scenario, the wrong configuration can be deployed and unforeseen scenarios can quickly happen where the whole infrastructure ends up in a thrashing state.

Third, one of the selling points of SDN is that an organization can push its network resources closer to their capacity, as was observed in [19]. As it was presented in this chapter, network resources (especially WAN links) are on purpose underutilized. If an organization starts utilizing its resources close to capacity then various contingency action plans need to be implemented in order to handle various failures. In [19] this was not an issue because the organization had complete control of the applications at the end-point and knew the semantics of these applications. However, this will not be the case for many of the scenarios presented in this chapter. Hence, an open question related to utilizing network resources at their limits is *are there any savings after the cost of the contingencies plans are subtracted from the savings of pushing the network resources closer to capacity?* Additionally, *how will the interaction be between the network controller and the applications hosted within an SDN-controlled infrastructure, in the face of failures when the network controller will make decisions of what data flows to disrupt and/or scale back?*

Last, but not the least, for most of the scenarios presented in this chapter, trust must exist between the interacting parties (cloud providers, organization renting resources controlled by the SDN, and the data traders). Many of these issues go beyond the technical realm, meaning regulations and legal frameworks have to be developed in order to create the proposed ecosystem presented here.

11.6   Chapter summary

This chapter presented the ways SDN adds value in Big Data. In order to start to dissect this area we considered four deployment scenarios. The deployment scenarios span through the following dimensions: the first dimension is whether or not the IT infrastructure (i.e., Cloud deployment) is private or public while the second dimension is whether or not the IT infrastructure is centralized (i.e., one cloud deployment) or distributed (i.e., multiple cloud deployments). A two-layered SND architecture is formed in the distributed deployments, having the first layer being the SDN controller that controls the inter-cloud network (WAN) among the different cloud deployments and the second layer involves the SDN that controls the intra-cloud network (LAN).

In order to investigate how additional value could be extract from Big Data, a categorization of the data was done. Three dimensions were used to classify the data: stored vs. streamed data, publicly available vs. privately owned, and a final category is that of dark data, which is data archived away and its content, structure, and usefulness may not be known.

Given the four deployment scenarios and the different data categorization we examined how organizations generate more value from their Big Data. First, we look at how the flexibility of being able to adapt the network resources (inter- and intranetworks) easily. Second, considering this adaptability, we examined the possibility to adjust the granularity of the data stream based on the priority of the streams, availability of resources, and the cost of renting those resources at the specific time. Third, we investigated the potential of retrieving archived data (referred to as dark data) and attempt to extract new knowledge from this data yielding new value for the company. The fourth and final approach we looked at is the option of creating new markets and ecosystems where organizations would be able to trade, sell, share, and broker data (both stored and streamed) due to the dynamic and flexible of the future SDE.

References

[1]   V. N. Gudivada, R. Baeza-Yates, and V. V. Raghavan, "Big data: Promises and problems," *Computer*, vol. 48, pp. 20–23, Mar 2015.

[2]   D. Kreutz, F. M. V. Ramos, P. E. Verssimo, C. E. Rothenberg, S. Azodolmolky, and S. Uhlig, "Software-defined networking: A comprehensive survey," *Proceedings of the IEEE*, vol. 103, pp. 14–76, Jan 2015.

[3]   N. Feamster, J. Rexford, and E. Zegura, "The road to SDN: An intellectual history of programmable networks," *SIGCOMM Computer Communication Review*, vol. 44, pp. 87–98, Apr 2014.

[4]   B. A. A. Nunes, M. Mendonca, X. N. Nguyen, K. Obraczka, and T. Turletti, "A survey of software-defined networking: Past, present, and future of programmable networks," *IEEE Communications Surveys Tutorials*, vol. 16, pp. 1617–1634, Third 2014.

[5]   A. Lara, A. Kolasani, and B. Ramamurthy, "Network innovation using openflow: A survey," *IEEE Communications Surveys Tutorials*, vol. 16, pp. 493–512, First 2014.

[6]   L. Cui, F. R. Yu, and Q. Yan, "When big data meets software-defined networking: SDN for big data and big data for SDN," *IEEE Network*, vol. 30, pp. 58–65, Jan 2016.

[7]   I. Monga, E. Pouyoul, and C. Guok, "Software-defined networking for big-data science – Architectural models from campus to the wan," in *2012 SC Companion: High Performance Computing, Networking Storage and Analysis*, pp. 1629–1635, Nov 2012.

[8]   G. Wang, T. E. Ng, and A. Shaikh, "Programming your network at run-time for big data applications," in *Proceedings of the First Workshop on Hot Topics in Software Defined Networks*, HotSDN '12, (New York, NY, USA), pp. 103–108, ACM, 2012.

[9]   R. Ahmed and R. Boutaba, "Design considerations for managing wide area software defined networks," *IEEE Communications Magazine*, vol. 52, pp. 116–123, Jul 2014.

[10] C.-Y. Hong, S. Kandula, R. Mahajan, *et al.*, "Achieving high utilization with software-driven wan," *SIGCOMM Computer Communication Review*, vol. 43, pp. 15–26, Aug 2013.

[11] S. Kamburugamuve and G. Fox, "Survey of distributed stream processing," Digital Science Center, Indiana University, School of Informatics and Computing, Bloomington, IN, USA, 2016.

[12] P. B. Heidorn, "Shedding light on the dark data in the long tail of science," *Library Trends*, vol. 57, no. 2, pp. 280–299, 2008.

[13] C. J. S. Decusatis, A. Carranza, and C. M. Decusatis, "Communication within clouds: Open standards and proprietary protocols for data center networking," *IEEE Communications Magazine*, vol. 50, pp. 26–33, Sep 2012.

[14] M. Chen, H. Jin, Y. Wen, and V. C. M. Leung, "Enabling technologies for future data center networking: a primer," *IEEE Network*, vol. 27, pp. 8–15, Jul 2013.

[15] D. Tuncer, M. Charalambides, S. Clayman, and G. Pavlou, "Adaptive resource management and control in software defined networks," *IEEE Transactions on Network and Service Management*, vol. 12, pp. 18–33, Mar 2015.

[16] S. Bouzghiba, H. Dahmouni, A. Rachdi, and J.-M. Garcia, *Towards an Autonomic Approach for Software Defined Networks: An Overview*, pp. 149–161. Singapore: Springer Singapore, 2017.

[17] C. E. Rothenberg, R. Chua, J. Bailey, *et al.*, "When open source meets network control planes," *Computer*, vol. 47, pp. 46–54, Nov 2014.

[18] W. John, K. Pentikousis, G. Agapiou, *et al.*, "Research directions in network service chaining," in *2013 IEEE SDN for Future Networks and Services (SDN4FNS)*, pp. 1–7, Nov 2013.

[19]   S. Jain, A. Kumar, S. Mandal, *et al.*, "B4: Experience with a globally-deployed software defined wan," in *Proceedings of the ACM SIGCOMM 2013 Conference on SIGCOMM*, SIGCOMM '13, (New York, NY, USA), pp. 3–14, ACM, 2013.

[20]   Z. Zheng, J. Zhu, and M. R. Lyu, "Service-generated big data and big data-as-a-service: An overview," in *2013 IEEE International Congress on Big Data*, pp. 403–410, Jun 2013.

[21]   H. Gjermundrød, C. Hauser, and D. Bakken, "Scalable wide-area multicast with temporal rate filtering distribution framework," in *2011 IEEE 11th International Conference on Computer and Information Technology*, pp. 1–8, Aug 2011.

[22]   C. Jentzsch, "Decentralized autonomous organization to automate governance," whitepaper, Slock.it, 2016.

[23]   S. F. Abelsen, H. Gjermundrød, D. E. Bakken, and C. H. Hauser, "Adaptive data stream mechanism for control and monitoring applications," in *2009 Computation World: Future Computing, Service Computation, Cognitive, Adaptive, Content, Patterns*, pp. 86–91, Nov 2009.

[24]   D. L. Tennenhouse, J. M. Smith, W. D. Sincoskie, D. J. Wetherall, and G. J. Minden, "A survey of active network research," *IEEE Communications Magazine*, vol. 35, pp. 80–86, Jan 1997.

[25]   H. Gjermundrød, D. E. Bakken, and C. H. Hauser, "Integrating an event pattern mechanism in a status dissemination middleware," in *2009 Computation World: Future Computing, Service Computation, Cognitive, Adaptive, Content, Patterns*, pp. 259–264, Nov 2009.

[26]   C. S. Li, B. L. Brech, S. Crowder, *et al.*, "Software defined environments: An introduction," *IBM Journal of Research and Development*, vol. 58, pp. 1: 1–1:11, Mar 2014.

[27]   A. Alba, G. Alatorre, C. Bolik, *et al.*, "Efficient and agile storage management in software defined environments," *IBM Journal of Research and Development*, vol. 58, pp. 5:1–5:12, Mar 2014.

Chapter 12

SDN helps other Vs in Big Data

Pradeeban Kathiravelu*,** and Luís Veiga*

Big Data is defined by a set of attributes or adjectives collectively known as the Vs of Big Data. Among these Vs, we discussed how Software-Defined Networking (SDN) helps Big Data achieve volume, velocity, and value in the previous chapters. Variety, volatility, validity, veracity, and visibility can be considered the "other Vs" that define Big Data. In this chapter, we will look into these other Vs in Big Data, and how SDN can be leveraged to achieve them. We will further discuss how SDN-based Big Data solutions are designed, and how SDN controllers are extended and exploited to create network, middleware, and system architectures for Big Data, focusing on these attributes.

Variety in Big Data can be attributed to both heterogeneity in data itself including the data type and storage format and media, as well as the variety in data producers and consumers. Volatility defines how long the data should be considered valid and/or how long should it be stored, maintained, or managed. Validity is a parameter that indicates whether the data is valid or invalid (correctness) which can be represented by a Boolean flag for each data object. Veracity defines the cleanliness or the quality of data (accuracy). Validity and veracity define the correctness and quality of data. Visibility of Big Data depends on who is permitted to access the data partially or completely, and how it is accessed.

Data centers and clouds should provide necessary separation of data among their multiple users. These users are called the tenants of the platform. Data centers and clouds can be made multitenanted through virtualization and softwarization of networks and systems. Software-defined data centers (SDDCs) [1] bring SDN to data centers, supporting multitenancy and virtualization in data centers. Similarly, Software-Defined Cloud Computing [2] extend SDN for softwarization of cloud computing networks and platforms. Figure 12.1 illustrates a multitenant SDDC network that guarantees these other Vs in Big Data. Variety in Big Data can be programed to be represented by various tenants of the controller deployment. Visibility to the data and insights can be ensured through virtual network allocation and tenant isolation in the control plane. On the other hand, workflows can have speed ups through

*INESC-ID Lisboa/Instituto Superior Técnico, Universidade de Lisboa, Portugal
**ICTEAM, Université catholique de Louvain, Belgium

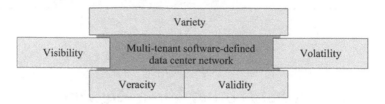

Figure 12.1   SDN shaping the other Vs in Big Data

distributed execution and scaling offered by SDN, supporting higher volatility and veracity, while ensuring validity in the data. These attributes are often interrelated to each other from an SDN-based architectural point of view, offering valid and accurate data, without compromising the privacy and isolation of the tenants. Ensuring variety, volatility, validity, veracity, and visibility in Big Data with SDN can be summarized as the requirement to have tenant-awareness, data isolation among the tenants, and horizontal scalability of the data and control planes of SDN.

In the remaining of the chapter, we will limit our focus to variety, volatility, validity, veracity, and visibility, when we mention the "other Vs in Big Data". We will further discuss the current approaches and open issues in achieving these other Vs in Big Data leveraging SDN in the upcoming sections. Section 12.1 offers an overall introduction to the other Vs in Big Data. We will discuss how SDN can be leveraged to achieve each of these other Vs in Big Data in Section 12.2. Section 12.3 discusses how SDN supports Big Data diversity, discussing various architectures and use cases of SDN in supporting heterogeneous Big Data to offer quality of service (QoS) and data quality, with multitenancy and data isolation. Finally, we will discuss the open issues and challenges in adopting SDN for Big Data in Section 12.4 with potential future work. We will conclude the chapter in Section 12.5 summarizing the chapter with current applications of SDN for the other Vs in Big Data.

12.1   Introduction to other Vs in Big Data

In this section we will look into the other Vs in a more detailed manner.

12.1.1   Variety in Big Data

Big Data can be of many types and formats. It can be structured, unstructured, semistructured, or ill-formed, as Big Data is often integrated from multiple data sources of different storage media. Data from a source such as a NoSQL data source may not confine itself to a predefined schema. Data storage in formats such as XML and JSON gives rise to flexible data schemas. Variety in Big Data in a multitenant environment poses new challenges to data storage, processing, and analytics platforms in terms of withstanding an increasing rate of heterogeneity in the data.

Large volume of binary Big Data consists of textual metadata that offers crucial information for indexing, accessing, and managing the data. Variety in Big Data consists of the metadata in addition to the data itself. Presence of such metadata is mandated by various data types of different application domains, such as DICOM (Digital Imaging and Communications in Medicine)[1] of medical imaging. The textual metadata present with the binary data is leveraged to embed the contextual information of the data, including the timestamps of data creation, last access, and expiry. By carefully analyzing the metadata of the stored data, existing platforms can be extended to scale and cater to the heterogeneous nature of Big Data. Metadata is thus leveraged to support constructing an efficient large volume of storage for heterogeneous Big Data, while assisting integration and access of the stored binary data.

We see the variety in Big Data as not just the type of the data itself, but also the nature of the data providers—the tenants that publish data and data consumers—the tenants that consume the data that has been published and maintained by the data providers. Data producers publish data to the data sources that can later be accessed. They create and share data in various forms, which is consumed by multiple data consumers. Data consumers play a pivotal role in the data variety, as the Service Level Agreements (SLAs) depend on the data consumers and their needs. They access and consume the data that has been shared by data producers. A tenant may also play both the roles of data producers and consumers, as the data producers themselves may access, analyze, and consume their own as well as others' data sources. The tenant that produces the data as well as the tenant that consumes them also determines the nature of the data, in terms of its significance and sensitivity. For example, data produced by medical practitioners tend to be more sensitive than the logs auto-generated by an executing software application. Therefore, the information on the source and target of the data is often included as part of the metadata of the data. The metadata also contribute to the variety of the data, in addition to the data itself. By isolating and segregating various types and qualities of data, data can be stored in a more compact manner and transferred more efficiently.

12.1.2 *Volatility in Big Data*

Frequent and rapid changes in data and its dynamic nature are emphasized as the volatility in Big Data. The change in data can be a change in contextual meaning, quality, state, and other custom data- or domain-specific modifications. The Big Data analytics platforms should be scalable and high performant to handle the volatile data real time. Moreover, each tenant may have specific requirements on how long the data should be kept in the servers. Volatility requirements of Big Data thus can be mandated by SLAs, where the data should be evicted beyond a certain time frame to ensure privacy, correctness, and other legal requirements. Any data analysis should be performed abiding to such time limits.

Big Data workflows also need to be executed within a certain time frame for the results to be useful. For example, a weather prediction workflow may take a considerable time to complete. Nevertheless, it should return the results before the time that it predicts the weather for. In other words, "predicting" weather for a time frame and returning the results after the certain time frame has passed is meaningless.

---

[1]dicom.nema.org/.

The output should be returned within the time frame and any intermediate data cached locally should be discarded afterwards for the sake of storage efficiency and privacy. Thus, volatility is often mandated by the nature of the execution.

Data validity depends on volatility, as beyond a certain period of time, data may become invalid. Correctness of data depends on the time since the data was produced and the nature of the data as well as the data processing workflows. Therefore, accuracy is a time function with an expiry time, as data may become dirty, invalid, less usable, or unusable with time. The volatility requirements are further driven by the privacy concerns. Data analytics and storage should be bound to these requirements, evicting any data beyond the specified time limit as invalid, if cannot be cleaned or transformed.

12.1.3 Validity and veracity in Big Data

Validity defines the correctness of the data. Data is integrated from various sources and stored in Big Data platforms such as data warehouses. These data platforms may host a share of invalid data, either by loading invalid data directly from a data source, or at the time of integration where valid data taken from multiple data sources become invalid in the integrated data repository at the given context. Invalid data makes the data analytic workflows expensive as it introduces a mandatory requirement of quality checks or increases the frequency and/or complexity of the existing data cleaning workflows. Invalid data may also be a result of data leakage where data of other tenants is taken out of scope or beyond their intended audience. Invalid data needs to be evicted to prevent wrong outcomes getting returned by the data execution workflows.

Presence of expired data reduces the correctness or validity and the overall quality or veracity of the data repository. This makes the volatility requirements a prerequisite for validity and veracity of Big Data. While validity is a correctness measure, veracity is a data quality measure. Hence, validity assumes a Boolean value per entry, either valid or invalid data, whereas veracity remains a continuous parameter. As data comes from multiple sources and formats, data quality may be reduced upon the integration. While invalid data may be an expired data that needs to be evicted, low veracity in data needs to be cleaned rather than being removed. Overall, data sources consisting of invalid, expired, or dirty data should be cleaned for a correct execution.

Veracity defines the trustworthiness or certainty of data while variety defines the diversity of data. Thus, validity is an absolute requirement for veracity. As the variety of Big Data increases, it gets harder to maintain certainty of data, as data comes in various formats, from various sources. Hence, variety and veracity are related to each other, where variety is often a defining character of veracity.

12.1.4 Visibility in Big Data

Cloud data centers and platforms are used by various users of multiple roles. To ensure an unobstructed usage of the platform by multiple tenants without interfering with each other, the platforms are designed with relevant abstraction and encapsulation of data. Thus, privacy is not compromised while providing multiple users with the same level of service through the multitenant architecture.

Multitenancy in Big Data platforms is defined by the visibility of data, as the data should be accessible only to the relevant audience. While having protected access to data, the storage media is often shared among the tenants. Big Data platforms should be protected and secured against unauthorized accesses. Visibility of data across the various data consumers is ensured along with privacy and multitenancy of Big Data platforms. In addition, analytic frameworks should have limited and protected visibility to the data without exposing the sensitive or private data. Various properties of data, such as storage efficiency, transportation over the network, and data characteristics should be visible to the Big Data analysis frameworks. Preserving the privacy of the tenant data contents will encourage and facilitate data producers to share them more willingly with data center administrators or service providers for data analytics, management, and optimization of the overall platform, network, or data center.

Visibility is highly related to authorization and authentication to the Big Data platform, in giving access to its contents. In addition, it also defines how data can be analyzed without compromising privacy. For example, sensitive data should be anonymized before the data is made visible to the data analysis platforms. Volatility, validity, and veracity determine performance, correctness, and accuracy of Big Data platforms, while visibility determines the privacy and access control of the data. Variety supports heterogeneity and multimodality in data and data sources.

12.2 SDN for other Vs of Big Data

SDN advocates a centralized control of the distributed data plane elements. In this section, we will illustrate how SDN can be leveraged to address the requirements of Big Data that we discussed in Section 12.1.

The SDN controller in an enterprise data center is a physically distributed cluster of high performance servers, albeit being logically centralized. Therefore, the controller is capable of handling large flows of data without causing a bottleneck, or becoming a single point of failure due to resource scarcity. Despite the volume, scale, and variety of the data flow, controller is communicated only for the control flows. Data flows happen at the data plane consisting of the switches and servers, as in any regular data centers. Thus, the controller in SDN manages to handle the large flow of Big Data efficiently, though it seems counter-intuitive as a centralized architecture. SDN has been extended for networks beyond data centers, and various architectures inspired by SDN are designed for storage, cloud, and data centers.

SDDC extends virtualization [3], SDN systems, software-defined storage [4], and middleboxes [5] to have programmable data center clouds with a better QoS. By extending the SDN paradigm to cloud, the infrastructure and platform that are the core of the cloud offerings are softwarized, making them easy to reconfigure and program through their software interfaces. There are several enterprise offerings of SDDCs such as Big Switch [6], Microsoft [7], and Plexxi [8]. Extending SDN beyond data centers, software-defined wide area network (SD-WAN) [9] offers a centralized control to manage and orchestrate a WAN, a much larger scale of networks compared to the traditional data center networks. Nuage [10] offers SDDC as well as SD-WAN.

Software-defined storage addresses the cost of scale native to the hardware-based storage solutions, following an approach inspired by SDN. VMware [11] offers SDDC and software-defined storage solutions. The increased scale and coverage of SD-WAN is significant as it supports efficient data transfer in a WAN. Combined with the support of software-defined storage, SD-WAN facilitates efficient data transfers beyond data centers. There are various software-defined storage solutions including Formation Data Systems, Hedvig, and Nexenta, and SD-WAN offerings including CloudGenix, VeloCloud, and Viptela.

12.2.1   SDN for variety of data

Data exists everywhere in various structure and storage media. Data is less useful in its native form, till it is transformed to provide valuable information. Multiple different data management systems are often necessary for analysis of data belonging to various research domains. The variety of data can influence its priority in the data transformation workflows such as data cleaning, data integration, or data transfers. Network flows in multitenant environments consist of packets of different priorities and deadlines from multiple users. Variety in Big Data can be translated into network priorities, which in turn can be managed efficiently with SDN where the network flows can be treated differently based on their priority or the tenant preferences.

Leveraging and extending recent middlebox and SDN research and developments, network flows can be tagged with custom data through a centralized controller. Thus information on SLAs, business rules, and policies can be included as custom headers with the packets. FlowTags [12] proposes an extended SDN and middlebox architecture that offers dynamic functionality to the SDN, by adding custom tags to the packets, to enforce network-wide policies, providing flow tracking capabilities. As FlowTags effectively enforces policies regardless of the presence of middleboxes that modify the flow headers in the network, an extended SDN middlebox architecture can be orthogonal to the presence of middleboxes. Furthermore, a SDN middlebox architecture with the capabilities to tag the network flows based on tenant application inputs enables a crosslayer communication between the Data-as-a-Service layer and the network layer in the Big Data platforms.

Traditionally, redundancy is viewed as either an undesirable element or a tradeoff to be exploited for reliability in storage and communication media. SDN enables research and implementation of architectures for Big Data to leverage redundancy at various levels of networking and system, to manage it without hindering the overall performance. Extended SDN architectures give the network administrators and users indirect ability to control and manage redundancy effectively for an improved QoS, by complementing the traditional network capabilities with SDN and middleboxes. Data flows can be differentiated based on the tenant preferences and the nature of the data and applications, by tagging the relevant network flows. *SMART* [13] proposes an architecture that tags the priority flows, and selectively deploys redundancy across those flows. It leverages SDN and middleboxes in partially replicating a subset of

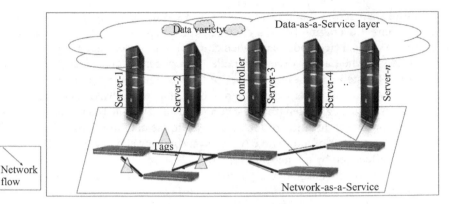

Figure 12.2   Variety-induced priority

selected flows, and hence exploiting redundancy in improving QoS of multitenant clouds, abiding to SLAs. *SMART* consists of two types of workflows—a regular workflow tags the priority flows, whereas a flow clone/divert workflow is invoked only when a policy is violated at any given SDN switch and triggers the extended SDN controller.

QoS can be guaranteed for specific tenant flows and data transformations as indicated in the application layer by the tenant applications themselves, by leveraging redundancy adaptively and selectively to adapt to the differentiated SLAs in place. Figure 12.2 depicts how data variety in Data-as-a-Service layer can be passed on to the network-as-a-service (NaaS) layer by tagging the first packet (or a subset of packets) of the network flows with metadata and other contextual information from the applications. In Online Analytical Processing (OLAP) servers, the data flows can be differentiated based on their priority, destination, or data types, which in turns is available to the switches and the SDN controller, as tags. The tags are read by the SDN controller extended with FlowTags capabilities for differentiated transfers of network flows, which belong to data of different application processes. Thus, based on the data variety, data can be ensured required separation and varying QoS guarantees at the network layer.

Though Figure 12.2 illustrates the differential treatment of network flows based on the tags inside a data center, this can further be extended to WANs, or scaled out to the Internet scale. When alternative routing paths exist in data centers and WANs — including the application scenarios such as content delivery networks (CDN) and the Internet exchange points (IXP)—they can be leveraged to route the data flows. Hence, the variety in data and data producers and consumers can be incorporated in offering a differentiated QoS at the network level.

12.2.2   SDN for volatility of data

To cope up with the increasing volatility of Big Data, executions and data transformations often need to be distributed to multiple parallel paths. Complex eScience workflows span across the globe, invoking services deployed in multiple geographical locations. Leveraging SDN, a data transformation workflow can be distributed to multiple web service nodes as service compositions and executed in parallel. This further assists when a few execution nodes or services in a data analytics platform becomes congested with a large number of service requests on the fly. Effectiveness of such service composition strategies based on SDN or SD-WAN depends on multiple factors including the length of the congestion in the route (how many nodes and links are congested), location of the congestion in the default network flow transfer path, and the number of alternative routes available between any two nodes—which is heavily influenced by the network topology.

Large scale Big Data analytics platforms can be designed as a composition of services. Data analytics with Internet-of-Things (IoT) devices comprise communication of a large number of sensors and actuators, in the Internet scale. If a service in an analytics platform is critical for various operations, it can be deployed in multiple servers inside a single data center network or in multiple geo-distributed data centers. Hence, the execution can be dynamically routed toward the service deployment, offering a load balancing to the service deployments. Leveraging the locality information readily available in the SDN-based approaches, distribution of service invocations is made bandwidth and cost efficient compared to a network-agnostic distributed execution that has limited or no knowledge of the underlying network deployment.

Locality data retrieved from SDN control plane can be leveraged for a quick virtual data integration of volatile data. Instead of integrating the entire data, the queries can load data dynamically from multiple sources, while constructing a partially replicated distributed data warehouse on the fly. Thus, volatile data can be virtually integrated to quickly produce and share the results among the peers. Such a partially replicated distributed data warehouse enables quick loading of volatile data before the data becomes invalid. This also facilitates easier eviction of expired or invalid data, since redundant copies are avoided unlike in the regular data warehouses where data is integrated and stored for a much longer time.

By leveraging network approaches such as Multiprotocol Label Switching (MPLS) [14], SLAs can be ensured to a certain extent in a WAN. SD-WAN leverages SDN to orchestrate various networks in a WAN, and support flow with various software-defined networks. SD-WAN transfers data between geographically distributed data centers using MPLS, long-term evolution (LTE), or broadband. Leveraging multi-wave length networks, SD-WAN achieves higher throughput and lower latency [9]. This enables volatile data to be handled well within the SLAs and time limits in a WAN.

The topology of network formed by the switches is referred as the network fabric. Presence of the network fabric supported by SDN can provide information on locality. Hence, distributed data warehouses are built and queried in an efficient manner. Instead of storing all the data integration in-house, data science researchers may share the data, which they have integrated amongst each others, on the same interests. If the integrated data is not present in the integrated data repository in a tenant's deployment, a colocated integrated data repository of another tenant will be accessed. The locality information retrieved from the network control plane ensures that closest neighbor is accessed. Hence, SDN can offer the best of both worlds on a high throughput similar to having an entire warehouse in-house, while offering storage efficiency of keeping minimal data in the storage.

12.2.3 SDN for validity and veracity of data

Validity of data can be confirmed and ensured with an additional overhead of a selective redundancy in the Big Data analytics platforms. The redundant bits can be leveraged to ensure correctness and validity of data. While the redundancy increases the volume of already large Big Data, validity and veracity can be ensured with minimal redundancy through efficient data-aware networks. Storage overhead caused by such redundancy can be ignored as storage is increasingly becoming cheaper. Furthermore, by leveraging commodity hardware through distributed file systems such as Hadoop Distributed File System and in-memory data grid platforms such as Infinispan and Hazelcast, storage and memory become more abundantly available.

The network distance between the physical node that hosts the data segment and the node that performs a data transformation workflow or execution may cause a bandwidth overhead due to data transfers between the nodes. This cannot be ignored unlike the storage overhead, as bandwidth is still scarce and expensive. The bandwidth overhead depends on multiple factors, including the data center topology, size of the network, and average length between any execution node pair in the network. Hence, the overall network information available to the controller can be utilized to ensure that the data is deployed respecting the colocated servers or data centers to minimize communication and coordination overheads, while executing data validity and veracity workflows. Execution is sent to the data from the nearest execution server, instead of pulling the data to the execution nodes. Thus, communication overhead is further minimized.

Quality checks such as near duplicate detection and ensuring data correctness should be done when constructing a data warehouse during the data loading phase, or periodically in iterations in existing data warehouses. Such data quality workflows lead to memory-heavy executions with a large execution time. Hence, the data quality workflows in Big Data platforms can be executed in in-memory data grid platforms instead of running in a single server, or directly on the storage itself. Enriched by the global network awareness of SDN controller, the data quality frameworks can scale seamlessly when required, minimizing the bandwidth overheads by keeping the related data objects closer. This enables an adaptive and context aware scaling out of the data cleaning workflows.

Typical data integration approaches used in-house for constructing data warehouses are not always suitable for data integration in much larger scale, or for integrating data from multiple online data sources. Not all the data in the chosen remote data sources is relevant for any research study. Study-specific researches require integration of only a well-defined set of data. Due to these limitations in the existing approaches to selectively load, integrate, analyze, and share data from distributed data sources, researchers often manually download selected sets of data of interest from the sources and integrate them in-house for their research studies. The researchers share the integrated data later with their peers. To automate this tedious integration process, data quality workflows need to be executed periodically in the integrated data repository to avoid duplicate or invalid data. The integrated data should be shared considering the locality to better utilize the bandwidth. SDN can be exploited in both the periodic data quality workflows as well as the bandwidth-aware sharing of the integrated data. Thus, SDN supports data integration and sharing with minimal redundancy and bandwidth consumption in the integrated data sets.

12.2.4   SDN for visibility of data

SDN was introduced with the promise of increased visibility to the network from the controller that controls the network. Visibility and management offered by SDN aid constructing large-scale networks and scaling them without making them unmanageable and complex. In addition to the enhanced control, visibility of the network (including control and details on switches, flows, and policies), supports innovation in the networks domain. While the underlying data center topology and network parameters can easily be monitored by the SDN controllers, Big Data visibility is more than what is addressed by a SDN controller. Avi Vantage [15] extends and leverages SDN, OpenStack, and container technologies to offer application insights. Thus it offers software-defined load balancing and automation to the data centers, along with application insights and enhanced visibility.

By exploiting flow table rules and middleboxes, various tenant data flows can be differentiated to have a controlled or partial visibility and performance guarantees in a data center network. The data flows can be monitored at the network and transport layers by leveraging SDN. NaaS [16] approach offers application-specific network services, in contrast to traditional application-agnostic approaches. Tenants may deploy services specific to them or specific to certain applications into the network. Through isolation of the execution space, NaaS allows tenant-specific network flows that do not hinder the performance of other NaaS and non-NaaS tenants. Visibility to the network plane and data isolation are achieved by leveraging programmable routers, SDN for the network control, and middleboxes for packet processing.

Network traffic flow monitoring systems such as OF@TEIN (OpenFlow@Trans Eurasia Information Network) [17] allow monitoring the network statics through visualizations. The real-time monitoring and statistics of small (mouse) and large (elephant) flows give visibility into the multitenant data, necessary to control the data flow, without being detrimental to the performance or privacy. OF@TEIN flow monitoring system builds upon Floodlight [18] SDN controller's northbound and offers a real-time visibility across the flows using Graphite dashboard. Since Big Data platforms mostly consist of a large number of elephant flows, overhead caused by per-flow statistics reporting at the network level is marginal. SDN and network traffic monitoring platforms limit statistics and monitoring to network level. They are incapable of monitoring the higher level parameters such as service requests served or the service requests currently executing, as they are agnostic to the applications that execute atop the network. Network traffic monitoring approaches should be integrated and extended with service, application, or data level monitoring and health statistics, with the help of SDN northbound integrated to the Big Data application.

Scientific Big Data workflows consist of data movement between data centers in geographically dispersed research labs. To avoid the bottlenecks introduced by the campus networks, parallel cyber infrastructures should be built for these data-intensive research network flows. The approach of using a dedicated network infrastructure for research data transfers is known as De-militarized Zones (DMZs) [19] of scientific data flows. SDN and OpenFlow [20] have been leveraged in building such research DMZs. Network monitoring on the DMZs requires protected access to the data flow in the WAN, comprising of on-demand and/or real-time data movements between remote collaborators. Hence, data analytics and eScience workflows are given special routing and data transfer paths, bypassing the firewalls and policies set up for regular in-bound and out-bound traffic to and from the research labs' data centers.

12.2.5 More Vs into Big Data

In addition to the Vs that, we discuss primarily in this chapter, there have been a few more Vs identified recently as deciding factors of Big Data. These include variability, visualization, and vulnerability. Interestingly, more and more attributes are identified to define Big Data and are fondly made to fit the group of "Vs." These attributes are often supported by SDN through its performance and scalability, following the same architectures that we discuss for the "other Vs in Big Data." By design, OpenFlow and other SDN protocols do not hinder the Big Data adoption. For example, vulnerability associated with Big Data is not significantly influenced by the SDN adoption.

Visualization defines how the Big Data should be able to be visualized, through a web service, RESTful, or a graphical user interface such as a web or a stand-alone application. While scaling is traditionally associated with the back ends, front ends also need to scale for complexity and number of terminals. The complexities and limitations in scaling the front end can easily be mitigated through a separation of the front ends from the cluster of back end, as in a client–server or a web service architecture. This approach facilitates the server to scale without tightly coupling itself to the visualization framework. This also permits multiple front ends to concurrently display the Big Data analytics outcomes, hence breaking the workload of the back end or server-side evenly among the clients.

Figure 12.3 illustrates a SDN-based architecture for Big Data visualization. The network fabric is the core of the network. Various servers are connected to the network fabric, which is coordinated by the SDN controller. Adapting web services architecture for Big Data analytics and visualization, we can separate it into a scalable distributed architecture. The SDN controller ensures that the front end and back end servers that serve the web service requests respect the data locality. The web service registry consists of all the service installations and thin clients/terminals. The storage/execution cluster consists of multiple nodes that contribute to the storage and execution of the service. The thin clients offer visualization to the Big Data applications and workflows. The servers and clients communicate through web service

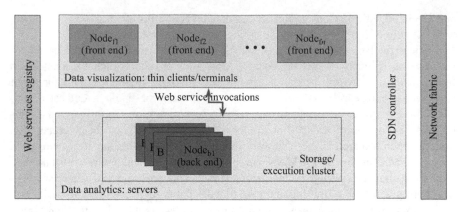

Figure 12.3   Big Data visualization with SDN

invocations assisted by SDN to ensure that minimal bandwidth overhead and communication delay are caused by the distributed architecture. Thus, this enables scaling of the Big Data visualization.

Variability defines the dynamic nature of Big Data, how the data changes itself and its model. This also refers to the inconsistencies in how fast data is loaded, and how it is loaded. Moreover, the definition of each object may change over time, per the nature of Big Data. The performance of ensuring variability in a distributed platform depends on the horizontal scalability, as with the case of veracity and volatility. Hence, ensuring data locality assisted by SDN is also beneficial for variability.

Due to the high volume of data, a security breach in Big Data may lead to a higher cost, adhering to the scale of economics. The larger amount of data often leads to an increased interest among the attackers, as in a honeypot. This property of Big Data is coined as vulnerability of Big Data. While SDN does not attempt to enhance the security of network or data plane, it does not introduce any new vulnerability into the system by design. Bad implementations of a centralized control may cause further vulnerabilities in the Big Data access as a single point of failure. However, this is an implementation challenge rather than a SDN issue.

12.3   SDN for Big Data diversity

SDN enables architectural enhancements for network flows allocation, routing, and control, which can be leveraged in data-centric applications and data centers. By exploiting OpenFlow rules, network flows can be discriminated based on their priority or other metadata attached by the tenants to the packets as indicated by the applications executing in the hosts/servers of the data center network.

12.3.1   Use cases for SDN in heterogeneous Big Data

The recent advancements in networks and systems research blur the distinction across the layers in the OSI model [21]. SDN provides a southbound API to communicate the control plane decisions to the data plane through protocols such as OpenFlow. Moreover, it defines a northbound API that is responsible for communicating and coordinating across the network control plane and the application layer. Thus, SDN offers flexibility and configurability to data center networks across multiple layers. This offers a coordination of data from the network control plane.

Software and hardware middleboxes provide specific custom functions and important features crucial to the enterprise data centers and clouds, such as load balancing, policy control, and security aspects in the data center networks [22]. They offer various functionalities to the Big Data frameworks such as firewalls, throttling, and access control. Hence, they cannot be eliminated from the data center networks. Research proposes efficient architectures to mitigate the potential overheads imposed by the middleboxes [5], and seamless middlebox deployments are enabled by SDN. Middleboxes can be part of a SDN architecture, exploiting the centralized control offered by SDN. Leveraging SDN, SIMPLE [23] offers efficient policy enforcement for middleboxes. Slick [24] proposes a control plane for middleboxes, extending the SDN paradigm and architecture to network middleboxes. Convergence of middleboxes and SDN [25] has provided many advantages including flexibility in middlebox placement, effective failure handling, scalability, and efficient policy enforcement. A network architecture consisting of SDN and middleboxes can be leveraged for an efficient extraction, transformation, loading, storage, transfer, management, and analysis of Big Data, in a secured and load balanced manner.

The model-driven service abstraction layer (MD-SAL) of OpenDaylight [26] controller implements a SDN framework following the Model-Driven Software Engineering principles. MD-SAL can be leveraged in integrating the controller extensions and middlebox controllers into OpenDaylight. Due to the loose coupling in the design, many extended SDN architectures can be made to work with other controllers with minimal changes in design. As another OSGi [27]-based OpenFlow controller, ONOS [28] may also be used to host OpenDaylight-based controller extensions with minimal to no changes for SDN Big Data applications. Algorithmic enhancements and extensions are deployed similarly in OSGi-based SDN controllers such as OpenDaylight and ONOS. The control plane components are developed as OSGi bundles and deployed in Apache Karaf [29] OSGi container, which is the core of these two SDN controllers. Due to their modular architecture, ability to customize and extend without modifying the code base of their core, strong industry backing, and the support from the Linux Foundation, OpenDaylight, and ONOS have been chosen as the primary controller in various enterprise-grade telecommunication frameworks.

12.3.2 *Architectures for variety and quality of data*

Enterprise clouds and data centers are designed to offer high-availability and fault-tolerance. Data locality in the networks is further driven by geopolitical and customer requirements. Data should be transferred abiding to the SLAs and customer policies. The complex customer requirements drive innovation in various levels from cloud middleware platforms to data center network topologies. Efficient and high performance network topologies such as small world data centers [30] are researched for the specific characteristics and requirements of the data center. Given the domain knowledge of data-centric big service deployments, custom topologies can be built to cater to the nature of the data flows. Traffic engineering research builds resilient architectures and proposes optimal approaches in failure detection and recovery on networks, which can be leveraged to ensure volatility and veracity in Big Data.

Network topology consisting of the network switches is collectively offered as a network fabric, where the components transfer data between them through interconnecting switches. With a multitenant controller deployment to control and orchestrate the network fabric, network can be virtually isolated and managed for multiple tenants. Offering multitenancy in network space, controllers hence enable scalability and enhanced control. Dynamic network fabrics can have their topologies dynamically configured, instead of a fixed hardwired network topology and configuration. Thus, SDN controllers orchestrating network fabrics make SDN adoption easier in data center and WANs.

eScience workflows consist of geographically distributed web-service deployments. Hence, they can be expressed as a service composition of various service deployments. Multiple implementations and deployments exist for the same service; each of these should be leveraged to avoid overloading any given service node. Such load balancing is made easy with software-defined approaches that exploit the global knowledge of service deployments available at the Data-as-a-Service layer, including the web-service engines and web-service registries, as well as at the network layer, such as the SDN control plane. Software-defined service composition thus aims to offer scalable and resilient service composition at global scale with congestion control at the service deployments and load balancing at the execution paths. Mayan [31] demonstrates how data quality workflows can be scaled out, improved and optimized for performance by componentizing the eScience workflows into web services and implementing a prototype of software-defined service composition.

12.3.3 QoS-aware Big Data applications

Big Data applications consist of multiple users of various roles, each executing applications of differentiated priorities that can be expressed as network flows in the network layer. Priority flows often have stricter SLA deadlines to be met. Traditional networks utilize routing algorithms that often do not consider any SLA, system policies, and user preferences. While many network flow routing algorithms exist, many of them fail to adapt to the dynamic nature of the data center and cloud networks and the enterprise requirements of their users and system. Traffic engineering approaches often are data-agnostic, and cannot dynamically change their behavior based on the data or application. To improve the efficiency of the Big Data applications, the existing traffic engineering approaches should be made data-aware. This is facilitated by the centralized access and control of the SDN controllers.

While typical network flows are smaller in scale with majority of the flows being classified as mice flows, Big Data consists of large data-heavy network flows known as the elephant flows. Therefore, SDN architectures should be adopted for elephant flows, catering the nature of network flows of Big Data applications. Due to the large fraction of elephant flows, time consumed by the flow table modifications can be neglected as data transfer takes much longer for each flow than regular network flows dominated by mice flows. Flow-level modifications to the routing tables become infrequent as each flow consists of a large number of packets in Big Data applications.

SDN research spans beyond data-center scale. Various improvements to IXPs are proposed for an efficient data transformation for Internet Service Providers (ISP) and CDNs, to scale and distribute at the Internet scale. Findings at data-center scale are currently extended to a much larger scale as research efforts. Following data center topologies, various large-scale topologies consisting of ISPs and IXPs are built. Extended SDN deployments at the Internet scale such as the software-defined Internet exchanges (SDX) [32] enable SDN to be leveraged for data transfers between the Internet regions. Bringing these different domains together gives more light to the Big Data solutions in the Internet scale.

Statistics when routing through each link in a data center can be monitored to offer fault-tolerance to the SDDC networks. Nodes or links that take much longer time to route the flows or packets than the average time to route, those who consume unconventionally large amount of energy or computing resources, or those who exhibit any other behavior that may lead to exceeding the threshold specified in the SLA, are considered to be functioning poorly, and acted upon depending on the policy action. Hence, service level guarantees can be offered based on the SLAs at the network level, instead of the typical application-agnostic network deployments. These SLA-aware data center networks can offer congestion control and load balancing among the service nodes and network paths. Moreover, economic aspects can be combined together with the service guarantees, offering higher profit to the network providers and a deadline-aware network transfers to the users. Fairness guarantees and differentiated QoS can thus be ensured in cloud and data-center deployments.

12.3.4   Multitenant SDN and data isolation

With multidomain deployments of software-defined networks, the networks can achieve isolation guarantees, offering service-aware networks. While the platforms and storage of clouds and data centers are multitenanted as in Infrastructure-as-a-Service (IaaS) and Platform-as-a-Service (PaaS), and let the tenants to use or host Software-as-a-Service (SaaS) on top of the platforms, network is often openly shared among the tenants in these environments. SDN can be leveraged to ensure that the network bandwidth is segregated based on the tenant preferences and policies; certain traffic such as mission-critical application data flows may be isolated from other bandwidth users. Such a data isolation, often mandated by the service guarantees or legal requirements, provide a virtual tenant network (VTN) for each tenant.

Leveraging SDN, research prototypes have been built to segregate the bandwidth virtually among the tenants of the network, hence offering virtual network embedding (VNE) algorithms for efficient resource allocation. ViTeNA [33] proposes and implements a VNE approach to allocate virtual networks among multitenant data centers. Such a virtual network allocation and isolation offered by ViTeNA offer enhanced privacy in tenant data and policy-based tenant network isolation. SDN thus enables a controlled visibility to a multitenant cloud or data center deployment in storing, accessing, and processing Big Data.

Figure 12.4 depicts how network can be multitenanted with the entire stack of a cloud platform. The federated deployment of controllers enables communication in the WAN while not compromising the tenant isolation at the data and network layers. CHIEF [34] designs a controller farm that builds a federated deployment of SDN controllers, enabling an intercontroller communication in a WAN with data isolation and privacy in the controller data space while offering control for data centers and clouds. It proposes community networks as a use case for such a federated controller deployment.

VTNs give the tenants control of network that is allocated to them. As multitenant networks, VTNs give a perception of having an own private network to each tenant. SDN controllers can be multitenanted themselves to control the virtual networks that belong to each tenant. OpenDaylight VTN[2] is a project that offers a multitenant virtual network deployment. Multiple controllers may be deployed as a federated controller deployment with protected access to each other to enable interdomain controller communication and coordination. These controller deployments can be completely independent while offering a controlled access to other controllers in a multidomain WAN environment. Thus traffic engineering and isolation among inter-data center traffic can be offered. Furthermore, with the global knowledge of the network, network traffic can be segregated based on the Big Data latency, throughput, or gitter. These separations allow efficient bandwidth usage while network flows with similar nature or service guarantees are colocated in the same network path.

12.4   Open issues and challenges

The scale of Big Data continues to rise beyond exascale. Controllers are logically centralized, yet physically distributed, entities. However, as the volume, variety, and velocity of Big Data increase further, the current centralized model offered by SDN and OpenFlow will certainly become a bottleneck. The on-going research efforts in SDN need to be on par with the rising dynamics of Big Data, with further innovation on protocols and implementations to match the scale and complexity of future data.

12.4.1   Scaling Big Data with SDN

Various research and industrial efforts leverage SDN for Big Data, at the data center and larger scale. While these efforts support the Vs of Big Data, there are multiple issues and challenges need to be addressed. The challenges are either those common to Big Data architectures or those specific to the SDN adaptation for Big Data. Currently, the industrial efforts are geared toward increasing the volume and velocity aspects of Big Data. Storage is getting bigger and bigger, whereas distributed execution platforms increase the efficiency of data analysis platforms to cater to the velocity

---

[2]https://github.com/opendaylight/vtn.

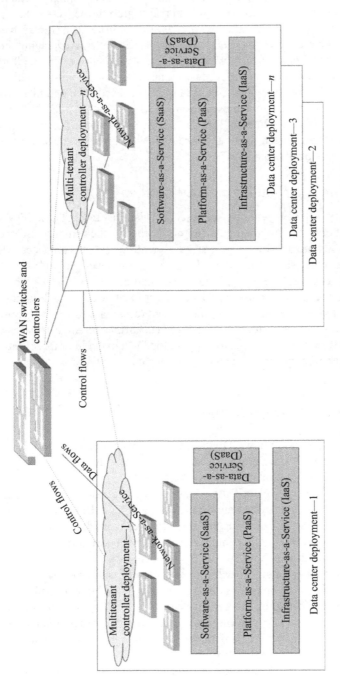

Figure 12.4 Multitenanting data centers and the network in a WAN

of Big Data. SDN-assisted enhancements to variety, volatility, validity, veracity, and visibility have significant impact on Big Data and require further research.

The research and implementation efforts at SDN and Big Data fronts have traditionally been orthogonal to each other. However, the research on leveraging them for each other is currently catching up. While there are a number of research efforts, the enterprise-level implementations on SDN integration aiming to boost the other Vs in Big Data remain relatively low. The Big Data platforms need to be optimized for efficient and locality-aware distributed execution with the assistance of SDN. Crosslayer optimizations with SDN would help Big Data in cost and carbon efficiency. The enterprise Big Data offerings need to focus more on how to leverage SDN appropriately to improve their performance and efficiency.

12.4.2   Scaling Big Data beyond data centers

To support variety, volatility, validity, veracity, and visibility in Big Data, SDN should be leveraged not only at individual data centers. Rather, as the complex eScience and Big Data workflows are distributed globally, they require design approaches extended to a much larger scale. Therefore, SDN should be further leveraged to WAN, CDNs, and the Internet for an efficient Big Data storage and processing in the global scale. IXPs may be leveraged to deploy SDN-based approaches to a much larger scale. The open challenge hence lies in how the current research efforts scale from local networks, to autonomous systems of the Internet. Further research is necessary to design and implement architectures to support Big Data in the Internet scale through the SDN-based approaches that currently exist at a data-center level.

12.5   Summary and conclusion

In this chapter, we discussed how SDN helps variety, volatility, validity, veracity, and visibility in Big Data. As the previous chapters discussed how SDN helps volume, velocity, and value in Big Data, we conveniently labeled these remaining attributes of Big Data the "other Vs in Big Data." We discussed research and industrial SDN approaches and architectures that help offer these other Vs in Big Data. We discussed background and related work for each of the attributes individually, and also collectively how multitenant SDN data center architectures support QoS, data quality, and diversity in Big Data applications.

SDN supports an efficient distributed execution of data processing workflows, with adaptive scaling. The awareness of data locality ensures bandwidth efficiency. This improves the performance of workflows ensuring Big Data validity and veracity. Faster executions ensure that volatile data is handled in a timely manner. Critical network flows belonging to volatile data can be given higher priority, enabling faster flow completion time for volatile data flows.

Leveraging SDN from the application plane, network flows can be tagged to represent the heterogeneous data. Hence, Big Data variety is ensured in a multitenanted environment with differentiated QoS for various data types or data flow origin and destination. Such a SDN architecture facilitates overall management view of the data center network without leaking the sensitive tenant data. In addition to controlled visibility of data to the relevant tenant, SDN offers monitoring capabilities for the data flows.

There are a set of challenges to be addressed to fully achieve a SDN-enabled platform for Big Data. Large-scale Big Data frameworks consist of data storage, execution, and flow between data centers, spanning a WAN. Big Data platforms also give rise to data-centric big services where the data is exposed and consumed through web service interfaces in an online deployment. SD-WAN brings SDN to WAN, as an interdomain controller network. Scaling up SDN from data centers to the Internet scale, bringing SDN close to IXP, is one of the many approaches that will enable SDN support Big Data at an even larger extent. The vast amount of research in Big Data, SDN, software-defined systems, and other related topics will certainly mitigate the open issues and challenges in fully achieving SDN-based approaches and architectures for Big Data inside and beyond data centers.

References

[1]   Fichera, R., Washburn, D., and Chi, E.: The software-defined data center is the future of infrastructure architecture. Forrester Research, Cambridge, MA (2012).

[2]   Buyya, R., Calheiros, R.N., Son, J., Dastjerdi, A.V., and Yoon, Y.: Software-defined cloud computing: Architectural elements and open challenges. In: Advances in Computing, Communications and Informatics (ICACCI, 2014 International Conference on, IEEE (2014) 1–12.

[3]   Chowdhury, N.M.K., and Boutaba, R.: A survey of network virtualization. Computer Networks **54**(5) (2010) 862–876.

[4]   Thereska, E., Ballani, H., O'Shea, G., *et al.*: Ioflow: a software-defined storage architecture. In: Proceedings of the Twenty-Fourth ACM Symposium on Operating Systems Principles, ACM (2013) 182–196.

[5]   Walfish, M., Stribling, J., Krohn, M.N., Balakrishnan, H., Morris, R., and Shenker, S.: Middleboxes no longer considered harmful. In: OSDI. Volume 4. (2004) 15.

[6]   Sherwood, R.: The promise of the software defined data center: Abstraction, hyper-convergence, and dramatically increased business agility (2016) [Available at: http://www.bigswitch.com/webinar/the-promise-of-the-software-defined-data-center-abstraction-hyper-convergence-and; accessed 19-April-2017].

[7]   Microsoft: Software-defined datacenter (SDDC) – windows server 2016 (2017) [Available at: https://www.microsoft.com/en-us/cloud-platform/software-defined-datacenter; accessed 19-April-2017].

[8]   Mathews, M.: Plexxipulse – 2017 software-defined data center 50 (2017) [Available at: http://www.plexxi.com/2017/03/plexxipulse-2017-software-defined-data-center-50/; accessed 19-April-2017].

[9]   Houle, A.C., Boulianne, L.P., and Dupras, L.: SD-WAN: A technology for
       the efficient use of bandwidth in multi-wavelength networks. In: Optical
       Fiber communication/National Fiber Optic Engineers Conference, 2008.
       OFC/NFOEC 2008. Conference on, IEEE (2008) 1–10.

[10]   Nuage: Nuage networks (2017) [Available at: http://www.nuagenetworks
       .net/products/; accessed 19-April-2017].

[11]   VMware: Virtualization and the software-defined data center (2017) [Avail-
       able at: http://www.vmware.com/be/solutions/software-defined-datacenter/
       in-depth.html; accessed 19-April-2017].

[12]   Fayazbakhsh, S.K., Chiang, L., Sekar, V., Yu, M., and Mogul, J.C.: Enforcing
       network-wide policies in the presence of dynamic middlebox actions using
       flowtags. In: Proc. USENIX NSDI. (2014).

[13]   Kathiravelu, P., and Veiga, L.: Selective redundancy in network-as-a-service:
       Differentiated QoS in multi-tenant clouds. In: OTM Confederated Interna-
       tional Workshops: On the Move to Meaningful Internet Systems, Springer
       (2016) 10 pages.

[14]   Davie, B.S., and Rekhter, Y.: MPLS: technology and applications. Morgan
       Kaufmann Publishers Inc., Massachusetts (2000).

[15]   Avi: Application services in any data center or cloud (2017) [Available at:
       https://avinetworks.com/; accessed 19-April-2017].

[16]   Costa, P.: Bridging the gap between applications and networks in data centers.
       ACM SIGOPS Operating Systems Review **47**(1) (2013) 3–8.

[17]   Rehman, S.U., Song, W.C., and Kang, M.: Network-wide traffic visibility in
       OF@TEIN SDN testbed using sflow. In: Network Operations and Management
       Symposium (APNOMS), 2014 16th Asia-Pacific, IEEE (2014) 1–6.

[18]   Wallner, R., and Cannistra, R.: An SDN approach: quality of service using big
       switches floodlight open-source controller. Proceedings of the Asia-Pacific
       Advanced Network **35** (2013) 14–19.

[19]   Debroy, S., Calyam, P., and Dickinson, M.: Orchestrating science DMZS for
       big data acceleration: Challenges and approaches. In: Networking for Big
       Data. Chapman and Hall/CRC, Boca Raton, FL (2015) 3–26.

[20]   McKeown, N., Anderson, T., Balakrishnan, H., *et al.*: Openflow: enabling
       innovation in campus networks. ACM SIGCOMM Computer Communication
       Review **38**(2) (2008) 69–74.

[21]   Briscoe, N.: Understanding the OSI 7-layer model. PC Network Advisor
       120(2) (2000).

[22]   Joseph, D.A., Tavakoli, A., and Stoica, I.: A policy-aware switching layer
       for data centers. ACM SIGCOMM Computer Communication Review **38**(4)
       (2008) 51–62.

[23]   Qazi, Z.A., Tu, C.C., Chiang, L., Miao, R., Sekar, V., and Yu, M.: Simplifying
       middlebox policy enforcement using SDN. ACM SIGCOMM Computer
       Communication Review **43**(4) (2013) 27–38.

[24]   Anwer, B., Benson, T., Feamster, N., Levin, D., and Rexford, J.: A slick
       control plane for network middleboxes. In: Proceedings of the second ACM

SIGCOMM workshop on Hot topics in software defined networking, ACM (2013) 147–148.

[25] Qazi, Z., Tu, C.C., Miao, R., Chiang, L., Sekar, V., and Yu, M.: Practical and incremental convergence between SDN and middleboxes. Open Network Summit, Santa Clara, CA (2013).

[26] Medved, J., Varga, R., Tkacik, A., and Gray, K.: Opendaylight: Towards a model-driven SDN controller architecture. In: 2014 IEEE 15th International Symposium on, IEEE (2014) 1–6.

[27] Alliance, O.: OSGi service platform, release 3. IOS Press, Inc., San Ramon, CA (2003).

[28] Berde, P., Gerola, M., Hart, J., *et al.*: ONOS: towards an open, distributed SDN OS. In: Proceedings of the third workshop on Hot topics in software defined networking, ACM (2014) 1–6.

[29] Nierbeck, A., Goodyear, J., Edstrom, J., and Kesler, H.: Apache Karaf Cookbook. Packt Publishing Ltd., Birmingham, United Kingdom (2014).

[30] Shin, J.Y., Wong, B., and Sirer, E.G.: Small-world datacenters. In: Proceedings of the 2nd ACM Symposium on Cloud Computing, ACM (2011) 2.

[31] Kathiravelu, P., Grbac, T.G., and Veiga, L.: Building blocks of Mayan: Componentizing the eScience workflows through software-defined service composition. In: Web Services (ICWS), 2016 IEEE International Conference on, IEEE (2016) 372–379.

[32] Gupta, A., MacDavid, R., Birkner, R., *et al.*: An industrial-scale software defined internet exchange point. In: 13th USENIX Symposium on Networked Systems Design and Implementation (NSDI 16), USENIX Association (2016) 1–14.

[33] Caixinha, D., Kathiravelu, P., and Veiga, L.: Vitena: An SDN-based virtual network embedding algorithm for multi-tenant data centers. In: Network Computing and Applications (NCA), 2016 IEEE 15th International Symposium on, IEEE (2016) 140–147.

[34] Kathiravelu, P., and Veiga, L.: Chief: Controller farm for clouds of software-defined community networks. In: Cloud Engineering Workshop (IC2EW), 2016 IEEE International Conference on, IEEE (2016) 1–6.

Chapter 13

SDN helps Big Data to optimize storage

Ali R. Butt*, Ali Anwar*, and Yue Cheng*,**

Distributed key-value stores have become the sine qua non for supporting today's large-scale web services. The extreme latency and throughput requirements of modern web applications are driving the use of distributed in-memory object caches. Similarly, the use of persistent object stores has been growing rapidly as they combine key advantages such as HTTP-based RESTful APIs, high availability, elasticity with a pay-as-you-go pricing model that allows applications to scale as needed. Consequently, there is an urgent need for optimizing the emerging software defined cloud datacenters to efficiently support such applications at scale. In this chapter, we discuss different techniques to optimize the Big Data processing and data management using key-value stores and software defined networks in virtualized cloud datacenters. Specifically, we explore two key questions. (1) How do cloud services users, i.e., tenants, get the most bang-for-the-buck with a distributed in-memory key-value store deployment in a shared multitenant environment? (2) How do tenants enhance cloud object store's capabilities through fine-grained resource management to effectively meet their SLAs while maximizing resource efficiency? Moreover, we also present the state of the art in this domain and provide a brief analysis of desirable features. We then demonstrate through experiments the impact of SDN-based Big Data storage management solution on improving performance and overall resource efficiency. Finally, we discuss open issues in SDN-based Big Data I/O stacks and future directions.

13.1 Software defined key-value storage systems for datacenter applications

Distributed key-value stores/caches have become the sine qua non for supporting today's large-scale web services [1,2]. Memcached [3,4], a prominent in-memory key-value cache, has an impressive list of users including Facebook, Wikipedia, Twitter, and YouTube. It can scale to hundreds of nodes, and in most cases, services more than 90% of database-backed queries for high performance I/Os. With the growth of cloud platforms and services, in-memory caching solutions have also found their

*Department of Computer Science, Virginia Tech, USA
**Department of Computer Science, George Mason University, USA

way into both public and private clouds. In fact, cloud service providers, such as Amazon, IBM Cloud, and Google App Engine, already support in-memory caching as a service. Amazon's ElastiCache [5] is an automated Memcached deployment and management service widely used by cloud-scale web applications, e.g., Airbnb and TicketLeap.

Similarly, the use of cloud object stores has been growing rapidly in recent years as they combine key advantages such as HTTP-based RESTful APIs, high availability, elasticity with a "pay-as-you-go" pricing model that allows applications to scale as needed. Cloud object stores, such as Amazon S3 [6], Google Cloud Store (GCS) [7], OpenStack Swift [8], and Ceph [9], have become the most widely used form of cloud storage in recent years. These stores combine key advantages such as high availability, elasticity and a "pay-as-you-go" pricing model, which allows applications to scale as the usage increases or decreases, and offers HTTP-based RESTful APIs for easy data management. The desirable features, coupled with the advances in virtualization infrastructure, are driving the adoption of cloud object stores by a myriad of applications. Examples range from web applications that store image and video files [10], to backup services that require large capacity for archival data [11], to Big Data analytics frameworks [12]. Similarly, object stores are increasingly being adopted by the HPC community as they provide efficient metadata management and scalability that helps in extreme-scale high-end computing, and allows for seamless adaptation to a wide range of general purpose and scientific computing file system workloads.

13.2   Related work, features, and shortcomings

A typical deployment of cloud object stores either opts to use a monolithic configuration or segmented storage setup [13] with a static configuration to handle different types of applications with evolving requirements. Using a monolithic configuration setup results in all applications experiencing the same service level, e.g., similar average latency per request, data transfer throughput, and queries per second (QPS).

From the cloud provider's perspective, supporting dramatically different workloads from different applications/users (tenants) through a single homogeneous configuration means that many optimization opportunities are lost. Each different application represents a workload with different characteristics. For example, a photo sharing application such as Instagram would have a large number of small–medium-sized files (e.g., kB- to MB-level image objects), with skewed access pattern where frequent read and write requests go for hotter/popular objects. In contrast, an enterprise backup application (e.g., Arq [14]) consists largely of write requests for large cold archive files with reads only sparsely arising. Using a homogeneous configuration prevents fine-tuning of the system to such varied needs and reduces overall system efficiency.

The situation is further exasperated by the fact that due to regular system upgrades and introduction of new storage architectures, datacenters hosting the object stores are becoming increasingly heterogeneous [15,16]. However, with either the

Table 13.1   Different types of workloads and application scenarios used for testing the behavior of object stores. G: GET operation; P: PUT operation; D: DELETE operation

Workload	Workload characteristics		App. scenario
	Obj. size	Operation distribution	
A	1–128 kB	G: 90%, P: 5%, D:5%	Web hosting
B	1–128 kB	G: 5%, P: 90%, D:5%	Online game hosting
C	1–128 MB	G: 90%, P: 5%, D:5%	Online video sharing
D	1–128 MB	G: 5%, P: 90%, D:5%	Enterprise backup

"one-size-fits-all" monolithic deployment or static storage segmentation policy driven partitioning, it is impossible to match specific types of hardware with the right type of application workload. For example, latency-sensitive small-object workloads would require low-latency storage devices and powerful CPU processing capacity, whereas large object write-only workloads can be supported with a combination of high network bandwidth across all layers (e.g., load balancer, proxy, object servers, etc.) and weaker CPU power. Under these scenarios, meeting SLA requirement for one of the workloads may require (1) adding hardware resources that may not improve the performance for other workloads and (2) software tuning that may decrease the performance for other workloads. Furthermore, the workloads seen by the object store are varied and fluctuate over time. Consider a scenario where the workload demand from one application (tenant) is spiking while the demand from another application that shares the same object store resources is dipping. In this situation, static policies need to be updated based on the changes experienced in the workload. This calls for a new object store architecture that can dynamically perform resource provisioning for driving online reconfiguration across multiple partitions of the object store.

13.2.1   Shortcomings

To motivate our approach and demonstrate the need for differentiated object stores, we study different types of representative practical workloads as follows. We examine four different real-world applications that use cloud object storage as listed in Table 13.1. We deploy and evaluate OpenStack Swift in a multitenant environment using COSBench [17] as workload generator configured for the four types of studied workloads. Swift is a popular object store implementation provided by OpenStack that is increasingly becoming the de facto cloud computing software platform. In these tests, we use three different Swift configurations (setups). We run COSBench clients on designated machines to saturate Swift. Each benchmark is run for 15 min after all data is loaded into the store. We use two nodes as proxy servers in each of the configuration. To simulate datacenter heterogeneity, one of the proxy server has 32 cores while the other has 8 cores. The proxy server running on the 32-core machine is connected to the storage nodes via 1-Gbps interconnect, while the proxy server on the 8-core machine is connected via 10-Gbps interconnect. In addition, four 32-core machines are used as storage nodes. Each storage node has 3 SATA SSDs. The storage nodes are well endowed and configured in such a way so as not to become a performance bottleneck for any of the studied configurations.

13.2.1.1   Default configuration

The default monolithic Swift setup is used where both 8-core and 32-core machines acted as proxy server. The workloads are handled by all resources and round robin DNS was used to distribute the requests to the proxies.

13.2.1.2   FavorsSmall configuration

The available resources are divided into two subobject stores, one configured for workloads with small objects and the other for large objects. One 8-core machine (connected via 10 Gbps) served as proxy for WorkloadA and WorkloadB, and another 32-core machine connected via 1-Gbps network served WorkloadC and WorkloadD.

13.2.1.3   FavorsLarge configuration

One 32-core machine (connected via 1 Gbps) is used as proxy for WorkloadA and WorkloadB , while one 8-core machine (connected via 10 Gbps) is used as proxy for WorkloadC and WorkloadD.

Figure 13.1 shows the comparison of performance achieved under the studied configurations. As shown in Figure 13.1(a), separating proxy servers for different workloads improved the overall QPS by 700% and 225% for FavorsSmall and FavorsLarge, respectively, compared to the default Swift setup. It is interesting to note that even though FavorsSmall resulted in very high QPS for small objects of (WorkloadA and WorkloadB), it is not the best configuration as it significantly affects the MB/s (dropped by from 350% to 500%, as observed in Figure 13.1(b)) for workloads dominated with large object (WorkloadC and WorkloadD). On the other hand, in FavorsLarge the throughput for large objects remained same.

Similarly, the latency of FavorsLarge is also less than that achieved by the default configuration for all the workloads (Figure 13.1(c)). FavorsSmall provides best and worst latency for small and large object workloads, respectively. We also observe that switching to different network connections on proxy servers in Default configuration results in similar results. These results demonstrate the need for a comprehensive study of the impact of different configurations on performance to ensure efficient cloud object store design. From our experiments, we infer the following: (1) Cloud object store workloads can be classified based on the size of the objects in their workloads. In case of small objects, cloud tenants are mostly interested in QPS and latency, whereas for large objects data throughput is considered more important. (2) When multiple tenants run workloads with drastically different behaviors, they compete for the object store resources with each other, the workload dominated with small objects experiences a dramatic loss in performance. This is because the

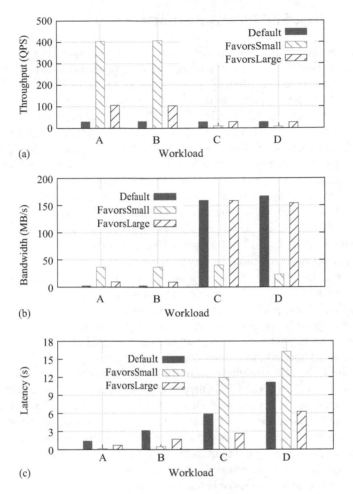

Figure 13.1 Performance achieved under various object store configurations in a multitenant environment: (a) Throughput (QPS), (b) Bandwidth (MB/s), and (c) Latency (s)

available network bandwidth is exhausted to transfer Transmission Control Protocol (TCP) packets containing payload for large objects, hence wasting the CPU power that would have been utilized to serve workloads with small objects on object storage nodes. That is why using a separate proxy server under FavorsSmall and FavorsLarge gives a fair chance to small object workloads to be properly handled by the storage nodes. Thus, cloud object stores need better resource management and dynamic support such as that enabled via modern SDNs to ensure that tenants are treated equally.

13.3   SDN-based efficient data management

A clear advantage of the cloud model is that it makes computation easy to deploy and scale. However, the vast variety of available storage services with different persistence, performance and capacity characteristics, presents unique challenges for deploying data-intensive computational tasks in the SDN-based virtualized cloud environment. For example, Google Cloud Platform provides four different storage options: ephemeral SSD (ephSSD), persistent SSD (persSSD), persistent HDD (persHDD), and software-defined object store (objStore). While ephSSD offers the highest the highest sequential and random I/O performance, it does not provide data persistence (data stored in ephSSD is lost once the associated VMs are terminated). Network-attached persistent block storage services using persHDD or persSSD as storage media are relatively cheaper than ephSSD, but offer significantly lower performance. For instance, a 500-GB persSSD volume has about $2\times$ lower throughput and $6\times$ lower IOPS than a 375-GB ephSSD volume. Finally, objStore is a RESTful object storage service providing the cheapest storage alternative and offering comparable sequential throughput to that of a large persSSD volume. Other cloud service providers, such as AWS EC2, Microsoft Azure, and HP Cloud, provide similar storage services with different performance –cost trade-offs.

The heterogeneity in cloud storage services [18–20] is further complicated by the varying types of jobs within analytics workloads, e.g., iterative applications such as K-means and Pagerank, and queries such as Join and Aggregate. For example, in map-intensive Grep, the map phase accounts for the largest part of the execution time (mostly doing I/Os), whereas CPU-intensive K-means spends most of the time performing computation. Furthermore, short-term (within hours) and long-term (daily, weekly or monthly) data reuse across jobs is common in production analytics workloads. As reported in [21], 78% of jobs in Cloudera Hadoop workloads involve data reuse. Another distinguishing feature of analytics workloads is the presence of workflows that represents interdependencies across jobs. For instance, analytics queries are usually converted to a series of batch processing jobs, where the output of one job serves as the input of the next job(s).

The above observations lead to an important question for the cloud tenants: How do I (the tenant) get the most bang-for-the-buck with data analytics storage tiering/data placement in a cloud environment with highly heterogeneous storage resources? To answer this question, we conducted a detailed quantitative analysis with a range of representative analytics jobs in the widely used Google Cloud environment. The experimental findings and observations motivate the design of a new system CAST [22], which leverages different cloud storage services and heterogeneity within jobs [19] in an analytics workload to perform cost-effective storage capacity allocation and data placement.

CAST does offline profiling of different applications (jobs) within an analytics workload and generates job performance prediction models based on different storage services. It lets tenants specify high-level objectives such as maximizing tenant utility, or minimizing deadline miss rate. CAST then uses a simulated annealing based solver that reconciles these objectives with the performance prediction models, other workload specifications and the different cloud storage service characteristics to generate a data placement and storage provisioning plan. The framework finally deploys the workload in the cloud based on the generated plan. We further enhance our basic tiering design to build CAST++, which incorporates the data reuse and workflow properties of an analytics workload. CAST consists of two major components: a job performance profiler, and a tiering solver. (1) The analytics job performance profiler module evaluates jobs execution time on different storage services using workload specifications provided by tenants. These specifications include a list of jobs, the application profiles, and the input data sizes for the jobs. The estimator combines this with compute platform information to estimate application run times on different storage services. (2) The tiering solver module uses the job execution estimates from the job performance estimator to generate a tiering plan that spans all storage tiers on the specific cloud provider available to the tenant. The objective of the solver is to satisfy the high-level tenants' goals such as achieving high utility or reducing deadline miss rates.

13.4   Rules of thumb of storage deployment in software defined datacenters

In this section, we present a detailed analysis of how object stores behave under various software and hardware configurations. Next, we use the study to develop rules-of-thumb for configuring object stores in software defined virtualized datacenters.

In the following analysis, we use a 32-core machine as a proxy node with two 32-core storage nodes each equipped with 3 SSDs (to eliminate the storage bottleneck), unless mentioned otherwise. For workloads dominated by small objects (at kB level) the metrics of interest are throughput in terms of QPS and response latency, while for workloads dominated by large objects (at MB–GB level), bandwidth in terms of MB/s or GB/s is more important.

Q1: How does object size impact performance?
First, we analyze the impact of object size on performance in terms of throughput (QPS) and bandwidth (GB/s). While QPS captures the object-wise throughput performance, the bandwidth serves as an important metric reflecting byte-wise performance. As shown in Figure 13.2(a), increasing the object size results in the throughput decreasing drastically. Specifically, when the object size is increased from 10 kB to 10 MB, we observe the increasing tendency of the network bandwidth. When the object size is increased further to above 128 MB, the bandwidth only improves marginally (from 0.97 to 0.98 GB/s), implying that the NIC is saturated. Figure 13.2(b) plots the corresponding latency distribution at each studied object size. At large object sizes (10–512 MB), the request response latency is more than 100× than that for small object sizes (10 kB–1 MB). From these tests, we can infer that, as long as the object size exceeds a certain threshold, network bandwidth becomes the limiting factor. Correspondingly, this again, explains why WorkloadA and WorkloadB achieve extremely poor performance when coexisting with WorkloadC and WorkloadD. Hence, the tests demonstrate that, in a multitenant environment with mixed workloads, individual

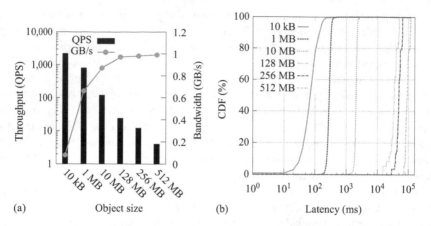

Figure 13.2   Impact of varying the object size on read performance. Note the log scale on the Y-axis of (a) (read performance) and the X-axis of (b) (read latency distribution)

workloads should be partitioned and serviced through disjoint object stores to reduce mutual interference and performance impact.

Q2: How does proxy server configuration impact performance?

Next, we study the effect of scaling proxy nodes on workload performance. We vary the computational capacity of the proxy node by increasing proxy's allotted CPU cores. Figure 13.3(a) shows the proxy tuning effect. As we increase the proxy workers in one proxy node the QPS is improved linearly until we reach 32 proxy workers. The observed CPU utilization reaches close to 85% (bounding the throughput) with both 32 and 64 proxy workers, implying that CPU becomes the bottleneck here. Adding one more proxy node (2×) almost doubles the performance (QPS increased from 2,200 to 3,700), clearly demonstrating that proxy's performance is constrained by the CPU capacity. Next, we repeat the test with large object workloads. As shown in Figure 13.3(b), the network bandwidth limit is reached as soon as the number of proxy workers reaches 4, with modest CPU utilization (about 25%) observed on the proxy node. This is because for large object workload, the performance becomes constrained by the network bandwidth before CPU can be saturated. Hence adding another proxy node (2×, i.e., doubling the available network bandwidth) results in linear increase in throughput. Thus, the takeaway is that a proxy's computational capacity can act as the bottleneck for workloads dominated with small objects, whereas the network bandwidth is the limiting resource for workloads dominated by large objects.

Q3: How does storage server configuration impact performance?

Next, we study the effect of scaling object storage nodes on workload performance. As shown in Figure 13.3(c), the peak QPS for small object workloads is achieved with 16 object storage workers, which is exactly the same as the number of proxy workers launched to achieve this QPS (recall that two object storage nodes are deployed behind

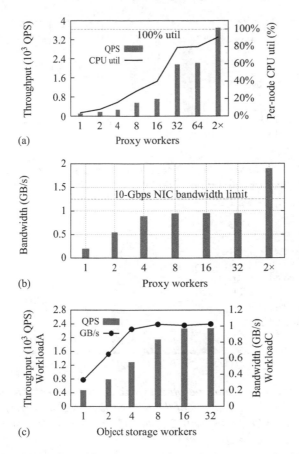

Figure 13.3 *Studied software/hardware configuration options. In (c), small-object workloads refer to bars (QPS) while large-object workloads refer to linepoints (GB/s). A:* WorkloadA; *C:* WorkloadC. *(a) Effect of varying proxy capability (A), (b) effect of varying proxy capability (C), (c) effect of varying object store server capability*

one proxy server node). This implies that the maximum performance can only be achieved when both the proxy and storage nodes are equipped with the same amount of CPU resources, which strengthens our observation that CPU capability is the limiting factor for small-object workloads. In contrast, for large-object workloads, the network limit is quickly reached with only 4 object storage workers. This is because, for large objects the performance is bottlenecked by the network (recall that each storage node has 3 SATA SSDs, thus disk bandwidth does not pose a limitation in our test).

Q4: How does network/storage affect performance?
In our next test, we study the effect of varying storage device and network connectivity on workload throughput. Figure 13.4(a) shows that faster network interconnect

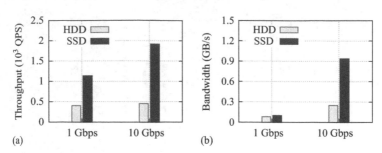

*Figure 13.4   Performance of the object store equipped with **homogeneous storage devices** as a function of the NIC bandwidth: (a)* WorkloadA *and (b)* WorkloadC

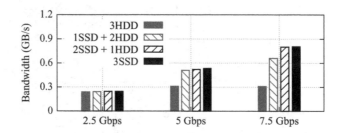

*Figure 13.5   Performance of large-object workload with **heterogeneous storage devices** as a function of the NIC bandwidth. The corresponding bandwidth (GB/s) with 2.5, 5, and 7.5 Gbps are 0.31, 0.62, and 0.93 GB/s, respectively*

(1–10 Gbps NIC) results in only 12% increase in QPS for small object workloads with HDD as storage medium, and 70% increase when SATA SSD is used. This observation shows that small-object intensive workloads are more sensitive to the storage devices rather than the network bandwidth. Thus, they may be efficiently handled using a lower-bandwidth network interconnect but by using high-bandwidth storage devices. On the other hand, increasing network interconnect improves performance by as much as 900% (using SSDs) in case for large-object intensive workloads (Figure 13.4(b)), which clearly indicates such kind of workloads can benefit from high-bandwidth network interconnects.

Q5: What is the impact of heterogeneous storage setup on performance of large-object workloads?
Finally, we study the impact of heterogeneous storage configuration on large-object intensive workloads. Here, we limit the network bandwidth using Linux traffic control tool tc. We measure the performance of the object store under a large-object workload, with four setups: two heterogeneous setups 1 SSD + 2 HDD and 2 SSD + 1 HDD;

and two homogeneous setups 3 HDD and 3 SSD as baselines. Figure 13.5 demonstrates that the choice of different storage device type combination changes based on the network bandwidth limit. We vary the network bandwidth limit to emulate the scenario where the network is partitioned in a multitenant environment. Note, when the network is limited to 2.5 Gbps, all four storage configurations achieve the same performance. Thus, the storage setup of choice under 2.5 Gbps is 3 HDDs. As the bandwidth limits increases to 7.5 Gbps, the 3 HDDs setup becomes the worst choice, especially when meeting SLAs is critical. Here, the 2 SSD + 1 HDD setup is desirable as it achieves almost the same performance as the 3 SSD setup, but with a higher resource efficiency. These tests necessitate the need for a workload-aware resource provisioning mechanism that selects the most efficient and high performing options under dynamically changing workloads and tenant requirements.

13.4.1   Summary of rules-of-thumb

It is fairly straightforward to manually tune the object stores by controlling all the other configuration variables. However, it is a challenging task to dynamically detect the workload shifts and meet the tenant goals while maximizing the resource efficiency at runtime, particularly when the service providers are faced with many software and hardware configuration options [23]. To this end, we develop the following rules-of-thumb that are helpful in guiding the online/offline performance tuning of object stores as well as the design of a micro-object-architecture-based storage system, MOS, for software defined datacenters.

Rule 1

Cloud object store design can benefit from (1) partitioning the monolithic object store architecture based on workload characteristics and (2) separately servicing interfering workloads in the multitenant environment. Object size distribution is a key factor for classifying workload characteristics.

Rule 2

CPU capacity of proxy servers is the first-priority resource for small-object intensive workloads. CPU becomes a bottleneck much earlier than the network for such workloads.

Rule 3

On the other hand, available network bandwidth plays a critical role in the performance of large-object intensive workloads.

Rule 4

The number of CPU cores used in storage nodes can be safely configured based on the number of deployed proxy workers, given that the storage devices provide sufficient disk bandwidth. This rule can be modeled using the following equation: $proxyCores = storageNodes * coresPerStorageNode$. For example, one 32-core proxy node may require four 8-core storage nodes.

Rule 5

The aggregated network bandwidth between proxy and storage nodes should be roughly the same as the link bandwidth used by cloud provider to connect to the proxies. Generally, this rule can be modeled as $bw_{proxies} = storageNodes * bw_{storageNode}$.

Rule 6

A faster network cannot effectively improve QPS for small-object intensive workloads. For tenants who do not impose strict Service Level Objective (SLO) requirements, the workload, if dominated with small objects, may be better served using a combination of low-bandwidth network (i.e., 1-Gbps NICs) with high-bandwidth storage devices (e.g., SSD delivering decent random and sequential I/O performance). This low-cost heterogeneous resource combination can effectively meet tenants' requirement while improving datacenter cost efficiency.

Rule 7

For large-object intensive workloads, we have to collectively consider the network bandwidth limits and the storage configuration. Given a certain network limit and SLA, a combination of slow and fast storage devices (e.g., HDD+SSD) may be able to serve the application needs in a resource efficient manner.

13.5 Experimental analysis

This section presents the experimental analysis using our especially designed workload-aware systems, CAST and MOS, in an SDN-enabled datacenter environment.

13.5.1 Evaluating data management framework in software defined datacenter environment

13.5.1.1 Overview of CAST framework design

CAST employs offline profiling of different applications (jobs) within an analytics workload and generates job performance prediction models based on different storage services. It lets tenants specify high-level objectives such as maximizing tenant utility, or minimizing deadline miss rate. CAST then uses a simulated annealing based solver that reconciles these objectives with the performance prediction models, other workload specifications and the different cloud storage service characteristics to generate a data placement and storage provisioning plan. The framework then deploys the workload in the cloud based on the generated plan. We further enhance our basic tiering design to build CAST++, which incorporates the data reuse and workflow properties of an analytics workload. CAST consists of two major components: a job performance profiler, and a tiering solver.

13.5.1.2 Methodology

Next, we present the evaluation of our workload-aware storage system, CAST and CAST++, using a 400-core Hadoop cluster on Google Cloud. Each slave node in our testbed runs on a 16 vCPU n1-standard-16 VM. We first evaluate the effectiveness

Table 13.2   Distribution of job sizes in Facebook traces and our synthesized workload

Bin	# Maps at Facebook	% Jobs at Facebook	% Data sizes at Facebook	# Maps in workload	# Jobs in workload
1.				1	35
2.	1—10	73	0.1	5	22
3.				10	16
4.	11—50	13	0.9	50	13
5.	51–500	7	4.5	500	7
6.	501–3,000	4	16.5	1,500	4
7.	> 3,000	3	78.1	3,000	3

Table 13.3   Characteristics of studied applications

App.	I/O-intensive			CPU-intensive
	Map	Shuffle	Reduce	
Sort	✗	✓	✗	✗
Join	✗	✓	✓	✗
Grep	✓	✗	✗	✗
K-means	✗	✗	✗	✓

of our approach in achieving the best tenant utility for a 100-job analytics workload with no job dependencies.

We compare CAST against six storage configurations: four without tiering and two that employ greedy algorithm based static tiering. We generate a representative 100-job workload by sampling the input sizes from the distribution observed in production traces from a 3,000-machine Hadoop deployment at Facebook. We quantize the job sizes into 7 bins as listed in Table 13.2, to enable us to compare the dataset size distribution across different bins. The largest job in the Facebook traces has 158,499 map tasks. Thus, we choose 3,000 for the highest bin in our workload to ensure that our workload demands a reasonable load but is also manageable for our 400-core cluster. More than 99% of the total data in the cluster is touched by the large jobs that belong to bin 5, 6 and 7, which incur most of the storage cost. The aggregated data size for small jobs (with number of map tasks in the range 110) is only 0.1% of the total data size. The runtime for small jobs is not sensitive to the choice of storage tier. Therefore, we focus on the large jobs, which have enough number of mappers and reducers to fully utilize the cluster compute capacity during execution. Since there is a moderate amount of data reuse throughout the Facebook traces, we also incorporate this into our workload by having 15% of the jobs share the same input data. We assign the four job types listed in Table 13.3 to this workload in a round-robin fashion to incorporate the different computation and I/O characteristics.

13.5.1.3   Effectiveness for general workload

Figure 13.6 shows the results for tenant utility, performance, cost and storage capacity distribution across four different storage services. We observe in Figure 13.6(a) that CAST improves the tenant utility by 33.7% – 178% compared to the configurations with no explicit tiering, i.e., ephSSD 100%, persSSD 100%, persHDD 100% and objStore 100%. The best combination under CAST consists of 33% ephSSD, 31% persSSD, 16% persHDD and 20% objStore, as shown in Figure 13.6(c). persSSD achieves the highest tenant utility among the four non-tiered configurations, because persSSD is relatively fast and persistent. Though ephSSD provides the best I/O performance, it is not cost-efficient, since it uses the most expensive storage and requires objStore to serve as the backing store to provide data persistence, which incurs additional storage cost and also imposes data transfer overhead. This is why ephSSD 100% results in 14.3% longer runtime (300 min) compared to that under persSSD 100% (263 min) as shown in Figure 13.6(b)).

The greedy algorithm cannot reach a global optimum because, at each iteration, placing a job in a particular tier can change the performance of that tier. This affects the utility calculated and the selected tier for each job in all the previous iterations, but the greedy algorithm cannot update those selections to balance the trade-off between cost and performance. For completeness, we compare our approach with two versions of the greedy algorithm: Greedy exact-fit attempts to limit the cost by not over-provisioning extra storage space for workloads, while Greedy over-provisioned will assign extra storage space as needed to reduce the completion time and improve performance.

The tenant utility of Greedy exact-fit is as poor as objStore 100%. This is because Greedy exact-fit only allocates just enough storage space without considering performance scaling. Greedy over-provisioned is able to outperform ephSSD 100%, persHDD 100% and objStore 100%, but performs slightly worse than persSSD 100%. This is because the approach significantly over-provisions persSSD and persHDD space to improve the runtime of the jobs. The tenant utility improvement under basic CAST is 178% and 113.4%, compared to Greedy exact-fit and Greedy over-provisioned, respectively.

13.5.1.4   Effectiveness for data reuse

CAST++ outperforms all other configurations and further enhances the tenant utility of basic CAST by 14.4% (Figure 13.6(a)). This is due to the following reasons: (1) CAST++ successfully improves the tenant utility by exploiting the characteristics of jobs and underlying tiers and tuning the capacity distribution. (2) CAST++ effectively detects data reuse across jobs to further improve the tenant utility by placing shared data in the fastest ephSSD, since we observe that in Figure 13.6(c) the capacity proportion under CAST++ of objStore reduces by 42% and that of ephSSD increases by 29%, compared to CAST. This is because CAST++ places jobs that share the data on ephSSD to amortize the data transfer cost from objStore.

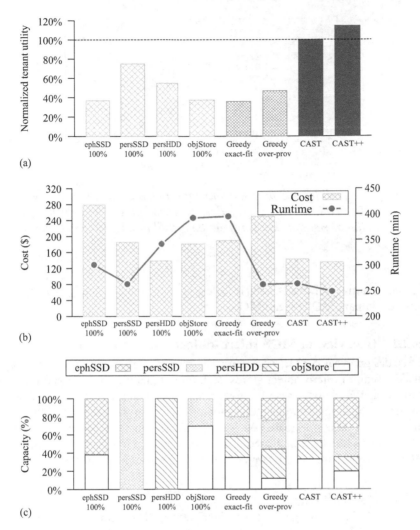

Figure 13.6   Effectiveness of CAST and CAST++ on workloads with reuse, observed for key storage configurations. Note: `Greedy over-prov` *represents* `greedy over-provisioned`*. Tenant utility is normalized to that of the configuration from basic CAST. (a) Normalized tenant utility, (b) total monetary cost and runtime, (c) capacity breakdown*

13.5.2 Evaluating micro-object-store architecture in software defined datacenter environment

In our next set of experimental analysis, we present the evaluation of our micro-object store, MOS++ using both a prototype implementation and simulations. We first use the prototype to evaluate a number of object store setups under multi-tenancy in both

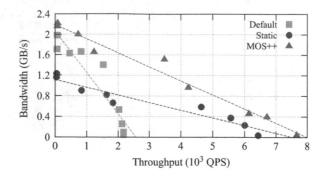

*Figure 13.7   Overall throughput vs. bandwidth observed under different setups.
Dotted lines are generated using linear regression, indicating the
linear relationship between the overall throughput and bandwidth*

static and dynamic workloads. This is followed by a simulation study of a large-scale
system to compare MOS++ and MOS.

13.5.2.1 Overview of MOS micro-object-store architecture

We have designed MOS [23], a novel micro object storage architecture with independently configured micro-object-stores each tuned dynamically for a particular type
of workload. We expose these microstores to the tenants who can then choose to
place their data in the appropriate microstore based on the latency and throughput
requirements of their workloads. We further enhance our basic resource provisioning
engine to build MOS++, which incorporates the container abstraction for fine-grained
resource management, SLA awareness, and better resource efficiency.

13.5.2.2 Methodology

We evaluate MOS++ using a 128-core local testbed. The testbed is connected using
a 10 Gbps switch, with a maximum bandwidth of 40 Gbps. We emulate a two-tenant
(client) environment, i.e., we run COSBench on two separate machines within the
same subnet. We use WorkloadA (small-object read-intensive workload) and WorkloadC (large-object read-intensive workload) for this purpose. We compare MOS++
against two different object store setups – Default, where we use off-the-shelf monolithic configuration of Swift, and Static, where we statically configure two micro
object stores designated for two tenants based on the rules-of-thumb of 6. The static
approach is more advanced than the default segmentation policies [13] and serves as
another point of comparison for our approach. Note that we focus on MOS++ for our
prototype evaluation as it also encompass the basic design of MOS.

The Default setup is launched directly on the physical machines. Static, like
MOS++, is launched inside containers. For Static setup, we tried several different
overall configurations and selected the best one. Specifically, 75% CPU cores, 30%

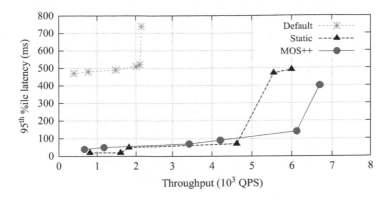

Figure 13.8   Throughput vs. 95th percentile latency under WorkloadA

of NW bandwidth, and 100% PCIe SSD with 30% SATA SSD are assigned to WorkloadA. Accordingly, 25% CPU cores, 70% NW bandwidth, and 70% SATA SSD are assigned to WorkloadC. MOS++ starts initially with the same configuration as Static throughout our evaluation. Regarding runtime parameters, we set slalow to be proportional to the workloads' load and slahigh 2× of slalow. We set utillow 65% and utilhigh 85%. We set epoch to be 3 minutes and utilthresh as 80%.

13.5.2.3   Performance evaluation

In this test, we evaluate MOS++'s ability to handle heterogeneous varying workloads. We vary the COSBench processes from 2 to 1,024 for WorkloadA to increase the throughput, while we decrease WorkloadC's load by varying the COSBench processes from 32 to 2. Figure 13.7 plots the overall performance of the two studied workloads in terms of both throughput (QPS) and bandwidth (MB/s). Default achieves significantly higher bandwidth compared to Static when WorkloadC dominates (the far left part on *X*-axis dimension). This is because the large-object workload consumes most of the network bandwidth to transfer packets containing payload for large objects. Guided by our rules-of-thumb, Static's statically provisioned micro store setup is able to balance the performance of both workloads to some extent. Hence, as WorkloadA gradually increases and eventually dominates, Static outperforms Default by as much as 2×. By leveraging workload-aware elasticity support, MOS++ combines the "best of both worlds", hence we see 10.4%–89.6% improvement in overall throughput and 7.6%–79.8% improvement in overall bandwidth, compared to both Default and Static. Thus, MOS++ is able to improve the overall performance for the two tenants with workloads exhibiting dramatically different characteristics.

Figure 13.8 depicts the 95th percentile read tail latency and throughput tradeoffs observed for WorkloadA. For WorkloadA, Default performs the worst and lies in the upper-left corner of the scatter chart. Static achieves comparatively similar performance with MOS++ as WorkloadA starts to increase. By adapting to the increasing load and adding more CPU power for WorkloadA, MOS++ eventually outperforms

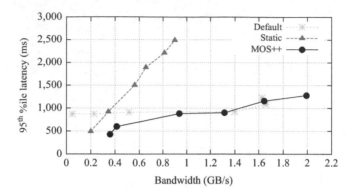

Figure 13.9   Bandwidth vs. 95th percentile latency under WorkloadC. *Average latency results show similar trend*

Static at peak loads (the right-most two data points) by up to 11.7% in throughput and up to 70.2% in tail latency. Figure 13.9 shows a similar trend under WorkloadC. Under the large-object dominant workload, Static is bottlenecked by its statically allocated network resource and hence limits the bandwidth for WorkloadC. Accordingly, we observe up to 79% improvement in bandwidth and up to 50.6% reduction in tail latency, compared to Default. Thus, MOS++ is able to improve the performance for both tenants, and effectively remove the performance bottleneck observed in Default and Static setups.

13.6   Open issue and future directions in SDN-enabled Big Data management

In this section, we discuss several future directions for the two proposed solutions of MOS and CAST. There are two limitations that are not fully addressed in our current implementation for both the solutions.

13.6.1   Open issues in data management framework in software defined datacenter

13.6.1.1   Analytics workloads with relatively fixed and stable computations

Analytics workloads are known to be fairly stable in terms of the number of types of applications. Recent analysis by Chen *et al.* [21] shows that a typical analytics workload consists of only a small number of common computation patterns in terms of analytics job types. For example, a variety of Hadoop workloads in Cloudera have four to eight unique types of jobs. Moreover, more than 90% of all jobs in one Cloudera cluster are Select, PigLatin and Insert. These observations imply that a relatively fixed and stable set of analytics applications (or analytics kernels) can yield enough functionality for a range of analysis goals. Thus, optimizing the system for such applications, as in CAST, can significantly impact the data analytics field.

13.6.1.2   Dynamic vs. static storage tiering

Big Data frameworks such as Spark [24] and Impala [25] have been used for real-time interactive analytics, where dynamic storage tiering is likely to be more beneficial. In contrast, our work focuses on traditional batch processing analytics with workloads exhibiting the characteristics identified above. Dynamic tiering requires more sophisticated fine-grained task level scheduling mechanisms to effectively avoid the straggler issue. While dynamic tiering in our problem domain can help to some extent, our current tiering model adopts a simple yet effective coarse-grained tiering approach. While we have designed a first-of-its-kind storage tiering methodology for cloud-based analytics, in the future, we plan to enhance CAST to incorporate fine-grained dynamic tiering as well.

13.6.2   Open issues in micro-object-store architecture in software defined datacenter environment

13.6.2.1   Limitation on number of microstores

Although MOS supports multi-tenancy and heterogeneous workload separation, we limit the number of microstores to be launched based on workload characteristics (i.e., object sizes) to reduce the implementation complexity and reconfiguration overhead. Consequently, the approach limits the kinds of different workloads the system can effectively handle. Should a workload change its inherent characteristics, e.g., the object size distribution changes dramatically, and no longer fit well with any provisioned microstores, the system may end up doing reconfiguration thrashing. This, in turn, will lead to reduced performance. A possible solution is to perform online workload analysis and profiling at the load balancer/redirector side, and using the information to compute an optimal number of microstores and perform workload-to-microstore mapping on the fly. Such a dynamic detect-and-map system can provide for high-impact future direction.

13.6.2.2   Online optimizations of microstores

Although MOS++ is able to meet the SLAs by leveraging offline workload profiling and online optimization, it does not currently consider the profit, i.e., revenue, for the service provider and tenant utility, i.e., perf /$, while provisioning the microstores. A feasible yet simple cloud-profit-aware solution can be to enhance our optimizer by incorporating the cloud pricing model and monetary profit. This aspect is orthogonal to our work, but can be easily incorporated into the design if needed.

13.7   Summary

In summary, we perform a detailed performance and resource efficiency analysis on identifying major hardware and software configuration opportunities that can be used to fine-tune object stores for specific workloads. Our findings indicate the need to re-architect cloud object storage specialized for the public cloud. We have presented an experimental analysis of cloud object stores and proposed a set of rules-of-thumb based on the study. The rules provide practical guidelines for service administrators and online resource managers to better tune object store performance to application needs. The resulting system, MOS, outperforms extant object stores in multitenant environments. Furthermore, we build MOS++ to enhance MOS by leveraging containers for fine-grained resource management and higher resource efficiency. Our experimentation reveals that it is possible to exploit the inherent heterogeneity within modern datacenters to better serve heterogeneous workloads across multiple tenants. Evaluation with our prototype implementation shows that MOS++ improves performance by up to 89.6% and 79.8% compared to the default monolithic and statically configured object store setup, respectively. Results show that, by utilizing the same set of resources, MOS++ achieves up to 18.8% performance improvement compared to the basic MOS.

Similarly, we designed CAST, a storage tiering framework that performs cloud storage allocation and data placement for analytics workloads to achieve high performance in a cost-effective manner. CAST leverages the performance and pricing models of cloud storage services and the heterogeneity of I/O patterns found in common analytics applications. An enhancement, CAST++, extends these capabilities to meet deadlines for analytics workflows while minimizing the cost. We present a detailed cost-efficiency analysis of analytics workloads and workflows in a real public cloud environment. Our evaluation shows that compared to extant storage-characteristic-oblivious cloud deployment strategies, CAST++ can improve the performance by as much as 37.1% while reducing deployment costs by as much as 51.4%.

We also discussed several future directions for the two proposed solutions of MOS and CAST in the emerging SDN-based datacenters.

References

[1]   "Facebook." http://facebook.com. Accessed on 18 January 2016.
[2]   "Amazon Web Services." https://aws.amazon.com/. Accessed on 18 January 2016.
[3]   "Memcached." http://memcached.org. Accessed on 18 January 2016.
[4]   Y. Cheng, A. Gupta, and A. R. Butt, "An in-memory object caching framework with adaptive load balancing," in *Proceedings of the 10th European Conference on Computer Systems*, p. 12, ACM, 2015.
[5]   "Amazon ElastiCache." https://aws.amazon.com/elasticache/. Accessed on 18 January 2016.
[6]   "Amazon S3." https://aws.amazon.com/s3/. Accessed on 18 January 2016.

[7] "Google Cloud Storage." https://cloud.google.com/storage/. Accessed on 18 January 2016.

[8] "OpenStack Swift." https://wiki.openstack.org/wiki/Swift. Accessed on 18 January 2016.

[9] "Ceph." http://ceph.com/. Accessed on 18 January 2016.

[10] A. Anwar, Y. Cheng, H. Huang, and A. R. Butt, "Clusteron: Building highly configurable and reusable clustered data services using simple data node," in *Proceedings of the 8th USENIX Workshop on Hot Topics in Storage and File Systems*, p. 5, USENIX, 2016.

[11] Y. Cheng, F. Douglis, P. Shilane, *et al.*, "Erasing belady's limitations: In search of flash cache offline optimality," in *Proceedings of the 2016 USENIX Annual Technical Conference*, p. 14, USENIX, 2016.

[12] A. Anwar, Y. Cheng, A. Gupta, and A. R. Butt, "Taming the cloud object storage with mos," in *The 10th Parallel Data Storage Workshop (PDSW'15)*, 2015.

[13] "Swfit storage policies." http://goo.gl/hRrySo. Accessed on 18 January 2016.

[14] "Arq." https://www.haystacksoftware.com/arq/. Accessed on 18 January 2016.

[15] C. Delimitrou and C. Kozyrakis, "Paragon: QoS-aware scheduling for heterogeneous datacenters," in *ACM ASPLOS*, 2013.

[16] J. Mars, L. Tang, and R. Hundt, "Heterogeneity in 'homogeneous' warehouse-scale computers: A performance opportunity," in *IEEE CAL*, 2011.

[17] Q. Zheng, H. Chen, Y. Wang, J. Duan, and Z. Huang, "Cosbench: A benchmark tool for cloud object storage services," in *IEEE CLOUD*, 2012.

[18] K. Krish, A. Anwar, and A. R. Butt, 'hatS: A heterogeneity-aware tiered storage for Hadoop," in *Cluster, Cloud and Grid Computing (CCGrid), 2014 14th IEEE/ACM International Symposium on*, pp. 502–511, IEEE, 2014.

[19] K. Krish, A. Anwar, and A. R. Butt, "[phi] Sched: A heterogeneity-aware Hadoop workflow scheduler," in *Modelling, Analysis & Simulation of Computer and Telecommunication Systems (MASCOTS), 2014 IEEE 22nd International Symposium on*, pp. 255–264, IEEE, 2014.

[20] A. Anwar, K. Krish, and A. R. Butt, "On the use of microservers in supporting Hadoop applications," in *Cluster Computing (CLUSTER), 2014 IEEE International Conference on*, pp. 66–74, IEEE, 2014.

[21] Y. Chen, S. Alspaugh, and R. Katz, "Interactive analytical processing in Big Data systems: A cross-industry study of MapReduce workloads," *PVLDB*, vol. 5, pp. 1802–1813, Aug. 2012.

[22] Y. Cheng, M. S. Iqbal, A. Gupta, and A. R. Butt, "Cast: Tiering storage for data analytics in the cloud," in *Proceedings of the 24th ACM Symposium on High-Performance Parallel and Distributed Computing*, pp. 45–56, 2015.

[23] A. Anwar, Y. Cheng, A. Gupta, and A. R. Butt, "MOS: Workload-aware elasticity for cloud object stores," in *Proceedings of the 25th ACM International Symposium on High-Performance Parallel and Distributed Computing*, pp. 177–188, ACM, 2016.

[24] M. Zaharia, M. Chowdhury, T. Das, *et al.*, "Resilient distributed datasets: A fault-tolerant abstraction for in-memory cluster computing," in *Proceedings of USENIX NSDI 2012*.

[25] "Impala." http://impala.io. Accessed on 18 January 2016.

Chapter 14

SDN helps Big Data to optimize access to data

Yuankun Fu* and Fengguang Song**

This chapter introduces the state of the art in the emerging area of combining high performance computing (HPC) with Big Data Analysis. To understand the new area, the chapter first surveys the existing approaches to integrating HPC with Big Data. Next, the chapter introduces several optimization solutions that focus on how to minimize the data transfer time from computation-intensive applications to analysis-intensive applications as well as minimizing the end-to-end time-to-solution. The solutions utilize Software Defined Network (SDN) to adaptively use both high speed interconnect network and high performance parallel file systems to optimize the application performance. A computational framework called DataBroker is designed and developed to enable a tight integration of HPC with data analysis. Multiple types of experiments have been conducted to show different performance issues in both message passing and parallel file systems and to verify the effectiveness of the proposed research approaches.

14.1 Introduction

Alongside experiments and theories, computational modeling/simulation and Big Data analytics have established themselves as the critical *third* and *fourth* paradigms in modern scientific discovery [1,2]. Nowadays, there is an inevitable trend toward integrating different applications of computation and data analysis together. The benefits of combining them are significant: (1) The overall end-to-end time-to-solution can be reduced considerably such that interactive or real-time scientific discovery becomes feasible; (2) the traditional one-way communication (from computation to analysis) can be bidirectional to enable guided computational modeling and simulation; and (3) computational modeling/simulation and data-intensive analysis are complementary to each other and can be used in a virtuous circle to amplify their collective effect.

However, it is a challenging task to integrate computation with analysis effectively. Critical questions include: How to minimize the cost to couple computation

*Department of Computer Science, Purdue University, USA
**Department of Computer Science, Indiana University–Purdue University Indianapolis, USA

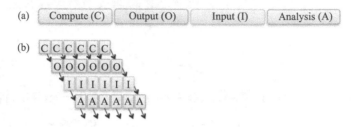

Figure 14.1   Comparison between the traditional process (a) and the new fully asynchronous pipeline method (b)

and analysis? how to design an effective software system to enable and facilitate such an integration? and how to optimize the coscheduling of different computation and data-intensive applications? In this chapter, we build an analytical model to estimate the overall execution time of the integrated computation and data analysis and design an intelligent data broker to intertwine the computation stage and the analysis stage to achieve the optimal time-to-solution predicted by the analytical model.

To fully interleave computation with analysis, we propose and introduce a fine-grain-block task-based asynchronous parallel execution model. The execution model utilizes the abstraction of pipelining, which is widely used in computer architectures [3]. In a traditional scientific discovery, a user often executes the computation, stores the computed results to disks, then reads the computed results, and finally performs data analysis. From the user's perspective, the total time-to-solution is the sum of the four execution times. In this chapter, we rethink of the problem by using a novel method of fully asynchronous pipelining. With the asynchronous pipeline method (detailed in Section 14.4), a user input is divided into fine-grain blocks. Each fine-grain block goes through four steps: computation, output, input, and analysis. As shown in Figure 14.1, our new end-to-end time-to-solution is equal to the maximum of the the computation time, the output time, the input time, and the analysis time (i.e., the time of a single step only). Furthermore, we build an analytical model to predict the overall time-to-solution to integrate computation and analysis, which provides developers with an insight into how to efficiently combine them.

Although the analytical model and its performance analysis reveal that the corresponding integrated execution can result in high performance, there is no software available to support the online tight coupling of analysis and computation at runtime. To facilitate the asynchronous integration of computation and analysis, we design and develop an I/O middleware, named *Intelligent DataBroker*, to adaptively prefetch and manage data in both secondary storage and main memory to minimize the I/O cost. This approach is able to support both in-situ (or in memory) data processing and postprocessing where initial dataset is preserved for the entire community (e.g., the weather community) for subsequent analysis and verification. The computation and analysis applications are coupled up through the DataBroker. DataBroker consists of two parts: a DataBroker producer in the compute node to send data, and a DataBroker consumer in the analysis node to receive data. It has its own runtime system to provide dynamic scheduling, pipelining, hierarchical buffering, and prefetching. This chapter introduces the design of the current prototype of DataBroker briefly.

We performed experiments on BigRed II (a Cray system) with a Lustre parallel file system at Indiana University to verify the analytical model and compare the performance of the traditional process, an improved version of the traditional process with overlapped data writing and computation, and our fully asynchronous pipeline approach. Both synthetic applications and real-world computational fluid dynamics (CFD) applications have been implemented with the prototype of DataBroker. Based on the experiments, the difference between the actual time-to-solution and the predicted time-to-solution is less than 10%. Furthermore, by using DataBroker, our fully asynchronous method is able to outperform the improved traditional method by up to 78% for the real-world CFD application.

In the remainder of the chapter, Section 14.2 covers the state of the art. Section 14.3 compares the efficiency difference between the message passing method and the parallel file I/O method for transferring data between applications. Section 14.4 introduces the analytical model to estimate the time-to-solution. Section 14.5 presents the DataBroker middleware to enable an optimized integration approach. Section 14.6 verifies the analytical model and demonstrates the speedup using the integration approach. Finally, Section 14.7 raises a few open questions, and Section 14.8 summarizes the chapter.

14.2   State of the art and related work

This section introduces the existing approaches to integrating computation with data analysis and compares our work with related work.

The conventional approach: As shown earlier in Figure 14.1, the computational modeling and simulation applications [4–6] will compute and output computed results to files. Providing that the file format is known, any data analysis application can be launched to perform various types of data analysis. The advantage is that independent software projects can be developed at the same time in separate organizations. Also, the computed results can be stored and analyzed later by other analysis applications. The problem is that it is strictly sequential, which results in long end-to-end time-to-solution.

The in-situ approach: In opposite directions of the conventional approach, the in-situ approach analyzes data when the data are still resident in memory. While the I/O cost is eliminated, it has three issues [2,7,8]: (1) It takes a lot of effort to couple the computation code with the analysis code. Developers have to place analysis functions to the address space of the modeling/simulation application, which requires data-format conversion and good understanding of both computation and analysis domains; (2) many real-world applications are already tight on memory. Allocating memory to in-situ analysis (together with other resource contentions) will slow down both computation and analysis processes. Since analysis applications are typically less scalable than computation applications, the computation applications will be stalled due to the limited in-situ memory space; and (3) it does not support preserving data for long-term studies and the entire community for different data analyses.

The data-staging approach: Unlike the in-situ approach, which requires writing custom code and sharing the same resources, a general approach is to use *data staging* to place analysis on an analysis cluster or a separate partition of a supercomputer. The data-staging approach has a flexible design, in which computation and analysis can execute on the same compute node, on different compute nodes, or on different HPC systems. The approach can also minimize resource contention (e.g., CPU, memory, bus, disk) between computation and analysis processes. To support transferring data from computation to analysis, a few I/O libraries and middleware have been implemented. FlexIO [9] uses both shared memory and RDMA to support data analysis either on the same or different compute nodes. GLEAN [10] uses sockets to support data staging on analysis nodes on an analysis cluster. DataStager [11] and I/O Container [12] use RDMA to provide staging on a separate part of compute nodes. DataSpaces [13] provides a distributed virtual space and allows different processes to put/get data tuples to/from the space.

We create a new computing framework called DataBroker that is, based on a data-driven data-staging service. It provides a unifying approach, which takes into account *computation, output, input,* and *analysis* as a whole, and performs global dynamic scheduling across computation and analysis to optimize the end-to-end time-to-solution. This approach also builds analytical models to estimate the performance of the integrated computation and analysis and optimizes the time-to-solution.

The new DataBroker is used to fasten analysis applications to computational applications. Different from the existing staging middleware, DataBroker can perform in-memory analysis or file-system-based analysis—adaptively—without stalling the computation processes. Moreover, DataBroker focuses on fine-grain pipelining operations. There exist efficient parallel I/O libraries such as MPI-IO [14], ADIOS [15,16], Nessie [17], and PLFS [18] to allow applications to adapt their I/O to specific file systems. We do not compete with these works. DataBroker is in the application level, which can use these techniques to optimize DataBroker's performance.

14.3   Performance analysis of message passing and parallel file system I/O

In a typical scientific workflow, there are two available data transfer methods. One way is to transfer data via Message Passing Interface (MPI) library, which is a widely used message-passing library on parallel computing systems. The other is to use file system via writing and reading files. Nowadays, file system has evolved a lot and becomes much faster than before. Current novel HPC systems mostly utilize high-speed Solid-state Drive (SSD) to store temporary data into local disk, meanwhile use parallel file system to store long-term data.

Naturally, one may think file system is slow to transfer data compared with MPI messages. But with the rapid development of parallel file system and the emergence of systems equipped with SSD, it is necessary to reconsider this issue. Thus, we compare the performance of transferring data using MPI and file I/O. In order to achieve the

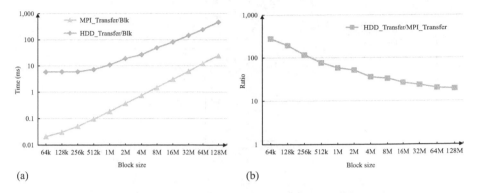

Figure 14.2   *Data transfer time and speedup for one block data on BigRed II: (a) data transfer time via MPI and HDD and (b) ratio of MPI/HDD*

goal, we design two sets of experiments. The first set is used to measure the time to transfer one block of data by one MPI message. The second set is used to get the time to transfer one block of data using file I/O.

The first set of MPI experiments is designed as follows. A producer process creates n blocks filled with random values and sends them to a consumer processes using n MPI messages. We measure the total time of MPI_Send function on each thread and assign it as the data transfer time T_{MPI}. Thus, the time to transfer a data block by MPI is $T_{\text{MPI/Block}} = \frac{T_{\text{MPI}}}{n}$.

The second set of file I/O experiments is described as follows. A producer process creates n blocks filled with random values and writes them to disk. After the producer process has finished, a consumer process will start reading the files. We measure the total writing time T_{Write} and reading time T_{Read} on each thread and use their sum as the data transfer time. Thus, the time to transfer a data block by parallel file I/O is $T_{\text{HDD/Block}} = \frac{T_{\text{Write}} + T_{\text{Read}}}{n}$.

The two sets of experiments are performed on BigRed II and Comet. BigRed II is a Cray XE6/XK7 HPC system in Indiana University. It contains a Gemini interconnect network and a Lustre parallel file system named Data Capacitor II (DC2). Comet is a dedicated XSEDE cluster in San Diego Supercomputer Center. It contains hybrid fat-tree interconnect network and a Lustre parallel file system. Besides, each Comet compute node has 320 GB SSD local storage. Thus, we conduct the two sets of experiments first on BigRed II to get $T_{\text{MPI/Block}}$ and $T_{\text{HDD/Block}}$, and then on Comet to get $T_{\text{MPI/Block}}$, $T_{\text{HDD/Block}}$ and $T_{\text{SSD/Block}}$.

Figure 14.2(a) shows the result of $T_{\text{MPI/Block}}$ and $T_{\text{HDD/Block}}$ on BigRed II. We can observe that MPI is faster than parallel file I/O on all block sizes. In addition, both $T_{\text{MPI/Block}}$ and $T_{\text{HDD/Block}}$ will increase as the block size increases. However, the performance gap between MPI and parallel file I/O becomes gradually narrower. We use the ratio of $\frac{T_{\text{HDD/Block}}}{T_{\text{MPI/Block}}}$ to measure it. Figure 14.2(b) shows that MPI outperforms parallel file I/O by 278 times on 64 kB, but the ratio falls to 19 times on 128 MB. This result reflects that MPI is excellent in transferring data on small block size, but the benefit loses as block size grows larger.

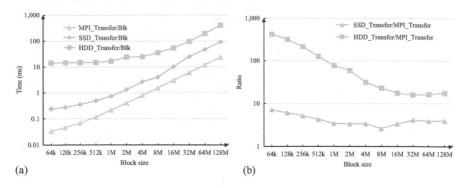

Figure 14.3 *Data transfer time and speedup for one block data on Comet: (a) data transfer time via MPI, SSD, and HDD and (b) ratio of MPI/SSD and MPI/HDD*

Figure 14.3(a) shows the results on Comet. We can find that the time to transfer a data block using MPI is faster than using local SSD, and using parallel file system is the slowest. Moreover, $T_{MPI/Block}$, $T_{SSD/Block}$, and $T_{HDD/Block}$ increase as block size increases. Again, we find that the performance gap among them becomes narrower. We still use the ratio of $\frac{T_{HDD/Block}}{T_{MPI/Block}}$ and $\frac{T_{SSD/Block}}{T_{MPI/Block}}$ to measure the trend. Figure 14.3(b) shows that MPI outperforms parallel file I/O by 419 times on 64 kB, but the ratio drops to 17 times on 128 MB. On the other hand, MPI outperforms SSD by 2.6 times on 8 MB, and up to 7 times on 64 kB. To transfer 128-MB data blocks, MPI is 2.9 times faster than SSD. This suggests that using SSD to transfer both small and large blocks is an acceptable choice.

From the above experiment results, we can summarize that MPI message is good at transferring small data size, but its performance drops when transferring larger data size. Moreover, on both machines, we find that MPI renders at most 19 times better performance when block size increases to 128 MB. Thus, parallel file system is not that slow in the case of transferring large file. Especially, when equipped with SSD, file system will be helpful in transferring both small and large data size.

14.4 Analytical modeling-based end-to-end time optimization

14.4.1 The problem

This chapter targets an important class of scientific discovery applications which require combining extreme-scale computational modeling/simulation with large-scale data analysis. The scientific discovery consists of computation, result output, result input, and data analysis. From a user's perspective, the actual time-to-solution is the

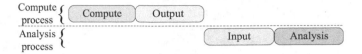

Figure 14.4   The traditional method

end-to-end time from the start of the computation to the end of the analysis. While it seems to be a simple problem with only four steps, different methods to execute the four steps can lead to totally different execution time. For instance, traditional methods execute the four steps sequentially such that the overall time-to-solution is the sum of the four times.

In this section, we study how to unify the four seemingly separated steps into a single problem and build an analytical model to analyze and predict how to obtain optimized time-to-solution. The rest of the section models the time-to-solution for three different methods: (1) the traditional method, (2) an improved version of the traditional method, and (3) the fully asynchronous pipeline method.

14.4.2   The traditional method

Figure 14.4 illustrates the traditional method, which is the simplest method without optimizations (next subsection will show an optimized version of the traditional method). The traditional method works as follows: the compute processes compute results and write computed results to disks, followed by the analysis processes reading results and then analyzing the results.

The time-to-solution (*t2s*) of the traditional method can be expressed as follows:

$$T_{t2s} = T_{\text{comp}} + T_o + T_i + T_{\text{analy}} \tag{14.1}$$

where T_{comp} denotes the parallel computation time, T_o denotes the output time, T_i denotes the input time, and T_{analy} denotes the parallel data analysis time. Although the traditional method can simplify the software development work, this formula reveals that the traditional model can be as slow as the accumulated time of all the four stages.

14.4.3   Improved version of the traditional method

The traditional method is a strictly sequential workflow. However, it can be improved by using multithreaded I/O libraries, where I/O threads are deployed to write results to disks meanwhile new results are generated by the compute processes. The other improvement is that the user input is divided into a number of fine-grain blocks and written to disks asynchronously. Figure 14.5 shows this improved version of the traditional method. We can see that the output stage is now overlapped with the computation stage so that the output time might be hidden by the computation time.

Suppose a number of P CPU cores are used to compute simulations, and a number of Q CPU cores are used to analyze results, and the total amount of data generated is D. Given a fine-grain block of size B, there are $n_b = \frac{D}{B}$ blocks. Since scalable applications most often have good load balancing, we assume that each compute

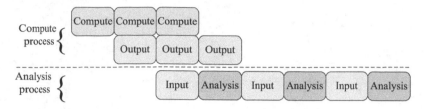

Figure 14.5   An improved version of the traditional method

core computes $\frac{n_b}{P}$ blocks and each analysis core analyzes $\frac{n_b}{Q}$ blocks. The rationale behind the assumption of load balancing is that a large number of fine-grain parallel tasks (e.g., $n_b \gg P$) will most likely lead to an even workload distribution among a relatively small number of cores.

Our approach uses the time to compute and analyze individual blocks to estimate the time-to-solution of the improved traditional method. Let t_{comp}, t_o, t_i, and t_{anal} denote the time to compute a block, write a block, read a block, and analyze a block, respectively. Then, we can get the parallel computation time $T_{comp} = t_{comp} \times \frac{n_b}{P}$, the data output time $T_o = t_o \times \frac{n_b}{P}$, the data input time $T_i = t_i \times \frac{n_b}{Q}$, and the parallel analysis time $T_{analy} = t_{analy} \times \frac{n_b}{Q}$. The time-to-solution of the improved version is defined as follows:

$$T_{t2s} = \max\left(T_{comp}, T_o, T_i + T_{analy}\right) \tag{14.2}$$

The term $T_i + T_{analy}$ is needed because the analysis process still reads data and then analyzes data in a sequence. Note that this sequential analysis step can be further parallelized, which results in a fully asynchronous pipeline execution model (see the following subsection).

14.4.4   The fully asynchronous pipeline method

The fully asynchronous pipeline method is designed to completely overlap computation, output, input, and analysis such that the time-to-solution is merely one component, which is either computation, data output, data input, or analysis. Note that the other three components will not be observable in the end-to-end time-to-solution. As shown in Figure 14.6, every data block goes through four steps: compute, output, input, and analysis. Its corresponding time-to-solution can be expressed as follows:

$$T_{t2s} = \max\left(T_{comp}, T_o, T_i, T_{analy}\right)$$

$$= \max\left(t_{comp} \times \frac{n_b}{P}, t_o \times \frac{n_b}{P}, t_i \times \frac{n_b}{Q}, t_{analy} \times \frac{n_b}{Q}\right) \tag{14.3}$$

The above analytical model provides an insight into how to achieve an optimal time-to-solution. When $t_{comp} = t_o = t_i = t_{analy}$, the pipeline is able to proceed without any stalls and deliver the best performance possible. On the other hand, the model can be used to allocate and schedule computing resources to different stages appropriately to attain the optimal performance.

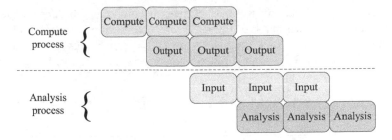

Figure 14.6   *The fully asynchronous pipeline method*

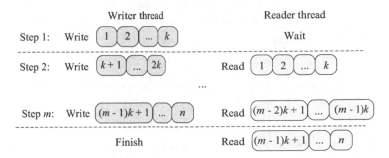

Figure 14.7   *The barrier microbenchmark*

14.4.5   *Microbenchmark for the analytical model*

To apply the analytical model in practice to predict the end-to-end time-to-solution, we need to know t_{comp}, t_o, t_i and t_{analy} on one block, respectively. Given an application's block size, users can get t_{comp} and t_{analy} simply by running their sequential kernel of computation and analysis on one block. The next step is to get t_o and t_i.

At first, we design a naive microbenchmark to estimate t_o and t_i. The microbenchmark contains P writer threads and Q reader threads. The mapping between writer threads and reader threads is static. Given a block size, each writer thread creates n blocks filled with random values and writes them to disk. After all the P writer threads have completed, the Q reader threads start reading the files one by one. We measure the total time of writing files as T_o and the total time of reading files as T_i on each thread. Thus, we get $t_o = \frac{T_o}{n}$ and $t_i = \frac{T_i \times Q}{P \times n}$.

However, the above naive microbenchmark does not consider the scenario where multiple writes and reads can execute concurrently and asynchronously. Thus, we propose a new version microbenchmark. Figure 14.7 illustrates its idea, each writer thread will generate n blocks in m steps. Thus, $k = \frac{n}{m}$ blocks are written into disk in each steps. Reader threads wait in the first step and start reading files in the second step and then reads the blocks generated by the writers in the previous step.

To achieve this idea, we use MPI_Barrier to synchronize between writer and reader threads. As shown in Algorithms 1 and 2, at the end of each step, all writers and readers will perform MPI_Barrier to control $k = n/m$ blocks to be written and read. With this approach, we can simulate the scenario that file writing and reading executed at the same time.

Algorithm 1 Writer thread in new microbenchmark

1: **for** $i = 0$ to m **do**
2:　　$blk\_id\_begin = i * n/m$
3:　　$blk\_id\_end = (i + 1) * n/m$
4:　　**for** $blk\_id = blk\_id\_begin$ to blk_id_end **do**
5:　　　　Write the block of blk_id to disk
6:　　**end for**
7:　　MPI_Barrier
8: **end for**

Algorithm 2 Reader thread in new microbenchmark

1: MPI_Barrier
2: **for** $i = 1$ to m **do**
3:　　$blk\_id\_begin = (i - 1) * n/m$
4:　　$blk\_id\_end = i * n/m$
5:　　**for** $blk\_id = blk\_id\_begin$ to blk_id_end **do**
6:　　　　Read the block of blk_id from the mapped writer processes
7:　　**end for**
8:　　**if** $i = m$ **then** break
9:　　**end if**
10:　　MPI_Barrier
11: **end for**

Then, we perform experiments by different P and Q configurations on BigRed II. After we get the t_o and t_i from the two microbenchmarks, we compare them with the t_o and t_i obtained from the real application. At last, we use the relative error of writing and reading (i.e., $\frac{|t_{Real\_app} - t_{Naive\_MB}|}{t_{Real\_app}}$ and $\frac{|t_{Real\_app} - t_{Barrier\_MB}|}{t_{Real\_app}}$) to reflect the accuracy for each microbenchmark.

The results for two version of microbenchmark with one writer and one reader are displayed in Figure 14.8. For the writing relative error, the two versions of microbenchmark have similar accuracy among different block sizes. But for the reading relative error, the new microbenchmark gets better accuracy than naive version on all block

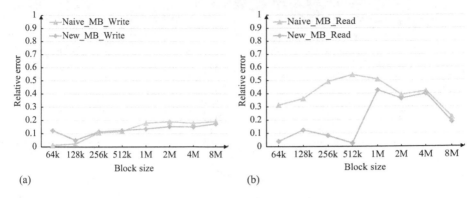

Figure 14.8   Accuracy of two microbenchmark compared to real application with one writer and one reader on BigRed II: (a) t_o relative error and (b) t_i relative error

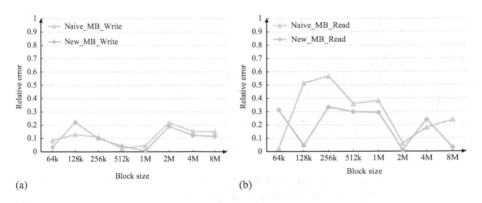

Figure 14.9   Accuracy of the two microbenchmarks compared to real application with four writers and one reader on BigRed II: (a) t_o relative error and (b) t_i relative error

sizes. The relative error of new microbenchmark is 20.5% on average among different block sizes, while 40.5% in naive version. In this case, the new one has similar accuracy on writing, but it has better accuracy on reading.

Figure 14.9 shows the relative error on writing and reading with four writer threads and one reader thread. For the writing relative error, the new microbenchmark has better accuracy with 10% on average among different block sizes, while the naive microbenchmark has 12% on average. For the reading relative error, the new microbenchmark also obtains better accuracy with 19.5% on average among different block sizes, while the naive microbenchmark has 29% on average. Thus, the new

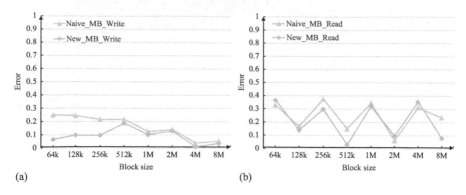

Figure 14.10   Accuracy of two microbenchmark compared to real application with 16 writers and 4 readers on BigRed II: (a) t₀ relative error and (b) tᵢ relative error

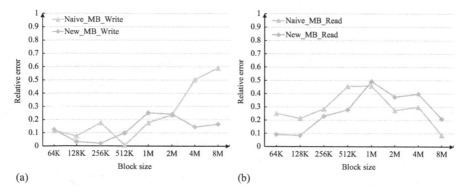

Figure 14.11   Accuracy of two microbenchmarks compared to real application with 32 writers and 32 readers on BigRed II: (a) t₀ relative error and (b) tᵢ relative error

version slightly outperforms naive version on writing, while has higher accuracy on reading.

Figure 14.10 shows the relative error on writing and reading with 16 writer threads and 4 reader threads. For the writing relative error, the new microbenchmark has better accuracy with 9% on average among different block sizes, while the naive microbenchmark has 16% on average. For the reading relative error, the new microbenchmark also obtains better accuracy with 21% on average among different block sizes, while the naive microbenchmark has 24.6% on average. In this case, the new version outperforms naive version on both writing and reading accuracy.

Figure 14.11 shows the relative error on writing and reading with 16 writer threads and 4 reader threads. For the writing relative error, the new microbenchmark has better accuracy with 13.5% on average among different block sizes, while the naive microbenchmark has 23.4% on average. Besides, the naive version even gets a relative error up to 59% on 8 MB. For the reading relative error, the new microbenchmark also obtains better accuracy with 27% on average among different block sizes, while the naive microbenchmark has 29% on average. Thus, in this case, the new version also outperforms the naive one on both writing and reading accuracy.

From the above experiment results, we observe that the new microbenchmark never gets a relative error of more than 50%. Besides, it gets an average relative error rate up to 13.5% for writing and up to 25% for reading among all cases and different threads configuration. Thus, we can conclude that the new version is more accurate than the naive version. The reason that the microbenchmark cannot sometimes predict the t_o and t_i accurately is that we do not consider network contention and sharing among the parallel file system between users into the microbenchmark model. And to add these two parts into the microbenchmark is not a trivial job, and we do not expect the microbenchmark too complicated. But we still can use the microbenchmark to get the trends and acceptable I/O performance to predict t_o and t_i in real applications.

14.5   Design and implementation of DataBroker for the fully asynchronous method

To enable the fully asynchronous pipeline model, we design and develop a software prototype called *Intelligent DataBroker*. The interface of the DataBroker prototype is similar to Unix's pipe, which has a writing end and a reading end. For instance, a computation process will call DataBroker.write(block_id, void* data) to output data, while an analysis process will call DataBroker.read(block_id) to input data. Although the interface is simple, it has its own runtime system to provide pipelining, hierarchical buffering, and data prefetching.

Figure 14.12 shows the design of DataBroker. It consists of two components: a *DataBroker producer component* in the compute node to send data, and a *DataBroker consumer component* in the analysis node to receive data. The producer component owns a producer ring buffer and one or multiple producer threads to process output in parallel. Each producer thread looks up the I/O-task queues and uses priority-based scheduling algorithms to transfer data to destinations in a streaming manner. A computational process may send data to an analysis process via two possible paths: message passing by the network or file I/O by the parallel file system. Depending on the execution environment, it is possible that both paths are available and used to speed up the data transmission time.

The DataBroker consumer is colocated with an analysis process on the analysis node. The consumer component will receive data from the computation processes, buffer data, and prefetch and prepare data for the analysis application. It consists of a consumer ring buffer and one or multiple prefetching threads. The prefetching threads are responsible for making sure there are always data blocks available in memory by loading blocks from disks to memory. Since we assume a streaming-based data analysis, the prefetching method can use the technique of *read ahead* to prefetch data efficiently.

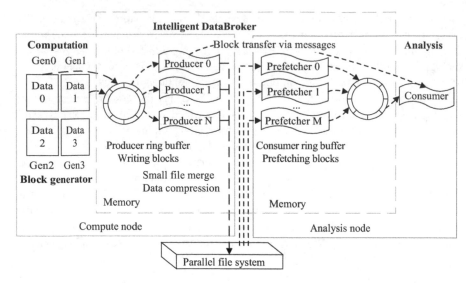

Figure 14.12   Architecture of the DataBroker middleware for coupling computation with analysis in a streaming pipeline manner. DataBroker consists of a producer component on a compute node, and a consumer component on an analysis node

14.6   Experiments with synthetic and real applications

We perform experiments to verify the accuracy of the analytical model and to evaluate the performance of the fully asynchronous pipeline method, respectively. For each experiment, we collect performance data from two different programs: (1) a synthetic application and (2) a real-world CFD application. All the experiments are carried out on BigRed II (a Cray XE6/XK7 system) configured with the Lustre 2.1.6 distributed parallel file system at Indiana University. Every compute node on BigRed II has two AMD Opteron 16-core Abu Dhabi CPUs and 64 GB of memory and is connected to the file system via 56-Gb FDR InfiniBand which is also connected to the DataDirect Network SFA12K storage controllers.

14.6.1   Synthetic and real-world applications

The synthetic application consists of a computation stage and an analysis stage. To perform these experiments, we use 32 compute nodes to execute the computation stage and use two different numbers of analysis nodes (i.e., 2 analysis nodes and 32 analysis nodes) to execute the analysis stage, respectively. We launch one process per node. Each computation process randomly generates a total amount of 1-GB data (chopped to small blocks) and writes the data to the DataBroker producer. Essentially, the computation processes only generate data but do not perform any computation. At the same time, each analysis process reads data from its local DataBroker consumer and computes the sum of the square root of the received data block for a number of iterations. The mapping between computation processes and analysis processes is static. For instance, if there are 32 computation processes and 2 analysis processes, each analysis process will process data from a half of the computation processes.

Our real-world CFD application, provided by the Mathematics Department at IUPUI [19], computes the 3-D simulations of flow slid of viscous incompressible fluid flow at 3-D hydrophobic microchannel walls using the lattice Boltzmann method [20,21]. This application is written in ANSI C and MPI. We replaced all the file write functions in the CFD application by our DataBroker API. The CFD simulation is coupled with a data analysis stage, which computes a series of statistical analysis functions at each fluid region for every time step of the simulation. Our experiment takes as input a 3-D grid of $512 \times 512 \times 256$, which is distributed to different computation processes. Similar to the synthetic experiments, we also run 32 computation processes on 32 compute nodes while running different numbers of analysis processes. For each experiment, we execute it four times and display their average in our experimental results.

14.6.2 Accuracy of the analytical model

We experiment with both the synthetic application and the CFD application to verify the analytical model. Our experiments measure the end-to-end time-to-solution on different block sizes ranging from 128 kB to 8 MB. The experiments are designed to compare the time-to-solution estimated by the analytical model with the actual time-to-solution to show the model's accuracy.

Figure 14.13(a) shows the actual time and the predicted time of the synthetic application using 32 compute nodes and 2 analysis nodes. For all different block sizes, the analysis stage is the largest bottleneck among the four stages (i.e., computation, output, input, and analysis). Hence, the time-to-solution is essentially equal to the analysis time. Also, the relative error between the predicted and the actual execution time is from 1.1% to 12.2%, and on average 3.9%. Figure 14.13(b) shows the actual time and the predicted time for the CFD application. Different from the synthetic application, its time-to-solution is initially dominated by the input time when the block size is 128 kB, then it becomes dominated by the analysis time from 256 kB to 8 MB. The relative error of the analytical model is between 4.7% and 18.1%, and on average 9.6%.

The relative error is greater than zero because our analytical model ignores the pipeline startup and drainage time, and there is also a small amount of pipeline idle time and jitter time during the real execution. Please note that each analysis process has to process the computed results from 16 computation processes.

Figure 14.14(a) shows the performance of the synthetic application that uses 32 compute nodes and 32 analysis nodes. When the block size is equal to 128 kB, the input time dominates the time-to-solution. When the block size is greater than 128 kB, the data analysis time starts to dominate the time-to-solution. The turning point in the figure also verifies the bottleneck switch (from the input stage to the analysis stage). The predicted time and the actual time are very close to each other and have

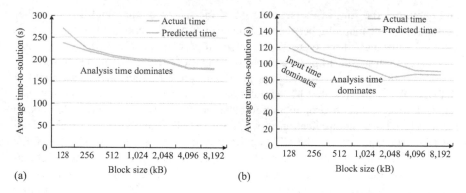

Figure 14.13   Accuracy of the analytical model for the fully asynchronous pipeline execution with 32 compute nodes and 2 analysis nodes: (a) synthetic experiments and (b) CFD application

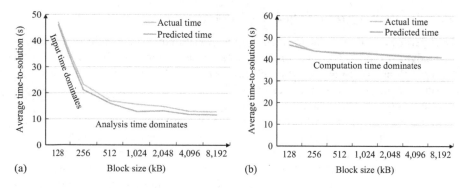

Figure 14.14   Accuracy of the analytical model for the fully asynchronous pipeline execution with 32 compute nodes and 32 analysis nodes: (a) synthetic experiments and (b) CFD application

an average relative error of 9.1%. Similarly, Figure 14.14(b) shows a relative error of 0.9% for the CFD application that also uses 32 compute nodes and 32 analysis nodes.

14.6.3   Performance speedup

Besides testing the analytical model, we also conduct experiments to evaluate the performance improvement by using the fully asynchronous pipeline method. The experiments compare three different approaches (i.e., three implementations) to executing the integrated computation and analysis: (1) the traditional method, (2) the improved version of the traditional method which builds upon fine-grain blocks and overlaps computation with data output, and (3) the fully asynchronous pipeline method

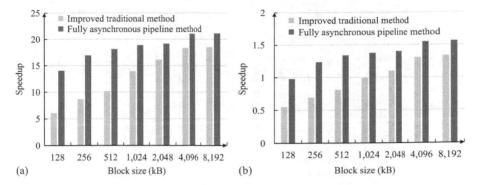

Figure 14.15   *Performance comparison between the traditional, the improved, and the DataBroker-based fully asynchronous methods using 32 compute nodes and 2 analysis nodes: (a) synthetic experiments and (b) CFD application*

based on DataBroker. Each of the three implementations takes the same input size and is compared with each other in terms of wall clock time.

Figure 14.15(a) and (b) shows the speedup of the synthetic application and the real-world CFD application, respectively. Note that the baseline program is the traditional method (i.e., speedup = 1). The data in Figure 14.15(a) shows that the improved version of the traditional method can be up to 18 times faster than the traditional method when the block size is equal to 8 MB. It seems to be surprising, but by looking into the collected performance data, we discover that reading two 16-GB files by two MPI process simultaneously is 59 times slower than reading a collection of small 8-MB files by the same two MPI processes. This might be because two 16-GB files are allocated to the same storage device, while a number of 8-MB files are distributed to multiple storage devices. On the other hand, the fully asynchronous pipeline method is faster than the improved traditional method by up to 131% when the block size is equal to 128 kB. Figure 14.15(b) shows the speedup of the CFD application. We can see that the fully asynchronous method is always faster (up to 56%) than the traditional method whenever the block size is larger than 128 kB. The small block size of 128 kB does not lead to improved performance because writing small files to disks can incur significant file system overhead and cannot reach the maximum network and I/O bandwidth. Also, the fully asynchronous method is consistently faster than the improved traditional method by 17% to 78%.

Figure 14.16(a) shows the speedup of the synthetic application that uses 32 compute nodes and 32 analysis nodes. We can see that the fully asynchronous pipeline method is 49% faster than the traditional method when the block size is equal to 8 MB. It is also 24% faster than the improved transitional method when the block size is equal to 4 MB. Figure 14.16(b) shows the speedup of the CFD application with 32 compute nodes and 32 analysis nodes. Both the fully asynchronous pipeline method and the improved traditional method are faster than the traditional method. For instance, they

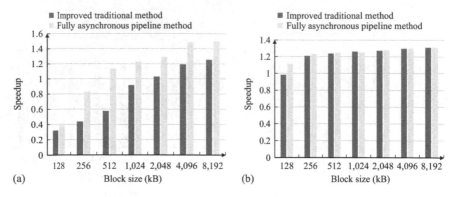

Figure 14.16 *Performance comparison between the traditional, the improved, and the DataBroker-based fully asynchronous methods using 32 compute nodes and 32 analysis nodes: (a) synthetic experiments and (b) CFD application*

are 31% faster with the block size of 8 MB. However, the fully asynchronous pipeline method is almost the same as the improved method when the block size is bigger than 128 kB. This is because the specific experiment's computation time dominates its time-to-solution so that both methods' time-to-solution is equal to the computation time, which matches our analytical model.

14.7 Open issues and challenges

This chapter presents a new way to accelerate scientific workflows consisting of computation-intensive applications and data-intensive applications. Although the current method has shown promising results, there are more open issues and challenging problems. Here, we provide a list of challenging problems as follows:

- Is it possible to design an adaptive data transfer method that can utilize both message passing and parallel file systems concurrently at runtime? Considering new file systems will utilize more nonvolatile memories (NVM), the performance difference between memory and file system becomes lesser.
- How to utilize the proposed analytical model to schedule computing resources more efficiently? It can lead to more efficient scheduling methods.
- Is it possible to extend the task-based pipeline approach to a general workflow model that consists of applications in a task graph?
- How to build a general-purpose workflow framework and programming tool to automatically combine different applications seamlessly at the fine-grain task level?

These open issues and challenges will require further research in SDN to facilitate faster data transfer and minimized time-to-solution in tightly coupled workflow applications.

14.8   Conclusion

To facilitate the convergence of computational modeling/simulation and the Big Data analysis, in this chapter, we study the problem of integrating computation with analysis in both theoretical and practical ways. First, we use the metric of the time-to-solution of scientific discovery to formulate the integration problem and propose a fully asynchronous pipeline method to model the execution. Next, we build an analytical model to estimate the overall time to execute the asynchronous combination of computation and analysis. In addition to the theoretical foundation, we also design and develop an intelligent DataBroker to help fully interleave the computation stage and the analysis stage.

The experimental results show that the analytical model can estimate the time-to-solution with an average relative error of less than 10%. By applying the fully asynchronous pipeline model to both synthetic and real-world CFD applications, we can increase the performance of the improved traditional method by up to 131% for the synthetic application, and up to 78% for the CFD application.

Acknowledgments

This material is based upon research partially supported by the Purdue Research Foundation and by the NSF Grant No. 1522554. Development and experiment of the software framework have used the NSF Extreme Science and Engineering Discovery Environment (XSEDE), which is supported by National Science Foundation grant number ACI-1053575.

References

[1]   G. Aloisioa, S. Fiorea, I. Foster, and D. Williams, "Scientific big data analytics challenges at large scale," *Proceedings of Big Data and Extreme-scale Computing*, 2013.

[2]   J. Chen, A. Choudhary, S. Feldman, *et al.*, "Synergistic challenges in data-intensive science and exascale computing," *DOE ASCAC Data Subcommittee Report, Department of Energy Office of Science*, 2013.

[3]   D. A. Patterson and J. L. Hennessy, *Computer organization and design: the hardware/software interface*. Boston: Newnes, 2013.

[4]   A. B. Shiflet and G. W. Shiflet, *Introduction to computational science: Modeling and simulation for the sciences*. Princeton: Princeton University Press, 2014.

[5]   H. Huang and L. L. Knowles, "Unforeseen consequences of excluding missing data from next-generation sequences: Simulation study of RAD sequences," *Systematic Biology*, vol. 65, no. 3, pp. 357–365, 2014.

[6]   S. Madadgar, H. Moradkhani, and D. Garen, "Towards improved post-processing of hydrologic forecast ensembles," *Hydrological Processes*, vol. 28, no. 1, pp. 104–122, 2014.

[7]   P. C. Wong, H.-W. Shen, C. R. Johnson, C. Chen, and R. B. Ross, "The top 10 challenges in extreme-scale visual analytics," *IEEE Computer Graphics and Applications*, vol. 32, no. 4, p. 63, 2012.

[8]   K.-L. Ma, "In situ visualization at extreme scale: Challenges and opportunities," *Computer Graphics and Applications, IEEE*, vol. 29, no. 6, pp. 14–19, 2009.

[9]   F. Zheng, H. Zou, G. Eisenhauer, *et al.*, "FlexIO: I/O middleware for location-flexible scientific data analytics," in *IEEE 27th International Symposium on Parallel & Distributed Processing (IPDPS)*, pp. 320–331, IEEE, 2013.

[10] V. Vishwanath, M. Hereld, M. E. Papka, R. Hudson, G. C. Jordan IV, and C. Daley, "In situ data analysis and I/O acceleration of FLASH astrophysics simulation on leadership-class system using GLEAN," in *Proc. SciDAC, Journal of Physics: Conference Series*, 2011.

[11] H. Abbasi, M. Wolf, G. Eisenhauer, S. Klasky, K. Schwan, and F. Zheng, "Datastager: Scalable data staging services for petascale applications," *Cluster Computing*, vol. 13, no. 3, pp. 277–290, 2010.

[12] J. Dayal, J. Cao, G. Eisenhauer, *et al.*, "I/O containers: Managing the data analytics and visualization pipelines of high end codes," in *Proceedings of the 2013 IEEE 27th International Symposium on Parallel and Distributed Processing Workshops and PhD Forum*, IPDPSW '13, (Washington, DC, USA), pp. 2015–2024, IEEE Computer Society, 2013.

[13] C. Docan, M. Parashar, and S. Klasky, "DataSpaces: An interaction and coordination framework for coupled simulation workflows," *Cluster Computing*, vol. 15, no. 2, pp. 163–181, 2012.

[14] R. Thakur, W. Gropp, and E. Lusk, "On implementing MPI-IO portably and with high performance," in *Proceedings of the Sixth Workshop on I/O in Parallel and Distributed Systems*, pp. 23–32, ACM, 1999.

[15] H. Abbasi, J. Lofstead, F. Zheng, K. Schwan, M. Wolf, and S. Klasky, "Extending I/O through high performance data services," in *IEEE International Conference on Cluster Computing and Workshops (CLUSTER'09)*, pp. 1–10, IEEE, 2009.

[16] Q. Liu, J. Logan, Y. Tian, *et al.*, "Hello ADIOS: The challenges and lessons of developing leadership class I/O frameworks," *Concurrency and Computation: Practice and Experience*, vol. 26, no. 7, pp. 1453–1473, 2014.

[17] J. Lofstead, R. Oldfield, T. Kordenbrock, and C. Reiss, "Extending scalability of collective IO through Nessie and staging," in *Proceedings of the Sixth Workshop on Parallel Data Storage*, pp. 7–12, ACM, 2011.

[18]   J. Bent, G. Gibson, G. Grider, *et al.*, "PLFS: A checkpoint filesystem for parallel applications," in *Proceedings of the Conference on High Performance Computing Networking, Storage and Analysis (SC'09)*, p. 21, ACM, 2009.

[19]   L. Zhu, D. Tretheway, L. Petzold, and C. Meinhart, "Simulation of fluid slip at 3D hydrophobic microchannel walls by the lattice Boltzmann method," *Journal of Computational Physics*, vol. 202, no. 1, pp. 181–195, 2005.

[20]   Z. Guo and C. Shu, *Lattice Boltzmann method and its applications in engineering*. Singapore: World Scientific, 2013.

[21]   P. Nagar, F. Song, L. Zhu, and L. Lin, "LBM-IB: A parallel library to solve 3D fluid-structure interaction problems on manycore systems," in *Proceedings of the 2015 International Conference on Parallel Processing*, ICPP'15, IEEE, September 2015.

Chapter 15

SDN helps Big Data to become fault tolerant

Abdelmounaam Rezgui, Kyoomars Alizadeh Noghani**,
Javid Taheri**, Amir Mirzaeinia*, Hamdy Soliman*, and
Nickolas Davis**

Cloud-based Big Data processing has become ubiquitous. Large cloud data centers (DCs) have proven to be a cost-effective, scalable platform to run data-intensive applications. As this computing model matures, cloud providers continue to face a number of challenges in handling Big Data applications on their DCs. One of those challenges is fault tolerance, i.e., ensuring that Big Data applications run properly on large-scale DCs despite failures.

Cloud DCs may contain hundreds or thousands of servers along with network switches, links, routers, firewalls, power supplies, storage devices, and several other types of hardware elements. Software that runs in a DC includes management and control software (e.g., virtualization packages), networking protocols, open-source code, customer-developed code, and various applications with known or unknown origins. This makes cloud DCs complex computing environments where it is extremely difficult to predict when and where the next failure in the DC will occur. For cloud providers, the ability to quickly detect and react to software and hardware failures is of paramount importance. For example, it is estimated that in a cluster's first year of usage, roughly 1,000 individual machine failures will occur.[1] Each minute of downtime can cost roughly $7,900 on average.[2] Moreover, fault tolerance helps avoid costly service-level agreement violations and preserve business reputation. Fault tolerance is therefore a crucial requirement in cloud DCs.

Systems often achieve fault tolerance through redundancy. In some cases, one redundant device is used to replace any of n active elements, e.g., switches or links. In other cases, one redundant device is used as a backup for each active element. The key challenge is to devise cost-effective solutions that minimize the number of additional redundant elements while satisfying key fault tolerance requirements such

*Department of Computer Science and Engineering, New Mexico Tech, USA
**Department of Mathematics and Computer Science, Karlstad University, Sweden
[1] http://www.datacenterknowledge.com/archives/2008/05/30/failure-rates-in-google-data-centers/.
[2] http://www.datacenterdynamics.com/content-tracks/power-cooling/one-minute-of-data-center-downtime-costs-us7900-on-average/83956.fullarticle.

as reducing recovery time, graceful degradation, etc. To achieve these objectives, it must be possible to quickly *reconfigure* the DC's network upon the detection of software or hardware failures. An even better alternative is to *predict* failures and to proactively reconfigure the DC's network so that faulty elements are not even part of the network when failures occur.

The ability to programmatically reconfigure networks has now become possible through software-defined networking (SDN). SDN is a new networking paradigm that enables network programmability. It decouples the forwarding hardware from the controller. In SDN, the network intelligence is logically centralized in software-based controllers, and network devices become simple packet forwarding devices that can be programed via an open interface [1,2].

The synergy between Big Data and SDN has now been established. For example, authors of [3] stated that good features of SDN can greatly facilitate Big Data acquisition, transmission, storage, and processing, and thus Big Data will have profound impacts on the design and operation of SDN. Aligned with this vision, in this chapter, we study how SDN can help achieving fault tolerance for Big Data workloads running in cloud DCs. Before that, we present the rationale behind running Big Data workloads in cloud DCs. Section 15.2 reviews common topologies for DC networks. Section 15.3 describes the principles involved in failure recovery. Section 15.4 discusses the conventional fault tolerance approaches. SDN-based fault tolerance approaches for Big Data workloads are discussed in Section 15.5. Finally, this chapter is concluded with some open issues followed by a summary.

15.1   Big Data workloads and cloud data centers

There are many reasons supporting the usage of clouds for executing Big Data workloads. The most outstanding reason is to derive a benefit from the massive amount of available resources that cloud DCs provide. The large volume of data and the high velocity of data generation are the two key characteristics of Big Data applications. These characteristics require storage capacity, computing power, and memory that can be quickly scaled to match the requirements of the application at hand. These requirements can be satisfied when running Big Data applications on cloud DCs. Cloud DCs offer resources (e.g., storage and processing capacity) that can be readily scaled as needed. The adoption of cloud DCs for Big Data processing is also due to the increased access to both Internet and public clouds. Companies like Google, Amazon, and Microsoft are leasing their massive cloud engines to users that require relatively hassle-free access to powerful computational resources.

As DCs grow, the probability of network failures and the consequent disruptions on the whole system will likely increase. Network faults impact network efficiency. Although certain types of applications are not sensitive to performance degradation, failure to accomplish Big Data projects can be very expensive. As such, it is incumbent upon DC providers to improve the availability of the underlying infrastructure and make it fault tolerant.

The codesign of a fault-tolerant network topology in conjunction with an agile recovery mechanism to detect and repair failures can dramatically help the network maintain adequate performance even in the presence of failures. First, the DC network architecture must be designed so that it can gracefully and quickly recover after failures—without any additional hardware. Second, in a case of failure, the recovery mechanism should react almost *instantaneously* and without imposing fatal workload on the other parts of the network. In what follows, we investigate common network topologies for DCs and elaborate on fault-tolerant mechanisms in legacy as well as SDN-based networks.

15.2 Network architectures for cloud data centers

The ability of the interconnection network to maintain a high operational efficiency, or at least to remain operational without disconnecting any computing nodes, strongly depends on the network topology and the routing function used to generate paths through the network. For the system to remain connected after a fault has occurred, there must exist a redundant path between every pair of computing nodes that avoid the failed element. Therefore, DC topologies are devised toward multipath topologies. Making use of multiple paths improves resource utilization and enhances resiliency against a subset of node failures. The most common DC network architectures are: (1) switch-centric DCs and (2) server-centric DCs.

15.2.1 Switch-centric data centers

In switch-centric DCs, the servers are considered as leaf nodes in the network hierarchy. The servers are connected to edge network switches, which in turn are interconnected to intermediate and core-level switches to transport traffic. The most common switch-centric topology is the *fat-tree* [4,5] topology. Fat-tree topology has hierarchical and scalable multilayer structure that has three layers of switches: edge, aggregation, and core switches. A fat-tree topology could have $n^3/4$ servers where n is a number of ports of switches in the topology. Figure 15.1 shows a fat-tree topology using 4-port switches to connect 16 servers.

15.2.2 Server-centric data centers

In server-centric DCs, servers, similar to switches, route network traffic. In this type of networks, servers have multiple network ports to connect to switches as well as other servers. These networks extend recursively using the lower level structures. Server-centric DCs support incremental expansion and are easily scalable to large numbers of servers (tens of thousands). BCube [6] and DCell [7] are examples of server-centric topologies.

BCube is a modular, recursive server-centric architecture. BCube networks are mainly designed to be used in shipping containers which are highly portable and quick to deploy. The portability feature of these networks helps change the network resource among different DCs as network resource demand changes. As it is shown

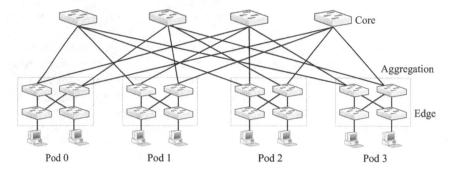

Figure 15.1   A fat-tree data center topology

in Figure 15.2(a), this topology uses eight switches to connect 16 servers where each switch has four ports. DCell is another expandable recursive server-centric DC. Compared to BCube networks, extending DCell networks requires fewer switches. However, servers in DCell networks have to spend more processing power in traffic rerouting than in BCube networks. Therefore, the decrease in performance due to traffic rerouting is more pronounced in DCell networks than in BCube networks. Figure 15.2(b) is an example of a DCell network that has four servers in each DCell0. This topology contains 5 switches and 20 servers.

Network topologies are comparable in various aspects including network diameter, the degree of servers, the number of servers, the number of switches, and the number of wires [8]. Herein, we mainly focus on how described topologies are fault tolerant. Thanks to various alternative paths between servers and network nodes, all aforementioned topologies are fault tolerant. Liu *et al.* [8] compared the fault-tolerant property of various topologies in more detail and introduced two metrics: (1) node-disjoint path (NDP) as the minimum of the total number of paths that share no common intermediate nodes between any arbitrary servers [8] and (2) edge-disjoint path (EDP) as the minimum of the total number of paths that share no common edges between any arbitrary servers [8]. In general, a higher NDP number means better fault tolerance to node failures while a higher EDP number means better fault tolerance to link failures. For fat-tree networks, the number of NDPs and EDPs is always equal to "1" since each server is connected to an edge switch with a single connection. Fewer ports on servers make the connections between servers and switches vulnerable to failures. On the contrary, for DCell and BCube networks, where k is the number of ports on each server, the number of NDPs and EDPs is $k + 1$. Unless each of the NDPs has a failure on it, two servers always remain connected. In fact, being more fault tolerant in server-centric topologies is achieved at the expense of having more redundant hardware modules.

The NDP and EDP approaches have been implemented in various network protocols. For example, the transport protocol may be designed to continue to work properly even when links are dynamically added/dropped to/from the network. An

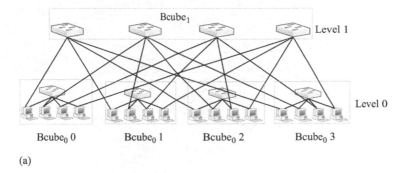

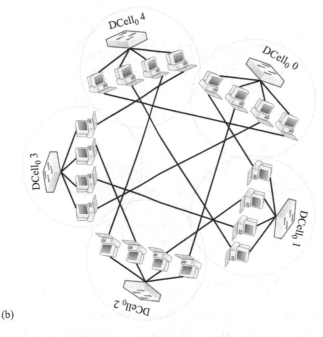

(b)

Figure 15.2   Server-centric topologies: (a) a BCube(4,1) data center topology and
(b) a DCell data center topology

example is the MultiPath TCP (MPTCP)[3] that aims to improve congestion control and
fault tolerance. It is worth noting that MPTCP was initially introduced to deal with
seamless TCP connections between WiFi and mobile networks. MPTCP was later
on extended to help multipath congestion control in DC networks [9]. In MPTCP,
multiple paths may be simultaneously active between a source and a destination. If
congestion occurs or if a link fails, a different link/path replaces the congested/failed
link or path. Figure 15.3(a) and 15.3(b) shows two MPTCP implementations on BCube

---

[3]RFC 6824: https://tools.ietf.org/html/rfc6824.

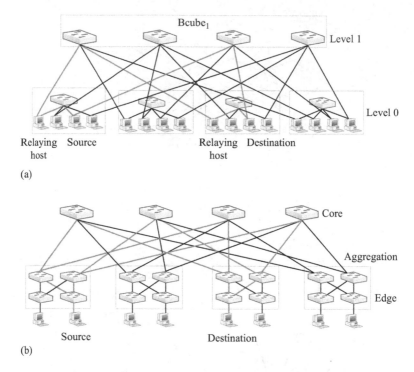

Figure 15.3   MPTCP in DC networks: (a) BCube DC and (b) fat-tree DC

and fat-tree networks, respectively. As it is shown, if one path fails, traffic can be seamlessly handled by the remaining active paths.

15.3   Fault-tolerant principles

Each network component may fail and affect users' applications catastrophically. Therefore, considering and addressing every possible malfunction are required for all network systems. Being fault tolerant consists of three steps: (1) detecting failures, (2) announcing failures, (3) recomputing routes and updating routing tables. The aforementioned steps form a recovery procedure. The ultimate goal is to decrease the running time of each step to minimize the total recovery time.

Detecting failures: The rapid detection of communication failures between adjacent nodes is important to quickly establish alternative paths. To speed up fault detection and improve fault detection efficiency, various protocols have been proposed including Bidirectional Forwarding Detection (BFD)[4] and MPLS Fault Management Operations, Administration, and Maintenance (OAM).[5] BFD is designed to

[4]RFC 5880: https://tools.ietf.org/html/rfc5880.
[5]RFC 6427: https://tools.ietf.org/html/rfc6427.

provide low-overhead, short-duration detection of failures in the path or between adjacent forwarding engines; it can be used at different granularity levels, that is, in (1) detecting path failures where a path is composed of multiple links and (2) establishing BFD sessions per link—including interfaces and data link(s) as well as the extending capabilities of forwarding engines. BFD first determines the state of a port by establishing a connection using a three-way handshake and then sends periodic control messages over that link. If no response message is received within a specified interval, the link is considered down. The time-out is determined by the control message interval T_i and typically has a value of $4 \times T_i$. Using a low control message interval, a faster reaction to the change in link state is possible.

Announcing failures: Failure announcement may happen in the form of broad-casting a specific message, triggering a message to a management entity (e.g., controller in the SDN architecture) or by distributing the updated table information to neighbors.

Recomputing routes and updating routing tables: Once the failure is detected and announced, the network must converge. Convergence is the event that happens within the transport network when the rerouted information flow merges back to a point in the error-free path. In legacy networks, convergence happens when devices that are directly connected to the faulty element update their routing tables and broadcast the updates to their neighbors. Broadcasting continues until all nodes in the network receive the message and update their table accordingly.

15.4   Traditional approaches to fault tolerance in data centers

Traffic and network restorations have been always key performance indicators in every network environment. DC networks should be fault tolerant to cope with any network faults in efficient time. Gill *et al.* [10] provide insight into the characteristics of DC network failures by analyzing the network failure logs collected over a period of around 1 year from tens of DCs. The authors showed that even when there is a 1:1 redundancy (one dedicated backup hardware for each network node), the network delivered only about 90% of the traffic in the median failure case. Performance is worse in the tail, with only 60% of traffic delivered during 20% of failures. This suggests better methods are needed for exploiting existing redundancy.

In another study, Liu *et al.* [8] propose a taxonomy for faults in DCs (Figure 15.4). Classifying the failures into fault models helps figure out the characteristics of different failures and methods to detect and deal with certain types of failures. The authors classified failure based on the following aspects:

Failure type: This attribute defines the level of failure. Either the whole component fails, or one of the links connected to it fails. The former is referred to as node failure, and the latter as link failure.

Fault region: When multiple related components are faulty, a fault region is a useful concept. For instance, in a DC, power failure of a rack disconnects all the

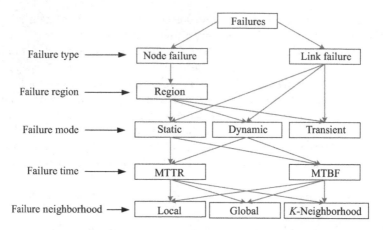

Figure 15.4   A taxonomy for faults in DC networks

components in the rack. If a routing protocol can figure out rack failures, it can bypass the whole rack.

Failure mode: This attribute shows the duration of failures. Failures are transient or permanent. Permanent failures are categorized into static or dynamic. The static failure exists since the system starts up, while the dynamic failure occurs during the operation of the system.

Failure time: This attribute shows the frequency of component failures. Two values, the mean time between failures (MTBF) and mean time to repair (MTTR), are used to evaluate the possibility of a failure and the time needed to recover from it.

Fault neighborhood: The extent of the dissemination of the fault information is identified by this attribute. Three different modes can be defined based on the distance from the faulty node to the selected node: (1) global; (2) local; and (3) k-neighborhood. In the global mode, every node in the network has information of all faulty nodes. In the local mode, only the adjacent nodes of a faulty node are aware of its information. Finally, the information of faulty nodes within distance *k* is tracked in the k-neighborhood mode.

The traditional approaches to have fault tolerant DCs can be classified into two categories: (1) reactive and (2) proactive.

15.4.1 Reactive approaches

A reactive fault-tolerant approach reduces the impact of failures, for example, by replacing the faulty element when failures occur. The two key issues to be considered in this context are the minimum redundancy requirement and the switching time.

Minimum redundancy requirement: In reactive methods, there should be some additional "standby equipment" (e.g., switches, routers, links) to replace faulty equipment when failures are detected. To reduce cost, network operators often opt for having one spare device for several active devices.

Switching time: The most simplistic reactive fault-tolerant method is to shut down the network that contains the faulty components and replace them. Although this method requires no complex mechanisms, the time to recovery might vary from hours to days, depending on the availability of replacement hardware. Considering the crucial importance of analyzing Big Data in the least possible time and enormous financial loss per each minute of downtime, this approach is absolutely infeasible. A slightly more complex mechanism is to shut down the faulty parts of the network and continue functioning at reduced capacity. Such methods are known as reconfiguration methods because the network is reconfigured once the fault is discovered. However, the reconfiguration method encounters a number of significant challenges including difficulties in deployment and a long recovery time. Local dynamic rerouting is the most expedient reactive way of handling a fault is to let the devices that are directly connected to the faulty element take care of the problem. For instance, if a switch learns that one of its neighboring switches is no longer available, it is responsible for forwarding packets on alternative paths that avoid the fault. Local dynamic rerouting requires a mechanism for rerouting packets around faults locally. This can be achieved either by using an adaptive routing algorithm [such as Open Shortest Path First (OSPF)] or by adding a rerouting mechanism to switches in the case of deterministic routing. Among all aforementioned reactive methods, local dynamic rerouting has, by far, the lowest time to recovery and so has the lowest number of packets lost when a fault occurs.

15.4.2   Proactive approaches

In proactive approaches, the network is designed in advance to cope with failures more systematically. With this method, resources have been preserved and backup paths have been worked out before the failure happens. Consequently, the protection paths could come into use immediately once the faults are detected. As a result, the fast recovery mechanisms provide an almost instantaneous response to a failure. A simple proactive way is to configure the network with alternative paths from start-up. In this approach, the network is configured with multiple paths between every source/destination pair. Therefore, when failure happens, the source node routes packets around network faults.

15.4.3   Problems with legacy fault-tolerant solutions

For Big Data applications, neither of reactive and proactive approaches in legacy networks are appropriate solutions to make the network fault tolerant. Reactive approach encounters several main problems. First, traditional routing schemes (like OSPF) may need tens of seconds to converge. During this transient time, from the time of a failure until all the nodes have new routing tables computed, applications can observe severe disruptions in service. This disruption of service during failure can be a serious problem for Big Data applications. Many Big Data applications do not tolerate long delays or delay jitters, and hence, they require low switching time with recovery time within milliseconds. Moreover, a large number of routing protocol packets need to be sent that consume noticeable network bandwidth and CPU resources. Second, since switches in legacy networks have no holistic view on the traffic load of other switches, they may utilize a suboptimal solution and redirect affected flows to heavily loaded switches and induce network bottleneck. Third, proactive recovery schemes require additional infrastructure to provide fast recovery from failures. This additional support includes extra routing table entries, extra fields or bits in the packet headers to indicate which links or nodes are failed, or extra addresses depending on the employed scheme. Furthermore, proactive recovery schemes may not employ some of the links of the primary path (before the failure) in the recovery/backup path (during the failure transient). This could result in increased backup path lengths and consequently increase the load on the network which can result in unbalanced load and increased delay. Finally, network providers have to install preconfigured paths on all the network nodes. These drawbacks make both reactive and proactive approach impractical for large-scale conventional networks.

15.5   Fault tolerance in SDN-based data centers

In the previous section, we discussed traditional approaches to achieve fault tolerance in cloud DCs. We now discuss how fault tolerance can be achieved in software-defined DCs. A software-defined DC is a DC where all elements of the infrastructure (networking, storage, CPU, and security) are virtualized and delivered as a service. Control of the DC is fully automated by software, meaning hardware configuration is maintained through intelligent software systems [11].

SDN global network traffic information in a central network controller and SDN data plane programmability help to control network traffic much better than traditional networks. We can summarize the benefits of SDNs in regard to fault tolerance in two key aspects. The first is related to the ability to exploit the global view of the network. In SDN, the controller has a global view of the network. In particular, it knows all alternative paths between any pair of nodes. This makes it easy to quickly converge to *efficient* paths when existing paths fail. This is particularly important in cloud DC networks where it is highly probable that several links/switches fail simultaneously. Existing paths may then need more than a few local corrections. Since SDN controllers are aware of the entire network, they can recompute efficient new paths quickly. Moreover, the availability of a global view produces new routes that are necessarily better than those that may be obtained using local information. Also, using the SDN programmable data plane, the newly computed paths can be activated seamlessly. The second aspect is related to the ability to route traffic based on the higher level information. With SDNs, network operators are able to use information from higher networking layers to reroute traffic when this is needed due to network maintenance or to a server failure. In traditional networks, it is not possible to route traffic based on higher layer information. For example, consider an HTTP application running in a cloud DC. For various reasons (e.g., when a failure occurs), the cloud DC operator may want to reroute the traffic destined to that application to a different server. In this scenario, using SDNs, the operator can use the (transport-level) information in the incoming packets to route traffic to the new server.

As SDN-based network devices are not intelligent, when a link breaks or a switch meets an outage in the forwarding plane, a controller is needed to help finding another valid routing path to continuously deliver packets. When initially designed, a controller in SDN architecture does not have the self-healing ability, and thus it must be equipped with the capacity of fault tolerance. The programmable nature of SDN provides network providers with the opportunity to develop and deploy various fault-tolerant mechanisms based on their requirements. Fault tolerance in SDN-based networks consists of two main phases: failure detection and failure recovery.

15.5.1 Failure detection in SDN

The controller entity in the SDN architecture can collaborate with existing failure detection mechanisms to detect and locate failures depending on the granularity of the failure detection mechanism that SDN controller collaborates with. For instance, BFD sessions could be established between two end points in a given path or among all adjacent nodes. In the former case, the controller can only detect a failure, while in the latter case, it can also locate failures. When the network node detects failure (e.g., through the BFD protocol), it sends a warning message to the controller for further processing. Detecting failures are also possible through other approaches. For instance, the authors in [12] proposed to use a circle that starts and terminates at the controller to monitor the status of a few links. Under normal circumstances, the control packet is transmitted along the loop and finally returns to the controller. If there is a failure inside the circle (i.e., link breaks), the second stage initiates where each switch in the loop is required not only to deliver the packet to the next hop but also send back to the controller. As a result, the failed link can be located.

15.5.2 Failure recovery in SDN

SDN and its OpenFlow implementation improve fault tolerance through the ability to dynamically reconfigure the network when failures occur. According to the difference in the version of OpenFlow protocol adopted, the methods based on the protection mechanism can be divided into two categories: approaches based on OpenFlow 1.0[6] and OpenFlow 1.1[7] [13]. For OpenFlow 1.0, Sgambelluri *et al.* [14] suggest to preserve the working path and backup path into two kinds of flow tables with different priorities. When the working path breaks, only if its corresponding flow table entries are deleted, the protection can be used. As a result, this method generates OFP_FLOW_RESTORE packet to inform the controller to recompute route if the primary one recovers. From OpenFlow 1.1, the concept of group table is proposed. Fast failover (FF) group is one of the proposed groups. FF works by executing the first live bucket in the group, meaning it will send the packet to the first port in the group where the port state is up. This allows the switch to perform a local failover instead of the SDN controller performing a centralized failover. Therefore, in this scenario, all the link failure detection

[6]http://archive.openflow.org/documents/openflow-spec-v1.0.0.pdf.
[7]http://archive.openflow.org/documents/OpenFlow-spec-v1.1.0.pdf.

and recovery happens in the data plane. As we will describe later in this section, a number of studies leverage OpenFlow FF group to make the network fault tolerant.

15.6 Reactive fault-tolerant approach in SDN

Akin to legacy networks, SDN architecture provides fault tolerance in two ways: reactive and proactive. Since reactive methods provide a longer recovery time, they have been the topic of fewer studies. Herein, we briefly describe the reactive method and elaborate on the proactive one in the next section.

The reactive approach in SDN architecture can be divided into three steps: (1) the relevant switches alert the controller about a fault, then (2) the controller starts the recovery process by either computing a new alternative path or looking up a precomputed alternative path, and finally (3) the controller generates certain commands to data plane in order to update their forwarding tables. Unlike reactive approach in the legacy network that may lead to a suboptimal solution, the SDN-based reactive scheme does not suffer from these issues because the centralized controller has a global view of the DC network; therefore, flow redirections are performed by taking into account the traffic load information of adjacent switches.

To mention a sample approach, the authors of [15] adopted the reactive approach that focused on an efficient failure recovery algorithm using cycle structure on mesh networks. This approach firstly computes a tree for the topology, then assigns a tie-set for each remaining link that is not contained in the tree. When the controller receives a notification of a failure in a link, it locates the link failure and chooses the minimum tie-set that includes a link that will restore connectivity. The controller then installs corresponding rules in the switch. Based on the flow tables, a tie-set switch can switch a communication path to a backup path upon detecting a link failure.

15.7 Proactive fault-tolerant approach in SDN

In order to provide fast failure recovery and reduce packet loss, the proactive fault-tolerant approaches are preferred. In proactive approaches (also known as protection approaches), the controller has worked out the backup path along with the primary path and stored the information into switches' forwarding tables [14], or packet headers [16]. Thus, when the working path is broken, data flows go through the protection path. SDN-based proactive failure recovery scheme for data traffic has been the topic of extensive research.

Van Adrichem *et al.* [17] propose to deploy link-based monitoring and protection to overcome topology failure. They introduce a failover scheme with per-link BFD sessions and preconfigured primary and secondary paths computed by a controller. Additionally, they adopt the FF group table implementation of the OpenFlow capable software switch to consider BFD status real time, hence eliminating the administrative processes of bringing an interface's status down. Initially, switches receive a preconfigured backup path along with the primary path in terms of FF rules. When the switch detects a link failure (through BFD protocol), it initiates the backup path immediately. Their implementation reduces the recovery time significantly—a path restoration time of 3.3 ms has been reported in this study—in various topologies. Segment protection based on the preplanned backup path was proposed in [14]. Instead of using group table, OF-based segment protection scheme employs flow entry priority and an autoreject mechanism to realize fast switchovers between working paths and protection paths. First, the controller precalculates backup paths for all possible link failure between adjacent nodes; it then installs corresponding flow entries to switches with different priorities by giving the primary path higher priority. Upon detecting a failure, the autoreject mechanism allows all affected flow entries using the failed links to be deleted immediately without waiting for the soft or hard time-out. Due to the preplanned backup paths installation, switch-over time is greatly reduced. The SlickFlow approach [16] provides resilience in DC networks using OpenFlow and is based on source routing. SlickFlow leverages the idea of using packet header space to carry alternative path information to implement resilient source routing in OpenFlow networks. Under the presence of failures along the primary path, packets can be rerouted to alternative paths by the switches themselves without involving the controller.

A number of hybrid solutions were also proposed. Authors in [18] designed a network restoration method for link failure in SDN-based networks. In this proposed method, the OpenFlow-enabled switches that detect the link failure for a particular flow inform the controller about the situation. Upon receiving this notification, the controller first examines if the *precompute* old path is affected by this change. If it is, the controller then calculates a new backup path for the affected flow and updates the OpenFlow switch about the new information. As another example, SDN has been used to mitigate disaster risks and cut down the investment and management cost in [19]. Their design consists of two modules: the proactive local failure recovery module running at the switches and the reactive global restoration module running at the controller. In the protection module, they adopt the multitopology routing to do local fast rerouting and consider the geography properties of the disaster failure to generate robust backup routes. In the restoration module, the controller reconnects failed nodes by rescheduling the preinstalled routes.

As discussed in previous sections, deploying proactive fault-tolerant method over the whole network is a very time-consuming and a resource-intensive procedure, if not impossible. This is because failure can happen at any part of the network, and thus, if network providers want to deploy proactive approaches, they have to anticipate all possible types of failures through the whole network. However, if a network provider can predict the potential points of failure, then the proactive approach is the best fault-tolerant solution. In such a case, the network provider only deploys proactive methods on certain parts of the network; this, in turn, will significantly reduce the configuration time and resource usage. Moreover, the proactive approach is not always in the form of finding a primary and backup path. Instead, deploying various mechanisms to *avoid* failures is also proactive. The SDN architecture can further enhance the usability of proactive approaches through helping network providers to dynamically deploy them in networks.

15.7.1   Failure prediction in cloud data centers

Due to the high cost of downtime for the average DC, operators always strive to minimize downtime as much as possible. A crucial requirement to reduce the downtime
is the ability to predict hardware failures. For example, Ganguly *et al.* [20] presented
a hard disk failure prediction model for usage in cloud environments. Using a two-
stage ensemble model and various data sources, they describe the techniques and
challenges associated with deploying an operational predictive model on cloud-like
environments. They also list the benefits associated with a predictive hardware model.
Bahga and Madisetti [21] detailed a framework that processes and analyzes data collected from multiple sensors embedded in a cloud computing environment. Using a
large set of information obtained from previous failure cases, they can predict failures
in real time before they occur.

Improving cloud functionality by applying neural networks is also a well-
researched topic. Chen *et al.* [22] applied recurrent neural networks to predict/identify
resource usage patterns. This allowed them to categorize the resource-utilization
time-series-data into different classes and predict when batch applications would fail.
This job prediction method improved resource savings cluster-wide between 6% and
10%. Duggan *et al.* [23] introduce a portable learning-based workload prediction tool
specifically tailored to analytical database applications deployed in the cloud. They
showed that their models were able to accurately predict the workload throughput
values of heterogeneous systems within a 30% margin of error. These types of predictive models focus on the application more than the physical hardware itself. Davis
et al. [24] leveraged neural network in FailureSim, a simulator based on CloudSim,[8]
to predict hardware failures in cloud DCs. In this approach, various performance data
are gathered from the cloud DC and fed into a neural network which then makes
predictions as to future potential hardware failures in the DC.

The collaboration between the prediction modules and SDN controller is beneficial for both sides. Through various available application program interfaces (APIs),
the prediction modules can communicate with the controller to retrieve underlying network information (traffic status, port utilization, etc.) and feed prediction results to the
controller. The controller then uses this information to deploy proactive fault-tolerant
methods in parts of the network to make it fault tolerant.

15.7.2   Traffic patterns of Big Data workloads

It is important to understand the characteristics of traffic patterns of Big Data workloads. These characteristics may be taken into account to improve fault tolerance using
the flexibility of SDN in terms of programmability, controller placement, etc. To this
end, we briefly discuss the networking behavior of Big Data workloads in DCs with
regard to their traffic characteristics and traffic distribution.

---

[8] http://www.cloudbus.org/cloudsim/.

There are two ways to classify DC network traffic patterns: (1) based on traffic size and (2) based on the numbers of senders and receivers. In the first classification, one can distinguish two types of traffic: elephant flows and mice flows. Elephant flows are extremely large continuous flows that take time and occupy network bandwidth to complete. Examples include VM migration and MapReduce applications. Mice flows are short-lived traffic such as emails, HTTP requests, etc. The type of network traffic that is traversing the network is very important to be distinguished by the network. For instance, elephant flows collision through a path may increase the probability of failures if the network nodes do not have enough capacity. Therefore, the network should be able to detect traffic and segregate them according to their characteristics. The second way to classify DC network traffic patterns is based on the number of traffic sources and destinations. Three types of patterns exist: one to one, one to many, and many to one. The latter type is particularly relevant in Big Data workloads, e.g., in a Map-Reduce application. In this type, there is a possibility of traffic conflict and buffer overflow at the destination or several intermediate points. This problem (known in the literature as the "Incast" problem) may have a significant impact on network performance and robustness [25]. Detecting and/or classifying flows, routing flows according to the network conditions, and resolving problems such as TCP Incast help avoid increasing the failure probability, and consequently make a network more fault tolerant. Achieving this goal is difficult in legacy networks due to the static nature of the network architecture. On the contrary, various studies have leveraged the intrinsic characteristics of SDN to develop dynamic traffic engineering methods in order to resolve problems such as TCP Incast or avoid collision of multiple elephant flows. A number of these studies have been investigated in previous chapters.

15.8   Open issues and challenges

In previous sections, we investigated the drawbacks of both reactive and proactive approaches in legacy networks. Although SDN can help mitigate a number of these problems, it also introduces new challenges.

15.8.1   Problems with SDN-based fault-tolerant methods

Both reactive and proactive approaches in SDN architecture encounter a number of problems. SDN-based reactive strategies imply (1) high restoration time due to the necessary interaction with the controller and (2) additional load on the control channel. The delay introduced by the controller may, in some cases, be prohibitive [2]. Although authors in different studies address this problem by reducing the number of flow setup messages, the proposed solutions are not comprehensive.

There are multiple concerns about the SDN-based proactive approach as well. First, since controller uses *old* information about the network to calculate the alternative path (backup path), this alternative may lead to the use of nonoptimal backup path. Second, the proactive approach provides FF capability by eliminating extra communication overhead between the controller and the switches, but it cannot handle cases where both working and backup paths have failed. As soon as both the working and protection paths face a failure, data flows cannot find another route to deliver packets even though there are other routes available. Third, the proactive approach has a scalability issue as the SDN controller must handle per-flow detouring that could overwhelm the controller.

15.8.2   Fault tolerance in the control plane

Although SDN could significantly help develop dynamic and agile methods of failure recovery in the data plane, it introduces the requirement of being fault tolerant in the control plane. In SDN architecture, network nodes need controller help to steer traffic flows. To guarantee the resiliency of the control plane, two aspects need to be considered. First, the controller must function properly, which means that the failure of the controller is not allowed. Second, switches can communicate with the controller even though OpenFlow channels break [13]. Providing resiliency against failure in the control plane is a vast topic which entails various issues such as controller placement, handover between controllers, controller synchronization, etc. Although a number of studies addressed the aforementioned problems (such as [26–28]), being fault tolerant in the control plane is yet an open issue.

15.9   Summary and conclusion

SDN networks would have many advantages to be used as fault-tolerant Big Data infrastructures such as programmability and global network view which help monitor and control the network behavior adaptively and efficiently. This chapter studied a number of requirements to provide fault tolerance in networks that Big Data applications perform upon. First, we studied the key requirements to be fault tolerant. The network topology design is crucial to provide resiliency against node or link failure. Second, we mentioned the principle concepts of fault tolerance and elaborated on reactive and proactive methods as two common approaches to deal with the failures in networks. Third, the fault-tolerant mechanisms in SDN architecture and their advantages were elucidated. Consequently, we investigated a number of studies that leverage SDN to provide fault tolerance. Finally, this chapter was concluded by introducing open issues and challenges in SDN architecture to provide a perfect fault-tolerant network.

References

[1]   B. Nunes, M. Mendonca, X. Nguyen, K. Obraczka, and T. Turletti, "A survey of software-defined networking: Past, present, and future of programmable networks," *IEEE Communications Surveys Tutorials*, vol. 16, no. 3, pp. 1617–1634, 2014.

[2]   D. Kreutz, F. M. Ramos, P. E. Verissimo, C. E. Rothenberg, S. Azodolmolky, and S. Uhlig, "Software-defined networking: A comprehensive survey," *Proceedings of the IEEE*, vol. 103, pp. 14–76, Jan. 2015.

[3]   L. Cui, F. R. Yu, and Q. Yan, "When big data meets software-defined networking: SDN for big data and big data for SDN," *IEEE Network*, vol. 30, no. 1, pp. 58–65, 2016.

[4]   C. E. Leiserson, "Fat-trees: Universal networks for hardware-efficient super-computing," *IEEE Transactions on Computers*, vol. C-34, pp. 892–901, Oct. 1985.

[5]   M. Al-Fares, A. Loukissas, and A. Vahdat, "A scalable, commodity data center network architecture," in *ACM SIGCOMM*, (New York, NY, USA), pp. 63–74, ACM, 2008.

[6]   C. Guo, G. Lu, D. Li, *et al.*, "Bcube: A high performance, server-centric network architecture for modular data centers," in *ACM SIGCOMM*, (New York, NY, USA), pp. 63–74, ACM, 2009.

[7]   C. Guo, H. Wu, K. Tan, L. Shi, Y. Zhang, and S. Lu, "Dcell: A scalable and fault-tolerant network structure for data centers," in *ACM SIGCOMM*, (New York, NY, USA), pp. 75–86, ACM, 2008.

[8]   Y. Liu, J. K. Muppala, M. Veeraraghavan, D. Lin, and M. Hamdi, *Data Center Networks: Topologies, Architectures and Fault-Tolerance Characteristics*. New York, NY, US: Springer Science & Business Media, 2013.

[9]   C. Raiciu, S. Barre, C. Pluntke, A. Greenhalgh, D. Wischik, and M. Handley, "Improving datacenter performance and robustness with multipath TCP," in *ACM SIGCOMM*, (New York, NY, USA), pp. 266–277, ACM, 2011.

[10] P. Gill, N. Jain, and N. Nagappan, "Understanding network failures in data centers: Measurement, analysis, and implications," in *ACM SIGCOMM*, (New York, NY, USA), pp. 350–361, ACM, 2011.

[11] Vangie Beal, "SDDC: Software-Defined Data Center." http://www .webopedia.com/TERM/S/software_defined_data_center_SDDC.html.

[12] S. S. Lee, K.-Y. Li, K.-Y. Chan, G.-H. Lai, and Y.-C. Chung, "Path layout planning and software based fast failure detection in survivable openflow networks," in *International Conference on the Design of Reliable Communication Networks (DRCN)*, pp. 1–8, IEEE, Apr. 2014.

[13] J. Chen, J. Chen, F. Xu, M. Yin, and W. Zhang, *When Software Defined Networks Meet Fault Tolerance: A Survey*, pp. 351–368. Cham: Springer, Nov. 2015.

[14] A. Sgambelluri, A. Giorgetti, F. Cugini, F. Paolucci, and P. Castoldi, "Openflow-based segment protection in ethernet networks," *IEEE Journal of Optical Communications and Networking*, vol. 5, pp. 1066–1075, Sep. 2013.

[15] J. Nagano and N. Shinomiya, "A failure recovery method based on cycle structure and its verification by openflow," in *International Conference on Advanced Information Networking and Applications (AINA)*, pp. 298–303, IEEE, Mar. 2013.

[16] R. M. Ramos, M. Martinello, and C. E. Rothenberg, "Slickflow: Resilient source routing in data center networks unlocked by openflow," in *Local Computer Networks (LCN)*, pp. 606–613, IEEE, Oct. 2013.

[17]   N. L. Van Adrichem, B. J. Van Asten, and F. A. Kuipers, "Fast recovery in software-defined networks," in *European Workshop on Software Defined Networks*, pp. 61–66, IEEE, Sep. 2014.

[18]   S. Sharma, D. Staessens, D. Colle, M. Pickavet, and P. Demeester, "Enabling fast failure recovery in openflow networks," in *International Workshop on the Design of Reliable Communication Networks (DRCN)*, pp. 164–171, IEEE, Oct. 2011.

[19]   A. Xie, X. Wang, W. Wang, and S. Lu, "Designing a disaster-resilient network with software defined networking," in *International Symposium of Quality of Service (IWQoS)*, pp. 135–140, IEEE, May 2014.

[20]   S. Ganguly, A. Consul, A. Khan, B. Bussone, J. Richards, and A. Miguel, "A practical approach to hard disk failure prediction in cloud platforms: Big data model for failure management in datacenters," in *International Conference on Big Data Computing Service and Applications (BigDataService)*, pp. 105–116, IEEE, Mar. 2016.

[21]   A. Bahga and V. K. Madisetti, "Analyzing massive machine maintenance data in a computing cloud," *IEEE Transactions on Parallel and Distributed Systems*, vol. 23, pp. 1831–1843, Oct. 2012.

[22]   X. Chen, C.-D. Lu, and K. Pattabiraman, "Failure analysis of jobs in compute clouds: A Google cluster case study," in *International Symposium on Software Reliability Engineering (ISSRE)*, (Washington, DC, USA), pp. 167–177, IEEE, Nov. 2014.

[23]   J. Duggan, U. Cetintemel, O. Papaemmanouil, and E. Upfal, "Performance prediction for concurrent database workloads," in *ACM International Conference on Management of Data (SIGMOD)*, (New York, NY, USA), pp. 337–348, ACM, Jun. 2011.

[24]   N. Davis, A. Rezgui, H. Soliman, S. Manzanares, and M. Coates, "Failuresim: A system for predicting hardware failures in cloud data centers using neural networks," in *International Conference on Cloud Computing (Cloud)*, IEEE, Jun. 2017.

[25]   S. U. Khan and A. Y. Zomaya, *Handbook on Data Centers*. New York, NY, US: Springer, 2015.

[26]   N. Katta, H. Zhang, M. Freedman, and J. Rexford, "Ravana: Controller fault-tolerance in software-defined networking," in *ACM SIGCOMM Symposium on Software Defined Networking Research (SOSR)*, (New York, NY, USA), pp. 4:1–4:12, ACM, Jun. 2015.

[27]   B. Heller, R. Sherwood, and N. McKeown, "The controller placement problem," in *Workshop on Hot Topics in Software Defined Networks (HotSDN)*, (New York, NY, USA), pp. 7–12, ACM, 2012.

[28]   S. Lange, S. Gebert, T. Zinner, *et al.*, "Heuristic approaches to the controller placement problem in large scale SDN networks," *IEEE Transactions on Network and Service Management*, vol. 12, pp. 4–17, Mar. 2015.

Part III

How Big Data helps SDN

Chapter 16

How Big Data helps SDN with data protection and privacy

Lothar Fritsch*

This chapter will discuss Big Data (BD) as a tool in software-defined networking (SDN) from the perspective of information privacy and data protection. First, it will discuss how BD and SDN are connected and expected to provide better services. Then, the chapter will describe the core of data protection and privacy requirements in Europe, followed by a discussion about the implications for BD use in SDN. The chapter will conclude with recommendations and privacy design considerations for BD in SDN.

16.1 Collection and processing of data to improve performance

BD and machine-learning (ML) technologies are expected to make significant contributions automated decision-making in a large number of application domains. SDN is a concept that promises dynamic reconfiguration of routers and other network equipment for the purpose of dynamic, flexible and reactive infrastructure management.

16.1.1 The promise of Big Data in SDN: data collection, analysis, configuration change

SDN offers new opportunities to dynamically configure networks based on automated decision-making based on ML algorithms, metrics and BD technology. As a presumption for such a scenario, we assume that a central controller configures all SDN components in its domain. The controller makes configuration decisions based on its configuration and on input signals. Input signals are provided, among others, by BD systems that consume data about network configurations, traffic patterns, status, possible attacks and other information. Within the BD systems, network data is collected, processed, aggregated or trained into ML algorithms. BD systems are then queried, often based on statistical models, for the retrieval of statistics, the generation

*Department of Mathematics and Computer Science, Karlstad University, Sweden

of forecasts or the making of decisions in various contexts. Important input to such queries are data sets, statistical or ML models, input signals and context.

In SDN, networking parameters are changed. The model of BD supported SDN presumes that SDN controllers by using BD systems that collect data on networking performance under various contexts will make better decisions about SDN configuration, and thereby improve network performance by whichever performance indicator important in a situation. Such performance indicators are, for example, network throughput, transmission time, load distribution, network resiliency against attacks or dynamic security decision-making against attacks.

16.2   Data protection requirements and their implications for Big Data in SDN

16.2.1   Data protection requirements in Europe

The European Union has a common framework for data protection, the Directive on privacy and electronic communications 2002/58/EC [1], and currently, in addition, implements the General Data Protection Regulation (GDPR) [2]. The GDPR will regulate the processing of personal data in a homogenized regulation in the EU from May 2018. The GDPR contains specific regulation for automated decision-making. The sections below will provide a brief summary of key elements of European data protection philosophy and describes a summary of the essential features of lawful processing.

16.2.1.1   European data protection philosophy

European data protection legislation bases legal processing of personal data on three principles: data subject consent, transparency of data processing and possibility of intervention for data subjects. Specific regulation applies in member countries for sensitive personal data. Such data is governed by specific regulation. An example is processing of personal data related to health.

In several European countries, privacy is considered to have a direct link to fundamental constitutional freedom rights. A general principle is that processing personal data is lawful, subject to conditions. The most important pair of conditions is the transparency of the collection and processing for the data subject, along with the requirement to collect explicit consent for data processing from the data subject. The European philosophy of data protection assumes an active, responsible individual who grants data processing rights to one or more data processors.

From the system owner and data processor perspective, EU data protection philosophy imposes responsibilities for managerial, organizational and technical measures [3]. Those responsibilities are anchored in organizations' management as well as in their technical operations departments. Data controllers the organization responsible for the personal data collected from data subjects are the legal entity obliged to comply with regulation.

16.2.1.2   Essentials of lawful personal information processing

In essence, all processing of personal data is legal if it is based on informed consent given by the data subjects. Generally, informed consent is given based on a declaration called a privacy policy of the data collecting entity. The processing of data then is expected to remain within the applications and entities specified in the policy. Data subjects then have extensive inquiry, correction and withdrawal rights.

Privacy and information security—a continuous process

GDPR now views information privacy management as a continuous process cycle. Most practical privacy management methods are inspired by the ISO27001-Plan-Do-Check-Act cycle for information security management [4]. Common elements are

- An inventory of personal data assets (data collection nodes, data processing nodes, types of personal data processed and processing policies),
- A privacy risk and impact analysis (targeting both organizational and data subject impact),
- The selection of controls and deployment (technical and organizational),
- The evaluation of system after change or in regular intervals.

Colesky *et al.* show a practical approach for privacy-preserving tactics in [5]. Here, basic transactions on personal data and an overall process for privacy by design are specified. The presented method is best applicable to new systems at the design phase. In contrast, an ongoing, cyclic privacy management process that is, usable on evolutionary software change processes is specified by OASIS in [6]. A complete cycle of privacy management as elaborated and detailed in their report.

New in the GDPR legislation are demands for information security, including integrity and confidentiality and general information security of the personal data. This includes protection against unauthorized or unlawful processing and against accidental loss, destruction or damage, using the respective technical or organizational measures.

Privacy by default

GDPR asks for the start-up configuration of IT systems to contain explicit support for privacy and data protection. As a generalized concept, we may think of the EU requesting any use of personal data in IT systems to be compliant with EU privacy regulation from the start, without opting out, setting privacy settings or deleting data collected without consent. Specifically, to implement and accommodate privacy-by-default, five properties must be present in IT systems that collect, process and store personal data:

- lawfulness, fairness and transparency of collection and processing of data;
- purpose limitation of data collection, e.g., through explicit policies, limited purpose and technical and managerial controls for purpose binding;
- data minimization to limit collection to the data required by the core business model;
- accuracy of the used data;

- storage limitation, setting a time limit for personal data storage in relation to the performed transactions.

With privacy audit in mind, system owners are advised to prepare credible evidence of the above features for all system components that process personal data.

Managing subject consent and privacy policies

Any collection of personal data shall be based on voluntary, individual and informed consent that is, acquired from the data subject before collecting or processing data. Informed consent is based on four adjectives: voluntary, individual, informed, demonstrable. Consent is expressed as any form of legally binding contract at the data subject's location, however, to fulfill the requirement of being demonstrable, the consent should get collected in a form that can get proven to auditors and courts, e.g., in writing or by using nonrepudiable electronic engagement forms such as electronic signatures. The burden of proof is with the data collecting entity! A privacy policy shall at least contain

- the period for which the personal data will be stored or the criteria used to determine this period;
- a reference to data subjects' rights;
- reference to the right to revoke consent;
- the existence of automated decision-making including profiling (automated individual decisions): information about the mechanisms involved, as well as the envisaged consequences of automated processing for the data subject;
- in case of intended further processing for purposes other than these for which the data were collected.

Managing data subject consent is a process that will need attention during the whole system lifetime. It is a per-data-subject process that governs the relationship between the data collector and the data subjects as long as identifiable personal information is remaining in the system. The relationship is managed in several phases:

- Collection of initial consent;
- Data subject initiated change or revocation of consent;
- Data collector or processor-initiated change of privacy policy causes renewal of consent; applies to: company mergers, change of business model, change of subcontractors, change of data model, possible change of hosting country and many.
- Termination of data, e.g., upon completion of transaction, retirement of business model, deletion requests and revocation of consent.

The demonstrable management of consent requires archival of a consent statement along with the privacy policy the consent was given to. It requires the handling of data subject identity top ensure legitimacy of future change, deletion or transparency requests over the whole lifetime of the stored data. Upon changes in privacy policies, versioning of consent-policy relationships will be the basis for determination of lawful processing of the acquired data.

Transparency and intervenability

An important feature of data protection regulation is transparency. As a complement to informed consent, data subjects have extensive rights for inquiry about the nature of utilization of their personal data. Intervention rights ensure data subject's rights to correct wrongful data, request data deletion and terminate engagement through withdrawal of consent.

Information requests and deletion requests must get timely answered. The data controller must react to erasure requests without undue delay. In scenarios where subcontractors provide data analysis, or data is being merged from various sources to accommodate analysis, information about such processing must get included in replies to information requests.

Data subject intervention is seen as any of the following actions: Data correction, data deletion and revocation of consent. In any case, the data controller has to ensure that the eligible person is demanding data access, correction or deletion. Deletion is to be final (concerning identifiable or person-relatable data). Revocation of consent implies the retirement of all identifiable and person-relatable data from processing, and its terminal deletion. It may be advisable to data controllers to keep a demonstrable log over deletion completion.

Audit evidence and breach notification

Audibility and breach notification are required. Audibility demands the production of audible evidence about the implementation of data protection procedures, controls and compliance that is, verifiable to inspecting auditor. Upon privacy breaches, the GDPR now sets stringent time demands on the data controller. Immediately, latest 72 h after the breach occurred, a national authority has to get informed about the data breach. In addition, the data subjects have to get informed. When the personal data breach is likely to result in a high risk to the rights and freedoms of natural persons, the data controller shall communicate the personal data breach to the data subject immediately. Is the person not reachable or is the breach of a magnitude that makes handling difficult, public broadcast channels have to be considered for informing data subjects.

Obligations with international and cross-border data transfer

Cross-border transfer of personal information, in particular to countries outside the EU, is subject to specific requirements. Explicit user consent is required. Exceptions are possible where the EU has signed data transfer agreements with third countries.

16.2.2   *Personal data in networking information*

In computer networking, many data sets are used that are directly or indirectly person relatable. Network addresses, adapter hardware addresses, static IP addresses, router addresses and other aspects of direct addressing may be related directly to an individual person's communication at the network protocol level. Even information about the content of communication may be accumulated, e.g., by the fact that particular addresses receive video streams at a particular time of the day. Typical person-relatable data is

- Directly person-relatable data: IPs, MACs and other static information is person-relatable data; communication peer addresses
- Indirectly person-relatable data: Traffic patterns, usage time, traffic destinations and media types form person-relatable patterns

   Dynamic configuration may break privacy policies, user consent and other regulatory laws. Dynamic and reconfigurable routing may accidentally export personal data into other legal spaces, breaching several laws.

16.2.3   Issues with Big Data processing

BD has several issues that need thorough consideration:

- Big Databases aggregate personal data that is, not bound to a well-defined purpose for processing personal data. Policy violations may occur with new models, contexts or data signals added to the system.
- Big Databases aggregate enormous amounts of personal behavior information on networks. They may cause a major problem in case data leaks out.
- It remains unclear what exactly ML algorithms learn when they automatically make connections between personal data. This creates two different kinds of privacy threats:
  - Profiling by combining prior not combined personal data about a data subject;
  - Falsely combining data with a data subject not related to the data, and in consequence, making wrongful decisions based on this data set.
- Transparency and audibility can be very difficult when training data for ML is not accessible. "Machines" will make decisions that will be hard to verify by anyone, based on "aggregated" or trained data.
- Data subjects may be treated as a member of a model-created group of other data subjects, and treaded based on group average information. However, such averages might not reflect the person's interests, data processing consent or customer relationship.
- SDN configuration actions to tackle certain security situations may unfairly put data subjects at a disadvantage due to algorithmic errors, wrongful models, improper input data or mismatching context.

16.3   Recommendations for privacy design in SDN Big Data projects

In ENISA's report on privacy by design for BD [7], the authors present design strategies for privacy. Further insight into privacy engineering for database applications is provided in [8]. In addition, they discuss important issues specific to BD processing, such as composability, streaming anonymization, decentralized anonymization and large data volume computability. The report proceeds beyond the notion of privacy by design and the known difficulties of their application as discussed in [9].

16.3.1 Storage concepts

Managing of the input data for BD analysis in SDN in a critical issue. The same holds for data protection and privacy issues. Input data for SDN is composed of static and historic data as well as real-time streams of data from current networking. SND BD applications' vision is to dynamically reconfigure networks based on historic statistics and current livestreamed status information. However, privacy legislation sets sharp limits on person-relatable data that is, processed by such systems. Storage concepts and architectures are an essential part of privacy compliance. Distributed data storage should be a major architecture feature from the start. Separation of personal data over various administrative domains protects against data theft, leakage and accidental release of all records. Any data not required in person-relatable form should get anonymized at the collection point and at storage by using appropriate algorithms that support the respective data application [10]. The origin of data may be important, for quality or legal reasons. Therefore, provenance information about the data source and the acquisition channel is relevant when selecting data for further processing. Per-purpose association of data sources, potentially with ad-hoc consent from data subject [11], may be one possible solution for the handling separated data storage on a per-case basis, as shown in Figure 16.1. A mechanism for generating audit and transparency records, preferably without creating new privacy issues on the way, should be in the core of all databases and processing nodes. Finally, database encryption, integrity protection, mandatory access control and the application of advanced techniques such as homomorphic encryption and encrypted search, and statistics computation should be considered. A number of storage strategies for privacy-respecting cloud applications have been presented in [12].

16.3.2 Filtration, anonymization and data minimization

An approach to avoid unmanageable complexity in privacy management is the reduction of the problem to the minimum size possible. The actual BD analysis should process only the data needed for the particular type of analysis. The data should not be communicated as raw data to the analysis data processing entity, but it should be transformed with privacy-preserving statistical data transformations. Such transformations preserve selected statistical properties that support a particular way of analyzing data, while through transformation, aggregation, homomorphic encryption and other methods hiding the data's links to data subjects. Such case-based analysis should ideally draw data from a distributed database approach, where each source database can transform the provided data sample according to the analysis case specification. Even the end users (data subjects) could manage and provide their own data through personal databases and data brokerage agents that offer, choose and transform their data.

Figure 16.1 shows a simple architecture of data subjects that, through their personal data brokerage agent, share filtered information with a BD system that, through

Privacy by design for Big Data

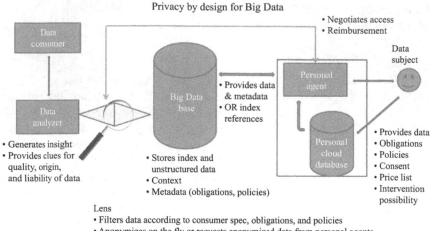

Figure 16.1   Privacy design for Big Data Analysis: User-centric data sharing, case-based filtration and anonymization

a specific analysis setup in the data analyzer component, delivers BD analysis services to a data consumer. Not that, in case of collaborating stakeholders such as competing network providers in SDN, each network provider could implement this architecture recursively and thus provide filtered data from their own domain to collaborative analysis systems that process data provided, for example, by all network providers into a specific analysis for a network threat situation.

16.3.3   Privacy-friendly data mining

In recent research, algorithms for privacy-friendly data mining, data anonymization and data transformation that preserve statistical properties while at the same time upholding confidentiality, and algorithms that preserve or enhance privacy through data transformations have been published in scientific literature. The book Database Anonymization [10] summarizes the state of the art in data transformation, in data analysis of privacy-transformed data sets and in general data transformation with the preservation of certain statistical and mathematical properties. The data architecture in Section 16.3.2 above will heavily rely on those algorithms for the filtering and analysis modules.

16.3.4   Purpose-binding and obligations management

Useful technology to enforce privacy policies and privacy obligations has been developed over the course of a decade, mainly led by researchers at Hewlett-Packard [13,14]. Two cornerstones of the technology are so-called sticky policies and obligations. Sticky policies are at the core of a system that encrypts personal data, amends it with processing policies and provides an infrastructure to retrieve decryption keys for data processing from a central party. The concept of obligations complements this by defining data–subject set policies for acceptable use of personal data. These rules are formalized as obligations that travel with the data in the same way the sticky policies travel with the data. The respective protocols and mechanisms provide very detailed control over how data travels and how it is processed. However, this comes at a cost, since policy processing imposes communication and cryptographic overhead.

16.3.5 Data subject consent management techniques

Documented data subject consent to both data collection and data processing is an essential precondition. However, in dynamic networking, it is often infeasible to foresee all possible future situations of data processing for dynamic networking, and thus, it will be impossible to provide precise privacy policies and supplementary information about data processing to the data subjects who may be profiled in SDN BD applications. Today's widely used practice is the formulation of maximally broad, flexible privacy policies that collect consent for all possible ways of data processing by all imaginable contractors. Such policies are not considered consumer friendly and will possibly create compliance issues with the EU GDPR framework. An approach suggested for such situations is that of recollection of consent when contexts change. One essential precondition is that there is a communication channel between the data subjects and the data processors that enables data processors to recollect consent for changed policies. Since such practices impose overhead on the data subjects, they should be reserved for situations such as large-scale internet attacks and similar large problems. An inverse perspective on this issue is the issuance of partial commitment for limited data processing, which in [11] enables arbitration between data subject and data processor for refining data collection policies later.

16.3.6 Algorithmic accountability concepts

Automated decision-making and ML concepts require a new set of governance rules to enable accountability. Approaches such as statistics, ML models, discovery of patterns and predictions based on stochastic models calibrated with historic data and other input signals make decisions about network configuration, service prioritization, and ultimately, people's access to network-based services. To ensure well-defined responsibilities in case of malfunctioning models, insufficiently trained ML systems or wrongful decisions, system owners will need to find out whether a model, an algorithm, the input data or any other component caused the malfunction to appear. The idea of holding algorithms accountable for their observable output, and to make the potential problems traceable, is called "algorithmic accountability" [15]. Any system that "learns" from personalized networking input data, and then is used to make automated decisions about dynamic network configuration, should be considered as being regulated by the GDPR. Data subjects should get informed about automated decision-making. However, beyond GDPR compliance, automated reconfiguration of networks may have consequences that call for audible evidence.

16.3.6.1   Dimensions of algorithmic accountability

We recommend particular focus on accountability by considering these dimensions of algorithmic accountability:

- Holding program code accountable: Program code should remain accessible for inspection. It should not be manipulated (e.g., through updates), modify itself, get declared as business secret or execute out of reach (e.g., in the cloud with unclear accountability relationships).
- Holding data usage accountable: Access to data shall be governed by defined policies. Actual access of algorithms to data should be logged. The version of data and the respective database should be logged. For detail inspection, access to the data used in a particular case at execution time may be necessary.
- Holding statistical models accountable: ML and decision-making systems use models to learn and to make decisions. Models can be updated. The archival and forensic availability of the used models and their specific parametrization in a particular situation are essential in cases of failure or disagreement. Retired models should become archived with integrity protection. An audit trail for the actual models used in decision-making should exist.
- Holding the application of algorithms accountable: The fact which algorithm has been used on what data for what purpose should be documented. In particular, in today's cloud paradigm, algorithms are hidden behind APIs, where they at any time become exchanged, updated or retired. An archival log over which version of which algorithm has been used is needed for algorithmic accountability.
- Holding decision-making accountable on all levels: Automated decision-making in SDN is not solely done by machines. The deployment of algorithms, the effect and outreach of automated decision-making, the mode of deployment of dynamic changes and the actual decisions to engage subcontractors, cloud services and input data are made with human interaction. Any system deploying automated decision-making, learning algorithms and extended BD capabilities should therefore have persons responsible for their operation, both on technical and managerial levels.

16.3.6.2   Preconditions for algorithmic accountability

Provision of and accommodating for algorithmic accountability has a number of preconditions. Access to source code and statistical models (authentic copies with time stamps) has to be granted at any time and for any version of the algorithm that was deployed in the SDN infrastructure. Since learning algorithms are only as good as their model and training data, access to input and training data (authentic through integrity-protecting cryptographic techniques) must be granted. To reconstruct the particular use of algorithms on a case, access to the specific computation transaction sequences should be possible ever in cases where the computation was carried out over several nodes. Finally, access to logs over interpretation and decision-making procedures for actions and reactions concerning dynamic network reconfiguration should be provided.

16.3.6.3   Dilemmas and issues with algorithmic accountability

Algorithmic accountability for BD and decision-making systems that process person-relatable data mat causes a number of dilemmas. Audible data and audible transactions and decisions require logging, which, if done naively, creates new person-relatable data in the logs. A number of dilemmas need to get resolved:

1. Authentic training data and other input data versus privacy and secrecy needs: Ensure that the access to authentic training data for learning algorithms does not violate privacy and secrecy rules.
2. Logging for accountability versus data protection and privacy needs: Ensure that the logging of transactions when processing personal data does not create new personal data on the way.
3. Incrimination created by prediction systems may be based on random patterns discovered in input data. Ensure that your analysis and decision-making systems react on solid data patterns, not on random patterns.
4. Algorithms can be designed with a bias (the same holds for prediction models). Make sure the designer bias is well understood before deployment!
5. Is an algorithm open AND understandable? Proven to function? Many vendors claim business secrecy and patents for their algorithms, and therefore, try to withdraw them from audit. Inspect accessibility to the algorithm and try to get evidence over correctness of the algorithms and of the underlying models.
6. What data went into the algorithm and how was it quality assured? Was there a selection bias? In particular, ML algorithms may learn specific patterns in the input data. Such patterns may become intentionally or unintentionally created upon filtering and selecting the input data. Untidy data measurement may induce such patterns, too. Provenance, acquisition quality, filter bias and data treatment should be assessed before admitting data into own learning models or decision-making systems.

16.3.7   Open issues for protecting privacy using Big Data and SDN

A number of open issues remain for standardization in SDN. First, the sufficient de-identification of network identifiers which are person relatable (such as IPs, MAC, frequently used access points) is an important issue. To enable privacy-friendly analysis, the distributed storage of information that can be selected, filtered and per-case joined for analysis is necessary. So far, standards for anonymized sharing of analysis data are missing. Technologies for purpose binding of data collections and log files exist; however, they are not feasible for the real-time SDN environments. A last, however, critically important arena is algorithmic accountability and data subject transparency. Audit trails, transparency tools and the conservation of historic algorithms and their data are widely unsolved issues.

16.4   Conclusion

SND and BD analysis are promising venues for improved resource utilization and increased security of network infrastructure. However, data subject security, privacy regulation and algorithmic accountability impose serious restrictions on data collection, machine-made decisions, and in addition create considerable customer management overhead. Data collection, analysis and ML projects should be specified and planned with great care to ensure their value will exceed their handling and compliance cost.

Acknowledgment

This work was funded by the ArsForensica project (project nr. 248094, Research Council of Norway, 2015–2019).

References

[1]   European Commission, "Directive 2002/58/EC of the European Parliament and of the council of 12 July 2002 concerning the processing of personal data and the protection of privacy in the electronic communications sector (directive on privacy and electronic communications)," report, 2002.

[2]   "Regulation (EU) 2016/679 of the European Parliament and of the council of 27 April 2016 on the protection of natural persons with regard to the processing of personal data and on the free movement of such data, and repealing directive 95/46/EC (general data protection regulation, GDPR)," 27-Apr-2016 2016.

[3]   L. Fritsch and H. Abie, "A road map to the management of privacy risks in information systems," in *Sicherheit 2008: Sicherheit, Schutz und Zuverlssigkeit. Konferenzband der 4. Jahrestagung des Fachbereichs Sicherheit der Gesellschaft fr Informatik e.V. (GI), Lecture Notes in Informatics LNI 128* (G. f. Informatik, ed.), vol. 128, (Bonn), pp. 1–15, Gesellschaft fr Informatik.

[4]   T. Humphreys and A. Plate, *Measuring the effectiveness of your IMS implementations based on ISO/IEC 27001.* London: BSI Business Information, 2006.

[5]   M. Colesky, J. H. Hoepman, and C. Hillen, "A critical analysis of privacy design strategies," in *Workshop on Privacy Engineering IWPE'16.*

[6]   A. Cavoukian, D. Jutla, F. Carter, *et al.* (eds.), "Privacy by design documentation for software engineers version 1.0 – committee specification draft 01," report, OASIS, 25-Jun-2014 2014.

[7]   G. D. Acquisto, J. Domingo-Ferrer, P. Kikiras, V. Torra, Y.-A. d. Montjoye, and A. Bourka, "Privacy by design in big data – an overview of privacy enhancing technologies in the era of big data analytics," Report 978-92-9204-160-1,

European Union Agency For Network And Information Security (ENISA), Dec. 1025 2015.

[8] G. Danezis, J. Domingo-Ferrer, M. Hansen, *et al.*, "Privacy and data protection by design-from policy to engineering," Report 978-92-9204-108-3, European Union Agency for Network and Information Security (ENISA), December 2014 2014.

[9] S. Spiekermann, "Viewpoint: the challenges of privacy by design," *Communications of the ACM*, vol. 55, no. 7, pp. 38–40, 2012.

[10] J. Domingo-Ferrer, D. Sanchez, and J. Soria-Comas, *Database Anonymization: Privacy Models, Data Utility, and Microaggregation-based Inter-model Connections*. Morgan and Claypool Publishers, 2016.

[11] L. Fritsch, "Partial commitment – 'try before you buy' and 'buyer's remorse' for personal data in big data and machine learning," 14-Jun-2017 2017.

[12] T. Pulls and D. Slamanig, "On the feasibility of (practical) commercial anonymous cloud storage," *Transactions on Data Privacy*, vol. 8, no. 2, pp. 89–111, 2015.

[13] M. Casassa Mont, S. Pearson, and P. Bramhall, "Towards accountable management of identity and privacy: Sticky policies and enforceable tracing services," 2003.

[14] S. Pearson and M. Casassa-Mont, "Sticky policies: an approach for managing privacy across multiple parties," *IEEE Computer Society*, vol. 44, pp. 60–68, 2011.

[15] "Workshop primer: Algorithmic accountability – the social, cultural and ethical dimensions of "big data," report, Data and Society Research Institute, 17-Mar-2014. Available at https://datasociety.net/output/algorithmic-accountability/ accessed on 14 November 2017.

Chapter 17

Big Data helps SDN to detect intrusions and secure data flows

Li-Chun Wang* and Yu-Jia Chen*

17.1 Introduction

Software-defined network (SDN) attracts a lot of attention from both academia and industry, but it also poses new challenges on security protection. As compared to the current network architectures, SDN is mainly characterized by its network programmability and centralized control of routing information. Programmability of the network can simplify the modification of network policies through softwares rather than low-level configuration. Besides, the centralization of the control plane provides a global view of the entire network, which can improve network management. However, the centralized design of SDN may lead to serious security concerns such as a single point of failure. Unfortunately, security protection is not enforced in the existing SDN standards due to the implementation complexity, thereby affecting the popularity of SDN in the long run. As a consequence, such security threats are becoming major attractions for malicious attackers.

Although facing new threats on its network infrastructure, SDN possesses the potentials to improve network security. Specifically, SDN brings the advantage of enhancing traffic monitoring with security software running on the application plane. In traditional networks, security services are manually implemented on network devices. Hence, the capability of security services is limited because of the inflexibility of updating network policies and the lack of network global information. In contrast, SDN can provide security services according to traffic statistics from the controller through the northbound interfaces. Afterwards, SDN security services can analyze big traffic data and develop appropriate security policies, leading to intelligent security protections.

In this chapter, we examine the security risks of SDN with the consideration of intrusions and abnormal data flows. Specifically, we discuss how SDN brings unique risks and threats to network service providers and customers. Then, we discuss the potential of integrating Big Data analytics into SDN for security enhancement and provide some examples to end this chapter.

*Department of Electrical and Computer Engineering, National Chiao Tung University, Taiwan

17.2   Security issues of SDN

The core concept of SDN is to integrate the control logic of the underlying distributed forwarding devices to a centralized controller. This centralized control intelligence can bring the benefits of monitoring the network behaviors. In particular, the forwarding intelligence and the network state in the control plane are separated from the data plane. The control/data split design enables the network control to become programmable while making the infrastructure abstracted from network devices and applications. However, the programmability and centralization of the SDN architecture also raise security concerns, especially on the control channel which has not been fully examined.

17.2.1   Security issues in control channel

Security is one of the key concerns when designing a new network architecture and its protocols. To ensure the availability of all the connected devices, network security protection must be incorporated into the architecture design. Although some SDN projects have discussed various approaches of enhancing the security and management for SDN [1], the security of SDN itself is afterthought. The advantages of SDN are mainly resulted from the programmability and providing a global view of the network. Nevertheless, these benefits can also bring unexpected threats at the same time. The capability of manipulating the network behaviors by the controller is susceptible to software errors and other possible vulnerabilities [2]. The separation of the control plane and the data plane increase the security protection burden on the controller. Such centralization of network intelligence could result in the single point of influences and the single point of failures. Therefore, the network can be compromised by the attackers seriously.

In the SDN control channel, the widespread failure of transport layer security (TLS) adoption has become a primary security concern. For the earliest OpenFlow specification (v1.0.0), the data exchange between the controller and the switches requires TLS connection. Nevertheless, TLS connection becomes an optional connection mode for the subsequent specification versions, such as v1.5.1. To save the CPU-intensive cryptographic operations, many vendors adopt plain TCP connection in their controllers/switches equipments instead of TLS connection. Table 17.1 summarizes the TLS adoption among controllers and switches for different vendors [3]. Aside from being optional in the specification, the TLS adoption failure is owing to the following reasons: (a) the high complexity of the configuration in generating certificates as compared to using plain TCP connection, (b) the lack of support from both controllers and switches vendors simultaneously, and (c) the rapid evolvement of SDN specification.

17.2.2   Denial-of-service (DoS) attacks

Without the security enforcement in the SDN control channel, it is possible to disrupt the legitimate communications between switches and the controller. The goal of a denial-of-service (DoS) attacker is to overwhelm the target's resources. For example,

Table 17.1   TLS/SSL adoption by controllers and switches for different vendors [3]

OpenFlow controller	TLS/SSL support	Switch vendor	TLS/SSL support
NOX	Yes	HP	No
POX	No	Brocade	No
Beacon	No	Dell	No
Floodlight	No	NEC	Partial
MuL	No	Indigo	No
FlowVisor	No	Pica8	No
Big Network Controller	No	OpenWRT	Yes
Open vSwitch Controller	Yes	Open vSwitch	Yes

a DoS attacker tries to use up the entire network resources for accepting connections, thereby resulting in legal network connection being denied [4]. This issue was discussed in [5] where a scanning tool is designed to test SDN networks. The scanning tool can monitor the response time of the requested packets. SDN networks can be identified by the obvious difference in response time between the new and the existing traffic flows. A DoS attack can be launched against SDN control plane once the SDN network is identified.

Now, we investigate the possible DoS attacks that can be launched on SDN networks. Generally, the effects of DoS attacks include limitation exploitation, resource consumption, and process disruption. Note that there are two types of DoS attackers, namely *outsider* and *insider*. An outsider attacker is regarded as an intruder by the authenticated network devices. On the other hand, insider attacker is originally authenticated to communicate with other nodes in the network [6]. DoS attacks against the SDN controller can be divided into several general cases.

17.2.2.1   Unauthenticated channel DoS (outsider)

Because of the absence of an authentication mechanism in the SDN control channel, switches basically communicate with the controller through the plain TCP connection. Thus, a node only requires the controller IP address and the port number for transmitting packet to the controller. An outsider can pretend to be a legitimate switch and flood the controller by sending huge number of packets in a short time. Figure 17.1 illustrates a DoS attack launched by unauthenticated channel to the SDN controller.

17.2.2.2   Man-in-the-middle DoS (outsider)

In this type of attack, the attackers try to disrupt the link from the controller to the individual switches. Figure 17.2 illustrates a man-in-the-middle DoS attack in SDN. For instance, a man-in-the-middle DoS attack on Floodlight SDN controller is shown in [8]. First, an attacker pretends to be a legitimate switch and obtains the data path ID (DPID) of the target switch. With the obtained DPID, the fake switch can communicate with the controller. As a result, the controller will terminate the connection from the originally legitimate switch, which is considered as a serious vulnerability in Floodlight controller. The network performance will be eventually

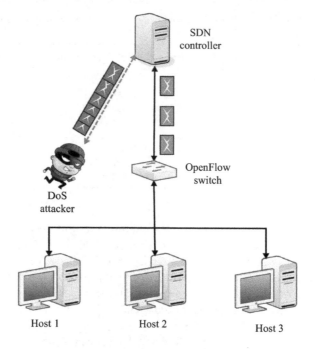

Figure 17.1   Illustration of unauthenticated channel DoS attacks [7]

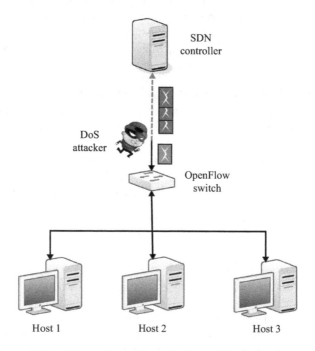

Figure 17.2   Illustration of man-in-the-middle DoS attacks [7]

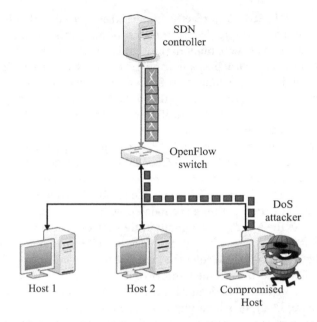

Figure 17.3   Illustration of compromised host DoS attacks [7]

degraded because of the expiration of the existing rules in the switch tables. This type of attack can cause process disruption and resource consumption. Due to the adoption of unsecured connection, it is possible that a man-in-the-middle DoS attacker can impersonate a legitimate controller.

17.2.2.3   Compromised host DoS (insider)

Network nodes being compromised may create the opportunities for insider to launch DoS attack. In this case, with the legitimate credential of an authenticated switch, an attacker can consume the controller resources by sending large amount of requests. A DoS attack launched from a compromised host is illustrated in Figure 17.3.

17.2.3   *Simulation of control channel attack on SDN*

In this section, we show some simulation results to illustrate the influence of the aforementioned DoS attack. In the existing SDN network, there are two modes for rule installation: proactive and reactive. In the proactive mode, rules are installed into the flow table for possible matches in advance. On the other hand, the rules in the reactive mode are installed by the controller in response to *Packet-In* messages. If a switch receives packets without any match in the flow table, a *Packet-In* message will be sent to the controller. Note that the *Packet-In* message is the only message to which the controller needs to respond.

Consider a SDN network in reactive mode, where the controller has to allocate resources to respond to the requests of *Packet-In* messages. A DoS attacker can generate large traffic loads with random flow attributes to trigger *Packet-In* events. In that way, every flow is regarded as a new traffic to the switch. Therefore, it requires an action command from the controller. Such a mechanism in SDN can lead to the following phenomenon: (a) saturation of the switch flow tables and deny of legitimate rule installation, (b) exhaustion of controller resources and thus failing to respond to legitimate switch *Packet-In* messages.

Controller benchmarking (cbench) [9] is commonly used to evaluate the controller performance and the DoS attack. Cbench can simulate a number of OpenFlow switches and evaluate the controller performance criteria in terms of response time, throughput, and latency. Figure 17.4 shows the number of controller responses with respect to the unit of time with eight emulated switches. In the emulation, cbench is used to compute the average throughput of the controller under normal operation. Additionally, with the same configuration, the controller throughput is compared during the DoS attack. The x-axis denotes the time in seconds while the y-axis denotes the throughput, which is defined as the number of controller responses per millisecond.

To relieve the threats of DoS attacks, it might seem applicable to adopt multiple controllers and applications which implement network policies [2]. In other words, the network architecture is converted from a centralized to a distributed one. However, it is shown that simply utilizing multiple controllers fails to avoid the single point of failure in DoS attack [10]. This is because that the load of the backup controllers can exceed their capability and thus eventually cause cascaded failures of controllers in the entire network.

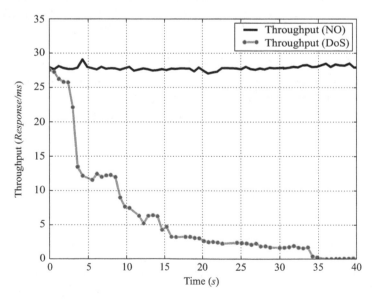

Figure 17.4   Comparison of controller throughput under normal operation (lined curve) and DoS attack (dotted curve) [7]

17.3   Big Data techniques for security threats in SDN

Although SDN poses new threats on the network infrastructure, there are still some potentials that can be exploited to secure network communications. For traditional network architectures, security services are implemented manually on network devices and regarded as added features. In this way, to update a network policy, a network operator needs to modify the low-level vendor-specific configurations at each network device. Not only is it hard to manage the network, but it is also likely to introduce configuration errors, thereby causing security vulnerabilities [11]. The inflexibility to implement network policies and the lack of network global information could limit the possibility of introducing new network services.

Compared to the traditional networks, the main advantages of SDN come from the centralization of the network controller and the network programmability. Programmability of the network can greatly simplify the modification of network policies through software updating rather than low-level configuration. Besides, the centralization of the control logic provides a global view of the entire network which can facilitate the management of complex networks [12]. Figure 17.5 illustrates a conceptual view of the SDN architecture between each layer.

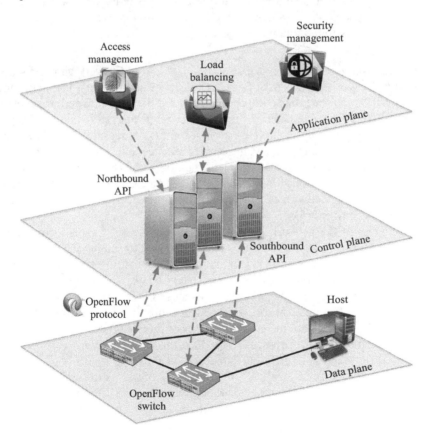

Figure 17.5   Conceptual view of SDN architecture [7]

In regard to network security protection, SDN can monitor the traffic flows and detect the malicious and suspicious intrusion patterns by analyzing the network statistics. In particular, recent Big Data analytics and machine learning can help the design and operation of SDN by obtaining some insightful information for smart decisions. For instance, the controller can perform traffic rerouting to avoid the suspicious network nodes based on big traffic data analytics.

17.3.1 Big Data analytics

The concept of Big Data analytics is closely related to the capability of storing and processing large amount of data sets. Big Data analytics have been successfully applied in many fields, such as cloud applications, health care applications, and scientific research applications. The benefit of Big Data arises from the capability of learning the diverse characteristics to decide the optimal system configurations.

Machine learning is known as one of the most powerful tools to achieve sophisticated learning and decision-making with Big Data analytic. By developing systems that are capable of learning from data, machine learning can intercept the data variations, classify the events, and predict future challenges in an autonomous fashion. Generally, Big Data analytic and machine learning can improve the next generation of network security in the following aspects.

- **Sensing**: Network intrusion detection requires sensing network anomalies from multiple network nodes. With Big Data analytics and machine learning, intrusion detection services can compare the collected flow data and perform anomaly detection in a real-time fashion. Support vector machines (SVMs) is one of popular machine-learning techniques used for intrusion detection [13]. SVM can construct a hyperplane that has the largest distance to the nearest recorded data point of any class, thereby classifying the network events based on the normal and abnormal network connection. In addition, hidden Markov model is also applicable for sensing network events by estimating the occurrence probability of the abnormal behavior [14].
- **Mining**: From the network usage information collected by the controller, the hidden patterns of network services can be deduced by mining the network traffic. Therefore, the network service operator can classify services according to the required provisioning resources. Unsupervised learning techniques are commonly used to deduce and explain key features of the sensed data. Based on the representative features, the network system can be configured to operate with high efficiency and with the ensured quality of service (QoS).
- **Forecasting**: Big Data analytics can facilitate the prediction of network behaviors (e.g., traffic requests of different services) and abnormal events (e.g., failure of network elements). As a result, the complexity of the network design and the network management can be reduced. For example, deep learning is a prominent method to predict the upcoming intrusion by automatically finding the hidden correlation of the traffic flow [15].

17.3.2   Data analytics for threat detection

Threat monitoring and incident investigation are essential for security protection in datacenter networks. The goal of threat detection is to identify hidden threats, trace attackers, and predict attacks. Two examples of how data analytic can help network security with respect to different dimensions are listed as follows:

- **Network traffic**: To strengthen the security in a datacenter network, it is important to monitor network behaviors and inspect data packets for detecting malicious activities. SDN controller can help collect the samples of data traffic from multiple switches and forward them to the security checkpoint such as the intrusion detection system (IDS).
- **Network nodes**: With the collected network statistics in the control plane, SDN can detect the abnormal behavior related to human or hardware. For example, abnormal access time or transaction amount can be detected and then the corresponding access will be denied in short time.

It is worthwhile being mentioned that security services in SDN can be easily implemented through software running on the application plane with security analytics. A security service in the application plane can obtain traffic from the controller through northbound application programming interfaces (APIs). In this way, the service can analyze the traffic and decide security policies for each traffic/node, which can then be applied on the switches.

17.4   QoS consideration in SDN with security services

Security services such as firewall and IDS are usually placed at choke points and rely on routing to the desired security deployment for network inspection. Specifically, if a data flow comes from an unidentified source, then it must be traversed to certain security devices according to security policies, which is called rule-based forwarding. A network user can also select the path or specify which choke point that his/her packets should traverse. The network provider can force the data flow through the requested sequences of security devices. Such a process is called security traversal. For example, a receiver R requests that all the data flows coming from the sender S need to be inspected by the firewall and the IDS sequentially. Hence, for the data packet sent by S, it must pass the firewall and then the IDS. However, these security services are likely to incur extra delay as well as traffic loads, thereby degrading the QoS of the network.

17.4.1   Delay guarantee for security traversal

Security services in SDN can be integrated in a software middlebox, which is implemented by distributed virtual machines (VM) dedicated to a set of security functions. These software middleboxes can provide dynamic flexibility to security services. However, since the security traversal path determined by these distributed security middleboxes is only based on nearby middleboxes and network condition information, the incurred delay of sending a packet may become very large. Specifically, for unexpected burst requests of security inspection or collapse of security middleboxes, the security traversal path cannot be dynamically changed by these distributed security middleboxes, causing security service delay.

17.4.1.1 Optimal security routing

In the literature, the aforementioned security traversal scenario can be modeled as a constrained shortest path (CSP) problem in order to achieve the optimal security routing [16]. Since the data flow is queued in the middleboxes, the delay performance is dominated by the middlebox loading. To achieve the delay requirements, the network conditions as well as the middlebox loading are needed to be further investigated.

We consider a network represented as a directed simple graph $G(N, L, M)$, where N is the set of network nodes, L is the set of all connected links, and M is the set of all security middleboxes. Denote link (i, j) as an ordered pair that is, outgoing from node i and to node j. Also, let R_{st} be the set of all paths from source node s to destination node t. Specifically, for any path $r \in R_{st}$, define cost function f_C and delay function f_D calculated as

$$f_C(r) = \sum_{(i,j) \in r} c_{ij} \tag{17.1}$$

and

$$f_D(r) = \sum_{k=1}^{m(r)} d_k, \tag{17.2}$$

respectively, where c_{ij} is the cost metric for the link (i, j), d_k is the delay metric for the kth security middlebox, and $m(r)$ is the number of security middleboxes on path r. Thus, we can model c_{ij} as the weighted sum of network congestion measure and middlebox loading measure as

$$c_{ij} = (1 - \beta)g_{ij} + \beta s_k, 0 \leq \beta \leq 1, \forall(i,j) \in L, \forall k \in M, \tag{17.3}$$

where g_{ij} denotes the network congestion measure for the traffic on link (i, j), s_k is middlebox loading measure of the kth middlebox, and β is the scale factor for the flexibility in different network conditions. In addition, g_{ij} is defined as

$$g_{ij} = \begin{cases} \frac{T_{ij} - 0.7 \times B_{ij}}{T_{ij}}, & 0.7 \times B_{ij} < T_{ij} \\ 0, & 0.7 \times B_{ij} \geq T_{ij} \end{cases}, \tag{17.4}$$

where T_{ij} is the total measured traffic amount in bps, and B_{ij} is the maximum of achievable bandwidth in bps on link (i,j). With the measurement of network congestion, one can avoid that a large number of paths in the same R_{st} share the same common link. We can select:

$$s_k = \frac{\lambda_k}{\mu_k},$$ (17.5)

which is considered as the intensity of middlebox loading. Hence, the expected waiting time for the M/M/1 queueing model [17] is

$$d_k = \frac{1}{(\mu_k - \lambda_k)},$$ (17.6)

where λ_k and μ_k are the input (arrival) rate and the service rate of the kth middlebox, respectively [18]. It's worth mentioning that if a security middlebox crashes, the service rate μ_k approximates to zero. Then, the CSP problem can be formulated as finding:

$$r^* = \arg\min_r \{f_C(r) | r \in R_{st}, f_D(m) \le D_{\max}\}.$$ (17.7)

The obtained minimum cost security traversal path r^* can satisfy a specified delay requirement by solving the CSP problem. Although the CSP problem is known to be NP-complete [19], some effective heuristic and approximation algorithms have been reported in the literature [20,21].

17.4.1.2 Optimal security traversal with middlebox addition

We present how SDN can help provide delay guarantee for security traversal. Figure 17.6 shows the system flow of the optimal security traversal with middlebox addition (OSTMA). First, a user requests the security and QoS requirements which specify the sequences of middleboxes and the delay constraints, respectively. Second, the network service provider dynamically monitors the traffic on each link and the loading of each security middlebox. This information is used to measure the delay performance of security traversal. After that, the network service provider adopts the heuristic algorithm to solve the CSP problem. If no path satisfies the delay requirement, a set of security middleboxes is added to the network for reducing latency of security traversal. Then, the optimal security traversal path is recalculated. At the end, the forwarding policy is set by the SDN controller.

The system process of the OSTMA can be classified into three stages: (a) network condition information collecting, (b) security traversal decision-making, and (c) traffic flow controlling. We detail these stages as follows:

- **Network condition information collecting**: In the first stage, the condition information of middleboxes and the network are collected by the middlebox monitor module and the network monitor module, respectively. The middlebox monitor module can record the CPU usage of each middlebox. This information can be implemented through the libvirt [22], which is an open source API used for managing cloud platform virtualization. The information of network topology and the network traffic flow can be collected by the network monitor module. One can

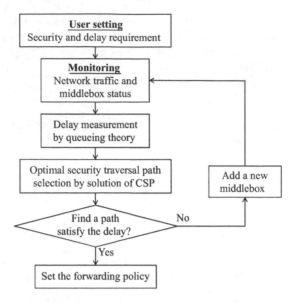

Figure 17.6   System flow of optimal security traversal with middlebox addition (OSTMA) [16]

Table 17.2   An example of host-port-switch table

Host IP	Host MAC	Switch	Port number
10.0.0.1	66:d3:c2:48:e4:af	00:00:00:00:00:00:00:06	1
10.0.0.2	72:50:cf:b0:2e:42	00:00:00:00:00:00:00:07	1

express the network topology via a host-port-switch table and a switch-link matrix. The host-port-switch table is applied to record the information that how end hosts connect to the SDN switches. Specifically, the host-port-switch table includes the IP address and the MAC address of the end host, the SDN switch ID, and the port number to which the end host connects. Table 17.2 shows an example of the entries stored in the host-port-switch table. The switch-link matrix, which includes port mapping information of each connected SDN switch, is used to record how the SDN switches are connected to each other. Table 17.3 shows an example of the entries stored in the switch-link matrix. The network traffic flow can be measured by the received and transmitted packets of each SDN switch port.

- **Security traversal decision-making**: In this stage, with the network condition information collected by the previous stage, the security traversal engine can analyze delay performance and then determines the optimal security traversal path. Recalling the SDN protocol, for the packet which comes from a new data

Table 17.3 An example of switch-link matrix

	Switch 1	Switch 2	Switch 3	Switch 4
Switch 1	×	3	×	2
Switch 2	3	×	4	5
Switch 3	×	3	×	4
Switch 4	2	3	4	×

flow arrives at the SDN switch, the switch forwards the packet to the controller since there is no match of installed flow entries. Hence, when receiving the packet, the packet header can be extracted by the security traversal engine in the controller and then checked for source/destination host addresses. Next, the security traversal engine evaluates the delay performance according to the network condition information. The optimal security traversal path is then determined by solving the CSP problem subject to the specified security and delay requirement. Finally, the optimal path decision is sent to the routing engine. To guarantee the delay performance, the system periodically updates the delay performance of the path based on the current network condition. In that way, the optimal security traversal path will be recalculated once the performance of the existing path violates the delay guarantee.

* **Traffic flow controlling**: In the final stage, the routing engine translates the logical path to the explicit network routes. All the routes are set by updating the flow table in the SDN switch. A path-to-route translator divides a path into multiple end-to-end network routes and computes the shortest route from one host/middlebox to another based on current network topology. Finally, the route operator converts the shortest path to flow entries and updates the flow entries to each SDN switch on the route.

17.4.2 Traffic load balancing

Burst traffic generated by massive network devices may result in heavy processing loading in the network server. Furthermore, traffic from different applications may demand various QoS requirements. A medium load balancer in datacenter networks can help relieve the heavy loading and satisfy the QoS requirements. The medium load balancer handles multiple connections and routes those connections to the request nodes, allowing the system to scale to serve more requests.

However, such a design in conventional load balancing technique has the following limitations. First, the medium server may cause service bottleneck and bring the single point of failure problem. Besides, the selection of routing path is static from the medium server and thus lack flexibility. Finally, the medium server is difficult to be scaled and the load balancing policy is not elastic.

Since the SDN controller can intelligently decide the forwarding policy of switches, SDN has the potential to improve the load balancing technique. By collecting the network condition information (e.g., network topology, link usage) and configuring the forwarding table of the switches, SDN can route the incoming traffic by some specific information in the header. Therefore, the SDN switch can operate as a load balancer. The service bottleneck and the single point of failure problem can be avoided due to the distribution of numerous switches in the networks. In addition, the network can route each traffic with all the possible paths in the networks. Finally, the load balancing policy can be updated elastically by simply reconfiguring the SDN controller.

17.4.2.1   Traffic-aware load balancing using SDN

We demonstrate how SDN can improve load balancing in machine-to-machine (M2M) networks by instant traffic identification and dynamic traffic rerouting. In M2M, network service capability layer (NSCL) serves as the cloud server of M2M services to handle the M2M requests. These NSCL servers can be deployed dynamically to satisfy the QoS requirements of various M2M services. Because these M2M services rely on the NSCL to establish a huge number of connections, balancing the loads of these NSCL servers is a critical issue.

With the capability of monitoring the network statistics and controlling the network routing, SDN can schedule the M2M traffic flow to avoid link congestion. System procedures for load balancing using SDN can be divided into four stages. In the first stage, the M2M service delay requirements are specified. This stage is essential when initiating a new service. A flag information to the new service is also assigned in this stage. One can use the type of service (ToS) which is a field in the TCP/IP packet header and is widely used to differentiate traffic types. In the second stage, the network loading and the workload of NSCL server are monitored. The workload information of the VM can be collected by the kernel application in the hypervisor. According to the ToS tag of each service, one can manage the traffic flow of a M2M service individually to satisfy different delay requirements. In the third stage, the SDN controller measures the delay and then finds the available path as well as the server combinations that can satisfy the delay requirement. In the final stage, the network setting can be updated by updating the flow entries of the SDN switches. For instance, the incoming packet header, such as the MAC address of destination and the IP address of destination, can be modified and forwarded to the NSCL server with low usage link. Note that it is suggested to reconfigure the network only when the server or network loading exceeds the predefined threshold to reduce the reconfiguration frequency.

We also introduce the system framework of the aforementioned load balancing method for SDN networks as shown in Figure 17.7. There are four components in the framework, including network monitor, server monitor, load balancing module, and routing engine. Network monitor collects network statistic information such as network topology and link usage from the SDN switches. These information can help understand the network condition and evaluate the delay performance of the network. Next, server monitor collects the workload information of the NSCL servers. This process can be achieved by the open source libvirt API [22] to obtain the CPU workload, memory usage, and disk status. After that, the load balancing module analyzes the collected information from the network monitor and the server monitor

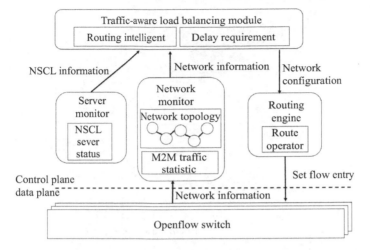

Figure 17.7   System framework of the proposed load balancing method for SDN networks [23]

to evaluate the delay performance of the overall network. Thus, the load balancing mechanism can determine the network configuration including the combination of the server and the forwarding path to satisfy the delay requirement specified in the ToS field. Finally, routing engine processes the network configuration and sets the routing policy by updating the flow entries of the SDN switches. As a result, the delay requirement of the M2M requests can be satisfied owing to forwarding the requests to the proper NSCL server.

17.4.2.2   Delay performance comparison

We compare the delay performance of three load balancing approaches: no load balance (noLB), CPU-based load balance (CpuLB) [24], and SDN-based traffic-aware load balance (TaLB). The performance index is the total response time, which is defined as the duration between the time that the data is sent by the end device and the time that the result of the request is received by the end device. The following two scenarios are considered in the experiments. In the first scenario, the end devices transmit a large volume of computation-intensive requests (e.g., face recognition) to the NSCL servers. On the other hand, in the second scenario, the requests are communication intensive (e.g., remote monitoring). For both scenarios, the response time is calculated for 30 continuous requests with a burst traffic occurring at the 20th request.

For the experimental result in the first scenario, the burst traffic causes severe performance degradation at the 20th request as shown in Figure 17.8. The CPU-based load balancing can reduce 10% of the response time compared with no load balance. For the SDN-based approach, huge improvement can be observed for about 30% of response time reduction. We note that the case without burst traffic (nBT) can be seen

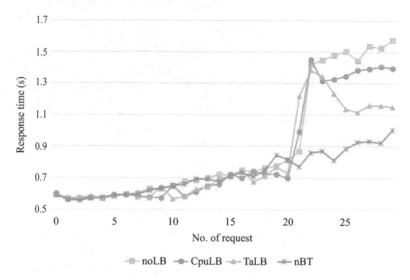

*Figure 17.8   Response time comparison of computation-intensive M2M
requests [23]*

as the optimal performance in the considered scenario. It is shown that noLB and
CpuLB have increased 60% and 45% of response time at the 30th request compared
to nBT, respectively. However, the SDN-based approach has only 20% increment of
response time.

Figure 17.9 shows the results for the second scenario. The CPU-based load balancer has no effect for communication-intensive requests, whereas the SDN-based
approach can reduce 50% of the response time of no load balance. Therefore, we conclude that SDN-based load balancing approach can effectively reduce the response
time, especially for communication-intensive M2M service.

17.5   Big Data applications for securing SDN

The potentials of Big Data analytics to mitigate security attack in network systems
have been widely discussed. By learning from data, Big Data analytics enable the
capture of timely and accurate insights related to network behaviors, which brings
the revolutionary change to network security protection. For example, inspection of
network packet can be more accurate and efficient compared to the existing deep
packet inspection (DPI) solutions.

17.5.1   Packet inspection

DPI is a popular network filtering technique examining the data and its header, which
can be used to identify the content type of packet (e.g., video, text). The capability

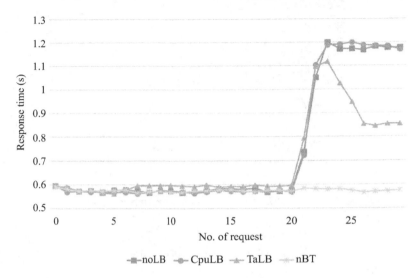

Figure 17.9 Response time comparison of communication-intensive M2M requests [23]

of DPI can be exploited to improve routing strategies in the network and quality of experience, which is a metric to evaluate application performance. However, the implementation of DPI in standard networks is usually time consuming and energy intensive.

Different from DPI, traffic-aware packet inspection technique can leverage the Big Data analytics to identify the flow content type and thus is not energy intensive and processor intensive. Moreover, traffic-aware packet inspection technique requires less knowledge and operating cost. Such a packet inspection technique can exploit the capability directly provided by SDN without using third-party tools, so it can be easily extended and deployed in the network.

Consider an example of video packet inspection, which is accountable for 64% of the total Internet traffic [25]. Figure 17.10 shows the distinct pattern of video traffic [26]. There are two phases in the video packet transmission including the buffering phase and the steady phase. The buffering phase is initialized at the beginning of a video streaming session. During this phase, a burst of video data is collected for a few seconds. After that, the rate of data receiving will be reduced and the system will enter the steady phase. During the steady state, video data are received periodically with blocks. The periodical receiving of data blocks results in ON–OFF cycles. Such an ON–OFF cycling traffic pattern for video streaming is different to other application activities (e.g., web browsing) [27]. By analyzing the size of the data transmission and the statistics retrieval time in controller, packet inspection can be designed to find which flag that appears to match the video traffic pattern.

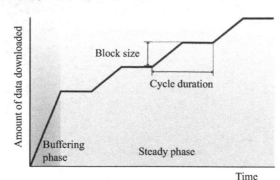

Figure 17.10   Traffic pattern of video streaming services [26]

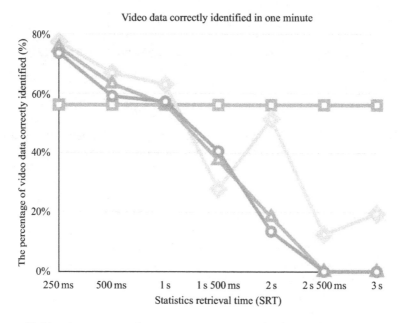

Figure 17.11   Accuracy performance comparison of video packet inspection [26]

Figure 17.11 shows the percentage of video data transferred in 1 min that can be correctly identified in terms of the success rate. In the DPI case, the result is obtained by using the average time for DPI to identify video streaming data. One can observe that 56.17% of the video data are correctly identified in 1 min. In particular, the cases with statistics retrieval time equal or less than 1 s outperform the case of DPI.

17.6   Open issues and challenge

Many issues on Big Data analytics for secure SDN remain open, which will be discussed in this section.

- **Controller management**: When SDN is applied with Big Data techniques, the frequent data access and large overhead in the control plane may degrade the network performance. Therefore, the scalability of control plane should be considered to relieve the extra traffic load from Big Data applications. One possible solution is to adopt the multicontroller network architecture. However, it is still an open issue to distribute network state to be logically centralized but physically distributed among different controllers.
- **Flow table management**: Current flow tables have around 8,000 entries [28], which are insufficient for Big Data analytics, especially for real-time applications. From the security aspect, the size of flow table can also be a critical vulnerability in SDN. A DoS attacker can exhaust the flow table in the targeted switch, thus disabling the switch functionality and eventually interrupting the network services. The design of flow table in the SDN switches should take these scalability and security issues into consideration.
- **Big mobile data analytics**: SDN can be applied in mobile networks to efficiently manage and orchestrate mobile network resources. SDN-enabled mobile networks have been considered as one of the most promising architectures in the next generation mobile networks and services. With the properties of continuous changing and updating over time, mobile data are particularly valuable for Big Data analytics to understand and predict network behavior. However, one primary concern of big mobile data analytics is the privacy leakage. Thus, more research should be conducted to study the privacy protection in SDN for big mobile data analytics.

17.7   Summary and conclusion

The core advantages of SDN result from the network programmability and management centralization. As such, SDN unleashes the potentials of network innovation through open controller applications. However, security vulnerabilities in the SDN control plane can introduce illegitimate access of network resources. Thanks to the collected network statistics in the controller, SDN security mechanisms can exploit Big Data analytics capabilities to detect network intrusions and secure data flows.

In this chapter, we investigated the security issues of SDN and gave some example of DoS attacks. We also discussed the potentials of Big Data analytics for protecting traffic flows in SDN. We further introduced the QoS issues when applying security services in SDN and presented the example of packet inspection using Big Data analytics. Finally, we suggest some open issues of Big Data techniques for secure SDN.

References

[1]   M. Casado, M. J. Freedman, J. Pettit, *et al.*, "Rethinking enterprise network control," *IEEE/ACM Transactions on Networking*, vol. 17, no. 4, pp. 1270–1283, 2009.

[2]   D. Kreutz, F. Ramos, and P. Verissimo, "Towards secure and dependable software-defined networks," in *Proceedings of the Second ACM SIGCOMM Workshop on Hot Topics in Software Defined Networking*, pp. 55–60, 2013.

[3]   K. Benton, L. J. Camp, and C. Small, "OpenFlow vulnerability assessment," in *Proceedings of the Second ACM SIGCOMM Workshop on Hot Topics in Software Defined Networking*, pp. 151–152, 2013.

[4]   I. Ahmad, S. Namal, M. Ylianttila, and A. Gurtov, "Security in software defined networks: A survey," *IEEE Communications Surveys & Tutorials*, vol. 17, no. 4, pp. 2317–2346, 2015.

[5]   S. Shin and G. Gu, "Attacking software-defined networks: A first feasibility study," in *Proceedings of the Second ACM SIGCOMM Workshop on Hot Topics in Software Defined Networking*, pp. 165–166, 2013.

[6]   M. Raya and J.-P. Hubaux, "Securing vehicular ad hoc networks," *Journal of Computer Security*, vol. 15, no. 1, pp. 39–68, 2007.

[7]   O. I. Abdullaziz, Y.-J. Chen, and L.-C. Wang, "Lightweight authentication mechanism for software defined network using information hiding," in *IEEE Global Communications Conference*, 2016.

[8]   J. M. Dover, "A denial of service attack against the Open Floodlight SDN controller." Research Report, December 2013.

[9]   A. Tootoonchian, S. Gorbunov, Y. Ganjali, M. Casado, and R. Sherwood, "On controller performance in software-defined networks," in *USENIX Workshop on Hot Topics in Management of Internet, Cloud, and Enterprise Networks and Services*, vol. 54, 2012.

[10]   G. Yao, J. Bi, and L. Guo, "On the cascading failures of multi-controllers in software defined networks," in *21st IEEE International Conference on Network Protocols*, pp. 1–2, 2013.

[11]   H. Hamed and E. Al-Shaer, "Taxonomy of conflicts in network security policies," *IEEE Communications Magazine*, vol. 44, no. 3, pp. 134–141, 2006.

[12]   S. J. Vaughan-Nichols, "OpenFlow: The next generation of the network?," *IEEE Computer*, vol. 44, no. 8, pp. 13–15, 2011.

[13]   W. Feng, Q. Zhang, G. Hu, and J. X. Huang, "Mining network data for intrusion detection through combining SVMs with ant colony networks," *Future Generation Computer Systems*, vol. 37, pp. 127–140, 2014.

[14]   C.-M. Chen, D.-J. Guan, Y.-Z. Huang, and Y.-H. Ou, "Anomaly network intrusion detection using hidden Markov model," *International Journal of Innovative Computing, Information and Control*, vol. 12, no. 2, pp. 569–580, 2016.

[15]   B. Dong and X. Wang, "Comparison deep learning method to traditional methods using for network intrusion detection," in *IEEE International Conference on Communication Software and Networks*, pp. 581–585, 2016.

[16] Y.-J. Chen, F.-Y. Lin, L.-C. Wang, and B.-S. Lin, "A dynamic security traversal mechanism for providing deterministic delay guarantee in SDN," in *IEEE 15th International Symposium on a World of Wireless, Mobile and Multimedia Networks*, pp. 1–6, 2014.

[17] M. Harchol-Balter, *Performance modeling and design of computer systems: queueing theory in action*. London: Cambridge University Press, 2013.

[18] D. Gross, J. F. Shortle, J. M. Thompson, and C. M. Harris, *Fundamentals of queueing theory*. New York: Wiley, 2008.

[19] Z. Wang and J. Crowcroft, "Quality-of-service routing for supporting multimedia applications," *IEEE Journal on Selected Areas in Communications*, vol. 14, no. 7, pp. 1228–1234, 1996.

[20] L. D. P. Pugliese and F. Guerriero, "A survey of resource constrained shortest path problems: Exact solution approaches," *Networks*, vol. 62, no. 3, pp. 183–200, 2013.

[21] H. E. Egilmez, S. Civanlar, and A. M. Tekalp, "An optimization framework for QoS-enabled adaptive video streaming over OpenFlow networks," *IEEE Transactions on Multimedia*, vol. 15, no. 3, pp. 710–715, 2013.

[22] Libvirt Team. Libvirt: The virtualization API. Available at http://libvirt.org. Accessed on 8 November 2013 [Online].

[23] Y.-J. Chen, Y.-H. Shen, and L.-C. Wang, "Traffic-aware load balancing for M2M networks using SDN," in *IEEE 6th International Conference on Cloud Computing Technology and Science*, pp. 668–671, 2014.

[24] M. Corici, H. Coskun, A. Elmangoush, *et al.*, "OpenMTC: Prototyping machine type communication in carrier grade operator networks," in *IEEE Globecom Workshops*, pp. 1735–1740, 2012.

[25] C. V. Networking, "Forecast and methodology, 2014–2019 white paper," *Technical Report, Cisco*, 2015.

[26] C. Hue, Y.-J. Chen, and L.-C. Wang, "Traffic-aware networking for video streaming service using SDN," in *IEEE 34th International Performance Computing and Communications Conference*, pp. 1–5, 2015.

[27] A. Rao, A. Legout, Y.-s. Lim, D. Towsley, C. Barakat, and W. Dabbous, "Network characteristics of video streaming traffic," in *Proceedings of the Seventh ACM Conference on Emerging Networking Experiments and Technologies*, p. 25, 2011.

[28] D. Kreutz, F. M. Ramos, P. E. Verissimo, C. E. Rothenberg, S. Azodolmolky, and S. Uhlig, "Software-defined networking: A comprehensive survey," *Proceedings of the IEEE*, vol. 103, no. 1, pp. 14–76, 2015.

Chapter 18
Big Data helps SDN to manage traffic

Jianwu Wang* and Qiang Duan**

Abstract

Traffic management plays a crucial role in achieving high-performance networking with optimal resource utilization. However, efficient and effective traffic management could be very challenging in large-scale dynamic networking environments. Software-defined networking (SDN) together with Big Data analytics offers a promising approach to addressing this challenging problem. We first provide an overview of the general process of network traffic management, in both conventional Internet Protocol (IP)-based networks and the emerging SDN networks. Then, we present an architectural framework of Big Data-based traffic management in SDN. We discuss some possible Big Data analytics applications for data analysis and decision-making in SDN for traffic management. We also identify some open issues and challenges that must be addressed for applying Big Data analytics techniques in SDN traffic management, which offer possible topics for future research and technology development.

18.1 Introduction

Software-defined networking (SDN) is an emerging networking paradigm that is, expected to play a crucial role in future networking. According to the well-received definition provided by Open Networking Foundation, SDN is a network architecture where network control is decoupled from forwarding and is directly programmable [1]. Traffic management is a key mechanism in networks for provisioning high-performance network services that meet various user requirements. Some of the new features introduced by the SDN architecture may greatly facilitate network traffic management. Because of its separation from the data plane, the centralized SDN controller makes it possible to assemble the network state information collected from data plane devices to form a global view of network topology. The flow-based packet forwarding in SDN allows switches to measure traffic loads with finer granularity

*Department of Information Systems, University of Maryland, Baltimore County (UMBC), USA
**Information Sciences & Technology Department, Pennsylvania State University Abington College USA

and allows the controller to obtain more precise information of traffic distribution across network topology. Network programmability supported by SDN through a standard application programming interface (API) on the controller facilitates the development of various application software that can utilize the network topology and traffic information to make traffic management decisions for provisioning high-performance services while fully utilizing network resources.

Although SDN offers a promising control platform for network traffic management, some technical issues must be addressed before such a platform can be fully exploited for optimal traffic management. The large amounts of data for a wide spectrum of network states and traffic loads that are collected by the SDN controller must be thoroughly analyzed in order to make appropriate decisions for optimizing both service performance and resource utilization. In a large-scale dynamic SDN, the diverse network states that need to be measured, the huge volume of measured data, and the fluctuation of traffic load on the network call for more sophisticated data analysis and decision-making capabilities that cannot be easily provided by the conventional methods currently employed for network traffic management.

Current Big Data analytics mainly deal with data which has one or more of the following features: large-amount data size (volume), high speed of data streams (velocity), various types and format of data (variety) [2]. Big Data analytics rely on and extend the current techniques of database, programing model, distributed computing, data integration, data mining, etc. A key goal of Big Data analytics is to be able to store and process data based on application requirement in an efficient approach. Main Big Data analytics techniques include NoSQL database for data storage and access [3], MapReduce programing model for parallel data processing [4], Lambda architecture for hybrid streaming and batch processing [5].

Big Data analytics makes it possible to analyze the massive, diverse, and dynamic network state data to obtain correlation between different key factors in network behaviors, including network topology, resource allocation, traffic distribution, and achievable service performance, thus may provide guidelines for network design and operation. Therefore, Big Data analytics offers a promising approach to addressing some of the challenges to data analysis and decision-making for network traffic management in SDN.

In this chapter, we discuss possible applications of Big Data analytics in SDN for addressing some of the challenges to network traffic management in this emerging networking paradigm. We first provide an overview of the general concept and process of network traffic management, in both conventional IP-based networks and the emerging SDN network. Then, we present an architectural framework of Big Data-based traffic management in SDN. We discuss some possible Big Data analytics techniques for data analysis and decision-making in SDN for traffic management. We also identify some open issues and challenges that need to be addressed for applying Big Data analytics techniques in SDN traffic management, which offer possible topics for future research and technology development.

Network traffic management is a key aspect of network control and operation that has been extensively studied in both academia and industry [6]. A wide spectrum of technologies have been proposed and developed for addressing different aspects

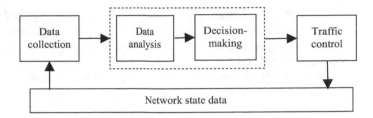

Figure 18.1 Key stages of network traffic management

of traffic management in various networking scenarios; for example, multiconstraint routing, load balancing, optimal resource allocation, congestion control, flow and packet scheduling, just name a few. The objective of this chapter is not to provide a comprehensive review of this broad field but focus on the data analysis and decision-making aspect particularly for the emerging SDN paradigm. We hope to provide the readers with a high-level picture of applying Big Data analytics in SDN traffic management and identify some topics for future research and development in this area.

18.2 State of art of traffic management in IP and SDN networks

18.2.1 General concept and procedure of network traffic management

In general, network traffic management manipulates traffic distribution in a network in order to fully utilize the network resources for accommodating traffic to meet user performance requirements. From a data analysis perspective, the key functions for traffic management can be organized into the following stages: data collection for monitoring network states; data analysis for examining traffic load, network behaviors, and service performance; decision-making based on data analysis results for adjusting traffic distribution and network operation; and traffic control to enforce the decisions made in the previous stage. In practical networking systems, data analysis and decision-making stages are often combined. The impacts on network states made by traffic control actions will be reflected through the collected data, which may then trigger new decisions after being analyzed. Therefore, the four stages of network traffic management form a cycle as shown in Figure 18.1.

Two types of data need to be collected from a network for performing traffic management: network topology data and network traffic data. The former includes information of network connectivity, i.e., how network nodes are interconnected, and network resource configuration, for example, switch capacity, and link bandwidth. The latter presents the traffic load on the network and their distribution with respect to network topology. Traffic monitoring collects statistics of traffic load and packet-forwarding actions in the network, for example, the duration time, packet number, data size, and bandwidth share of a traffic flow. Network topology is relatively static and could be changed either by network administrator through configuration or due to network device failures (e.g., broken links). Network traffic is much more dynamic and highly influenced by user behaviors and application features, for example, online gaming applications will generate traffic that is, quite different from what typical e-commerce applications generate.

Distribution of traffic with respect to a network topology is determined by the traffic control mechanisms employed in the network and has a significant impact on utilization of network resources and the performance achieved by the network. Essentially, the objective of network traffic management is to achieve optimal traffic distribution with respect to a network topology in order to fully utilize network resources while meeting all user requirements.

18.2.2   Traffic management in IP networks

18.2.2.1   Data collection for network measurement

Network topology
In an IP networks, each router relies on a routing protocol to exchange network state data, typically including status of routers and transmission links, in order to obtain network topology information. Each router constructs a network topology view based on the obtained routing information. Since routers cooperate with each other through a distributed routing protocol without a centralized controller, the network topology views built at individual routers may not be complete and consistent.

Traffic measurement
Possible mechanisms for traffic monitoring in an IP network include network management system (e.g., SNMP) and routing protocols extended with link states (e.g., OSPF-LS). Traffic monitoring can be performed at either packet level or flow level. A traffic flow in an IP network is defined as a set of packets passing an observation point in the network during a certain time interval, such that all packets belonging to a particular flow have a set of common properties [7]. Currently, flow-level traffic monitoring has been widely adopted as a main mechanism for collecting traffic load information in IP networks [8].

18.2.2.2   Data analysis and decision-making for traffic routing

Individual routers maintain their own network topology and traffic state information; therefore, data analysis and decision-making for traffic management in an IP network are performed distributedly on individual routers. Each router runs some sort of algorithm to analyze the network topology, which is typically modeled as a weighted graph, and decide the path from the router to each destination. The lack of a global network view in data analysis and decision-making leads to local optimization in IP routing—any node simply selects a path that is, optimal from its own perspective. The assumption here is that one node's decision has no or little impact on the overall system, which is generally not true. Routing decision-making needs to take into account the overall system objective and have a global view of the network in order to optimize overall network resource utilization and service performance.

Basic IP routing decision is mainly destination based; that is, all packets whose destination addresses share the same prefix have the same next hop at the router

Table 18.1   Comparison between traffic management in IP and SDN networks

	Data acquisition	**Data analysis and decision-making**	**Traffic control**
IP network	Distributed data collection at individual routers using routing protocols and network management tools	Independent data analysis and local decision-making on individual routers	Update local routing table for controlling single-hop packet forwarding
SDN network	Centralized controller collects data and assembles data to form a global network view	Data analysis and decision-making based on a single network view to achieve global optimization for resource utilization and performance	Update flow tables at multiple switches to set up end-to-end flow path

thus have the same path through the network. With destination-based routing, it is often difficult to take advantage of the diverse connections available in the network; therefore, traffic distribution in the network tends to be unbalanced and causes low-resource utilization. Routing decision in an IP network is often based on shortest path selection that mainly considers only topology information. Network administrators may assign metrics that reflect traffic load on network topology, for example, available bandwidth on links. Such metrics may impact routing decision but metric assignment is typically performed offline due to lack of real-time traffic monitoring and analysis mechanism.

18.2.2.3   Traffic control

The main traffic control action taken by a router after making a routing decision is to update the routing table at this router and then forward packets by following the routing table. Traffic control is distributed in an IP network without end-to-end flow control.

18.2.3   Traffic management in SDN networks

As summarized in Table 18.1, traffic management in SDN networks are different from that in IP networks in all four stages. We will explain the differences in detail in this sub-section.

18.2.3.1   Data collection for network measurement

Network topology

Earlier SDN deployment often employed link layer discovery protocol to collect network topology information. More recently, border gateway protocol with link states [9] provides an approach to constructing global network topology with better scalability. The centralized SDN control also allows the topology states collected from data plane switches to be assembled and represented in a standard format, thus being accessible by various SDN applications that may perform various data analysis and decision-making functions. For example, application-layer traffic optimization (ALTO) [10] can expose network state information to SDN applications via a RESTful Web service interface. The information that ALTO provides is based on an abstract or logical map of a network, which comprises two parts: a network topology map that shows the connectivity among network nodes and a cost map that gives the costs of the connections shown on the network map.

Traffic measurement

Individual SDN switches collect and store local traffic statistics in their own storage, which then can be either retrieved by a controller in a *pull* mode or proactively reported to a controller in a *push* mode. In the pull mode, a controller collects the statistics of a set of flows that match some specification from chosen devices. In this way, the controller may limit the communication overheads introduced by traffic monitoring but may not be able to provide timely responses to events occurred in the data plane. In the push mode, switches send traffic statistics to the controller either periodically or triggered by events, e.g., a flow counter reaches a predefined threshold. This model allows the controller to obtain real-time monitoring of network traffic but causes more communication overheads between the controller and the switches.

SDN enables a logically centralized controller that may greatly facilitate data collection of both topology and traffic states. In SDN, network states are measured at switches, and measurement results are all sent to the controller. Therefore, SDN controller is able to assemble the collected data to form a global view of the topology and traffic load distribution for the entire network domain. SDN control also supports traffic measurement on multiple levels, including both packet level and flow level. Meters supported by the currently available SDN southbound protocol, for example, OpenFlow [11], offers an effective method for flow-level traffic monitoring. SDN allows a wide variety of flow identification through flexible flow table matching mechanisms; for example, a flow may be identified by combination of MAC addresses, IP addresses, transport layer port numbers, protocol types, etc. By specifying different flow identifiers, flow-level traffic measurement may be performed with various granularity levels.

18.2.3.2   Data analysis and decision-making for traffic routing

The topology and traffic distribution of the entire network domain collected and assembled by the SDN controller allow data analysis and decision-making to be performed based on one single global view of the network, which may greatly facilitate the performance of traffic management through approaches that are not feasible in IP networks. For example, routing decision made based on the global network view can achieve global optimization of the overall network resource utilization and end-to-end service performance, thus avoid the local optimization issue caused by the distributed routing in IP networks. In addition, all data analysis and decision-making will be made based on the same global network view; thus solving the problem of possible inconsistent decisions made separately by individual routers in IP networks [12].

Another advantage of SDN—network programmability—also offers great potential to significantly enhance data analysis/decision-making for network traffic management. The northbound interface in the SDN architecture is expected to provide a standard API through which various control/management applications may access the global network states for analysis and specify their decision-making results (typically in the form of policies for network operations). In this sense, SDN architecture decouples data analysis/decision-making functions, which is performed by applications, from data collection performed by the controller cooperating with switches. Such decoupling allows novel data analysis/decision-making software to be developed and deployed upon a standard control platform without being constrained by implementation specifics of the underlying network infrastructure.

18.2.3.3 Traffic control

The key action of traffic control in SDN lies in updating the flow tables in SDN switches, which serve as an abstract interface between the controller and data plane devices for simplifying network operations in the latter. Unlike routing table updates performed independently by individual routers in IP network, the SDN controller is responsible for setting up end-to-end flow paths by installing flow table entries at all the switches that the flows traverse. Therefore, SDN enables global traffic flow management as well as global routing decision (Table 18.1).

18.3   Potential benefits for traffic management in SDN using Big Data techniques

18.3.1   Big Data in SDN networks

We will discuss the features of traffic-related data in SDN networks in terms of volume, velocity, and variety, which will be incentives/requirements for traffic management in SDN networks using Big Data analytics.

18.3.1.1   Bigger volume of network state data

SDN has been rapidly adopted in various networking scenarios, including wide area backbone networks as well as data center networks, which typically consist of a large number of network devices. In addition, network function virtualization (NFV) enables multiple virtual network functions to be hosted on the same physical network device, which further increase the amount of network state data that will be collected. SDN networks have been applied for service provisioning to a large group of users running a wide variety of applications. Therefore, a large amount of data of network topology states and traffic loads need to be collected and analyzed in order to make decisions for effective traffic management in SDN.

18.3.1.2   Higher velocity of network state changes

SDN for future service provision will be very dynamic. Network programmability supported by SDN allows control applications to reconfigure network topology. Application of virtualization in SDN enables virtual network functions to be easily migrated in the network. Various traffic flows may be established and terminated dynamically to meet the highly diverse user requirements. All these factors call for more advanced data analysis techniques to handle the much higher velocity in network state changes.

18.3.1.3   Broader variety of network state data

A wide spectrum of different network devices may be installed in current and future SDN networks. NFV brings in the possibility that virtually any network function, existing or emerging, to be realized as software instances running on virtual machines. On the other hand, SDN is becoming the network core for a general network service platform upon which various applications with highly diverse traffic loads may be deployed. Therefore, a much broader variety of network state data, including both network topology and traffic data, must be processed by SDN traffic management.

18.3.2   How Big Data analytics could help SDN networks

The centralized and programmable control platform enabled by SDN offers great potentials to enhance network traffic management; however, such potentials are still to be fully exploited. Although network programmability supported by standard northbound APIs in SDN allows creative approaches for data analysis/decision-making to be realized, currently available network control/management applications are mainly based on traditional methods. An example is graph theory-based modeling and optimization, which were originally developed with the IP network architecture in mind [13].

Big Data analytics-based technologies offer new approaches to addressing such challenges. Traditional methods for network design typically first formulate as optimization problems, which often are NP hard, then propose some algorithms that are typically heuristic to achieve close to optimal solutions. Next, they conduct simulations and/or testing experiments to evaluate performance of the proposed algorithms in order to validate their effectiveness and efficiency. Big Data analytics makes it possible to analyze the massive network-related data to obtain correlation between different components that offer guidelines for network design and operation. The trend is to transform some NP hard problems for network design and optimization to practical solvable problems using correlation inferred from data rather than causality determined by traditional mathematical analysis [14]. Table 18.2 summarized how Big Data analytics could help SDN traffic management in its stages.

18.4   A framework for Big Data-based SDN traffic management

A general framework for Big Data-based traffic management in SDN network is given in Figure 18.2. The framework comprises three planes: a data plane that consists of SDN switches, a control plane that has the centralized controller, and an application plane where network control and management programs run.

Table 18.2 Benefits of applying Big Data analytics in SDN traffic management

	Data acquisition	**Data analysis and decision-making**	**Traffic control**
SDN with Big Data analytics	Be able to collect more diverse, real-time data about network topology and traffic load	1. Parallel data analytics 2. Realtime data analytics 3. Data mining on existing pattern (descriptive statistics) 4. Data mining on future prediction (inferential statistics)	Better (more optimized) control based on historical data and future prediction

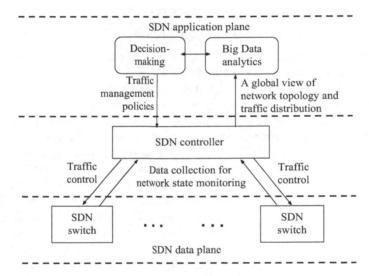

Figure 18.2 Framework for Big Data-based traffic management in SDN

The data plane comprises devices (switches) for forwarding packets in SDN networks. In addition to packet forwarding, these devices also perform data collection functions that measure network device states and traffic load distribution. The measurement results are provided to SDN controller through a southbound protocol (e.g., OpenFlow protocol) with either a pull or a push mode as we discussed in Section 18.2.3.

Key functionalities of the SDN control plane can be categorized into two processing directions. The upward direction includes functions for collecting and synthesizing network states to form a global view of network topology and traffic distribution and then presenting this network view to the application layer. The downward processing direction is to translate application requests, which are typically presented in the form of policies for traffic control and network operation, into action rules for packet forwarding in the data plane and then update the flow tables at SDN switches in order to realize such action rules.

The application plane is where all the control and management applications run in the SDN architecture. Such applications together can be regarded as the "brain" of SDN that can analyze data collected and assembled by the controller to make decisions regarding what traffic control actions should be taken. SDN applications interact with the controller through northbound interface to obtain data from the controller and send action requests (the results of decision-making) to the controller.

18.5   Possible Big Data applications for SDN traffic analysis and control

18.5.1   Big graph data analysis for SDN traffic analysis and long-term network topology improvement

We can utilize Big Data techniques to efficiently calculate the load of each switch of the network topology from the massive monitoring traffic data in SDN. The first technique is to utilize distributed graph databases, such as Titan [15], Neo4j [16], and ArangoDB [17], to store and manage the monitoring traffic data for each switch in SDN. The interconnected switches in SDN can be naturally described in graph by modeling the switches as graph nodes and the pair-wise switch connections as graph edges. We can record the traffic load of each switch (comparing with processing capability) and each pair-wise switch connections (comparing with transfer bandwidth capability) for each monitoring time stamp in a distributed graph database for long-term storage. Distributed graph databases are database systems specialized for scalable graph data storage, analytics, and query. The second technique is to utilize big graph data programing model, such as Bulk Synchronous Parallel (BSP) [18], to parallelize analysis of graph data via graph partitioning. Many Big Data systems, like Spark [19], can already support parallel graph analysis. The above two techniques could work together seamlessly. For instance, we can develop big graph data analytics algorithms on Spark GraphX which processes data stored in Titan-distributed graph database in a parallel and scalable approach. We could write spark program to calculate the distribution of traffic load of every switch of the SDN in the past month/year and rank switches based on traffic load. This can help identify bottlenecks for network performance and underutilized network links; provide guidelines for network design, e.g., increasing/decreasing switch capacity and link bandwidth of certain parts of the network.

18.5.2   Streaming-based Big Data analysis for real-time SDN traffic analysis and adaptation

Besides the batch-based statistical SDN traffic analysis and long-term network topology improvement explained in Section 18.5.1, Big Data techniques can also help analyze the most recent network traffic data for real-time SDN traffic analysis and adaptation. Big stream systems like Storm [20], Flink [21], and Spark Streaming [22] are designed to efficiently analyze high-speed streaming data from various sources. For instance, Spark Streaming can take incoming streaming data for each time window (such as 1 s), partition it across available computing nodes, and process the partitions in parallel. By utilizing these systems, we can monitor each switch's load in real time. Once a switch's load reaches a certain threshold, SDN controller can decide how to reroute the current and future flows to avoid the overloaded switches. We need to design new network scheduling algorithms that can utilize the big stream systems and achieve real-time flow-level adaptation.

18.5.3 Big Data mining for SDN network control and adaptation

Using data mining techniques, we could learn the temporal patterns of switch workload from historical monitoring data and utilize the pattern for SDN network control and adaptation. Traffic load often fluctuates during different time periods such as weekend vs weekdays and daytime vs night. There have been many systems supporting data mining on top of large volume of datasets including Spark MLLib [23] and Mahout [24]. By utilizing these systems, we can do temporal correlation mining and regression of acquired time series traffic data of each switch in parallel and model how the switch's load changes over time. We can then predict future network performances using the learned models. It provides proactive guidelines for temporary capacity adjustment through data plane reconfiguration (enabled by the network programmability provided by SDN) or virtual network function migration (supported by NFV) in order to improve network resource utilization and energy efficiency.

18.6 Open issues and challenges

18.6.1 Data acquisition measurement and overhead

Real-time acquisition of sufficient data that may accurately reflect network states and their changes in a certain time period forms the basis of applying Big Data analytics in SDN for traffic management. However, such data acquisition in a large-scale dynamic SDN network is challenging. Both the number of switches and number of traffic flows increase dramatically with network scale thus requiring a large volume of data to be measured at different switches. The measurement results need to be sent to the SDN controller where collected data are preprocessed to form a global view of network topology and the current traffic distribution across the topology.

Both data measurement and measured data transportation cause extra overheads in the network and potentially degrade network performance due to their consumption of the processing capacity at switches and transmission capacities on network links. Therefore, how to achieve a balance between accurate data acquisition and extra overheads for data measurement/transportation is an open issue that deserves thorough study. The objective is to meet the data acquisition requirement for Big Data analytics with the minimum amount of overheads, such as the minimum number of network states need to be measured, the lowest sampling rate for measurement, and the least consumption of transportation and processing capacity. We also note that different Big Data analytics applications (such as the ones discussed in Section 18.5) have different data acquisition requirements.

18.6.2 SDN controller management

Another challenge to Big Data acquisition in large-scale SDN networks is related to distributed deployment of SDN controllers. Large-scale SDN networks typically employ logically centralized but physically distributed controller in order to enhance network scalability and reliability. There are a variety of deployment schemes for distributed SDN controller, for example, duplicated controllers with replicated network states or a cluster of controllers each controlling its own part of the network. A key issue that must be addressed is to assure a consistent global view of network to be presented to Big Data analysis and decision-making functions on the application layer. On the other hand, data is often distributed in Big Data systems. If we could utilize available data management techniques of Big Data systems, such as partitioning, duplications, and consistency management, for distributed SDN controller, we may offer a promising approach to addressing the challenges brought in by distributed controllers in SDN to improve network performance.

18.6.3 New system architecture for Big Data-based traffic management in SDN

Big Data analysis needs proper software and hardware environment to reach its full potential. Computers with high I/O capacity and performance (such as SSD storage) and fast interconnection (such as InfiniBand) can greatly reduce the processing times of Big Data analysis applications. The hardware environment in a SDN is normally optimized for data transfer, which can bring challenges on Big Data system's deployment and performance. To achieve Big Data-based traffic management in SDN, we need both network management capability and data analytics capability. It could mean a hybrid hardware architecture design that provides the best integration and interaction of the two capabilities. For system architecture, one possible solution is to leverage the infrastructure virtualization and NFV that are common in data centers. This full spectrum resource virtualization can help on-demand scalability required by both Big Data analysis and traffic management in SDN. For SDN that is, deployed in a nondata-center environment, such as WAN, there will be additional overhead on data transferring between SDN controller and Big Data execution platform. The overhead will limit the advantages of using Big Data techniques for SDN.

18.7 Conclusion

In this chapter, we investigated the general process of traffic management and how it is done without and with SDN. Then, we discuss how Big Data techniques can work with SDN, and what potential benefits it could bring. We then provided system designs for three possible Big Data applications that may be employed for better SDN traffic management and discussed the remaining open challenges. We believe SDN could work together with Big Data analytics in order to offer better traffic monitoring, analysis, decision-making, and control in SDN networks. In the future, we believe there will be a growth of interests and support from Big Data techniques for SDN traffic management.

References

[1]   Open Networking Foundation, "Software-Defined Networking: the New Norm for Networks," ONF White Paper, April 2012.
[2]   Kambatla K, Kollias G, Kumar V, and Grama A. Trends in big data analytics. J Parallel Distrib Comput. 2014/7;74: 2561–2573.
[3]   Cattell R. Scalable SQL and NoSQL data stores. SIGMOD Rec. New York, NY, USA: ACM; 2011;39: 12–27.
[4]   Dean J, and Ghemawat S. MapReduce: simplified data processing on large clusters. Commun ACM. ACM; 2008;51: 107–113.
[5]   Marz N, and Warren J. Big data: principles and best practices of scalable realtime data systems. 1st ed. Greenwich, CT, USA: Manning Publications Co.; 2015.
[6]   Akyildiz IF, Lee A, Wang P, Luo M, and Chou W. A roadmap for traffic engineering in SDN-OpenFlow networks. Comput Netw. Elsevier; 2014;71: 1–30.
[7]   Claise B. Trammell, B., Ed., and P. Aitken," Specification of the IP Flow Information Export (IPFIX) Protocol for the Exchange of Flow Information. STD 77, RFC 7011, Sep 2013.
[8]   Hofstede R, Čeleda P, Trammell B, *et al.* Flow monitoring explained: from packet capture to data analysis with NetFlow and IPFIX. IEEE Commun Surv Tutorials. 2014;16: 2037–2064.
[9]   Gredler H, Medved J, Previdi S, Farrel A, and Ray S. North-bound distribution of link-state and traffic engineering (te) information using bgp [Internet]. 2016. Available: https://www.rfc-editor.org/info/rfc7752.
[10] Alimi R, Yang Y, and Penno R. Application-layer traffic optimization (ALTO) protocol. 2014; Available: https://tools.ietf.org/html/rfc7285.txt.
[11] McKeown N, Anderson T, Balakrishnan H, *et al.* OpenFlow: enabling innovation in campus networks. SIGCOMM Comput Commun Rev. New York, NY, USA: ACM; 2008;38: 69–74.
[12] Agarwal S, Kodialam M, and Lakshman TV. Traffic engineering in software defined networks. 2013 Proceedings IEEE INFOCOM. 2013. pp. 2211–2219.
[13] Karakus M, and Durresi A. Quality of service (QoS) in software defined networking (SDN): a survey. J Netw Comput Appl. 2017;80: 200–218.
[14] Cui L, Yu FR, and Yan Q. When big data meets software-defined networking: SDN for big data and big data for SDN. IEEE Netw. 2016;30: 58–65.

[15] Titan: Distributed Graph Database [Internet], 2017. Available: http://titan. thinkaurelius.com/.

[16] Neo4j: The World's Leading Graph Database. In: Neo4j Graph Database [Internet], 2017. Available: https://neo4j.com/.

[17] ArangoDB – highly available multi-model NoSQL database. In: ArangoDB [Internet], 2017. Available: https://www.arangodb.com/.

[18] Gerbessiotis AV, and Valiant LG. Direct bulk-synchronous parallel algorithms. J Parallel Distrib Comput. 1994/8;22: 251–267.

[19] Apache Spark Project [Internet], 2017. Available: http://spark.apache.org.

[20] Apache Storm Project [Internet]. Apr 2016. Available: http://storm.apache.org.

[21] Apache Flink Project [Internet]. Apr 2016. Available: http://flink.apache.org.

[22] Spark Streaming [Internet]. Apr 2016. Available: http://spark.apache.org/ streaming/.

[23] Meng X, Bradley J, Yuvaz B, and Sparks E. Mllib: Machine learning in apache spark. J Mach Learn Res. jmlr.org; 2016; Available: http://www.jmlr.org/ papers/volume17/15-237/15-237.pdf.

[24] Apache Mahout: Scalable machine learning and data mining [Internet], 2017. Available: http://mahout.apache.org/.

Chapter 19

Big Data helps SDN to optimize its controllers

Daewoong Cho, Saeed Bastani**, Javid Taheri**,
and Albert Y. Zomaya**

19.1 Introduction

The paradigm of separating control and data planes in software-defined networking (SDN) facilitates network abstraction and programmability features, which in turn foster fast service innovation. These features are enabled by an architectural element of SDN referred to as the *controller*. It provides a global yet abstract view to network applications such as traffic management and load balancing. Also, the control policies mandated by applications are enforced by the controller by means of creating and updating flow-level rules in the forwarding tables of devices in the infrastructure network, whether it be a data center or a wide area network. With these central roles of controller element in mind, it is crucial to sustain its performance in a satisfactory level. Notably, in a centralized controller architecture, key performance metrics including scalability and resiliency of the controller are potentially vulnerable to severe degradation, due to the following reasons. First, with the growth of network size or the rate of changes in the network state, the processing demand in the controller increases, potentially to a level that cannot be handled in a timely manner (scalability issue). Second, with insufficient number of controllers, or ineffective placement of the controller(s) in the network, a set of network devices may not be able to reach any controller. Even if the network devices can physically reach a controller, intolerable delay must happen (resiliency issue). The worst case scenario would be using a single controller which also happens to be placed ineffectively. In such a case, the controller becomes a single point of failure.

An immediate solution to scalability and resiliency of SDN control plane would be using multiple controllers in a distributed fashion. However, subtle challenges must be addressed including the number of controllers, their placement in the network, and the assignment of network devices to controllers. The right solutions to these challenges depend on the network state, which as we mentioned earlier is dynamic in

*School of Information Technologies, University of Sydney, Australia
**Department of Mathematics and Computer Science, Karlstad University, Sweden

nature. For SDN to be adaptive to the network state, it must rely on the surrounding information in the network itself and use it to self-optimize its control behavior. However, the surrounding information can be large in size and fast in terms of change rate. This qualifies the network state as a Big Data scenario, and thus Big Data analytics are necessary to be employed in order to support SDN to make optimal decisions about its control plane topology and behavior, which is the topic of this chapter. Specifically, we propose a number of feasible scenarios of using Big Data analytics in SDN controller optimization. These scenarios cover a rich set of use cases ranging from controller placement to flow aggregation and back-up path identification. The chapter also presents a number of open issues that need to be addressed by academia and industrial practitioners.

19.2   What is a SDN controller?

In this section, we present a brief overview of SDN controller and its roles in a SDN-based networking environment.

The SDN controller acts as a brain in SDN which manages flow control to enable intelligent networking. SDN controllers rely on southbound protocols such as OpenFlow to guide switches how to forward traffic. The SDN controller lies between network devices at one end and applications at the other end. Therefore, all communications between applications and network devices should pass through the SDN controller. It provides applications with an abstract view of the underlying forwarding plane and enforces application-driven optimal policies for traffic forwarding. By analogy with a computer system, the SDN controller acts as an operating system for the network. With the SDN paradigm, the control plane is decoupled from data plane (i.e., forwarding devices). Therefore, the controller facilitates automated network management and make it easier to integrate and administer business applications [1].

The primary functions of an SDN controller are maintaining the network topology and inventory including the list of connected devices and their capabilities. Also, it collects network statistics, performs analysis, and orchestrates new rules throughout the network [2]. We can summarize the main roles of the SDN controller as follows:

- global management of network devices and their capacities;
- collecting and maintaining resource state information;
- performing analysis on the collected network statistics; and
- making new rules and updating flow tables of the forwarding devices.

The ultimate effect of SDN controller is to determine per-flow forwarding path in a network. To this aim, SDN controller should be agile in reacting to network dynamic and should be consistent in the enforcement of flow forwarding policies throughout the network. The SDN controller achieves these goals in interaction with other architectural elements of SDN, as demonstrated in Figure 19.1. The Big Data analytics component is added to the control plane to help support SDN controller to materialize its goals in an effective way. We elaborate this new feature of SDN architecture in further details in the following sections.

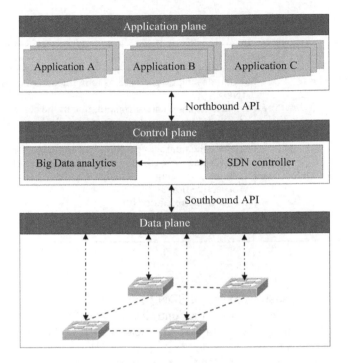

Figure 19.1   Software-defined networking architecture

19.3   SDN controller-related issues

Most, if not all, advantages of SDN paradigm over the traditional networking are brought by its promise of providing a global view of the underlying network and using this global view in making decisions about per-flow traffic forwarding. This, however, raises several challenges that need to be addressed in order to realize a full-feathered SDN solution. Table 19.1 demonstrated major challenges related to SDN controller and describes a number of solutions proposed in the literature.

The SDN controller-related issues can be classified in two broad categories: (i) scalability and (ii) resiliency. In the sequel, we discuss these issues in more details and present some solutions based on controller placement strategies.

19.3.1   Scalability

As mentioned before, SDN has many advantages compared with the traditional network. However, with its centralized control, scalability is an issue when the scale of a network grows. It should be carefully considered that how to link geographically distributed network domains efficiently [11]. According to NOX benchmark, the SDN controller cannot handle beyond 30k requests/s [12]. Apart from size problem, high flow initiation rates can cause another major issue in SDN environments [13].

Table 19.1   Controller-related issues and their solutions [3,4]

Issues	Solutions
Load concentration	• To upgrade single-core systems to multicore systems, scale-up (NOX [5])
	• To distribute state and/or computation of the control functionality to multiple controllers, Scale-out (Onix [6], HyperFlow [7], Kandoo [8])
	• To reduce the number of requests forwarded to the controller by forwarding only larger flows to the controller (DevFlow [9])
Flow initiation overhead	• To set up forwarding entries before the initiation of actual flows (proactive flow initiation design)
	• Flow table aggregation [10]
Resiliency to failures	• Synchronized slave controller (backup controller)
	• Distributed/multiple controllers

When the network size grows, the SDN controllers should handle more events and requests. Beyond a certain load, the controllers may not be able to process all the incoming requests within a required time threshold [3,14,15]. This can be explained by the following reasons:

- With large amount of control messages arriving at a controller, the bandwidth, memory, and processing resources of controllers become a bottleneck [16].
- When the network size grows large, some forwarding devices in the data plane will encounter long flow setup latencies regardless of controller location [17,18].
- With the size, and thus the demand of the network growing, flow setup times can increase significantly because the system is bounded by the processing power of the controller [14]. The processing load induced by network events is generally considered as the most significant part of the total load on the controllers [5,19].

Arguably, a single controller may not have enough capacity to manage the entire network, and thus it could become a bottleneck in terms of processing power, memory, or input/output bandwidth. This calls for distributed control architectures [16]. To this end, several approaches have been proposed in the literature to physically distribute the controllers to improve the scalability of SDN. We will address this in more details in Section 19.3.3.

19.3.2   Resiliency

A centralized controller architecture is vulnerable to network faults such as network device, controller, and link failures because when a network device fails, it causes a chain of device-to-controller communication failures. Specifically, it can affect all the network devices that include the failed device in their control path [16].

Control plane

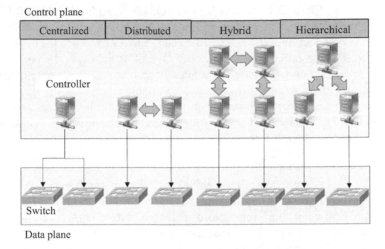

Figure 19.2   Different controller placement strategies

According to the OpenFlow standard specification, a controller can also have backup controller(s). In this context, the decision on where in the network to place the controller(s) will drive the achievable resiliency in the control plane [16].

19.3.3   Solutions

To enhance the SDN performance in terms of scalability, latency, and reliability, different SDN controller placement strategies should be used depending on the given situation. Otherwise, performance degradation will be experienced when solely relying on random controller deployment [20]. In other words, controller placement strategies are the key to address the scalability and resiliency challenges faced by the control plane. Controller placement problem consists of two joint subproblems: (i) how many controllers are needed and (ii) where in the network the controllers should be placed [21].

In the sequel, we describe different SDN controller placement strategies (see Figure 19.2) proposed to enhance the scalability and resiliency of SDN control plane.

19.3.3.1   Centralized placement

A centralized placement has a single entity that manages all forwarding devices in data plane. Naturally, single network connection between control planes and data planes is vulnerable to a node failure [22]. NOX, Maestro [23], and Beacon [19] are examples of centralized controllers. To gain an enhanced scalability, the controllers are materialized by multicore computer architecture.

19.3.3.2   Distributed placement

A distributed placement can be scaled out to meet the requirements of dynamic environments from small to large-scale networks. Examples of distributed placement are

Onix, HyperFlow, Fleet [24], DISCO [25], ONOS [26], and PANE [27]. Distributed controller placement offers an enhanced fault tolerance, i.e., when a controller node fails, another controller node will perform its tasks corresponding to the devices originally assigned to the failed controller node. Overall, it enhances the control plane resiliency, scalability and decrease the impact of problems [28]. Despite its undeniable advantages, distributed controllers are vulnerable to consistency issues due to the inherent delay of state synchronization among the controllers. This causes some controllers to rely on stale (and potentially invalid) information which in turn may result in invalid flow forwarding policies.

19.3.3.3   Hybrid placement

In this scheme, a logically centralized global controller manages network-wide state in a top layer, and a group of controllers residing in a bottom layer. Kandoo [8] is an example of hybrid controller architecture where the bottom-layer controllers do not need to have any knowledge about peer controllers. This helps reduce the load in the global controller by filtering new flow requests while also providing the data path with faster responses for requests that can be handled by a local controller residing in the bottom layer.

19.3.3.4   Hierarchical placement

The hierarchical approach has a centralized controller (master) to manage the activity of all underlying controllers (slaves) [29]. In distributed controller approach, controllers are connected to each other to maintain recent network state but in hierarchical approach: slave controllers are not connected, and they only communicate with their master controller. Unlike the hybrid approach that could have more than one master controller, hierarchical approach has only one master controller.

19.4   Big Data for SDN controller optimization

There are a couple of reasons why we should use Big Data analytics to address the SDN controller scalability and resiliency problem. As growing the size of network and its traffic, network-related data became large data sets compared to the past, hence a traditional approach cannot efficiently handle such large scale of data sets. Since network should maintain high availability all the time, real-time decision-making based on collected Big Data is required to dynamically adapt a new environment. General system capacities are however constrained to process ever-increasing network data in real time.

In the context of SDN-based networking, a lucrative benefit offered by Big Data analytics is the support it can provide for creating/updating traffic forwarding policies using the historical and trend data while minimizing human intervention. In this respect, we motivate/argue that Big Data analytics can benefit SDN controllers in terms of making a right decision for efficient resource management in SDN environments including improving/maximizing network utilization, efficient network load balancing, and controlling flow table for a reduced latency. The basic principle is that a Big Data analytic application exists in the control plane to support decisions of the SDN controller.

In this section, we illustrate the Big Data analytics system architecture, Big Data analytics techniques for optimizing the SDN controller, and present problem formulations with derived algorithms for controller placement. Finally, we propose scenarios where SDN controller functions can be optimized by means of Big Data analytics.

19.4.1 System architecture

While SDN controller acts as the "brain" of SDN, the Big Data analytics system acts as the brain of the SDN controller. It can help the SDN controller make sophisticated/holistic decisions about network resource management. The detailed system architecture for the Big Data analytics is described in Figure 19.3. The processes for the Big Data analytics can be organized in order as follows:

- Data collection: the data related to the SDN controller optimization is accumulated in this process. This includes information about the traffic of the controller as well as the forwarding elements, flow path, controller energy usage, response time, link capacity, and controller resource state, to mention a few.
- Data cleaning: the collected data is processed to extract meaningful information and key factors required for decision-making. Data preprocessing techniques are used to clean and validate the collected data.
- Analysis: optimization algorithms are used to carry out analysis on the information extracted in the previous step.
- Suggestion: the Big Data analytics provides workable suggestions for SDN controller optimization.

19.4.2 Big Data analytics techniques

There are many techniques that can be used to analyze data sets [30]. Among them, two major Big Data analytics techniques can be used to predict key metrics such as expected network traffic in any given region and use it for optimizing the SDN controller. We describe these techniques in the following sections.

19.4.2.1 Descriptive analytics

This technique uses historical data to find pattern(s) which can best illustrate the current situation. Association analysis, clustering, and classification are example methods exploited in descriptive analytics. Examples of information types provided by this technique are as follows:

- the amount of network traffic occurred during last week;
- the frequency of network devices or links failure during last year;
- the amount of energy used by the SDN controller during the last month; and
- the average network latency incurred by switch-to-controller communications during Christmas time.

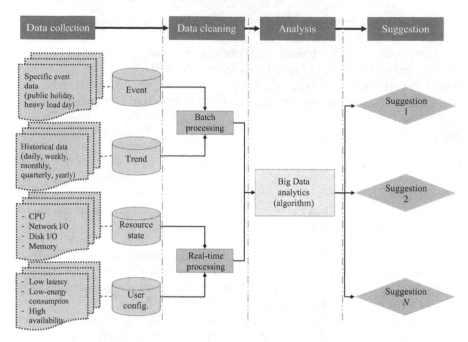

Figure 19.3   Architecture of Big Data analytics system

19.4.2.2 Predictive analytics

This technique aims at predicting the likelihood of future outcomes given a set of historical data. The predictive analytics can provide the best possible countermeasure against the future events. Example use cases of predictive analytics are as follows:

- predicting the expected network traffic at a special time period;
- using the expected network traffic to determine how many controllers and where they should be placed;
- building network backup paths to cope with issues arising from sudden failure of network devices or links in the future;
- determining the amount of resources required for the SDN controller to maintain a response time threshold; and
- using the predicted load to determine the energy usage of any given controller.

19.4.3 Problem formulation

We design a model to show how key metrics such as traffic demand and energy usage can be used by the Big Data analytics. Table 19.2 describes the notations we use to formalize the problem statement introduced in this section.

Table 19.2   The model parameters and variables

	Basic parameters
S	Set of switches
C	Set of controllers
E	Set of network flow
c_m	A controller, $\forall c_m \in C$
s_l	A switch, $\forall s_l \in S$
$e_{i,j}$	Traffic flow between switches s_i and s_j, $e_{i,j} \in E$
$e_{i,j}^b$	Backup traffic flow between switches s_i and s_j, $e_{i,j}^b \in E$
	Current resource state
$c_m^{l,cpu}$	CPU resource limit of controller c_m
$c_m^{l,mem}$	Memory resource limit of controller c_m
$c_m^{l,bw}$	Bandwidth resource limit of controller c_m
c_m^{cpu}	CPU resource utilization of controller c_m
c_m^{mem}	Memory resource utilization of controller c_m
c_m^{bw}	Bandwidth resource utilization of controller c_m
c_m^{tf}	Network traffic (consumed bandwidth) of controller c_m
s_l^{tf}	Network traffic of switch s_l influencing its controller
c_m^{eg}	Energy usage of controller c_m
$e_{i,j}^{lt}$	Network latency between switches s_i and s_j
c_m^f	The number of failures of controller c_m in a specific time frame (e.g., a week)
s_l^f	The number of failures of switch s_l in a specific time frame (e.g., a week)
$e_{i,j}^f$	The number of failures of $e_{i,j}$ in a specific time frame (e.g., a week)
	Expected resource state
$c_m^{e,tf}$	Expected network traffic of controller c_m
$s_l^{e,tf}$	Expected network traffic of switch s_l influencing its controller
$e_{i,j}^{e,lt}$	Expected network latency between switches s_i and s_j
	Decision variable
bv_{s_l,c_m}	"1" if switch s_l is assigned to controller c_m; "0" otherwise
	Output variables
$PL(e_{i,j})$	Path length (in number of hop)
$CD(x1, x2)$	Communication delay between $x1$ and $x2$ where x is one of switches (s_l) or controllers (c_m)

Let's denote by $S = \{s_1, s_2, \ldots, s_l\}$ the set of forwarding elements (e.g., switches), $C = \{c_1, c_2, \ldots, c_m\}$ the set of controllers, and $Q(c_m)$ the set of switches controlled by controller c_m. Network flows are represented by $e_{i,j} = (s_i, s_j) \in E$. Table 19.3 shows the flow path list derived from the SDN example topology depicted in Figure 19.4. Network traffic stands for consumed bandwidth of network devices.

Table 19.3   Flow paths for the SDN example topology in Figure 19.4

Flow	Fastest path	Path length (PL($e_{i,j}$))
$e_{1,3}$	$(s_1, s_2), (s_2, s_3)$	3 hops
$e_{1,7}$	$(s_1, s_2), (s_2, s_3), (s_3, s_4), (s_4, s_5), (s_5, s_6), (s_6, s_7)$	7 hops
$e_{1,10}$	$(s_1, s_2), (s_2, s_3), (s_3, s_{12}), (s_{12}, s_{13}), (s_{11}, s_{10})$	10 hops
$e_{1,12}$	$(s_1, s_2), (s_2, s_3), (s_3, s_{12})$	4 hops

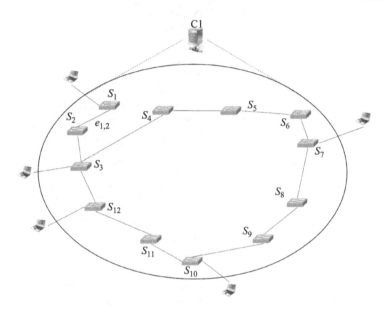

Figure 19.4   SDN example topology

Parameter values for SDN example topology (Figure 19.4)

- Controller elements : $Q(c_1) = \{s_1, s_2, s_3, s_4, s_5, s_6, s_7, s_8, s_9, s_{10}, s_{11}, s_{12}\}$
- Controller traffic: $c_1^{tf} = \{s_1^{tf} + s_2^{tf} + \cdots + s_{11}^{tf} + s_{12}^{tf}\}$
- Flow path $e_{i,j}$ is described in Table 19.3
- Controller energy usage: c_1^{eg}

19.4.4   Optimization algorithm

This section details an example algorithm to optimize the SDN controller operation in terms of how many controllers are needed in accordance with current network traffic, and where the controllers are placed for low latency and fault tolerance.

Algorithm 1 represents the pseudocode of controller optimization algorithm. The main role of the algorithm is to guide the SDN controller on how/when to apply

---

Algorithm 1 Controller optimization algorithm

    Input : Links (E), switches (S), controllers (C)
    Output: Controller optimization
1: **foreach** *controller c_m in C* **do**
2:    | Calculate controller traffic c_m^{tf}
3:    | Calculate switch traffic s_l^{tf}
4:    | Calculate expected controller traffic $c_m^{e,\text{tf}}$
5:    | Calculate expected switch traffic $s_l^{e,\text{tf}}$
6:    | **if** *controller traffic (c_m^{tf}) is above HIGH_THRESHOLD* **then**
7:    | **if** *horizontal expansion is allowed* **then**
8:    | | Place a new controller c_{m+1}
9:    | **else**
10:   | | Allocate more resource to controller c_m
11:   | **if** *controller traffic (c_m^{tf}) is below LOW_THRESHOLD* **then**
12:   | Shut Down c_m controller
13:   | **if** *controller failure is expected* **then**
14:   | Place a backup controller
15:   | **if** *link/node failure is expected* **then**
16:   | Build backup paths ($e_{i,j}^b$) for switches influenced by link/node
               failures
17:   | **if** *the expected communication delay (CD(x1, x2)) between controllers*
          and switches is above AGREED_THRESHOLD **then**
18:   | Place a controller to meet the agreed response time between
               controllers and switches
19:   | **if** *exists flow rule redundancies* **then**
20:   | Aggregate flow rules

---

solutions. For instance, the algorithm suggests a solution on a specific phenomenon such as heavy/low controller traffic, communication delay, or flow rule redundancies. Also, the algorithm presents countermeasures against expected network failures in the future.

19.4.5 Applicable scenarios

In this section, we present a number of scenarios that can benefit from Big Data analytics to optimize SDN controller. Common to all scenarios, using Big Data analytics can help make decisions more quickly and accurately compared to manual intervention. This property is most needed because network environments are dynamic in nature, which mandates the SDN controller optimization strategy to be responsive in adaptation to the fast-paced network dynamics. Our proposed scenarios introduced in the following sections cover a rich range of optimization objectives ranging from scalability and resiliency to energy efficiency, low latency, and controller load reduction.

Scenario 1. Controller scale-up/out against network traffic concentration (Figure 19.5)

- The Big Data analytics predicts controller network traffic ($c_m^{e,\mathrm{tf}}$) based on accumulated historical data.
- If controller network traffic is expected to be above a threshold, the Big Data analytics system will suggest controller scale-up or scale-out in accordance with the amount of expected traffic.
- Scale-up: The resource for controller c_1 is scaled up by A
  - $c_1^{l,\mathrm{cpu}} = (c_1^{l,\mathrm{cpu}} \times (100 + A))(\%)$
  - $c_1^{l,\mathrm{mem}} = (c_1^{l,\mathrm{mem}} \times (100 + A))(\%)$
  - $c_1^{l,\mathrm{bw}} = (c_1^{l,\mathrm{bw}} \times (100 + A))(\%)$
- Scale-out: Load distributions to multiple controllers (here, three controllers)
  - $c_1^{\mathrm{tf}} = (s_1^{\mathrm{tf}} + s_2^{\mathrm{tf}} + s_3^{\mathrm{tf}} + s_4^{\mathrm{tf}})$
  - $c_2^{\mathrm{tf}} = (s_5^{\mathrm{tf}} + s_6^{\mathrm{tf}} + s_7^{\mathrm{tf}} + s_8^{\mathrm{tf}})$
  - $c_3^{\mathrm{tf}} = (s_9^{\mathrm{tf}} + s_{10}^{\mathrm{tf}} + s_{11}^{\mathrm{tf}} + s_{12}^{\mathrm{tf}})$

Scenario 2. Controller scale-in for reduced energy usage (Figure 19.6)

- The Big Data analytics detects controllers whose traffic (c_m^{tf}) and resource utilization are below a given threshold.
- If traffics for a controller can be managed by other controllers, the Big Data analytics advises to decrease the number of running controllers for energy efficiency.
- If a controller $c3$ is to be turned off, its assigned switches are reassigned to a controller $c2$.
- Turn off the $c3$ controller to save energy usage.
- Controller energy usage before scale-in: $c_1^{\mathrm{eg}} + c_2^{\mathrm{eg}} + c_3^{\mathrm{eg}}$
- Controller energy usage after scale-in: $c_1^{\mathrm{eg}} + c_2^{\mathrm{eg}}$

Scenario 3. Backup controller placement for fault tolerance and high availability (Figure 19.7)

- The Big Data analytics predicts future network latency ($e_{i,j}^{e,\mathrm{lt}}$) and possibility of controller failure (c_m^f).

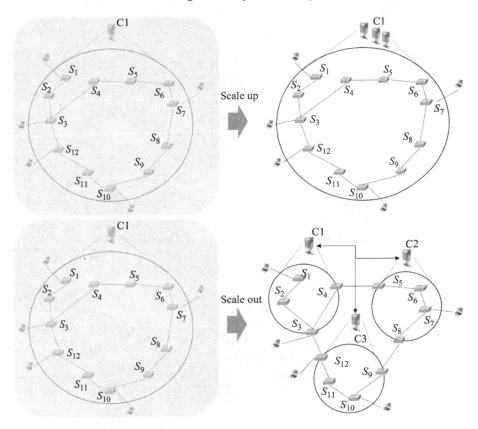

Figure 19.5   Controller scale-up vs. scale-out to manage network traffic

- The Big Data analytics can guide to place a new controller (c_2) and isolate the current controller (c_1) to process data that has already received.
- New traffics are forwarded to a new arranged SDN controller (c_2).
- When the isolated controller (c_1) completes processing data, it can receive data again or be removed if this is useless.

Scenario 4. Creating backup paths to improve fault tolerance (Figure 19.4)

- The Big Data analytics detects spots where switch failures (s_l^f) and link failures ($e_{i,j}^f$) are likely to occur.

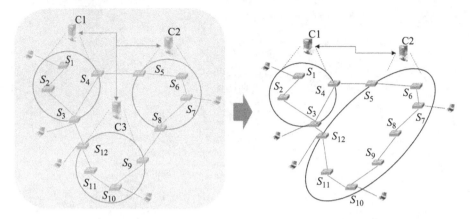

Figure 19.6   Controller scale-in to reduce energy usage

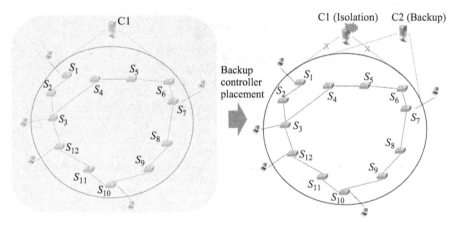

Figure 19.7   Backup controller placement for fault tolerance and high availability

- The Big Data analytics suggests a backup path between nodes to counteract link or node failures.
- When link or node failure happens, the SDN controller immediately updates a flow table with a backup flow path.
- If there is no backup path established before (such as between nodes 1 and 3 in Figure 19.4), the Big Data analytics can suggest the controller to add a new link $e_{1,3}^b$ between $s1$ and $s3$.
- The controller maintains the table of backup paths suggested by Big Data analytics (Table 19.4).

Table 19.4 Backup flow path

Flow	Backup path	Path length (PL($e_{i,j}$))
$e_{1,3}^b$	N/A	N/A
$e_{1,7}^b$	$(s_1, s_2), (s_2, s_3), (s_3, s_{12}), (s_{12}, s_{11}), (s_{11}, s_{10}), (s_{10}, s_9),$ $(s_9, s_8), (s_8, s_7)$	9 hops
$e_{1,10}^b$	$(s_1, s_2), (s_2, s_3), (s_3, s_4), (s_4, s_5), (s_5, s_6), (s_6, s_7), (s_7, s_8),$ $(s_8, s_9), (s_9, s_{10})$	10 hops
$e_{1,12}^b$	$(s_1, s_2), (s_2, s_3), (s_3, s_4), (s_4, s_5), (s_5, s_6), (s_6, s_7), (s_7, s_8),$ $(s_8, s_9), (s_9, s_{10}), (s_{10}, s_{11}), (s_{11}, s_{12})$	12 hops

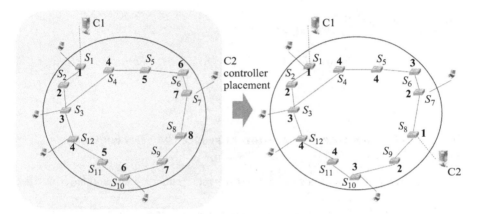

Figure 19.8 Controller placement to lower latency between controllers and switches

Scenario 5. Controller placement for low latency between controllers and switches (Figure 19.8)

- The Big Data analytics decides the best location where a controlled should be placed to meet the agreed response time.
- Assuming that agreed response time: $CD(x1, x2) \leq 4$ hops
- Controller $c1$ is connected directly to the switch $s1$.
- The further away from the switch $s1$, the bigger other switches' communication delay.
- By placing additional controllers, communication delay between switches and controllers can be reduced.
- By placing a controller linked to the switch $s8$, communication delay is significantly decreased (e.g., $CD(controller, s10) = 6 \rightarrow CD(controller, s10) = 3$).

No	Flow match	Action
1	1111	Fwd 1
2	1110	Fwd 2
3	1101	Fwd 1
4	1100	Fwd 3
5	*110	Fwd 2
6	11*1	Fwd 1
7	0100	Fwd 3
8	*100	Fwd 3
9	**10	Fwd 2

Flow rule aggregation

No	Flow match	Action
1	11*1	Fwd 1
2	**10	Fwd 2
3	*100	Fwd 3

Figure 19.9   Flow rule aggregation to reduce SDN controller's traffic

Scenario 6. Flow rule aggregation to reduce the SDN controller's traffic (Figure 19.9)

- The Big Data analytics detects flow rule redundancies and advises the controller to optimize flow rules.
- The size of flow table can be reduced as it is demonstrated in Figure 19.9.

19.5   Open issues and challenges

This section discusses open issues and challenges which need to be addressed in order to adopt Big Data analytics for the SDN controller optimization. We summarize the key challenges as follows:

- Detailed statistics collection for Big Data analytics can enable better decisions of the controller while it can cause heavy network load, which leads to another communication delay.
- Standardized interfaces between the SDN controller and the Big Data analytics are needed in heterogeneous environments.
- It is essential to define how to collect and process large amount of data generated by thousands of devices in the SDN environments.
- We need sophisticated analytics algorithm to make the best decisions for the SDN controller optimization.

19.6   Conclusion

In this chapter, we first discuss the basic features and recent issues of the SDN control plane, notably the controller element. Then, we present feasible ideas to address the SDN controller-related problems using Big Data analytics techniques. Accordingly, we propose that Big Data can help various aspects of the SDN controller to address scalability issue and resiliency problem. Furthermore, we proposed six applicable scenarios for optimizing the SDN controller using the Big Data analytics: (i) controller scale-up/out against network traffic concentration, (ii) controller scale-in for reduced energy usage, (iii) backup controller placement for fault tolerance and high availability, (iv) creating backup paths to improve fault tolerance, (v) controller placement for low latency between controllers and switches, and (vi) flow rule aggregation to reduce the SDN controller's traffic. Although real-world practices on optimizing SDN controllers using Big Data are absent in the literature, we expect scenarios we highlighted in this chapter to be highly applicable to optimize the SDN controller in the future.

References

[1]   M. Rouse, "SDN controller (software-defined networking controller) [online]. 2012. Available from http://searchsdn.techtarget.com/definition/SDN-controller-software-defined-networking-controller [Accessed 6 Mar 2017]."

[2]   "What are SDN Controllers (or SDN Controllers Platforms) [online]. Available from https://www.sdxcentral.com/sdn/definitions/sdn-controllers [Accessed 6 Mar 2017]."

[3]   S. H. Yeganeh, A. Tootoonchian, and Y. Ganjali, "On scalability of software-defined networking," *IEEE Communications Magazine*, vol. 51, no. 2, pp. 136–141, 2013.

[4]   E. Borcoci, "Control Plane Scalability in Software Defined Networking," in *InfoSys 2014 Conference, Chamonix, France, 2014*.

[5]   A. Tootoonchian, S. Gorbunov, Y. Ganjali, M. Casado, and R. Sherwood, "On controller performance in software-defined networks," *Hot-ICE*, vol. 12, pp. 1–6, 2012.

[6]   T. Koponen, M. Casado, N. Gude, *et al.*, "Onix: A distributed control platform for large-scale production networks," *OSDI*, vol. 10, pp. 1–6, 2010.

[7]   A. Tootoonchian and Y. Ganjali, "Hyperflow: A distributed control plane for openflow," in *Proceedings of the 2010 Internet Network Management Conference on Research on Enterprise Networking*, pp. 3–3, 2010.

[8]   S. Hassas Yeganeh and Y. Ganjali, "Kandoo: A framework for efficient and scalable offloading of control applications," in *Proceedings of the First Workshop on Hot Topics in Software Defined Networks*, pp. 19–24, ACM, 2012.

[9]   A. R. Curtis, J. C. Mogul, J. Tourrilhes, P. Yalagandula, P. Sharma, and S. Banerjee, "DevoFlow: Scaling flow management for high-performance

networks," *ACM SIGCOMM Computer Communication Review*, vol. 41, no. 4, pp. 254–265, 2011.

[10] S. Luo, H. Yu, and L. Li, "Practical flow table aggregation in SDN," *Computer Networks*, vol. 92, pp. 72–88, 2015.

[11] T. Huang, F. R. Yu, C. Zhang, J. Liu, J. Zhang, and J. Liu, "A survey on large-scale software defined networking (SDN) testbeds: Approaches and challenges," *IEEE Communications Surveys and Tutorials*, Vol. 19, No. 2, pp. 891–917, 2017.

[12] A. Tavakoli, M. Casado, T. Koponen, and S. Shenker, "Applying NOX to the Datacenter," in *HotNets*, 2009.

[13] T. Benson, A. Akella, and D. A. Maltz, "Network traffic characteristics of data centers in the wild," in *Proceedings of the 10th ACM SIGCOMM Conference on Internet Measurement*, pp. 267–280, ACM, 2010.

[14] Y. Jarraya, T. Madi, and M. Debbabi, "A survey and a layered taxonomy of software-defined networking," *IEEE Communications Surveys & Tutorials*, vol. 16, no. 4, pp. 1955–1980, 2014.

[15] M. Jammal, T. Singh, A. Shami, R. Asal, and Y. Li, "Software defined networking: State of the art and research challenges," *Computer Networks*, vol. 72, pp. 74–98, 2014.

[16] Y. A. Jimenez Agudelo, "Scalability and Robustness in Software-Defined Networking (SDN)," PhD Thesis, Polytechnic University of Catalonia, 2016.

[17] M. Reitblatt, N. Foster, J. Rexford, and D. Walker, "Consistent updates for software-defined networks: Change you can believe in!," in *Proceedings of the 10th ACM Workshop on Hot Topics in Networks*, p. 7, ACM, 2011.

[18] M. F. Bari, A. R. Roy, S. R. Chowdhury, *et al.*, "Dynamic controller provisioning in software defined networks," in *Network and Service Management (CNSM), 2013 9th International Conference on*, pp. 18–25, IEEE, 2013.

[19] D. Erickson, "The beacon openflow controller," in *Proceedings of the Second ACM SIGCOMM Workshop on Hot Topics in Software Defined Networking*, pp. 13–18, ACM, 2013.

[20] S. Guo, S. Yang, Q. Li, and Y. Jiang, "Towards controller placement for robust software-defined networks," in *Computing and Communications Conference (IPCCC), 2015 IEEE 34th International Performance*, pp. 1–8, IEEE, 2015.

[21] B. Heller, R. Sherwood, and N. McKeown, "The controller placement problem," in *Proceedings of the First Workshop on Hot Topics in Software Defined Networks*, pp. 7–12, ACM, 2012.

[22] P. Vizarreta, C. M. Machuca, and W. Kellerer, "Controller placement strategies for a resilient SDN control plane," in *Resilient Networks Design and Modeling (RNDM), 2016 8th International Workshop on*, pp. 253–259, IEEE, 2016.

[23] E. Ng, Z. Cai, and A. Cox, "Maestro: A system for scalable openflow control," *Rice University, Houston, TX, USA, TSEN Maestro-Techn. Rep., TR10-08*, 2010.

[24] S. Matsumoto, S. Hitz, and A. Perrig, "Fleet: Defending SDNs from malicious administrators," in *Proceedings of the Third Workshop on Hot Topics in Software Defined Networking*, pp. 103–108, ACM, 2014.

[25] K. Phemius, M. Bouet, and J. Leguay, "Disco: Distributed multi-domain SDN controllers," in *Network Operations and Management Symposium (NOMS), 2014 IEEE*, pp. 1–4, IEEE, 2014.

[26] U. Krishnaswamy, P. Berde, J. Hart, *et al.*, "ONOS: An Open Source Distributed SDN OS," [Online]. 2013. Available from http://www.slideshare.net/umeshkrishnaswamy/open-network-operating-system

[27] A. D. Ferguson, A. Guha, C. Liang, R. Fonseca, and S. Krishnamurthi, "Participatory networking: An API for application control of SDNs," in *ACM SIG-COMM Computer Communication Review*, vol. 43, pp. 327–338, ACM, 2013.

[28] D. Kreutz, F. M. Ramos, P. E. Verissimo, C. E. Rothenberg, S. Azodolmolky, and S. Uhlig, "Software-defined networking: A comprehensive survey," *Proceedings of the IEEE*, vol. 103, no. 1, pp. 14–76, 2015.

[29] A. So, "Survey on Recent Software-Defined Network Cross-Layer Designs," Carleton University, 2016.

[30] J. Manyika, M. Chui, B. Brown, *et al.*, "Big Data: The Next Frontier for Innovation, Competition, and Productivity," McKinsey Global Institute, 2011.

Chapter 20

Big Data helps SDN to verify integrity of control/data planes

Qingsong Wen*, Ren Chen*, Yinglong Xia*, Li Zhou**,
Juan Deng***, Jian Xu***, and Mingzhen Xia***

20.1 Introduction

Traditional non-SDN (Software Defined Networks) are vertically integrated, where the control plane that decides packet routes and the data plane that forwards packets are tightly bundled. The control over the path that a packet traverses is distributed to network devices, which run vendor proprietary distributed routing protocols. Such architecture makes traditional networks stiff and hard to manage and hinders network innovations [1,2]. SDN aims to overcome these limitations by separating the control and data planes. Network control is logically centralized to SDN controller or network operating systems. Network devices become simple common packet forwarding devices. Programmability is enabled and allows for the control and management of networks through open interfaces. Compared to traditional networks, it is much easier to introduce new network services and networking protocols in SDN networks. In addition, SDN is better suited for cloud computing which has been widely adopted. Constant instantiation, deletion, and migration of VMs (Virtual Machines), and services in cloud environment create unprecedented network dynamics. Fast, reliable, and optimal traffic engineering is required to cope with the network dynamics. The programmability nature of SDN offers the potential to fulfill the traffic engineering needs in cloud environment. Cloud providers (e.g., Amazon, IBM, Google, and VMware) have deployed their own SDN solutions.

The centralized SDN controller periodically collects from the network large volumes of data including various information on network devices, hosts, links, bandwidth, traffic, flows, failure, and a variety of statistics information. The global view of the network and traffic engineering decisions is based on the insights gained from analyzing the collected data. Traffic engineering becomes difficult when the numbers of hosts and network devices in a SDN network are large, and the hosts have service-level agreements (SLAs) on bandwidth requirements. The wide adoption of

*Cloud Computing Competence Center, Huawei Research America, USA
**Department of Computer Science and Engineering, The Ohio State University, USA
***Huawei Research Center, Huawei Technologies, China

cloud computing poses even larger challenges on traffic engineering. First, the instantiation, deletion, and migration of VMs, and services occur frequently in cloud, and each occurrence calls for the required connectivity to be provisioned immediately while still maintaining the SLAs. Second, the volume of traffic in cloud is highly dynamic and reaches its peak shortly, and thus traffic engineering must be able to perform fast path replanning in order to fulfill SLA requirements.

In this chapter, we apply the Big Data analytics from graph computing perspective to help traffic engineering in SDN networks. Specifically, we propose a high-speed top K shortest paths (KSP) algorithm to calculate routes, develop several efficient schemes for routing errors detection, and present a novel edge-set-based graph processing engine to deal with large-scale graph data from SDN. Compared to existing solutions, the experiments show that our proposed KSP algorithm brings 3–6× speedup, and our graph processing engine achieves 3–16× speedup.

20.2   Related work

SDN and Big Data have gained significant attentions from both academia and industry. They facilitate each other in several ways [3]. Current research literature has witnessed research efforts to leverage SDN to help Big Data applications [4–10].

On the other hand, how Big Data can facilitate SDN is scarce. The authors in [3] summarize that Big Data can help SDN in three aspects: (i) traffic engineering, (ii) attack mitigation, and (iii) cross-layer design in SDN. A traffic engineering system architecture is proposed in [3] that utilized Big Data application to output traffic engineering guidance. This architecture adds two components, *Big Data Application* and *Traffic Engineering Manager* to the SDN application layer. The SDN switches/routers at the data plan report their big traffic data and failure status to the SDN controller, which then summarizes the collected big traffic data information and send it to the *Big Data application* in the application layer. The *Big Data application* uses Big Data analytics to obtain insights from the big traffic data then gives guidance to the *Traffic Engineering Manager*, which derives the traffic engineering policies. This work in [3] provides a very high level description of a system where Big Data helps SDN. The implementation of the two newly added components, *Big Data Application* and *Traffic Engineering Manager*, is however not presented. The authors in [3] also explain how Big Data analytics can help mitigate attacks in SDN. Attacks can target different layers in SDN, namely SDN applications, SDN controller, and SDN switches/routers, as well as the communication channels between two adjacent layers. The attacking traffic come from various resources and present in different formats. Applying Big Data analytics to the attacking data to detect anomaly is expected to combat attacks in real time. The machine-learning methods used in Big Data analytics may also be used for real-time anomaly detections.

20.3   Finding top-K shortest simple paths

In the emerging SDN networks, no specific routing protocol is predefined, and any shortest path algorithms can be adopted to help traffic engineering in SDN networks.

In practice, SDN network controller needs to perform shortest path query for every flow. Often, multiple shortest paths of each flow are calculated to satisfy various constraints and Quality of Service (QoS) requirements. Thus, finding shortest paths can be extremely time consuming in SDN controller especially for large-scale network.

Finding the shortest path/paths in a network is a fundamental problem or subproblem of many practical applications, which has been extensively investigated in the literature. Given a graph, different shortest path/paths variants can be formulated according to the corresponding application scenarios. The simplest one is the single-pair shortest path problem, where a shortest path from a given source to a given destination is calculated. Another problem is to find the single-source shortest paths (SSSPs), where we want to find a shortest path from a given vertex to every other vertex in a graph. Both the problems can be efficiently solved by Dijkstra's algorithm [11]. The more general problem is to find the top K ($K \geq 1$) shortest paths (KSP) for a given source–destination pair in a graph. In this paper, we focus on the general top KSP algorithms, since the performance of such algorithms has become a critical challenge in many practical applications.

Given a graph with nonnegative edge weights, KSP algorithm ranks the top-KSP from source vertex to destination vertex and enumerates them in increasing order of length. In many real applications, the shortest paths generated by KSP algorithm are usually required to be simple, i.e., no loops containing two or more vertexes exist in each path.

20.3.1 MPS algorithm for top K shortest simple paths

MPS algorithm [12] (named after the authors) is a high efficient top KSP algorithm especially for finding shortest loopless paths, which exhibits much faster speed than other top KSP algorithms [13,14]. Let $G = (V, E)$ be a directed/undirected graph with $n = |V|$ vertices and $m = |E|$ edges. The main idea of MPS algorithm is to improve the shortcomings of the original Yen's algorithm [13]. Specifically, the computational complexity of Yen's algorithm was improved from $O(Kn(n \log n + m))$ to $O(m \log n + Kn)$ by MPS algorithm, when a worst case analysis is considered.

We define the following notations for Algorithm 1, which presents the MPS algorithm for ranking paths:

X: a set containing distinct paths which are ranked to select the shortest path in kth iteration.

T_k: a pseudotree composed of shortest path candidates.

T_t^*: a graph having the same topology of G, where minimal cost of each vertex has been calculated using SSSP algorithm.

c_{ij}^*: precomputed reduced cost [12] for any edge $(i, j) \in E$.

p_k: shortest path found in the kth iteration.

$p_{v_k t}^k$: a subpath from v_k to t in p_k, also called as a deviation path of p_k.

$p_{v_k t}^*$: the shortest path from v_k to t in T_t^*.

p_{sv}^k: the path from s to v in p_k.

$p \diamond q$: the concatenation of two paths p and q.

(u, v): the edge connecting a pair of vertices u and v.

Algorithm 1 The original MPS algorithm for finding top K shortest simple paths [12]

    Input: $G = (V, E)$; **Output:** $p_k, k = 1, 2, \ldots, K$
1: Compute T_t^*
2: Compute c_{ij}^* for any edge $(i,j) \in E$
3: Rearrange the set of edges of (V, E) in the sorted forward star form
4: $p_1 \leftarrow$ shortest path from s to t
5: $k \leftarrow 1$
6: $X \leftarrow \{p_k\}$
7: $T_k \leftarrow \{p_k\}$
8: **while** $k < K$ **and** $X \neq \emptyset$ **do**
9:     $p \leftarrow$ shortest path in X
10:    $X \leftarrow X - \{p_k\}$
11:    **if** p is loopless **then**
12:       $k \leftarrow k + 1$
13:       $p_k \leftarrow p$
14:    **end if**
15:    $v_k \leftarrow$ deviation node of p_k
16:    **for each** $v \in p_{v_k t}^k$ **do**
17:       **if** p_{sv}^k is not loopless **then**
18:          break
19:       **end if**
20:       **if** $E(v) - E_{T_k(v)} \neq \emptyset$ **then**
21:          find the first edge (v,x) in the set $E(v) - E_{T_k}(v)$, such that $p_{sv}^k \diamond < v, (v,x), x >$ is loopless
22:          $q \leftarrow p_{sv}^k \diamond < v, (v,x), x > \diamond p_{xt}^*$
23:          $X \leftarrow X \cup \{q\}$
24:          $q_{vt} \leftarrow < v, (v,x), x > \diamond p_{xt}^*$
25:          $T_k \leftarrow T_k \cup \{q_{vt}\}$
26:       **end if**
27:    **end for**
28: **end while**

$< u, (u, v), v >$: the path containing vertex u, edge (u, v), and vertex v.

$E(v)$: the set of edges whose tail vertex is v.

$E_{T_k}(v)$: the set of edges in T_k whose tail vertex is v.

In Algorithm 1, set X containing path candidates for ranking shortest paths is used and initialized with the shortest path p_1. In the kth step, the shortest path candidate in X is selected and popped out as p_k. Then, some new path candidates to obtain the $(k + 1)$th shortest path are generated. For this purpose, for each node v in $p_{v_k t}^k$, the shortest path $p_{v_k t}^*$ from v to t whose first edge is not an edge of $E_{T_k}(v)$, will be computed. In Algorithm 1, $p_{sv}^k \diamond p_{vt}^*$ denotes a new candidate for p_{k+1}. Note that p_{vt}^* has been precomputed when generating T_t^*, which can be used to find the shortest path from any vertex $v \in V$ to t. When all deviation paths for node v have been determined, $E(v) - E_{T_k}(v)$ becomes an empty set.

The MPS algorithm works similarly to Yen's algorithm. Note that T_t^* can be easily computed with classic SSSP algorithms by reversing the orientation of all the edges and considering t as the initial node. The total time complexity of MPS algorithm

---

Algorithm 2 The improved MPS algorithm for finding top K shortest simple paths

---

Input: $G = (V, E)$;   **Output:** $p_k, k = 1, 2, \ldots, K$
1: Compute T_t^*
2: Compute c_{ij}^* for any edge $(i, j) \in E$
3: Rearrange the set of edges of (V, E) in the sorted forward star form
4: $p_1 \leftarrow$ shortest path from s to t
5: $k \leftarrow 1$
6: $T_k \leftarrow \{p_k\}$
7: Insert(Q, the last vertex's internal ID of p_k)
8: **while** $k < K$ **and** $X \neq \emptyset$ **do**
9:    $a \leftarrow$ Extract-min(Q)
10:    $p \leftarrow$ find the path whose last vertex's internal ID is a
11:    **if** the last vertex (denote as m) of p is not t **then**
12:       $p \leftarrow p \diamond p_{mt}^*$
13:    **end if**
14:    **if** p is loopless **then**
15:       $k \leftarrow k + 1$
16:       $p_k \leftarrow p$
17:    **end if**
18:    $v_k \leftarrow$ deviation node of p_k
19:    **for each** $v \in p_{v_k t}^k$ **do**
20:       **if** p_{sv}^k is not loopless **then**
21:          break
22:       **end if**
23:       **if** $E(v) - E_{T_k(v)} \neq \emptyset$ **then**
24:          find the first edge (v, x) in the set $E(v) - E_{T_k}(v)$ such that $p_{sv}^k \diamond < v, (v, x), x >$ is loopless
25:          $T_k \leftarrow T_k \cup < v, (v, x), x >$
26:          Insert(Q, the internal ID of x)
27:       **end if**
28:    **end for**
29: **end while**

---

is $O(m \log n + Kn)$, where determining T_t^* takes $O(m \log n)$ time using the classic Dijistra shortest path algorithm, and ranking KSP needs $O(Kn)$ time. In fact, in the worst case, no more than n different vertexes will be considered after the deviation node, when new candidate paths are being added to the set X. To produce only simple paths, a potential candidate path is examined if it is loopless when constructing the pseudotree (see Lines 11–14, 17–19, and 21 in Algorithm 1). Those candidate paths will be dropped if they are not loopless.

20.3.2 *Improved MPS algorithm with efficient implementation*

The original MPS algorithm works well in the case of small networks with small values of K. However, the original MPS algorithm would consume excessive amount of memory in case of large networks with large values of K due to storing all candidate paths, which increases the execution time and even stalls because of running out of memory space. Therefore, we propose an improved MPS algorithm (see Algorithm 2)

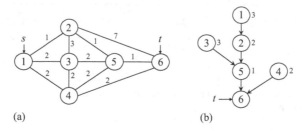

*Figure 20.1   (a) An example network where edge cost is located beside each edge;
(b) the corresponding T_t^* calculated by SSSP where the number beside
each vertex denotes the minimum sum cost to the destination vertex*

which significantly reduces the memory space to increase execution speed without affecting the final output paths. The main improvement comes from the following two novel designs.

20.3.2.1   Pseudotree with pruning

The majority of memory consumption of the MPS algorithm comes from constructing the pseudotree T_k of shortest path candidates. Since most of path candidates would not be in the final top KSP in large networks, we propose a novel scheme to add only one path to the pseudotree in an iteration, while the original MPS would add a path for each vertex on the deviation path in an iteration. To illustrate the proposed scheme, let us consider a simple network shown in Figure 20.1, where the T_t^* (shortest paths of all vertices to the destination vertex t) is also provided. Based on the aforementioned MPS algorithm, we can obtain the pseudotree of candidate paths after the first two iterations as shown in Figure 20.2. At the second iteration with $k = 2$, the MPS will add a path to destination vertex 6 for each vertex v on the deviation path (i.e., vertices 1, 2, 5). In contrast, our scheme only needs to add one path by designing a tree-pruning scheme. First, at each vertex v on the deviation path, our scheme only needs to add one vertex x instead of one path as shown in Figure 20.3 (also see Line 25 of Algorithm 2), where the shaded vertices would not be added in the pseudotree unless they are on the top KSP. Even though we only add one vertex each time instead of a candidate path, its final path cost can be obtained based on the information of T_t^*. Next, based on all path costs, the "path" with minimum cost is selected and the corresponding full path is then added in the pseudotree (see Lines 9–13 of Algorithm 2), which is the shortest path in current iteration. It can be seen in Figure 20.3 that the proposed scheme brings reduced memory consumption. This memory reduction would be significant and brings impressive speedup in large networks, which will be demonstrated in the following experiment section.

20.3.2.2   Pseudotree with internal ID and reversed order

The second source of major memory consumption in MPS algorithm comes from storing the set of candidate paths (see X in Line 23 in Algorithm 1). Since all the information about the candidate paths is available in the constructed pseudotree, we

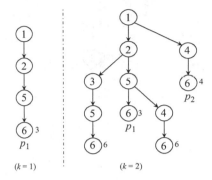

Figure 20.2 *The constructed pseudotree from the first two iterations of MPS algorithm. The number beside the leaf vertex denotes the path cost. p_1 and p_2 denote the first and second shortest paths, respectively*

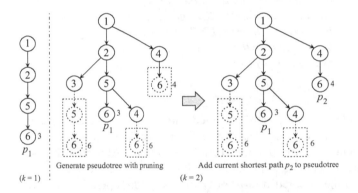

Figure 20.3 *The constructed pseudotree from the first two iterations of the improved MPS algorithm with tree pruning. The number on the right hand side of the leaf vertex denotes the path cost. p_1 and p_2 denote the first and second shortest paths, respectively. The shaded vertices would not be added*

do not need to explicitly store these paths. Here, we propose a simple yet efficient way to retrieve the candidate paths without actually storing them. In the original MPS algorithm, each vertex points to its child vertex/vertices in the pseudotree as shown in Figure 20.2. We adopt a reversed order such that each vertex points to its parent vertex. Furthermore, we add a distinct internal ID for each vertex as its property. By doing so, we can obtain the whole path from any leaf vertex's internal ID by repeated proceeding from child to parent in the pseudotree. This reversed order with internal ID scheme combining with tree pruning in the pseudotree is depicted in Figure 20.4. During the construction of the pseudotree (with or without our proposed pruning scheme), the

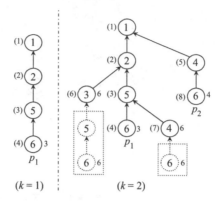

Figure 20.4   The constructed pseudotree from the first two iterations of the improved MPS algorithm with tree pruning, internal ID, and reversed order. The shaded vertices would not be added. The number inside parenthesis on the left hand side of each vertex denotes its internal ID. The internal IDs are distinct, so any path can be fetched based on its last vertex's internal ID. The number on the right hand side of the leaf vertex denotes the final path cost (the cost from s to t), even though the path is pruned

final cost of each added path or pruned path is also available. Therefore, we can just store the key-value pair (path cost, leaf's internal ID) of each added path or pruned path into a min-priority queue Q (see Lines 7, 26 in Algorithm 2) instead of storing the whole path as in the original MPS algorithm (see Lines 6, 23 in Algorithm 1).

Due to the adopted min-priority queue Q, the operation of finding the leaf's internal ID of the shortest path can be finished in $O(1)$ time (see Line 9 in Algorithm 2). Once the leaf's internal ID is found, the whole shortest path in current iteration can be easily retrieved from the reversed-ordered pseudotree as shown in Figure 20.4 (also see Lines 9–13 in Algorithm 2).

20.4   Routing check and detection

Due to the network dynamics in the SDN, it is desirable to detect routing errors quickly and efficiently. In this section, we illustrate how to detect routing errors in SDN networks through a map-reduce-based framework equipped with embedded graph computing engines. Three common types of errors including loops, black holes, and inconsistent snapshot can be found in forwarding tables. For large subnetworks, it is impractical to check forwarding rules one by one as it would be slow and inefficient. For example, it takes more than 1 h to check 120 million forwarding rules in the INET having 315 switches and 1,900+ links; this is not desirable considering limited response time constraint. To scale to large data center network, it is necessary to

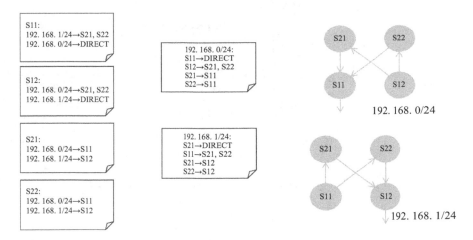

S11:
192. 168. 1/24→S21, S22
192. 168. 0/24→DIRECT

S12:
192. 168. 0/24→S21, S22
192. 168. 1/24→DIRECT

S21:
192. 168. 0/24→S11
192. 168. 1/24→S12

S22:
192. 168. 0/24→S11
192. 168. 1/24→S12

192. 168. 0/24:
S11→DIRECT
S12→S21, S22
S21→S11
S22→S11

192. 168. 1/24:
S21→DIRECT
S11→S21, S22
S21→S12
S22→S12

192. 168. 0/24

192. 168. 1/24

Figure 20.5   Subnet forwarding rules partition

partition the forwarding rules to utilize a map-reduce-based framework to speed up detecting errors in SDN networks.

20.4.1   Subnet partition

To verify forwarding tables in large networks, two partition strategies are proposed in [15]: partition on switches and partition on subnets. Partition on switches does not scale well on large networks since a forwarding rule will be checked on a number of partitions, thus resulting in significant communication overhead between servers due to frequent data synchronization. Since each server holds a set of forwarding rules to reach a subnet, we can organize the sets of forwarding rules into a forwarding graph. As a result, the routing error checking problem can be transformed into a graph problem by checking the three common types of errors on the forwarding graph. Figure 20.5 illustrates the concept of partitioning the forwarding rules based on the subnets, as well as the corresponding forwarding graphs. In Figure 20.5, each of the four servers is first initialized with a list of subnets assigned with several forwarding rules. The forwarding rules are then organized into two groups, corresponding to two subnets 192.168.0/24 and 192.168.1/24. The forwarding graph for each group is calculated and checked in parallel. This process can be easily mapped to a map-reduce-based framework, which is shown in Figure 20.6, where we take a map-reduce-based framework using Spark [16] to partition the forwarding rules. In Figure 20.6, the set of forwarding rules is first partitioned into small shards and delivered to mappers [17]. Each mapper checks a full set of subnets and generates intermediate keys and values, which are then shuffled by map-reduce-based framework. The reducers compile the values that associated to the same subnet and produce final results.

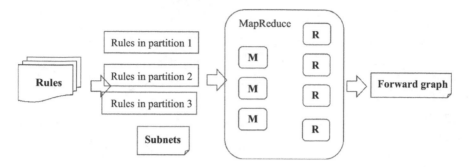

Figure 20.6   Workflow of map-reduce-based framework

20.4.2   Loop detection

A loop is a path (with at least one edge) where its head vertex and tail vertex overlap to form a closed chain in the graph. A simple loop in the graph is a cycle with no repeated edges or vertices (except the requisite repetition of the first and last vertices). A loop in SDN is a cyclical path through the network switches that trap some packets in a closed chain. This self-loop forwarding behavior leads to increased latency, power consumption and exposes the network in potential attacks. To solve this problem, strongly connected components (SCC) algorithm has been widely used [15,18]. In a directed graph, an SCC is a subgraph where each vertex is reachable by another vertex through a path within the subgraph. To find SCC, we employ the famous Tarjan algorithm [18] in time complexity $O(m+n)$, where $m = |E|$ and $n = |V|$. Algorithm 3 provides pseudo code of the Tarjan algorithm.

20.4.3   Black hole detection

A black hole is a network condition where the flow graph ends abruptly, and the traffic cannot be routed to the destination, for example, a switch in the flow path drop packets, thus preventing the flow from reaching the destination. There are conditions when a switch may forward a packet to the destination even when the destination switch is not directly connected to it. When this happens, the packet might keep bouncing up and down between switches. This would continue until the packet Time to Live (TTL) expires, at which point the packet is discarded and the packet fails to reach the destination node. A black hole can be generated by an inconsistent configuration of one or more routing tables in the network. A black hole can also be an artifact of a routing policy, such as the use of default routes for specific input ports or prefixes, where routes to failed destinations are not withdrawn while the aggregated prefix is still alive. Zen *et al.* [15] identify two types of black holes: implicit ones and legitimate ones. Legitimate ones include the switch which is the last hop in the network, and the packet dropping rule is explicitly specified. Implicit drop rules need to be checked. In graph terminology, black holes refer to the vertices with no outgoing edges.

Algorithm 3 Tarjan algorithm for finding strongly connected components

---

Input: A graph given as $G = (V, E)$**;   Output: Set** R **having strongly connected components**
 1: Initialize $i = 0$, $S = []$
 2: **for each** $v \in V$ **do**
 3:       **if** v not visited **then**
 4:             SCC(v)
 5:       **end if**
 6: **end for**
 7: **function** scc(v)
 8:       $v.idx \leftarrow i, v.link \leftarrow i, i \leftarrow i + 1$
 9:       S.push(v), $v.inS \leftarrow$ True
10:      **for each** (v, w) in E **do**
11:            **if** w not visited **then**
12:                  SCC(w)
13:                  $v.link \leftarrow min(v.link, w.link)$
14:            **else if** $(w.inS =$ True) **then**
15:                  $v.link \leftarrow min(v.link, w.link)$
16:            **end if**
17:      **end for**
18:      **if** $(v.link = v.idx)$ **then**
19:            **repeat**
20:                  $w \leftarrow S$.pop(), $w.inS \leftarrow$ False, R.add(w)
21:            **until** $w \mathrel{!}= v$
22:      **end if**
23: **end function**

20.4.4   Reachability detection

Switch w is defined reachable from switch v if there exists a directed path from v to w. In this work, reachability refers to the subnet in the network can be reached from any other switch, thus it is a single-source reachability problem. This problem can be represented as a graph problem which exposes the similarity between reachability problem and the class of well-known problems such as transitive closure and shortest path computation. Therefore, it allows us to use existed efficient graph solutions [19,20] to solve the reachability problem. A straightforward approach is to conduct a reverse DFS/BFS from the destination switch and check if the source vertex set contains all the switches in the network. This reachability verification takes $O(|V| + |E|)$ time where $|V|$ is the number of switches and $|E|$ is the number of links.

20.5   Efficient graph engine

The aforementioned routing planning and routing error detection from SDN networks can be dealt with through graph analytics perspective. To efficiently solve these graph problems especially at large scale, we need an efficient graph processing engine. Compared to many other Big Data subsystems, the graph processing system imposes

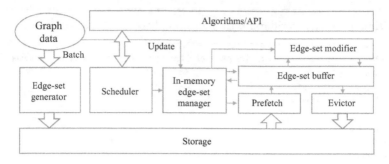

Figure 20.7   System architecture

significant performance challenges that adversely impact the adoption of the useful technology in SDN Big Data scenarios. For example, one of the challenges is poor data locality due to irregular data access. Therefore, graph processing is not bounded by the computational capability of a platform, but the IO latency [21]. This motivates some single machine solution for relatively large-scale graph processing, where both the disk and memory resources are leveraged for processing, such as GraphChi [22] and XStream [23]. Our system leverages some ideas in this field but achieves much better performance. Such work paves an approach for large-scale graph computing; however, those solutions still face challenges that traversal along the graph structure, such as the breadth-first search (BFS).

The architecture of the proposed graph processing system is shown in Figure 20.7. The edge-set generator converts graph data into a set of edge-sets, each consisting of a group of edges. Graph analysis algorithms are implemented using the same programing model as that in GraphChi, and the scheduler will load/preload corresponding edge-sets for processing. If modified in the edge-set modifier, the resulting edge-set will be persisted onto the storage by the evictor. The in-memory edge-set manager maintains the edge-sets that are currently cached in the edge-set buffer and decides which to evict according to an alternated LRU policy that considers the edge-set to prefetch. The edge-set buffer hosts the edge-sets under processing and those prefetched.

20.5.1   Edge-set representation

The edge-sets are naturally related to the parallel sliding window (PSW) in [22], but more flexible. For example, in Figure 20.8, an input graph is represented as three edge lists known as *shards*, each consisting of all the edges with the destination vertex in a certain range. We show the ranges on top of the shards. To traverse a graph, the PSW works in an iterative manner. The yellow zone covers the data to be processed in the current iteration. It is worth noting that, at the ith step, the yellow zone exactly corresponds to the ith row plus the ith column of the blocked adjacency matrix. Therefore, to traverse a graph, it is equivalent to simultaneously scan the blocked adjacency matrix top-down and left-right. Such regularity implies an approach to efficiently prefetch data. Note that the graph sharding in [22] corresponds

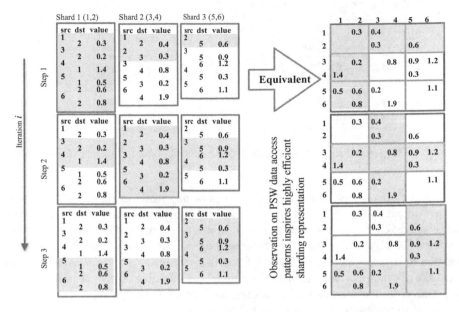

Figure 20.8 PSW in terms of edge-sets

to the vertical-only partitioning of the adjacent matrix, which is incapable to address celebrity vertices with extreme dense incoming edges, but such an issue does not exist for our edge-set-based approach where the matrix is partitioned both vertically and horizontally.

Since all graph algorithms can be implemented using PSW under the gather-apply-scatter (GAS) model (or its variants) [22] and PSW is nothing but all the edge-sets on the same column in the blocked adjacency matrix, we conclude that the edge-set representation of a graph is generic. To generate the edge-sets, it is even more straightforward than that in GraphChi where a global sorting is required. In our case, we scan the edge list once to determine the vertex degrees and then we divide the vertices into a set of range by evenly distributing the degrees. Then, we scan the edge list again and allocate each edge to an edge-set according to the ranges where source and destination vertices fall into. Note that both scans can be conducted in divide-and-conquer manner. Thus, given p parallel threads, the complexity under PRAM is given by $O(m/p)$, where m is the number of input edges. In contrast, GraphChi sorts all edges and then generates the shards. Given sufficient memory (i.e., a single shard for GraphChi), the complexity is $O(m \log m) > O(m/p)$. Note that GraphChi actually utilizes the radix sort with complexity $O(km)$, but theoretically $k \leq \log m$. In practice, we also observed improved parallelism and performance for our proposed approach.

20.5.2 Consolidation

The edge-set generator shown in Figure 20.7 can merge small edge-sets. The sparsity nature of real large-scale graph can result in some tiny edge-sets that consist of a

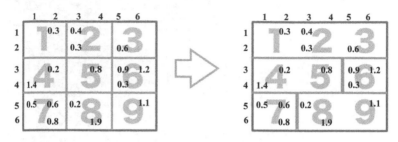

Figure 20.9   Horizontal consolidation of logical edge-set to improve data locality

few edges each, if not empty. Loading or persisting many of such small edge-sets is inefficient due to the IO latency. Therefore, it makes sense to consolidate small edge-sets likely to be processed together, so that we can potentially increase the data locality. Consolidation can occur between edge-set next to each other horizontally, vertically, or both. We consolidate edge-sets using the following heuristic method. For the sake of simplicity, we look at the horizontal consolidation only. First, we determine a bound B for the merged set as follows: let k denote the page size of the platform, in terms of the number of bytes, and s the size of an edge, then the bound is given by $\lceil \frac{k}{s} \rceil$, which ensures that the resulting set is aligned with the system page, leading to improved IO efficiency. Second, for each edge-set $s_{i,j}$ smaller than the bound, i.e., $|s_{i,j}| < B$, where i,j are the indices of the edge-set in the corresponding adjacency matrix with $N \times N$ blocks, it identifies its horizontal neighbor that minimizes the size of the resulting set if merged:

$$\tilde{s} = \min_{j' \in \{j-1, j+1\}, 0 < j < N} (|s_{i,j}| + |s_{i,j'}|) \tag{20.1}$$

If $\tilde{s} < B$, it proposes to merge with the selected neighbor. If two edge-sets select each other, then they are merged. The neighbors of the merged set are the union of the neighbors of the two. We continue the consolidation process repeatedly until no merge occurs anymore. In Figure 20.9, we merge the neighbor sets as long as the size of the merged set is no more than the given bound (e.g., four edges). As a result, edge-sets 1, 2, and 3 are consolidated. Similarly, edge-sets 4 and 5 are merged, and also 8 and 9.

The horizontal consolidation improves data locality especially when we visit the outgoing edges of vertices. We can also merge the edge-sets vertically, which benefits the information gathering from the parents of a vertex. Note that if all the edge-sets in a row (column) are merged, it is equivalent to have the outgoing (in-coming) edge list of the vertex. Note that the edge-set consolidation is transparent to users, that is, the users will still see nine edge-sets when implementing graph algorithms; but physically, there are only five edge-sets stored on disk. The proposed system maintains the mapping between the logical edge-sets and the physical edge-sets. Once a logical edge-set is prefetched, the system is aware that all logical edge-sets coexisting in the same physical edge-set become available in memory, which are likely being processed immediately. Thus, the temporal data locality is improved.

20.5.3   Multimodal organization

We allow multimodal data organization for the edge-sets, because of the impact of organization formats on particular graph computing algorithms. We take two formats as an example: The coordinate format (a.k.a. COO) in our context is simply a list of edges, each having a source vertex ID, a destination vertex ID, and some attributes on the edge; while the compressed sparse row (CSR) in our context sorts COO according to the source vertices and then compresses the list by eliminating the repeated source vertices. Both can be found in literature of sparse matrices and graphs. The impact of COO and CSR on performance varies according to the graph processing algorithms. Specifically, for the same input graph, we observed better performance for performing PageRank using COO than CSR, although CSR helps the IO a little bit due to the compression. However, for performing BFS, CSR shows higher noticeable advantage. The reason is that the CSR allows us to locate a vertex quickly as it is sorted, while for COO, we have to filter the edge-set when seeking a particular vertex. Although due to high sparsity, COO may help save the memory required to present a graph than CSR where each vertex has a pointer. Note that in PageRank, we visit all the edges in each iteration of the algorithm, regardless the order of the edges, while in BFS, we must follow the graph topology to visit the neighbors of the vertices visited in the last iteration.

20.5.4   Scheduling and prefetching

The scheduler shown in Figure 20.7 applies the user-defined vertex program to the graph and coordinates with the *in-memory edge-set manager*. The manager maintains buffer of edge-sets. The scheduler notifies the manager which edge-sets will be processed, according to the data access pattern discussed in Section 20.5.1, and the edge-set manager informs the prefetch component to load those edge-sets, as long as the buffer is not full. In the meanwhile, the *evictor* dumps the edge-set that are least recently used. The *edge-set modifier* updates edges and/or its property. Note that the scheduler is aware of the spatial/temporal data locality. If an edge-set is already loaded, it will not be loaded again.

20.6   Experiments

20.6.1   Performance evaluation of finding top-K shortest simple paths

In this section, we compare the performance of our improved MPS algorithm against the original MPS algorithm. To minimize the running time, we implement both algorithms in C++ on top of the GraphBIG, since GraphBIG is an open-sourced efficient graph framework similar to the IBM System G library [24] and covers major graph computing types and data structures. The experiments are performed on a desktop with Intel i7-6700 CPU (3.4 GHz), 64-GB memory, and Ubuntu 16.04 operating system. Note that both algorithms do not benefit from multicore parallel computing due to no parallel implementations at current stage. It is expected that similar results can

Table 20.1 The number of vertices and edges for each generated grid network

Grid network	32 × 32	128 × 128	512 × 512	2,048 × 2,048
Vertex number $|V|$	1,024	16,384	262,144	4,194,304
Edge number $|E|$	1,984	32,512	523,264	8,384,512

be obtained in parallel computing since the two algorithms follow similar execution flow. The running time of each algorithm is measured between the input graph is loaded into memory and all shortest paths are written into output files.

Without loss of generality, we consider synthetic square grid networks similar to [14] for ad hoc networks, where each vertex is connected to its four neighboring vertices with random edge weight uniformly distributed in (0, 10). Four grid networks with different sizes, from thousands to millions vertices and edges, are generated in the experiments, which are summarized in Table 20.1. For each experiment of searching top KSP, we randomly select 50 pairs of source and destination vertices, located on the opposite sides of grid networks, to record the total running time.

Running time: First, we consider the case of finding top 10 shortest paths under different grid network configurations. The total running time of 50 pairs under different grid networks is depicted in Figure 20.10. In all grid networks, our improved MPS algorithm brings around 3–4× speedup over the original MPS algorithm. Second, we evaluate the total running time of 50 pairs of finding top KSP under different K values in a 128 × 128 grid network, where the value of K is selected from 10 to 10,000. The results are depicted in Figure 20.11 by log–log scale. It can be seen that our improved MPS consistently provides 4–6× speedup over the original MPS algorithm.

Similar speedup can be obtained in the case of other grid network and K value configurations. However, when the network and the value of K are large to some extent, the original MPS slows down rapidly. For example, in a case of finding top-100 shortest paths of 50 pairs under 2,048 × 2,048 grid network, the improved MPS algorithm requires about 13-min running time while the original MPS algorithm needs over 50 h. This is due to the excessive amount of space requirements of storing all candidate paths in the original MPS algorithm which may exceed the 64-GB memory in the desktop computer.

Memory: To measure the improvement of memory consumption for our improved MPS method, we perform experiments by utilizing the massif tool in *Valgrind* [25]. In our experiment, we compare the memory consumption of the original MPS and our improved MPS under different grid networks and different K values. As shown in Figure 20.12, compared to our improved MPS, the original MPS consumes up to 6.7× memory when $K = 100$ and 2.5× when $K = 10$. With the increment of network size, the memory consumption of both cases grows dramatically. For example, with the original MPS, 32×32 grid network consumes

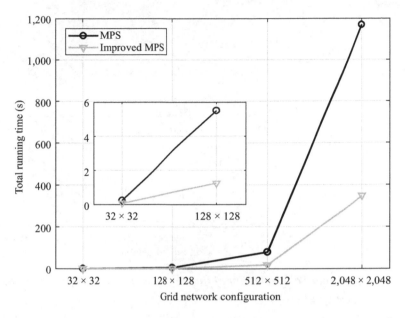

Figure 20.10 *Total running time of 50 pairs of finding top 10 shortest simple paths under different grid networks*

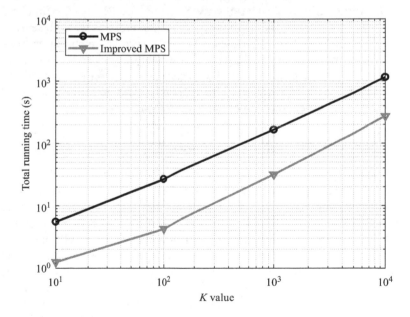

Figure 20.11 *Total running time of 50 pairs of finding top K shortest simple paths under different K values in a 128 × 128 grid network*

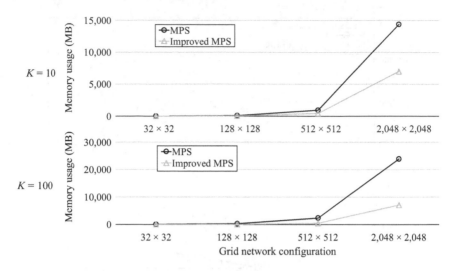

Figure 20.12   Memory consumption of finding top K shortest simple paths under different grid networks and K values

only 17-MB memory when $K = 100$. However, when the grid size gets to $2,048 \times 2,048$, the memory consumption of the original MPS even exceeds 23 GB, while our improved MPS only consumes 6.9-GB memory in this case. In real-world use cases, the memory consumption problem would be even more severe when processing larger networks. If the memory footprint exceeds the available memory capacity, we have to inevitably introduce the overhead and complexity of disk storage or distributed computing. Therefore, compared to the original MPS, our improved MPS significantly reduces memory consumption and enables the processing larger network in a single machine.

20.6.2   Performance evaluation of the efficient graph engines

We observed highly promising performance improvement against our baseline methods in our preliminary experiments. In Figure 20.13, we illustrate the execution time of our workload against GraphChi. The efficiency improvement was quite significant, approximately 3.6–10.4× faster. We achieved such speedups because (1) our system eliminates vertex-centric graph reconstruction in GraphChi that results in significant memory allocation and release repeatedly; (2) our system explores data parallelism in an edge-set by processing multiple vertices simultaneously. Our system achieved 10%–30% performance improvement over GraphChi on the preprocessing phase, primarily because our system requires no global sorting. To combine the preprocessing and the workload of 10-PSW-based traversal, we achieve 1.5–3.4× overall speedup as shown in Figure 20.14.

In Figure 20.15, we illustrate the execution time of PSW-based SSSP against GraphChi. We implemented Bellman–Ford algorithm which computes the shortest

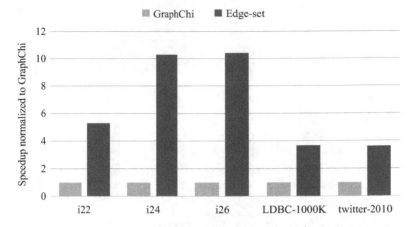

Figure 20.13   Performance of PageRank against GraphChi

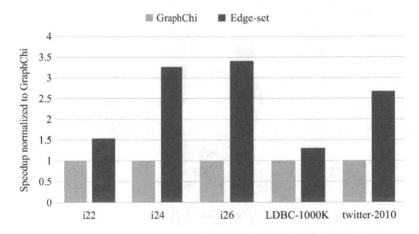

Figure 20.14   Performance of PageRank against GraphChi including preprocessing

paths from a single source vertex to all of the other vertices in a weighted graph. It traverses all the edges $|V|-1$ times where $|V|$ is the number of vertices in the graph or ends when no vertices distance are changed since last iteration. The source vertices were randomly chosen, and the average execution time was calculated and compared with GraphChi. The efficiency improvement was quite significant, approximately 3.7–16.2× faster over the baseline. The speedups vary since the iterations required to end may vary with different source vertices. To combine the preprocessing and the workload of PSW-based SSSP, we achieve 1.5–2.9× overall speedup as shown in Figure 20.16.

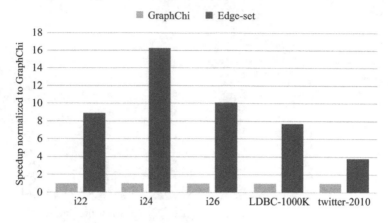

Figure 20.15 Performance of SSSP against GraphChi

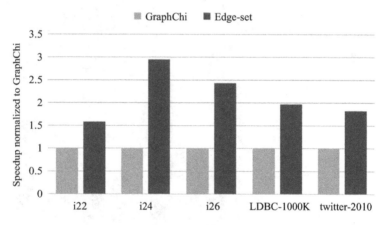

Figure 20.16 Performance of SSSP against GraphChi including preprocessing

20.7 Open issues and challenges

Despite that the Big Data analytics and processing through graph computing can help deal with emerging problems in SDN networks, we also face many new challenges. One challenge is to address the network dynamic of SDN in real time. In SDN networks, when new computing or storage devices are added, all network services should be available for use as soon as possible. To achieve this goal, the SDN systems need monitor the whole network and immediately update the infrastructure once the network changes. This indicates that the processing of dynamic graphs also needs real time for SDN system, which brings challenges especially in large SDN networks. Another challenge is to efficiently deal with extremely large-scale graphs

from emerging SDN networks. Modern processors are inefficient for graph computing under either vertex-centric or edge-centric models for large-scale graphs. This
mainly comes from the bad cache performance due to large memory footprint. In
future, we will extend the proposed edge-set-based system onto distributed computing environment to address extremely large-scale graphs and further improve the
performance of our system from computer architecture aspects. Last but not least,
challenge comes from how to design efficient interactive graph analytics for SDN
networks, which can put the human in the loop for exploring the SDN graph data
by visualizations. However, the human recognition capabilities and the screen size
would limit the effectiveness of this approach. Furthermore, few existing solutions
provide the functionality to explore large distributed graph data and the evolution in
dynamic networks.

20.8 Conclusions

The emerging SDN decouples the control and data planes to overcome the short-
comings of traditional networks. This decoupling makes control plane possible to
control the data planeâL™s traffic of an entire network, bringing much flexibility
even through the network is dynamically changed. However, the centralized SDN
controller requires fast and reliable traffic engineering to cope with the large number of nodes in the network as well as the network dynamics. This challenge can be
leveraged from Big Data area in the perspective of graph computing. Two critical
functionalities of traffic engineering in SDN controller are fast routing calculation
and reliable routing errors detection. To deal with these two problems, we developed efficient graph-commuting-based schemes in this chapter, which demonstrated
much faster speed than the existing solutions. Furthermore, we present a novel edge-
set-based graph processing engine to deal with large-scale graph problem in SDN
networks, which also achieves much faster speed than the state-of-the-art solutions.

References

[1] D. Kreutz, M. V. R. Fernando, P. Verissimo, C. E. Rothenburg, S. Azodolmolky,
and S. Uhlig. Software-defined networking: a complete survey. *Proceedings
of the IEEE*, 103(1): 14–76, 2015.

[2] T. Benson, A. Akella, and D. Maltz. Unraveling the complexity of network
management. In *Proceedings of the 6th USENIX Symposium on Networked
Systems Design and Implementation*, pages 335–348, 2009.

[3] L. Cui, F. R. Yu, and Q. Yan. When big data meets software-defined networking:
SDN for big data and big data for SDN. *IEEE Network*, 30:58–65, 2016.

[4] W. Hong, K. Wang, and Y.-H. Hsu. Application-aware resource allocation
for SDN-based cloud data centers. In *Proceedings of 2013 International
Conference on Cloud Computing and Big Data*, pages 106–110, 2013.

[5]   Y. Han, S.-s. Seo, J. Li, J. Hyun, J.-H. Yoo, and W.-K. Hong. Software defined networking-based traffic engineering for data center networks. In *Proceedings of the 16th Asia-Pacific Network Operations and Management Symposium*, pages 1–6, 2014.

[6]   P. Samadi, D. Calhoun, H. Wang, and K. Bergman. Accelerating cast traffic delivery in data centers leveraging physical layer optics and SDN. In *Proceedings of 2014 International Conference on Optical Network Design and Modeling*, pages 73–77, 2014.

[7]   A. Sadasivarao, S. Syed, P. Pan, C. Liou, and I. Monga. Bursting data between data centers: case for transport SDN. In *Proceedings of IEEE 21st Annual Symposium on High-Performance Interconnects*, pages 87–90, 2013.

[8]   G. Wang, T. E. Ng, and A. Shaikh. Programming your network at run-time for big data applications. In *Proceedings of the 1st Workshop on Hot Topics in Software Defined Networks*, 2012.

[9]   I. Monga, E. Pouyoul, and C. Guok. Software defined-networking for big-data science – architectural models from campus to the wan. In *2012 SC Companion: High Performance Computing, Networking Storage and Analysis*, pages 1629–1635, 2012.

[10] P. Qin, B. Dai, B. Huang, and G. Xu. Bandwidth-aware scheduling with SDN in Hadoop: a new trend for big data. *IEEE Systems Journal*, PP(99):1–8, 2015.

[11] E. W. Dijkstra. A note on two problems in connexion with graphs. *Numerische mathematik*, 1(1):269–271, 1959.

[12] E. de Queirós Vieira Martins, M. M. B. Pascoal, and J. L. E. D. Santos. Deviation algorithms for ranking shortest paths. *International Journal of Foundations of Computer Science*, 10(03):247–261, 1999.

[13] J. Y. Yen. Finding the k shortest loopless paths in a network. *Management Science*, 17(11):712–716, 1971.

[14] G. Feng. Improving space efficiency with path length prediction for finding *k* shortest simple paths. *IEEE Transactions on Computers*, 63(10):2459–2472, 2014.

[15] H. Zeng, S. Zhang, F. Ye, *et al.* Libra: Divide and conquer to verify forwarding tables in huge networks. In *Proceedings of the 11th USENIX Conference on Networked Systems Design and Implementation*, NSDI'14, pages 87–99, Berkeley, CA, USA, 2014.

[16] Y. Luo, W. Wang, and X. Lin. Spark: A keyword search engine on relational databases. In *Data Engineering, 2008. ICDE 2008. IEEE 24th International Conference on*, pages 1552–1555. IEEE, 2008.

[17] J. Dean and S. Ghemawat. Mapreduce: simplified data processing on large clusters. *Communications of the ACM*, 51(1):107–113, 2008.

[18] R. Tarjan. Depth-first search and linear graph algorithms. *SIAM Journal on Computing*, 1(2):146–160, 1972.

[19] A. V. Aho and J. E. Hopcroft. 1974. The design and analysis of computer algorithms (1st ed.). Addison-Wesley Longman Publishing Co., Inc., Boston, MA, USA, 1974.

[20] T. H. Cormen, C. E. Leiserson, R. L. Rivest, and C. Stein. Introduction to algorithms, Third Edition (3rd ed.). The MIT Press, 2009.

[21] Y. Xia, I. G. Tanase, L. Nai, *et al.* Explore efficient data organization for large scale graph analytics and storage. In *IEEE Big Data*, pages 942–951, 2014.

[22] A. Kyrola, G. Blelloch, and C. Guestrin. Graphchi: Large-scale graph computation on just a PC. In *Proceedings of the 10th USENIX Symposium on Operating Systems Design and Implementation (OSDI)*, volume 8, pages 31–46, 2012.

[23] A. Roy, I. Mihailovic, and W. Zwaenepoel. X-stream: edge-centric graph processing using streaming partitions. In *Proceedings of the Twenty-Fourth ACM Symposium on Operating Systems Principles*, pages 472–488. ACM, 2013.

[24] L. Nai, Y. Xia, I. G. Tanase, H. Kim, and C.-Y. Lin. Graphbig: Understanding graph computing in the context of industrial solutions. In *Proceedings of the International Conference for High Performance Computing, Networking, Storage and Analysis*, page 69. ACM, 2015.

[25] N. Nethercote and J. Seward. Valgrind: A framework for heavyweight dynamic binary instrumentation. In *Proceedings of the 28th ACM SIGPLAN Conference on Programming Language Design and Implementation*, PLDI '07, pages 89–100, New York, NY, USA, 2007. ACM. ISBN 978-1-59593-633-2.

Chapter 21

Big Data helps SDN to improve application specific quality of service

Susanna Schwarzmann*, Andreas Blenk**,
Ognjen Dobrijevic***, Michael Jarschel[†], Andreas Hotho*,
Thomas Zinner*, and Florian Wamser*

21.1 Introduction

Managing the quality of real-time multimedia services, such as video streaming and networked virtual reality, still poses many technological challenges. For instance, data-rate demand of video streaming services is dramatically increasing. At the same time, virtual reality applications call for low user-to-server latency. These opposing demands are dictated by the evolution of the quality concept, which has been transformed over the past decade from more technical, network-level quality of service (QoS) into user-centric quality of experience (QoE) [1]. Going beyond QoS, which commonly involves network performance in terms of measurable parameters like throughput and delay, QoE identifies additional factors that influence service quality as perceived by end-users. These QoE influence factors (QoE-IFs) may, for example, include user-device screen resolution and previous service-usage experience.

Recently, many research results have exploited the paradigm of software-defined networking (SDN) [2] as means to implement QoS-/QoE-oriented network control and management (CaM). The respective "CaM loop" aims at customizing the network configuration to reflect the specified quality improvement target, e.g., reducing the number of video-stream stalling events. SDN, with its separation of network control logic from data plane devices into distinct controller entities, provides architectural blocks to realize QoS-/QoE-centric CaM [3]. Well-defined communication interfaces, as advocated by SDN, enable network applications that work with SDN to communicate information about multimedia application states to the network controller. On the other hand, SDN facilitates the acquisition of network-wide performance statistics from the controller entities by means of, for instance, OpenFlow [2]. As a result, SDN

*Institute of Computer Science, University of Würzburg, Germany
**Institute for Communication Networks, Technische Universität München, Germany
***Faculty of Electrical Engineering and Computing, University of Zagreb, Croatia
[†]Nokia Bell Labs, Munich, Germany

is able to maintain a global application state across the network, supported by the fact that it can cooperate with both service and network providers.

Furthermore, with the introduction of QoE as a CaM objective, which calls for (1) measuring and collecting QoE-IF data, (2) processing and analyzing this data, and (3) producing and enforcing action decisions, network CaM faces the challenges of dealing with large data sets, i.e., "Big Data" [4]. Recent network-level solutions were only provided for small data-scale scenarios, since they lack Big Data-related technologies that are able to handle huge data sets. In the QoE CaM context, a respective SDN system might consider a vast number of QoE-IF data sources (i.e., *data variety*) that produce large data quantities (or *data volume*) on different time scales (referred to as *data velocity*). New developments of Big Data technologies, e.g., Deep Learning or MapReduce, allow for an efficient processing of such large data. Moreover, Big Data techniques facilitate efficient execution for most of the state-of-the-art machine learning (ML) and data mining (DM) algorithms. Combining SDN control logic with methods of Big Data analytics, e.g., by integrating them into an SDN controller, would enable taking into account a wide range of QoE-IFs and, thus, "more precise" decision-making that conforms to the specified CaM goal. Moreover, Big Data techniques could be used, e.g., for customizing QoE estimation models during service run-time to consider categories of end-users with different demographics.

This chapter first provides an outline of the current results in the domains of: (1) QoS/QoE CaM for real-time multimedia services that is supported by SDN, and (2) Big Data analytics and methods that are used for QoS/QoE CaM. Then, three specific use case scenarios with respect to video streaming services are presented, so as to illustrate the expected benefits of incorporating Big Data analytics into SDN-based CaM for the purposes of improving or optimizing QoS/QoE. In the end, we describe our vision and a high-level view of an SDN-based architecture for QoS/QoE CaM that is enriched with Big Data analytics' functional blocks and summarize corresponding challenges.

21.2　Classification of SDN-based context-aware networking approaches

In the following section, we discuss various approaches that use SDN for QoS/QoE-oriented network CaM of multimedia services (QoS/QoE CaM). Since, in particular, *data variety* and information gained by monitoring, as well as *data analytics* and related control actions play an important role in the Big Data context, we consequently classify the presented approaches based on QoE-IFs, the control actions triggered by this information, and the resulting implications. An overview of the investigated approaches with their classification is shown in Table 21.1.

In the area of SDN and QoS/QoE management, video streaming is currently one of the main drivers, as it is generating most of the Internet traffic [5] and has a strong influence with representatives such as MPEG Dynamic Adaptive Streaming over HTTP (DASH) and HTTP adaptive streaming solutions. For that reason, the solutions discussed in the following section focus on video streaming or video conferencing.

Table 21.1 Classification of SDN-based context-aware networking approaches

Source	Monitored QoE-IFs	Control action	Implication
[6]	Packets in the network (DPI)	App-aware path selection	Prevention of video stallings
[7]	Application type, packet loss rate, network latency	App-aware path selection	QoE enhancement of a multitude of applications
[8]	Network congestion indication	Flow prioritization	Quality enhancement of live video transmission
[9]	YouTube video buffer	App-aware path selection	Prevention of video stallings
[10]	Network throughput, video buffer	Flow prioritization and quality adaptation	Prevention of video stallings
[11]	Available bandwidth, network latency, client properties	Dynamic resource allocation	Fair QoE maximization
[12]	Available bandwidth, packet loss rate, jitter, initial delay, buffer	Change of routing paths and transport nodes	QoE enhancement for video streaming
[13]	Active DASH streams, network resources, client properties	Bitrate guidance, bandwidth reservation	Fairness with respect to video quality
[14]	Available bandwidth, video buffer	Network resource allocation	Fair QoE maximization

21.2.1 Monitoring of QoE influence factors (QoE-IFs)

We begin with a classification of selected management approaches according to the monitored parameters. Each SDN-based CaM approach monitors at least one QoE-IF. These factors can be classified in terms of quantity/frequency and location of monitoring, whereas our classification considers four dimensions of monitoring. There are commonly mechanisms that perform (1) monitoring in the network at packet level, (2) monitoring at flow level, (3) monitoring of application information that are available within the client software, and (4) mechanisms that perform monitoring at network- and application-side, i.e., monitoring of network parameters as well as application-side QoE-IFs updates.

Monitoring at packet level in the network. An approach that exploits network information on packet level is [6] by Jarschel *et al.* for QoE management of web and video traffic. By means of Deep Packet Inspection (DPI), packets are inspected on their way from their source to destination. Based on significant packet fields, the application can be identified. The challenge is that a wide range of information has to be collected at different points in the network so as to get a holistic insight into the application and the network. The latter approach also discusses whether a Northbound interaction between an application and SDN controller is more beneficial than packet DPI, since encrypted traffic poses another major challenge with regards to end-to-end encryption. The approach in [7] collects information about packet loss and packet latency, refraining from inspecting application information based on a packet payload. There, a major challenge is the collection of packet- and flow-level statistics at different locations in the network. The efficiency of such approaches and the associated detection of the network bottlenecks strongly depend on the possibility of comprehensively monitoring the network.

Monitoring at flow level in the network. Besides the approaches that monitor the network on packet level, there are also approaches that examine the network at the flow level. For this purpose, no individual packets are analyzed, but the whole flow through the network is considered. In [8], for example, monitoring is performed to quickly detect network congestion based on network flow statistics.

Monitoring of application information. An example where application information is used as a basis for control actions is [9]. This proposal relies on the client's buffer state as QoE-IF. In this case, the client buffer state is only one QoE-IF example, which is investigated for the considered video streaming use case. A further development of collecting information on application level might reveal that a targeted monitoring of specific application parameters is desirable for each active application and for each client so as to optimize QoS/QoE management in the network.

Monitoring at network- and application-side. Unlike the previously mentioned mechanisms, which either rely on network monitoring or application monitoring only, the mechanisms presented in [10–14] consider both, application, and network information, to decide about control actions. This may include, upon others, the number of active video streams, current network throughput, capabilities of the user-devices in terms of screen resolution, and QoE-IFs like current buffer or the number of media quality switches. Thereby, a new challenge arises in multi-application scenarios, where information on other applications' traffic must be gathered at a large scale as well. This requires to monitor variety of data, but it also offers an added value, as it is possible to make decisions for the benefit of all applications. All the above-mentioned challenges lie in the direction of Big Data and machine-based data analysis, because data variety and volume are crucial for the success of these approaches.

21.2.2   Control actions of management approaches

The presented mechanisms are based on various adaptations in the network in order to meet the requirements of an application. In addition to the control actions implemented in the network, some of the approaches also take into account additional control actions within the application. However, in the following subsection, we are only going to detail the network-side adaptations, since the focus of this work is on SDN, which naturally performs the adaptations on the network level by using, e.g., the OpenFlow interface.

As the presented classification table shows, several proposals employ the same or similar control actions. Dynamic application-aware path selection is performed in [6,7,9,12], whereby [12] additionally performs a dynamic selection of the transport node. Having the knowledge from the monitoring entities and QoE models, an algorithm decides about the network path for the specific flows in order to meet the application requirements. The challenge in this context is to make coordinated, fine-grained decisions. Granularity of the information, hereby, improves the decision-making process. Fine-grained information can be used to carry out more targeted actions on the network level. If ML is used on the massive data, it is possible to better estimate the required application parameters that influence the control actions, such as clients' video buffers. For all approaches, the amount of data is essential to make efficient decisions and not to discriminate against other applications in the network.

The mechanisms of [8,10] temporarily prioritize specific flows in the network so as to prevent QoE degradation. This is realized by implementing at least two queues in network switches, whereby one is set up as a best effort queue, while the other one processes packets of the prioritized flows. Packets in the high-priority queue are preferably scheduled as opposed to packets in the best effort queue.

Dynamic allocation of resources, e.g., bandwidth reservation, is considered in [11,13,14]. What these mechanisms have in common is that they take into account fairness aspects. This can either mean that all video clients—which possibly have different device capabilities (e.g., screen resolution) and, hence, different network demands—have a fair video quality, or that the QoE is maximized whilst fairness constraints are considered.

Big Data and ML approaches have potential to support these CaM mechanisms in the decision process. For example, it is easy to imagine how reinforced learning can be used. An algorithm learns from the impacts triggered by specific control actions. Hence, the algorithm continuously optimizes its decisions and is aware of the currently best-fitting control action. The basis on which the algorithm decides which control actions to perform, i.e., the feature set considered for learning, is extensive and includes, among other things, network and application behavior. By employing user-defined data obtained through monitoring of the user behavior (e.g., video-stalling duration or initial delay thresholds that provoke a user to abort service), it is even possible to react in a user-centric manner.

21.2.3 Potential of Big Data for SDN QoE management

The applicability of Big Data for SDN-based QoE management approaches is indisputable as discussed in the previous subsections. The trend for more data and more monitored QoE-IFs dictates the use of Big Data in this area. Nevertheless, current approaches do not exploit this potential and avoid the use of Big Data, since the approach and the way of thinking are different with this massive data.

In contrast to the traditional approaches, Big Data helps in evaluating information in three different directions. First, Big Data supports the statistical analysis of encrypted traffic, which is important in today's networks. On the basis of privacy issues, traditional approaches refrain from packet analysis and rather collect statistics on network and packet throughput so as to get information about the applications. Second, Big Data can help to analyze data within the whole network at different points of presence. Many CaM approaches can improve their optimizations by taking into account information about the entire network. Third, Big Data also helps at application level, where all applications need to be considered and, consequently, a lot of information needs to be gathered.

Besides the collection and analysis of the huge amount of data, Big Data can help with its analytical methods. Feasible are, for instance, algorithms that facilitate learning and predicting appropriate control actions based on the given data. Some ongoing work in the context of Big Data and QoS/QoE management is presented in Section 21.3.2, also including examples where network control decisions rely on the outcomes of Big Data analytics mechanisms. The challenge in the context of control actions is to make coordinated, fine-grained decisions. For all approaches, the amount of data is essential to make efficient decisions and not to discriminate against other applications in the network, especially with respect to fairness in the network.

21.3   Big Data analytics to support QoS/QoE management

In this section, we focus on the potential of Big Data analytics to support QoS/QoE management. We first give a short overview on Big Data analytics approaches and, afterwards, present current work that applies those techniques in the context of QoS/QoE management.

21.3.1   Big Data analytics

This subsection provides a short overview on typical Big Data analytics techniques. We will not discuss Big Data in general, as it focuses not only on ML and DM approaches, but also addresses a broad range of data handling aspects [15]. Data handling aspects are only of limited importance here, since we have to deal with the "3Vs": *volume*, since we need to handle a large quantity of data, *velocity*, as we need to deal with the incoming data just in time, and partially with *variety*, when we bridge the gap between the network flow data and the application level. We ignore the other "2Vs" of Big Data. Therefore, we will focus on typical ML and DM approaches which form the basis for an analysis of the collected data, with a special emphasis on Big Data aspects. An in-depth discussion of the combination of Big Data and SDN can be found in [16].

The goal of ML is to learn from a given set of examples and to build models from it. This model can be later applied on newly and unseen data. A second goal is to gain new insights about present data by means of those models. DM includes this model learning step in a bigger process, which includes data handling and application of learned models as other important steps. Due to this data-centric view, a lot of new "DM" techniques have been developed in the past. The most prominent example is the association rule mining approach, which is part of a more general class of methods known under the term *pattern mining*. In general, ML and DM techniques are broadly classified into *Supervised learning*, *Semisupervised learning*, or *Unsupervised learning*. An introduction to ML can be found in [17,18] and to DM in [19].

When supervised learning is applied, the classification rules (model) are learned based on labeled data. Labeled data, or training data, indicates the desired output or the correct feature value, depending on the given input. Hence, the model builds a function that relates input parameters to the output feature. This model is then applied to unlabeled data and the output is predicted based on that. Typical supervised learning algorithms are Support Vector Machine (SVM), Decision Tree, Naive Bayes, k-Nearest Neighbor (k-NN), and Random Forest. These techniques are often superordinated as *Classification*. In contrast to the classification, where the output variable is a predefined class, *Regression* predicts continuous values. Other learning approaches like bagging, boosting or ensemble learning combine either weak or strong learners to a new model.

The term *Clustering* denotes the unsupervised learning methods, where no labeled data is given in advance. Typical clustering techniques include density-based methods like DB-Scan, as well as standard statistical approaches like k-Means, k-Medoids and expectation–maximization. More methods are mentioned in the survey article [20]. More recently, methods like Latent Dirichlet allocation become popular in many areas. The basics are already addressed in text books like [18]. Semisupervised learning is a part of supervised learning, with the difference that it makes use of both labeled and unlabeled data. In this way, fewer labeled data is needed, but as larger quantity of the available data is used, a more general model can be learned.

ML and DM approaches discussed so far typically need to be able to access all data during the model learning or pattern detection phase. Storing all the Big Data is sometimes impossible and, therefore, classical ML and DM methods cannot be applied. Stream DM refers to a set of methods adopted in such a way that models can be learned, or patterns can be detected, directly from a stream of data. Besides adopted standard methods like tree learner, one can find special methods such as time series analysis, which inherently rely on data streams in this area. An overview of stream mining algorithms is given in [21]. As there is no longer a need to store the data, we can address the Big Data issue of volume and velocity within our network analysis setting. We can directly stream the data to a learning machine, which computes new models "on the fly." These models can be deployed on network devices or controllers, and take care of the network flows. The Apache Storm framework[1] provides a distributed stream processing framework, which can be adopted to efficiently learn from a data stream.

Reinforcement learning is another ML paradigm (cf. [22]), where an agent autonomously learns a strategy. It can be seen as a kind of weak supervision, as minimal feedback is provided which is used to learn the strategy. The agent is not trained in terms of actions to take, instead, it is rewarded (positively as well as negatively) for its decisions. Typical examples are game playing (the feedback is winning the game or getting a higher score) or controlling machines, such as a robot moving through a labyrinth. The benefit of such a system is that it learns continuously, even if it is in practical application.

With the advances of deep learning methods, reinforcement is becoming more and more popular and successful, as shown by examples of game learning for Atari computer games [23]. The main idea is the use of a deep neural network to do different

---

[1] http://storm.apache.org.

processing steps on the corresponding layer. This includes the image processing, which in a classical learning step would be a kind of feature engineering, but also the judgment of the reward over long time. Without going into details on how deep learning methods work, one could apply similar deep learning approaches on network traffic, with the goal of controlling the flow through the network. A neural network could learn reconfiguration of the network by directly analyzing the network traffic. This could also be done in a stream stetting, by utilizing one of the stream frameworks.

If one is not able to do stream mining, there is the need to store and process Big Data for learning. In the past years, a few of typical paradigms were developed. Among them are the MapReduce approach implemented in Hadoop[2] (disk focused) or Spark[3] (memory focused) mainly developed by search engine vendors to process web-scale data. MapReduce is a method to efficiently process large datasets [24]. Two functions *map* and *reduce* form the key of the approach and call each other iteratively. During the map phase, the input data is filtered or sorted with respect to some criteria implemented as a user-defined function in parallel. The results are distributed and sent to the reducers. The reducers summarize the values, in order to obtain a smaller set or even the final result set, and return it. If the data is stored in a distributed fashion, the first map job will directly access this distributed data, which allows to easily work on a big network dataset in parallel.

Another paradigm developed in the past years to store a large amount of data is NoSQL databases. In contrast to classical relational databases, NoSQL databases follow different main principles when storing data, such as columns, documents, key-values, graphs, and multimodels. Besides the change of the storage model, such databases favor speed over traditional properties like consistency. An introduction to the new, often distributed storage models can be found in [15].

21.3.2 Current and ongoing work

Mestres *et al.* [25] present a new paradigm called knowledge defined networking based on the idea of a Knowledge Plane for the Internet [26]. Their idea is to learn from network behavior and automatically operate the network accordingly, via a loop of constant learning. An SDN controller analyzes the network and provides the information to an analytics platform that transforms this information into knowledge. To this end, several ML techniques are applied: supervised learning, unsupervised learning, and reinforced learning. The knowledge is provided to the controller, which can find appropriate control instructions based on this knowledge and its global network view. Information about performed control actions and impact on the network behavior are again provided to the analytics platform. The authors present two use cases for the proposed Knowledge Plane. The first one focuses on routing in an overlay network, while the second one targets resource management in a Network Functions Virtualization scenario.

---

[2] http://hadoop.apache.org/.
[3] http://spark.apache.org/.

In [27], six classifiers (Naive Bayes, SVM, k-NN, Decision Tree, Random Forest, and Neural Networks) are compared with respect to their applicability to estimate the QoE from QoS parameters. The authors present a framework in which users can rate their satisfaction with the quality of a YouTube, during video playback and after the video is finished. Simultaneously, the framework monitors the video characteristics (QoS parameters). The framework is used within a large-scale crowd-sourcing study in order to obtain training data which map video QoS to QoE values. Besides the crowd-sourcing approach, the authors conduct experiments in a controlled environment. Hence, the objective Mean Opinion Score (MOS) can also be matched with network QoS parameters, such as packet loss, jitter, and latency. Based on this data, models are trained for the six different classifiers. With regards to the mean absolute error, the Decision Tree yields the best classification result for a 4-fold cross-validation benchmark. In terms of the correctly classified share from the test set, Random Forrest and Decision Tree outperform the other techniques.

A methodology for estimating YouTube QoE based on statistical properties of encrypted network traffic is presented in [28]. The authors set up a testbed where several YouTube videos are played back. During playback, the network traces are stored. These traces provide information like packet length, size of transferred data within a fixed interval, packet count statistics, and TCP flag count. Further, application-level data is captured during video playback. The latter data includes the number of video stallings, stalling duration, and playback time on a certain quality level. Based on these QoE-related parameters, each video instance is classified into one of three QoE classes: low, medium, and high. Several experiments with varying video durations and bandwidth configurations provide 1,060 videos and associated network traces in total. Using WEKA, this data is used for feature selection and model building with several classifiers (OneR, Naive Bayes, SMO, J48 and Random Forest). Again, Random Forest outperforms the other methods with respect to accuracy, when the model is trained and tested using 10-fold crossvalidation of the whole dataset.

Traffic classification is also targeted in [29]. However, unlike the previous approach, the authors do not aim at predicting a QoE value, but at classifying network traffic into one of several QoS classes. A QoS class comprises applications that have similar QoS requirements, e.g., voice, video conference, streaming, bulk data transfer, and interactive data are considered as different QoS classes. To learn the classifier, network traces are stored and labeled as one of these classes. The knowledge about an application's QoS class can then be used to perform a QoS-aware traffic engineering in order to satisfy the application's needs. The authors propose to apply the classifier within a framework that is located in an SDN controller so as to take advantage of its global network view, programmability, and computation capacity.

The feasibility of different ML algorithms for traffic classification is investigated in [30]. The authors use the OpenFlow protocol to gather information about the traffic in an enterprise network. They store several features of the TCP flows and the corresponding packets. These features include flow duration, packet time stamp, interarrival time and packet count. To obtain labeled data, the authors run applications in a controlled-experiment environment and store the traffic traces produced by different applications. This data set is used to train models for predicting applications based on network data with three different classifiers: Random Forest, Stochastic Gradient Boosting, and Extreme Gradient Boosting. Their results indicate that each of this supervised learning techniques can obtain a high traffic classification accuracy.

Statistical regression analysis is used in [31] to determine the relationship between several QoS parameters and the resulting QoE for video conferencing on a MOS scale. The authors consider packet loss rate, round trip time, bandwidth, and jitter to produce the regression coefficients. These coefficients are analyzed for several access technologies (e.g., Wi-Fi and 3G) in order to predict the QoE depending on the chosen technology, with the goal to dynamically select the technology providing the best QoE. One more approach for estimating the QoE from QoS parameters is presented in [32]. The authors propose to use the predictions to find the input network parameters which obtain QoE that satisfies a user's needs and to decide about appropriate network management actions.

The focus in [33] is on user QoE in an enterprise environment. The authors evaluate the potential of several ML algorithms to predict the worker satisfaction based on objective measurements (waiting times). They use results from a subjective user study and technical data from the system monitoring to learn three models, namely, SVM, Gradient Boosting, and Deep Neural Networks. The resulting classification accuracies reveal that none of the examined algorithms is reliably applicable for QoE prediction based on nonintrusive, application monitoring data. However, when modeling on a per-user scale, there is a share of about 5%–10% of all users, whose models can classify with over 80% accuracy. Hence, the QoE may be predicted with good accuracy for specific users, if personalized prediction models are applied.

21.4   Combining Big Data analytics and SDN: three use cases to improve QoS/QoE

In this section, we present three use cases which illustrate the envisaged benefits of combining Big Data and SDN. The first use case is an extension of classical network QoS monitoring to achieve improvements and adjustments in the network due to certain network settings. The second use case assumes a business agreement between a video on-demand provider and an SDN-based network operator to exchange values of QoE-IFs, which are then processed by Big Data applications. The final use case, as opposed to the second one, assumes no direct communication between the video service provider (SP) and the network operator, while Big Data applications are utilized in order to infer the service-level QoS/QoE.

21.4.1   Use case 1: improving the operation of networks

This subsection deals with the use case of improving network operation by combining Big Data and SDN. In particular, we discuss compliance of network performance with the QoS requirements for Voice-over-IP (VoIP) traffic.

Traffic flows and their mutual influence within networks are highly complex and unpredictable in today's networks. Network-level actions, like queuing, traffic shaping, selective dropping and link-efficiency policies, provide a network operator with control over how these flows transition over the network. This is especially critical for VoIP and video streaming traffic, since the operator needs to improve network operation and maintain the specified QoS requirements, such as maximum allowed latency and minimum required throughput. From a technical perspective, this means that in cases where network virtualization is not possible—or the use of technologies such as virtual local area networks is not adequate—network settings and QoS optimizations can be used in the network to enable a robust traffic flow.

For VoIP networks, a telephony application typically requires the one-way latency less than 400 ms. This must apply to the entire network, if VoIP traffic is being transported. In this case, layer 3 markings (preferably Differentiated Services Code Point, or DSCP) or layer 2 prioritization with the Class-of-Service (CoS) markings are commonly used for this purpose, in the outbound direction of each network link.

A continuous measurement and monitoring of the important quality features in the network forms the basis for the VoIP QoS management. In the network, switches and routers are currently being used to generate NetFlow statistics on packet latency and to perform active tests on how to meet the current QoS requirements for VoIP. In terms of Big Data and Big Data analytics, two general paradigms can be applied in addition to the traditional monitoring and testing: (1) the collection, storage, and processing of the data on a high detail-level using Big Data mechanisms and (2) the analysis and evaluation with Big Data learning methods to provide better insights, detect failures, predict future critical situations and usage trends without direct operator interaction.

Collection, storage, and processing of the data according to the Big Data principles. Through large-scale collection and storage of data, QoS statistics can be collected across the entire network. It is even possible to add application information (*variety*) as additional source to do a better network control. Big Data provides means for efficient data storage, e.g., NoSQL databases, how the storage cluster needs to be scaled based on the data volume, and how the data needs to be processed to meet analytical engines such as Hadoop. The new data allows not only for more detailed statistics due to the higher *volume* of the data. Even more, this data is the basis for learning new models and extracting hidden knowledge about the usage patterns of the network. Due to the new size, the insights are more fine-grained and the control action will allow for more specific and timely (*velocity*) reaction with respect to users' need. This could even reach a level where personalized traffic requests can automatically be met by the network when learning is used.

Analysis and evaluation with Big Data learning methods. By analyzing the collected data and learning QoS models from it, conclusions can be drawn about the QoS-compliance. It can be checked whether the QoS requirements are enforceable or not, and whether the QoS should be adapted based on the models learned from historical data. Daily patterns and traffic situations can be estimated, appropriately handled, and evaluated for the network control purposes. It is even possible to predict future traffic situations and to take long term actions based on the collected data. Examples of successful ML applications on network traffic are described in Section 21.3.2, which show what is currently possible with state-of-the-art models. With the adoption of stream DM and deep learning models, we expect self-adaptable SDN controllers given some high-level strategy of the network provider, which show the full potential of Big Data analytics in this area.

The implementation and configuration for QoS management takes place in the entire network with the help of SDN. With SDN, for instance, the control actions are passed to the devices and dynamic adjustments can be made based on the output of the Big Data analytics engine. In the end, the use of Big Data in QoS management means the logical continuation of the idea, in which data is evaluated to enforce QoS requirements for special types of multimedia services.

21.4.2   Use case 2: improving the quality of video-on-demand streaming based on business agreements

This subsection gives another example of how the integration of Big Data applications into an SDN-based network environment can enhance QoS/QoE. The example assumes that a video-on-demand (VoD) streaming SP, e.g., Netflix or Amazon Prime, has negotiated with a future SDN-based network operator (SNO) to exchange service-level and network-level information relevant to QoS/QoE control. Such a business agreement between SPs and SNOs may provide mutual benefits: SPs offer improved QoS/QoE to their end-users, while SNOs can utilize their network resources more efficiently. The business agreement encompasses varying points. The SNOs agree to provide "prioritized" traffic treatment for the SPs' customers.

Further, SPs and SNOs agree on the exchange of values for the relevant QoS/QoE-IFs. In case of VoD streaming, we identify the following parameters to be reported by the SPs:

- (anonymized) user demographics data (e.g., user age range), which is reported during the video session establishment phase;
- previous service usage experience (beginner/advanced user), which is reported during the video session establishment phase;
- service cost (flat rate, cost per video, etc.), which is reported during the video session establishment phase;
- user device type (e.g., smartphone, tablet, and laptop), which is reported during the video session establishment phase;
- user device characteristics (screen size, OS, CPU and RAM features, etc.), which are reported during the video session establishment phase;
- video client statistics (e.g., buffer status, number of video freezes), which are reported periodically for the session duration;
- service features (MPD information), which are reported during the video session establishment phase; and
- server statistics, which are reported periodically for the session duration.

However, this constitutes a large number of QoE-IFs, which need to be efficiently monitored and provided by SPs. Here, Big Data applications can be utilized by the SPs in order to efficiently process and compress the monitored data on end-users and VoD service.

In order to put such an architecture into effect, further implementation steps are necessary. As a first adjustment, the VoD clients and servers would be extended so as to report QoS/QoE-IFs, e.g., by piggy backing HTTP traffic. For the information exchange between SPs and SNOs, an orchestrator may be used that serves as the collection and extraction point for the data on relevant QoS/QoE influence factors. To interact with the SDN control plane, the orchestrator can use a Northbound interface provided by one of the open source SDN controllers.

To make use of Big Data services, two ways are possible. Either the orchestrator interacts with a Big Data infrastructure via another interface or it integrates Big Data applications directly. Furthermore, the operation of the orchestrator might be optimized on run-time with the help of Big Data applications. For instance, latency information is extracted, which helps to improve the network optimization. In addition, Big Data applications lower the burden of extensive data processing on SDN controllers, or even relieve them of the processing raw information completely.

On the SNO side, SDN controllers periodically collect network-wide statistics on the performance of the data plane elements. Based on the received information from the orchestrator and the monitoring data on the network, the control plane can make the best possible decision according to the business agreement and the overall network optimization goal. The SDN controller can use VoD service and end-user information to make decisions. This information allows the SDN controller to make distinctions, e.g., between advanced users and beginners ("a beginner is less likely to be annoyed with video flickers than an advanced user"). Other end-user information can be the service cost. Here, an end-user paying for each video expects more value-for-money than a flat-rate end-user. Such insights and metrics can be delivered via Big Data applications running on the SP side. Furthermore, other Big Data received information can provide insights into the reasons of video freezes. Here, end-user information allows to differentiate between video freezes due to poor client performance, e.g., a stressed end-device running too many applications, or video freezes as a result of misconfigured network operations. Other service information can be frequent changes in video quality. Thus, the SDN controller can support video traffic to provide a more stable delivery and, thus, reduce quality switches. In case of general over-utilization, information retrieved from Big Data applications allows to distinguish end-users based on their previous usage experience, i.e., history of application use.

21.4.3 Use case 3: improving the quality of applications without business agreements

In a setup where no direct negotiation and information exchange between SNOs and SPs exist, Big Data applications can still help to improve the overall service and network performance. In this case, the incentive for an SNO is to serve end-users with the best possible network performance, as they would most commonly blame the SNO for poor service quality.

The challenge is to identify reasons for service performance degradations, in particular for encrypted network traffic. Thus, the goal of an SNO would be to establish a network monitoring infrastructure with an SDN controller that is making decisions based on the efficiently monitored data. In order not to burden the controller with intensive data processing, the monitoring infrastructure incorporates Big Data techniques. Big Data applications then provide statistics of video streaming traffic based on, e.g., average packet size, interarrival packet time and average throughput. Since this, again, might be a large amount of data, it is of immense importance to efficiently provide low-dimensional data presentations, which can be provided by Big Data unsupervised learning techniques or auto encoders. Besides directly connecting and monitoring SDN infrastructures via OpenFlow, other techniques such as Simple Network Management Protocol (SNMP) or sFlow can be used.

However, as video traffic may be encrypted, such an approach demands for models that are capable of estimating values of the respective QoS/QoE metrics solely based on the monitored traffic parameters [28]. While these models are currently derived based on tests with human subjects, a future Big Data-based network optimization may even incorporate automatic QoS/QoE model creation and user inquiry. Furthermore, end-user information about the service usage can be obtained from test volunteers, who use client-side monitoring solutions or even provide feedback on QoS/QoE directly. These kind of solutions would result in a massive amount of data, which demands the efficient processing in a Big Data infrastructure. Such models would be updated on run-time and used by the SDN controllers.

21.5   Vision: intelligent network-wide auto-optimization

With millions of transactions and events happening per second in an operator's network, the goal of leveraging this information for the purpose of quality optimization and efficiency is truly a Big Data application. Through the scalability of the cloud and new developments in analytics, for the first time it is feasible to handle this vast amount of information and gain insight into the global network state "on the fly." The global network state is an accumulation of the entire network information at any point of a defined period of time. In particular, recent trends in Big Data technologies, such as distributed DM and information retrieval systems like Hadoop or Spark, support such a distributed state collection and efficient processing. Adding distributed sites connected through SDN-based networks to form a Telecommunication Company (Telco) cloud system enables to automatically act on those insights, gained both globally and locally.

Figure 21.1 represents a high-level overview on how a Big Data analytics engine (BDAE) interacts with a distributed Telco cloud network. An exemplary Telco cloud might be structured into three tiers, namely, micro points of presence (micro-pops), central offices, and central data centers. The network functionality of such Telco cloud is provided by virtual network functions running inside the data centers of each tier. The access networks connect the micro-pops and central offices, while the backbone networks interconnect the central offices to the central data centers. The architecture follows the notion of the global–local cloud as described in the Future X Network [34]. All instances in the three tiers follow the same basic structure, consisting of computing,

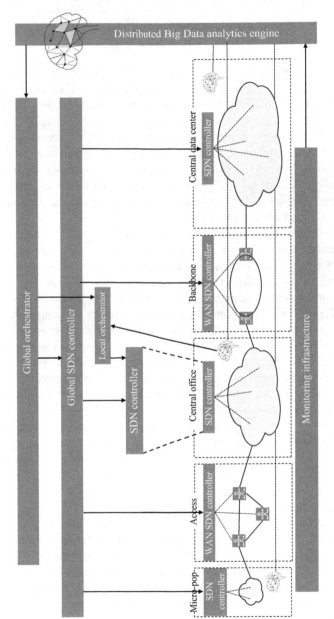

Figure 21.1   Big Data analytics in a Telco cloud network

Figure 21.2 Steps to Big Data-enabled local network optimization

storage, and networking resources. The difference lies within the size and number of each category, e.g., a micro-pop might only consist of one or two servers and a small storage system connected via a small SDN network, whereas central data centers may consist of thousands of servers, as well as the corresponding storage and networking equipment. Accordingly, micro-pops are large in number, while there are only a few central data centers in the network. Each of instance of every tier has its own local orchestrator as well as local SDN controller, which is shown in detail for the central office. The central office consists of several racks and is traditionally located in metro areas. For the few hyper-scale data centers, the individual data center locations are connected via high-speed optical networks.

While this structure enables high bandwidth and flexible relocation of virtual functions between locations, a real-time optimization of user experience in a single session requires the following subsequent steps among all tiers (Figure 21.2): real-time measurements, real-time analytics, real-time decisions, and real-time actions. In particular, the information exchange between tiers is important to enable a global optimization of the network operation. However, even with the increasing processing capabilities of Big Data applications, the overhead of exchanging every piece of information would be too large. Thus, comprehensive and compact representations are needed, which could be provided by Big Data applications preprocessing the information first locally in each tier. Further, with such a concept, even latent variables of the monitored networks, i.e., the state information, could be efficiently detected via Big Data applications. This is enabled by the Telco cloud, since all functions can be performed in any of the local data centers. The local monitoring system feeds information to the local analytics engine, which generates a recommended action for the local orchestrator. The orchestrator's task is then 2-fold. On the one hand, it optimizes, according to the analytics results, the deployment of the involved virtual functions in its domain, while on the other, it instructs the SDN controller to steer the network traffic accordingly.

Apart from the local optimization in every tier, the local analytics engine also identifies and compresses information that is relevant to the network on a global scale. Which information this entails and how often it is communicated to the global analytics engine depends on the preferences and optimization goal of the global orchestrator. Both the global orchestrator and analytics engine, as well as their redundancies, are located in the central data centers. Together, they optimize the whole network based on macroscopic trends and longer time-scales than the local measures. By preprocessing and preselecting the information at the local sites, the network is not congested with monitoring data and the global engine only has to deal with actually relevant information. The proper granularity of information needed for such a global optimization system remains an open research question. However, if the right abstraction can be found, an operator can facilitate fundamental changes within the network, e.g., core network reconfiguration, and prediction of necessary changes to and failures of the hardware infrastructure, in an automated fashion. That way, the operator can minimize the operational cost, as well as the error introduced by human configuration of the network.

An intrinsic challenge is the identification of information that is of global interest, as well as the interaction of network elements, controllers, orchestrators, and the Big Data analytics engine. Accordingly, an intelligent and well-designed information exchange between Big Data applications and SDN controllers among all domains is needed. The ideal interfaces and interactions are still an open question and may vary between different scenarios. The following section will discuss two possibilities for the access network domain in relation to the challenges.

21.6 Challenges and discussions

Following the previous sections and the presentation of our vision for the Big Data-supported SDN architecture, we consider the important challenges in this section. It has been shown that challenges arise both in management and Big Data directions. Many today's challenges of SDN-based QoE management can be addressed by the Big Data paradigm. Nevertheless, as a result of the previous discussions, it has become clear that Big Data itself poses further open questions that should be considered. In the first part, we briefly discuss the challenges of SDN-based QoE management. We explicitly highlight the possible applications of Big Data in that case. In the second part, we discuss outstanding issues of the Big Data-supported SDN architecture with respect to the information exchange between Big Data applications and SDN controllers.

21.6.1 Challenges of SDN-based QoE management

SDN-based QoE management is a far-reaching and promising concept, which also entails challenges. The monitoring of information currently shows that encrypted traffic impairs the retrieval of information. Consequently, encrypted traffic represents a challenge for traditional SDN-based QoE management approaches. To go more into detail, it makes it difficult to use DPI procedures. Instead, more statistical methods based on a lot of data need to be used that fosters Big Data approaches. Patterns in network traces can help to train models so as to specify application classes, although traffic is encrypted. Furthermore, it is of the utmost importance that network-wide monitoring is established in order to implement QoE management efficiently. A network-wide overview of key QoE-IFs is necessary. To control the network (e.g., path selection), it is necessary to know the complete network. This requires a lot of information from different devices throughout the whole network, which in turn can be addressed again by Big Data.

What applies to the network level also applies to the application level. At the application level, the challenge is to monitor all applications with appropriate granularity. When monitoring is performed on application layer (e.g., to support QoE fairness), it is not sufficient to monitor one client or application instance. One must be aware of all relevant applications running and their requirements so as to allow fine-grained and targeted decisions. For fine-grained and targeted control actions in the network, additionally information from all areas must be known. For all approaches, the amount of data is essential to make efficient decisions and not to discriminate against other applications in the network with respect to fairness. Another challenge for management approaches is the processing of the large amount of data. The question arises on how to store, handle and structure different information with respect to the desired outcome. Additionally, subjective studies on QoS/QoE mapping, which are needed to train models in order to automatically identify the resulting QoE, are very costly.

The key derivation must therefore be, that in order to counter the challenges of QoE management in the present time, the network and application status must be learned and the effects of the actions on the network must be examined. Next, the resulting model must be set up with the help of unsupervised or supervised learning methods to automate network/application control actions in an efficient way.

21.6.2   Challenges of a Big Data-supported SDN architecture for enhancing application quality

The application of Big Data also includes challenges as discussed in the previous section. It is important to take these into account in order to consistently implement the use of Big Data. An intelligent and well-designed information exchange between Big Data applications and SDN controllers among all domains is needed.

With regards to the Big Data-supported SDN architecture, Figure 21.3(a) outlines the interaction between SDN and Big Data as presented in [16]. All available monitoring data on application and network levels are gathered by the SDN control plane and forwarded to a remote analytics engine. If necessary, additional flow rules can be added to the data plane in order to gather specific monitoring information on demand. Based on this monitoring data, stream processing approaches as outlined in Figure 21.3 can be applied to deduce context information or control instructions. Exactly this information is essential to support the QoE management.

The information is then passed to the control plane and can be used to enhance the application quality. Moreover, control actions may be reported back to the BDAE and used for updating QoS/QoE models, e.g., by using reinforcement learning. In this scenario, the SDN control plane may constitute a bottleneck resulting in a limited number of monitoring information and control actions being forwarded to the Big Data analytics engine.

A less controller-centric solution featuring the interaction between the BDAE and the SDN controller is highlighted in Figure 21.3(b). Apart from the monitoring data provided by the SDN controller, the BDAE is able to collect more data from an additional monitoring system or from the network elements using management

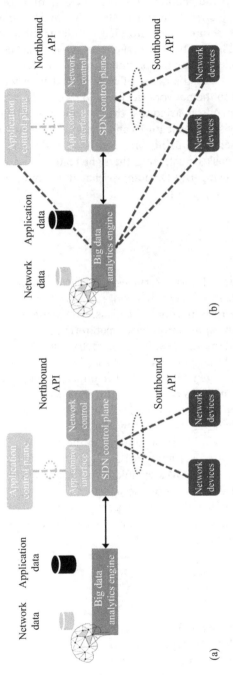

Figure 21.3 *Architectural options for an integrated Big Data/SDN architecture: (a) controller-centered interaction between the Big Data analytics engine and the SDN controller and (b) data-centered interaction between the Big Data analytics engine and the SDN controller*

protocols like SNMP, NetFlow or sFlow. Further, the BDAE may also be connected to the application control plane enabling a direct access to monitoring data of corresponding applications. This might result in the availability of more fine-grained application data and, thus, a more accurate view on the applications using stream processing techniques. Additionally, reinforced learning approaches may be used to enhance the QoS/QoE models based on the impact of control actions on the application quality. Nevertheless, the total amount of exchanged data may be limited due to capacity constraints between the network devices and the Big Data analytics engine.

To overcome such capacity restrictions, the network devices require additional knowledge to forward only selected features and examples needed for the analysis in the BDAE. This can be facilitated using ML models on SDN switch and controller levels just for the special task of selecting the right features and examples. These models can be learned by using Big Data approaches in learning clusters, based on the gathered monitoring information.

21.7   Conclusion

The diverse demands of today's Internet services, combined with an increasing number of end-users, call for a more efficient network resource control and, hence, for a network capable to enforce resource control actions. Due to the necessity to correlate large amounts of network and application-based monitoring data, Big Data approaches are promising solutions to derive context information like QoS/QoE mappings, which help deciding about control mechanisms for enhanced application quality.

This book chapter is a step toward a better understanding on how Big Data approaches and Big Data analytics can be used, together with SDN architectures, so as to enhance the overall application quality. Therefore, we present several SDN-based approaches that aim at enhancing user QoE by monitoring QoE-IFs and performing appropriate control actions within applications or in the network. Subsequently, we highlight the potential of Big Data analytics to support QoS/QoE management by outlining several works that exploit ML techniques in the context of QoE. We extend this presentation toward a vision on how networks can optimize themselves in the future, facilitated by Big Data and ML approaches. Finally, we focus on challenges and open research questions with respect to an SDN architecture that leverages Big Data for improving the user QoE.

Acknowledgments

This work was partly funded in the framework of the EU ICT project INPUT (H2020-ICT-2014-1, Grant no. 644672). Ognjen Dobrijevic acknowledges support of the project "Information and communication technology for generic and energy-efficient communication solutions with application in e-/m-health (ICTGEN)" cofinanced by the European Union from the European Regional Development Fund. The

Deutsche Forschungsgemeinschaft (DFG) supported this work with the Grant "SDN-enabled Application-aware Network Control Architectures and their Performance Assessment" (ZI1334/2-1, TR257/43-1).

References

[1]   "Qualinet White Paper on Definitions of Quality of Experience (2012)," Mar. 2013. European Network on Quality of Experience in Multimedia Systems and Services (COST Action IC 1003), Patrick Le Callet, Sebastian Möller and Andrew Perkis, eds., Lausanne, Switzerland, version 1.2.

[2]   D. Kreutz, F. M. V. Ramos, P. E. Verssimo, C. E. Rothenberg, S. Azodolmolky, and S. Uhlig, "Software-defined networking: a comprehensive survey," *Proceedings of the IEEE*, vol. 103, no. 1, pp. 14–76, 2015.

[3]   R. Schatz, M. Fiedler, and L. Skorin-Kapov, *QoE-Based Network and Application Management*, pp. 411–426. Springer International Publishing, Quality of Experience: Advanced Concepts, Applications and Methods ed., 2014.

[4]   V. N. Gudivada, R. Baeza-Yates, and V. V. Raghavan, "Big data: promises and problems," *Computer*, vol. 48, no. 3, pp. 20–23, 2015.

[5]   Cisco, "Cisco Visual Networking Index: Forecast and Methodology, 2015-2020 White Paper," Tech. Rep., Cisco Systems, Inc., San Jose, USA, 2016.

[6]   M. Jarschel, F. Wamser, T. Höhn, T. Zinner, and P. Tran-Gia, "SDN-based application-aware networking on the example of YouTube video streaming," in *Proceedings of the 2nd European Workshop on Software Defined Networks (EWSDN 2013)*, (Berlin, Germany), pp. 87–92, 2013.

[7]   O. Dobrijevic, M. Santl, and M. Matijasevic, "Ant colony optimization for QoE-centric flow routing in software-defined networks," in *Network and Service Management (CNSM), 2015 11th International Conference on*, pp. 274–278, IEEE, 2015.

[8]   J. Zhu, R. Vannithamby, C. Rödbro, M. Chen, and S. V. Andersen, "Improving QoE for Skype video call in mobile broadband network," in *Global Communications Conference (GLOBECOM), 2012 IEEE*, pp. 1938–1943, IEEE, 2012.

[9]   B. Staehle, M. Hirth, R. Pries, F. Wamser, and D. Staehle, "Yomo: A YouTube application comfort monitoring tool," *New Dimensions in the Assessment and Support of Quality of Experience for Multimedia Applications, Tampere, Finland*, pp. 1–3, 2010.

[10]   S. Petrangeli, T. Wauters, R. Huysegems, T. Bostoen, and F. De Turck, "Network-based dynamic prioritization of HTTP adaptive streams to avoid video freezes," in *Integrated Network Management (IM), 2015 IFIP/IEEE International Symposium on*, pp. 1242–1248, IEEE, 2015.

[11]   A. Bentaleb, A. C. Begen, and R. Zimmermann, "SDNDASH: improving QoE of HTTP adaptive streaming using software defined networking," in *Proceedings of the 2016 ACM on Multimedia Conference*, pp. 1296–1305, ACM, 2016.

[12]   H. Nam, K.-H. Kim, J. Y. Kim, and H. Schulzrinne, "Towards QoE-aware video streaming using SDN," in *Global Communications Conference (GLOBECOM), 2014 IEEE*, pp. 1317–1322, IEEE, 2014.

[13]   G. Cofano, L. De Cicco, T. Zinner, A. Nguyen-Ngoc, P. Tran-Gia, and S. Mascolo, "Design and experimental evaluation of network-assisted strategies for HTTP adaptive streaming," in *Proceedings of the 7th International Conference on Multimedia Systems*, p. 3, ACM, 2016.

[14]   V. Joseph and G. de Veciana, "Nova: QoE-driven optimization of dash-based video delivery in networks," in *INFOCOM, 2014 Proceedings IEEE*, pp. 82–90, IEEE, 2014.

[15]   A. Bahga and V. Madisetti, "Big data science & analytics: a hands-on approach," VPT, 2016.

[16]   L. Cui, F. R. Yu, and Q. Yan, "When big data meets software-defined networking: SDN for big data and big data for SDN," *IEEE Network*, vol. 30, no. 1, pp. 58–65, 2016.

[17]   T. Mitchell, *Machine learning*. Boston, MA: McGraw-Hill, 1997.

[18]   K. P. Murphy, *Machine learning: a probabilistic perspective*. MIT press, 2012.

[19]   J. Han, J. Pei, and M. Kamber, *Data mining: concepts and techniques*. Elsevier: Morgan Kaufmann, 2011.

[20]   P. Berkhin, "A survey of clustering data mining techniques," in *Grouping multidimensional data*, pp. 25–71, Springer, 2006.

[21]   J. Gama, *Knowledge discovery from data streams*. CRC Press, 2010.

[22]   L. P. Kaelbling, M. L. Littman, and A. W. Moore, "Reinforcement learning: a survey," *Journal of Artificial Intelligence Research*, vol. 4, pp. 237–285, 1996.

[23]   X. Guo, S. Singh, H. Lee, R. L. Lewis, and X. Wang, "Deep learning for real-time Atari game play using offline Monte-Carlo tree search planning," in *Advances in Neural Information Processing Systems*, pp. 3338–3346, 2014.

[24]   J. Dean and S. Ghemawat, "Mapreduce: simplified data processing on large clusters," *Communications of the ACM*, vol. 51, no. 1, pp. 107–113, 2008.

[25]   A. Mestres, A. Rodriguez-Natal, J. Carner, *et al.*, "Knowledge-defined networking," ACM SIGCOMM Computer Communication Review, vol. 47, no. 3, pp. 2–10, 2017.

[26]   D. D. Clark, C. Partridge, J. C. Ramming, and J. T. Wroclawski, "A knowledge plane for the internet," in *Proceedings of the 2003 Conference on Applications, Technologies, Architectures, and Protocols for Computer Communications*, pp. 3–10, ACM, 2003.

[27]   M. S. Mushtaq, B. Augustin, and A. Mellouk, "Empirical study based on machine learning approach to assess the QoS/QoE correlation," in *Networks and Optical Communications (NOC), 2012 17th European Conference on*, pp. 1–7, IEEE, 2012.

[28]   I. Orsolic, D. Pevec, M. Suznjevic, and L. Skorin-Kapov, "YouTube QoE estimation based on the analysis of encrypted network traffic using machine learning," in *Globecom Workshops (GC Wkshps), 2016 IEEE*, pp. 1–6, IEEE, 2016.

[29] P. Wang, S.-C. Lin, and M. Luo, "A framework for QoS-aware traffic classification using semi-supervised machine learning in SDNs," in *Services Computing (SCC), 2016 IEEE International Conference on*, pp. 760–765, IEEE, 2016.

[30] P. Amaral, J. Dinis, P. Pinto, L. Bernardo, J. Tavares, and H. S. Mamede, "Machine learning in software defined networks: data collection and traffic classification," in *Network Protocols (ICNP), 2016 IEEE 24th International Conference on*, pp. 1–5, IEEE, 2016.

[31] M. Elkotob, D. Grandlund, K. Andersson, and C. Ahlund, "Multimedia QoE optimized management using prediction and statistical learning," in *Local Computer Networks (LCN), 2010 IEEE 35th Conference on*, pp. 324–327, IEEE, 2010.

[32] H. Du, C. Guo, Y. Liu, and Y. Liu, "Research on relationship between QoE and QoS based on BP neural network," in *Network Infrastructure and Digital Content, 2009. IC-NIDC 2009. IEEE International Conference on*, pp. 312–315, IEEE, 2009.

[33] K. Borchert, M. Hirth, T. Zinner, and D. C. Mocanu, "Correlating QoE and technical parameters of an sap system in an enterprise environment," in *Teletraffic Congress (ITC 28), 2016 28th International*, vol. 3, pp. 34–36, IEEE, 2016.

[34] M. K. Weldon, *The future X network: a Bell Labs perspective*. CRC Press, 2016.

Index

Printed in the USA
CPSIA information can be obtained
at www.ICGtesting.com
JSHW011507221024
72173JS00005B/1234